Also by Alanna Nash

Dolly

Golden Girl: The Story of Jessica Savitch

A Note About the Author

Alanna Nash is the author of *Dolly*, a biography of Dolly
Parton, and *Golden Girl: The Story of Jessica Savitch*. Her
articles on music, film, and gangsters of the 1930s have
appeared in *Esquire*, *The New York Times*, *Ms.*, *Working
Woman*, and *The Saturday Evening Post*. A former pop
music critic for the *Louisville Courier-Journal*, she is a
contributing editor and monthly record reviewer for *Stereo
Review* and a program reviewer for *Video Review*. She has
also written and produced a number of country radio
interview shows, including two nationally syndicated series,
and specials for the Mutual Broadcasting System. In 1982,
Esquire named her one of "Country Music's Heavy 100."

Behind Closed Doors

Behind Closed Doors

Talking with the Legends of Country Music

Alanna Nash

Alfred A. Knopf
New York
1988

THIS IS A BORZOI BOOK
PUBLISHED BY ALFRED A. KNOPF, INC.

The title, "Behind Closed Doors," copyright © 1983 Warner
House of Music (BMI). Used by permission, Warner House
of Music, and Kenny O'Dell.
Owing to limitations of space, all other acknowledgments
of permission to reprint previously published material will
be found following the text.
Front cover photographs of Dolly Parton by Beth Gwinn/
Retna; Loretta Lynn by David Redfern/Retna; Emmylou
Harris, Willie Nelson, and Rodney Crowell by © Jim
McGuire. Back cover photographs of Chet Atkins, Bill
Monroe, Reba McEntire, Rosanne Cash, Brenda Lee by ©
Jim McGuire; Tammy Wynette by Darlene Hammond/
Pictorial Parade; Conway Twitty by Beth Gwinn/Retna;
Charley Pride by David Redfern/Retna; Hank Williams, Jr.
by © Leonard Kamsler.

Library of Congress Cataloging-in-Publication Data

Nash, Alanna.
  Behind closed doors.

1. Country musicians—United States—Interviews.
2. Country music—United States—History and criticism.
I. Title
ML385.N37 1988   784.5'2'00922   87-46321
ISBN 0-679-72102-9

Manufactured in the United States of America
First Edition

Composed by Dix Type Inc., Syracuse, New York

Printed and bound by the Murray Printing Company,
Westford, Massachusetts

Designed by Julie Duquet

For Elizabeth Barnes, William Livingstone,
and the regulars at the Mosey On Inn.

Keep a-goin'.

Music is moral law. It gives a soul to the
universe, wings to the mind, flight to the
imagination, a charm to sadness and a gaiety
and life to everything. It is the essence of order
and leads to all that is good, true and beautiful.
—Plato (427–347 B.C.)

Oh Lord, I got 'em . . . I got the honky-tonk blues.
—Hank Williams (1923–53)

Contents

Acknowledgments

Through the last dozen years, literally hundreds of people conspired to make this book possible. Some of them helped to set up interviews, or offered to publish them, while others filled in the gaps in my knowledge of country music, and taught me how things work the Nashville way.

I will always be indebted to Jerry Seabolt, who in 1975, while working as a publicist for United Artists Records, served as an unofficial "good will ambassador" on my first trip to Nashville. He not only picked me up at the plane and took me to dinner, but gave me a tour of Music Row. The UA Tower was still under construction, and I was surprised that the famed 16th Avenue seemed so small and self-contained. But then we've both grown since then. And Seabolt, who is something of a legend himself, is still my friend.

As the years went by, three other people could always be counted on to give me the straight story on any situation, and just as often, companionship over a meal. In time, I began to think of Elizabeth Thiels, of Network Ink, Inc., Cindy Leu, formerly of CBS Records/Nashville, and Clarence Selman, dinosaur-at-large, as my guardian angels. And Elizabeth, whom I hope to know in many more lifetimes to come, always made me feel as if her guest room were ready and waiting.

For professional help and friendship, I would like to thank: Biff Adams, Bob Allen, Janice Azrak, Jerry Bailey, Debbie Banks, Bobby Bare, Christie Barter, Jenny Bohler, Louise Boundas, Woody Bowles, Bonnie Bramlett, Eleanor J. Brecher, Allen Brown, Tony Brown, Hal Buckley, Tony Byworth, Coyote Calhoun, Debbie Campbell, Maggie Cavender, Jim Chapman, Marshall Chapman, Guy Clark, Elizabeth Costello, Bobby Cudd, Fran Dalton, Brenna Davenport-Leigh, Kelly Delaney, Joan Dew, Larry Dixon, John Dotson, Nancy Dunne, David Elrich, Marshall Fallwell, Jr., Donna Fargo, Helen Farmer, Jim and Teresa Fergusson, Danny Fields, Kathy Gangwisch, the late Don Gant, Melodie Gimple, Randy Goodman, Bob Gordon, Emory Gordy, Jr., Doug Green, Steven J. Greil, Cindy Grisolia, and Cathy Gurley.

Also: Stacy Harris, Julie Henry, Sally Hinkle, Henry Horenstein, Mike Hyland, Loretta, Loudilla, and Kay Johnson, Gene King and King's Record Shop, Paul Kingsbury, Kip Kirby, Fred Koller, Betsy Kronish, Pam Lewis, Bill Littleton, John Lomax III, Cheh Nam Low, Ronni Lundy, Rocco Matera, Milton Metz, Bob Millard, Liz Meyer, Peter Mikelbank, Ron Mitchell, Rudy Moeller, Martha Moore, Ed Morris, Erin Morris, Dave Mulholland, Frank Mull, Michelle Myers, Sim Myers, Sandy Neese, Tracy Nelson, Susan Niles, Kenny O'Dell, Robert K. Oermann, Paul Randall, Bonnie Rasmussen, Tandy Rice, Susan Roberts, Ronna Rubin, LaWayne Satterfield, Karl Shannon, Vivien Sheldon, David Skepner, Cynthia Spencer, Raymond L. Snell, Chuck Thompson, Paulette Weiss, Kay West, Tim Wipperman, and Robin Wolkey. I offer sincere apologies to anyone I've overlooked.

And as someone who came to country music rather late in life, I am grateful to the following people who tried to talk sense into me years before: my uncle, Warren Nash, who knows more about country music than I ever will; another uncle, Richard H. Nash, who introduced me to Johnny Cash's "I Walk the Line" in 1956, when, as a first-grader, I had other things on my mind; Sheila Pyle, who, in the early '60s, sparked my interest in the folk origins of old-time country music; Rick McCarty, who, in 1972, wouldn't stop playing his Flatt and Scruggs records even when I got down on my knees and begged; and Florence King, whose essay "Red Necks, White Socks, and Blue Ribbon Fear," in *Harper's* magazine in July 1974, inspired me to take a closer look at a genre I had largely overlooked.

I also owe special thanks to Joan Tewkesbury, the writer of Robert Altman's *Nashville*. Had I not seen the movie—and then discussed the country music culture at great length with her over several years—this book probably would not exist. It was Joan who made me see beyond the obvious, and want to know more.

But there are other people who really made this book happen: Lee Goerner, my very patient editor, who happens to have impeccable taste in country music; Jane Ziegelman, his assistant, who hunted high and low for the 70 manuscript pages I mistakenly said I didn't have; Diane Alexander, Jane Burke, and Joanne Tingley, all of whom transcribed interviews at one time or another, and my parents, Allan and Emily Kay Nash, who fought country music as long as they could, but eventually gave in to Emmylou Harris, Rosanne Cash, and Sweethearts of the Rodeo.

And finally, I want to thank Mia Grosjean, my former agent, who believed in the project when no one else did; my current agent, Charlotte Sheedy, for her continuing hard work and good faith; and my interim agent, Gloria Safier. I can only guess how Gloria felt about country music, but I will always remember her with fondness. The contract for this book was one of the last she wrote before her sudden, premature death in 1985. To everyone who knew her, she was an extraordinary human being.

I just learned how to yodel
I sure can play guitar
I love to sing them country songs
And I wanna be a star.
If I don't make it pretty soon
I don't know what I'll do
'Cause I just saw John Travolty
Now he's a cowboy, too.

> —Skeeter Davis, "Everybody Wants a Cowboy"
> (copyright High Harmony Music)

*F*or me, it started not with John Travolta and the "urban cowboy" boom but with Pee Wee King. Not in the '50s, when King was riding tall in his own saddle, but in 1974, when the Country Music Association saw fit to induct him into the Hall of Fame.

I had just gotten out of journalism school then, and was scouting around for stories to free-lance to national magazines. Pee Wee King not only lived in my hometown of Louisville, but coincidentally, my earliest memory of television was of King, circa 1953, squeezing a country polka out of his accordion. And so, after consulting the *Writer's Market* for some kind of periodical that might find Pee Wee as fascinating as I did, I fired off a letter to *Country Music* magazine. They went for the idea, I slowpoked over to Pee Wee's, and the story appeared in the magazine. That, I thought, was that.

In no time, however, the magazine's English editor and Singapore-born art director were on the phone talking to me about going to Nashville to do a "sisters" story, or profiles of the sisters of Loretta Lynn, Dolly Parton, and Tanya Tucker, who hoped to follow in their siblings' footsteps.

What I knew about country music at that point would have filled a one-gallon cowboy hat (give or take a liter). But in comparison to the rest of the magazine, heck, I was at least from the right *country*, and to top it off, I was from Kentucky, home of the Renfro Valley Barn Dance and the birthplace of untold numbers of hillbilly stars. And so, with fourteen years of private classical violin lessons behind me, and feeling, as Knight-Ridder columnist Tom Hennessy would one day write, that "anyone who liked [country] music was poor, sad, uneducated, non-liberal, rural, drank whiskey to excess, and would probably wind up in a tarpaper asylum in the Ozarks," I made my first trip to Nashville in October 1975. There, in addition to Crystal Gayle, Stella Parton, and La Costa, I interviewed Marty Robbins, Minnie Pearl, and a rising young star named Emmylou Harris.

My aunt, Iona Fagan, an amateur genealogist, claims that we Nashes are descended from General Francis Nash, the founder of Fort Nashborough, later rechristened Nashville. Don't ask me to prove it—especially since both my parents are Tennesseans who moved to Kentucky "to get away from country music and everything that it stands for." But there must be something in the genes: after that first trip, I was hooked.

The next twelve years would be the most dramatic and turbulent time in the history of the music—years that saw the "outlaw" phenomenon of Willie Nelson and Waylon Jennings, the pop-crossover stampede of Kenny Rogers, the Charlie Daniels and Alabama brands of Southern rock, the rise of the progressive traditionalists such as Emmylou Harris and Ricky Skaggs, the urban-rural sensibility of Rosanne Cash, the Las Vegas-tinged soul of Lee Greenwood, the New Traditionalists such as George Strait, Randy Travis, and Dwight Yoakam, the indestructibility of George Jones and stone-hard honky-tonk, the filigreed harmonies of the Judds, and the rock roots of Steve Earle. During those years, I would interview almost every significant country performer of the last several decades for books, magazine articles, and network and syndicated radio shows.

"Country stars are symbolic ordinary figures," movie critic Pauline Kael wrote in her *New Yorker* review of Robert Altman's *Nashville*. So in almost every case, in addition to gleaning more information about a uniquely American form of music, I was interested in finding out why these particular artists chose to lead *extra*ordinary lives—the incessant traveling in the back of a Silver Eagle, the estrangement from family and friends, the toll it takes on their health—in order to sing about the virtues of rural existence and the pain of heartbreak, or, in short, ordinary life.

What I was not fully prepared for was the workings of the country mind, and, as such, the set of values that places country musicians on a different plane from their counterparts in pop or rock. Take, for example:

● George Jones, who once rode a lawn mower to a liquor store when Tammy Wynette, in an attempt to keep him sober, hid the keys to the cars.

● Jeannie C. Riley, who turned to gospel music after "Harper Valley PTA," and whose dining room boasts a photo of herself and her daughter dressed and posed as Madonna and child. An outtake from the session, I am told, shows the Madonna reaching for a cup of coffee.

● David Allan Coe, the ex-convict turned country star, who sports a tattoo of a spider on his principal private part.

● Barbara Mandrell, who charges a fee to view her honeymoon nightgown, on display at the Mandrell Country Museum.

● And Mr. and Mrs. Hank Williams, Sr., who remain colorful figures in death. At Audrey's funeral, for example, Bob Harrington, the "Bourbon Street Preacher," stood next to the open casket singing "Hey, Good Lookin' " to the deceased. And a few years ago plans were under way to unearth Hank Sr. and rebury him in the toe of a mammoth cowboy boot. The top of the boot was to be a revolving restaurant with a panoramic view of Montgomery, Alabama.

Since country performers customarily create their music out of their own lives and experiences—and since country singers have traditionally come from working-class roots, allowing the auto mechanic of today to become the honky-tonk hero of tomorrow—it seemed obvious early on that these artists had a great deal to say about their art: how they came to write particular songs, what their triumphs and tragedies have been, and if they are happy in a life that seems so grand and unimaginable to almost everyone.

That, in essence, is why this book came to be, and why I chose the question-and-answer format, one that provides the opportunity for thoughtful ruminations about the culture, the music, and the musicians' personal lives. In the best of these interviews, the questions unmask the public persona and get to the heart of the man or woman behind the music—the private person behind the official personality. I also hope the interviews occasionally provide the give-and-take of good conversation, and that they dispel the stereotypical "dumb hillbilly" image that country performers have suffered for decades. In today's big-business country music industry, no artist makes it to the top without an exceptional talent, a keen mind, and a perceptive overview of a complex and highly competitive marketplace.

However, this anthology is not definitive, by any means. In selecting the people whose words fill these pages, I have chosen artists who were, first of all, available and willing to contribute, who were able to express themselves easily and with candor, and whose interviews are the most memorable or revealing. In some situations, I have included interviews that may seem dated, but which, in the case of Dolly Parton, for example, explore a career in transition and what went into making Parton an international superstar. It also presents a woman whose talent is matched only by her perseverance, something not always discernible in her bubbly presentation.

All in all, the dozen years that went into this book have been delightful ones for me. I have learned a lot. I have come to appreciate the depth and soul of a music easily dismissed by some as "corny" and shallow. And I have met some unforgettable people, many of whom will never be household names.

Not long after I first started going to Nashville, I bought a secondhand jukebox as a birthday present for a friend. It hit me early in the day I was to give it to her that it would be fun to have the jukebox "announce" itself when it was plugged in. I had an old boyfriend tape-record a message ("Happy birthday! This is your jukebox speaking . . ."), which I wanted to get pressed onto a 45 and placed in the rotation of the records.

But in Nashville at least, the old-time voice booths, where a lacquer can be yours for a few dollars, have gone the way of Hadacol. And so I walked into Masterphonics, a record-mastering company, and found Tom Casassa, a former Grand Ole Opry engineer and a man who has helped literally thousands of musicians sound their best on records. I told him my name and what I wanted to do, adding that I needed the thing by five o'clock—and that I didn't have any money.

"Let's start over," he said.

"My name is Alanna Nash, and . . ."

"No, no," Tom said, "I mean your real name."

"That is my real name."

Tom fixed me with a wary stare.

"Let me see your driver's license," he demanded, and then handed it back, satisfied. "I thought you'd just taken two good music towns—Atlanta and Nashville—and made yourself a name." And then he cut my record—for free.

What follows is not a tale of two cities, but a collection of stories of remarkable people, people who have become legends for their talent, for their lifestyles, and—through the efforts of the Tom Casassas of the business, who have helped them shape their craft—their performance, and their stamp upon the industry, the commerce, and the culture. For the most part, they were country when country wasn't cool. And chances are they will remain so long after John Travolta has forgotten the name of Gilley's.

Alanna Nash
June 1987

Behind Closed Doors

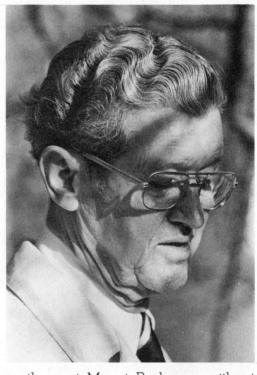

When the Japanese attacked the Marines at Okinawa in 1945, journalist Ernie Pyle reported that a banzai battalion yelled what they believed to be the most injurious of insults: "To hell with President Roosevelt, to hell with Babe Ruth, and to hell with Roy Acuff!"

Now eighty-five, Roy Acuff is still a premier symbol of America, so much so that his craggy features could probably be carved alongside the others at Mount Rushmore without the slightest hint of public protest. The reigning elder statesman of country music and the Grand Ole Opry's most revered star, Acuff is also known as the "King of Country Music," a title that was updated from the one Dizzy Dean originally gave him—"King of the Hillbillies"—during World War II.

In the beginning, however, Acuff wanted to be a professional baseball player, making it as far as the New York Yankees' rookie instruction camp before a series of sunstrokes put an end to his plans. Turning to music, he served his apprenticeship on medicine shows before forming a band and earning his own regional radio programs. When he finally got an audition on the Opry, in February of 1938—after weeks of trying—he was so nervous he forgot the words to "Great Speckled Bird," one of his best-known numbers, along with "Wabash Cannonball" and "The Precious Jewel." He quickly became a regular, though, and before long, Acuff would be influential in changing the thrust of the Opry from string bands to singers—in his case, with his own self-contained Dobro-flavored band, the Smoky Mountain Boys. In 1962, Acuff became the first living performer to be elected to the Country Music Hall of Fame.

Although he is reported to have sold 30 million records, his recordings were always secondary to his spot on the Opry, mainly because he recycled the same melodies all too often. Never better than a mediocre fiddler—he would end up doing balancing tricks with his violin just to keep it in the act—and hardly the best of singers, Acuff nonetheless had an uncommon delivery. Full of emotional zeal and sincere showmanship —not unlike the preaching he heard from his father's pulpit—he would often weep onstage when he sang a mournful song. But as he is reported to have said, "I'm a seller, not a singer."

In 1981, a year after this interview, Acuff's wife, Mildred, died, and not long after, beset by loneliness, poor hearing, and a chronic heart ailment, he sold his mansion overlooking the Cumberland River and moved to a small house specially built for him on the edge of Nashville's Opryland theme park—near the Roy Acuff Music Hall and Museum. A man of staggering wealth—through his co-ownership of the Acuff-Rose Publishing Company, considered the first music publishing firm to be headquartered in the South, and his many real estate investments— Acuff could probably afford to reside anywhere, and not be a sort of "living relic," constantly on display in Opryland's carnival atmosphere, constantly within earshot of the tourist train whistle. Acuff likes trains, though, and he likes it when people who ride them ask for his autograph.

I arranged our interview over the telephone, through a member of Acuff's band who supposedly handled such things. But when I arrived on time, I was told that Acuff had left for lunch and wouldn't be back for several hours. I left Acuff a note, reminding him of our appointment, and asked him to call. When he did, he apologized, but hinted that he really didn't want to do the interview after all. I pressed him on it, and told him I had been looking forward to it. "Well," he said, "I hope you'll try to think up some new questions. All you people ask me the same things, over and over." Just before we hung up, Acuff asked how much time the interview would take. I said an hour. "Oh, Miss Nash," he said with a haughty laugh, "I wouldn't give the President of the United States an hour of my time."

Just the same, we met in his dressing room at the Grand Ole Opry—dressing room No. 1. He insisted on leaving the door open, even when I objected to the noise from a nearby marching band. When the interview was over, I noticed that he had given me fifty-five minutes. I reminded him of what he'd said about an hour, and he told me, in a poignant sort of way, that he had just been nervous. After all these years, he said, it still makes him anxious to talk to strangers.

Q You had a heart attack a few years ago. Did that make any big changes in your life?

A Well, it maybe has changed my way of living. I'm not going at the speed that I once went with. I used to go in a rush all the time. I was going at everything in a hurry, like I was fighting a fire. And I've changed my life to slow down and take life easier, and try to go at my business much quieter and not let things excite me quite as much as they used to. I am a very nervous person, though. I've always been that way, all my life. When I played baseball back when I was a young man, I was an energetic, highly strung person. I played to win, but if I lost I was a good loser. But I still played to win. And when I came here to Nashville, I came here to win, not to lose. (Laughter) So the heart attack has slowed me down some, yes. I don't make as many appearances as I did. I've slowed them down considerably. But I'm still on the Opry, and I will be here as long as I'm well received, I hope.

Q Do you still get stage fright?

A Well, you can call it stage fright if you wish. I would call it a nervous sensation. But I wouldn't give you a dime for a person that could walk on the stage and tell you that he wasn't at all nervous. Because he's most likely a drone. And he's not likely to succeed. If you want to go on that stage, if you want to do anything, go at it with a determination. Go out there to win, go out to please your audience. When the curtain goes up, it's just like the whistle blowing on the football field or the basketball court. Or the umpire hollerin', "Play ball." The fright is all over after that, but before that time, you stay tense, you walk the floor, you twirl your fiddle bow, and you play another tune. Waitin'. But to say that I'm afraid or nervous, no. I have overcome all those things, I hope. But I am very tense before I go on the show—any kind of a show. Here at the Grand Ole Opry, I've been on it for forty-two years now, and I'm just as tense. I'm not as nervous as I was when I first went on, because I really was a nervous young man. But now, just about thirty minutes before show time, I'll start walking the floor and wonderin' what I'm gonna do and what's gonna happen, and try to figure my show out, if I can.

Q You ran for governor of Tennessee a few times in the forties, winning the Republican nomination in 1948. Would you have been a good governor, do you think?

A Oh, I don't know. I'm proud that I didn't have to try to prove that to anybody. I had some of the finest people in the state backing me, and I would have had good advice. And I suppose back in those days it wasn't quite as hard a job to be governor as it is now. There's so much *business* to the government now. It's a *hard* job now. Back when I made the race, I think anybody with good, ordinary thinking could have made decisions and would have been beneficial for the people. And that was what I made the race for, for the people. The people *asked* me to make the race, and I made it. I don't regret that I did, and I don't regret that I lost, either. Because it would have possibly changed the life of Roy Acuff, and I'd rather have the life I've lived than to have been governor for as many years as I could have. If I'd'a still been governor, I wouldn't have been happy. Not as happy as I am now.

Q Why?

A Well, because country music and entertainment is a great life to live. I've had the opportunity of meeting so many people and going so many places. I've visited around the world with country music. I've been, not a *pioneer* altogether, but somewhat of a pioneer to other parts of the world. I have carried country music where country music was never carried before. And it's been rewarding to me in every respect that I know of, except, as I told you a while ago, I had a flare-up with my heart. I was just going too fast. Just tryin' to do too much. So I found out you can get things done just as well by going slow and approachin' it in a different way.

Q In 1974, President Nixon came to the opening of the new Grand Ole Opry House and yo-yo'd with you onstage. You even wore a red, white, and blue outfit for the occasion. How do you look back on that night?

A Well, first of all, I view Mr. Nixon with tears in my eyes. I loved Mr. Nixon. I had known him before I ever introduced him on the stage. I worked for him when he was running for vice president with Mr. Eisenhower. So I had known him for a long, long time—not so personally, but I had been around him, and then I got acquainted with him and his family. And I knew them as well as I have ever known any of the Presidents. And it grieves me to think that he let this [Watergate] happen to him. But when he was here, all this was brewing, and I knew it was bothering him on the stage. But it didn't show on him. He went through with his part just like a pro. And he was kind enough to say to me, "Uh, Roy, what do I do next?" You know, I was leading him around to all the different places on the stage and all. And I'd say, "Well, Mr. President, just go back over there and sit down with your wife till we get ready, and after a while I'm gonna have you play the piano." And he was just wonderful that night. He played three songs on the piano—"Happy Birthday" to his wife, and "God Bless America," and "My Wild Irish Rose," I believe. But he was just as easy to work with as it is for me to sit here and talk with you right now. I loved it.

Q That would have been difficult for a lot of people. How do you think of yourself? What's your self-image?

A How do I think of myself?

Q In other words, what kind of person are you?

A Well, I'm not a deceiving person. If I tell you something, you can pretty well bet that it's true. I made a policy many years ago not to be a person that people mistrusted. Not to lie. It's better to tell the truth and let it hurt than it is to lie and to have to think about it all through your life. If I don't lie, I'm truthful in what I say to you. And I'm truthful in what I say to my boys, and my boys ought to know that. And the people that know me know that I have that character. As far as my ability to perform, I have no more ability than a lot of others. A lot of others perform just as well or better than I do. As far as my understanding people, I don't know that anyone understands people any better than I do, 'cause I usually study a person if I'm gonna be around 'em. I don't make up with strangers very easily. No, not very easily. Because I'm always curious that I may be getting in with the wrong company. So I'll go slow as far as going to a stranger. I'll make sure that I have found out something about his character—who he is, what they are, what they're doing, what their background might be—before I ever become what you might call real friendly. Friendly enough to invite 'em into my home. And if I invite somebody into my home, you can bet that I trust them.

Q Minnie Pearl told me that she'd never been to your home just to visit, although she'd been there for parties. That's surprising, since you two have worked together for decades and always seemed to be so fond of each other. Does the "family" of country music treat each other more like distant cousins? Is it not as chummy as it appears?

A Well . . . (long pause), now a lot of people think that because we are here in Nashville and we're on the Grand Ole Opry together, that all of us boys and the girls, too, know one another and visit with each other in their homes, and everything. That is far from true. I only know where three or four of them live. We meet here at the Grand Ole Opry, we play the Grand Ole Opry, and we go home. Each goes to their individual home, or they're supposed to, anyway. And as far as saying to Minnie Pearl, or to Jeanne Pruett, or Jeannie Seely, or Jeannie C. Riley, or to Ernest Tubb, or Hank Snow, or Bill Monroe, or any of those boys, "Come on, go over to the house with me," I don't do that. And neither do they. They have their little social affairs with whoever they have their friendship with, and I have mine. But we don't associate together but very little. Now, if there's a party, that's a different thing. I may be invited to a party that maybe Ernest Tubb might have. I don't recall ever being invited to one of his parties. I don't know if he ever threw a party or not. But I used to have parties ever' once in a while at my house, and I usually invited Minnie, because Minnie was the type of person that I knew could get along with everybody. When you invite in a group of people like that, you want to make sure that all of them are pretty well acquainted, so they can have a good time. It's hard for a stranger to have a good time among strangers. So people are misled that think that here is a family of Grand Ole Opry people, of say sixty to eighty of us, and that we go around visiting. Now I'm not speaking of young and old. I'm speaking of both. The young, they have theirs that they associate with, but they don't associate with others on the Opry. Very, very few of them ever associate with others on the Opry. They go their way, and we go ours. And the real truth of the matter is that we see one another so little that some of us are really not acquainted with each other. Because they're out on the road all the time. I spent all my life on the road. About the last three years of my life is all I've spent here in Nashville, since I had the heart attack and quit traveling on the road like I did. Right now, while you and I are talkin', as many of those boys and girls as can possibly find jobs are either traveling to that job or comin' from a job, or headin' in to Nashville now. 'Cause I'm talkin' with you on a Thursday evening, and as many of 'em as can make it through are comin' in for the Friday-night Opry. Some of 'em won't be able to make it. They'll call up our head-quarters here and talk to Mr. Hal Durham, who takes care of things. Maybe some of them have troubles on the road and won't be able to make it, and they gotta change the program 'round. Oh, it's all kinds of troubles in this business. But we don't associate with one another like I'd like to see it done. I'd like to see us have more parties and gatherings, and be more sociable, but it's just [not] that way.

Q With all the changes in country music of late, can we still really call it "country" music? Where is the music headed now? Where is it going?

A Not goin' anywhere. No, country music is still country music. Some of them play things they *call* country music, but it's not country music. But country music will stay right where it is. It's up to the person what type of music they want to play. And if they want to play contemporary music, why that's their business. If they want to go back and sing folk songs, *that's* their business. If they want to play what they term bluegrass, that's their business. If they want to play pop, same thing. It's usually your instruments and the way you present it as to what it is. I can sing you "The Wabash Cannonball," and it's called country. Bill Monroe can play it with his band, and they call it bluegrass. One of these marching bands that play at a lot of football games, they play it in band-type music. So it's accordin' to the way you present it as to what it is. But as far as I'm concerned, the Grand Ole Opry hasn't got too far from it yet. It's far enough, don't get me wrong. I don't want to see it go any farther. I hope it will start backing up, and from what I see, I think they *are* backing up. I think they're coming back to the acoustical instrument. I think they're gonna watch the songs that they sing more closely, [so] that their songs haven't got the vulgarity in them that some of 'em carry. And I think they'll go back gradually to the better way of country music. I don't mean to go back like when I first come here. I was a very green young man when I came to Nashville. I'd had five years' experience in Knoxville. But I don't have to go back to what they call the "hillbilly." They could call me hillbilly now if they wished. Some of 'em call me a mountain music singer, which possibly I am. I don't care whether they call me country. I don't care what they call me. It makes no difference what they call Roy Acuff, because whatever it is, that's what I am. If they want to say I'm singin' a bluegrass number, I'll possibly be a-singin' a bluegrass number. If they want to say I'm doing a folk song, I'll possibly be doing a folk song. But I'll be doing it in my own style, and the only thing that I know is that I brought it from the country here, I brought it from the mountains, and that's just exactly what I still do today. With the same instruments, exactly. No change.

Q Your father was a Baptist minister, as well as a lawyer and a judge, and you've recorded a number of religious songs through the years. Do you have a feeling God put you here for a specific purpose?

A Yes. He put you here for the same reason. Each person is put here for a purpose. And He'll be the one to take you away, too, when the time comes. It's time all of us were thinking more about the hereafter than just living today. I think that we should prepare ourselves for death, because death is gonna come to you one day. And I hope that I will be prepared to go in the right way. And I hope you will be, too.

Q Minnie said you've bought your cemetery plot, and that sometimes you just go out there and sit and think.

A My father and mother are laying out there, and a brother. And it don't bother me to go out there and look at it. I look at it with peacefulness. I look at it as a place of rest. When my father passed away, we didn't have any money, and we shared a stone with a person out of Knoxville. Then after I got to where I felt I could afford to have a little plot of ground ourself, why, I called my family in and told 'em what I'd like to do and they all agreed to it. We moved my father to this place out here, to Springhill Cemetery. And then Mother was buried there—Mother knew where she was going to be buried. My brother knew where he was going to be buried. And I know where I'm going to be buried, but only the body will be put down there, dear. Their souls are somewhere else. They're back of that black dark curtain. There's a dark curtain we all gotta walk through. There's never been anybody come back. Nobody knows. Some people maybe think they do, but they don't. It's just a mystery, and it's one that you can study on, and hope for, and pray for, and someday we'll all know.

Q What do you think your purpose is?

A What my purpose is? I'm doing what, I presume, God would like for me to do. I'm trying to bring happiness into homes, and I'm trying to do it in just as clean a way as I possibly can to stay in country music, and to sing the type of songs that I think families enjoy. I sing a lot of hymns. I love gospel music, and I include a lot of it in my programs. And I always have, all my life. I was raised in a Christian home, but that's not gonna send me to heaven. I've got to be a Christian myself. So there's a lot to think about, and a whole lot to hope for. You've got to put your trust in the good Lord and go on. You can't stop and worry about it. There's more insane people carrying a Bible around in their hand today and thinking they're preaching to somebody. And they can't even *see* somebody. But they think they can. It's not good to start worrying about religion. Worry about your life, take care of yourself, live a good clean life, and Christianity will come along with you.

Q What have been the highest and lowest moments of your life?

A Well, I told you to think of somethin' to ask me that had never been asked, and you are. (Laughter) I have had a lot of high spots in my life. I've had a lot of them. I would have to say that having the privilege of introducing the President of the United States was one of the highlights of my life. And I was invited to the White House [in 1973] to entertain the prisoners of war. I think those were real highlights. I've been around the globe, almost, entertaining our boys and girls in the military. Those were enjoyable moments. Those are some of the high points of my life. One of the very low ebbs in my life was when I was knocked out of an athletic career when I was a young man. I was knocked out with a sunstroke, and I thought the whole world had turned on me. I couldn't see where I would go. But I reckon the good Lord kindly laid His hand on me and showed me a different direction than playing ball. I wanted to make a career of baseball. I played football and basketball, too, but I wanted to make a career of baseball. And I was hoping after that that I might be a coach somewhere, in a high school, maybe. But that all turned dark, and after that point, I started playing country music. My father played country music, and I had an uncle that played country music. We all sang, all of us children. And I just started seein' a different world to live in, in country music. There wasn't any money in country music at that time. Money had nothing to do with it. I did it for free, because I loved it. And I got a lot of experience on radio before I ever asked WSM here for a job. I had five years of experience in carryin' programs. And I was well prepared to carry programs. My principal in school, she saw the talent I had. She got me to lead chapel, to lead singing, and she meant a lot to me. She taught me a lot about how to turn correctly onstage, and how to do things that so many of our country music performers had no training about whatsoever. But those were things that helped me. And they've helped me to go as far as I have. But the high spots and the low spots, I couldn't tell you what the real high spot or the real low spot was. There's just so many things in between that have happened in my life and brought a lot of happiness and a lot of tears. I've lost some of my very dearest friends. You're very low when those things happen, when you lose your father and mother, your brother, and your close friends. I've seen so many of my close friends out here on the Grand Old Opry pass away. But I'm still around. And I'm grateful for it.

Q You had a bad car wreck in 1965. You tried to pass a car and realized you couldn't do it, threw on the brakes, skidded out of control, and hit the oncoming car. You had two pelvic fractures, a crushed rib cage, and a broken collarbone. What did you learn from that?

A I learned that you can get killed right quick. And you can leave here before you know it. (Small laugh) Well, it taught me a lesson in driving. I think I'm as good a driver as can hit a road. I've driven hundreds and hundreds of thousands of miles. I used to put a hundred thousand or a hundred twenty-five thousand miles on ever' car I got. Ever' year. We'd ride ever'where. And I did the greater part of the drivin'. But the accident . . . it just taught me that you can get killed real quick in an automobile when you're really not thinkin' about it. I had no *thought* of an accident. But I come very near killin' one of my very best friends, and I like to have killed myself. And it taught me just how quick your life can be taken away from you. As you and I sit here in this room, we're not both sure we're gonna see home again. Did you know that? It's true. You don't know when you leave home if you're comin' back. You don't *think.* You expect to, but you don't know. So many little girls and boys, or men and women, have left home with all good intentions of ever'thing. But first thing you know the telephone rung, and the message is that So-and-So's in the hospital. But they never come back home. Don't let it happen to you.

Q What do you think the strengths and weaknesses of your performance are? Do you ever wish you could improve a certain part of it—your fiddling, or singing or writing?

A Oh, I do that every time. Every time. I'm usually happy with my performances, but I can look back on them, and I can see where I could have improved them, and I try to do that the next time. I keep trying to improve myself ever' time I walk onstage in front of an audience. I try to present myself in a way that I will capture that audience. You've got to capture an audience. You don't go out there and just sing, or just play. If you can't capture an audience, you might as well not be out there. You're just a dumb lump walkin' around on the stage. When you walk in front of 'em, you've got to take 'em in your hand, and hold 'em, then immediately say thank you and goodbye. That's the way to hold an audience. You don't do it just by goin' out there and singin' a song of love, or a song of fun. You've got to go out with the determination to put on a program that the crowd is gonna enjoy. And hoping that you can do it. I fail 'em a lot of times, but I still keep trying. I'm not a quitter. And I'm not a loser. I'm a winner. I've been a winner all my life. But you have your ups and downs in country music, the same as in anything else.

Q Did you ever doubt your ability to make a living playing country music?

A When I started in country music, there was nothing [no other rewards] to country music, except to play it. I said a while ago, there was no money. There were many times when I was down to my last dollar. When I first came here, all the bands that were on the Grand Ole Opry had other jobs. Or they worked on a farm. They made their living that way. But when I came to Nashville, I brought a group of boys with me. I *had* to make a living out of country music. And there wasn't nobody else making a living out of country music alone. Now, there may have been some, but I wasn't acquainted with them. So I had to work my way into it. And after I got into it, and I got to makin' money, other people saw that I was doin' good, and that money could be made out of country music. But I come out of the country, and I had never seen anybody else perform a country music show. I built my own show, and I perform my own show today. I'm not a blueprint—I'm an original. And I could be nothing else but original now. It's too late. I've seen others try to copy me, and I've told 'em, "I appreciate you singing my songs and trying to copy me. And go ahead, sing my songs. But don't try to sing 'em like Roy Acuff. Sing 'em like *yourself.* Put *your* stuff into it." Hank Williams used to copy me, but after he did the "Lovesick Blues," my partner [Fred Rose, Acuff's partner in Acuff-Rose Publishing Company, which published Williams' songs] told him, "No more Acuff. Let's be a Williams." And I was proud for Hank, because Hank Williams made a big success. But I've seen a lot of 'em. George Jones sung a lot of my songs. Ray Price sung a lot of my type stuff. But they did it in their own style. They made their own way. I don't say that I was a leader to them—please don't misunderstand me. I've just seen those things happen. But you are not gonna be successful if you are a carbon copy. Because they're gonna say you're tryin' to sound too much like Jim Reeves, or Hawkshaw Hawkins, or Cowboy Copas. You can't do it. Do your own thing. I sing a lot of Hank Williams' songs. I love 'em. I sing Stonewall Jackson's songs, too. But I don't sing 'em like Stonewall does. I sing 'em like Roy Acuff. And I sing all of my songs like Roy Acuff. I don't copy nobody.

Q Columbia Records tried to get you to change your style, and you left the label rather than do it. Were you ever tempted to change it to sell more records?

A No, I would have been completely lost. And I wouldn't have been successful, because I wouldn't have been able to put my heart and soul into it like I do now. They don't impress me with that type stuff. Money never changed me. I just do my own, and I go on and forget about it. I'm sure there was a lot of the boys that saw what I was doing with country music, and went into it in their own style, and started doin' real well. And a lot of them fell by the wayside. Some of them found another field to work in, and they've done good. I admire them for it. I respect them. But you have to be an original.

Q Do you still write songs?

A No, I haven't written a song in quite a while. I guess songwriting is kind of like sellin' sugar out of a sugar barrel at an ol' grocery store. You finally scrape the bottom dry and sell all the sugar you got and say, "Well, I don't think I'll buy any more," and forget about it. I possibly could, but I have no reason to write songs now, because I don't record but very little, and when I do, I just pick up some songs that some of the other boys write for the company, and some that I like to do. I don't know whether I'll ever record anymore or not. I've not made my mind up on it. I'll make my mind up later about that.

Q You never seemed to write much from personal experience. Except for your religious songs, the songs you wrote were more about things than innermost feelings.

A Yes, and it's awful hard for me to write a song and not bring Christianity into it. Now, don't forget—I am not a saint. And I'm far from a sinner. But I can start writin' a song, and my mind gets to thinkin' about love, and God, and Christianity. And it's hard for me to stay right on a ballad like some of these boys write today. They don't think of Christianity in their writing. I hope they do when they go home and get their mind off things. But in their writing they just don't think in the right direction. They think in an opposite direction. They think of vulgarity. And I can't write on that type of stuff. My songs are all train numbers and things that move me. I worked at a railroad company for years. I was a callboy and played baseball for the L & N Railroad for about two or three years, and I learned to be around railroaders. I loved railroaders. That's what makes me think so much of Boxcar Willie. He's playing the part of a hobo, and singin' hobo songs, and he dresses like a hobo. And I've seen many a one looks just like him, down on the railroad track. I think he's a great person, and I think one day he'll be a great entertainer. He loves to sing train songs. He was raised on a railroad track. He's doin' his character. He's not tryin' to copy anybody. He sings my songs, but he don't copy me. He sings 'em like he knows to sing 'em. And that's the reason I admire him. But as far as my writing, I might write one like George Burns, "I Wish I Was Eighteen Again." (Laughter) He didn't write that one, but it was very fitting for him, and I'm so glad to see him doing well with it. He's taken a liking to country music, and he's found out in his older days that there *is* something to country music. There's a love in country music. You've got to listen to it—you've got to be around it. You don't just jump up and say, "I love country music." You've got to be exposed to it.

Q Do you wish you were eighteen again?

A No, I would take the challenge of going through life again as I have, and just to sing the song as he sung it is wonderful. But to wish you were eighteen again is just an unthought-of thing. I'm satisfied that I can never be again, and have no reason to want to. I'd rather look forward to something else now. I'm looking forward to another home someday, as I go on. I wrote a song one time, "I'm Building My Home." [He quotes:] "As I travel life's highway / I'm building a home." I was building my home in heaven, and that's the way the song goes.

Q Are you happy?

A Sure. I have no reason to be unhappy. I'm making a living. We've got our home paid for, and we've got everything in our home paid for. My cars are all paid for. My equipment that I keep up my grounds with is all paid for. I don't owe one man one cent. Anywhere. I only owe one person, and that's my life to God. But I don't go around cryin' and preachin'. And I sometimes say the wrong things. I speak up sometimes. I sound off! If I get mad, I'm liable to use a bad word! But I am always apologetic about it. I don't mean it. Maybe I've got enough education to think of another word I could use, but it seems like them other words fit just a little stronger. And they just put a little more *emphasis* just to say one real *bad* one, and then say, "I'm sorry." (Laughter)

Q Do you have a quick temper?

A Yeah, I'm liable to fly off anytime. Not in here with you, though. (Laughter) I don't think I have as quick a temper as I used to. I think I have settled my life more for that. But I can get irritated. There's not any real reason for me to. As I say, my wife and I are happy. And our grandchildren are happy. We have so much to be thankful for. I shouldn't have any reason to ever fly off of the handle and get mad, but I'm just that quick-tempered type of person, and might. (Small laugh)

Q What makes you angry?

A I don't know anything in particular that might make me angry. I don't like to see people overbearing, and out raisin' sand and cursin' everybody out just because they might be a bully. If there's anything I always like to whip it's a bully. Show me a man that thought he was some great fighter and was a-bullyin' somebody around, and I'll show you a man that would take him on. I've had a lot of fights in my younger days. I *loved* to fight. I didn't fight 'cause I was mad. I fought 'cause I just loved to fight. I'd defend myself, and I'd defend anyone else. If the person I saw didn't take somebody on, I'd take 'em on for 'em, just to see how strong and good a man he was. Then get up and apologize and go on.

Q Do you still do that today?

A No, my age would not permit me to do that, but even with my heart condition as it is, should I get mad and somebody fly up at me right quick, he'd possibly get a-hooked on the jaw with a fist before I could ever keep myself from it. I don't want to. I hope it never happens. But I would, I guess, because I'm that type person. But I am a guy, too, that will apologize very quickly. And if I harm anyone, or hurt anyone's feel-. ings, I wouldn't sleep good at night until I apologized or found out if I had done them wrong in some way.

Q Your career has covered the entire spectrum of country music, from traveling on medicine shows in the thirties, to your own traveling tent shows, which drew ten to fifteen thousand people at a time, to perform- ing at the Ryman Auditorium and the new Opry House as the kingpin of the Grand Ole Opry. In one way, I imagine the medicine shows, with the vaudeville act, were some of your most enjoyable days. What were they like?

A They were great days. I learned a lot on a medicine show. I played all different kinds of characters. I played the part of a little boy, and of a little girl, I played the part of an old woman, of a colored man—I played the part of every kind of character you could name. And after the plays, I'd go out and sing a couple or three songs for the doctor [Dr. Hauer, who sold Moc-A-Tan elixir], and then he'd make his pitch. And after we got through sellin' medicine and ever'thing that we had to do, why, me and Jake and another boy would put on a show for them. We'd put on what we called an afterpiece, which took fifteen or twenty minutes to perform. We were the only ones, so one night I'd be an old man, and the next night I'd be a little girl. The next night I'd be a blackface. Whatever we wanted to do. So it gave me a wide experience to under- stand comedy. And I think that was my biggest thing when I came to Nashville—my shows that I traveled on the road with. I taught my boys. I showed them what I wanted them to do. And I would do it in slapstick style. We'd tear an audience all to pieces. But then after we'd make 'em laugh for a while, I'd sing one of my tearjerkers, and I'd bend 'em down to their knees. I've seen 'em sittin' down on the front seats, or back in the back, cryin', wipin' their eyes. And then as soon as I got through with that, I'd bring 'em out of it—put some effort to it, do a fiddle tune, brighten 'em up, do a square dance, do *somethin'*. Don't keep 'em cryin'. Do something to lighten 'em up again! Tell a joke! Make 'em laugh! Put 'em back down! Let 'em cry again! Bring 'em back up and make 'em laugh! (Pause) That's *show* business.

*I*n 1984, two weeks after the release of the video for Alabama's "(There's a) Fire in the Night," the group's management withdrew the clip in fear of director David Hogan's main character and drawing card: a comely witch who seduces her young Romeo and then kills him with a poisonous tattoo.

"There was a little bit of sexual explicitness," Hogan was reported as saying, "and even though there wasn't anything satanic about it, I know the group was concerned about the witch and her tattoos. I saw it as a fairy tale for grownups . . . But I'm dealing with a Bible Belt audience."

If Alabama's management hoped to preserve the band's wholesome image—and the notion that their music appeals to the masses, except those of the black magic variety—the censorship served its purpose: the following year, a *People* magazine poll found the band—comprised of three guitar-playing cousins, Randy Owen, Jeff Cook, and Teddy Gentry, and a drummer, Mark Herndon—to be the most popular group in contemporary music.

Without the magazine's sanction, however, Alabama was already the country music success story of the '80s, making history in 1982 when it became the first group ever to win the prestigious Country Music Association's Entertainer of the Year award. In succeeding years ('83 and '84), it went on to set a CMA record as the only act to capture the award three times in a row, beating Barbara Mandrell's two-year streak of '80–'81.

To date, Alabama has sold more than 14 million LPs, won two Grammy awards, and as of mid-1986 charted eighteen consecutive number one singles—all staggering statistics, considering that in the summer of 1980 they were still playing for tips in a Myrtle Beach, South Carolina, bar. No one was more surprised at their success than RCA, the band's own record company. When the label signed them that same year, RCA's executives said they'd be happy if Alabama's first album sold 60,000 copies. It ended up going platinum, selling more than a million units. Every other Alabama album would do at least the same, the group's biggest-selling LP, *Feels So Right,* having sold nearly five times that amount.

But if Alabama has its legions of die-hard fans, it also has its share of detractors, who say that the group may be the most popular act in modern music but it is likewise the most overrated. Industry heads, fearing the obvious criticism that Alabama has been overhyped—and overrewarded—with an eye toward bringing in the free-spending youth audience, claim that the boys from Fort Payne, Alabama, are the saviors of Southern rock and, among other things, family unity—a band whose sound appeals to parents and kids alike.

In truth, Alabama's music is an amalgam of country, rock, and pop, a commercial sound originally dominated by up-tempo country-rock material such as "Mountain Music" and "Tennessee River," which earned the group its youthful devotees, and which was later tempered for the mainstream country-pop audience with romantic ballads such as "Feels So Right," "Old Flame," and "Close Enough to Perfect." But in recent years, Alabama has billed itself as "the people's band," recording albums with working-class American themes and turning out such songs as "Roll On" and "40 Hour Week," which celebrate truckers and factory workers—the backbone, along with farmers, of the traditional country music constituency.

In the early days of the group's success, much was made of the band's close harmony vocals, the fact that they provide their own instrumentation—Cook, the only real picker among them, plays the lead guitar and fiddle, while Gentry and Owen play the bass and rhythm guitar—and the fact that they write much of their own material. Predictably, as soon as Alabama began to dominate the charts, Nashville record executives —after decades of saying that an act with the structure of a rock group would never work in country music—nearly tripped over one another in finding a similar group (i.e., MCA's Atlanta, CBS's Exile, Capitol/EMI's Sawyer Brown, etc.) to share a piece of the Alabama pie.

The real success of the group, however, rests almost entirely on Randy Owen, without whom the band would certainly still be playing Myrtle Beach. While the band eschews the idea of a leader, not only is Owen the focus of Alabama's musical and visual appeal—with his strong, soulful voice, his maturing songwriting abilities, his anchoring rhythm guitar, his rugged good looks, and his shiny-eyed exuberance onstage—but it was Owen who spearheaded the business decisions that led to Alabama's RCA signing. Owen is likewise the lead spokesman in interviews, seeming to have the best perspective on the group's past and future and proving to be the most skilled at tactfully avoiding questions the group doesn't want to answer.

From the beginning of Alabama's success, interviewers, frustrated at the difficulty in getting much substantive repartee out of the group—especially with Jeff Cook's one-liners and wisecracks—jokingly said that talking with Alabama was something akin to watching an episode of the old Monkees TV show. Comparisons to the manufactured pop group became embarrassingly apt when it was discovered that Owen, Cook, and Gentry contribute extremely little to the instrumental accompaniment on their records (Herndon does not appear at all), leaving those duties to seasoned session musicians. Virtually all country music performers do the same these days, but the idea of Alabama was always that the group was a self-contained, all-inclusive *band.* One could not imagine the Charlie Daniels band, the Allman Brothers, or even the late Lynyrd Skynyrd doing the same thing. However, as musicians, Alabama has improved immeasurably since the first album, as demonstrated by the concert recordings of "Tennessee River" and "My Home's in Alabama" on the *Greatest Hits* LP, and the 1988 release *Alabama Live.*

None of this has daunted Alabama's huge fan following. The band has been so successful, in fact, that the concert grosses alone for dates between May 13, 1981, and August 15, 1983, totaled $14,352,739.51. When the group took two weeks' vacation in the summer of 1983, their manager, Dale Morris, told *Music City News* that it cost the organization "about $450,000." The individuals have invested their money well: Owen and Gentry in cattle farms, Cook in a recording studio, a building construction firm, a radio station, an apparel store, an abundance of gold jewelry—much of which he wears at the same time—and, he admits good-naturedly, $5,000 for new teeth "so I can smile."

In addition, the group runs Alabama gift shops in Nashville, Myrtle Beach, and their hometown of Fort Payne, Alabama, a community of 14,000 nestled between Lookout Mountain to the east and Sand Mountain to the west ("the Sock Capital of the World," because of the town's numerous textile mills), where the band still lives.

The story of the group's creation is fairly well known—"cousins meet cousins, find the right drummer, and finally hit the big time." In the beginning, music was merely a pastime for Gentry and Owen, who grew up on adjacent cotton and dairy farms. They joke—in all seriousness—that their situations were so dire that their families couldn't even afford an outhouse. Since Owen's family didn't get a radio until he was twelve, their exposure to music—mostly gospel—came from the Lookout Mountain Holiness Church, where snake handling was de rigueur.

In contrast, Jeff, a middle-class boy from the "city," began playing in bands at an early age, even working as a rock-and-roll disc jockey. The three didn't discover that Cook, too, was a cousin until they had already formed a band. Their kinship has been somewhat exaggerated: Owen and Gentry, related through Owen's father, are second cousins, with Cook showing up as a fourth or fifth cousin somewhere down the line.

After appearing on a local talent show in 1969, the band began to work together in earnest the following year, when Cook, an electrician, Owen, a student, and Gentry, a carpet layer, became the house band at Canyonland, a nearby amusement park. When Cook moved to Anniston, Alabama, in the early '70s for a government job, feeling that a music career wasn't going to materialize, Owen and Gentry followed him there, serious about building a future in music and determined to sharpen their skills. With their day jobs leaving them little time to practice, they became roommates, rehearsing their vocal harmonies in bed at night before they drifted off to sleep. In '73, using the name of Wildcountry, they moved to Myrtle Beach, South Carolina, to pursue a full-time life of music, eventually becoming a mainstay at the Bowery, playing six nights a week for seven years. Despite the solidarity of the three guitarists, the band had trouble keeping a drummer until 1979, when the Massachusetts-born Mark Herndon signed on, admitting that he knew nothing about country and that his roots were in rock and roll. The choice turned out to be a wise one for the group: not only is Herndon merely a salaried employee, and thus not an equal partner in the tremendous Alabama fortune, but his youthful blond looks and trendy clothing draw a large fan following.

It wasn't until 1980, though, after years of club dates and a few mildly successful singles on small labels, that the group—calling itself Alabama since 1977—finally attracted a major record company. RCA noticed their hit, "My Home's in Alabama," which was originally released on MDJ Records, climbing to number sixteen on the national charts, and signed them in the spring of that year. In August—when the movie *Urban Cowboy*, with its country-rock soundtrack, was winning new country fans all across the nation—Alabama's first RCA single, "Tennessee River," went to number one.

The Alabama phenomenon is still puzzling to a great deal of the music industry, as well as to the majority of music critics, although their last studio album, *Just Us*, received comparatively favorable reviews. But the band has consistently kowtowed to music business politics, showing up for all the award ceremonies and accepting their truckloads of citations with humble speeches and tears. They also cater to their fans, charging no fees for membership in their fan club and throwing the June Jam— their own version of Fan Fair—in Fort Payne. In 1986, they dedicated their North American tour to their following, and even wrote a love song for them, "Fans." But perhaps more important, they have tapped into the knee-jerk patriotism of country music, with such songs as "If It Ain't Dixie, It Won't Do." To some, these songs have helped revive the Southern pride that Jimmy Carter's disastrous presidential administration nearly obliterated.

The following transcript is the product of two interviews. The first, recorded in a Nashville hotel room, was done in June 1980, only two months after the group signed with RCA. The second interview took place in October 1981, at RCA Records, in Nashville. By the second interview they were the hottest act in country music, having just won their first CMA awards, for Vocal Group of the Year and Instrumental Group of the Year. At the first meeting, Randy and Teddy were surprisingly unguarded, good-natured, and naïve in their dealings with the press and in their attitude toward the music business. A year later, things had changed. Randy, who had been so open and enthusiastic in our first interview, immediately laid down the rules. "Fire away," he said wearily, but with definite assertion, "just as long as we don't talk about our wives and our kids." Mark Herndon, who is said to be outspoken and somewhat surly during interviews, was not present at either meeting.

In the years since then, the conviviality of old has been replaced by a decided cautiousness. According to someone at their record company, their new attitude stems mainly from the fact that having grown up with nothing and come into vast amounts of money overnight, they are terrified it will all end tomorrow. Indeed, in 1986, the band failed to be nominated in a single category for the all-important Country Music Association awards.

Q You've had quite a year [1981].
A Randy: Yeah, it's been a great year.
Q What's been the biggest surprise about all of this?
A Randy: The biggest surprise for me is havin' two gold and one platinum [record].
Q You didn't expect that?
A Randy: Not in one year. I kind of expected and hoped that we had a shot at bein' the Vocal Group of the Year, or winnin' some kind of an award. But that's a lot of records, and this is a bad time for record sales, as far as the recording industry goes.
Q But you certainly were hyped as the Next Big Thing.
A Randy: Yeah, I don't want to call any names, but I know a lot of people that's been talked about as bein' the upcoming people to look at. And they kinda fizzled away, you know.
Jeff: The thing that surprised me was gettin' the Instrumental Group of the Year [award]. Because I always felt like our strong point was our vocals. And that was like icing on the cake to get that one.
Q Have you run into any resentment that you've come so far so fast?
A Teddy: I don't think so.
Randy: I haven't experienced that at all.
Teddy: I think everybody that's known our group knows how we came by success. Most of 'em feel proud for us.
Jeff: And if there is anybody that resented it, they don't say anything to us about it.
Randy: We're real sensitive to people's feelings, too, and I haven't felt anything like that at all. I think once people do get to know us, like Teddy said, and they understand that we've been workin' real hard for eleven years to make somethin' happen, it doesn't seem so quick. [In later interviews, the group would refer to what they considered harsh treatment from music critics and members of the country music industry.]
Q What's been the reaction back home?
A Teddy: We haven't been back home, really, to find out. My wife tells me she has more people comin' up to her at the supermarket and sayin' "Congratulations," but I think a lot of people think that since they know

you, and you grew up there, they really don't know how to approach you or what to say to you. But I think most of 'em are really proud of it. Like this lady said earlier today, "I used to say I'm from Fort Payne, Alabama, and people would say, 'Where's that? Never heard of it.' " And now, she said, "people have heard of it for sure." So people are startin' to associate where we're from. Which is good, because it is our home.

Q They haven't had an Alabama Day?

A Teddy: They have an Alabama Week, which is the first week in June. [Beginning in 1982, the band would host its annual June Jam in Fort Payne to raise money for local charities and organizations.]

Q Is there a lot of pressure on you now to follow up this current success?

A Randy: Yeah, there is. (Loud sigh) I feel a lot of pressure within my own self to do especially good work on the album, and probably above and beyond all that, to do a fuller stage show than we've been doin'. We want to be able to have people come see our show and say that they haven't seen but four or five that were better. We'd like to say the *best* show they've ever seen, but as long as we're in the top five, like in the nominations for Group of the Year, we'll feel like we'll have won in our fight to put on a great show.

Teddy: I think, like the old saying goes, you have to work harder to stay on top than you do to get there. And I really believe that, because once you get to this point, people expect you to get lazy and take things for granite . . . or is it "granted"? Which is it, Jeff?

Jeff: (Silence)

Teddy: Well, you know what I'm talkin' about. To most people, the people who make it start sittin' around sayin', "Well, everybody's supposed to help me now, because we no longer have to get out and work the [radio] stations, and work the record stores, and make all the phone calls to say thanks like we used to." But we feel it's more important now than ever before.

Q What about writing? Do you have time to write anymore?

A Teddy: Very little.

Jeff: I tried writing in the back of the bus while we were riding along, and everything I wrote had to be in the key of the diesel. So I gave up the idea.

Q What do you think your songs say about you as a group and as individuals? Are you concerned about a personal vision coming through?

A Teddy: I think we try to look at a positive song. We try to stay away from real negative songs. We look more for the quality of a song, and how it relates to us, and [whether] the feeling is right for our group. And whether it has the right harmonies and if it fits our group musically. That's really what we try to choose our material from.

Q What's your objective when you sit down to write a song?

A Randy: First of all, I have to have something to write about. I can't just sit down and say, "Today I'm going to write a song." It's got to be something that turns me on, or something I'm real bothered about, or something I'd just like to say. When I write a song, or when we collaborate writing together, we always try to think about our group. Because our time is so short. See, used to be we had all kinds of time to write, and now that time's not there. But now I think you'll be seeing other artists do tunes that we wrote several years ago. They're good rock songs, or they're good country songs. I think they're tailor-made for some other artist, but not for us right now. When I set down now, well, me and Teddy wrote a song the other day. And we try to make the chord progression, and the beat, and everything about it so we can have harmony on it. So that it sounds like a group doing it, rather than just something with a vocal range that only one person could sing.

Teddy: I used to try to force-write. I'd say, "I've got to write a song today, so I'll get my guitar." And I think that helps you in a way, because the more you write, the better you get. For some writers, I guess, the first song they ever write is a hit. Then they write another song, and it's a hit, too. But now, I get to write less. But like Randy said, I write only when I've got something that really has to come out.

Randy: That really sounds like a big old lie, because we'd like to write every tune on our albums. It's a simple thing of economics, if nothing else, in our careers now. Maybe later on, when we have it made . . . but it just might be impossible to do that. We don't ever want to cut ourselves out of a hit record that someone else has written. When we go in the studio to cut a record, we try to make a single out of every record. In other words, if we cut a song, we think it has possibilities of being a single.

Teddy: If not, why cut it?

Q Randy, you look exhausted—beat.

A Jeff: We beat him regular. Or "regularly." Which is correct, Teddy? "Regular" or "regularly"?

Teddy: I know what you're talkin' about.

Jeff: We used a wet squirrel on Randy the last time he was beat.

Randy: Well, I am tired. We left Nashville, flew from here to Los Angeles to do the "Rock Concert," and we were delayed about five hours, due to the fact that some of the other acts on the show were barkin' at us like dogs, and we got scared and ran off the stage. I'm tellin' the truth, now. And we left Los Angeles and went to Louisiana State University and did a homecoming there, and we got to do our show about eleven-thirty that night, and then we flew from there to Toronto, and did our first CBC show, and then from there to New York, and we did two shows at Madison Square Garden. Then we went from there to Mobile, Alabama, and today I'm in RCA Studios talkin' to you. I slept real good last night . . .

Teddy: But it just wasn't enough.

Randy: It just wasn't enough.

Jeff: (Laughter) For the whole thirty minutes.

Q Overall, what has all this success done to your life? Rearranged things? Allowed you to have things you wanted that you couldn't have?

A *Teddy:* Well, I think my wife has showed up with a couple of new outfits on . . .

Jeff: (Laughter)

Teddy: . . . but outside of that . . . Naw, it's more than the money. Somebody said the other day that when we walk into a place now, to the people who follow country music, or country-rock music, we have the respect of the people, even though we're still dressed in jeans and a T-shirt, or whatever, while we're out travelin' on the road. We get the respect now. We haven't been thrown out of any places . . .

Jeff: Lately! (Laughter)

Teddy: . . . recently. It's just nice when people come up in the airport, or wherever you're at, and say, "Congratulations on your award." It really makes you feel good that you've just accomplished something. It gives you a feeling that the last ten and a half years was really worth it. It's finally startin' to pay off. And, of course, my family are not havin' to do without things, too. That's a big thing with me, 'cause when they get older, I guess they'll be on their own. But while they're young, I'd like to have enough money to take care of 'em.

Q What do you say to all the bands out there who are hanging on, who've struggled the way you did for years and years?

A *Teddy:* Well, I'd like to think that what we've done is helped open up the door. I think probably Marshall Tucker and Charlie Daniels helped open up the door for us to be able to move into the country field and perform as a group. But you've got to stick together, and you've got to have some good material, regardless of whether you write it yourself or find other writers and cut some of their songs. I think hangin' in there and approachin' it from a business standpoint, tryin' to organize yourself with good credit, and formin' a corporation and workin' for the good of everybody is the only way you can ever make it. And then it's a long shot. You have to try to be the best at what you're doin' and be the hardest worker and get the most done. It's like anything else, I guess. You have to get into it and do things by trial and error, a lot. You can do a lot more by yourself than you think you can. We used to manage ourselves, book ourselves . . .

Jeff: Drive ourselves . . .

Teddy: . . . we were just about totally self-contained, as far as everything that we did. But that's the cheapest way in the long run. Until you get to need an agent, or need a manager. Unless you've got somethin' to manage, you really don't need one.

Randy: You definitely don't need a manager if you're just workin' night-clubs.

Teddy: That's right.

Jeff: Don't need a bookkeeper for a long time, either.

Randy: Really, because you know as much about how to book your-self, and you can take that money and live on it durin' the week, like we did.

Jeff: Or you can take that ten percent or fifteen percent you'd pay an agent and use it to promote yourself, rather than just sit back and answer the telephone.

Q So you became businessmen as well as musicians.

A Randy: Got to be, yeah.

Jeff: Organization, I think, is the key to all of it.

Q The night you won the awards, you said something about a tape you'd gotten from a songwriter. What was that?

A Randy: Well, I think Donny Lowery and Mac McAnally are two of the most gifted songwriters that I've heard in a long time. I really don't know the partnership they had as far as the writing, who wrote the most, or if it was an equal thing, or whatever. But I do know what "Old Flame" did for our career. And I'm very grateful to Donny, because he's the one who brought the song to us personally. We were sittin' on the bus, and this guy came on and said, "I write songs, and I'd like for you to listen to some of our music." So we listened to 'em, and all the songs were great, but we only cut "Old Flame." You know, we feel like now that everything we put out has got to be a number one single, and it's got to be up to that quality. And we have some more songs that Donny has been a part of writing that we haven't cut yet, but more than likely, we will. [As of 1986, they had not.] I think it only goes to show what we were just sayin' previous, that you've got to keep pluggin' away, you know. As far as I know, "Old Flame" was the first song that Donny had ever had cut by anybody. And it was an instant smash. I mean, that was a *big* record for the group Alabama, because it established us . . . well, it was one of the nominations for the CMA awards [for Single of the Year]. And you don't take that lightly, you know. That's a very important nomination. Course, had it not been for [the Oak Ridge Boys'] "Elvira," I believe that "Old Flame" would have won. You can't take the impact of a song like "Elvira," a big crossover record, away from "Old Flame." "Old Flame" was a country record, and "Elvira" was a crossover, so it doesn't have as much impact. But for our group, it was an incredible success. And we don't forget things like that, either.

Q Is there a certain image that you want the band to have, or you think it does have?

A Jeff: Good music.

Randy: I think the image that we have, of just bein' people who get out and do things, and not bein' so recognizable everywhere [is what we want]. I honestly think that's part of the appeal of our group. Because everybody don't know who we are. When they see us, they don't know for sure that it's us. Because apparently, we look different ways at different times. Sometimes we really dress up, and sometimes we're very casual. And I feel at ease either way, myself—dressed up, or with tennis shoes and a T-shirt. We do shows both ways. As long as we're comfortable whatever we're doin', I think the audience will be the same way. We don't play games with the audience, and try to have a certain image so that we try to look the same way every night, so that we get stereotyped.

Jeff: I like the fact that we can still go out to a restaurant and not be harassed. We like for people to ask for our autograph. That's flattering, but you can still go out in public, and not have to have your meals sent in. You don't have to hide from people. And I don't think we ever want to lose touch with the crowd.

Q Where do you want to see all this go? Do you want to go on *Hollywood Squares* and be movie stars, or is that beneath your dignity?

A Jeff: Why not?

Teddy: Well, I think you can only do so much. If you're gonna be a number one group, and go out and tour, then you have very little time for anything else. It's like Dolly [Parton]. She's gettin' into the movies now, and I think that has to slow your record career down. But if that point ever comes, it'll be a good choice to have to make, if you make so much money on one that you have to give up the other one.

Jeff: We don't want to spread ourselves too thin for the time being, though.

Teddy: I guess in the future we'll have the opportunity to do somethin' like that, and I guess we'll have to wait and decide at that time what we want to do.

Q Are there any misconceptions about the group, do you think?

A Teddy: The only thing people get confused about is the fact that the group Alabama is just four musicians and singers. I mean, we don't have a backup band. Even at the CMA awards show, this lady was on me to hurry up and get the band up there so she could take a picture of 'em —the guys that backed us up in the group. It's just us, you know. [The group added a keyboard player, Costo Davis, in the years after this interview.]

Q "My Home's in Alabama" was your first big hit, and now it's your signature tune. What was the incentive for writing that?

A Randy: Well, it's a long story. Back in 1977, our band was real good, as far as the material that we were doing. We had a tight group. But the drummer that was playing with us at the time decided he wanted to leave the group. Then Teddy was thinking about moving to Nashville, too, and trying to make it writing songs. So I set down one day and thought about myself, and my career, and what I wanted to do. And the line "My home's in Alabama," and our band "Alabama," just kept coming to me. So I wrote down that line. Then Teddy came down to my trailer one day. We was livin' in Myrtle Beach, South Carolina, at the time. And we wrote the chorus and the verse. We were real happy about the way it came off. The music came out of a jam that we worked up, and then we worked up the music with the words. It just fit perfectly, as far as the way we wanted it to sound. Then we done it that way—just one verse and a chorus—for quite some time. Then we decided to record it. It was gonna be on our third road album, which we never released to distribution. And we finished up the second verse just before we recorded it. It's pretty much an autobiography, really, of me and Teddy's lives. The only thing about it that's kind of different is the "L.A." in the song stands for "lower Alabama." That was a joke, in a way. Where we're from, see, we consider ourselves "Yankees." You know, we're from northern Alabama.

Teddy: Or U.A.—"upper Alabama."

Randy: But we never thought anything would happen to the song. It was originally about ten minutes long. We just got into a jam on the end of it. And then, after MDJ [MDJ Records, based in Dallas] got "I Wanna Come

Over" to thirty-three on the charts, they said, "We think 'My Home's in Alabama' is the song we want to do next." But I didn't think the song would ever be a hit. I thought it might be a hit in Alabama, but it turned out to be a lot bigger hit in a lot of other states than it was in Alabama. Anyway, they shortened it down [to six minutes and twenty-four seconds]. They went in the studio and edited it, over, and over, and over. We went in and redid the vocal tracks.

Teddy: They added strings and—

Randy: We redid practically the whole track, is what it amounted to. And just left the feel the way it was, the tempo and everything. And then we started to get a lot of reaction from that song.

Q Has it become an anthem for Southerners?

A Randy: I wouldn't think so. Not yet. It hasn't had time. But maybe I'm wrong. [The song is now the state's official song.]

Teddy: Well, that lady I told you about paid us one of the highest compliments we've ever had. She said that before she heard the song, she was kind of ashamed of being from Alabama. But after she heard the song, she was proud to be from Alabama. That's a great compliment.

Randy: The part of the song that really comes from my heart is "I'll speak my Southern English as natural as I please." Because I've been through that. When I was in college, people would make fun of the way I talked. Even Southern people would. Maybe it was just hard for them to understand the way I pronounced things. Or maybe I pronounced 'em wrong. But I knew what I was saying. That had always been a pet peeve of mine, and I got a chance to put it in a song. It sure fit right in that one.

Teddy: See, Wildcountry was the name of our band for the first two albums that we cut and sold off the stage. We had a thousand pressed up, trying to get a demo album to get a deal with. And we finally got a deal with GRT for a single, in 1977. Then we changed the name of our band. After checking around, we found there were several Wildcountry bands around. That was the biggest reason we changed the name. We had hundreds of names, and Alabama was the last one we didn't throw out. We had to call ourselves something, I guess.

Q Are you pleased that's what you chose?

A Teddy: Yeah, I think it was a good choice. It's easy to remember, and our record is on the front of the record rack, usually.

Q So "My Home's in Alabama" was a hit on a small label, MDJ Records, where you went in '79, and then you were signed to RCA in 1980 as a result.

A Randy: Yeah, I think that's a direct result of "My Home's in Alabama."

Because the average person that listens to music really understands that song. But I know a lot of musicians who bought that record, too. And, you know, the comments and compliments that they've given us really make it all worthwhile. Course, when your brother musicians tell you that they like the song, that means something. You feel like you've accomplished something.

Q How far did "My Home's in Alabama" get on the charts?

A *Randy:* I think it got to sixteen. But they told us at RCA that they could take it to number one! (Laughter) But see, our problem at MDJ was distribution. It's the same with any small label. When you get in that bracket, the sales, as you well know, account for a lot of the movement up the charts. And they just couldn't get the records out. They done an excellent job, considering. I mean, MDJ had only been in the business for a year, I guess. And for them to take a song that was as long as that . . . See, so many stations plugged the long version of that song. And for them to take it that far, and to get it played that much, was great for us. It was a turning point. It turned everything around for us.

Teddy: It was a reasonable gamble for RCA. By making a showing like we did on an independent label, it made them say, "Well, what would they have done if *we'd* had 'em?"

Q How gregarious is this group, really? Do you play good-natured tricks on each other, for example?

A *Teddy:* Oh, yeah. One of the best ones I ever pulled on everybody in the band was just before Christmas one time. Everybody had been gettin' things on me, and I said, "Well, I'm going to get somethin' on them." So I sat around and thought about it. I came up with the idea for us to draw names and buy each other a present. So I wrote down my name four times, and wadded it up in little pieces of paper. (Laughter) And then I dropped them in this hat, and I said to everybody, "Now, don't tell whose name you got, because it won't be a surprise. It won't be any fun that way." And I said, "We'll hold what we spend on one another to about twenty dollars." So everybody went along with me. And everybody drew, and everybody had my name, of course. (Laughter) I let it ride for about a week. And our drummer at the time got together with Jeff, and somehow they decided to swap names. And this is the only thing that blew it for me. I'd'a had all these Christmas presents. (Laughter)

Randy: Yeah, both of them had the same name. You should have seen the looks on their faces! (Laughter)

Teddy: That's not as funny as what happened to Randy one time, though. We was up at a club in Winston-Salem, North Carolina. And the drummer that was playin' with us at the time had this show he done where he'd do a drum solo and set off fireworks and flash pots and all this kind of stuff.

Randy: And the fire marshal didn't like it. Threatened to close the place down.

Teddy: But one night after we had finished playin', Randy stayed over there talkin' to the guy that owned the place, and they decided to listen to the jukebox. And Randy didn't know that our drummer had reloaded everything. And he walked over to plug in the jukebox, and he accidentally got hold of the cord that plugged up the flash pots.

Randy: I'd been drinking a few.

Teddy: And he plugged it up, and he was standing right on top of one of the flash pots. Needless to say, it was a shocking song he heard on the jukebox.

Randy: Burned my hair and my beard . . . I was lucky to come out of it without burnin' everything I had. Course, another thing, we've had, you know, six or seven drummers that's played with us over the years. And drummers are more unusual people, for some reason. Anyway, we had this one drummer, the first one we ever had after Teddy quit playing drums. We was playin' near Gadsden, Alabama. And this club was like a VFW. And the guy who managed it was the bouncer, too. He had so many black eyes, and so many black-and-blue places on him where people had beat him up every Saturday night. He would approach the fella and say, "Okay, I'm gonna throw you out!" And the guy would go to work on him, and just beat the hell out of him. And he never threw *anybody* out! But anyway, we was playing, and the drummer had a stage that he sat on. We stood out in front of it, you know. And the drummer had a problem. He loved to sip the, you know, stuff, and he sipped it pretty heavy. So we looked back there, and he was real bad. Course, that's the reason why he's not playing with us now. But I looked, and the last thing I saw was his heels. He was goin' off the stage, backwards. (Laughter) And, you know, we lost the drummer for a while.

Teddy: Well, that happened to Mark, too. Not 'cause he was drinkin', though. We were doin' the Ralph Emery TV show here in Nashville early one mornin', and we were gettin' down on "Tennessee River." And when we got to the chorus, Mark's stool broke on him. (Laughter) Last thing we saw was his rear hittin' the floor and his feet goin' up in the air!

Jeff: But he kept playing! (Laughter)

Teddy: But onstage we usually try to be sober enough not to fall down and stuff.

Q So you've paid your dues.

A Randy: Oh, yeah. We did a show with Sammi Smith up in Hartford, Connecticut, one time. And she didn't make the first show, 'cause her plane made a belly landing in New York City. And Waylon [Jennings] was late getting there. So we were the only people there, and we had to play for an hour and a half. And the front of the stage was just old boards that had been just slightly nailed up. And I kind of reached out and touched the front of it, and the whole damn thing just . . . I'd'a fell off thirty-five feet on my head, out on the floor. And then, like I said, we had to play for an hour and a half. And this guy kept saying, "Come on, these people are getting restless." But they couldn't go anywhere, because there was about fourteen inches of snow that had fallen. So Waylon finally got there, and he played his first show without a drummer. His drummer couldn't make his flight. And then Sammi got there, and she decided not to go on to the next place. So we were stuck there in Hartford. I think she got scared because of the flight. And she decided to ride back to Nashville with Waylon. So we were left up there, but she paid us for the show in Massachusetts, even though she didn't make it. Anyway, we came back, and this was during the gas shortage. (Laughter) We stopped at every station between the New Jersey line and Hartford, Connecticut, and got a dollar's worth of gas. And we finally got down to Virginia, and things started getting a little better.

Teddy: I remember one of the guys went to get gas that morning, and he was gone four hours. They would only let you have two dollars' worth at the most. We had to go from one station to the other and set in line before we could start back to Alabama with a full tank. It was rough.

Q When was this?

A Randy: This was in '73, I guess, '73 or '74. It was really something, you know. It was awful.

Q Who else did you back up during these days?

A Randy: Bobby Bare . . .

Teddy: Jerry Wallace . . .

Randy: Ray Pillow, Narvel Felts, Mel Street . . . Boy, so many, it's hard to remember exactly.

Q What kind of band do you think you are? How would you classify yourselves?

A Randy: Country. Progressive country, I guess. Southern country, or—

Teddy: Modern country.

Randy: Well, what we do is, we write our songs. If we get somebody else's song that they've written, we take that song and we do it the way we can perform it best onstage. Whatever people classify that as, you know, that's left up to the radio people and the press. To me, it's country. It's not rock 'n' roll, that's for sure. And I don't think it's rock. Maybe there's some bluegrass there. Maybe MOR [middle of the road] a little bit, because we have some harmonies that aren't just straight country. I think that was probably a problem with our music for a while, because people couldn't just take it and classify it and say, "Well, that's country." Even though the songs that we got on our albums could have been done differently to match a certain kind of music, like rock or country.

Teddy: A country artist could have cut it, and it would have been a country song. Or a pop artist could have cut it, and had a pop song.

Q You said earlier that you look for positive songs. There are a lot of romantic love songs on your albums, but "Feels So Right" has been your first positive love song released as a single. Your hits have been with different types of material, either the personal, Southern material, with "My Home's in Alabama," and "Tennessee River," or the songs about unhappy love affairs, "Why, Lady, Why" and "Old Flame." Was it a conscious choice to stay away from upbeat love songs as single material?

A Randy: Well, that's basically what we write about. But in the past, when we started picking songs to do, I tried to get completely out of that. You know, love songs are great. But you have to have a love song that's unreal to get in the Top 10. And I think it's easier for us to have something that's successful if ours is different. "Tennessee River" is a real good example of what I'm talking about. It's got a little bluegrass, and it's just different. There aren't a lot of songs that sound like that song. And, of course, "My Home's in Alabama" is different. Course, now, we work on these things over and over, to try to *make* 'em different. Because it's really a crush to an artist, or a writer, for somebody to say, "That sounds just like something that I've heard." But you can't get too far out with it, because if you go too far, the average person don't know what in the hell you're doing. If it's real crazy chords and stuff, nobody's going to buy the record.

Q How do you work out the harmonies? I read that you used to lie in bed at night and sing until you dropped off to sleep.

A Randy: Yeah, that's really true. I was going to school at Jacksonville State University, there in Alabama, and I was living with Jeff, who was working for the government at the Anniston Army Depot. And Teddy was working in Cookeville, Tennessee, in a carpet outlet up there. He quit his job and came to Alabama. And we took three beds and put 'em in this big room.

And I'd go to school and they'd all go to work, and we'd come in and practice and write in the afternoons. Then we'd all go to bed and we'd turn out all the lights, and we'd start workin' on it. We'd sing and harmonize till three or four o'clock in the morning, and get up and tear out the next day to school or work or whatever. We had this song—I don't know whether you ever heard "Shelly's Winter Love" or not—and we just hit that cold. So I'd come in, countin' off, "One, two, three . . ." And Jeff would be in a dead sleep, and he'd rise up out of the bed and start singing his harmony part. (Laughter) We done him that way all the time. We'd go out and stay out late, and we'd come back in, countin' off the song.

Teddy: But the way we went about it, to rehearse with no music, in the dark, just layin' there flat on your back, using nothin' but vocals to work out your parts, is a pretty different way to go about it. I think it was good, though.

Randy: Yeah, another thing, I sang most of the lead, and the lead singer has to give up that voice change. When you sing, you've got to sing straight. You've got to follow a pattern. You can't do all those neat tricks that people do with their voice. Because if you do, there's no way you can follow that with harmony.

Teddy: Like, it would be impossible for me and Jeff to sing harmony with Willie Nelson, you know, crazy [singing before and behind the beat] like he does.

Randy: That's right.

Teddy: But that's where your good harmony feels right, is in that pattern. And Randy has a real strong voice to carry it through.

Randy: See, people like Willie don't really need harmony anyway. But for us, that's always been a big thing, 'cause we tried to make it as a group.

Q The three of you are cousins.

A *Teddy:* Right.

Q Were you playmates as kids, too?

A *Teddy:* Me and Randy were. We were raised right across the field, well, a couple of fields from each other. We lived about three-quarters of a mile apart, I guess. His father's farm and my granddaddy's farm were joined. And we learned to pick guitars in church. That's where I first started to get interested in music—playing the guitar and singing.

Q You seem to even think alike. When I was flipping the tape over, you just automatically went into a little routine. Are you so in tune with each other after all these years that you don't have to communicate with each other in words?

A Randy: Oh, definitely. We've been together a long time. Maybe politically or spiritually we don't think alike, but as far as music we do.

Teddy: We know each other well enough that we can read each other without saying a whole lot. You kind of know what the other person's thinking.

Q What's the motivation for this group? Why do you want to do this?

A Randy: For me, personally, it's the whole scope of my family. I have relatives that are musicians and singers, and, course, they never made it. They never really pursued it as far as they could have went. They got married and had a family, and went to work somewhere. They had to do that. And, of course, now, I have a much greater goal. I just lost my father. I lost him at the time we were signing with RCA. And it was like the worst part of my life happening with the best. Just yesterday, I was sitting across the table from Chet Atkins. He was always one of my daddy's idols. He idolized the way Chet Atkins plays guitar. And if I could tell him that I set across the table from Chet Atkins, it would be great. But I want to make my wife and my family proud. They've sacrificed for me. And I want them to know that I was serious. That I meant to be, or tried to be, number one. Whether I ever made it to the charts or not, I tried to be number one.

Q [to Teddy and Jeff]: How about for you?

A Teddy: I guess it's the same thing. My mother played and sang—her and two of her sisters used to sing on the radio back when they were girls. And my father was a big lover of country music. He played a little guitar and sang some himself. But I was raised by my grandfather, mostly. And I think it's more of a pride thing, especially since some of the things that happen to you in life make you more determined to succeed. Like, somebody tries to talk you out of it. They say, "What are you doing playing music? Why don't you move back here to Fort Payne and get you a job down at Wendy's? I think I can get you a job as assistant manager."

Randy: (Laughter)

Teddy: Which is like saying, "I have no faith in what you're doing."

Randy: And they say, "Why don't you shave or cut your hair?" This isn't right now. But when we first started, we caught hell for the way we looked. And, of course, we looked more clean-cut then than we do now. But it was really strange. I know my family were always supportive of my career. Now, they never approved of some of the clubs that I had to play in to make a living. But as far as supporting me in doing what I wanted to do, they were behind me. It's real important.

Q What changes do you notice in yourself when you're back home on Lookout Mountain?

A Randy: When I go back home, that's when I really get the desire to succeed, even more than when I left there. Because I see these kids that I grew up with. I see the girls that used to be so beautiful to me, and they're now "old ladies." They've let themselves go, because they've had to work so hard to survive in this hectic world. And the boys that used to weigh a hundred fifty-five pounds and be muscular, well-built guys, now weigh two hundred and fifty, and they look a whole lot older than what they really are. And they've got four or five kids, and the children aren't clothed properly. And their wives are wearing horrible clothing. And they're living in a . . . I hope I don't sound conceited, but do you know what I mean? I like to have something just a little bit better. It makes you want to push on, and it makes you realize that you've been doing something right, too—that it wasn't a big mistake. I don't think that I would have ever fit in, living like that, 'cause I worked a few jobs, like workin' in a factory. Now, I love to work with my hands, but I never could have fit in working in a factory in eight-hour shifts. I done it one summer, and it almost drove me crazy. For those people, that's a way of life. They'll work there twenty years, eight hours a day. And they can live that way. If they can do it, more power to 'em. Somebody's got to do it. But I could never do it. We was talkin' the other day, when we were doin' the RCA show. Jeff asked Teddy if this wasn't better than layin' carpet. And, course, Teddy said, "It's a lot easier, too. I don't hurt my back, or my knee." But, you know, it's not that you care for the work. It's just that you want something that people can say, "Hey, that guy has *accomplished* something." And, at the same time, you're doing what you want to do. Music is a God-given talent. You can't just say, "I'm going to make it in music," and not have any talent. If you could, you can imagine how many people would be in music, because most people look at it as being very easy. And there would be millions of people trying and never succeeding, because the public can pick out someone that don't really have the talent to do it. And they don't ever get to that point. But when you have the talent, I think you should hook it.

Teddy: It's definitely not an easy life, though. Like, not too long ago, we played twenty-nine straight days, seven days a week, without a night off. The bad thing about playing with a group is, when you're sick, you can't leave everybody else hanging, so you go ahead and play anyway. I've played sitting onstage with a flight jacket on to keep the chill factor down. You sit there and shake and shiver and have a high temperature, but you still go ahead and give it your best effort, because the other guys can't afford not to play, for one thing, especially in the early days.

Randy: But it pays off in other dividends, working as a band.

Teddy: Yeah, one thing I feel real good about is our success as a band. For so many years, people would say, "Well, yeah, Randy's got a good voice there, a good lead voice. Maybe we can sign him," you know. But Randy always stuck with us to say, "No, you have to take us as a group." There's not a whole lot of groups that get into the country charts. I know there's the Charlie Daniels band, but there's still Charlie. As far as a band, one of the few who were successful at it was the Eagles, when they started their country stuff. But it's quite a good feeling to know that you're giving hope to other musicians who play in a group. I just hope we don't let any of 'em down.

$\mathcal{S}$everal years ago, when he and his wife went on a Caribbean cruise, Chet Atkins, "off duty" for the first time in a while, decided to grow a beard and try to relax. But, as Atkins, otherwise known as the "CGP," or "Certified Guitar Player," mentions here, he hardly goes anywhere without his guitar. One night Atkins and songwriter John D. Loudermilk were sitting around the ship trading licks, and a small crowd began to gather. "You sure can play that guitar," a fellow told him afterward, "but I'll tell you one thing—you ain't no Chet Atkins."

That Atkins' name is a household word speaks enormous testament to the man born Chester Burton Atkins in 1924 in the Clinch Mountain community of Luttrell, Tennessee, about twenty miles from Knoxville. Although music was all around him—his father, James, was a classical musician and music teacher, and his brothers and stepfather also played guitar—his was less than an ideal childhood. His father deserted the family when Chet was a child, and the boy, poor, malnourished, and asthmatic, was often confined to bed, where he concentrated most of his physical and mental energy on the guitar. "I was, like a lot of musicians," says Atkins, whose face resembles that of a friendly Cherokee Indian, "very introverted, very shy, and I wanted atten- tion. I could get it with the guitar."

At eighteen, Atkins found employment playing his second instrument, the fiddle, on WNOX in Knoxville. From there, he toured with Archie Campbell and Bill Carlisle, backing on both the fiddle and the guitar. In time, he took a succession of jobs in country and pop radio, but both his personal ambition and the musical perfection he expected in himself and those around him led to numerous sackings. ("I was always getting fired. My mother used to tell me, 'You'll never hold down a job. You're always telling everybody what to do.' And I was! I only knew four chords, but the group leader usually only knew three.") In 1944, for example, he auditioned—unsuccessfully—for a spot with Roy Acuff's Smoky Mountain Boys and later lost his job at Chicago's WLW in 1945.

The following year, Atkins came to Nashville as part of the Red Foley band, with whom he made his Grand Ole Opry debut. Soon, however, he was talking with people about making his own records—against Foley's wishes. "He said, 'I want you to just work with me. I don't want you recording with anyone else,' " Atkins remembers. "And I said, 'I don't want to be working in a band all my life. I want to be a star just like you. I want to be famous like you.' " Shortly thereafter, Atkins lost his solo guitar spot on Foley's radio show and quit the group altogether.

Finally, in 1950, when Mother Maybelle Carter and the Carter Sisters "adopted" him and he became a regular on the Opry, Atkins settled down in Nashville. In short order, he began playing in some of Music City's earliest modern recording sessions, his dexterity quickly making him one of the busiest studio musicians. Today, while those who know the unassuming Atkins sometimes lose sight of the fact, it is generally ac- cepted that Atkins is the most versatile, if not the best and most famous, popular guitar player in the world—a man who has mastered not only country guitar but also classical, blues, flamenco, and jazz, or, as his press release boasts, "every musical form from bluegrass to Bach."

As a musician, of course, Atkins is best known for his unique finger- picking style—the thumb sounding out the rhythmic bass notes and three fingers picking out the melody—which has influenced every guitarist who came after him. But Atkins' contribution goes beyond that. From starting out as the top session guitarist for RCA's Nashville sessions, he moved up to the post of A & R (artist and repertoire) assistant under Steve Sholes in 1952, assisting Sholes on Elvis Presley's "Heartbreak Hotel" sessions in 1955. The first country music star to become a major record company executive, Atkins was named manager of Nashville operations for RCA in 1957, at the age of thirty-three. As he moved through the ranks there, becoming A&R director in 1960 and a company vice president in 1968, he developed what has come to be known as the Nashville Sound—the production style that, whatever its critics may say, kept country music alive during the heyday of rock and roll.

As such, wrote William Ivey in *Stars of Country Music*, "Atkins' career is unique in a single respect: Every stage in his development as a musician has been matched by an increased impact on the business side of music. Chet has thus possessed an opportunity afforded few artists, that of consistently imposing his personal interpretation of country music upon a major corporation (RCA) and upon many significant country entertainers"—including Dolly Parton, Charley Pride, Don Gibson, Bobby Bare, Jerry Reed, Waylon Jennings, Eddy Arnold, Dottie West, Floyd Cramer, and the Everly Brothers, all of whom he either discovered, recorded, or signed to the label.

In 1977, Atkins marked his thirtieth anniversary as an RCA recording artist, with more than 100 albums to his credit. But as "Mr. Guitar" readily admits, his own career as an artist suffered during the quarter of a century he oversaw the RCA Nashville operation. ("I've done all my [own] albums half-assed at home in the basement," he told writer Paul Hemphill.) Partly for that reason—and because he dislikes the way today's music moguls run the industry ("spending way too much money to make records, making a lot of money for themselves at the expense of the artist")—he resigned his executive position with RCA in 1981. Late in '82, he moved his artist affiliation to CBS Records—RCA's chief rival.

From the beginning, though, Atkins' CBS output raised eyebrows. First came an exercise LP (*Work It Out with Chet*) that hardly seemed like anything worth leaving RCA for. But what Atkins was really aching to do was to try a contemporary jazz album, and in 1983 CBS released *Stay Tuned*, a jazz-fusion effort with fellow guitarists Larry Carlton, Earl Klugh, George Benson, and Mark Knopfler of Dire Straits. The album made the Top 20 on the jazz charts, and two other fusion LPs, *Street Dreams* and *Sails*, followed.

With the jazz division now marketing Atkins' albums, in some ways his Grand Ole Opry days seem a lifetime ago. For a brief moment recently, that idea gained credence when Atkins—steamed over the change of criteria for nomination for the Country Music Association's Instrumentalist of the Year award, an honor he has won eight times—sent in a letter of resignation from the organization, only to be talked out of the notion by Jo Walker-Meador, the CMA's executive director.

Still, the awards and the honors keep coming, not only for his artistry but also for Atkins' help in making Nashville the recording center it is today. Several times the winner of *Playboy* magazine's jazz poll, as well as the recipient of similar honors from *Downbeat, Guitar Player,* and *Frets* magazines, Atkins, a frequent performer on National Public Radio's *A Prairie Home Companion,* has also collected seven Grammy awards. In 1973, at forty-nine, he was inducted as the youngest member of the Country Music Hall of Fame, and in 1983, the Academy of Country Music gave him its Distinguished Pioneer Award. Before the latter presentation, Buck Trent summed up the thoughts of several generations of musicians: "Thank God he doesn't play a banjo!"

The following interview took place over a span of months in 1981, and was recorded in Atkins' Nashville office, backstage during the rehearsal of a TV show, and on the telephone. In person, as Bill Ivey has noted, Atkins "projects the image of a country boy who has never quite grown comfortable with his accomplishments."

Q Why, after all those years, did you decide to leave RCA, where you'd had your whole career?

A Well, I worked for a wonderful man named Steve Sholes for many, many years. He discovered me and signed me up, and I owe him everything. The problem was, I worked too hard. I'm sure that if he hadn't died in 1967, I would have. But when he died, I made up my mind that I was going to slow down, so I started hiring people, and gradually I turned all the artists over to other A&R men, with the exception of Hank Snow and Jerry Reed. I recorded them for quite a few years after I had turned Dottie West and Hank Locklin and people like that over to someone else. I did that because I realized that the stress was getting to me. I was pretty ill ten years ago [with colon cancer, which recurred again in the early '80s], so I've been backing away from it ever since. The last three or four years I was with RCA, I just had an office over there. They paid me a salary, I went in and told people, "You're talking to the wrong guy. You've gotta talk to Jerry Bradley and Joe Galante downstairs. They handle that." So that was all I did. I never really liked being an executive. You know, I'm a guitar picker, and trying to do something else was stressful for me because I never learned how to say no to songwriters and artists who wanted to record for me. So, anyway, I got to feeling kinda guilty taking the company's money and not doing anything for it.

But they used to tell me, "Well, consider it pay for years gone by when we didn't pay you enough money." And I said okay, and I accepted it for quite a few years. But then I looked around, and I had so much junk, and I didn't have any place for my awards. I'd always kept them down in the basement hidden away. So I bought an old house just down the street from RCA, and now I have room for all my junk and my guitars, my photographs and my awards, and it's fun. Somebody got out the rumor that I was starting a museum, but I'm not. No museum. I wouldn't do that, but Red O'Donnell [the late columnist for the Nashville *Banner*] printed that as a joke, and a lot of people believed it.

Q When you first left RCA, you said you were leaving as an employee, but not as an artist. Then not too long after that, you signed with CBS. At the time, you said the reason was "enthusiasm," that at CBS "they still feel that there's life after thirty in the record business—one can still sell records after thirty."

A Yeah, well, there was a little lack of interest at RCA. You have regimes running most record companies that are youth-oriented, and they aren't interested in the old artists, so they drop them. I saw what was happening, and I felt I had to go where I could keep developing my career. I didn't have anything to do with the running of the operation at RCA for many years, but I didn't approve of them dropping a lot of the artists who'd been with the label a long time. I thought they should have kept people like Hank Snow. He'd been with RCA since 1936, and I think that's a hell of a record. I'd like to have seen him stay around longer, not because he'd been with the record company so long, but because I think he's a great artist and a great singer, and I think he can make hit records. But, you know, if the people running the companies don't think so, then it's just futile to keep them around. And he's not the only one. There are many, of course. And it's happening in all the record companies, not just RCA. I hired people over there to run the place and that's what I wanted, and they run it their way, and I didn't complain. I'm not complaining now. I'm just saying that's the way it is. I wouldn't do it that way, but that's the way they do it, and I had to approve. Because I didn't want to be running the company. I wanted to get out of all that stress and work and let them worry and lose sleep like I used to do.

Q You mentioned your awards a while ago. You've been nominated for the CMA Instrumentalist of the Year every year since the awards have been in existence, and you've won it many times. Do you become jaded after a while?

A You know, I should be in the damn *Guinness Book of Records*. I've been nominated ten or eleven times and *not* won it. For a while, I won it about three or four years straight, and then I never expected to get that again. Never. Well, I quit goin' for a while in 1980. I said, "Hell, I'm tired of going down there and not winning. I've lost long enough." [After his awards in 1967–69, he did not win again until 1981, after which he won every year through 1985. He failed to be nominated in 1987, due, he says, to a mix-up in the new rules for eligibility.] You know, they put the camera on you and you lose. For ten damn years—that's too long.

Q But *Cashbox* magazine named you Best Instrumentalist of the Year something like eighteen years in a row. And *Playboy* gave you the same award, with the *Playboy* readers giving you top honors in the jazz poll three or four times, not to mention the Grammy awards. How many of those have you won as an artist and as a producer?

A I've won seven or eight, I think. Isn't that amazing? I gave Shel [Silverstein] one of 'em.

Q You gave away a Grammy?

A Well, he won one, and he gave it to a girlfriend, and then he wanted one to give to his mother. So he said, "I'll just take one of yours," and I said, "Okay." You're not really allowed to give them away, I found out later, but Shel's got one of mine. I won mine 'cause there wasn't any competition back then, I guess.

Q I'd like to get your thoughts on some of the people you worked with or discovered. Let's start with Dolly Parton.

A Well, the first time I ever heard Dolly Parton was many years ago. She was nine or ten years old, and she came over and did a talent show that was on WSM on Friday night. They used young people on there. Margie Bowes was also a part of that. But anyway, she appeared, and an announcer up there, Grant Turner, liked her and brought me a tape on her and said, "She's sensational." And I listened to it and I said, "Yeah, she's all right, but she's only nine or ten years old. She needs to go to school." I think I told him to talk to me about her later, or something like that. But she sounded entirely different than she does now, the best I remember. It was a little young voice, kinda low, not high like it is now, the best I remember. She must have been trying to sound more mature. Really, she sounded like a little man. I've gotta ask her about that sometime and see if she's had a sex-change operation since then. But in essence, I guess you could say I turned her down that time. I didn't the next time, of course. That's what's important. But one time we were rehearsing a TV show out at Opryland, and I was sitting there waiting for something to happen. She came walking across the stage with a pair of real tight pants on, and she walked up to me and said, "I saw you lookin' at my crotch." And it embarrassed the hell out of me, and I said, "Well, it was only a glance. Damn, I'm sorry!" And I really didn't realize I had done it. But she accused me, and I suppose I did. And I said, "Well, you do that, too, once in a while, don't you?" And she said, "Oh, sometimes," and she went giggling off. She loves to tease, Dolly does.

Q You also have a cigar story to tell about her.

A One night we were doing another show out at Opryland, and we were leaving, I guess, and she was with one of her girlfriends. And she said, "If that SOB doesn't get away from me with that cigar, I'm gonna die." And, of course, she was talkin' about me, and I heard her, and I said, "Dolly, it's me." And we had a laugh out of it. She didn't know who I was. I apologized, because I would have put it out or gone off by myself and smoked it if I'd known it bothered her that much. But she called me an SOB, and she didn't abbreviate it, don't you know. And it hurt my feelings. But I'm over it now. (Laughter)

Q You told me one time that Porter Wagoner's story of how Dolly came to be signed with RCA is not entirely accurate. His version is that when he brought you a tape, you refused to sign her at first, saying, "Porter, I don't think she'd sell, because she just cannot sing!" He says he talked you into taking her on the strength of their duets, and promised that if she lost RCA any money, you could take it out of his royalties.

A Well, the truth about how Dolly was signed is very simple. Porter had had a girl singer named Norma Jean, who got married and left, and I said, "Who are you gonna get to replace Norma Jean?" He said, "Well, I'm thinkin' about Dolly Parton." I said, "Who's that?" And he said, "She records for Monument, and she writes songs, and she's great." And I said, "Well, good." He was gonna use her on his TV show, and I said, "Can you get her off of Monument and get her over to RCA when her contract runs out?" And he said, "Yeah, I think so." So he brought her over, and I sent off to New York for a contract, and we signed her up. That's the story on it. There are other stories that contradict that, but I know the truth, and the truth has set me free. Really, that's the truth. When Porter brought me her tape, I listened to it and I said, "She's fine." I suppose Porter just told Dolly I didn't like her to strengthen himself with her, and it ended up at my expense. But anybody who knows me knows I'm not that type of person. I never have done that to anybody. When I was recording people, I let all the artists do as they wanted to do, and if they were wrong, we didn't do that anymore, you know. But that's exactly what happened. If I had felt that way and said I couldn't stand her singing, I wouldn't be able to face that girl. But I've always loved Dolly, and I am telling you the truth. I guess it is true that she got her contract on the strength of the duets, and through his TV show, because he needed somebody to replace Norma Jean and do duets with him. But I can't remember saying anything like "Well, I like Norma Jean better," because Dolly wrote the songs, and I thought, "Yeah, she's a good writer." There was nothing that I said that put her down in any way that I can remember, but it's been quite a few years, you know, and you forget. The reason I mention that is, I heard her on the radio one day doing an interview, and she said, "Chet didn't use to like my singin', but now he does." And I thought, "What in the world is she talking about?" So the next time I saw her, I asked her. And she told me this story that Porter told her about how I signed her. And I said, "Well, as the years go by, you'll find out that it isn't true." I think she's found out now. But I wondered how in the hell she'd been able to face me thinkin' that all these years.

Q What sort of memories do you have of Hank Williams?

A Hank I knew very well. We tried to write songs together a couple of times, and he always smelled very strong of bourbon. He was a very funny guy. I think people think of him as a sad, melancholy sort of guy, but he was very funny, and always speaking his mind, hurting somebody's feelings. But he could be very nice, too. Hank didn't have too much education, and he was ignorant in a lot of ways, but he was very bright and clever. He recorded for MGM, you know, and one time they kept calling down, wanting him to go into the studio and make some records. And he kept saying, "My throat's sore. I can't record right now." And they kept calling, wanting him to record something, and finally they said, "What the hell's it gonna take to cure you of your sore throat?" And he said, "I think about twenty-five thousand dollars would do it." (Laughter) So they sent it down, and he recorded. But Hank was quite a guy. I played on some of his records, and the last song I recorded with him was "I'll Never Get Out of This World Alive." I remember thinking, "Hoss, you're not just jivin'," because he was so weak that all he could do was sing a few lines and then just fall in the chair. When I was with the Carter Sisters, Hank had his band, and we played Kansas City together for a few days. He was straight at the time, and I remember seeing him buy a stack of comic books at night and take 'em up to his room to read. That was his reading material. I often wondered if that's where he got his ideas for songs.

Q What about the rest of the Carter Family? Did you know them, too?

A Not really to tell any anecdotes about. I knew the old Carter Family, but

I never saw them work together. I knew A. P. and Sara and Maybelle, and I loved Maybelle very much. I used to go see her a lot before she died.

Q Elvis?

A Elvis was a very shy sort of person, especially around older people, like myself. I was eight or ten years older, I suppose. It was "Yes, sir" and "No, sir" all the time. But he was very talented, and I respected him a lot. We all knew he was going to be a very big star, because he had gotten so hot in Louisiana and Arkansas and around. But when Mr. Sholes first signed Elvis, he was afraid he had made a bad deal, because right away Carl Perkins got a smash out called "Blue Suede Shoes." And Steve called Sam Phillips and said, "Did I buy the wrong boy?" And he thought a minute and said, "No, you bought the right boy. Don't worry about it. Elvis is the one." And, of course, he was. But Mr. Sholes called me and said, "We're gonna record Elvis, so get a band together and hire some singers and rent the studio." And we worked together two or three times, and then he started those all-night recording sessions, and I dropped out. But the first sessions with Elvis were done over on McGavock Street, in that studio that RCA built there with the Methodist Church. And I remember one time Elvis started jumping around and he split his pants right in the seat, don't you know, and he asked somebody to go back to the motel and get him another pair. I'll never forget them—they were pink with black piping on the sides. Anyway, when he changed pants, he left his old ones laying around someplace, and the next day, this girl who worked for the Methodists found them. She said, "What am I supposed to do with these pants?" I said, "Keep 'em. They'll be worth a lot of money one day." And she thought that was very funny. But six months later, I heard she was trying to get on *I've Got a Secret.* Her secret was gonna be that she got Elvis Presley's pants. (Laughter)

Q You and Owen Bradley created what has come to be known as the Nashville Sound. The general definition of that is country music done up with pop instrumentation and pop attitude, aimed toward the crossover market. Has there been confusion over that term through the years? How do you think of it?

A The Nashville Sound? That's just a sales tag, I guess. If you record in Memphis, they call it the Memphis Sound. If you record in L.A., they call it the L.A. Sound. But I did an interview with a German the other day, and he said, "Do you know the Nashville Sound, what it is?" And I said, "No." And he rattled some coins in his hand, and he said, "That is the

Nashville Sound." (Laughter) And I said, "Okay." But it's a sales tag, and I suppose anytime you have background singers and musicians who are primarily from the South, they will sing with a certain sound to their voices, and musicians will play in a certain manner. If there's a Nashville Sound, that's what it is. But I've always just thought it was sort of a sales tag and didn't amount to much.

Q But what about its connotation as a pop approach to making country records?

A You mean it's not pure country? I suppose when it was really in vogue was back when I was recording people like the Browns and Jim Reeves —a lot of records that were country and crossed over to pop. Owen Bradley, as you mentioned, was doing the same thing with some of his people. So that's what came to be known, I think, as the Nashville Sound. And if there *was* a Nashville Sound, it had to be, of course, Floyd Cramer, who played a different piano style that changed the whole world, and the Anita Kerr Singers, who were one of the greatest vocal groups of all time. She was a great, great woman, and had more to do with bringing great artists to town, I think, than anyone. Because she was such a great background singer and arranger, and people loved her because she was such a beautiful and nice lady. But as I say, though, it's just a sales tag, and doesn't mean much to me.

Q I've read where you've apologized for bringing the pop sound to country records.

A That was quite a few years ago. I'm not apologizing anymore. It's gone so far pop now, that anything I did was very minuscule—very insignificant. But we had to do that, because when you're making records, you try to keep your job. And the way you keep your job is to sell records. And the way to sell records is give those friends and neighbors something different all the time. They demand it. Anytime you put out a record, it's gotta have a hook in it—some little surprise that they didn't expect. And the way you do that is maybe put strings on a record, and if that sells real well, then you do that again. And then you try some other background—voices, or harmonica, electric guitars in harmony, and you experiment around. And whatever sells, that's what you use. So maybe once in a while you'll use horns in the background, and if that sells, you do that again. Just trying to make hits for the artist, and trying to make yourself secure with a job with a company, and of course, the DJs are doing the same thing—they're playing records that they think will get listeners for them, so all the music takes a certain direction. Maybe it's uptown. Maybe it's back to the country, we hope. I think also that once you get into those things, then you have everybody else in the business conforming. And they'll say, "Well, So-and-So is selling records—let's do this." So you get an awful lot of conforming. You get conformity in the radio station programmers, because they say, "Aw, that's not what's hitting—that's not it." And I think a lot of great records don't get played because they don't conform. I don't produce much anymore, but if I did, I would look around, and when everybody's going North, I'd go South. I'd do something different, and get attention. Because that's the way you start trends. That's the way you sell millions of records, as opposed to thousands. You come along with an artist who is very different, or you come up with some sound, like I did with the Floyd Cramer sound, if I can be so immodest. But I knew that was a smash sound, you know. Why conform and do what everybody else is doing when you can come up with a brand-new thing and sell millions of records?

Q So if you were producing now, what would you do? Come up with something totally new?

A I'd be more enterprising and experimental than the people are. I'd try all kinds of new sounds and new things to try to get million-sellers. And maybe I would fall on my face, but I'd give it a try. That's the advantage I had back when I was making a lot of records. I was a guitar player, and I could play concerts and make a living. So I didn't care that much if I got fired. You know, I loved the money I got, but it didn't matter that much to me, so I experimented a lot. And then after I had a little success, I really experimented, because it gave me confidence, and I knew I could try a lot of different things. And because I was square, the people would like it, because the people who buy records are pretty square. So I felt pretty secure in my job.

Q Do you still think you're square?

A Yeah. I like the melody. I can play you the melody on the guitar, I'll bet, fifty different damn ways. And I used to sit around when I was a kid and figure out how to do that. See, Ernest Tubb came along when I was a kid, and his guitar player played the strict melody, and I knew that's what people liked. They used to have a sign in the King Records studio in the forties that said, "Where the hell's the melody?" So I learned to play the melody all kinds of different ways, and I learned to phrase in many different ways, which has always been an advantage to me.

Q It's curious how some guitarists name their instruments after women. Do you ever think of your guitar as a woman?

A I used to do that. I used to call my guitar Betsy, or something, and then B. B. King started doing that a few years ago. And I thought, "Boy, I had that idea!" I've had so many similar ideas and didn't use them. Yeah, the guitar has always been with me everywhere I go. It's my security thing. I hardly ever take a trip without it, and a lot of times, I'll take it and won't even play it. But I feel very uncomfortable when I don't have it with me. It's like I left home without my shorts on, or something. So I always take it with me.

Q As a child, you were marked by poverty, malnutrition, and asthma, without much opportunity to change things. You've said that you were "from so far back in the sticks, I didn't know anything of the world. I didn't know how to dress. I didn't know if green went with blue. I didn't know how to order food in a restaurant. I'm still very ignorant. I still learn things." With such humble beginnings, do you feel that you were fated to do what you've done with your life?

A No, I don't believe in things like that. I think you kinda shape your own destiny. I had a father who was a musician, and my brother was a good musician, and the neighbors played, you know. When you're a kid, you want to be like your idols, and in my case, my idols were my father and brother, so they inspired me to play music. I also admired inventors when I was a little kid, and people who could write and draw pictures. So years later, when a guy would come in to see me with a great song, I admired him so much and I was nice to him because he did something that I would like to have done.

Q But your father never really approved of your style of music until years later, right?

A Yeah, he didn't think much of the guitar. He wanted me to be a violinist or a piano player, and I rebelled, like all kids do, and played guitar because he didn't like it, I suppose.

Q You have a laid-back, easygoing manner about you, and yet a lot of people are in awe of you. They snap to attention whenever you walk by.

A It's all PR.

Q Why do you think that is?

A I think you gain that probably by being around a long time, and being known a long time. You kind of become a legend in your spare time, and people look up to you because they've heard you so long. I do that with certain people, I suppose. People I've idolized for years and years. I feel kind of uncomfortable around them, and I don't open up the way I should. I think that hurt me a lot when I was producing, because a lot of the artists couldn't relate to me too well. They maybe felt uncomfortable around me, because they thought I was a better musician, or more famous or something. And I think that probably hurt me with some artists who are very, very sensitive. I can understand that, because I would be the same way around somebody that I idolize.

Q Have you always been secure about your talent?

A No, not at all. Every time I go out it's Amateur Night, I feel. But I practice, and struggle through it. Every time you go out, you take a chance on embarrassing yourself, and sometimes I do, but the applause comes a lot more often than the boos. I've only been booed about one or two times in my life, and that was many years ago, so it's worth it all.

Q How do you think the history books will record what you've accomplished up to this point?

A I don't know. I told somebody the other day that I didn't think I'd contributed a hell of a lot. I knew a good song when I heard it, and I knew when to keep my mouth shut and let the artists and musicians come up with good arrangements, and occasionally I made a suggestion or two. But I think just about any good musician could have done that. I was just lucky. I was in the right place at the right time, and I was fortunate enough to be Mr. Sholes's friend.

Q How would you *like* people to remember you?

A I never know how to answer that question. I was up in New Hampshire one time, and I was strolling around and found this old graveyard behind the motel there. And I saw an epitaph that read, "As you are now, I once was. As I am now, you soon shall be." That got my attention, don't you know. But to answer your question, I guess I'd like for people to say I played in tune, that I played in good taste, and that I was nice to people. That's about it.

Rosanne Cash

*R*osanne Cash crashed into country music in 1980 like a Roller Derby queen at a square dance. With her New Wave clothes and spiky punk hair—sometimes orange, sometimes eggplant—she seemed more California than country, even if her daddy did happen to be the Man in Black, perhaps the quintessential symbol of post-World War II country music.

Born in Memphis as her father's career was just getting under way, Cash was reared on the West Coast, her parents divorcing when she was eleven. "A total hybrid artist," as she calls herself, she grew up, like Wynonna Judd, with an amalgam of cultural influences, balancing the music of her beehive-hairdo relatives with Joni Mitchell and the Rolling Stones. From her CBS debut album, *Right or Wrong*—deemed "the first real country album for the Eighties" by *The New Rolling Stone Record Guide*—it was apparent that her music was rock-oriented and progressive and that she would fit no existing female country mold. In later years, *Newsweek* would name her "the most intensely modern of Nashville's new women."

Now thirty-three ("I don't think I'm old enough to be in a book about legends"), Cash is a complex and strong personality, her sometimes formidable verve and intelligence tempered by warmth and quick humor. Married since 1979 to singer-songwriter-producer Rodney Crowell, Cash has based much of her songwriting on their often volatile relationship, producing what critic John Morthland has called a "mature new kind of country love song—romanticism with a hard edge."

That element of Cash's music was never better expressed than on 1985's *Rhythm and Romance*, an album that challenged the boundaries of modern country music in form, content, and even language, Cash insisting on one cut that "I can't live like a whore." Written during "a tough year where everything changed drastically for me personally," the album reached the number one position on the country charts and earned her further serious appraisal from the pop ranks. *King's Record Shop*, coming along in 1987, offered a smaller sound, devoid of synthesizers, with a back-to-basics production approach. "I wanted a real simple, guitar-framed record . . . to try to make the sound get close to the real person," she explains. The LP was hailed as another exemplary blend of traditional and progressive country, ballad and biting rock.

Despite such achievements, Cash, the mother of three, puts family life ahead of her career, refusing to tour very often or very long. The pitfalls of celebrity exist even in Nashville, however, where autograph-seeking fans consider her fair game at the post office and the grocery store. "I just hate it," she sighs. "It makes me feel like I have something on the back of my skirt."

The following interview is a compilation of four sessions that took place in 1981, '82, '84, and '86, at CBS Records-Nashville, at a Music City recording studio, and on the telephone.

Q Rhythm and Romance is by far the most personal album you've ever done. What made you decide to write about such intimacies in your life, and why did you wait three years between albums?

A Well, when I did *Somewhere in the Stars*, I really wasn't ready to make a record. I was seven months pregnant when I was doing vocals, and I just wasn't feeling aggressive or uninhibited, or willing to take risks. Now, of course, Rodney says I made it against his advice. (Small chuckle) But I was feeling pressure from the record company to go in and make a record. I hadn't written hardly anything. But I did it, and it was a mistake. And I paid for its being a mistake. It wasn't that great of a record, and it didn't sell as well. So after that, I made a decision that I wasn't gonna go back in until I had proved myself as a songwriter, or until I had written an album. And in the meantime, I had another baby, and then my drug use got out of hand, and I ended up going to treatment. That takes up space in your life.

Q This album is about your marriage, your drug abuse, and your relationship with your father, right?

A Maybe from an outsider's point of view. From my point of view it's more about the process of what Jung called "individuation." It's just an internal process. And the record is about the issues I was dealing with at the time I was writing it. So, yeah, those three issues are part of it. Not all of it, but they're part of it.

Q One song on the album, "Second to No One," is probably the first record ever played on country radio with the word "whore" in it, from the line "I can't live like a whore."

A Yeah, and I think it's hurting me.

Q Why?

A Some stations didn't want to play it because of that.

Q That's one of the songs about the stabilizing of the marriage.

A Yeah. That was just a painful process that Rodney and I went through—trying to learn how to love each other in a real way, and not always trying to demand that the other respond to you on your terms.

Q "Second to No One," where the woman talks about the man having an affair, was supposedly very hard for you to write. In one verse, you say, "She thinks she's got the key to your heart, now I've got to wait by the door." That's a lyric that you wrote years ago and just held on to. Is that a common practice with you?

A That particular line I had written, like, eight years ago. And when I was writing "Second to No One," I was going through my old stuff, and that line was there, and it worked. I'm always saving little notes to myself.

Q Musically, a song like "Never Gonna Hurt" is derivative of a group like, say, the Kinks, but the lyrics are extremely personal. The press material quotes you as saying you wrote it when you and Rodney were fighting, going on to say, "It just shows how lucky you are when you're a writer, because you have a way to release that ugly emotional buildup."

A Yeah, that was just out of anger.

Q What was Rodney's reaction to all these songs?

A Well, I think the first ten or twenty times he heard "Never Gonna Hurt," he got pissed off! (Laughter) But then again, he's an objective songwriter, so he was able to give an opinion that didn't include his own feelings.

Q How were you and Rodney able to repair the marriage?

A We started being honest with each other. We came close to breaking up. But we just love each other a whole lot. And we had to get back in touch with that fact.

Q "Halfway House" is supposed to be your favorite track on the album, with a melody you'd been trying to write for ten years. Reviewers can't decide whether it's about your drug rehabilitation or your relationship with your husband.

A It's about both. And it's about that same internal process of finding your own truth. I wrote it when I got out of treatment. And I was fresh out of treatment, so that was definitely making itself felt in the song. I had just finished reading [Shirley MacLaine's] *Out on a Limb*, too, and I was concerned with trying to get back on a course of finding some kind of spiritual significance in my life that I had been separated from by drugs for so long. So that was real prevalent in my mind when I was writing it, and it was also just capturing what Rodney and I had been going through.

Q What's "so long"? How long were you on drugs?

A Well, my God, I started taking drugs when I was fourteen.

Q Regularly?

A Yeah! I have the emotional maturity of an eighteen-year-old girl.

Q How did this start?

A Oh, recreational. I was growing up in Southern California, and it was just all there, you know. So, I mean, you do it off and on for several years recreationally, and then one day you wake up and it's not recreational anymore. It's the key emotional element in your life. And that's fuckin' scary.

Q How long did the treatment last?

A A month. I learned a lot in four weeks.

Q This was voluntary treatment? You checked yourself in?

A Well, I didn't want to go. But by that time I had gotten so . . . I committed myself, and Rodney insisted I go through with it. I didn't want to be there.

Q Rodney said he had problems, too. Did he go first?

A No. He did it on his own. He's a strong person. And we help each other.

Q How rough was it for you there?

A I don't want to sound self-pitying about it, but at the same time, to be honest, it was excruciating to be away from my kids and my husband for a month. My kids were babies. I was forced to come to terms with a lot of anger and stuff I didn't know that I felt. It's very intensive therapy. It's group therapy and individual therapy from seven in the morning until nine at night, every day. A drug addict is a con artist. And when you have to let go of all those defenses, it's painful. But it's great. I'm just so glad it happened to me. Because I can finally be in touch with myself and find some kind of center. And I like my life a whole lot better.

Q You don't seem as moody now as you used to.

A I'm not as moody, no. I really saved my life. I think I'd be dead now. I really do.

Q It had gotten that out of hand?

A Yeah, it was pretty bad.

Q The song on *Rhythm and Romance* that probably spawned the most speculation is the one about your father, "My Old Man." You've said you had real reservations about putting it on the album, but that Rodney strongly wanted it to come out, and that it means a lot to your father. You also said you wrote it so people would stop asking you questions about him.

A Well, it's just so obvious to me. I don't know why people ask about it. It's awkward for me, because it *is* very personal. It's almost like if you give a gift to someone and people want to know how much it costs. It's embarrassing. I feel like the song is its own statement.

Q David Malloy produced *Rhythm and Romance.* This was the first time you made an album without Rodney. How did you feel about that?

A I was excited and scared. Even part of that German record [on the Ariola label] was with Rodney. But he wants to concentrate on being an artist himself now, and not produce so many records. He produced some of this album. But I was looking forward to workin' with David. I wanted to see what I could learn from somebody else. And I wanted to quit being a pushy bitch.

Q Most people know Malloy only from producing Eddie Rabbitt's records, which is not a sound I associate with you.

A Yeah, but he's grown as a producer. He made great records with Eddie, but the stuff he's doin' now is incredible. Still, this album is a little bit too pop for me. Not pop meaning as opposed to country, but pop as opposed to rock. It's a little bit too layered, too textured. I would prefer to do the next album more spare. But it was still a good process, and I learned a lot from David and I enjoyed working with him.

Q Let me run another quote past you. You've said, "On the first three albums, I was constrained, fearful, and a bit neurotic about making records, because I felt I had to have total control. But this time, I was relaxed and confident."

A Ummm . . . I wasn't very relaxed. I was more confident, but I had just gotten out of treatment two months before, and I was still having anxiety attacks. I don't know. It was different. Before, I was just neurotic about making records and I was insecure. This time I had written almost all of the songs, so I felt I had a certain validity going in. That yes, I should be makin' a record. Before it was, like, "Why the hell should I be makin' a record? I'm not exactly Maria Callas, and I haven't written the whole thing. Although I do think I have a good song sense, and I put together a good group of songs. But is that a good enough reason to make a record?" So I was being really hard on myself. This time I had written almost the whole album. I said, "Okay, I've got a good reason to make a record."

Q Let's talk a little about the album *Somewhere in the Stars.*

A I'm not happy with that album anymore. I wanted to surpass it by so much. It had some good things on it. You know, it was the continuation of this woman's saga of her love life from *Seven Year Ache.* She left him, and he left her, but most of *Somewhere in the Stars* was her just reaffirming her love for this guy.

Q I don't suppose either of these people bear any correlation to anybody we know?

A (Laughter) Well, I guess it's somewhat autobiographical. (Pause) I guess it's *a lot* autobiographical.

Q So even before *Rhythm and Romance,* there were definitely clues to your personality and your life in your songs?

A Oh, sure. I mean, I have to pick songs that I feel relate to me personally. I don't think I could ever just do a song for ulterior motives. It's a real emotional process with me. *Somewhere in the Stars* was the first time Rodney and I wrote a song together—"Looking for a Corner," which was a real sad song, a real introspective song. Actually, I wrote most of it, and he finished it for me. He wrote the bridge.

Q You also wrote the title song.

A Yeah, that was a fantasy waltz through the heavens. (Laughter) Meeting your lover in the heavens, because you're separated from him geographically. It was just this image I had of looking up at the stars and thinking that he was looking at them, too, which I'm sure that lovers throughout the centuries have thought. But then I took it a step further and imagined meeting him up there and dancing around in the galaxies. (Much laughter)

Q How did you think of that?

A Well, I did an interview with a girl named Carol Caldwell, and we were talking about astronomy, because I have a great interest in it, and I was reading books like crazy. And she said, "Why don't you write a song about it?" And I said, "How?" And she said, "I don't know. You figure it out." So it really intrigued me, and for weeks I was thinking, "Space country . . . hmm. How do I do this?" And it finally hit me to just write a love song, only in the heavens somewhere.

Q Was it difficult to write with Rodney?

A No, not this song, because I really had written all of the verses. Then I said, "I can't come up with a bridge," and he just wrote it. But I'm lazy, you know.

Q Was it tough for Rodney to be your producer?

A No, it wasn't tough for him. He's real organized, and he's secure about his own abilities. And he has a broader view of my abilities than I do most of the time. Rodney can be tough on *me,* but only because he wants the best. He's easy to work with in the sense that he's kind and diplomatic, but he's tough in that he gets it out of you. He can be relentless. You know, it can be discouraging to keep doing something and not have it accepted.

Q But on the whole there's been no emotional turmoil in working together so closely?

A The first two [albums] were an emotional turmoil. There was a lot of arguing, and I felt I really had to stand my ground, and stand up for what I wanted, and fight for it every inch of the way. And I just realized that I do trust him, and I don't have to fight for everything. He's not going to steer me wrong, and if there's something I do feel strongly about, he always lets me have my way, because the artist is the customer, as he says, and the customer is always right. (Laughter)

Q Will he produce your next album?

A I don't know. I want to co-produce it, whoever it is. I did want Rodney to do it, but then we're still discussing it. We're not sure that will happen. I've written a couple of songs, and I'm just waiting for my kids to get back in school next week so I can have some time alone to write. [Crowell did in fact produce her next album, *King's Record Shop.*]

Q *Rhythm and Romance* made it to the number one spot on the country charts, but didn't CBS treat it as a pop album, handled out of New York instead of Nashville?

A No. New York didn't give me help. They said they were going to, and they didn't. And I'm not naïve anymore.

Q Why didn't New York promote it? All the publicity came out of there.

A Because that's how record companies operate. They tell you one thing, and then they do another.

Q So how did it get where it got?

A Where has it gotten? It's gotten to the top of the country charts!

Q Where did it get in the pop charts?

A Zero! Well, I think it got into the Top 100 for two weeks or something. But I'm not complaining. I'm not bitter. I create my own destiny.

Q Some of the rock critics gave you a hard time about it.

A Yeah, I got slammed. But, you know, I was expecting it. It was my turn to get slammed—fourth album, they've been nice to me before. It was just my turn. I told Rodney that before the record came out—that they were gonna fry me this time, and a lot of 'em did.

Q Is four the magic number?

A I don't know. I just think it was time, or I had taken too long, or whatever. I don't know. This year, I've really tried to stop letting that stuff get to me.

Q It must have been some consolation when it won a Grammy.

A Yeah, it was.

Q Do you think you and Rodney have suffered in general for your ideas about music and record making, especially in Nashville? Let me read you something you told a Nashville trade magazine: "We've been trend-buckers. We've banged our heads against the wall a lot, and ended up feeling on the fringe in a lot of ways. We approach things in different ways. We sound and look different, and we end up getting shit for it." Is that an accurate quote?

A Yeah. But they should have prefaced it by saying that the reporter said, "Do you consider yourself trendsetters?" And then I said, "No, I consider that we're trendbuckers."

Q What are some specifics of this?

A Well, you know, there's a formula in Nashville about how you should make records, how you should relate to your audience, how much you should tour. The whole thing is a package deal. They might as well turn it into a handbook and give it to you as you enter the business. And I *just don't buy it!* I don't buy it at all! I think there's individual ways to approach life and success. And that's what's caused people to . . . see, I hate to set myself up by saying "rejection," because I don't accept that anymore. I don't think people judge me anymore. But, in a way, it's been brought into relief that we're not the same, we don't do it the same way.

Q What do you mean, "brought into relief"? That it's been a plus?

A Well, it's been a plus in my mind, because I'm more comfortable with my life. But I think maybe there's some resentment outside of us. But I don't want to be negative about this.

Q It's amazing that you can sell records the way you do, because you hardly ever tour.

A Never. Well, I did four dates for this album. But I do tons of TV. God, I do enough TV to make up for tours. But I don't think that I have to tour to sell records. I just don't. Maybe I'd be sellin' five times as many if I did tour, but I don't know that, so it doesn't irk me.

Q That same article, in *Music Row* magazine, quotes you as saying that there are three kinds of country music on the scene today, the neo-traditional, the neo-progressive, and a homogenized blend called neo-Velveeta. Did that just pop into your head?

A (Laughter) Yes. I'm plagued by thoughts like that. They just keep popping in all the time.

Q Do you still write mostly in bed?

A Yes, I love to write in bed.

Q A couple of people have pointed out that in an interview you seem very sunny and upbeat, but that your music is almost the opposite.

A Well, Rodney said once that I was a complex person, but my needs were simple. So I think that pretty well defines my musical being, too. (Laughter) Rodney's pretty smart. Rodney's smarter than I am.

Q When you recorded *Seven Year Ache*, did you think people were going to see it as a radical departure from the first CBS album *[Right or Wrong]*?

A Well, I remember feeling real close to it and real insecure about it after we finished it, 'cause I'd been listening to it for too long. I wouldn't say it was a radical departure, but I would say a definite progression. There's some new groundbreaking on it, I think.

Q The New Wave stuff?

A New Wave-influenced. Maybe a couple of things New Wave-influenced. I didn't strike a pose. I'm not a New Wave singer, but I do listen to it. But it's a country record. With *Right or Wrong*, everybody was saying, "It's a country record." And I was saying, "It's *not* a country record." And then I started realizing that it really was. I mean, no matter what I did, because of my roots and my background and my influences, it's a country record. So was *Somewhere in the Stars*. It's not what you're gonna hear on country radio all the time, but it's New Country.

Q Country punk?

A Punktry! (Laughter) That's what we called it in the studio.

Q Both of the songs you wrote on *Seven Year Ache*, the title song and "Blue Moon with Heartache," went to number one. Before that happened, though, critics singled them out as the best songs on the album. Did you think that was true?

A Well, "Blue Moon with Heartache" is kind of a cop from Tom Robbins' book, *Still Life with Woodpecker*. (Laughter) I love Tom Robbins. But I don't know. That one song on the record, "I Can't Resist," Rodney and Hank De Vito wrote. And it's a beautiful ballad. But I had this concept. I love Judy Garland. And I had this concept of it being one of these sultry, big-band type of things. We were gonna put horns on it, and it has this bedroom saxophone all over it that's just gorgeous. It evokes all these images of "High Atop the Starlight Ballroom," you know, ballroom dancing and everything smoky and your boyfriend just home from the war. All that stuff. I love big bands. And that's what that's like.

Q You wrote a song on your first album called "This Has Happened Before."

A Yeah, I wrote that one when I was in Germany. I was making my first record, for Ariola, which wasn't released here. And I was so depressed. I was living in Munich for two months, just away from everybody. And I laid on the floor for nine hours and wrote it. (Laughter) I was missing Rodney, too. We had a fledgling romance going.

Q What specific input to the records did you have when Rodney was producing you? Did you intend to just let Rodney do it all?

A *No*, I wouldn't let him do it all! (Much laughter) Are you kidding? At that time, I would *never* turn my record over to someone and just go in and put my voice on. *Never!* I mean, I'm a very stubborn woman. I get my way. From the very beginning, from song selection to mixing, it was the two of us, a mutual effort, a communal thing. I mixed the vocals, and he mixed the instruments. That's the way we usually did it. And we chose the songs together from the beginning. He'd find songs and show 'em to me, and we'd decide, and some I found myself. But like on *Seven Year Ache*, there's this song by Leroy Preston from Asleep at the Wheel, called "My Baby Thinks He's a Train." It's a difficult song to sing, and Rodney wanted me to do it, and I was real unsure about it. But we did it, and I just love it. Rosemary Butler and Emmylou [Harris] and I did it in three-part harmony, these Andrews Sisters-type things. [She sings, "Do-do-do-do-do"] (Laughter) It's great!

Q What kind of person would you say Rodney is?

A [loving tone]: Oh, Rodney's shy, and intelligent. He's the most intelligent man I know. He's very honest. And he's got the best ear for songs of anybody in the world. About songs for a specific person, you know? That's where his true talent lies as a producer. He knows what songs are good for me, and he knows where to find them.

Q How did you meet him?

A I met Rodney at a party at Waylon Jennings' house in 1975. Emmylou was there, and he was playing guitar for her. She was singing "Leavin'

Louisiana [in the Broad Daylight]." He had just written it, and she was just about to record it. And I was there sitting under a pool table, being excruciatingly shy. I thought he was great. I thought he was wonderful. And I was watching him, and I thought, "Who *is* this guy? He's so cute." But my first impression of him was, well, I had heard about him, and I thought he was a scoundrel. I thought he was a philandering womanizer. But then when I saw him I thought he was so cute. I didn't know who he was, and yet I did know who he was. It's really strange. The first time I ever saw his name, I got an Emmylou Harris album and I saw his name in the credits on the back. And when I read his name, I just went, "Ding!" Like a little bell went off in my head. It was a real premonition that he was gonna be somebody special to me, you know. And then I met him the first time at that party, and he didn't notice me at all. But I kept seeing him again and again occasionally after that. I don't know. (Uneasy laughter) That was embarrassing to talk about.

Q So what did you do? Did you finally go up to him and say, "I read your name on the back of an album and a bell went off in my head"?

A No, no, no. I was very shy. I mean, I'm still pretty shy, but I was even more shy then. We started noticing each other, you know, and started liking each other. And when I went to Munich, we started a correspondence, and it led to a romance that led to a marriage that led to a baby. (Laughter) And then another one. [She also is mother to Rodney's daughter by a previous marriage.]

Q Did motherhood change you at all?

A Drastically. Because my priorities were totally rearranged, you know? My ambitions for my career became secondary, and my kid became primary.

Q Did you expect that?

A No, I did not expect it. But I mean, having a baby is just wonderful. It's drama—nature's high drama. I think it's gotta change you. You never expect that you'll feel that way about your child, but you do. That you would throw yourself in front of a train for someone, you know? I love having kids. It's the neatest thing in the world. When I get with other young mothers, we just talk about babies constantly. Hours on end. Baby talk. When Rodney was producing Sissy's [Sissy Spacek] album *[Hangin' Up My Heart]* she was pregnant with Schuyler. She was very much into her pregnancy, but she was very composed about it, too. Then when the kid was born, everything broke loose, like, "I can't believe how much I love this child!" I'd bring my kids to the studio, and I remember one day when one of the kids threw up in my hand, I said, "Oh, God," you know, and started bitching. But Sissy said, "It's an *honor* to have your kid do that!" She has the attitude that a child is the most precious thing in the universe. And it is.

Q You wanted to be an actress for a while. Would you have been good if you'd stuck with it?

A I hope I would have been a good actress. I hope I still will be. When I grow up, that's what I want to be. (Laughter) Maybe sometime in the future I can still do it.

Q It's often reported that you studied with Lee Strasberg, but you really only studied at his studio.

A Right. I didn't actually study with Lee Strasberg. I did audit his class. I just sat there. I was too scared to really take a class with him, to sign up for his class, but I did audit it so that I wouldn't have to have him yell at me. But I took a class under one of the other guys at the institute, who did yell at me anyway. But it was great. It was a fabulous experience. It was like therapy.

Q How so?

A Well, the first scene I ever did, I was absolutely terrified. I mean, I was in tears before I went on, I was so frightened. And I went up, I did the scene, and I thought, "Well, that was pretty good." And my teacher paused at the end of the scene, and he lit into me for forty-five minutes. He did not stop yelling at me. He told me everything I did wrong. But to my partner he said *nothing*. Absolutely *nothing!* I mean, I went home and went to bed and I just stared at the ceiling. I was destroyed for a week. And I went back, and he said, "You've got to do the scene over." So the next week, or a couple of weeks later, I went back, and I was absolutely petrified. I did it again, and he just looked at me and said, "Very nice, Rosanne." And I thought, "This guy's playing with my head! I don't know what he wants out of me. He's trying to make me go *crazy!*" The next week after that, he didn't say anything. Then finally he gave me a good review, and I didn't know whether to believe him or not. But they try to provoke you into doing your best work, and it works. He was trying to make me bring those things out of myself, and eventually I did. I learned, you know. But it intimidated the *hell* out of me.

Q Aside from that, why did you quit?

A I didn't quit. I was interrupted. Ariola wanted a demo, and so I went to Nashville and made it. And then they bought the demo, and they wanted me to come make the record in Munich, so I had to quit Strasberg's. I still want to go back. I loved it. My kid sister went. I talked so much about it that she finally went for a few months. She really liked it, too.

Q Would you want to do some acting now, maybe a movie with your father?

A You know, it's funny, because everybody knows that I went to Lee Strasberg, and everybody also knows that I've never done any acting. And so for me to say, "Oh, yeah, I really want to be an actress," it just piles this tremendous thing on me to where eventually if I *do* do it, everybody's gonna be watching. Because I've talked about it so much, and then I'd be confronted with it and I'd have to live up to my own big mouth. I don't know if I could do it. You know, "Well, she's been saying she wants to do this for so long, she'd better be good at it!" So now I'm gonna be too scared to do it, I think. (Laughter) I don't know.

Q But you've had pressure all your life, just being Johnny Cash's daughter.

A Yeah, I know. And I always plowed through it. If I was already real scared to do something, I always made myself do it. Because I figured that bein' scared was the first sign that you *should* do it. And being Johnny Cash's kid has been a pressure. People expect things of you that they ought not expect of you. But I tell you, I expected more resentment from the people in this industry than I got. It's a fact of life that people resent famous people's kids. And I expected it to hit me full force, and it really didn't. I mean, I got some of it when I put my first record out.

Q In what form?

A In reviews. Some reviews were a little bit . . . Basically I got very good reviews, very good press about it, and I was real happy. But some reviews were a little catty. I'd say ninety percent of the critics were objective. They listened, and they critiqued the album for themselves. And I didn't get near as much resentment as I expected. I was real happy about that.

Q What's your objective now?

A To make myself a better singer. That's my immediate goal. I think it's the most honest goal. Instead of trying to make myself a star, I think I should make myself a better singer. Because at this point, I'm not a great technical singer. I think I'm an emotional singer, basically, and I want the technical stuff, too, because I think having that technical ability breeds confidence. And I want that confidence.

Q You don't have much now?

A I have confidence, but I have stage fright, and I want to get rid of it. I don't want to get sick before I go onstage anymore.

Q Tracy Nelson had an earlier recording of "Couldn't Do Nothin' Right," which you also did. I asked her once what she thought about onstage when she was singing those powerful ballads of hers. She said, "I'm thinking, 'Did I put out enough food for the dog?' And 'What am I going to fix for dinner?' "

A (Laughter) That's funny.

Q What do you think about onstage?

A I think about what I'm saying. That sounds trite, but I do. I learned something in acting about emotional recall. When you're doing a scene, you have to think of something from your own past life that will help you evoke the emotion you need in that scene. And I just apply it to singing. If I've gotta sing something really sad, man, I dig down deep in my guts and come up with something and stick it onto that song. I try to. It doesn't always come across, but I try to.

Q What's an example?

A If I told you, then I would probably lose it.

Q How did you feel when your father was inducted into the Country Music Hall of Fame?

A I was never so proud in my life. I was so happy. And he was so happy, too.

Q His speech was very moving.

A His speech was great. I was so happy he said what he did about young people and the stylists. I felt like part of that was meant for me. It was really good. That was a good week for me. My husband got five ASCAP awards, and my dad got elected to the Hall of Fame.

Q What's your father like?

A He's funny! He's got a great sense of humor. When Rodney and I got married, my dad gave me away. And just as we were starting to walk down the aisle, he said, "You want to blow this off and go to a movie?" (Laughter) But he's a gentle man. He loves children, you know. My favorite things are to see him with my baby or with other kids. He's so great with kids. When John Carter [Johnny's son with June Carter] was little, he'd just get himself a carful of kids and go to the movies with them. I mean, eight or ten kids, by himself, and he'd never lose his patience. He still does those things. I've never seen him lose his patience with children.

Q I read that you said he was a bad driver.

A *Lousy* driver! (Much laughter) Oh, *God!* Like I said, it's like his foot's tied to a yo-yo.

Q Did you get your sense of humor from him?

A Part of it, I think. Yeah, we have the same sense of humor in a way. You know, after he got elected to the Hall of Fame, there were all these telegrams and flowers coming to the house. And he came in and he was looking through all this stuff, and he said, "Open that telegram there and see who it's from." So I opened it up, and I said, "Oh, this one's from God." (Laughter) It kind of broke it, because there was just too much goin' on.

Q You were influenced by Joni Mitchell and a lot of other people in addition to your father.

A Yeah, I listened to her quite a bit when I was in my teens, and Crosby, Stills, and Nash, Tom Rush.

Q You grew up in California. Do people tell you that you can't be a country person because of that?

A Yeah. "Well, you're not country!" Well, maybe I am.

Q Do you think of yourself as a country person?

A Ummmmm . . . in a way I think of myself as a country person, with some worldly knowledge, maybe. I mean, I can't strike any poses. I didn't grow up in Tennessee, but I was born in Memphis. And I grew up with all those people around, those [she goes into a country twang] "country sangers," and bouffant hairdos, and goin' to the Palomino and all that stuff. I had some diverse influences growing up. But I really feel my roots are firmly based in country music, and that the music I'm doing is a natural progression of where country music is going. It's lyrically oriented, which is what country music has always been, it's logical music, it's simple . . . maybe some of it does have a harder edge, but I consider myself a country artist.

Q Did your parents meet in Memphis?

A No, they met in Texas at a roller-skating rink. My mom lived in San Antonio, and my dad was based there. He was in the Air Force. And she was skating, and I think he made a bet with a friend that he would ask her out, and he did.

Q Her name is Vivian Liberto. Is that Spanish?

A Italian.

Q You haven't talked about your childhood very much in interviews.

A I don't like to talk about my childhood. In fact, I don't remember much of it. And the things I do remember aren't very happy. So I don't really like to talk about it.

Q How do you see yourself fitting in with other women singers today?

A Not very well. (Small laugh) I don't know. I'm kind of in a no-man's-land of music sometimes, because I don't really fit in with the traditional women country singers. And I don't really fit in with the women rock singers, either. But it's still honest. That's what I think is the most important. If you're honest about what you're doing, then people are going to recognize it, and even if they don't know what to label it, they're going to have to respect it, because it's sincere. In a way, I feel like I'm breaking some new ground that people like Emmylou started. But she's followed a different course than I think I'm going to follow. I think I'm part of the New Country. I don't know if anybody else does, but I do. I think

Rodney and I are both part of that—maybe erasing some of those lines between musical styles.

Q Is that what you mean by New Country?

A The New Country, punktry. (Laughter) Yeah. But I'll tell you the women singers I admire. Mainly Rosemary Butler. She sings with Jackson Browne and Linda Ronstadt. She does mostly backup work. She's a fabulous singer. She's my favorite. And I love Emmylou, but I don't see myself as fitting into a bag with any other women right now. Certainly not Pat Benatar, certainly not Barbara Mandrell. Somewhere in between those two.

Q When you came back from Germany, you played guitar for a while in Rodney's band, the Cherry Bombs. What was that like?

A I was doing these bar gigs with the Cherry Bombs as the rhythm guitarist. And I mean, Albert Lee's in the band, and I have my little electric guitar, and I'm supposed to be playing rhythm guitar to *him!* So I just turned my amp off. In fact, there were many nights I just turned it off. But I'd turn it up just a little bit for the songs I knew really good, you know. It was a great experience. Lot of fun. The Cherry Bombs were high energy, goin' for it.

Q So how did you get your confidence up?

A That was one way I got my confidence up. Another thing was just realizing that everybody in the world is insecure, and it's just a matter of how good your cover is. (Laughter) So you just have to work on that. I mean, I finally just accepted that. And also, I took a couple of voice lessons. Just the fact of him telling me how to connect the diaphragm to the throat, instead of just singing from the throat, helped. That's given me more confidence.

Q Has Emmylou tried to help you much?

A Well, she has been one of my prime encouragers. She's great. Emmylou will play me all these obscure songs, and I'll say, "Oh, Emmy, I want to cut this song!" And she'll say, "No, *I'm* cuttin' it. I just wanted you to hear it." (Laughter) But there have been a couple of times where Emmy and I were gonna cut the same song. Neither one of us has ever gotten *mad,* you know. It's just like with [Crowell's] "I Don't Have to Crawl." She had that on hold for a *long* time. And I thought, "She's not gonna cut it," you know. I said, "Emmy, I wanna cut it." And she said, "Nope, I got it!" And it came out on her next album. And then [Tom Petty's] "Hometown Blues." When I cut it, she said, "I was gonna cut that song!" She said, "You don't mind if I do it on my live album, do you?" I said, "No." [Harris ended up not recording it.] And there have been a couple of others. I mean, it's a natural thing, I think, when you have similar taste. You're gonna come across the same song. But Emmy has been a friend. When she heard my first record, she called me up from the road and she said, " 'No Memories Hangin' Round' is the best thing I've heard in a long, long time." And that gave me a lot of confidence.

Q Are there any misconceptions about you, do you think?

A My hair isn't purple—eggplant—anymore. (Laughter) No, I don't want to talk about that.

Q Anything else?

A Nooooo! I want to keep my mystery.

Q Really?

A Yeah. I'm a believer in mystery. I'm a believer in not giving too much away. If you do, then they don't come looking for it themselves.

Q So when people hear the name Rosanne Cash they should think Greta Garbo?

A No, Judy Garland. I love Judy Garland, like I said. I would like to be thought of as an emotional singer, as she was.

Q An emotional singer—maybe you'll end up in Las Vegas.

A Oh, dear! That's the *last* place an emotional singer should go!

Q Would you play Las Vegas?

A Why not? I'm not afraid of Las Vegas. I love blackjack. I can win at blackjack, too. I'll tell you, the last time Rodney and I went to Las Vegas, we sat down and played blackjack, and we were losing and losing and losing. And then Rodney had to go back to L.A. And by myself, I won back everything we had lost, plus a couple hundred more. Yeah, I can play blackjack.

Q Despite your recent difficulties, you and Rodney are often spoken about as "the ideal couple," and not just in the *People* magazine way.

A Well, we are well suited to each other. I didn't want to settle down before I met him, and he didn't want to settle down before he met me. Some people are just supposed to be together.

Q Opposites attract?

A I think so, yeah.

Q And couples fill voids in each other?

A I think that's true in a lot of ways with us. Because, for example, socially, he's not a real outgoing person. He's not a real party guy. And when we go out socially, I'm the flirtatious one, and he thinks it's cute that I flit from person to person and do all of this glib stuff. (Laughter) But there are a lot of ways we're different like that.

Q Was there a point when you were intimidated by Rodney?

A Yes. I was . . . oh, for a long time. Especially as a writer. I would feel intimidated about showing him stuff I'd written. But I don't feel intimidated by that anymore. Only when he gets mad do I feel intimidated. (Laughter)

Q Did Emmylou ever intimidate you?

A No, Emmylou never intimidated me. I always had a great deal of respect for her, and I still do, because I think she has a whole lot of integrity, musically. But no, she never intimidated me. It was always real easy to talk to her, because she has a real eclectic taste in music. She would play this weird stuff for me sometimes, like Bavarian folk choirs. (Laughter) I would really get off on it, and all the guys would be throwing up.

Q You talk about Judy Garland frequently. Why are you so taken with her?

A I don't like her self-destructiveness. I think that was real wasteful. But she had an artist's soul. I mean, it was just so apparent. She just lived for her art, and all the pain in her life went into her art. She channeled it into that. And also she stirred something in other people on that emotional level. She said, "If the audience reacts the way that you feel inside, then you're doing it right." And I think that's true.

Q Have you had moments onstage when that happened for you?

A Yeah. Not as many as she did, but moments. I'm still a student. I still consider myself a student. I want to learn more. I just read Maria Callas' book, and I was really taken by her, too. She obviously had a gift for that. I mean, I've only heard her sing on record. I was too young to really see her live. Because she quit performing back in the early sixties. But on record it comes through, too—that great dramatic quality. When it gets to those emotional dimensions, then it really becomes noble. That's when it becomes art, and stops just being a workman's skill.

Q Do you think of yourself as an artist now?

A Yeah, I do. I feel that I'm an artist. I mean, like I said, I'm still a student, though. I'm a student artist! (Laughter) I just want to learn more about the art itself. About the mode of expression through singing. And song interpretation. Song choice is just as important, too. You have to look hard. God, good songs are startin' to get few and far between.

Q In the *Esquire* profile that Carol Caldwell wrote, you told her a dream you had about talking with John Lennon.

A Oh, you know, I was almost sorry I told her that dream. Because it seemed like it cheapened it a bit. It was real to me. And to see it in print, all of a sudden it becomes . . . A lot of times I'll see something in print about myself and it separates it from my life in a way. Do you know what I mean? You see it objectively for the first time, and you think, "Oh, God, the image is getting away from the person." I don't know. I feel strange sometimes when I read things in print that I've said or done. I think, "I'm a *mockery* of myself!" (Small laugh) But it's true that I had a dream about talking with John Lennon after he died. It was a real moving dream. I mean, I didn't know John Lennon. And I had no reason in the world for him to talk to me when he died, but it was great. It gave me a bit of comfort, because he said he was going to hang around and finish his work here.

Q You appeared on *Every Man Has a Woman,* the tribute album to Lennon where various artists—Harry Nilsson, Elvis Costello, Roberta Flack, Eddie Money, and others—performed songs written by Yoko Ono. How did your participation in the project come about?

A Well, I read about it, and I said, "God, this sounds great! I'd love to do that." And the next day, David Sheff, who's a friend of Yoko, a writer, called me. And he said that Yoko liked my work, and she wanted to invite me to be on the album. So I was just knocked out. And then she sent me all of her albums, with the suggestion that "Nobody Sees Me Like You Do" would be the right song. And after listening to everything, we agreed. And Rodney [who co-produced the track with Rosanne] and I went in and did it.

Q Was she there?

A No, she stayed out of the production completely. She just gave us a budget and let us do it. And then when we finished it, we sent it to her, and she really loved it. She said she was listening to it all the time. And then we got to go to her house for dinner on John and Sean's birthday the year it was released. That was just a mind-blowing experience.

Q Why?

A Well, this is a person I've read about my whole life, and I just admire so much, you know, her and John. It was just incredible. Walter Cronkite was there! (Laughter) I mean, how much more prestige can you ask for? Walter Cronkite and Andy Warhol!

Q Getting back to what you were saying about the John Lennon dream and how talking about it cheapened it a bit, I would think it would be very strange to have your personality marketed and presented to the public for the purpose of selling records, which every record company tries to do with every artist. Isn't that what we're also talking about here?

A Yeah, there are some aspects of it that I don't like. It seems sometimes that when you're a public figure, or when you provide a service that is *very* public, like making records or movies, or "mass art," as it were, the public who buys your product thinks that you, too, are public, and should be available to them at all times. I don't think that at all. Montgomery Clift said, "The only thing I owe 'em is a good performance." (Short laugh) Sometimes I feel like that.

Q Where do you draw the line?

A I don't know. Because there *is* a responsibility of artists. I feel very seriously that if you're in the public, then you ought to be an example, and not just be self-indulgent. But there is a point where you've gotta draw the line to preserve yourself—save some for your husband and kids.

Q Did you ever talk with your father about this?

A Yes. My father gave me an excellent piece of advice. He just got out of the hospital, you know. He has ulcers. He has a tremendous amount of stress, which he's just realizing and trying to get rid of. He said that a ninety-year-old woman took him through her house just before she died. And she said to him, "I want to tell you something, and I want you to remember it. Every material possession you acquire becomes a stick to beat you with. Live simply." And I believe it. Live simply, and you'll be happy.

Q What kind of old woman do you think you'll be?

A A writer. When I'm old and I can't get around, I want to just write all the time.

Q Like the short stories you wrote when you were at Vanderbilt?

A Yeah, short stories, novels, exposés . . . (Big laugh) I don't know. I really admired Lillian Hellman. I think she was a great old lady. As far as old ladies go, she would be my role model right now. She wasn't sweet, she didn't jive anyone, she was really straightforward, and a superb writer.

Q Do you have a dark side, as Hellman had?

A A *very* dark side, yeah. But I don't give it away to strangers. That's something I save for the important parts! (Much laughter)

Q You've said you were a tough kid, but do you think you're a tough adult, a tough person? Do you have a strong enough ego to sustain yourself?

A I'm tougher than I used to be! I remember one of the first few nights when I was living in London. Some people invited me out to go to the theater with some actresses who were, like, real struggling London street actresses, who had to scrounge for every break. And those girls were *tough.* They talked tough, and they didn't cut any ice with anybody. And I thought, "God, I'm a *pansy* here! I'm not tough at *all!* I'm so *soft!*" (Much laughter) But I think since I've gotten quite a bit tougher. I think if you have a baby you get tough in certain ways.

Q Which ways?

A Well, it requires a great deal of physical and emotional energy to have a baby. Sometimes, even going onstage when I'd be overcome with stage fright, I'd think, "Well, I had a *baby,* so I can do this. It's not gonna be *that* hard."

Q Is having a baby a sign of maturity to you?

A I don't know about other people, but I don't think I grew up until I had a baby. It made me settle down some.

Q What were you like before?

A More selfish. I mean, your point of view shifts from yourself outward. You want to protect your child and nurture your child, and be an example. You don't want to hurt your kid, and you don't want to be reckless with your child's future.

Q You don't ever resent the hours the kids take away from your creative time?

A They add to my creative time. When you have the ability to add on a whole new room to your heart, it adds to your creativity. You have boundless creativity when you have boundless love. And *that's* a big plus for the future. If you can always draw on that love as a source of creativity, then it'll never run dry. Besides, you can't resent somebody you love that much. If you do it dissipates so quickly. I mean, mother love is incredible. One of my kids still gets in bed with us every night, in the middle of the night. Rodney and I both love it. I think it makes a difference if the husband is there at the birth. It does. You get that instant bonding.

Q When you wake up in the morning and look in the mirror and see that person there . . .

A I think, "Oh God, I'm getting fat!" (Laughter)

Q Are you vain?

A Isn't every woman vain? I think every woman is to a certain extent. Nobody wants to go out of the house lookin' like a dog. (Laughter) Nobody wants to look old at thirty. It's part of the human condition. I'd be lying if I said I wasn't vain.

Q If your record company wanted you to do something that you thought was outrageous, and they said, "Rosanne, if you don't do this, your career is going to go down the tubes . . ."

A Then let my career go down the tubes. I still have to look at myself in the mirror. And besides, that's not true. There's never going to be some stunt or some show that my whole career depends on. It doesn't happen that way, and I'm in it for the long run.

Q You've sort of paved the way for such people as Sweethearts of the Rodeo and Marty Stuart to come on the scene.

A I *have?*

Q Yes. In fact, James Dickerson of the Memphis *Commercial Appeal* says, "Of the New Wave, Rosanne Cash was the first out of the starting gate." Do you feel like a pioneer of some sort?

A Well, you see, I don't like to think of myself as establishment, that I'm back in the ranks, smiling down at all the people I paved the way for. I don't think of myself in those terms at *all*. If anything, I think that I'm more willing to take risks than I ever was, and more willing to step outside of any kind of perception that anybody has. I'm more willing to change than I've ever been, and less afraid of what people think than I've ever been. So I don't consider myself a smiling benefactor. Forget it. I don't buy it. I don't accept it.

Q Why are you less afraid to take risks now?

A Because I'm more comfortable with myself. I let fear take over my life for a long time. And I think a lot of the things I did were just a reaction to my own fear, just a struggle against it. But now I'm just more comfortable.

Q This is a result of the treatment and all the soul-searching you went through?

A Well, I mean, it's all a process that keeps going on, once you start it.

Q So this was a wonderful, cathartic breakout for you?

A Yeah. Definitely.

Q But you still don't feel like a role model in any way?

A I just don't want to set myself up. That's dangerous.

Q What's your motivation right now? What keeps you going?

A What keeps me going is that thing inside that's always pushed me. I guess it's ambition. I don't know. I hope that in its more noble aspects it's just a quest to better myself, to become a better person. Again, to really expand all the potential that's there. I think that's every person's responsibility. I think the greatest sin is wasted potential. I'm writing a song for a film called *Square Dance*, which Michael Nesmith's producing, and I'm writing a song for a children's album, and I've written a song for a play. So I'm starting to write outside of my own little box. And that's something I'm real interested in pursuing.

Q Do you ever think about where you'll be in, say, thirty years?

A No, I never wonder about that. Except I think, "God, I hope I don't get wrinkles in my neck!"

David Allan Coe

$\mathcal{D}$avid Allan Coe has a problem.

Yes, he has a compelling voice, one that's supple, emotional, and full of nuance. And although the cuts on his albums typically run the gamut from the sublime to the ridiculous, he has a gift for writing songs that are more complex and defiant than most, songs such as "Would You Lay with Me (in a Field of Stone)," a number one hit for Tanya Tucker, and "Take This Job and Shove It," a chart topper for Johnny Paycheck.

His problem is his appearance. No, it's really his image. At first glance—and even second—David Allan Coe comes across as a grandmother-raping, motorcycle-riding, black-leather hoodlum, becoming, as Bill C. Malone has suggested, the only performer of the "outlaw" genre to take the label beyond fantasy, beyond association with the Old West, and into the underworld of modern urban society. Tall and wide as a grizzly, the 49-year-old Coe often carries a walking stick guaranteed to pulverize a smart-ass name caller, sports a gallery of tattoos, including one of the devil on his chest, and almost always wears earrings—sometimes the Indian-bead type, or the more pirate-oriented blade-and-anchor variety. And then there's his gold-plated, rhinestone-inlaid fingernail, the whole effect topped off by an avalanche of wavy blond locks, cascading down below the hip pockets of his leather pants. The hair, in fact, resembles a cape, and it's enough of a showpiece to give Crystal Gayle an anxiety attack.

All of this conspires, however, to keep Coe from becoming the mainstream star—or at least the *radio* star—that he desires to be. While his LPs currently sell around the 250,000 mark—a hefty number in country music—Coe has yet to score a number one single, coming as close as number four in 1983 with "The Ride," the story of a hitchhiker's ghostly encounter with Hank Williams, and 1974's "Mona Lisa Lost Her Smile," which peaked at two. His *Greatest Hits* album, released in 1979, eventually "went gold" (selling a million dollars' worth), but with the exception of the aforementioned hits, he rarely hears his records on the air.

"Them radio people don't want no real outlaws," he complains in a frequent gibe at Willie Nelson and Waylon Jennings, "just somebody that looks like one." In that respect, Coe is his own worst enemy, of course, since he has concocted a number of identities for himself through the years, the most famous incarnation being the mysterious Rhinestone Cowboy, replete with black mask. But Coe has retired the Rhinestone Cowboy persona now, at least for the moment. "To tell you the truth," he said in 1984, "I want to be just a person without the flash and the rhinestones and all."

Just who Coe really is—and wants to be—is anybody's guess, but it doesn't help his case that he says he's "into close-up magic and large illusions." The unlikely product of Akron, Ohio, Coe claims to have spent his youth, beginning at the age of nine, in various reform schools and jails, for offenses ranging from possession of burglary tools to car theft and, later on, violations related to membership in motorcycle gangs.

The first time Nashville paid any attention to him was in the late '60s, when he'd parked a hearse with his name plastered on it in front of the Ryman Auditorium and pretended to be a star. When that failed to draw the attention he wanted, he circulated the story that he spent time on death row in the Ohio State Penitentiary for murdering a fellow inmate who smiled at him in the showers—a story that journalistic research failed to corroborate.

Signed to the independent SSS and Plantation labels in the early '70s, Coe initially wrote songs about prison, in an impressive, if derivative, country-flavored white blues style. In 1974, Columbia Records came courting, partly because of the success Tanya Tucker had with "Would You Lay with Me" the previous year. Here, with *The Mysterious Rhine-*

stone Cowboy, Coe began to develop his personal stance, putting a beat behind the traditional country sound and eventually acquiring a strong sense of melody. He also showed his penchant for parody—now part of his stock-in-trade—with his 1975 version of Steve Goodman's "You Never Even Called Me by My Name." The song became his first Top 10 hit.

In short order, Coe began to be lumped with the progressive country movement of Willie Nelson, Waylon Jennings, and Jerry Jeff Walker. But while other leaders of the movement, particularly Nelson, aimed for a mainstream audience, Coe remained an outsider. In concert, he turned in lengthy and often brilliant sets, covering an expansive range of material, such as songs by John Prine, James Taylor, Bill Monroe, ZZ Top, Jimmy Buffett, and the Righteous Brothers, usually altering the tempo of the originals and stringing them together at the verse or chorus. But he also dwelled on eccentricity for its own sake, opening shows in a white bishop's robe and a beret and stripping to other costumes to fit his various personas, followed by impromptu magic acts and the appearance of a roving stagehand wearing white tails and a cowboy hat.

If that meant that Coe really occupied no specific niche in country music, he nevertheless earned a rabid cult following and quietly sold records, even if his recordings took on an increasing and disturbing sense of braggadocio, self-pity, and megalomania. His outrageousness on record became a deliberate and sometimes embarrassingly intimate reflection of his personal life, a life that further placed him outside the bounds of acceptable social behavior, even for a country star. The kicker came when Coe, a practicing polygamist who says he's ordained in the Confederate Nations of Israel, a radical splinter group of the Mormon church, moved up to Tennessee from Florida in 1982, taking up residence with his wives in a compound of houses at Ruskin Cave in Dickson. In addition, his behavior was so unpredictable—and his language so littered with unprintable profanity—that label executives grew nervous when he turned up for industry events. When one Music Row publicist introduced him to her new account executive and began extolling the woman's professional virtues, Coe looked unimpressed. "Yeah," he inquired, "but can she suck a———?"

Today, however, Coe insists he's turned over a new leaf. No more cursing on live TV. No more singing songs off his X-rated "adult" albums. And if he won't exactly give up his polygamy, at least he's cut back on his wives, from seven, at one juncture, to four.

"People seeing me for the first time don't realize that I've cleaned up my act," the outlaw's outlaw said in 1980, tapping his walking stick on the floor of a Louisville radio station, where we did this interview. "I'm conservative now compared to what I was." Well, yes and no. His 1987 album, *A Matter of Life . . . and Death,* features a photo of the artist's father reposing in his casket.

Q When people think of David Allan Coe, they have a tendency not to think of the music so much, but rather your image.

A That's very true. The music is hardly ever talked about. It's always every-thing *but* the music. And I think the music is important, and if I didn't think so, I wouldn't do the things I do. I don't want people to like me because I comb my hair a certain way. I want 'em to like the music. And that's why I've always been so outrageous, so they couldn't possibly like me as a person. I've always wanted 'em to just say, "Boy, he's an ass-hole, but his music is great." But they never did. It was a totally different thing, and it wasn't accepted that way.

Q Was there a certain point when you realized that you'd made a mistake, that this wasn't the way to go?

A Yeah, but by then it was too late. Once I had stepped out there and took that stand, then it was too late to ever take a different stand. It's like Johnny Cash findin' Jesus. He may have found Jesus, but he sure lost an awful lot of people, as far as his career was concerned. I don't ever want to lose those people that were with me from the beginning, but I also want to gain a larger audience. And anybody that leaves David Allan Coe because he has a hit record, I don't need those people anyway. I have an international fan club, and I read every piece of mail that comes through, so I know what those people are thinking, and how they feel, 'cause they tell me. And without fail, if I had to sum up my fan mail as to what people thought about David Allan Coe, I could say that the reason they like me is because I am singing about truth, I am singing about reality, and I am livin' in the streets and singin' about the streets. Even though I've lived in a million-dollar mansion with three swimming pools, I still rode my motorcycle with a bunch of dirty, greasy bikers, and slept on the ground in a tent. I still had the best of both worlds. And I never forgot where I came from, and I never will. I'll always be David Allan Coe, ex-convict, till the day I die.

Q How do you go about turning around an image like that?

A Well, the liner notes on the last couple of albums are explaining to people that I'm forty years old now. I'm not an eighteen-year-old kid knockin' out drunks in bars anymore, you know? I'm a forty-year-old man that has responsibilities, that has a family, that has bills to pay, and that has new ideals. Nobody stays the same. Nobody thinks the same. My basic philosophy is the same, but I've changed my opinions about a lot of things. My music has changed to reflect the lifestyle that I'm livin' at the time, but even at that—I mean, I've had people come up to me and say, "I don't like them ocean songs." Well, that's fine, if they don't like the ocean songs. But I live part of my life on the ocean, and I'm expressin' that part of my life. There's a lot of people that do like the ocean songs, and they might not like the desert songs. But the fact remains, if you look inside David Allan Coe's music, there's something for everybody. From eight to eighty, there's somethin' in there, if you'll just listen. 'Cause it's about people, and life.

Q How would you characterize the change in your music?

A I would say that I've gotten less preachy, more philosophical; I've gotten to the point now where I feel like I've got twenty albums that I can be artistically proud of, so I want to start makin' some albums now that I can be commercially proud of as well. So I'm doing songs that I feel can be played on the air, that could become hit songs, and yet I'm not singing "Does Your Chewing Gum Lose Its Flavor on the Bedpost Overnight?" I'm still singing about things that matter, and count, I think. I'm not ashamed of anything that I'm doing, or that I have done. There's only one song that I've recorded recently that I did for someone else, and that was "The Great Nashville Railroad Disaster (A True Story)," which Billy Sherrill, my producer, told me he felt was a hit song, and he thought I should sing it. I said, "Okay, Billy, I'll take your word for it, and I'll take a chance, and I'll do it." But if I had it to do over again, I wish I hadn't done it. I felt it was a cop-out for me to do it.

Q One song off that album *[I've Got Something to Say]* that did get a lot of air play was "Hank Williams Junior-Junior." How did that song come about?

A Dickey Betts and I were sitting in a hotel room in Nashville, and we were talkin' about the [Allman] Brothers gettin' back together. Then we started talkin' about different people and started playin' songs for each other. And he had a couple lines for this song about Hank Williams, Jr., and I said, "Dickey, that's great!" And he said, "Well, I didn't know whether it was good, or whether someone would think it was a put-down." And he said, "Bonnie Bramlett and I were tryin' to write it one night." So we called Gregg Allman's house. Bonnie was livin' there at the time, and she gave us the lyrics over the phone. So Dickey and I sat there and put the whole song together. And I said, "Dickey, there's already two of you on there as writers, and it was really your idea. I just sorta put it together and arranged it." I said, "You can put 'arranged by David Allan Coe' on there if you want." So that's how that came about. Plus the fact that I feel like Hank Jr. has really changed a lot. I think he's come of age, and that people should let him be his own person, and let him sing his own music. There's some things that I'd like to see Hank Jr. do. As David Allan Coe, a fan of Hank Williams, I think that if Junior sings a Hank Williams song, that he should sing it respectfully, you know? And I don't think he should take "Your Cheatin' Heart" and jazz it up. Because people who come to hear his daddy's songs, that's what they come to hear. Me included. But when he's singin' his own songs, then I think he should have the freedom to do whatever he wants to do. I feel that he's comin' into his own, but I still don't feel that he's found himself. I feel like he's been influenced by the Marshall Tucker band, and the Allman Brothers band, which is all new to him, you know? And I think that he still can take those things and apply 'em to his music, and that he'll eventually outgrow that. He's real influenced by the people he's around at the time. Now, he can be around Waylon [Jennings], and you can see that in his music. Or if he's around Marshall Tucker, you can see that in his music. But I think he's a good entertainer, and I'd like to see people just let him be on his own, and not make him keep walkin' in the shadows of his daddy. 'Cause that's awful hard to do.

Q That would be a lot of psychological baggage to carry around.

A Yeah, I think so. But you gotta understand the way he was brought up by Audrey. I knew his mother real well, and when he was old enough, she had him out there dressed up in them little cowboy suits, singin' them Hank Williams songs, man, and that took a toll on that boy's brain, you know? That was expected of him to do that, and it's real hard. I have another friend, named Jim Owen, who does a Hank Williams impersonation show, and it's scary sometimes. Shelby Singleton [of Sun Records] is like my foster father. And Shelby has a kid named Orion who sounds so much like Presley it's frightening. Well, Shelby cut a song with Orion and Jim Owen called "I'm So Lonesome I Could Cry." Right? So he's got Orion singin' like Presley, and he's got Jim Owen singin' like Hank. And then he's got Orion comin' back doin' a recitation thing, where he says, "You know, there's so many people, that if they could have just heard Hank's songs . . . ," talkin' like Presley. He sounds just *like* Presley! And it's scary! It's almost like them two suckers have come out of the grave and are talkin' to you. It just brought chill bumps all over me. And I said, "Man, you all are messin' around with these people's corpses. There's gonna be somethin' bad happen here eventually."

Q You have a host of guest artists on your *I've Got Something to Say* album, including George Jones, who helps you sing a song called "This Bottle (in My Hand)." Wasn't that a rather obvious choice for him?

A I remember when they said George Jones couldn't sing, and they would only let him be a songwriter. George is the greatest living country singer I've ever heard in my life. There is nobody who can sing a song better than George Jones. And they can say what they want to about him, but as I put on my liner notes, when George and I sang together, there's nobody in the world who can ever tell me George Jones can't sing because he's drinkin', or because he's doin' drugs. I've never picked up a guitar, no matter how long he'd been drinkin', or whatever, that he couldn't sing and stay right with me. I've never been ashamed of George Jones in my life, and I never will be.

Q Did you write that song with him in mind?

A No. I didn't write the song with George in mind at all. George and I wrote a song together called "Whole Lot of Lonesome in Me," that's on the *Family* album. And a lot of people don't realize it's him. When they see "David Allan Coe and George Jones," they think it's somebody else, that it's not *the* George Jones. But it is *the* George Jones that wrote the song with me. I've been with George a long time. I think some people are gonna be surprised when they find that the people in the music industry like David Allan Coe probably as much as they do. It's just that I'm a pretty well kept secret.

Q As far as surprises on that album, the real zinger was Bill Anderson dropping by to do a song. Most people can't imagine any two singers more philosophically apart than Whispering Bill Anderson and David Allan Coe.

A We intended it to be a surprise. But I also intended to show that if Bill Anderson can accept David Allan Coe, why can't you? If Bill Anderson can sing with him, surely you can play the record. And it worked. We got on the charts. Really, I don't know why so many people think it's unusual that Bill and I sang together, but they do. First of all, when I lived on my houseboat in Nashville, Bill Anderson's houseboat was on one side, and Billy Sherrill's was on the other side. I was the only one that lived at the lake all the time, so I watched their boats for 'em durin' the wintertime, and we became good friends. I've known Bill since 1967, and he's just a real sincere, good person. I mean, he did things for David Allan Coe that nobody else would do in that town. As an example, when we had the single "Get a Little Dirt on Your Hands," he called me up and said, "I want you to do the Grand Ole Opry with me." And I said, "Well, you'd better call somebody and make sure it's okay to do that, you know?"

And he said, "Why?" I said, "Bill, it ain't like askin' George Jones to go to the Opry with you. You're talkin' to David Allan Coe. You'd better go find out what them people's feelings are." So when he went over there, and they started sayin', "Well, Bill, listen, the show's pretty booked up now . . . ," Bill said, "Well, fine, I just won't play this week, then. I'll play next week, and I'm tellin' you a week in advance that David Allan Coe's gonna be my guest, or there's gonna be no Bill Anderson show." So when I went out to the Opry, I ended up getting a standing ovation, and all the executives from the Opry came around and said, "We're really impressed, and we're surprised. We heard you would do this and that, and say this and that . . ." I said, "Listen, man, I would never do anything to embarrass the Grand Ole Opry and what it stands for. And if you people thought that I would, then you've really underestimated a professional entertainer, because that's what I am." So they all wanted their pictures taken with me, and I just charged 'em five dollars apiece.

Q Are you still the Mysterious Rhinestone Cowboy?

A Well, I will probably always be the Mysterious Rhinestone Cowboy. It might be hard for people to understand that in country music nobody except Porter Wagoner was wearin' rhinestone suits when David Allan Coe went to Nashville. They was all wearin' three-piece suits. When I went to Nashville, I had long hair, I was wearin' earrings, I had a beard —I was everything that they are against. And I could sing better than any one of 'em. And they resented me to no end. And they did everything they could to keep people from hearin' me. A lot of other younger kids started comin' to Nashville—the Country Cavaliers, for example. They had hair down to their waists, you know? They never made it. Only a few filtered through. There's a few, like Kris Kristofferson, Mickey Newbury, but the majority of 'em fell by the way, man. And when I saw this last Country Music Awards show, and all them people were wearin' Levi's and cowboy hats, and dancin' like they do down at Mickey Gilley's place, that just blew me away. Because three years ago, they would not let any of us wear our Levi's into the Country Music Awards. That was an insult to them. And like everything that we stand for—Willie Nelson and David Allan Coe and Waylon Jennings—everything that we have built up to this point, them people have now taken it and said, "This is ours." Lynn Anderson is an "outlaw" now. She's got an album out called "Outlaw Is Just a State of Mind." I mean, it's amazing to me, you know? I'm reading stories where it says, "Loretta Lynn was the first outlaw country singer because she sang a song about the pill." It's like, whatever is fashionable at the time—if there's a number one song about roses, there'll be five hundred songs out about roses in the next month. And to me, that's wrong. I don't ever want anybody to package David Allan Coe up like that, as anything that I'm not. They can package me up and say, "Here's David Allan Coe, ex-convict." If they want to sell me like that, then that's fine with me. Like, I'm a Mormon, but I don't want people sellin' me from the angle of a Mormon, because when you say Mormon, you think of Donny Osmond. And the Mormons don't want you to think David Allan Coe when someone says Mormon. They *want* you to think Donny Osmond.

Q For the record, Don Williams always wore jeans to the CMA show and got away with it. But back to the Rhinestone Cowboy for a moment. He was one of your two distinct personalities. There was the Mysterious Rhinestone Cowboy, and there was David Allan Coe, right?

A Yes. First of all, my first two albums are blues albums. Black-oriented blues. Because that's the kind of music I was into. When I went on the road with Kris Kristofferson I became interested in country music as an entertainer. And I went back and I researched everything I could find about country music. I listened to every old record. I knew everything about everything. I could do impersonations of any country artist that there was. I got into it a hundred percent. I realized at this time that everybody was tryin' to be pop, and everybody was wearin' three-piece suits. So I said, "Okay, my game plan is I'm gonna wear rhinestone suits." But I wasn't only gonna wear rhinestone suits. And I'm gonna tell you somethin' now, that of all these country-and-western big shots that are supposed to know about their music, never once has one of 'em said that the rhinestone suit that is on David Allan Coe's *Greatest Hits* album is the exact replica of the suit that Hank Williams had on the night that he died. And the suit was made for me by Nudie, the same person that made Hank Williams' suit. It is *exact*, to the same number of rhinestones, the exact design of the suit that Hank Williams had on when they found him dead. And the last show that he sang, he wore that exact suit. None of 'em has ever realized that. And they've always made it out as a disrespectful thing, when it's always been a respectful thing.

Q Didn't Mel Tillis give you several rhinestone suits?

A Mel Tillis gave me my first rhinestone suit. I would come to his office, and the secretary would say, "Who is it?" Then she'd tell Mel, "David Allan Coe is here." And he'd say, "Oh, you mean the Rhinestone Cowboy?" And that's how that started—the Rhinestone Cowboy. And then I would go down to the Grand Ole Opry. Tootsie's Orchid Lounge had a back door that you could come out of, and you could walk into the Opry. I would wear my rhinestone suit, and I would go over there, and I'd go up into the back of the Opry, and I'd stand in the hallway there and talk to the guard. And then I would go out where the guard couldn't see me. I'd stand there and run in place until I was hot and sweaty. And then I would walk out like I'd just come off the Opry stage, and all them people would ask me for my autograph. Then they would start sayin', "Well, I never saw him on the Opry, did you see him?" And they said no. So they started callin' me the Mysterious Rhinestone Cowboy, because no one ever saw me on the Opry stage, but they always saw me signin' autographs. And that's how that came about. I spent over half a million dollars havin' clothes designed by Nudie for the Mysterious Rhinestone Cowboy. I created the whole thing. And then I had a fella named Larry Weiss bring me a song called "The Rhinestone Cowboy" in 1973. And I told him, "Man, I think it's a good song, but I think it would be too egotistical for me to sing the song." So I didn't do it. I put out an album on Columbia Records called *The Mysterious Rhinestone Cowboy*. He put an album out on another label called *The Rhinestone Cowboy*. And four years later, Glen Campbell sang that same song, and it became a number one record. He went to Nudie's and rented him an outfit to wear on his album cover. And they started callin' him the Rhinestone Cowboy. And he was very much aware of who David Allan Coe was. And Glen Campbell never once said, "Hey, I'm not the Rhinestone Cowboy— David Allan Coe is. I just happened to sing this song." He totally ripped me off, as far as I'm concerned, everything that I had ever done. To the point where when I'm on the CB radio sayin', "This is the Rhinestone Cowboy," they say, "You're not Glen Campbell." So I put on my album that the Rhinestone Cowboy was dead. The Rhinestone Cowboy, to me, was an alter ego, which gave me room to sing songs like "When She's Got Me (Where She Wants Me, She Don't Want Me)" and "Another Pretty Country Song." And all those hard-core country songs like George Jones and Hank Williams and them guys sing. And David Allan Coe left me the room to sing "Willie, Waylon and Me" and "House We've Been Calling Our Home" and "Crazy Mary" and all those songs. I used to do seven clothing changes in my show. I would come out and do part of my show dressed like an Indian, with a wig and whiteface makeup like KISS. And then I would do part of my show dressed like a pirate, part of my show dressed in country-and-western clothes, and then I would come out with my motorcycle jacket on and my hat, and sing the rest of my show. And all that came to an end. But in recent years, the Mysterious Rhinestone Cowboy has made some very mysterious appearances. He made one in Los Angeles with Johnny Lee at the Palomino Club, and had his picture in all the newspapers, singin' six songs with Johnny Lee. So he's still around.

Q You've said you were the first to do quite a few things that you never got credit for, especially concerning Willie Nelson and Waylon Jennings.

A That's true. It's just very unfortunate for me. Those guys became stars, and I didn't. Like, I was the first one to go in and use my band in the studio, and not use studio musicians. But when Waylon became famous, everybody said Waylon was the first one ever to do that. Took me six months to talk Waylon into even doin' it with his own band. I said, "Waylon, you don't sound like your records. You've got to start soundin' like your records."

Q My impression was that Waylon brought his band into the studio the first time Chet Atkins produced him, but that Chet thought the band was too rough, and replaced them with the studio musicians.

A See, I don't understand why they don't want to give me credit for the things that I do. Are they really that intimidated by me? Are they that afraid? There's a voice inside of me that says, "Why do you think they killed Malcolm X? Why do you think they killed Martin Luther King?" I'm sayin', "Yes, but I'm just a musician. I'm just a singer. I'm not a prophet. I'm not tryin' to turn people against anything." I'm not saying you should or should not go against your government. I'm not a politically minded person. I'm not involved in that at all. I don't understand why they consider me such a threat, why they're so afraid of the truth, of the things that I say.

Q It seems to me that when this "outlaw" stuff started, the term really meant "brotherhood."

A That's exactly what it means. But the only people in the world who know that are you and me and the rest of the outlaws.

Q That evaporated fairly quickly, though.

A Well, it evaporated because some record company executive said, "Oh, that's neat!" And they started packaging it up and selling it. So what they did was say, "Okay, let's take these two guys here, because we control them." Or "Let's take these five people and say, 'The Outlaws.' And we'll package them, because we know that if we tell 'em to do somethin', they will." It's like Kenny Rogers. They can say, "Kenny, you're gonna have to take your earring out of your ear tonight, because it's not gonna look right on this show," and he'll take his earring out of his ear. But he's still got long hair and a beard, so they can still pass him off as being a new breed of country singer and an outlaw. Right? They can do that with Waylon and Willie. They can do it with Tompall [Glaser]. But they don't want the real thing. You know? And that's what makes the difference. For years and years, the thing was, when you'd call a radio station and say, "Why aren't you playing David Allan Coe's record?" they'd say, "Because he did an interview and he cussed on the air." First of all, I have never cussed on the air, on any live radio station, in my life. On a television station, I did, in Dallas, Texas. And the things that I said on the station could not even compare with the things that I've heard Richard Pryor say on television. It's like in 1955 my sister was considered a bad girl because you could see her knees, because her dress was above her knees. Different times, different places. Changing times. I mean, who would have ever thought that you could pick up a David Allan Coe album and hear "Honey, Don't You Lay That Shit on Me" on Columbia Records? Five years ago, it would have never happened. But I've brought them people that far, where I've showed them. The difference in Tammy Wynette sayin' "damn" and David Allan Coe sayin' "damn" is when she says it, you know it's because someone told her, "Tammy, if you say 'damn,' it'll sell a hundred thousand." And you can see that when she says it. But David Allan Coe says it because he means it. There are some times when there's just no other word that can take the place of the word you're using. And if it's considered a bad word by some people, then that's fine. I'm writing a new book called *The Book of David,* and that book has a lot of religious overtones in it, in the respect of what I believe, see? I don't believe that there's a language between me and my God. I don't believe that there's certain words that I can't say to Him. Because I believe that if there was, He would never let 'em come out of my mouth. I believe that's all man's laws. It has nothing to do with God. So as long as you and God have an understanding, I don't think you have to go to church and give men ten percent of your money. That's why I fell out with the Mormon church, because I won't give 'em a percentage of the money that I make. And I said, "If that's a part of your church, then I think that's wrong. I'd rather take my money and give it to a dope dealer. I know what he's gonna do with it. I don't know what you're gonna do with it. Are you gonna build more TV stations that I can't perform on because you own 'em? Are you gonna have more radio stations that won't play my records because I have long hair and I'm Mormon, and you're ashamed of me?" So I went round and round with them, you know.

Q I can imagine.

A Man, there's so much that I wish people knew. You try to talk to people about the Avenging Angels, when you start talkin' about Mormons, and they say, "Avenging Angels?" I say, "Yeah, that's the Mormon Mafia. That's the people that go murder you in your sleep if you ever say anything bad about Mormons. That's the Mormon Mafia that comes in the middle of the night and rapes your wife and kills your daughter because they heard you say somethin' bad about Mormons." And people say, "Well, how can that be possible?" How can anything be possible? Just open your eyes, man. You're livin' in a world where things are possible, you know?

Q So why haven't you spoken about this before? You've had a cult following for a long time. It would have been easy for you to tell people.

A Well, you know, Jesus had an occult following when He first started, and then He had a hit record, and He started having more people following Him around the country, and then He had disciples that were goin' around sayin', "Jesus is coming." And when He got there, He had a crowd. Well, it's sorta like that with David Allan Coe. I don't have fans. I've got disciples. If you believe in David Allan Coe, you tell somebody about him. It's like John Prine, or Kris Kristofferson. When you hear them people, you believe in 'em, man. You know? I am the master of my fate and the captain of my soul. That's what my album *Invictus Means Unconquered* is about. I don't know how long I can go on being unconquered, but at this point, I am the most unconquered musician in country music. Nobody has packaged me up and said, "Here's David Allan Coe. Don't you want to look like him? Don't you want to dress like him? Don't you want to sound like him?" It's never been that way. It's been, "He sings dirty songs." And I don't sing dirty songs. I sing a *few* dirty songs, but I also sing some very good songs. And speaking as David Allan Coe's manager now, not as David Allan Coe the entertainer, I see David Allan Coe as I looked at Bob Dylan in the sixties, when nobody knew who Bob Dylan was, but they were listening to people sing Bob Dylan songs. And I think people are gonna find out in the eighties that the reason the term "outlaw" country music came about was because David Allan Coe was a member of the Outlaws Motorcycle Club, and he got up on stage at a Waylon Jennings concert with his Outlaws colors on, and his picture was taken by a photographer and was in every newspaper in the country. It said "David Allan Coe," and you saw his back where it said "Outlaws." And some guy writin' the story said, "The Outlaws came to town." And that's how it started. David Allan Coe was the first person to ever use a phase shifter in country music. I was the first country-and-western person to be into theatrics and wear makeup and wigs onstage. I was the first country-and-western entertainer to have semi-trucks to carry my own PA instead of just singin' on whatever they had in the house. I was the first one that cared enough about music to have my own lights at no matter what cost. I was the first one to have a bus for my band and a bus for myself. I was the first one to own my own limousines and not rent 'em. But everybody else has been given credit for that. I was the first country-and-western singer to make movies in this generation, in 1970. I've made nine movies, I've got twenty-seven albums out, I've written one book about my life, and I've got another one comin'. I was also the first country-and-western singer to have an all-girl band, Ladysmith. I had the first male-chauvinist all-girl band. And they're doin' pretty good today. In fact, Carol Grace [Anderson] and I wrote a song called "Million Dollar Memories" that's on Mickey Gilley's *That's All That Matters to Me* album. I've had over two hundred songs recorded by other singers. I've had four number one records in England and Australia. They tell me I'm a big star over there. I'm fixin' to go over and find out. All my movies have been released in foreign countries, and almost all my albums. Probably the most famous of my albums overseas is *Nothing Sacred*, the adults-only album, which made every newspaper in England because the Queen banned the record because of my reference to her in a song called "I Made Linda Lovelace Gag."

Q You've also written a song called "I've Got Something to Say," with a stanza about drafting women. Your stand on women is somewhat confusing. Why did you write that?

A Well, people kept sendin' me songs, and I kept sayin', "I don't sing other people's songs. I sing my songs." And they said, "Why?" And I said, "Because I think I've got somethin' to say." So I went back home, and my little five-year-old daughter said, "Daddy, why don't you write a song called 'I've Got Somethin' to Say'?" And I said, "Okay, I will." And I did. But I'm still not sure they got the message. Yeah, people are *really* confused when I take a stand for women. They were confused when I had an all-woman band, and they were confused when I made a stand about women bein' drafted, because they know I'm a biker and a male chauvinist. But it's not so much that I'm takin' a stand for women's rights. I'm takin' a stand for people's rights. You know? I think women are people. If they're not, let's shoot 'em all. That's the way I feel. If they're not people, let's just kill 'em and get rid of 'em. You know? Who needs it? If they're people, let's start treatin' 'em like people.

Q A lot of people aren't aware that you wrote Johnny Paycheck's big hit, "Take This Job and Shove It."

A That's right.

Q You've had your differences with Johnny.

A See, my differences with Johnny stem from the fact that, well, I don't watch television, but my mother called me one night and told me that Johnny Paycheck was on the *Merv Griffin Show,* and that he'd just sung "Take This Job and Shove It," and that they were talkin' about it. So I turned it on, and I heard Merv say, "Well, tell me, John, did you write this song?" And he said, "No." And Merv said, "Well, who did?" And he said, "A friend of mine." And he never mentioned my name. And I was really hurt by that, you know, because to me Johnny Paycheck was over. I mean, the record company told my producer that he had one more chance at Johnny Paycheck, and then they were droppin' him off the label. See, I manage David Allan Coe, and I book David Allan Coe, so I have to play different roles. And as David Allan Coe's manager, I had been tryin' to change some of the things that people thought about him, to get his records played on the radio. And it was working. I knew if I put out "Take This Job and Shove It," it would be right back to another David Allan Coe controversy. And I didn't want that to happen. So I felt it was better for me to let Johnny put the song out, but I thought that they would give me credit for writing it. But the record company's campaign was: "Don't mention the name David Allan Coe, because if you do, Johnny Paycheck's no longer gonna be the workingman's hero, David Allan Coe is."

Q But why would they do that? Did they have more money tied up in Johnny at that point?

A They didn't want the split air play. They didn't want to give them disc jockeys no choice. And to me, it's wrong. I used to love radio, man. When I started, I put my first record in the trunk of the car and I drove to every radio station in the country. I went in there and talked to them disc jockeys, and they played my records, and it was great. Them people had personalities. Now they got some guy in L.A. that programs seventy-three radio stations, tells you what to play, and you're like a puppet. There's no radio personalities anymore. And it's bad. I don't like it. But to answer your question, the reason that Johnny sang the song was because my record company was tryin' to change David Allan Coe's image with radio, so his records would be acceptable. Well, the music has always been acceptable. It was the image. Right? A lot of people seein' me for the first time don't realize that I've cleaned up my act. They still think I'm to an extreme. But I was probably really to an extreme before. I'm conservative now compared to what I was.

Q So you and Johnny made up?

A Yeah, Johnny and I have patched up our differences. He always thought I was mad at him because I wrote another song, a follow-up song to "Take This Job and Shove It," called "No Farmers, No Future." This was at the time when the farmers were drivin' their tractors to Washington, D.C. And CBS Records told me they didn't think there was enough interest in the farmers' cause for Johnny to sing the song. And I said, "Well, I believe it's a national issue here. I mean, I think you maybe ought to turn the news on, pal." I said, "I think it would be a good song for John, since he's callin' himself the workingman's hero, and farmers are workingmen." But he thought that's why I was upset. And he called me one day and he said, "You know where I am?" I said, "No, I don't know where you're at, Paycheck." He said, "I'm in L.A." I said, "Well, that's great." He said, "With Merle Haggard." I said, "Oh, really?" He said, "Yeah. Merle wants you to come out here, but I told him you and I didn't get along." I said, "Paycheck, Merle Haggard is there and he wants me to come out there?" I said, "Put him on the phone." So Haggard gets on the phone and he says, "Let me play you this tune me and Paycheck just did." So he played me a song, and he said, "What do you think?" I said, "Well, it's all right, man. Let me hear somethin' else." So he put another song on, and when he got back on the phone, he said, "How'd you like that one?" And my old lady said, "He's not here." And Haggard said, "What?" And she said, "He's not here." And Haggard said, "Well, where is he?" And my old lady said, "I don't know. He said somethin' about goin' to the airport." So I flew out to L.A., and when I got there, me and Merle went to a hotel room—just me and Merle—and we sat down for four hours and played each other songs. 'Cause he told me, "Man, I never listened to none of your music, because everyone told me you were runnin' that ex-convict stuff to the max." So I sat down and talked to him about it, and then I said, "Man, you should let people know you been in prison, 'cause them people need someone to identify with." And I went through my rap about that, and I played my songs. So when we got through, he took me out to his bus and he said, "I want everybody to listen to me." He said, "I want to introduce you to David Allan Coe. I know I introduced you to him earlier, but I want to do it again. Because this is the greatest living songwriter in the world today. I mean, better than me, or anybody that you think is good." He said, "This man's got ten songs to their one that is great." I thought he was drunk, right? I get home, and I call the record company, and they say, "Merle Haggard called here, and he wants every one of your albums. He wants everything you've ever recorded, he's doin' a whole album of your songs, he wants to go on a tour with you, and he thinks you're the greatest thing there ever was." So I called out to L.A., and his manager said, "Oh, don't think nothin' about it. Merle's like that. He went to see *Bonnie and Clyde* once, and he had his band dress like gangsters for six months." So he busted my bubble. Here I thought he really liked me, and I found out I'm just a passing fancy. (Laughter)

Q Interesting that Haggard wanted to do a tour with you. In some instances, there must be a problem with billing when you appear with another artist. After the 1976 Willie Nelson picnic, for example, the newspapers reported that you stole the show.

A That's what the headlines said: "David Allan Coe Steals Willie Nelson Picnic." And on that show was the Pointer Sisters, Leon Russell, Waylon, Willie, everybody. The paper said they didn't even know why Willie showed up. They said, "After David Allan Coe sang, they could have folded the tents and gone home." The climax is, I've never been on another Willie Nelson concert. (Laughter) They won't follow me, and I can't be an opening act. Like, Loretta Lynn's people called once and said they'd like to have me open up for Loretta. I said, "Really?" I said, "Okay, I'd be glad to do it, but she's gonna look awful silly when my two semi-trucks and two buses and two limousines pull in, and she's supposed to be the star of the show. And I've got a half million dollars' worth of diamonds on, and she's sittin' there in her little 'Coal Miner's Daughter' bus." I said, "I think there's gonna be a problem here, pal." They put me on a show with Freddy Fender once. They paid me twenty-seven thousand dollars to do the show, and they gave Freddy fifteen hundred. He told 'em he would not go onstage before me, because he'd had a number one record and I'd never had one. And the promoter came back, and he was just berserk, man. He said, "What am I gonna do?" I said, "Hey, pal, I don't care when I play. All you have to do is just give me my money, and I'll play right now. What time is it now? Four o'clock in the afternoon? I'll go do my show right now. It doesn't matter to me, man. You're payin' me to play. I'm not on no ego trip about bein' no star." So he said, "You mean you're really goin' before him?" I said, "Definitely. Of course I will." So I went out and played first. And when I got through, I said, "Now, how many of you people came out to see David Allan Coe?" And they all started clappin'. I said, "I want you to do me a favor. I'd like you to get up and leave right now. And I want all the people who came to see Freddy Fender to stay here, because Freddy's havin' a big-star attack, and he thinks everybody came to see him."

So when they left, there were six people in the audience—two nuns, two of Freddy's cousins, and two other Mexicans that had come to see him. That was it. So he's never been on another show with me.

Q You're into magic and ventriloquism a little bit.

A Yeah. (Laughter) I'm into close-up magic and large illusions, and one of the things that I eventually want to do is to make my shows an incorporation of magic and music. Say, I walk out and sing and throw my microphone up in the air and it turns into a pigeon. I'm thinking seriously now about doin' a special. But right now, I've sort of set the ventriloquism and the magic aside, and decided to concentrate on the music and the movies, until I can get to a point where I can incorporate those things.

Q How do you want people to think of you?

A I always want to be thought of—and you might think this is funny—as David Allan Coe, ex-convict, because that's what I am. And to me, for the rest of my life, I can only be called two things. I can either be called David Allan Coe, convict, or David Allan Coe, ex-convict. And as long as you're callin' me ex-convict, that means I'm on the streets. And that's all I ever want to do, is be on the streets.

Q You were once quoted as saying that you felt everybody in music had sold out the people they represented, which were the people on the streets.

A Yeah, I did make that statement. I said that Willie had sold out, that Waylon had sold out, that Kristofferson had sold out. But what I didn't realize at the time was that they really hadn't sold out, but that the people from the streets had abandoned them when they started havin' hit records. And that's the difference.

Q In your quest for radio play, has anyone accused you of the same thing?

A I don't know. I'm sure that there's gonna be people that might say that, but anybody that tells you that they're not in this business to make money is a liar. And anybody that tells you that they're not making records to have hits is a liar. Otherwise, there's no reason to make records. If you're not makin' records to have hit records, then you shouldn't be makin' records. You should be making albums, and sellin' 'em at your concerts. That's how I feel about it. I'm making records to be played on the radio, so that more people can become familiar with David Allan Coe. And so they'll buy the albums that's got the songs on it that they can't play on the radio, to learn more about David Allan Coe. That's what it's all about.

Q In reference to that, did you once say that you're your own worst enemy?

A I probably *am* my own worst enemy, because I won't do the things that people expect me to do. I don't see people after concerts—not even my own family. When I walk offstage, I go right to the bus. Or I take a car, and I leave. I don't stay there.

Q Why?

A Because that's not what I want to be. I don't want to be that kind of a person. I want you to come there to hear the music and to see me. And I can deal with that from the stage, but once I walk off that stage, then I go back to bein' David Allan Coe, farm boy, ex-convict. And I feel like my total lifestyle and the things that I believe in are so foreign to the masses that I have nothing really to communicate with them, on any kind of level. I don't feel like standin' out there and havin' people pull at me, or shout at me, or ask me questions. It's nothing that I enjoy doing. I enjoy singing. And I feel that's what people pay to hear, and that's what I do. I'm not a comedian. I don't tell jokes. I sing. And when I get through singin', I gave you what you paid for, and I leave. It's like when you walk in a store and buy a television set, you pay your money and you take your TV home. You don't sit there in the store and watch it. And if you're a mailman, you don't take a walk on your day off.

Q So while you really want commercial success, you're not about to compromise yourself for it, is that it?

A When I say commercial success, all I mean is that I want 'em to play my records. I think if they'll play my records, people will buy 'em. But I mean, you gotta understand—I'm selling 100,000 albums, and gettin' no air play. If I wasn't, I wouldn't have been on Columbia Records for eight years. I'm selling records, and I'm doing it because of my personal appearances, and because of my disciples that believe in me.

Q In your opinion, does anybody else have the kind of following that you have?

A No. I think everything else is very faddish. I was with Willie Nelson when there wasn't three people that would come and see him, you know? And all these people that are Willie Nelson fans today, they'll be somebody else's fans tomorrow. I think Willie has a hard-core following of people that will always be Willie Nelson fans, but it ain't the masses.

Q Let me read you something he said about you. "David Allan Coe is as good a songwriter as any of us. But he goes to an extreme to be extreme. He calls a lot of attention to himself at any cost. David Allan Coe reminds me of a white Muhammad Ali. I think he puts himself down by overpromoting himself. Everything's carnival, circus ballyhoo, the old street hustle."

A He said I do everything to extremes? But so does he. I saw him in *Honeysuckle Rose* with his hair in pigtails, down to his waist, and a headband on. I read in the paper where Willie Nelson made the statement that they can arrest him for smokin' marijuana anytime they want, because he always has it on him, and he's always smokin' it. I mean, is that an extreme? Is it an extreme to have in the newspaper that it says on your bus "If you're wired, you're fired," and in the next breath you're tellin' people you got marijuana? (Laughter) You know? That's an extreme. Willie Nelson is an extreme. If you don't think he is, you go back and buy one of them pictures of him with that flattop haircut and them white buck shoes on. (More laughter) But you never see a picture of David Allan Coe like that, 'cause I've been like this since the day I got out of prison. And I'll be like this till the day I die.

Q What did you learn about yourself in prison?

A Everything. I learned everything about myself in prison. I think David Allan Coe is probably the Billy Graham of my generation. I could have been that kind of preacher, or the kind of preacher that I am. But it's all the same. Not to get into a real religious thing, but I sorta feel like the Blues Brothers—that I'm on a mission from God, or the devil, or whatever that is that's in my head tellin' me what to do. There's a voice in there, and I respect that voice, and that voice to me is my inner voice, and the inner voice to me is God, or the devil, or whatever name you want to put on it. It doesn't matter to me. You can call it Joe, or Fred, or Ralph. It doesn't matter. God or Satan. But it's that voice inside me that says, "Pick up that pen and write down these words." And there ain't nothin' I can do to stop them words from bein' written on that paper.

Q Is it automatic writing?

A It's automatic writing. I've never had to write any other way. Or to speak any other way. When you ask me a question, the voice answers. I'm just a tool. This is just a shell that carries the voice.

Q Do you have any idea where all this will go? Is it building to a climax?

A I think so. If I'm not assassinated, and I live long enough, I think that I will be the most famous ex-convict that this world has ever known. I really believe that.

Q But the purpose is?

A The purpose is . . . I'm not sure it's time to say the purpose. But what it amounts to is organized religion is bullshit. That's what it amounts to.

Q But if you're on a mission, how could you write in your book that your first mistake was being born?

A In the eyes of my mother, my first mistake was being born. I don't think there's anything greater than life, and freedom. I have never taken a depressant pill in my life. I have never been depressed about life. I feel great about life. I hope I can live to be eighty. I'm happy every day that I'm here on earth. I don't understand why people are takin' drugs these days, and sayin' they just can't live like this, and they are just so depressed with life. It's just totally baffling to me how people can take downers and stumble over themselves and choke on their own puke and die in their sleep. But rather than say those things, I sing songs about those things. Instead of saying, "This is right and this is wrong," I would rather say, "This is what happened. You take your choice."

Q Is there any one song that you think explains your philosophy best?

A If there was ever only one song from David Allan Coe that people would listen to, I would like it to be a song called "Heavenly Father, Holy Mother." I think that that song right there sums up what David Allan Coe stands for. But if there was ever two songs that they would listen to, then there's a song called "I Still Sing the Old Songs," which is probably my favorite song of all time, next to "Jody Like a Melody." The songs that I like myself are not songs that anybody's heard on the radio, but they're on my albums.

Q Johnny Cash has been a terrific influence on you, and since we started this interview talking about him, let's end up that way, too. How would you say he's affected your career?

A Johnny Cash is probably the greatest influence I've ever had. I've been involved with John in several things. I wrote the liner notes on one of his albums, *Johnny Cash Sings Precious Memories.* He sang a song with me that I wrote called "Cocaine Carolina," on his *J. R. Cash* album. I was on John's twenty-five-year "Silver Anniversary" [TV] show. And I've got a tape recording that we play every night before our concerts, with Johnny Cash introducing me. I think that he is the greatest living human being that I've ever met in my life, bar none. He is totally honest in the things that he believes in, and the things that he does. I've never met a more sincere person in my life. And I just wish that I could someday have him look at me and see me the same way that I see him, and respect me for the things that I believe in.

Q You don't think he respects you?

A I think he respects me in the things that I believe in to a degree, but I also think that he sees me as a threat. Because I have been to prison, and he hasn't. And I really do know what it's like, and he doesn't. Because I'm David Allan Coe, ex-convict. And I always will be.

Rodney Crowell

Although his intention was always to make a mark as a performer, throughout his career Rodney Crowell has found far greater success as a songwriter than as an artist.

The irony for Crowell, of course, is that while he has never achieved the status he desired as a record seller, his albums have consistently contained songs that went on to become important records for other performers—"Shame on the Moon," for Bob Seger, "I Ain't Living Long Like This," for Waylon Jennings, "Leaving Louisiana in the Broad Daylight," for the Oak Ridge Boys, "'Til I Gain Control Again," for Willie Nelson and Crystal Gayle, "On a Real Good Night," for Gail Davies, and "Sharecropper's Dream (A Long Hard Road)" and "Voila, An American Dream," for the Nitty Gritty Dirt Band. In addition, both Emmylou Harris, in whose Hot Band Crowell once played guitar, and Rosanne Cash, who is also Crowell's wife, have built a large part of their repertoires with Rodney Crowell tunes.

At the same time Crowell was earning a reputation as one of Nashville's finest songsmiths, he began forging an additional, if accidental, career as a producer. Aside from producing several of his own albums, he turned out critically acclaimed LPs for other progressive artists, particularly for Rosanne Cash, working on all her projects from her debut LP on Germany's Ariola label to her Columbia albums—*Right or Wrong, Seven Year Ache, Somewhere in the Stars, Rhythm and Romance* (sharing production duties on the latter album with David Malloy), and *King's Record Shop.*

All the while, though, and from the time an eleven-year-old Crowell banged the drums in his father's hillbilly band, playing Houston's grimy portside bars, he yearned for success as a recording artist and live performer—the same kind of success other singers enjoy with his songs, his arrangements, and his production.

That success—and the promise of a recording contract—is what lured Crowell to drop out of Stephen F. Austin College in Nacogdoches, Texas, and move to Nashville in the early '70s. As it turned out, the recording contract was nonexistent, and Crowell ended up washing dishes and playing Happy Hour at the Steak and Ale. But the serious songwriter had already taken shape. In 1973, Crowell was a regular, along with Guy Clark, Townes Van Zandt, Steve Young, Richard Dobson, and John Hiatt, at Bishop's American Pub on "writer's night." And, for a short time, he signed on as a staff writer with Jerry Reed's Vector Music.

Crowell's real break came in 1974, when Emmylou Harris got hold of his demo tape, recording his songs, and, in time, put him in her band. From there, in 1978, Brian Ahern, then Harris' husband, produced Crowell's first solo album, *Ain't Living Long Like This.* The LP moved fewer than 20,000 copies, but as a writer's demo, it was gold: two years later, three songs on the album would sell a total of a million singles for other artists.

In 1980, things began to look up for Crowell the performer when "Ashes by Now," a single from his second album, *But What Will the Neighbors Think,* went to number thirty-seven on the pop charts. But soon Crowell began settling down into cult status, becoming known as something of a freewheeling wunderkind. In the studio, he appeared to have one eye on the trends about to spring in Los Angeles—where Crowell and Cash lived for a time—and another on progressive Nashville.

A few years ago, after finishing albums with Sissy Spacek and Larry Willoughby, Crowell called it quits as a producer to concentrate on his solo career. In 1984, he delivered an LP called *Street Language* to Warner Brothers, for whom he had recorded his previous three albums. The company rejected the LP as being devoid of hit singles and as a record that was neither country nor rock, falling through the commercial cracks. Crowell, a man who believes in doing things his way, took his contract to Columbia, culling four songs from the earlier version and rerecording them for the new album with the same name. In the meantime, with no product on the market for five years, his career lost momentum, but the distance gave Crowell the advantage of being able to court a larger, rock-oriented audience while retaining his country base.

Produced by Crowell and Booker T. Jones, the updated *Street Language* was solid in material and performance, presenting Crowell at the top of his form. Like fellow Texan Buddy Holly, Crowell, 38, has always had one foot in country and another in rock 'n' roll, but here he points both shoes toward the fast lane. In contrast to the low-key atmosphere of Crowell's previous LPs, *Street Language* boasts a relatively uptown production—a couple of tracks even cutting loose with screaming sax and sassy chorines.

Aside from that, the biggest surprise on the LP was that Crowell, who in the past admittedly leaned on his songwriting prowess instead of stretching his limits as a performer, emerged as a remarkable vocalist, reminiscent in spots of the youthful Roy Orbison. In 1988, he followed it with an all-out country approach, *Diamonds and Dirt*, which he co-produced with Tony Brown. Critics hailed it as his finest effort, Steve Hochman of *Rolling Stone* congratulating Crowell "for being able to recognize his own qualities and finally get them on record."

The following interview was drawn from five sessions conducted in 1981, 1985, and 1986 at Warner Brothers Records in Nashville, at a CBS Records showcase in Atlanta, at RC Square (the Nashville office Crowell shares with Rosanne Cash), and on the telephone.

***

Q As a songwriter and producer, you've been responsible for some of the most memorable songs and enduring records in contemporary country music. How do you think you fit into the scheme of things as a performer?

A From what I see, I'm part of that new element in country music. Katy Bee, a journalist here in Nashville, calls it "neo-progressive." And I think a lot of the record companies are anticipating that as a trend—that particular kind of progressive, modern image combined with country music. I talked with three record companies before I signed with CBS, and they seem to think I may have potential to work in that area.

Q Some people see you as the leader of the pack. Do you see yourself that way?

A No. If I did, I wouldn't be the leader of the pack. (Laughter) Well, okay, I'm not being totally honest. I do think that I am *one* of the leaders of the pack. I do think that. But if I dwell on that and overexpand what that really means, I'd lose out quickly. I try to keep that in a real healthy place.

Q Who else would be in that pack?

A There's tons of people doing good stuff.

Q In the neo-progressive vein, though.

A Well, there's too many to mention. I mean, there's Guy Clark, and Keith Sykes, and John Prine, and there's Willie Nelson. Now *he* would have to be the leader of the pack, as far as just getting in sync with himself and doing what he does. But see, whenever I talk music, I have to go beyond country. I have to talk about people I admire. At the present, I admire Bruce Springsteen the most, I admire Prince, I admire Randy Newman, and I admire John Fogerty. Not for what kind of music they make, necessarily, but I feel that they're really in sync with themselves. I say "in sync with yourself" a lot these days. And I think I can spot it when someone is just making music for themselves, even if they do have a certain style. Like, Prince has a style, but he's in sync with himself and with his music, and that's why it's working for him so well. And in this little area of music [country], I admire the songwriters more than the artists. I admire Ricky Skaggs, because, again, I think the reason he's been so successful is that he's making the kind of music that's *him*. It's easy for the listeners to reach in to his records and pull out the man, and say, "This is what he is."

Q Your new album, *Street Language,* has been a long time coming. What do you hope to achieve with it?

A Work. (Laughter) The bottom line? I hope to achieve an audience. That would be good. Right now I'm rehearsing a band, and we're going out on the road for a long time. We're opening for the Hooters, and doing some co-bill shows with the BoDeans. It's mostly rock-market stuff. So I'm just hoping to create an opening for myself to eventually get into the concert-artist realm. That's what I want to do. If this record does it, that's great. If it doesn't, well then I'll try it again. I don't put everything on one record. The rest of my career, as I'm designing it, is to be a writer and performer.

Q Why did you choose Booker T. Jones to produce this with you?

A Because I've known Booker T. for a long time, and we'd talked about makin' a record together as far back as right after my first album. But for one reason or another, we didn't get it together until this one.

Q Did he bring the horn sound to this album? Is that one reason why you wanted him?

A Well, no, actually the horns were my idea. It was more of a personal chemistry between me and Booker. He's a real sweet soul. And he just inspires me personally. He inspires almost everybody he comes into contact with. He's a real creative, real gentle, low-key guy who brings out the creativity in musicians. The draw was that I knew that I could work with him and feel good about things.

Q You sing your tail off on this album.

A Yeah! I'm proud of that. That was a goal that I really wanted to achieve. Because on all of my other records, I kinda sloughed off on that. In all honesty, I had such a high opinion of myself as a songwriter that I failed to realize I needed to deliver that much as a performer. But with the time that I've had away from that, and with growing personally and spiritually and every other way that you grow as you get older, it became obvious to me that I wasn't being really honest with myself about all of my talents.

Q Your father was an amateur musician. What does he think of your success?

A He loves it. My dad was a product of the Depression, and he grew up in Murray, Kentucky, the son of a sharecropper. That song I wrote [recorded by the Nitty Gritty Dirt Band], "Sharecropper's Dream (A Long Hard Road)," was really me writing through my father. It was his life, and what he went through. He grew up dirt poor, you know, on a farm. And the Depression came along, and it was just such a heavy thing that a lot of the country people in their twenties or so went to places like Detroit, and got jobs on the auto assembly line, or Pittsburgh, or Houston, where my dad went—places where industry and construction work was on the rise again. My dad had [musical] talent, but he went for something else. He went for that construction job, where he could make some money, and that kept him there. So he never did really pursue his dream to be a singer, or a country music star. But I know that he really wanted to, had circumstances been different. So I think he enjoys it through me. I came along at a different time, so I wasn't worried about keeping a job. I didn't mind moving to Nashville and sleeping in my car for a while. That was an adventure to me. The first time I moved to Nashville, in '72, I slept in my car for the first two months I was here. And I was having a ball. I wasn't worried about security at all. The world was my oyster.

Q So your father never said, "Oh, Rodney, don't fool around with that"?

A No way! Because music was a big part of both sides of my family. It was the real escape valve. They worked hard all week long, and the way they celebrated and rejoiced in life was by making music on weekends. And the music was country music.

Q As a kid, were you conscious of wanting to better yourself?

A Yeah, I was conscious of the fact that we were basically poor people, and that I wanted to do something to get myself out of there.

Q "Ballad of Fast Eddie," on the new album, is dedicated "in memory of Peter Sheridan, the Real King of Hollywood." Who was that guy?

A He was an acquaintance that Rosanne and I had out in L.A. He was a real character. He rode with the Hell's Angels and Merry Pranksters. A real intense guy, about six feet four, and he liked to intimidate people. But for some reason, he liked me. He got on Willie Nelson's bus and stayed there for two years one time, and nobody asked him to leave. And he hung around me and Rosanne a lot, just kinda kept the spooks away. Well, Rose and I got married, and her dad was throwin' a big party at the Bel-Air Hotel for us, and we were talkin' about people to invite. And we came to Peter's name, and we said, "God, are we gonna invite Peter and have him come and intimidate everybody, and be an asshole, and ruin the whole thing?" And we said, "Yeah! Let's do it. It'll make it interesting." So we were all prepared for him to come and be a jerk, but he showed up with this six-foot model on his arm. The thing about Peter was that he was from somewhere around Hyannis Port [Massachusetts], probably next-door neighbors to the Kennedys. You know, private prep school kind of guy. So at the party he was the perfect gentleman. He just charmed everybody off their feet. And Rose and I were just fallin' over ourselves. We knew he had it in him. He was just so intelligent that he intimidated people, and we were really knocked out by that. And then two weeks later, he went and picked up his motorcycle at the shop. And he ran through a stop sign, and he didn't have his helmet on, and he got hit by two cars. And, of course, it killed him. Then shortly after he died, Rose and I had a series of dreams about him. And it wound up with me writin' that song.

Q So is this his story?

A Well, vaguely. A lot of the stuff is [verbatim]. Like, when I first met Peter, I said, "Peter, where are you from?" And he said, "A little place called lonely, man." I said, "Hmmm, yeah." Then I did something one time, and I said, "Oh, I'm sorry." And he said, "Hey, don't be sorry. Just be careful." So most of the stuff in the song is things that he said, or images that he evoked.

Q Emory Gordy, Jr., is credited as the co-writer. Did Emory know him?

A Yeah, Emory knew him. Emory helped me put the music together. I wrote all of the lyrics before I even had music for it. I just wrote it in free form. And the song is exactly the way I wrote it down the first time. I didn't even rewrite it. I said, "God, this is it. I'm gonna leave this just like it is."

Q "She Loves the Jerk," the John Hiatt song on the new album, is a more commercial sound than you've ever gone for.

A Yeah, but you know, when we went in to record the album, that was the first thing we did. We just bashed it down. We said, "Let's take a shot at this one." I think the commerciality of it—and that's probably the way it is with a lot of commercial things—is that we just took a bash at it, and then kind of tidied it up. Just the way it went, you know?

Q Your vocal is especially sturdy on that. Was it easy for you to lay down?

A No, that's a hard song to sing, and I waited until the end. I had a pretty good live vocal that I kept, because I knew it was gonna be so hard to do. I kept sayin', "Well, I think I'll keep the live vocal. It's pretty good." And then I got all of the other vocals done, and I listened to the live one as opposed to the ones I'd worked on. And I said, "Oh, shit, I'm gonna have to do something to this one." So I rolled up my sleeves and went to work, and dug around in there and found a way to do it.

Q What was the way to do it?

A Just close your eyes and sing your ass off.

Q Did you have to punch in much [use sections of other takes of the same song]?

A Well, I would try to get a good one, or try to find a track that was pretty good all the way through, and then punch in the weaker moments.

Q You wrote "When the Blue Hour Comes" with Roy Orbison and Will Jennings. How did that come about?

A Well, I've known Orbison, but that was the first time I ever worked with him. And that was really Will's [doing]. He was the chemistry for that. Because Will was tryin' to help Orbison get some tunes together, and so Will called me up and said, "Hey, let's go write a song with Roy Orbison." And I said, "Let's *go*." So we wrote that song, and Orbison seemed real happy with it. He was gonna record it and everything. But then at the last minute, he backed out on the whole deal. And since we wrote the song for him, I wasn't gonna do it. But when I realized that Orbison wasn't goin' through with the project, I called Will and said, "I'm gonna do the song." And he said, "Yeah, go ahead." It was the next-to-the-last song I recorded.

Q Who came up with the theme of the song?

A Will did. He said, "I wanna write a song called 'The Blue Hour.' "

Q That's real Orbison-like, though, the idea of a "blue hour."

A Yeah. Well, originally we had toyed around with writing that song for the first version of *Street Language*. And Will had the idea then, but we didn't really do it. Orbison should have done it. But his loss is my gain.

Q Is it mostly one writer's lyric, or everybody's lyric?

A Well, it's Will's idea, and basically Will and I wrote the song. The verses were more my writing, and the chorus was really Will's writing.

Q So what did Roy do?

A He just kinda sat there and nodded. (Short laugh)

Q Well, that's important.

A Yeah, *very* important. I mean, more important than who came up with the key ingredients is the fact that it was shaped around his aura. It really was. And he came up with that bridge, "I will always be there for you / When the blue hour comes." Which was a part of the song that we were scratchin' our heads over, sayin', "How do we tie all of this up?" And then just at the right moment, Orbison said, "Well, you could do this . . ." And it was perfect.

Q You did a lot of co-writing for this album.

A Yeah, it's the first time I ever really put a full effort into co-writing.

Q Why did you decide to do that?

A Well, I'd done it on my own until I was blue in the face. It was just something I wanted to do. You know, you go along and you do things, and then an idea comes to you, and you say, "Well, God, it's time that I collaborate."

Q Do you like the process?

A For the most part. I like it with Will Jennings. He's great. And Keith Sykes. And Rosanne, too.

Q You're apparently not interested in recording duets with Rosanne.

A No, only because we didn't want to get into the husband-and-wife performing-duo syndrome. I think we would prefer to keep our marriage and relationship off the stage, and just in the studio. We can work to-gether privately, and be mad at each other, and nobody would ever know. But I just never wanted to go on the stage with Rosanne when I was mad, or when she was mad at me and we were arguing. You know, go up there, talkin' under your breath about how bad the other one is, but smiling and kissing each other and putting on a show for the audi-ence. That just ain't real, and I don't want to put my marriage in that situation. [They have since recorded a duet, "It's Such a Small World," which became Crowell's first number one single as a performer.]

Q You met Rosanne during your touring days with Emmylou, but you didn't really get to know her until she came to you for help on her German Ariola LP. What was she like then?

A Rose was real insecure then. She's like night and day from then. She's changed a hundred percent. When I first met Rosanne, she was way deep into a shell. But once she got a little bit of acceptance and approval, she just came *bursting* out of that shell. And Rosanne is in an all-time good place now. One thing I've learned about this relationship is that it's teamwork from sunup to sundown.

Q Did you like her immediately?

A I was very much taken by her. Really intrigued. I thought she was incredibly gifted, as far as what she knew. She was kinda young when I met her. She's still young, as far as that goes. But we just became friends, with no romantic attachment. I was ending a marriage, and we just knew each other casually until she called me out of the blue one day and said, "I want you to produce some tapes for me." I was flattered, you know. And I think that opened me up to wanting to get to know more about her. Then when we started gettin' to know each other real well, all of the walls came tumblin' down, and we had to accept the fact that we needed each other. After I'd been through one marriage, I swore I'd never do it again. I wanted my time for myself. But as soon as you say something like that, then somebody comes along and proves you different, turns it all around. And that's what Rose did for me. She's still doing it.

Q She wrote "Seven Year Ache" after an argument with you.

A Yeah, we had a great argument. That was just before we were gonna get married, and we were out to dinner, before going to work in the studio, actually. I was having a hard time making that commitment, saying, "I'm really gonna get married in the proper perspective, and this time to stay." And it just finally blew up. 'Cause I knew Rosanne had made the decision and the commitment, but it was left up to me. And I had to go kinda crazy before I could finally accept that. So I went crazy and made it real hard on her, but luckily she wrote a real good song out of it. And after I came down off my high horse, I realized what an ass I was being. So as it turned out, I learned a lesson and she wrote a great song, and made some money. And we *did* get married.

Q In the beginning, were you intimidated by the fact that Johnny Cash was her father?

A It wasn't as intimidating as it was interesting. Because it made Rosanne a much more interesting person, really. Rosanne had traveled worldwide by the time she was twenty-three, and knew things and was really learned in certain situations that, because of my limited experience, I knew nothing about. And I was only too glad to learn about these things from her, you know? And I took into consideration that a lot of the reason she was as experienced in the ways of life as she was, was because the opportunities were given to her because of her dad. And I've seen how those opportunities can be for the good and the bad. And to me, they weigh up pretty equally. But Rosanne knows how to use the good parts and keep the bad in perspective.

Q I read an interview with Johnny Cash in which he was talking about what he had learned from his sons-in-law—how he had opened up and experimented musically. What do you think he learned from you?

A Well, I don't want to say that he learned anything from me. I may have reacquainted him with some things that he had learned a long time ago that he wasn't using anymore.

Q Such as?

A Well, those kinds of things are hard to pinpoint. They're really attitudes. But if Johnny Cash learned anything at all from me, it's about the way I use drums. I'm particular about drum sounds and drum feels, and for a long time, I pretty much just used one drummer, Larrie Londin, because he can play any style. I think after I started hangin' with John a little more, he started payin' a little more attention to what was going on with the drums, and the sound. And I think he might have started thinkin' about getting a little bit of that muddy sound out of the drums and bringing back a little more of the snap, crackle, and pop, as I call it. But I couldn't take credit for teaching Johnny Cash anything, because he's been in this business all these years, and anything I've learned in the last ten, he knew fifteen or twenty years ago.

Q Do you want superstar status as badly as you used to?

A I don't know if I want it as bad. I still want it, but I want it in a more healthy way. I mean, if I had had it five years ago, I wouldn't have been able to handle it. I just wasn't emotionally ready. I feel like I'm a lot more myself now, and stable, and solid with what I want to do. So the timing wasn't right then. I could spout off about how bad I wanted to be a superstar, but someone was looking out for me. Because I wasn't ready.

Q And you are now?

A I don't know. I will be, if it happens.

Q Will you be terribly disappointed if it doesn't?

A Probably not. I thought I would be, but now I'm beginning to think that I wouldn't. That experience with the album I made with David Malloy [the first *Street Language*] is a small scale of what that's like. That record didn't come out, and I worked hard with high hopes that this was gonna be it. But it wasn't it. And it didn't bother me. So if superstardom never happens for Rodney Crowell, then I don't think it will devastate me, because I'll still have a creative life.

Q You also have a cult following. And if you wanted to, you could just stay home and write songs and make several hundred thousand dollars a year, couldn't you?

A Yeah. And that's success, I guess. You know what I'm just learning to do? The difference in me now and a few years ago, when I really wanted it bad, is that five years ago I could not enjoy success. I could have two songs that I wrote in the Top 10 at the same time, and I *could not* enjoy that success. I guess it has something to do with the way I was raised. A man growing up in Texas, you know, nothing's ever good enough. I mean, I've been very successful as a songwriter, and five years ago I wanted to be a success as a recording artist so bad that I couldn't enjoy the success that I was having. It's just in the last while that I've begun to enjoy what I do, and enjoy my success for what it is, without trying to project it into something bigger. And I want to stay on that train for a while. To me, that makes a lot more sense. Or, it's starting to feel comfortable. So if I don't ever become a big superstar, if I continue to learn how to enjoy the success that I do have, then I'll be happy.

Q How did you turn that around?

A I think it's just a process of getting older, growing up emotionally. Getting off drugs, for one thing.

Q Why did you do drugs?

A (Chuckling) Because I'm not that smart.

Q Did you think they would make you a better songwriter?

A I guess I did. I mean, it's water under the bridge. And I don't want to go on about drugs. But I'll say this. Drugs keep you from growing emotionally. And since I've been straight, I think my emotional growth is starting to catch up with me.

Q How long did you do drugs?

A Oh, for *years*. And I got lots of work done. But when I was in my twenties, I could *do* that and get lots of work done. I was stoned for a long time. Maybe that had something to do with my not getting in sync with myself. But I don't want to go on about that. That's over now.

Q How long have you been straight?

A A couple of years, three years.

Q Do you think your songwriting would suffer if you reached that superstar level and toured all the time?

A It might. I don't know. You never know.

Q That wouldn't bother you?

A It probably would.

Q Do you feel as if you can rest on your laurels from what you've written before?

A No, shoot. What I've written before no longer exists.

Q Paul McCartney said the other day that if he never wrote another song, he's comfortable with what he's done.

A Well, that's good. I'm glad he said that. Because he's in his forties, and maybe when I'm in my forties, I'll have enough acceptance of myself to be able to say that. But at this point, I don't feel like that. I've written some songs that I'm really proud of, and I'm proud of my volume of work. But it still ain't what I'm here to do. You asked me if I still want that superstar stuff. In one way, that's distasteful, you know? To say, "Hey, I'm vain enough to want everybody to love me." But at the same time, I'm gettin' more comfortable with the idea of "Of *course*, I want everybody to love me. Of *course*, I want a giant audience to admire me." Then again, tomorrow morning, it's still work.

Q Do you not have a sense of satisfaction?

A Oh, well, yeah. The one thing that I've gotten over the past five years that I didn't have before is that I enjoy my work, and I'm satisfied with my work. I never was satisfied with my work before. That doesn't mean I'm gonna rest on my laurels. It just means that I can now do a day's work and be pleased that I've done a good day's work, and leave it at that. And then tomorrow, I'll try with all of my talents and all of my abilities to do another good day's work. That's the way I want to finish my career. Just workin', and workin', trying to achieve satisfaction, but never contentment.

Q A couple of years ago, you decided not to produce other artists anymore, because you wanted to concentrate on your own career as a performer. Have you totally turned your back on producing other people, even Rosanne?

A Well, I never turned my back on Rose, and I don't turn my back on anybody else. I mean, I'll always work with Rose. But David Malloy produced *[Rhythm and Romance]* too. I'm just no longer in the arena as a producer. I'm a writer and a performer. And that's the way I've geared my mind. I was never satisfied with a day's work as a record producer. I would think that it would behoove Rose to find herself a producer who really has a passion for producing, and who knows that that's where they belong, and that's their niche. Because I'm gonna pursue writing and performing with a passion.

Q You have a good reputation as a song finder.

A I think that's my whole thing in producing records. I learned to produce records just following the book. I mean, if you just want to learn how to do it, it's easy to do. But what I want to bring into it that adds a little more dimension of creativity is good songs. And I think we've had pretty good success finding different kinds of tunes for Rosanne to do—songs that are still within the framework of what country fans can relate to.

Q Such as "My Baby Thinks He's a Train"?

A Yeah, that would be an example. That's got a theme that's been used for a good while in country music—trains, and what trains mean to people. I think that song is just a new treatment of an old theme. And the record we got with Rosanne takes the rock-'n'-roll sensibilities for recording and applies them to that old rockabilly-country feel of the song.

Q Is it tough to produce records for your own wife?

A No, Rose is easy. You should ask Rosanne, "Is it hard to be produced by your husband?" You know, I have a vision, and sometimes in the long run my age and experience prove me to be right in a good number of situations that come up between us when we're working. But there are times when I'm wrong, and it's really a learning process when she makes me realize I'm wrong and I have to accept it. Because to keep your relationship with your mate going on a real positive keel, you've got to be honest. Every once in a while, all of the walls have to come tumbling down so that you're right back to the letter "A" with each other. And sometimes these rivalries or volatile situations happen in the studio, and with your marriage at home, you can't let 'em go any further. If you do, they sit on the back burner and become poison later. So you have to stop and deal with the problem then and there to get it out of the way. And that has made our relationship stronger, I think. We had to throw away the bad aspects of us workin' together so that we didn't ruin our relationship. Because that's the most important thing—that and our kids. It's far above everything else in importance.

Q Rosanne is very strong-minded.

A Incredibly! And right for being that way, you know?

Q Is there an example of a song that you thought should be done one way and she thought it should be done another?

A No, it's never been anything that clear-cut. Because when Rosanne and I agree on a song and decide that we want to do it, then we're usually pretty much in sync about what it should be like. There are subtle little things that can come up, like the way the drum feel should be, or the way a guitar sound should be, and we can argue about that for a while, and then eventually get over it. But we try to keep a professional attitude going in the studio. Nothing can be more embarrassing for a real good musician than to be on a session and have to sit through a family argument. And I'm really for the musician. Part of what I do is to make life better for musicians, I think. So we try to keep it at a professional level so that we don't fall down to that family-quarrel business in front of other grown adults, you know. You've got to behave with a certain amount of decorum. But working with Rosanne is a gas. I love it. Because she's so hip, for lack of a better word, that she always makes it to where it's fun and challenging.

Q That's a great thing for a man to say about his wife.

A Well, I wouldn't be married to her if I couldn't say that about her. I mean, if you're going to be married to someone, the minute you get into that syndrome where love turns to hate, the relationship's over. You may live together for the rest of your life, but the relationship ended a long time ago. The only way to keep a relationship alive, I think, is to recognize in the other person what it is in you that wants to be an individual. And if you understand that your wife, or your husband, is equally entitled to express their individualism, you're going to be pretty much in harmony with each other. It's when one or the other gets dammed up and can't express themselves to the other, I think, that you fall in trouble.

Q How do you rate yourself as a producer of other artists?

A You could ask Sissy Spacek, or Guy Clark, or Rosanne about this, but I think the best thing that I bring into a relationship as a producer is that after we're through, I'll be their friend. I don't make any enemies in the studio. I mean, even if the creative relationship goes, we usually remain friends. I don't rate myself as a producer anymore. I feel like it's the past. I don't feel compelled that way at all anymore. I feel much more compelled to grow emotionally, and to write, and to perform.

Q The image you have in the industry is that of a man who has stuck to his guns, but who has also paid a price. You haven't had the commercial success that other people have enjoyed with the songs that you wrote. Why is that?

A Timing hasn't been right. I haven't been right in my soul and mind. I haven't done the proper work at the proper time to get that kind of recognition. I mean, I've certainly written the songs for it, but it never jelled for me as a recording artist at the right time.

Q I was listening to that first album again the other day. It was way ahead of its time.

A Well, you know, that was before I started thinking. I put out that record and it didn't do very much, and I started scratching my head, going, "I wonder why that didn't work." And once I started thinking too much, then I started experimenting in areas that maybe weren't quite right for me. And so it's a process of elimination. I like to think that now I've gone through a full cycle, and I can get back to where I was then. Because if I start thinking about something, I paint myself into a corner. And that may be one of the reasons why it didn't click for me, whatever it was. And to be honest, you know, when someone comes to talk to me about what I do, this always comes up, and I'm getting tired of it. I mean, it's old to me. It's just a matter of timing. I'm sure if I stay in this business long enough I'll do something right, and it'll work.

Q What kind of overall image do you think you have?

A I really don't know. I know what kind of image I'd *like* to have. I'd like to be thought of as a creative songwriter, and a good performer—an honest performer.

Q Do you think you've paid a price for your integrity?

A Probably. I've thought at times I could have sold out and been a success, but then that's not what I'm here to do. I'm not here to sell out and be a success. I'm here to be a success at what I do best. And I just happen to think that I haven't done what I do best good enough yet. That keeps me going.

Q Have any of your albums sold more than 75,000 units?

A No. Probably not even added together. (Laughter) I think I probably have what they call a base of 50,000 album sales. But I learned a long time ago that you can't really measure your artistic achievement by the commercial acceptance of it.

Q I think people have this idea about you that you don't really want to be an artist so much, or that you don't want to have to stay on the road all the time.

A I think they're wrong. Why not?

Q Because they think you have too much integrity to get out and sign autographs at record stores, and do all those things that artists have to do.

A What's integrity got to do with it? Why can't I take my integrity to that arena?

Q Few people are able to do that.

A I know that. And that's why I admire Willie Nelson so much. Some people may question his integrity about all these records that he makes, but maybe he's going around helping people who've helped him. He made a record with Faron Young. Now, Faron Young ain't had a record in *years*, right? But Willie has a soul big enough to go back and help. Faron Young once had a giant hit with "Hello, Walls." Which helped Willie. So Willie goes back and helps him. I think the man has personal integrity. But probably [Bruce] Springsteen is the prime example of integrity right now, making it work in the marketplace. And Emmylou's record *The Ballad of Sally Rose* is an example of integrity. She's out there plugging away. She's always had integrity, and she's always worked at it. I think it's a misconception to think that I have too much integrity to deal with all of the low-intelligent-factor stuff. It's not true.

Q You mentioned Guy Clark a while ago. He's been a good friend of yours for some years now. How did you first meet him?

A Well, I was livin' with Skinny Dennis Sanchez and Richard Dobson, and Townes Van Zandt was, like, crashed out on our floor. I was the only one who had a regular job at the time, and I paid the rent on this house. And I came in from my dishwashing job one day, and it was the first time I ever saw Guy Clark. He was passed out on my bed, all six feet two of him, with his big ol' cowboy boots just hangin' over the edge.

Q Townes Van Zandt and Richard Dobson are well-known songwriters. But who is Skinny Dennis Sanchez?

A He's another dead guy. He died onstage in California, playing his up-right bass. He was this character who lived out behind me in this little extra apartment. He turned the power on illegally, and he lived out there with a hot plate for a long time. But he had a heart attack onstage. He went out in a blaze of glory.

Q How old was he?

A He was twenty-six at the time. Guy wrote about him in "L.A. Freeway," the part where he says, "Here's to you, old Skinny Dennis," and goes on for a verse or so.

Q It sounds like a drug death.

A No, it wasn't a drug death, although he did take drugs. He'd had a heart problem since birth. He was just lucky he made it as long as he did.

Q How did you hook up with Brian Ahern?

A Oh, God, that's too complicated to tell. The capsule version is that he was gonna produce Emmylou's first record, and they were lookin' for songs. But they weren't havin' any luck finding songs, and they got hold of a tape of my stuff, and "Bluebird Wine" and "'Til I Gain Control Again" was on it. And those were the first songs they found that they liked. So they found out where I was, and called and asked me to come to Canada, where they were. And then I went on down to Washington, D.C., where Emmylou lived at the time, and Emmy and I just really struck a chord with each other. Then they took me out to L.A., and got me in her band.

Q And then you put a lot of songs in Ahern's publishing company.

A Right. That was in about '74.

Q Did you essentially fill Gram Parsons' spot as Emmylou's singing partner? Were you sort of the surrogate Gram, as well as Emmy's rhythm guitarist and bandleader?

A Well, people have called me that, but there's too much romanticism attached to that, I think. Gram was a talented guy, and he died. He should have stayed alive, you know? And I was just another musician who could sing and had some real roots in music—somebody Emmylou hit it off with. So I was no surrogate Gram. He was who *he* was, and I was who *I* was. I've never been comfortable with that, because that's not a real picture.

Q What was Emmylou like in those early days when you were touring with her? I remember interviewing her for the first time in 1975, and she seemed terribly nervous, maybe frightened, insecure.

A Oh, she was great. She's still great. But in the early days, Emmylou was like a deer. Just real full of earthy energy. And real sweet, real loyal, real trusting, and just full of innocence. But not stupid innocence. The kind of innocence that allows you to be open with everybody. At the same time, though, she was real intimidated by the hoopla of her success, and, as you say, a little bit insecure. Actually, it wasn't that she was insecure. She was just so sensitive. But she was really fun. And, of course, I had a crush on her. But that mellowed into a real deep friendship. She inspired a real loyalty in me. While I was workin' with her on the road, it was the most important thing in the world to make sure that this thing happened for her. And she was really generous with her experience and her time with me. I would have to say I owe one of my biggest debts of gratitude to Emmylou for taking me around with her, and letting me gather up a lot of experience for myself while she was forging her own career. With her generosity, and her belief in my talents that were, at that time, really way down deep, and not really surfacing, she thrust me into a situation where I could grow. She let me get in touch with my talents. A lot of people wouldn't have done that. But she knew that there was a writer in there somewhere, and I think that's why she did it.

Q Did those years with Emmylou teach you anything specific that you grew from?

A Yeah, I got involved with Emmylou at a very formative stage in my career. It could have gone in any direction at the time. But there's a sort of dignity that Emmylou had about what she did that I kind of absorbed. Personal pride in her work, you know? I think she believes very strongly that what she's doing has a quality. She did back then, and I picked up on that. And I've turned that into my own form of expression as to how I go about doing the things I want to do in music.

Q When you left Emmylou's Hot Band, were you scared? Was it hard to leave?

A No, it wasn't hard to leave, because Emmylou made it real easy. She just said, "Well, I'm gonna hate to see you go, but I've expected this as long as we've been associated." She was real helpful. And she also created a situation where I could move on to other things. I was kind of afraid, though, because I was dropping out of a happening thing, to get into something that wasn't a happening thing, other than the fact that I wrote songs that a few people would record. But I'm glad I did it, because I've just been digging my own way out ever since.

Q She told me once that you would be lackadaisical when you'd play a song of yours for her—that you'd just sort of casually mention something, and it would turn out to be a song like "Leaving Louisiana in the Broad Daylight" or " 'Til I Gain Control Again."

A I never did give Emmylou the hard-sell treatment. The truth is, I never really did write songs specifically for an artist. I did that one time, and that was with Emmylou. She probably doesn't even remember it, but after she recorded a couple of my songs in the very beginning, I thought, "Well, this is great," you know. So I said, "I'm gonna write another song for Emmylou." And I wrote a song called "A Woman Needs Love (And Not Things to Live In)." And I really worked hard on it one day, and finished it up and took it over. And normally I would just play a song around Emmylou and she'd hear it and like it. But I said, "Emmy, I wrote you this song. Listen to this." And I played it for her. And she kind of smiled and said, "Well, that's real nice. But I heard this tape the other day that I didn't even know you had, and there's two songs on there I really want to do." So that just said one thing to me, which is you'd best just write songs for the sake of writing songs. Write 'em for yourself. Don't try to fit 'em into a pattern that someone else might use. Or at least that's the way it works for me. I know that there are a lot of other writers who can go in and knock something out for somebody and have it work perfectly. But that never worked for me. And, by the way, that song never got recorded by anybody.

Q Other than "Ballad of Fast Eddie," do you sometimes write a song as if you were writing poetry and then write music for it?

A I *have* done that—written more of a lyrical thing, and then put it to music later. But usually when I write poetry, I leave it as that. Because I've found that the songs with the most continuity and the best flow are the ones that I write when I'm not really thinking about it. Those are the kinds of songs where you're just grooving along with whatever the day has to offer, and then all of a sudden you stumble onto a piece of inspiration. Those tend to be the better songs for me than the ones where I actually sit down at my desk and say, "I haven't written a song in a few weeks. I've gotta write something to keep my hand in." I call those the intellectual songs, and they don't mean as much to me as the emotional ones.

Q Which of your songs are intellectual and which are emotional?

A Of mine? I won't tell you the intellectual ones, but I'll tell you some of the emotional ones—"I Ain't Living Long Like This" and " 'Til I Gain Control Again" for starters. "Leaving Louisiana in the Broad Daylight" is not really an emotional song, but it came to me and my friend Donivan Cowart, who helped me with it, in that good ol' way, where I just happened onto it. I didn't have any preconceived notions about how any song I might write that day was gonna be. So I try to keep a real open mind to it, you know. That leaves the possibilities open.

Q Is "Leaving Louisiana in the Broad Daylight" patterned after a true happening?

A It's not patterned after a specific event, but it's patterned after a type of event that might have gone down. You had to be twenty-one to buy alcoholic beverages in Texas, where I grew up, but you could go across the state line to Louisiana and buy it when you were fifteen, if you had the nerve to just walk up. And I was always after that weekend of fun, so we used to go to Louisiana and spend weekends over there, goin' to the Big Oaks Club in Lake Charles, Louisiana, and listenin' to the Boogie Kings play, tryin' to meet girls. And I met a lot of young women who were in that situation where they were dominated by their fathers, or an uncle, and I knew there were a lot of young girls who would like to get in their car or get in a car with some stranger and just drive off. Right in broad daylight. And wave goodbye at everybody, and really feel free. I think there are a lot of people who want that feeling. And I never forgot that.

Q How do you feel about the way other people have recorded your songs? Have you liked their versions?

A When I first started gettin' songs of mine covered, I heard a few records that I didn't like, you know? And I was vocal about it, and word got back to the people who I put down. And I felt really bad about that when I got to thinkin' about it. Because, you know, I write songs, and I have an idea about how I think they ought to go, but for me to take that any further and expect people who record my songs to do 'em the way I think they ought to be done is silly on my part. Once you've written a song, you've just got to let it go. And I try not to judge what other people have done. I've been a bit jealous that, like, the Oak Ridge Boys have had hit records with songs I did. But, you know, at the same time, I don't take nothin' away from them. Because they worked for years to get to where they are today, and they deserve the success they're having. I just think I deserve it, too. But I try not to be bitter about it. I just try to recognize that I'm a bit disappointed that they had hits with the same songs I recorded, and I thought I had better records. But I'll also say that I spent the money well.

Q I read where you said that you wanted to reach younger audiences "as an entertainer, antennae poet and musician. I think I might be something different to them." What did you mean by that?

A Well, I know there are a lot of kids out there between twelve and twenty who are turned off to the various forms of country music because of a stereotyped image that was presented to them a long time ago. And that image isn't really true. There can be a quality in country music that's just a little bit more than the prevalent cheating situation. Now, I really enjoy good cheatin' songs. And I enjoy wholesome country for what it is. But with the youth of today, it's got to be a little bit more ambiguous, and entail something that may seem a little greater than the simplicity that country music has meant in the past. I think there are a lot of young people who've felt like there's no intellectual challenge in country music. And I felt that what I was offering was at least valid, because they might be able to see that something extra that I'm trying to put in there. I could simplify what I'm doing a lot, and probably get more success in the marketplace. But I think if I hold out, and just continue doing what I'm doing, the rewards may be even bigger. Then again, I may miss it all.

Q You did a few dates opening for the Pretenders several years ago. Do you think people see your music as a fusion of several styles—of New Wave and country, for example?

A Well, every style of music that I like I adapt some qualities of it. I incorporate that into my act, as they say. I mean, R&B, and country, and going back, the Beatles came along, and finally New Wave got on there. I never did really incorporate disco into what I was doing. I didn't see nothin' there. But there were aspects of the New Wave thing that came on in '78, '79, that really appealed to me. Mainly Elvis Costello, because he was a writer. Out of all of that New Wave stuff, I went for "Who's the writer in this movement?" And that was the best material I could find out of it. So I incorporated a bit of that sensibility, or tried to understand how I could use that. I thought there were great aspects of what

New Wave meant—you know, the urgency. I was tired of the laid-back image.

Q When you incorporate different styles, how do you know where to draw the line?

A The only place you draw the line is where the song dictates. What you should do with every song is explore its musical possibilities. Some songs offer more opportunity for experimentation than others. But I think experimentation, for what it is, can have a field day in country music. If it ever gets started.

Q It's confusing to me whether you want to be a pop artist or a country artist.

A Hey, you hear me talking. I sing like I talk. I'm from the South, and the word "pop" means popular to me. And I certainly would love to be a popular artist. But it's gonna have to be doing what I do natural. I mean, I'm Southern. I grew up on country music. But I also grew up on the pop counterculture. So if I make a record that warrants those kinds of returns, then it'll happen. But I can't sit here and say I'm gonna be a pop artist, or I'm gonna be anything. I'm just gonna be a songwriter, a singer, and a performer. And I'm gonna do that as good as I can. I want to do something that is poignant and that expresses a reality that comes from your heart, as opposed to your mind. And then the results of that will be seen.

Q So you're not consciously going to try to make a record that doesn't fall through the cracks?

A No. I'm not gonna consciously try to make a record to do anything except be successful at getting me on record, the way I should be recorded.

Q In 1980, you told *Rolling Stone* that you have a "paranoia of being a wash-up."

A Oh, yeah. Doesn't everybody? I mean, I'm a pretty confident person when I'm on an up, but I think everybody has those times when you don't feel very good about what you're doing, and really can't understand how anyone else could see anything in it, either. I get those. Rosanne's been real helpful to me, because occasionally I'll get on that down syndrome, and start putting down what I do, and pretty soon I'll start believing it. And I think at those times I feel like "Oh, gee, I'm never going to write another song again, and I've only faked it this far, right?" It's just insecurities that we've got to deal with, and I end up saying it in print somewhere. I don't think it's true, but it's a real feeling that I think needs to be acknowledged and dealt with. Now I've dealt with it. (Chuckling)

Q *Street Language* may be a big success.

A Yeah, but Rose has turned me on to an old saying, which is basically my feeling about this: "You can't judge an artist's career by one painting." Once all the work's finished, then you have to set it all up and look at it. That's when you get a good picture of what an artist has done. And, you know, this is just one more. But I hope it's all heading uphill. It's always been heading uphill. It's just a few more steps up the ladder for me.

Q Well, in some ways, this isn't the easiest life you've chosen—trying to write good songs, being a recording artist, staying true to yourself, and then having to sell records and keep the label happy, and live a semi-nomadic lifestyle all at the same time.

A The gist of this thing that you wanted to get at—why my insistence on doing things my way has been a price to pay . . . I think it's because my insistence on doing things my way hasn't been exactly the right thing for me to do, and I think it's because I didn't know myself well enough. I mean, I was insecure enough to the point where I would let minor failures just throw me off in a big way, and send me down blind alleys. And I would like to think that now I'm secure enough that I can start making records and *not* be thrown off by small failures. It's like I said earlier, and I keep coming back to this, because this is the theme of my life right now—I want to know how to enjoy the successes I *do* have, no matter how big or small they are. I think that's the key. That's the ultimate thing to me.

Lacy J. Dalton

*I*t's show time at the Wild Times Corral, the meanest cowboy bar to be found anywhere in St. Louis' Chase—Park Plaza Hotel. A few latecomers straggle in past the eight-foot-high white Styrofoam cacti, some of them genuine drugstore outlaws, most of them conventioning librarians. Over by the window, waiting to go on, sits Jill Croston, a.k.a. Lacy J. Dalton, the grainy, gritty-voiced singer dubbed everything from the country Janis Joplin to the female Waylon Jennings.

Dressed in a sparkly red overblouse and jeans, Dalton drinks a beer and watches the customers' faces. Some of them smile, and she smiles back, but just now she's a hillbilly girl with the blues. Last night, somebody stole her equipment truck, getting away with "everything," including her thirteen-year-old Martin D-28, a sentimental favorite. To top it off, she spent the morning at a local hospital for treatment of a bruised vocal cord.

"I feel old, fat, and broke tonight," says the diminutive Dalton, nursing her beer. "I might even get maudlin." A moment later she steps up to the mike, and her fears are both confirmed and dispelled. The high notes prove too often shaky and bottom-heavy, with an outright croak here and there, and Dalton apologizes to the audience. But the crowd isn't paying that any mind, because whatever vocal deficiency Dalton may have tonight she makes up for in spirit, taking the stage like a sassy, old-time dance-hall girl, prancing and strutting, pointing her finger in the air like an imaginary six-shooter. Dalton has gotten out of tighter situations than this in her life, and in part, perhaps, it is her ability to make such a recovery that moved the Academy of Country Music to name her Best New Female Vocalist in 1979.

Although she is regarded as one of country music's most unique and versatile artists, Dalton would be the first to admit she took a circuitous route. In fact, Lacy J. Dalton of Santa Cruz, California, started life out in the farm community of Bloomsburg, Pennsylvania, as Jill Byrem, the daughter of a beautician-waitress and a guide on a hunting preserve. After dinner, her father picked guitar, banjo, and mandolin, but young Jill, more interested in art than music, drifted off to visions of becoming a great painter—"one of the ones who did the masterpieces."

Surprisingly, Dalton's musical talent slumbered until her late teens, when, after a short stay at Brigham Young University, she took off for Brainerd, Minnesota, with a friend to become a folksinger. There, she worked as a cook, listened to Joan Baez records, and "sang awful protest songs" in local clubs. On a trip back home, another friend loaned her his bluegrass, Leadbelly, and Robert Johnson records, and helped her become more proficient on guitar. Before long, she was hanging out in New York and performing in the Village.

In 1966, Dalton's life was to change drastically when she met a psychedelic poster salesman and headed west to California. There she fell in with the hippie movement and formed an acid-rock band. Despite regional success, the band broke up, but Dalton eventually married the group's manager, John Croston, and had a child.

Jill Croston might have remained just a regional favorite had it not been for a freak accident that left her a widow at twenty-seven. In 1971, her husband dove into a pool and, pushing up from the bottom, hit his neck against another swimmer. He was totally paralyzed. A week after the accident, Dalton discovered she was pregnant. She took her husband and baby to a cabin in the mountains around Santa Cruz, applied for food stamps, and took some late-night singing jobs. She also began writing country music.

After her husband died in 1974, Dalton, then a crepe flipper in a California eatery, returned to her "best moneymaking skill" and recorded an album in a Santa Cruz garage. She mailed a copy to her friend David Wood, a Los Angeles attorney, who had spent four years as a country disc jockey. Wood found the album scattered, with no real musical focus, but thought Jill Croston could be a top female country artist and arranged for a demo tape.

At CBS Records in Nashville, producer Billy Sherrill recognized Dalton's music—an amalgam of country, blues, rock, pop, and ballad—as being far more progressive than what any other female country singer was doing. But the name Jill Croston, vague and somehow unmemorable, would have to go. Considering a name change both a commercial necessity and an assault on her dignity, Dalton built her new name by borrowing those of friends and influences. The irony, she says, is that people often misread "Lacy" as "Lucy," prompting her to sign letters to intimates as the tongue-in-cheek "Lucille."

With the release of her first CBS album, *Lacy J. Dalton,* in 1980, the former Jill Croston was hailed as an impressive and original new talent, receiving such accolades as a full-page story in *Time.* Possessing a voice that sounded as if she'd spent too many years shouting orders over the din at the local diner, Dalton was more than just a novelty, however. She also knew how to deliver a song with aching believability.

Still, what made Dalton's debut enormously exciting was the quality of her writing. Much of her early work, especially, slices out vignettes of beer-and-bologna existence rooted deep in her own experience. For instance:

And then there's ol' Dottie

Down at the truck stop,

Been there since we was sixteen.

The only thing different

Twenty years later

Is the hip size on ol'

Dottie's jeans.

"Beer Drinkin' Song" © 1980 Algee Music Corp.

In the years since she wrote that song, Dalton has continued to teeter on the rim of major stardom, never quite realizing the level of success almost universally predicted for her. At times, during which she was revamping her career, finding new management, and experimenting with new producers, it looked as if she might be down for the count. After her rocket-hot launch, she made several solid albums with producer Billy Sherrill—their collaboration yielding such hits as "Crazy Blue Eyes,"

"Hard Times," "Takin' It Easy," and "16th Avenue"—before the unmistakable Nashville formula began creeping into her work.

Part of the problem was that as Dalton became a bigger star, she had little time to write the kinds of songs with the peephole poetry and back-booth philosophy that made her debut album sparkle. And as Sherrill took on more acts to produce, he had less time to find material to suit Dalton's strong but sensitive persona. In addition, Dalton's record company, with whom she frequently fought, had no idea how to market a woman who sang as much rock as she did country, a woman who dressed in jeans and work shirts and muddied the waters by wanting to sing songs *about* something.

Finally, in 1985, after a two-year hiatus from recording, Dalton began a strong comeback with *Can't Run Away from Your Heart,* produced in Nashville by Marshall Morgan and Paul Worley. But with her 1986 LP, *Highway Diner,* produced in Muscle Shoals, Alabama, by Walt Aldridge, Dalton, now forty-two, was apparently back on the trail proper—back to songs of substance and integrity ("Working Class Man"), the kind she wrote when she wasn't having to worry about her career as a performer. There she addressed the working-class ethic with a freshness that has gone stale for so many others. And as a woman with a real-life stint as a short-order cook in her past, she sings (in her self-penned "Changing All the Time") with unsentimental realism about a waitress who has seen, as someone once put it, "too many dawns creeping over dirty windows."

The following is the culmination of perhaps a dozen interviews conducted from the summer of 1980 to the fall of 1986. They took place in various places around the country—in a St. Louis hotel room, in a cab speeding to the Los Angeles airport, in a Nashville recording studio, in the bowels of a "honky-tonk disco" in Louisville, and on the telephone.

Q When you first came on the scene, critics described your voice as "whiskey laced with honey" and "cigarettes and tequila," and used a lot of other overblown phrases. It *is* a different voice, however. Have you always liked it?

A No. I still don't a lot of the time. When I first heard my voice on tape, I wanted to throw up. But I've gotten used to it now on record. I have a very strange voice. There are a lot of tones in it. There's a lot of bottom, a lot of mid-range, and a lot of high. If the sound system isn't set properly,

I can literally drive people out of the room with my voice. You know, if it's too piercing, with all that vibrato. I'm working on having less vibrato. But it's a natural part of my voice. It just happens. And sometimes it's irritating. My voice has changed a lot over the years, and a lot of that is because I wanted different textures. It's like using different colors in a palette. Sometimes I use a little too much red. But I don't know many singers who use textures. Getting a horn quality, or a flute quality, or an oboe quality—that's the kind of thing I like to do with my voice. Nina Simone and Phoebe Snow are examples of singers who consciously use textures.

Q In 1980, everybody was saying that you were the Next Big Thing. You've certainly had your success, but it must be frustrating not to have your career measure up the way everyone predicted.

A Well, it is frustrating. But I really figure that I needed every minute of the delay. I am an artist. I had absolutely no conception—and I still have a long way to go—about being a good business person. I'm still sort of *allowing* things to happen to me. And what allows you the freedom to be really creative is control. The price of freedom is eternal vigilance, and I'm only just beginning to know what and who to watch out for.

Q How much of an issue is being a woman in this business?

A I really think being a woman is a major issue in most any business. Because we're always taught to be the peacemakers. I hope that when an aggressive country album emerges from me, there are some songs on it for women. You know what I mean? In the way that "God Will" [the Lyle Lovett song] could be for women. But I think singer-songwriters, male *or* female, have a tougher time anyway. Hell, it took Willie [Nelson] twenty years! And it's hard for women, period. Promoters and club owners look at the *Billboard* charts, and they don't hire women who aren't in the Top 10. I think men can get away with a little more, but if you're a woman and you're not in the Top 10, you might as well be in Siberia. At least for getting the kinds of bookings that you need to survive.

Q This is one of Gail Davies' problems, that she is seen as an assertive, aggressive woman. The country audience, or at least the good ol' boy network in Nashville, will probably never accept that.

A Well, I don't believe the country audience won't eventually accept that. Because one half of the country audience is women. And some of these women come up to me at my shows and they say, "God, you got me through my last divorce," or "Thank you, your music pulled me through when such-and-such happened." And they're my age, maybe a little younger, or a little older, some are single, and they're raising a couple of kids by themselves, and they *need* strong statements. They appreciate them. And I think it's just the ultraconservative music machine that's force-feeding us all this soft, easy stuff. Maybe that's why most women don't sell records. But I'll bet you, by God, with the right promotion, someday I *will* sell records. And I'll be able to draw in a coliseum the way that a man does, *if* I stay true to what I believe people need and want to hear. Because women buy most of the records. And just because some folks want to see women as victims forever and forever does not mean that that's what they will always be.

Q "Everybody Makes Mistakes" is one of your favorite songs, isn't it?

A Yeah, it is. But when I wrote it, I hadn't even planned to show it to Billy, because it's the kind of song that I write a lot of, with an unusual melody and a message that's a little heavy. But I was sitting in Billy's office after I had showed him a bunch of the songs I had written for the *Takin' It Easy* album. He left the office and I began to play "Everybody Makes Mistakes," because it's fun to sing. And he walked back in the office and he said, "What in the devil is that?" He said, "Is that yours?" And I said, "Yeah, I didn't show it to you 'cause it's not country, and it's not rock 'n' roll. I really don't know what it is." He said, "I love it. I think you ought to record it." That's the kind of guy Billy Sherrill is. We knew it wouldn't be a huge commercial hit. But it's probably one of the most real things I've ever recorded. It says what I want to say. And it frames it in the way that I like to frame things. I've been surprised at how many people come up to me and say they connect to it somehow.

Q Did that song grow out of a personal experience?

A Yeah. Well, it's about a love affair, but it's about more than just a love affair. It came from being disappointed in people. That song grew out of a whole lot of thinking about how people, particularly in business, take advantage of each other. How we misrepresent ourselves. Because people do a lot of things for money that they might not do in a personal relationship. But maybe some of that is even flowing over into personal relationships. We're not as good as we ought to be right now. We're not as good as we know how to be. And we need to know we're all in the same boat—we all blow it sometimes. That's what "Everybody Makes Mistakes" is all about. I made the song grow out of a personal relationship because that's an easy way to communicate a message. We can understand everybody taking too much in a love affair. We can understand people faking in a love affair. And it only takes a little bit of thinking to expand that into the whole world. Because everybody *does* make mistakes. But that's not the problem. The problem is when everybody takes too much, and everybody fakes, and everybody fools everybody all the time, and the end justifies the means. The end *never* justifies the means in my life. The means justify the ends. In other words, I want to live my life so that if I die tomorrow, I've conducted myself in such a way that I feel good about what I've done. I haven't been greedy, or if I have I've confronted it. I haven't lied, or if I have I've confronted it. I've been as assertive as I can be. I've tried to let everybody know how I really feel. There's a line in "Hillbilly Girl with the Blues" that goes, "I've never tried to hide / How I really feel inside." And I hope that's always true of me.

Q Do you feel that you write better for yourself than if you go out and pick somebody else's songs?

A Not necessarily. The biggest hits I've had, like "Working Class Man" and "16th Avenue," have been written by other people. I like other people's writing. And I like co-writing. I do a lot of it. Co-writing to me doesn't mean copping out. It means a real sharing takes place. And if you're writing with a really great writer, you can always feel it. You both know what the right thing is, and you both know when you hit it. And there's no compromise. A lot of times I'll give a co-writing credit to someone who just wrote one line. But that one line may have changed my idea about the whole song. So I give that person their due.

Q Exactly how did that name change happen?

A Well, the last thing I ever wanted to do in my life was change my name. My legal name is Jill Croston. But nobody could remember it. And finally, Billy Sherrill, who is big on name changes, looked at me and said, "I can't get anybody to remember your last name. Find another one." Well, I couldn't find a name that I liked with Jill. It just didn't—Jill Parrish—I mean, I couldn't find anything that would stick. So I took the last name of a woman I learned a lot from, who is one of the most incredible singers I've ever heard. She has the best phrasing other than Billie Holiday I've ever heard. In fact, she may be better than Billie Holiday. Her name is Karen Dalton. Lacy was my ex-guitar player's *wife's* name, and I always thought it was catchy. So I said, "All right, I'll be Lacy Dalton." The "J" is so I can still be Jill to myself. But it was a very painful thing, diametrically opposed to everything I stand for. I almost broke up with my manager over it. It was just horrible for me. It was part of that "I'll go to Nashville, and they'll give me some sickening name, and make me bleach my hair, and give me a boob job, and make me lose twenty pounds. Then I'll be just like everything else—a homogenized version of Lacy J. Dalton that's somebody else's idea about me." You know what I mean? But I relented. I'm not a marketing expert. I don't know that stuff, and I *am* in this to make some money. I have a son to raise. To be perfectly honest with you, if I were independently wealthy, I would sit on a farm somewhere and play for my friends and leave music as an avocation. But it's the best skill I have to earn money with, so that's why I'm doing it on the level that I'm doing it. I just want to make some real good music, and make some real good money, and buy a farm with enough space around me so that I don't have to be staring at the neighbors taking a bath. Or so I can sit naked on my front porch in a rocking chair. And praise the Lord and pass the jar. When I was growing up, there was always this threat of "Oh, if we can't come up with the rent, we'll have to move." I would just like to see what it's like not to have that feeling.

Q A lot of people have the feeling you don't really want to be singing country music—that you'd rather be singing folk or rock or blues.

A They're wrong. No, I enjoy singing country music. I enjoy singing lots of different kinds of music. I don't ever want to limit myself to one type of music. In fact, you can tell that's not the case from as early as my first album. There's a blues song on there, and even a rockabilly tune. I like the country framework, because it allows you to have that mobility between styles. I mean, I can even sing an old jazz standard, and if I'm Willie Nelson, it'll be a hit. People don't hear Willie Nelson and say he's not country. But he does songs like "Stardust." Willie Nelson *is* really country. And he's really pop. But he's a jazz musician, too. [Guitarist] Django Reinhardt was a big influence in Willie's life, and Willie is making Django an influence in all our lives. He's gone over all these areas, and we're getting to experience, through Willie, a lot of music that we might have turned our noses up at. I can sing a rock-'n'-roll tune on my album, and the country audience, which is very progressive now, will like it. I like country because I don't feel restricted. If I were singing rock 'n' roll, and I put a country tune on the album, it would probably be passed over. In country music, when you do that, it's sort of *noticed*. Which is another advantage to singing from a country framework. I don't ever want to not be able to sing country songs. And I also don't ever want anybody to say, "You can't sing this blues song, or this folk song, on your album." I don't believe that's happening anymore, anyway. I mean, Charlie Daniels did a lot for that. A song like "The Devil Went Down to Georgia" is essentially a song with folk roots, country instrumentation, and rock-'n'-roll rhythm. It's a modern-day folk song. It's not even so modern-day, if you've studied folk music at all. The lyric to "The Devil Went Down to Georgia" is a classic theme in folk music. That's another reason why I like country music—it's the current folk music of the American people.

I'm gonna make music the way I see it, and write songs the way I feel them, and sing them the way I think they should be sung. I have never been the kind of person who would fit into anybody's pigeonhole about anything, and I don't ever intend to be. I'm just going to sing music, and I don't care what you call it.

Q How do you feel about the comparisons with Janis Joplin?

A Well, I loved Janis Joplin. But I do not want to be her reincarnation. I don't want to be the hard-livin', hard-drinkin' mama. That isn't me. Sure, I have a beer once in a while. But I am not a self-destructive, drug-wasted individual. You know, I have a feeling that a lot of people think, "Well, Janis was so honest and so real that the world just broke her." And I don't think you have to break. I don't intend to break.

Q So you resent the comparisons?

A I do resent the self-destructive stuff. And then I also understand that people are really looking for that kind of a person. They want Janis Joplin back so bad that if they could dig her out of the grave and hook her up to some machine and make her run again, they'd do it. Because she was so honest and strong. And we had someone like that to believe in for a while.

Q You knew her, didn't you?

A I met Janis a couple of times. But my husband knew her well. I've been approached twice to do a Janis Joplin movie, and I have refused both times, because I don't like the script. They have the rights to her original music, which is great, but I am not gonna play Janis Joplin as a weak, misguided nitwit. Because that's not who she was, and that's not the lady I met. She was witty and intelligent, and we were all doin' that stuff. We were all nuts, and takin' a lot of drugs back then. And that was just what was happening. The script implied she drank too much because she thought she was ugly. She drank so much because we *all* were drinking that much. That was what an artist *did*. Those were the last days of the artist/loser. You know what I mean? If you weren't a junkie or an alcoholic, you weren't a great artist. Because you didn't really know what the pits were.

Q Before I met you, I had the feeling somebody created the character of Lacy J. Dalton, and that there was an image built around her, and to some degree, songs written around that image.

A I don't think that's true. Because a lot of the songs on the first album were written five and ten years before the album came out, "Late Night Kind of Lonesome," for example. But, you know, nobody has a clear idea about me. *I* don't even have a clear idea about me. (Laughter) It's crazy. You know, that's the one thing about Dolly Parton. She's truly one of my favorite performers. I respect her as a musician because Dolly *feels* her licks with her mind and her soul. When Dolly sings a musical lick, it's not something she's necessarily learned, it's something she's grooving into. When she sings, " . . . can't hold a candle to you-oooooou"—that "you-oooou" is Dolly going: "Oooh, didn't that feel *good!*" And that's important to a singer. But Dolly has also learned a really important skill that I don't have yet. Dolly has learned to have the "Dolly persona," the happy-go-lucky, sweet, blue-eyed, "you better love my wigs and my big boobs 'cause I don't care if you do or you don't" persona. I mean, I'm sure Dolly Parton gets depressed, but we'll never know it. I'm sure Dolly Parton wants to throw up her hands in despair and scream, but we're not going to know it, because the "Dolly persona" is happy and positive. I think she's a great metaphysician, because she puts out an example of positive thinking. Now, I'm not sure that Lacy J. Dalton will do that. Underneath Lacy J. Dalton, Jill Croston has great periods of depression, and periods of being real uncomfortable with things. I'd like to find a stage persona, a constant, positive image. And I think the reason I admire that is because it's the hardest thing for me.

Q This must pose a problem for your record company.

A It shouldn't. Lots of people are lots of things, and can *do* lots of things. I would hope CBS would see it as an advantage. Because I think I probably have twenty-five or fifty separate and distinct personalities, any one of which is ready to crop up on any different day. (Laughter)

Q Early on, there was some attempt to project you as a hard-living, honky-tonk person, a female outlaw.

A Well, if there was, that was definitely not the whole picture. My stage persona was like that when I was playing bars. I pick up the ambience of the place I'm in and try to entertain people. But it was different in concert. I don't know about just being a honky-tonk performer. I don't even know if I like that. I'm uncomfortable when anyone tries to put a label or an image on me. Besides, there's a whole other side of me that isn't like that at all. I would like to see that emphasized a little more. There actually is a sensitive human being here with some intelligence, a person who doesn't want to throw her life away with drugs and alcohol. I think the last thing the young people of this world need is somebody else exhibiting wanton and ridiculous destruction of their body for the enjoyment of the masses. That's not where I'm at. I drink beer occasionally because it relaxes me, and it relaxes my throat. I may look like some kind of a drug addict, because I wear blue jeans and I'm forty and I have strange-looking hair. But I don't take drugs at all. Ever. In fact, I very much disapprove of them. I think people think that I'm very hard. Writers like to play up the idea that I'm an outlaw. Well, I'm not hard. And I'm not tough. I fall to pieces as easily as anybody. And I don't want to be thought of as the kind of person who's just hell-bent and whiskey-bound, and all that crap. I mean, I don't want to be another Hank Williams and die when I'm . . . well, I'm already older than he was. (Laughter) I'd just like this image—if I have an image—to be a little closer to the truth. I don't want people to think all I ever do is drink beer and ride motorcycles and get tattoos. That's just not how it is. What I always say to my manager is that I'm a middle-aged housewife who's having a fling. There's also that part of me, as well as the creative person. But the composite has never really arrived. Maybe I *am* a bad girl. Maybe I *am* just a hideous wreck of an old outlaw. But I don't feel like that. I feel a lot younger. And a lot more positive. On the other hand, there's definitely a side of me that's wild and crazy, but it's not evil, and it's not satanic. I never even break the law anymore. (Laughter) I try real hard to be good.

Q A friend of yours told me you used to sing on the street in Santa Cruz.

A Um-hum. Not for very long. Sometimes there'd be fairs in Santa Cruz, and I'd dress up like a gypsy and go with my friend, who was a bagpiper. And she'd call the crowd together with her bagpipes, and then I'd sing some songs and she'd collect the money. Then she'd play a bagpipe tune, and I'd run around and collect the money in a hat. Used to make a lot of money like that. It was really a wonderful experience, in a way. It gave you the feeling of what it must have been like to be a gypsy. I mean, you learn how to size people up. It's a strange thing to walk around in gypsy garb and do that. You learn to play fast songs when you pass the hat. You learn a lot of old carny tricks. (Laughter) It'll come in handy if I ever become a bag lady on the streets someday.

Q You were also a topless dancer for a time.

A (Embarrassed laughter) Yeah. But talking about it is really too gross. A person will do many things in desperate straits.

Q On the opposite end of the spectrum, you often talk about speaking with God. There's the famous story of God telling you to record "The Tennessee Waltz" when you prayed for a hit record. What I want to know is, when He talks to you, what does it *sound* like?

A Believe me, you know. It sounds like the truth.

Q It's an audible voice?

A It depends on what you're talking about. Sometimes it's just a prodding of my conscience. But yes, once or twice in my life, I have heard an actual voice. Well, maybe it's an audible non-voice. I don't know how to explain it. It's small and quiet, but you can hear it really clearly, and it's absolutely distinguishable. Sometimes it sounds like your own voice, but not quite. It doesn't sound like, you know [big theatrical voice], Moses. It's just sort of a normal, inside-your-head kind of voice. Okay, so maybe I'm crazy. I hear voices. Oh, please, I'm starting to sound like those people on television who say [deep voice], "And the Lord said to me . . ."

Q You use a Southern accent in some of your songs, but it doesn't show up in others. And it usually doesn't show up in your normal speaking voice, although sometimes it does. Why is that?

A Because sometimes I talk like that. Sometimes I *feel* like that. You're right, I don't always have it. It's terrible. I'm such a phony. Well, let me re-phrase that. I'm such a *mimic*. When I'm in Nashville, I suddenly find myself with a Southern twang that isn't there any other time. I'm not even conscious of it. London was interesting that way . . . I'm a chameleon. I'm not *real* fond of that. But it just happens sometimes. And occasionally when I'm having fun with a song, I'll do it on purpose. It's just like painting with another shade of color.

Q There's another song on your first album that is generally overlooked, but which is one of your best pieces of writing—"Beer Drinkin' Song," with Dottie the waitress. How did you come to write that song?

A "Beer Drinkin' Song" was written about people in small towns all over the United States. I wrote it about a friend writing me from Texas, but I was thinking about Pennsylvania. When I was growing up, my folks al-ways went to the local neighborhood bar. And there were lots of Polish people there playing accordions. They played polkas, but they inter-spersed the polkas with country music. My mother played guitar, and my dad played mandolin, and guitar, and banjo, and they always sang. And I was talking with my manager, David Wood, one night, and he was telling me how wonderful Germany is, and what a great time they always had in the big beer halls over there, where people would link their arms and sing a great beer-drinking song, you know, "oompah-pah, oom-pah-pah." And I was thinking, "Why hasn't anyone written an American beer-drinking song?" So David Wood and I sat down and wrote one.

Q The best verse in the song is the one about "ol' Dottie's jeans" and her expanding hip size.

A Well, that was definitely my line, because I have *lived* that one. (Laugh-ter) There was a time in my life, when I was a cook at a greasy spoon in

Brainerd, Minnesota, drinking beer and taking birth-control pills, when I weighed one hundred eighty-seven pounds. And I am five feet one and a half inches tall. So I just sort of *watched* my hip size expand. Being fat was one of the greatest lessons, though. I got to see what it was like to be a Big Mama. I got to feel what it's like to be ol' So-and-So down at the truck stop. It was like this whole other personality developed. And it was very good for me. Because I'd always been the Cute Little Thing, and all of a sudden I wasn't. I couldn't just bat my baby blues and get anything I wanted. I had to earn acceptance with the sheer force of my personality. And I knew the pain of being separate, of not being cool. Because it's very painful not to look like Farrah Fawcett, and to have a big nose. And it's even more painful to be one hundred eighty-seven pounds. But it makes you more compassionate. I often wonder what I would be like if God had made me five-nine and willowy. I might have drunk myself to death by this time. Or, truly, I think if I had stayed in Bloomsburg, Pennsylvania, the hip size in my jeans, which is not small, would have been a great deal larger. (Laughter) And it wouldn't have mattered to anybody. In a small country town, people don't seem to worry as much about externals. They don't care if you're a size forty or a size twenty. Country people aren't as concerned with the Body Beautiful as with the person beautiful. And I think we've got to get back to that. I praise God every day for that experience. First of all, I never would have studied nutrition, I never would have known anything about vitamins, and I never would have gotten into exercise. I run two to four miles every day. But what I'm saying is, let's not let that get in the way of how we feel about each other. We only have these bodies for eighty to ninety years. What are we going to do when we lose them? What if we die and become pure energy? *Then* how are we going to relate? (Laughter) Think about it! You aren't going to look at this energy blob and say, "Hey, look at that energy blob with bigger than major-sized yaboos." You know, it's not going to *happen*. Hopefully, of course, there is some kind of continuation. I haven't had anybody come back and tell me there is, but I'm definitely looking forward to something other than just plain blackout time. Although, if it's blackout time, it's blackout time. You've got to be realistic. But if there's reincarnation . . . (Sigh) Oh, God, please don't let me come back as a hillbilly singer.

Q Let me ask you about your mother. She's credited as the co-writer on "Living in the Fast Lane." You and she seem to be close, since she travels with you sometimes.

A Yes, we are close. My mother is really one of the most remarkable people in the whole world. But we also drive each other *totally* crazy. Let's establish that right away. (Laughter) She is, after all, my mother. Mothers and daughters just do things differently.

Q Were you always close, or have you just become close as adults?

A Well, first of all, I will never, ever be more grateful to any other human being in my life. My mother is the most completely honest person who's ever lived on the planet. I've never known my mother to tell a lie, not even to herself. And she's had a very, very hard life. She's been widowed twice. But she's incredible. She's sixty-some years old and still goes hiking and shoots archery and rides horses. Drives a diesel truck when she has to. She's a very competent, wonderful human being, and I've learned a lot from her. I'll never be able to repay her for the values that she taught me. And yes, I've always been close with my mother, even though I was a horrible daughter when I went to California. I mean, I never wrote to her. I was just *gone*. But I guess she must have understood. I couldn't have a better friend than my mother. I never had to be afraid to talk to her about anything. My mother, and my father, actually, instilled it into me that it doesn't matter what anybody thinks. They said, "What other people think is *not important*. It's what *you* know is right." And the basic things that my mother taught me are pretty much right on. But she never restricted me. I was given a lot of freedom. If I wanted to do something that she didn't approve of she'd say, "Well, I usually tell you how it is. If you want to go ahead and do this, it's up to you. But just know that I don't approve." She put a lot of trust in me as a kid.

Q But didn't you tell me once that you moved out when you were fourteen?

A Yes. I moved out and went to live with my mother's best friend—mostly because of my relationship with my father, whom I loved dearly. But my dad and I were too much alike. As the years pass along, I see just how much like him I really am. A lot of the behavior that he saw in me as a kid was behavior that he had a very hard time conquering himself, and he was real intolerant of. I could call things that he really didn't want me to call, and he knew me too well. He knew when I was being lazy and not being real. That's the one thing about my father that I'm grateful for. He was an absolutely unaffected person. And probably the only person he couldn't get along with was me. Because I can be real manipulative. It's something I have to fight all the time. I have to confront being emotionally dishonest, and I have to fight like crazy not to be lazy. I mean, basically, left to my own devices, I could very easily become a couch potato. (Laughter)

Q What was it like living with your mother's best friend?

A Well, she had about nine kids. I helped her take care of them, and cleaned the house, and I was able to make it. And then I moved in with one of my girlfriends, whose parents were like a mother and dad to me. Completely different situation than my situation at home. They had plenty of money and were both professional people, and I got a lot of support from them. I had a lot of different influences growing up. Then when I graduated from high school, I left for college, at Brigham Young University.

Q Were you reared as a Mormon?

A No. When I was a child, we went to a Protestant church. People just seemed to go there to socialize and do this little ritual on Sundays. And when I was nine, I told my mother, "I'm not going back there anymore. That's not where it's at for me." First I went to a Baptist church, and I took Baptist instruction, because some friends of mine did that. But I didn't find anything there. And then I took Catholic instruction, because my friend Mary McFadden, with whom I wrote "Crazy Blue Eyes," was a Catholic. Well, I did find something I liked in the Catholic church. I liked the ritual and the incense. I'll never forget going there one Christmas Eve and hearing those nuns sing. I thought it was like the angels in heaven. On the whole, though, it's just the trappings of religion that are such a turnoff. The actuality of God is a whole other ball game.

Q So why did you go to Brigham Young University?

A Well, at that time I was investigating the Mormon religion. I had gone through a few dozen others by that time, and I had a friend who was Mormon. And she had this brother who went to Brigham Young, and he said it was a wonderful place to go to school, with a great art department. Also, it was cheap. I hadn't really planned on going to college. I wanted to go to art school, but I didn't have the money. Art school is more expensive than university. Anyway, at the last minute, I sent in my application to Brigham Young, and they accepted me, and I borrowed two hundred dollars from my grandmother to get there. I stayed for a semester and a half, cleaning toilets from three in the morning until seven, putting myself through. I left with a fiddle-playing Mormon named Yvonne Squires. We went to Salt Lake City and got jobs playing music. From there, I went to Brainerd, Minnesota, where I got fat and played at folk clubs around the lake there. I sang all these sweet, sad Joan Baez songs and dyed my hair black. I sounded foul, and looked worse. My mother came up and got me. She kept looking at my feet and crying. It was *deep*. (Laughter) She cried all the way back to Bloomsburg.

Q What were you like in high school?

A Very responsible. A good student, not a great student, because I don't like school. But I have always had this sort of sick desire to please, so I would get good grades for that reason—not because I cared much about what I was learning. I wasn't pretty, but I was very wholesome-looking. Very small. I think the people in my class liked me. But I was definitely one of the weird kids in high school. I'm sure I freaked some of the people out, because I never could get it through my head why it was so important to be in a clique, and wear a certain kind of clothes, and toe the line in any way. I remember going to our youth center one time and saying, "Why won't any of you guys talk to me? I realize I'm not in your clique, but what's the difference?" I would confront them with these things, and they'd go, "Well, God, you're really *weird,* you're really *strange.*" And it's true. I *am* really strange. (Laughter) And I imagine I was probably pretty hard to take sometimes in being that direct. But I had a lot of friends, and I had a lot of good times. I had a lot of *awful* times, too.

Q Such as?

A Well, in the sixth grade, they elected me May Queen. And I thought, "This is going to cause a lot of people to be jealous of me." So I had very mixed feelings about being elected May Queen. I remember having thoughts like that from early on. It's not easy to think that hard when you're that young, and you don't have any answers.

Q But in 1980 your hometown held a "Lacy J. Dalton Day." That must have been gratifying to some extent.

A Well, I arrived at my mother's house after having driven almost all night from a gig we did in some other town in Pennsylvania. I got an hour and a half of sleep, and then German TV came, and also the local branch of *P.M.* magazine. So I'm just *dying,* I'm so tired. And we do this interview. The girl was *totally* unprepared. She asked me questions like "Where were you born?" (Laughter) And then it was time for the "Lacy J. Dalton" parade. (Laughter) Somebody in my hometown got a horse for me to ride. And it was the most beautiful thing you have ever seen. But they neglected to tell me that the horse had *never* been in a parade, was a three-year-old *stallion,* and was not really well trained as far as signals —you know, right, left, stop, start. But he really had a wonderful disposition, and that helped, and even though he was scared and trembling, we got through the parade all night. But there was another girl on a pinto horse leading the parade, and she looked like she knew what she was doing, because at least her horse was responding to the commands. A lot of people thought *she* was Lacy J. Dalton, you know? (Laughter) People still don't know what I look like. CBS did a market study on me and what they discovered is that people basically like me, and they want to see me get ahead, because they think of me as an underdog. But they don't know what in the hell I look like. (Laughter)

Q What are the biggest misconceptions that people have about performers?

A Well, first of all, everybody always thinks that if you're on TV, you're fabulously wealthy. Wrong! That is a myth I have to dispel. I mean, I probably make less money in a week than most secretaries. Of course, I'm not Kenny Rogers, either. And trying to buy outfits and keep up with the dry cleaning and the stuff you have to do with the little money you clear is just crazy. I think that what people don't understand about show business is that you get maybe—let's take an average price for a gig, say four to six thousand dollars. After the booking agency takes fifteen percent, and the manager takes ten or twenty percent, you're left with a little less than half to pay all the traveling expenses, the salaries, and the rooms and meals for yourself and the band. And what you wind up with, unless you're very smart or commanding big fees, is not a great deal.

Q What's the biggest misconception you had before you went into the business?

A The one misconception *I* had about being a performer was "What's so hard about the road?" Because when you think about the road, you automatically think, "There they are traveling in their big, fancy bus, eating at the very best restaurants, having their clothes ready for them . . ." It's not like that. You get there in a thirty-five-foot bus that you share with ten other people, sometimes for six weeks at a time. You have things happen like somebody throwing the clothes that you had cleaned at the Holiday Inn into the equipment truck and they're all wrinkled, and the bass player borrowed your iron at the last place and you haven't seen it since. The road isn't easy. You're in a different bed every night, and the demands on your personal time and space are enormous. Most human beings respond to having some sort of routine in their lives, and on the road there's no routine. One day you get up at four-thirty and the next day you get up at noon. The next day you have to leave right after the show at eleven o'clock and catch a plane, so that at four in the morning you're sitting in Chicago for two hours to save money on plane flights. You fly out again at six a.m. and you arrive at eight a.m. and you spend half an hour waiting for your rent-a-cars with your eyes bleeding all over the airport floor. Then you get in the rent-a-car and you go to the hotel, and the air conditioning doesn't work, and it's a hundred and ten degrees. And you can't get any sleep, and you have a show to do at two o'clock in the afternoon at somebody's fair. You wake up at twelve-thirty, take a bath and get ready, and it's one-thirty and you haven't had time to eat. You jump in the car, you get to the gig, and what do they have as refreshments? Pink meat and American cheese, which is all kind of melted together into a pizza-shaped gob, with nuts glommed in the middle of it, and which has been sitting in the sun for a couple of hours. Try being a vegetarian on the road. Good luck! There are people out there who *love* the road, and I wish I were one of them. But most of the time, I *hate* the road. (Laughter)

Q Have you always thought you were destined to have this career?

A Well, all my life I have known that I was going to do this, because I've always felt that everything in my life has been for a reason. Everything— the heartaches, the fat, my husband's broken neck. All of that was for a reason, and that was to prepare me to try to heal people, to bring joy to people, to uplift them and make them happy. And to be able to relate to them. On the other hand, I never particularly wanted to do this when I was a kid. But I've known since I was seven years old that I was going to do it. It's the craziest thing in the world. And I've never been able to say it in such a way that it doesn't sound like [big voice] "Well, I knew what I was going to—" You know what I mean. But I remember sitting in a bathtub when I was seven, looking down at my legs in the water. I had skinny little bow legs, and I was really worried that my thighs would never meet at the top, because I was so bow-legged. And I had seen *Snow White and the Seven Dwarfs.* And all of a sudden I sang, "I know you / I walked with you / Once upon a dream." And I remember looking around at the bathtub kind of glowing, and I thought to myself, "Wow, I can *sing!* I can make all these noises with my throat!" It was like this sense of wonderment. Like a light bulb going on—an incandescent feeling. But I didn't *care* that I could do that. I didn't particularly *want* to do that. I just knew that I *could* do that. And in fact, never during high school or grade school did I ever want to be a singer. And I certainly never thought about being a *star.* Stars weren't interesting to me. Dolls weren't interesting to me. I liked cowboys instead. And fuzzy-faced old hunters that my dad would bring in from the game farm. Those were the kinds of heroes that I had. People like Zsa Zsa Gabor just never quite got it for me. But, God . . . It's weird. I never wanted to be "Ra ta ta ta ta ta," you know? (Laughter) Because to me, getting up on a stage and going through the motions of being an entertainer is a very hollow thing.

I don't want to wind up at the end of my life being a smile—a big row of teeth that somebody remembers. I want to have said something to people. I'm not just up there like a trained seal, bouncing a ball off my head. But there are times when I feel like that.

Q Do you think that's your purpose—to say something to people?

A Well, my purpose is to get to know myself and God. Good grief, I'm beginning to sound like the Billy Graham Crusade, or some kind of wild religious fanatic! But I mean, becoming a singer is, I think, my destiny. I don't know what my purpose is. It's whatever happens along the way to finding myself.

Q This is an extraordinary life you've lived.

A Yeah, if I died today, I would have seen an awful lot, I think, for my forty years. Seems like a million lifetimes. And I've been a million people, or at least four or five, within this one life. The little segments of my existence have been so extreme, from the crazy psychedelic sixties era to the very straight Brigham Young University days to all my adventures in Gnashville. I've seen so many sides of life. Now, the only one I have left to experience is being very, very rich. I'm determined to do that one before I croak.

Steve Earle

$\mathcal{T}$he morning after his two sold-out showcase appearances in Nashville, country-rockabilly artist Steve Earle is being made up for a television interview in a studio off Music Row.

"Oh, boy, I'm a lovely shade of green," says Earle, admittedly hung over and "industrial-strength nauseous." Dressed in jeans and a black T-shirt with the sleeves rolled greaser style,

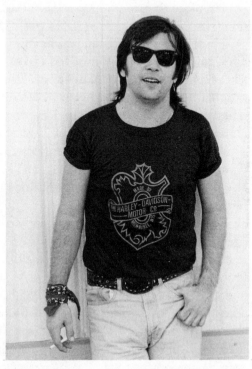

Earle throws a look at his publicist and smiles a capped-toothed grin. "I'm doing my Keith Richards impersonation today," he cracks.

Although Earle insists that he's a country singer ("This is just eighties hillbilly music"), he looks more like John Cougar Mellencamp than Porter Wagoner. ("Actually, he looks like the kind of guy who might carry a switchblade in his back pocket," says his producer, Tony Brown.)

No matter what he looks like, Earle, 33, has accomplished a rare feat. His debut album, *Guitar Town,* a stunning synthesis of country, rockabilly, and root-level rock 'n' roll, went to the top of the country charts, scored high on the pop charts, and earned him glowing critical reviews and respect not only from the country audience but from some of the biggest names in rock. In a matter of months, Mellencamp began performing "Guitar Town" in his concert set, *Billboard* reported that Bruce Springsteen was seen buying Earle's LP at Tower Records, Elton John sent his limo to deliver Earle to his concert, and Elvis Costello requested an audience.

Yet, as is often the situation, before the showcase concerts, where Earle and his longtime band, the Dukes, performed *Guitar Town*—the title is CB talk for Nashville—in its entirety, the singer was hardly a prophet in his own land. In fact, a number of industry honchos who attended the first Earle performance came, according to one publicist, "to see if he could really pull it off."

After that night, however, even Nashville had to agree with reviewers in New York, Houston, Los Angeles, and Atlanta who said that Earle was one of the most exciting—and perhaps important—new artists of the decade.

"Yeah," Earle would say the next day. "Things are startin' to look pretty good for a change."

It was, admittedly, a long time coming, since Earle has been bouncing around Nashville off and on for twelve years now without attracting much attention as an artist. From 1982 to 1985 he cut some rockabilly tracks for Epic and the independent LSI label, showing up in his jacket photos in pink-and-black outfits with string ties. Like the photographs, the early records never quite seemed "real," sounding more like the product of a record company hunch that if the Stray Cats could do it, Nashville could too. But at the same time that Earle allowed himself to be shrink-wrapped and delivered to the public, he had begun to build a name around town as a writer of merit—even if the early records failed to show it.

With *Guitar Town*, Earle lives up to that reputation, the record proving him to be not only a first-rate writer, but a singer of far greater depth and sensitivity than any of his previous records hinted. In a voice that recalls the wry, plaintive sparseness of John Prine and the tender tough-guy bravado of Mellencamp, Earle moves through the personal sagas of small-town dreamers, big love losers, and day-to-day existers, hanging on by their fingernails and praying for change.

All ten songs deal, in one way or another, with the lure and the loneliness of the road, and with the hope, the disappointment, and the salvation it brings. There's the small-time rocker of "Guitar Town" who tires of his "two pack habit and a motel tan," the gas pump attendant of "Someday" who spends his life counting out-of-state plates, the Southerners who take the "Hillbilly Highway" north to find work in the factories, and the father who calls home to talk to the "Little Rock 'n' Roller" who is growing up without him. On the whole, the songs paint a bleak portrait of disillusioned white working-class America. And most of them are also more autobiographical than they seem.

Born in Fort Monroe, Virginia, where his father was stationed in the Army (his Texas grandfather sent a can of Lone Star dirt to be placed under the delivery table so the boy could be close to his roots), Earle grew up seventeen miles northeast of San Antonio, in Schertz, Texas, from all accounts, the kind of dead-end town he describes in "Someday." The oldest of five kids, he quickly fell under the spell of what would become his two main influences: the music his uncle Nick Fain hammered out of an old guitar and the Elvis Presley records Earle started buying in grade school. His first guitar came along when he was eleven—an acoustic model, since his family couldn't afford an electric.

At fourteen, Earle ran away from home to play music in Houston, eventually hooking up with such songwriters as Townes Van Zandt ("a real good teacher and a real bad role model") and Richard Dobson— performers who had achieved cult status in the region for their lyrical, literate writing. In 1974, he hitchhiked to Nashville, where he played in various bands, among them that of Texas expatriate Guy Clark, and eventually wrote songs recorded by Carl Perkins ("Mustang Wine"), Johnny Lee ("When You Fall in Love"), and others. His big break came —and went—when Elvis Presley chose one of Earle's tunes, but failed to show for the recording session.

Earle's career as an artist still looked doubtful, and every few years, like the characters in his music, he would take to the road again, hoping whatever he'd find would "boost the low signal" of his self-esteem. The songs on *Guitar Town* were written in Nashville, in Alabama, in Mexico, in Los Angeles, and in San Antonio while Earle was getting the second of his three divorces and living with friends. As a result, he "appears to be the very guy he's singing about," as one critic noted.

In delineating the trouble with today's country music, *Time* magazine declared in September 1986 that "at least one . . . trouble is . . . there is only one Steve Earle . . . An old-fashioned engine, maybe, but built for speed and just the thing to get country music back on track." MCA is betting that it's so—the company has given him a seven-album contract.

The following interview was recorded in May 1986 in a Nashville restaurant. Since then, his follow-up album, *Exit O*, has been released to excellent reviews.

Q If you compare the Steve Earle on MCA with the Steve Earle on Epic and LSI records, you might think they were two different artists. Why is that?

A Well, there was quite a bit of time in between there. It wasn't like I turned around and did something different overnight. The first two Epic singles were originally cut for LSI in '82. That's four years. Also, we were cutting some outside material. I just wasn't writing up to my potential. I think I was a better writer when I was twenty years old than I was in that period. Then I started writing again for some reason.

Q What brought on that pause in writing?

A The business just started to get me. I had a publishing situation where I really didn't get any feedback. Now I'm in a publishing situation [with the Oak Ridge Boys' Silverline-Goldline publishing firm] where they make writers feel good about themselves. Because every time you finish a song, the fear that you'll never write another one is the first thing that comes to mind. See, I don't ever remember the process of writing a song. It's like they just all of a sudden exist. It's real strange. That's why I've always had trouble when people ask me, "Well, how do you write a song? Do you write the lyrics first, or do you write the music first?" People try to nail you down to that process, and I don't know. I really don't have any idea. None whatsoever.

Q You mean, when you wake up in the morning, there's a song next to the pillow?

A Almost. The good song period. That's like Webb Wilder's line: "This is a little song that me and Bobby wrote, but the good lyric fairy didn't choose to visit us on this one." (Laughter) It really is still sort of a mystery to me. But the main thing is I got to a point where I was feeling good about myself as a writer again, and I was determined to make a record that you could put on the turntable and listen to. It was sequenced before it was recorded. I wanted it to all hang together, and so I sat down and wrote it in one time frame. And I write under pressure pretty well. I needed a kick in the butt, and this project was just the thing. The next one will be more political. I'm halfway through writin' it now. But "Someday" and "Hillbilly Highway" were written two or three weeks before the session, so I'll write right up until the last minute.

Q There's a definite road theme that runs through *Guitar Town*.

A Yeah, sort of two things. The first two things I wrote were "Guitar Town" and "Down the Road," because I was looking for an opening and an ending. So I wrote 'em like bookends, and then filled in the spaces in the middle. And the album's kind of about me. It's kind of personal. But a couple of songs were written in the later stages, and "Someday" and "Good Ol' Boy" were more about regular people. "Someday," though, was part of the road theme to the album. Because we did 77,000 miles in '83, so there was no way that the road couldn't seep into this record. But I've always had problems with road songs. People don't want to hear you feelin' sorry for yourself because you're ridin' around in a bus that costs more than their house.

Q It's not that kind of road song, though.

A No, it's not. And I was adamant about that. I thought, "This record's not going where I want it to, because I don't think people will want to hear that." But it really was something that I had to get out of my system, and it helped me, sort of like therapy. I got to feelin' real good about myself and what I do for the first time in years. The next record will probably have more things like "Someday" and "Good Ol' Boy."

Q "Someday" is the portrait of the gas attendant caught in small-town isolation. Did that come out of your own experience to some degree?

A Well, I did live in a small town outside of San Antonio, but that's not coming from that end of it as much as it is traveling on the road and seeing these people. Interstate highways are like a tunnel that runs through the country. You're not really in Texas, and you're not really in Ohio. It's like federal property, and you don't see the towns. I remember getting feedback from people that we met, and they didn't know what to think about us. All these people pile off a bus or out of a van in the middle of the night, and it was really . . . I slopped it around to assume that character, but the town in "Someday" is Jackson, Tennessee. And there *was* a particular person, a kid who was workin' on his car. It was about two o'clock in the morning, and not that many people were stoppin'. We'd always gas up before we'd cross the state line into Arkansas, because gas was a lot more expensive in Arkansas. So we stopped in Jackson to top off the tank, and when we pulled up, there was nobody in the gas station. The kid was up under his car. And there was a little bit of an attitude there. He didn't like us very much. I'm not exactly sure why, but one theory was that we were just passin' through and he was sorta stuck there. And that stayed with me for a long time—almost a year and a half—before I wrote the song. And "Someday" is a song that all the critics seem to pick out. It's been quoted more than anything else. And

I'm enjoying playing that more than anything else in the show. It's the one song where I like to get on real solid ground, plant my feet, and just nail nearly every night. It nearly always goes well, because it's all attitude, you know.

Q Even more than "Hillbilly Highway," which has that jaunty rhythm?

A Yeah. "Hillbilly Highway" is probably the hardest thing on the album to do live. It's very tough to play, and if the monitors aren't good, it's tricky.

Q How autobiographical is that tune?

A Not very. I start out saying, "My granddaddy was a miner," but mining was probably the only thing my grandfather *didn't* do. On the other hand, my father is an air traffic controller, and he's the only one of his brothers who got out of Jacksonville [Texas]. But I got that song basically from *Coal Miner's Daughter* [the Loretta Lynn autobiography]. That's where the term came from—in the first chapter, she talks about the hillbilly highway. That's the only place I've seen that term. And it was just because of all the people comin' up North from the coalfields to work. But the parts of the song about the relationship between the third generation and the other two generations are autobiographical, and the rest of it's not.

Q What ties the song together is the recurring line about the woman crying when the man or the boy leaves home—"never heard such a lonesome sound."

A Yeah, that was really weird. After we [Earle and Jimbeau Hinson] wrote the line in the first verse, I just kept singing it [in the next verses] because I was stuck for a line in that position. And before it was over with, I thought, "Well, hey, it's kinda cool to have that line come through every time." But that song is probably more of a hybrid than anything else on the record.

Q Emory Gordy, Jr., your co-producer along with Tony Brown, told me you've had a bit of opposition from some of the radio stations—some of them don't want to play "Hillbilly Highway" because of the negative connotation of the word "hillbilly."

A Yeah, it's just silly. You know, before the record companies came to Nashville, guys came down from New York and brought masters and recorded. Originally they called it folk music, and then they called it hillbilly music. The term comes from Detroit. It was a derogatory term aimed at people who were goin' up there and taking jobs. But they needed the work. So it was real common when the mining was slow. And also when people got to a certain age, they started worryin' about black lung [disease]. So they would go up North and look for jobs. Or they'd go just to get out of the mines. And now they're comin' back down because GM's built that Saturn plant outside of town [in Smyrna, Tennessee]. And the people who've got priority on those jobs are first- or second-generation Tennesseans that went up there for work. Anyway, I looked up the word "hillbilly" in the dictionary, and it said "a Michigan farmer." (Chuckling) But Ernest Tubb meant well when he said, "Don't let's call it 'hillbilly' music anymore." You can take it a couple of ways. There's the Lenny Bruce theory, you know. He had the routine where he said "nigger" about fifty times when he first walked onstage. So you can take a negative term and turn around and use it to your advantage, make it stronger. I have more of a problem with country music, 'cause there's been so many contrived crossover records tagged with the word "country." That's why we have a problem bringing in anybody new, and bringing in the younger audience. They assume that's what it's gonna be. My record's racked "country" in the stores, and there are people who are gonna dismiss it before they hear it, because it's country. My manager [Will Botwin] also manages Rosanne Cash. And MTV won't play her videos, even though Rose is essentially a pop artist. But they're gonna penalize her just because she records in Nashville. It's ridiculous. I don't understand that.

Q You've also had to go back in and recut "Guitar Town" for the radio version, changing, "Everybody told me you can't get far / On thirty-seven dollars and a Jap guitar," to "cheap guitar."

A Yeah. Well, I don't want to alienate the vast Japanese-American country audience, you know. They made Lyle Lovett take the word "nigger" out of one of his songs. So Lyle and I sent Tony [Brown] a memo saying we'd solved the problem. We'd put "nigger" in "Guitar Town" and "Jap" in his song.

Q You had a number of other things going on in your life while you were writing this—you were getting a divorce, for example.

A Oh, yeah. I didn't live anywhere when I wrote this record. I didn't even have an apartment. I was just sort of doin' a couch tour. The record was writtten here in Nashville, at [Oak Ridge Boy] Bill Golden's house in Gulf Shores, Alabama, in San Miguel de Allende in central Mexico, and in San Antonio. Oh, yeah, and also in L.A., at [guitarist] Richard Bennett's house, 'cause we wrote two of the tracks—"Good Ol' Boy" and "Think It Over"—together. Which was nice. I almost moved to L.A. during that period. I hadn't signed with MCA yet, and I got the idea that I could make a better hillbilly record out there than I could here. And I went out there and hung out long enough to find out that that was probably not true.

Q "Little Rock 'n' Roller," the song about a father's phone call home to his son, is obviously a true story.

A Yeah. I wrote that in Mexico. It was really hard to write. And it's not that much fun to perform. The better it comes off, the harder it is on you. Because at that point, my ex-wife and I weren't even speaking, and I really had doubts whether I was going to be J.T.'s father anymore [referring to his son, Justin Townes, named after Townes Van Zandt]. I mean, she could have kept me from seeing him. She could have done lots of things. And I was down in Mexico with friends, and I was bummin' *everybody* out. I was industrial-strength morose. But I couldn't figure out what was botherin' me. I couldn't put my finger on it. And then finally it dawned on me, and I wrote the song, and I was okay after that. So it served its purpose.

Q Your son is four now. You've been quoted as saying one of the deepest hurts you ever had was when you came home from a tour one time and he didn't know who you were.

A Yeah. That hurt a lot. He was a year old the first time I went out, and I was gone for twenty-eight days. That's a long time to a little kid. It's the equivalent of ten years to an adult. I mean, they change so fast. And he didn't recognize me. I can't think of anything that's hurt me more, and I've been hurt *a lot*, you know? That was real, real hard to take.

Q The life of an itinerant musician is a lot more difficult than it's cracked up to be.

A Well, I don't think it's really that hard. It's hard on you physically, but that's something you get used to. I love it. It's harder on me stayin' in town for extended periods of time.

Q You've been friends with Townes Van Zandt and Guy Clark for a long time. What do they say about your album?

A I haven't talked to either of 'em about it. I talked to Guy last night, and he didn't mention whether he had heard the record or not. So I don't know. And I haven't seen Townes since he was in town here about six months ago.

Q Guy and Townes were role models for you, and while they've both achieved cult status as writers, neither of them have approached the commercial success you've attained with just one album.

A Yeah. It sort of bothers me. Townes just came along about three or four years too late. 'Cause his first album came out in '68. And he was a pretty serious folksinger. I think things would have been a lot different for Townes if he had come along just a little earlier. I think he would have received the recognition that a lot of people in the folk boom did. Because there's certainly no one who writes any better in that whole crop of Cambridge and New York folkies. And there will always be a demand for Guy Clark. Guy could be writing a lot of things besides songs. It just happened to be songs. It's almost incidental.

Q It's obvious that your writing is influenced by hanging out with those guys, and wanting to do quality, literate work. But you've managed to fit intelligent lyrics to an upbeat and rhythmic style of music that gets you played on the radio—something they haven't been too successful at doing.

A I think it's just that they're comin' from bein' folksingers. But I'm less pure, and more ambitious. And I've been called an opportunist son of a bitch.

Q By whom?

A By other writers. When I first came to town. But I believe in populist art. I believe in making things as accessible as possible, strictly because I've got an eighth-grade education, and I don't know how to do anything else. Springsteen's sales figures before *Born in the U.S.A.* were the best-kept secret in the record business. Nobody knows *what* he was selling, but he wasn't selling [a lot of albums]. As good as he was writing. And with *Born in the U.S.A.*, he got out of that eastern seaboard, inside-joke thing. I know some people who had been fans for a long time were disappointed in *Born in the U.S.A.* I can't understand that, because it's really the strongest set of songs he's ever had. And they're so simple. Lyrically, there's a lot more economy of words, and the sound is more stripped down. He's reaching a wider audience because it's a very universal record. That's why it works.

Q It's usually harder to write something simple than something complex.

A Oh, yeah. Townes's best song is "If I Needed You." It's the simplest thing he ever wrote. I mean, the ones I really tear apart are things like "Lungs" and "Mr. Mudd and Mr. Gold." I'm one of the few people besides Townes who knows "Mr. Mudd and Mr. Gold" and can perform it. I ruined my copy of the album pickin' up the tone arm and puttin' it back down again, tryin' to learn that lyric. But I really did it as an exercise, trying to understand that type of writing.

Q The jackets for the Epic singles show photographs of you dressed in rockabilly clothing.

A Yeah. Wasn't that cute?

Q Whose idea was that?

A The art department at CBS's. And mine.

Q Did you walk around town wearing that stuff?

A Naw. I walked around lookin' like I do now. But I did wear that sort of stuff for shows durin' that period. I think Nashville was lookin' for a rockabilly act, because Stray Cats were happenin'. And I had that [LSI] EP out, and I sort of turned out to be it. I was seduced by it myself. All I knew was I had a record deal, and no one had ever paid any attention to me as an artist before. It wasn't until much later on that I realized that there just wasn't any room for me as a writer in that format. So it's as much my fault as it is theirs.

Q The rockabilly format?

A Yeah. The three-piece band. We never did ballads. We couldn't.

Q Do you think you needed that as a steppingstone?

A Well, whatever, I have no regrets about it. But I don't think I'd have this record deal if it hadn't been for that one.

Q Is that what you meant by the other songwriters calling you opportunistic? Did they think you were jumping on the nearest bandwagon?

A No, because the EP was cut before [Stray Cats'] *Built for Speed* was released in the United States. When I made that record, I'd never heard Stray Cats, and didn't even know who they were. My interest in rockabilly goes back to everything I've ever done. Because of my age—I was born in '55—I did things like that sort of backwards. I got into [novelist Jack] Kerouac from reading *The Electric Kool-Aid Acid Test*, by Tom Wolfe, and backtracking. I got into rockabilly by listening to Credence [Clearwater Revival] and Beatles records, and tracin' it back. 'Cause I'm too young to have heard those records when they came out. But, no, I had a genuine interest in it. I'm a real good rhythm guitar player. I've got a strange sense of rhythm, and when I converted that over to electric guitar, it just lent itself to that style. There's still a lot of that in what I'm doing. And it'll always be there.

Q "Think It Over" is probably the most authentically rockabilly of the tracks. It sounds a lot like the old Elvis Presley song "I'm Left, You're Right, She's Gone," with a little Buddy Holly and Carl Perkins thrown in.

A Yeah. Richard and I wrote that one. But to me, "Hillbilly Highway" is a rockabilly record. And then there are other things that stylistically don't have anything to do with rockabilly. That's one of the things that I'm most pleased about with this record—we found a little slot in the sound, and we're able to duplicate it onstage, 'cause it's the same guys. That's real important to me.

Q The record company has invited comparisons to John Cougar Mellen-camp.

A Yeah. Well, they were happening anyway.

Q How do you feel about that? And about the comparisons with Spring-steen?

A It doesn't bother me. The Cougar and Springsteen comparisons are just because of "Someday" and "Good Ol' Boy." And because there's a tendency toward lyric-oriented American music.

Q And small-town vignettes.

A Well, small-town motifs are not what I'm about. I'm about songs. And I'm gonna do a whole album of historical songs one of these days, 'cause I think that's the only way "The Devil's Right Hand" would fit into my albums, the way I'm doing 'em. It would seem out of place, stuck in the middle of this record.

Q You're not afraid the Cougar stuff is going to hurt you—that people will call you "a country John Cougar" and stop there?

A Well, I don't know if it's gonna hurt me or not. I wish they wouldn't do it. But the Midwest is real AOR [album oriented rock]-oriented. That's the big radio format there, and that's what Cougar appeals to. And Spring-steen built his base from the Northeast, because they're very Top 40-radio-oriented in the Northeast. He's also got a huge influence of beach music in his music. I'm from the Southwest, and I live in the Southeast. So that's where I'm coming from. The similarity's there, and I understand the comparisons. But I think they're irrelevant.

Q Well, you also dress something like Cougar, with the denim jacket and the bandanna tied around your wrist.

A Yeah, but I've been dressin' like that for a long time. I'm sure I'm gonna catch some flak. [Critic] John Lomax made a big deal out of the fact that he thought our album covers were real similar. He said *Guitar Town* looked like *Scarecrow*. I never thought about it. They're both black-and-white, but that's about the only thing. So I don't know. It may hurt, but I think that the music holds up enough on this record that it'll overcome any of that. About categorizing what I do, you know . . . Emory [Gordy, Jr.] says it's white contemporary music. (Laughter)

Q At your showcase last night, the audience was singing along with "My Old Friend the Blues." Everybody seems to identify with it. Where did that song come from?

A I was in San Antonio, but I wasn't livin' anywhere. And I was sort of industrial-strength in love. It was a real weird deal, though. I was flyin' down to San Antonio to see this girl every time I had some time off, but it just wasn't clicking. I don't know whether it was me and the place I was in at the time, or just the combination of the two of us. But it was a real strange sort of relationship. She lived in a part of town that I got my "street legs" in. And I got up one morning and I was pretty bummed out, and I started walkin' around, hoping that sheer geography would anchor me. But even that didn't work. So I went back, and that melody had been laying around for six months, and I had the guitar lick, and I wrote it in literally about twenty minutes. It was just one of those deals. It's the real thing. It didn't require any work at all. That was it. As a writer, I was told for years and years to write up-tempo and positive. 'Cause that's what radio wants. But life's not always up-tempo and positive. And you need songs like that. Sometimes people need to cry as much as they need to laugh, and the end result is the same. In the show, if contact with the audience is marginal, I've discovered that when we hit that song I've usually got 'em from then on. 'Cause it drops down, and it makes 'em listen.

Q You mentioned "The Devil's Right Hand," which Waylon Jennings has recorded on *Will the Wolf Survive?* That's a very different kind of song from what we hear on *Guitar Town.*

A Yeah. It's eight years old. I was living in Wimberley, Texas, for about three months, decompressing after living in Mexico for a while. I'd been down there sittin' out a publishing contract. There was no office to take the songs to, and I could live cheaper down there. So rather than move straight back to Nashville, I rented a trailer in Wimberley for a while. And I had about sixty guns. I was mobilized for Iwo Jima. Sat on my front porch for the whole three months. Probably went through fifty or sixty rounds a day. I wasn't writing that much, but that was one of two things that I wrote.

Q Why sixty guns?

A It was just my hobby. That's the only time in my life I've ever had a hobby. It was just something that I got into. Shot a lot of black-powder weapons, for the most part. They're cheaper to shoot. I was just sorta into 'em, and it was a lot of fun. I killed many, many cans from my front porch. Some people think that's a gun-control song, which is really strange. I was a member of NRA [National Rifle Association] when I wrote that song. The only reason I'm not now is because all my guns were stolen about four or five years ago. I went on a guitar-buying binge after that. Now I've got twenty-five or twenty-six guitars. So, you know. It was my hobby.

Q That's a song that demonstrates your ability to create a character.

A Well, that's real important.

Q Did you learn that from Townes and Guy, or from reading books?

A Both. When it comes to books, my favorite form is probably the historical novel, and biography. Historical novels fascinate me because of the research that they require. Anything that's in a particular setting like that works for me, for some reason. When I was a kid, what probably impressed me more than anything else, and had a real profound effect on my life, was *Lust for Life*. I like Gore Vidal's books. Right now, I'm reading *Lincoln*. And I loved *Burr*. That's one of my favorite books. That's a neat form. And I went through a period where I was writing songs that were really sort of the same thing. I had to do research to get 'em together, but then you assume a character, and you create a whole other little history within the history that's yours. That's what folk music's all about. I really enjoy it. One of these days, I do want to do a whole album of songs like that.

Q Now the story about your grandfather sending a can of Texas dirt up to the hospital in Virginia sounds a little bit like folklore.

A No, that's true. My dad was in the Army at Fort Monroe, and my grandfather couldn't stand the fact that I was gonna be born in a foreign land. So he put his youngest son, who'd never been out of Jacksonville, Texas, in his life, on a train with a Prince Albert can full of dirt from his pasture. Scared him to death. The kid was fifteen years old, and all of a sudden, bam, he's goin' to Virginia.

Q So was the can of dirt actually placed under the delivery table?

A Well, no. A great big ol' Army nurse with a mustache prevented that. So they settled for makin' sure I didn't touch any foreign soil before they got me home. They stuck my feet in it. I've got a picture of it. I did the same thing with my boy. J.T. was born about six in the evening. I called my grandfather, and he left in the rain and went out to the San Jacinto Monument, where Santa Ana was captured, and got the dirt from there, and we stuck J.T.'s feet in it. I've still got the dirt in a jar. And I've got the pictures of both of us in the same frame. Texans are into that sort of thing.

Q So you consider yourself a native Texan?

A Oh, yeah. Well, you know, the Army doesn't count. That's suspended animation. It has nothing to do with nativity. Any dependents that are born while you're stationed elsewhere are from wherever you're from. And I grew up there. I mean, I was less than a year old when we moved back to Texas.

Q Before we started taping, you said that when you were a kid, you didn't want to be a fireman, you didn't want to be a cowboy, that this was it. From what age, though?

A When I saw my first Elvis Presley movie. I was a big Elvis fan, went to all the movies, even after they were bad. I mean, I even paid to see *Spinout*, you know? (Chuckle) And I started listening to music, and noticing music . . . I was buying records when I was in the first grade. That's what I spent any money I got my hands on on. I bought whatever singles came out—I mean, *lots* of 'em. I didn't start buying albums until the Beatles, around my thirteenth birthday.

Q So Elvis was the biggest influence?

A Yeah, and my uncle [Nick Fain], my mother's half brother, who's only five years older than me. I was real close to him, and he played, and I really don't remember wantin' to be anything else. I never really had a chance to. Nick was always just sort of there, and he was my hero. That's what he wanted to do, so that's what I wanted to do, too.

Q Is he still around?

A He's still around. He's havin' a rough time of it. He pretty much made his living playing in clubs. And he wrote some incredible things.

Q Has your success been frightening in any way?

A It was for a while there. This tour allayed any fears that I had. Like I said, I never wanted to do anything else. So it doesn't scare me a bit. I'm a horrible hypochondriac, and I'm even starting to get over that. If I survive this tour, I can survive anything.

Q A horrible hypochondriac?

A Oh, yeah. I'm terrible. I mean, I've been so bad to myself. If I'd known I was gonna live this long, I probably would have taken a lot better care of myself. (Chuckle)

Q You're just thirty-one.

A Yeah, but I was convinced I was only gonna live to be twenty-six or twenty-seven, and all of a sudden, I discovered I was twenty-eight. It's just one of those deals. I think I'm wrapped pretty tight. I can be pretty hard on myself internally. But now I'm startin' to cool out a little bit, to the point where I don't worry about it so much. I think I became aware of my mortality a little younger than most people do, because I've been in the music business up here since I was nineteen, and I've been doin' it for a livin' since I was sixteen. We've got a pretty high mortality rate. I've lost a lot of friends. You become acquainted with death at a real early age in this business, and I think I was preoccupied with it for a long time.

Q How so?

A Well, I've got a hiatal hernia which causes real bad chest pains. For a long time, anytime I'd get any gas, which happens to you on the road, not eatin' right, I would sort of panic. And I'm sort of borderline hypoglycemic, just because of my diet. There's nobody with normal blood sugar in this country, I don't think. So I used to just worry about it a lot. I picked it up from my mother. She keeps several medical books and the PDR [Physicians' Desk Reference] close at hand at all times. But now I've gotten back to the point of thinking I'm gonna die when I'm gonna die, and there's not anything that I can do about it. I've relaxed about it a little bit. I think it's just anxiety. There are so many things that I felt like I didn't have control over in my career, and my life. And when you can't do anything about those things, you start lookin' for something else to worry about. That's really all it was. Just classic anxiety. About everything in general.

Q Your writing talks about restlessness a lot, but not necessarily about anxiety.

A No. One of the reasons I think I feel better is because I'm writing better again. There was a point at which I was absolutely fearless, until I was about twenty-five or twenty-six. I drank a lot. When I was twenty-three, twenty-four, twenty-five, I drank a quart of liquor every day. God bless Townes. He's my favorite writer, but one of the best things that ever happened to me was realizing that I wasn't Townes Van Zandt. And there was a lot of pressure on me to be a folksinger. I hitchhiked to Nashville. I mean, I didn't know you could get here any other way.

Q Pressure from whom?

A Well, from Townes and other people. Townes saw me as the last folksinger. Because I would do almost anything. Whatever I had to do. I used to hitchhike to most of my dates in Texas before I moved up here. It seemed ridiculous to me to pay for transportation when I could stick my thumb out and get it for free. And it was real easy to get rides in those days. I made the trip back and forth to Nashville several times before I ever drove it in a car or flew it in a plane. I tried to hitchhike to L.A. several times, but I never could get past Muleshoe, Texas. It's against the law to hitchhike on the interstate highway, and for some reason they enforce it in Muleshoe. I've been in the Muleshoe jail three times, always for hitchhiking. My only crime. My father wired the money out, and they let me go.

Q Any other interesting hitchhiking experiences?

A Well, there are a lot of 'em. 'Cause I was real young. I can't imagine doing it anymore. I had some close calls. I ran away from home when I was fourteen and went to Houston. This was in the early seventies, and I remember a car coming up and asking me if I wanted a ride one night.

Years later, when the Dean Corrll–Elmer Wayne Henley [homosexual abduction-murder ring] story came out, I realized I had been in that part of town then, walking around the city in the middle of the night. 'Cause what I'd do. I wasn't staying anywhere, and you didn't want to go to sleep at night, because it wasn't safe. So you'd stay up all night, and just walk around and find things to do. And in the daytime, you'd go to a park and lay down in the grass and go to sleep, because nobody would mess with you as long as it was broad daylight. So it was pretty weird.

Q You said in the car that you're so close to your family that your father has used up all his sick days traveling to see you perform.

A Right.

Q If you're so close to your family, then why did you run away from home?

A Just to play music. And I didn't want to finish school. That was the main thing. I did *not* want to stay in high school. I didn't feel like there was anything I could learn there. And I knew what I wanted to do—what I wanted to be. My parents and I went through about two years of . . . well, I put 'em through hell for several years. 'Cause I grew up in a weird part of San Antonio. It's real strange socially. Because the high school was built to be a college preparatory school, because there were all these new subdivisions. No vocational training whatsoever. And then through rezoning, we ended up bordering on one of the poorest barrios in the city. So we had a lot of real poor Mexican kids and a lot of kids from out on the edge of town—farm kids and ranch kids. We're talkin' about small ranches, you know, and they didn't have the money to go to college. So we had the highest dropout rate in San Antonio, and one of the worst juvenile delinquency and drug problems in the city. They used to come through with dogs and search every locker in the school at least twice a month. We also had a real strict dress code. And I warred with 'em about the length of my hair. Then, you know, the rednecks . . . I got beat up for havin' long hair. Pickup truck would stop, three or four guys would jump out and beat the shit out of me, cut my hair off with a pocketknife, and then take my cowboy boots. And the kids with long hair thought I was strange because I wore cowboy boots. So me, and Charlie, my road manager, and two or three other people felt like we were fairly intelligent, but that we really weren't gettin' what we needed out of school, and we all dropped out. We were sort of our own little group, and we didn't really fit in anywhere. It was strange. It was a weird place to grow up.

Q It's fairly common for creative people, or people who have achieved something on their own terms, to have been social misfits most of their lives.

A Yeah. I've always wondered about that. Because my family is real important to me. I get incensed when people misspell my name, because my father went through too much hell for anybody to get the name wrong, once I start to amount to something. So I have no idea why I ran away from home and why I rebelled against them. Because they loved me, and they never had any trouble showing love. My family's real affectionate. On the other hand, I think the reason I've had such bad luck with women is because I always gravitated toward women with fucked-up family lives. So I don't know. Maybe running away from home was just practicing. You gotta rebel against something.

Q Well, of course, there's also a romance in taking off like that, particularly for a young man who aspires to be a folksinger. It's the old Woody Guthrie—Bob Dylan legend.

A Yeah, and I just equate that [staying in one place] with complacency, and I cannot allow myself to become emotionally complacent. As long as I'm not quite satisfied with what's going on, I'll always write. And continuing to write is the most important thing to me.

Q In your case, the more personal the song is, the more powerful.

A Yeah. Of course, you can't put in too many inside things that no one else understands. But if you can write something that's ultra-personal, then you're puttin' a big piece of yourself out there. And people pick up on that. "Little Rock 'n' Roller" is like that. So is "My Old Friend the Blues." And "Fearless Heart." You can feel it click. Recently, I've got more control over audiences than I've ever had before, for some reason. I don't know whether it's the songs, or whether I've just gotten better at it. I mean, we did the Jamboree, in Wheeling, West Virginia, where the median age was probably fifty, and the shows went great. And we opened for George Jones, and it was the same thing. The median age was probably forty-five on that show. I have a theory that older audiences in the Midwest and in the North will accept me more readily than older audiences in the South. I don't know why, except they're not closed to the idea that this is country music. You know what I mean? There aren't so many preconceived ideas about what I must be because of the way I look. It's different in the South.

Q It's always amazed me just how many country music fans there are in the North. People tend to think most of them are in the South, and I'm not sure that's true.

A Well, the Midwest is real strong. It's almost like playin' Europe there, in that they're so polite. They applaud after the numbers, and it's over with. It's real different from playin' the South. In New York, though, they *are* hillbillies. They just don't know it.

Q You said earlier today, "The days of winging it off the numbers charts in this town are over." Why do you say that?

A Well, the Nashville numbers system [a form of musical shorthand used by session players] is a real unique thing, and it's great. But now we're getting into A&R [artist and repertoire] people who are musicians again. Like Emory and Tony. [Jimmy] Bowen [president, MCA/Nashville] has put together an incredible staff, like [bassist] David Hungate [formerly of Toto]. In a way, their background is Los Angeles. I mean, Emory's from Georgia, and he used to play with Emmylou Harris and with Elvis, but he's also played on films. And if you're gonna produce an act, I think you're gonna need to have some knowledge of music theory. It's just speaking the language of music. It's a more critical language than the Nashville numbers system is, when you actually get into musical notation. But I think that a producer in Nashville in the future is going to need that background.

Q You said that Nashville's been cheating record buyers for a long time, packaging one or two hits with eight fillers. Do you really think that's going to change?

A Yeah, I do. Because otherwise, we're going to be a ghost town. We're in the business of selling albums. We're not in the business of . . . well, look at radio. [Warner Brothers Records executive and producer] Jim Ed Norman went out on the road to talk to radio, and he got his tail in a crack. He was gonna come back with the information Warner Brothers needed to get their songs on the radio, and he said, "Hey, man, we're behind you. You just let us know what you need and what you think your listeners want to hear." And the guy said, "What makes you think we care? We're in the radio business. We sell advertising. If country music doesn't sell advertising, we'll go to talk." And by the same token, we're in the business of selling albums, not supplying music to radio. We need them, and they need us, but they shouldn't dictate the situation any more than we should. There has to be a place in the middle. I think things are gonna change. Because there is a stigma attached to country music— that the albums are not worth buying.

Q Why is that, though?

A They don't spend enough money on records, for one thing.

Q Let's face it, up until a very few years ago, the country music audience was not that discriminating or sophisticated about what they accepted on their records.

A But being sophisticated and being stupid are two different things. I don't think there's anything on my album that people of average intelligence can't understand and relate to. I'm trying to make records where people don't feel cheated. Nashville has been guilty of insulting the country music audience for years and years. And they're a lot smarter than they get credit for.

Q I'm just saying that it never occurred to them to expect more than one hit and the rest fillers, or that the producer also had the publishing on nine of the ten songs.

A Well, of course, they don't know any of that. There's no reason for them to know that. But those things always come back on people when they practice that sort of thing. I've seen it happen. Plus, Tony Brown and Emory Gordy are here. The guard has changed.

Q Well, at MCA, at least.

A It has at MCA, and it's changing other places, too. Nobody else is gonna be able to compete with MCA if they don't change. I really believe that. We have one of the biggest-selling acts in country music, George Strait. And we have the best track record as far as selling albums on our developing artists. They're selling more records on Steve Wariner than have ever been sold on him. It's not marketing so much as it is they're just delivering records that people will buy. People aren't disappointed in the records when they buy 'em.

Q Where do you want to see all this go for you?

A That's probably dictated by whatever the audience turns out to be. I really don't think it's a matter of country or pop or rock. You can accuse this record of being a rock-'n'-roll record, but you can't accuse it of being a pop record. There's a difference, and there's nothing pop about it. I consider myself a country singer. That's why I signed with the Nashville division of MCA. But I just want to reach the largest audience that I can, and that also means a rock-'n'-roll audience, which I believe I can reach without changing the music. There's a twelve-inch version of "Someday" goin' out to AOR radio. That's the West Coast's decision, and we in Nashville really don't have anything to do with it. It's a sampler, with "Someday" on the A side and "Fearless Heart" and "Good Ol' Boy" on the other side. So we'll see what happens with that. It's shipping the week after "Guitar Town" ships to the country stations. But country music is where strong and topical lyrics originally came from. It was always the most important thing in country music. Lyrics are important in music in general these days, and I'd like to be a part of bringing it back. It'll change in a few years, and we'll be back to songs where lyrics aren't important anymore. Because sometimes people want to dance, and sometimes they want to listen. And right now there is a movement toward lyrics again. I think of myself primarily as a songwriter. If I didn't write, I'd blow up. It's very important for me to succeed as an artist, but it's more important for me to succeed as a writer. I really think that I was born to do this.

Merle Haggard

The bus, an hour behind schedule, heaves a puff of black smoke as it limps to the curb outside the auditorium and collapses. Quick as a bus door can open, it does, and three stiff-jointed pickers crawl out and disappear onto the sidewalk, leaving the vehicle's premier occupant rummaging around inside.

Finally, the door opens again with its customary swoosh, and the drawn face of Merle Haggard, his blue eyes vacant and cloudy, comes into view. He surveys the situation for a moment, scowls, runs a hand through thinning hair, and then slumps off the bus, a wrinkled gray duffel bag of a human. Haggard walks a short way up the sidewalk, stops to light a cigarette, and then turns back around and ambles into the building, seeming somehow like an old sailor gone to seed.

"The finest American singer-songwriter of the post-Hank Williams era," as writer John Lomax III was to dub him, Merle Haggard, 51, is also perhaps the most charismatic of the country music luminaries. Moody, uncompromising, and unpredictable in his personal life, he wears the scars of life's battles as badges of survival. His power, assesses country music journalist Ronni Lundy, "is in the pain he serves with no excuses, no plea for understanding or a second chance." In his classic songs of drink, defeat, and heartbreak, he seems hell-bent on living out a romantic-loner image gleaned early in his youth, or in making good on a public relations tag of the new Woody Guthrie, fighting for the plight of the working-man and the socially disenfranchised.

A complex and thoughtful man, Haggard at once expresses a hard masculinity and a tender inner core. Many of his most memorable songs —"Today I Started Loving You Again," "If We're Not Back in Love by Monday," "Tonight I'll Kick the Footlights Out Again," and even the songs chronicling his childhood, "Mama Tried" and "Hungry Eyes"— ache with the anticipation of a fulfilling relationship with a woman, and of longing for the security of hearth and home.

In his private life, of course, Haggard, the restless, conflicted, dislocated, itinerant poet, has eschewed an array of wives and children for the lure and the loneliness of the road. He admits that "my character will probably pay in the end for not experiencing those soft and beautiful parts of life I've heard other people sing about in their songs."

Born in Bakersfield, California, a dry, flat, oil-and-agriculture town he and Buck Owens would later help develop as a notable country music center ("Nashville West"), Haggard, the son of Okie migrants, grew up in wrenching poverty, a converted railroad boxcar serving as the family home. ("When Merle sings 'Hungry Eyes,' " his mother once said, "almost every word of it really happened like that.") The boy was nine when his father died, and the loss sent him spiraling into confusion and self-doubt. From running away from home and hopping freights, he soon graduated to trouble with the law, mostly for burglary and auto theft.

At twenty, Haggard ended up in San Quentin State Penitentiary (turning twenty-one in prison, as he would later sing), for trying to burglarize a tavern he mistakenly believed had closed for the night. A stay in solitary confinement—where he was able to converse with convicted murderer Caryl Chessman through the ventilation system—shocked him into straightening out his life, and he was paroled in 1960, at age twenty-two. A dozen years later, Ronald Reagan, then governor of California, granted him a full pardon.

Back in Bakersfield after his parole, Haggard, strongly influenced by the recordings of Lefty Frizzell and Jimmie Rodgers, began picking up work as a guitar player and occasional singer in the town's rough-and-ready back-street bars. There he met Fuzzy Owen, an Arkansas musician, who eventually became his manager and who helped him secure his first recordings in the early '60s. By the end of the decade, he had written a number of his now classic songs—"The Bottle Let Me Down," "Mama Tried," "Hungry Eyes," and "Workin' Man Blues." His timeless and now well-covered standard "Today I Started Loving You Again" (co-written with his second wife, Bonnie Owens) came along in 1970, as did his most controversial song, "Okie from Muskogee," which had hippies and right-wingers arguing over the singer's intent.

In the early '70s, Haggard shifted his concentration from hit singles to experimentation with various musical forms and tributes, including a two-record salute to Jimmie Rodgers, *Same Train, A Different Time* (where he would explore the Depression-era motif that would later become a theme), and *A Tribute to the Best Damn Fiddle Player in the World*. The latter LP—for which Haggard learned to play the fiddle in three months—paid homage to the dying Bob Wills and sparked new, wide-ranging interest in western swing. A tribute to Dixieland music, *I Love Dixie Blues*, followed in 1974.

In the late 70's, Haggard moved his label affiliation from Capitol, where he'd been for twelve years, to MCA. The MCA albums were often uneven, but they also contained a number of brilliant sides, including "I Think I'll Just Stay Here and Drink," "Red Bandana," "It's Been a Great Afternoon," "If We're Not Back in Love by Monday," "I'm Always on a Mountain When I Fall," "The Way I Am," "Ramblin' Fever," "My Own Kind of Hat," and "Leonard." A 1980 LP, *Rainbow Stew/Live at Anaheim Stadium*, showcased his backing group, the Strangers, as one of the most exemplary bands in country music.

The following year, Haggard changed labels again, to Epic. Here, instead of simply making good records, he seemed to have something of substance to say once more, particularly with "Big City," which again addressed the unrest of the workingman. Duet albums with George Jones (*A Taste of Yesterday's Wine*) and Willie Nelson (the superlative *Poncho and Lefty*, which won them the CMA Vocal Duo of the Year award in 1983) quickly followed, while his solo recordings (*Going Where the Lonely Go* and *That's the Way Love Goes*) found him reflective and seemingly resolved to heartache.

By the mid-'80s, however, his LPs *It's All in the Game, Kern River*, and *A Friend in California* indicated a personal and artistic stagnation, if not disintegration, something he would not begin to pull out of until 1987, with *Seashores of Old Mexico*, another duet album with Willie Nelson, and *Chill Factor*, a magnificent display of both his writing and performance skills. A cursory look at his private life revealed he was $3 million in debt, his 1978 marriage to singer Leona Williams had broken up, and he had entered into a fourth matrimony that seemed shaky. Upon rumors of other personal problems, he had begun missing dates.

That's about where Haggard was when his bus pulled up outside the Louisville auditorium in September 1986. What I remember most about this interview was how easy he was to talk to. He seemed totally unguarded and genuine in his responses, and if he hadn't had a show to do in a couple of hours, I imagine we'd be there still.

Q Where do you figure you are in the scheme of things these days?

A At this point? Well, I'm just right where I was probably about 1965—every day you start over. There's a lot of sayings to cover it—"You're as good as your last record," or "You're as good as your last performance," or even "What have you done for me lately?" That's about where I'm at.

Q You've had more peaks than valleys in your career, however. You and Conway Twitty hold the record for the most number one singles, for example, although right now he's a few ahead of you.

A I really don't know. I've heard that.

Q Do you feel pressure to try to keep that lead?

A No, I never set out to do that. You know, a lot of people, I imagine, set out to become whatever they become. I just kind of eased into it sideways. I've been unaware of a lot of things. And I really didn't want a lot of things that's come my way. But life has a way of giving you what you don't want, you know. Had I wanted this, I probably never would have gotten it.

Q What did you not want? What would you give back, for example?

A Well, there's some areas in the business that I would like to have steered clear of. You talked about the peaks and valleys a minute ago. I guess the valleys are necessary so you can distinguish the peaks. I mean, life has been overwhelmingly good [to me] in the way that other people measure it. But no one knows, really, how much Conway Twitty likes what he's doing. And there's no way for Conway to even know whether he likes it, because he has nothing to compare it with. So there's no way for anyone else to know, except to guess, and say, "I wonder if I wouldn't enjoy that?" But there's no way for you to tell me what you do, and how your life is. I guess there are people who enjoy being looked at. And there's people who enjoy the cries and the screams. And there's people who enjoy the admiration and the praise that one gets. Part of it I enjoy. If I do something that I feel is good, I like people to applaud for it. But if I do something that I don't feel is good and they applaud, I don't like it. Because then I wonder whether they can even tell [what's good]. One time, I got mad at my guitar player, and we did a real bad show on purpose. And they stood up.

Q You did a bad show on purpose?

A Yeah, we did it on purpose. I was pissed off. I was tryin' to get a point across to him. He was doing little funny endings, and so I started singing like a little funny guy, you know? And most people didn't even know the difference.

Q Do you have contempt for your audience at times like that?

A Well, it makes you wonder, "What in the hell's the use of tryin' to do what you're doin'?" I mean, if they're gonna go for that. And it makes you feel kinda ignorant. Because whatever it is they liked all these many years, you don't even know what it is. You can't even give it to 'em, because when you give 'em what you thought was the direct opposite of what was good, and they go for it, then that leaves you totally in the dark.

Q Does that tempt you to let down on the quality of your writing or your performance?

A No, I keep writing and singing for the people who know what I'm doin'. There's just a few friends and critics, and other songwriters, and other guitar players. I keep workin' for those people. And that's probably why I've never been any bigger than I am. Because I never did cater to the autograph set. You know, they make up about four percent of all the people who come to the show. And they're the people who want more than their ticket gives 'em. If you gave it to them, they'd want somethin' else, you know. I never did do that. I didn't even do it when I was a young artist, touring by myself. It wasn't because I was overwhelmed by it, or had too much of it. It was just something I never did dig doin'. I just always went to the stage, and got off the bandstand, walked across the dance floor, out the door, and got in the car and left. That's the way I've done it all my life. I think there are people who understand that, and appreciate the fact that we're not tryin' to sell a bill of goods.

Q People also talk about you as the last authentic outlaw—somebody who doesn't pander to trends or submit to "high-gloss packaging." Do you think of yourself that way?

A Well, "outlaw" has a dual meaning with me, because of the fact that I had some real run-ins with the law earlier in my life, you know. Every time they say "outlaw," I have to stop and think about what they're talkin' about. You know, are they talkin' about "outlaw" outlaw, or are they talkin' about a guy that don't do it the same way everybody else does it?

I think they mean the latter part. I was lucky in the beginning, because I had a guy named Fuzzy Owen, who was my personal manager, and a guy named Ken Nelson, who was the representative of Capitol Records and who gave me the green light in the studio and allowed me to construct my very first record. That was an unusual thing. Because most people who want to help somebody bring 'em in and show 'em how it's done. Well, some years later, I asked Ken, "How come you let me do those things when I was so young and inexperienced?" And he said, "I don't sign people that I have to produce. I sign people who are capable of producin' themselves." And I said, "Well, I'm sure glad you did it that way, so I could find out who I was." There was a lot of luck involved in the fact that that happened in the early years—that I run into a good guy when I needed to. I've run into so many of the other kind over the years that I've had my share of that, too. But I keep on trustin' people, and havin' faith. But I'm also a little more gun-shy, or a little more aware of the people that are in the business to rip you off. They're standin' on every corner, you know? I've got to where I can pick 'em out pretty good.

Q Ken Nelson is, in a way, almost a forgotten man, but as a producer, he gave a lot of people the freedom to develop their style and their sound without trying to mold them into anything artificial. In fact, he was probably country music's finest producer during that time.

A Ken was a guy who just did not interfere. He listened for an out-of-tune instrument, he wouldn't let songwriters come in during the session, and he kept people off your back. When you were recording, he'd just doodle on a piece of paper. He'd say, "All right, Master 45,265, Take 1." And he'd go to doodlin'. And then when the song was over, he'd either say, "Merle, I think we should do it one more time," or he'd say, "It's a master and a joy to behold. Come in and be proud." He always used those words, you know.

Q Fuzzy Owen probably taught you more than anything, though, didn't he?

A Oh, yeah. Fuzzy taught me how to write songs.

Q How so?

A Well, I was well into the effort of writing songs. I've been doin' it since I was as young as nine or ten, and I didn't meet Fuzzy until I was twenty-four. But Fuzzy had written a couple of number one songs, which gave him, in my mind, the credentials to say yea or nay when I would present him with something. And he was very upsetting to me in the beginning of it all, because he wouldn't ever give. I'd sing him something, and he'd say, "That's good." And I'd say, "Well, do you think it might be a hit?" "Naw." And finally one day I sang him a song, and I said, "What do you think?" He said, "I believe it might be a number one song."

Q What was it?

A "Swingin' Doors." And it was. Same thing with the very first song we recorded, which was "Sing Me a Sad Song." We'd been two years waiting for a session. I got to thinkin' that Fuzzy was maybe a little bit phony, or maybe he didn't have the money, or something, you know? Every time I'd bring him a song, he'd say, "Naw, I don't believe this is the one we want." So I had this unique thing happen to me. I was workin' for Wynn Stewart in Las Vegas. Wynn had a chain of number one songs about eight or nine long, and he'd just written a new song called "Sing Me a Sad Song." We were gettin' ready to go on the stage one night, and I said, "Wynn, would you make me a star if you could?" I wasn't really serious, you know, about halfway jokin', and he said, "Well, sure I would." I said, "Well, you can do it." He said, "How's that?" I said, "Let me have that song." And he said, "You've got me. It's yours." Well, that was a great favor, 'cause he could have said, "I can't do that." But he was kind to me. So at intermission, I went directly to the phone. Fuzzy was still livin' in Bakersfield. I said, "I've got that song," and that was the first time I'd ever told him that, you know. And he said, "Is it really good?" And I said, "I believe it's the one. Wynn wrote it, and he was gonna do it for his next single." So we set up the recording session, and went down and cut it. The thing came in [the charts] at nineteen, I think, and then went to twenty-one. Then it went back up. And it went bobbin' up and down for a while. It was only on there about three or four weeks, and it fell out, you know. But it went in the charts, and we were on a small label.

Q This was on Tally?

A Yeah. And I think we sold twelve or fifteen thousand singles out of Fuzzy's apartment, just shippin' 'em ourselves. Then we had another chartmaker called "Sam Hill," and then we had "My Friends Are Gonna Be Strangers."

Q The Liz Anderson song that really got you on your way.

A Yeah. We sold like forty or fifty thousand of those out of the apartment, shippin' 'em ourselves to different distributors. And we'd been in touch with Capitol—they were aware of our operation. And the minute we had three in a row—"My Friends Are Gonna Be Strangers" went to number four in *Billboard*—they came in and offered us a long-term contract.

Q Did you think you were set for life?

A Actually, our very first record on Capitol didn't do that well. I think we sold, like, six thousand records on "I'm Gonna Break Every Heart I Can." We just kinda chunked it away, and went on back and did "Swingin' Doors." And it was a funny-actin' record, too. The thing went to fifteen, and then it fell back to thirty, or something like that. And my heart went right into the ground. I told Fuzzy, "This thing's fallin'. You were wrong." He said, "Don't worry about it." I said, "Fuzzy, it's already goin' down in the charts." He said, "Awww." I said, "I *saw* it." He was doin' something in the camper we was in, and he didn't pay no attention to me. So I just quit. And then the next week, it jumped from thirty back to fifteen again.

Q What happened?

A I was tryin' to think . . . it went all the way to number one, and ended up bein' the most played song of the year 1966.

Q It's unusual for a record to drop and then come back up. Did the record company have a change of heart and decide to promote it?

A I don't know why it did that.

Q How else did Fuzzy help you?

A Well, he was my sounding board. Like I say, I would write something, and he would say, "Naw, it's good writing, but I don't believe it's a hit." I'd say, "Well, what the hell makes a hit, then?" And we would take the *Billboard* charts and tear 'em apart. We'd say, "Looky here, this one here's a hit because it says this, and it has this good melody, and it has all the pieces of the pie." And Fuzzy'd say, "And this song you've written over here, it's got this and that, but it doesn't have this." And pretty soon, he began to make a lot of sense. I got to thinkin' about the unreality of the songs that I was writin', and maybe my lack of credibility to sing about a certain subject. I had a song called "If I'd Left It Up to You." It was really a good song. I still sing it. I've recorded it three times over the years. It's sold well every time. But it never was a hit. And Fuzzy said, "I think the reason the first record on that wasn't a hit is because people just didn't believe you were old enough to back up that bit of philosophy." And I think it's true. It's only happened once or twice in history where a twenty-one- or twenty-two-year-old guy was able to have that much credibility. Lefty Frizzell is the only one I know of that ever did it— maybe Elvis and him.

Q The lyrical quality of your early records was fairly surprising, however. I know Frizzell was your biggest musical influence, along with Bob Wills, but who influenced the way you put words together and expressed yourself poetically?

A Well, no one except Fuzzy and Bonnie [Owens]. Bonnie, of course, came after that period you're talkin' about. I guess I must have come by that honestly, because there's a couple or three songs that I wrote while I was a teenager that I still sing. In fact, I was thinkin' about openin' the show with one of 'em tonight, if I can remember it. The name of it is "If

You Want to Be My Woman." Glen Campbell used to open his shows with it a lot. I wrote that when I was sixteen, somethin' like that.

Q How does a kid with that much poetry in him end up getting into trouble with the law?

A Well, I got into it because I wanted to. My idols were the wrong people. I idolized Jesse James, Bonnie and Clyde, and those people, I presume because of the movies and the way that people like that were dramatized and made out to be heroes. I went for it as a youngster, I guess.

Q The romance of it.

A Yeah. I guess subconsciously I felt the need to do these things so that I could say I done 'em. And maybe so I could write about 'em. I didn't know that, but that might have been subconscious, too, to justify and authenticate what I needed to write about. You know, Jimmie Rodgers rode freight trains and then wrote about it. And at a very early age, I did see the necessity to write your own songs. Some things you notice and you don't even realize why you notice 'em. But I remembered that people like Bing Crosby, for example, sang a song that Hoagy Carmichael or Irving Berlin wrote, and it didn't mean anything to me. I liked the record, and I remember it now, but it didn't make me like Bing Crosby.

Q He was actually one of your favorite singers, wasn't he?

A Yeah, I liked his voice. But it didn't make me like *him,* or make me interested in him. Whereas Jimmie Rodgers, Lefty Frizzell, and Hank Williams—their names were down there in little, bitty letters as the writer. So I began to wonder about this guy. Why would he write "Take These Chains from My Heart," for example? I realized the importance of that.

Q At about what age?

A Probably fourteen, fifteen years old. And I just started tryin' to write. I did it all the time. I was *always* tryin' to write somethin'. And there was a lot of garbage. But Fuzzy was able to sharpen my ear to the point where I could recognize my own good and bad, maybe. And he never really did anything other than that. He would irritate me to the point where I'd have to go back and do somethin' better. He didn't butter me up. He didn't say, "That's really good." He'd say, "Awww, that's all right." Well, that wasn't what I wanted to hear, of course. Because I really respected him, really liked him, and I couldn't get him to lie. (Laughter)

Q You co-produced several of your albums with various other people, including Fuzzy, but you produced *A Friend in California* by yourself.

A Yeah, not that that's really what they want me to do right now. They would like me to go and have some young producer produce me, I think. And I don't know why. They seem to like what I do. A friend of mine had dinner with one of the executives at CBS [and he told him] that dollar for dollar I was the best act they had. And why a record company will not come and tell you that theirself, I don't know. Some kind of deal like Fuzzy, I guess. They're afraid to tell you you're doin' good—afraid you'll slack off, or something.

Q The CBS executives are cagey fellows.

A Yeah, that's right. They keep suggesting things . . . they want me to do somethin' with some young producer, a guy [David Malloy] who did good with Rosanne Cash, or this one or that one. But then they come back to me, in the same conversation, and say, "You've got to write somethin' like 'Big City.' You've got to come up with another 'Big City.' " I said, "Ricky Skaggs is doin' all old songs. Why can't I do all old songs?" "Well, they don't want old songs from you." I said, "Okay, I understand that. But I can't use a kid in there producin' me on my own stuff. I've got to do it my way, 'cause I'm the only guy that knows how it's supposed to be done. I'm the guy that wrote it."

Q I would guess they probably don't want you to use your band, either.

A No, they don't want me to use the band, but the band's on all the big hits. (Much laughter) My band was on Willie's [Willie Nelson's] last two hits. I think the band is capable of doin' anything I could ever come up with.

Q There's a rhythmic sense in the songs you wrote and recorded for MCA in the late seventies and early eighties that doesn't appear in your CBS material. Why is that?

A You know what we were doin' then that might have been a little different? We was doin' the two-drummer scene.

Q Even on the recording sessions, not just in concert?

A Yeah, I think so, on the stuff you're talkin' about, like "Ramblin' Fever"?

Q Well, especially the *Serving 190 Proof* and *Back to the Barrooms* albums.

A Yeah. *Back to the Barrooms* was two drummers. A funny thing happens there. [He makes a noise to imitate how two drummers shadow each other.] It could be done with overdubs. In other words, you play the song through once, and you go back and lay another drumbeat in there. But it's not the same energy as havin' two guys sittin' across from each other, one of 'em hittin' on one side of the beat and one of 'em hittin' on the other. It makes the singer perform different.

Q You really feel a drive behind you.

A Yeah. I like that stuff, too. I know what you mean there.

Q Your CBS work seems more reflective than your MCA material.

A Well, the MCA stuff . . . I was living in Nashville. Two years I lived down there, '76 and '77. I think most of the stuff you're talkin' about—"Great Afternoon," "Ramblin' Fever"—was done in '77 down there. And '78, *190 Proof* was done down there. A lot of it wasn't really that good.

Q Why not?

A Because I was down there in the studio all the time. Since I lived there, it seemed like every time they opened the doors, they would call me to come down and record. And a lot of the session players were personal friends of mine, and I got a small case of what they call "studio-itis." I just got to cuttin' everything, and writin' songs on the spot. It was the most critical period of my career. I think if I'd stayed there one more year, I'da killed myself completely. In fact, I was really bumfuzzled about '78 or '79 as to what to do. I moved back to California, and I moved to a different place than I'd ever lived, over on the coast, where my mother was livin'. She'd only been livin' there about a year herself. And I recorded a session I was very disappointed with, on a record called "If We're Not Back in Love by Monday." That was the first thing I did when I went back out on the coast. And we couldn't get that record in tune. I hate that record right now when I hear it. It was a pretty good song, though. But my ex-wife, Leona [Williams], can probably be charged with the blame of my success over the last seven or eight years.

Q Why is that?

A Well, because she was wantin' to get big in the business, and she'd been wantin' to get big in the business ever since she was a little girl. But she was not using what I thought was the right method to obtain what she was goin' after. And I made a statement to her one day. I said, "Why don't you do this the right way? Why don't you get a band, and get your own little sound, and go out on the road and work real hard and play a lot of rhythm guitar, and try to polish up your art and quit worrying about getting a big-name producer to do you?" I said, "Why don't you just get real good?" And we didn't communicate very well, and she said, "Well, you know, it's not like it was when you started. It's not as easy now." And me being the way I am, I said [lofty tone], "Are you saying that I couldn't make it now if I wanted to make it now?" And she said, "I don't think you could." And that's probably the reason I'm here right now. 'Cause I was coolin' off saleswise, and was not at all happy with things. It would have been easy for me to have just slowed on down and went into something else, and forgot about it, probably. Because I'd been doin' it long enough. But she brought out the competitive nature in me, and I went after it. Funny thing about it was that I went down and got me a big producer. (Laughter)

Q Just what you told Leona not to do.

A Well, my situation was different than hers. A big producer is no good to you unless that big producer is excited about doin' you. Jimmy Bowen wouldn't be good for her, because Jimmy Bowen did a session on her at the same time when we did the *Back to the Barrooms* album. We got some hits out of that. And one album led to the other, and probably the most successful session we've had, the *Big City* session. We did about twenty-four sides. Two albums—*Going Where the Lonely Go* and *Big City*—was done in the same forty-eight-hour period. We did all those songs, just bam, bam, bam. And *Big City* is still a big seller. So the importance of the song is still predominant. There's the proof of it. Anybody coulda sung "Big City," I think, and had a hit on it. It just said what people wanted to hear. They're tired of the slums, and the big scabs, you know? I was, and I was down there in the middle of that session when we wrote "Big City." We was down in L.A., and Dean Holloway, the other writer on it . . . well, he actually didn't write any of it, but Dean and I are friends. Anyway, Dean said, "We ought to write somethin' about this nasty son of a bitch, you know?"

Q About the city, you mean?

A Yeah, L.A. I said, "What do you want to call it?" And he said, " 'Big City.' " I said, "*Damn*, Dean, that's a dynamic title!" And I wrote that thing in about twenty minutes, and I went in there and cut it, and put that good ol' shuffle beat to it. I'd never done a shuffle. I used to hate shuffles, because we had to do 'em all the time in the clubs. That was one of the things that I didn't do when I first started out, was 4/4 shuffles, because I'd done so many of 'em. Ray Price songs for years were shuffles. So that's what I didn't want to do. Well, this was the first one I'd done in my whole career, I guess, and it worked.

Q Now that you're not married to Leona anymore, what gives you that kick? What motivates you?

A Well, I lost it pretty well about six or eight weeks ago. I guess I got burnt out, as you would say. I didn't have any motivation left, didn't have any reason to do anything. I'd done everything you could do. And I was workin' in Hemet, California, doin' double shows. And the band wasn't soundin' right, and I didn't have the energy to figure out what was wrong. It was in a dusty, thrown-up little arena that somebody'd made the day before, and I thought, "Man, I've been in this business all my life, and look here. I'm down in Hemet, California, right where I started twenty-five years ago, and the only difference is the size of the check." And that was pretty discouraging. Because I don't have enough money to retire, or the energy to do it again. I got beat out of most of the money I made in the last six or eight years.

Q Bad investments and alimonies?

A Yeah. And thieves. Theft is the biggest problem. So I was just really disgusted with it all, and about the last fifteen minutes of that Hemet show, I was like the guy in the parachute. You know, "If I ever get my feet on the ground again, I ain't never goin' up." I hated it. And that fifteen minutes was the hardest thing I ever did in my life. But I knew it was the last one. When I walked off of there, I felt really good. Because everybody kept sayin', "Aw, you'll feel all right tomorrow." And I said, "You don't seem to understand. I don't *give* a shit. (Laughter) I am *not* going on-stage tomorrow. I don't give a shit if they *eat* me."

Q Is this when you canceled a bunch of dates and the wire services carried the stories?

A Yeah, and nobody sued me. I don't guess, did they?

Q What about the fair manager in Roseburg, Oregon? The one who said you canceled two hours before show time, and then turned down your offer to make up the date?

A Well, somebody started to sue, and we sent him a nice letter. But I just didn't really care. All you can get is turnip juice out of a turnip, you know? So I went home, and got to likin' it a little better every day.

Q Staying at home, you mean?

A You bet. And the only reason I'm out here tonight is because we figured out the problem a couple nights ago. We had a problem with the music, and the music was the only reason I'd been out here for the last two or three years. Because I like to play. And there was a couple problems in the band, but I didn't know what to do about 'em, and I didn't have the energy to figure it out. But we finally got a good show. Had three in a row now, I guess. And I wrote a couple of songs. I thought the well had run dry. And I didn't really mind, because the well has really been a great well. What can a guy expect? You know, how many songs can you write? Well, all of a sudden, they've begun to come again. I've got the inspiration to write. And I'd lost that. And without that, there is no surprising the band. Any songs you've got will begin to get old. Part of the way that we conduct our shows is by laying the new songs on the band and on the audience at the same time. That way you grab the enthusiasm of everybody in the room. And without that, I was like a comedian without any jokes. And I just couldn't stand it. Well, we've gained a lot of that back, and I'm still holdin' my breath, hopin' that it's not just an Indian summer, or somethin'.

Q But how did you turn that around?

A I was tired. I guess I gained a little strength back. And I drove around in my car a lot. Did a lot of thinkin'. And I found a couple things that I wanted to buy. And I guess the need to do it . . . there was a lot of desire. I hated to see it end, because I enjoy it. And somebody gives you those songs, you know. (Low chuckling) And I don't think they give 'em to you if you're not gonna use 'em right. And I just couldn't get any songs.

Q Mel Tillis says he thinks a writer only has a certain number of songs in him, and when they're gone, they're gone.

A I got a couple more. I've got at least two that I'm real proud of. And I found a couple other ones. Freddy Powers has been writin' good songs. I think we've gotten together, oh, probably fifteen or so really good songs, and we're goin' down to Willie's studio this week, and we're gonna record again.

Q What do you think of this last album of yours?

A *A Friend in California?* I don't know. I'll give it a five.

Q A five out of ten?

A On a scale of ten. It was average. It was different in some ways. I liked the instrumentation on it. I liked a couple of the songs real well. But, like, "I Had a Beautiful Time" was a song that I'd written ten or twelve years ago. So there wasn't the enthusiasm of the new song with that. There wasn't a lot of my solo writing on that album. It was mainly Freddy and I. I've been guilty of doin' . . . see, there's two different kinds of songs. There's the kind that you construct, and there's the kind that come to you. And I'd constructed a lot of songs on there. And the ones that I didn't finish I'd just turn over to my ace writer. I'd say, "Fred, finish this." Well, that's good. That'll work a little bit, in some ways. But it left me short of the necessary pride, or whatever a person has. Didn't build my ego any. And I've written at least one good song, I know for sure. We tried it out on the audience night before last.

Q What's it called?

A It's called "I Don't Have Any Love Around." The title's the weakest part of the song. I'm proud of it. And I've got some other good ideas for construction projects, but the fact that this other good song came, and it came like they used to, makes me suspicious as to maybe the well ain't dry, after all.

Q Every writer is terrified of running out of material. When that happens, though, you usually just need to sit back and rejuvenate.

A Yeah, sometimes that's just what it is—physical and mental fatigue. And boredom, or complacency, or whatever—doin' the same thing. A lot of people don't realize that what goes along with this glamour and these high points that the people witness—the big nights at the CMA and this and that—are just a small percentage of the life that's involved. The main part of this life is a twenty-year bus ride. I've had people come back in the back of my bus, and in twenty minutes they say, "Oh, my God, I've got to get out of here. I couldn't stand this!" Well, it really does get claustrophobic, and it got to me real seriously this year. I wasn't worried about anybody suin' me, because I knew that I had a valid reason for doin' what I did. In fact, I went down and talked with a psychiatrist to prove it.

Q You did see a psychiatrist?

A Yeah, I went down and talked to a guy for a couple of sessions. And he said, "There's nothin' wrong with you. You're just tired." I really just went in case of a lawsuit. There was no use goin' sayin' I had a stomachache, or whatever, which I did have in one show. I missed one show, and then I came back and missed seven or eight more. Well, a stomachache don't last seven or eight shows, you know. And I couldn't go to a stomach doctor for that, so I went to a head doctor. And I just told him. I said, "The reason I'm here is because people want me to do somethin' I can't do anymore, and I've got contracts and obligations. And you've got to help me find out why I can't do 'em." I wasn't drunk, and I wasn't doped up, and I wasn't off partyin' somewhere. I was home, cryin'. You know? Or wishin' I could cry.

Q When was this?

A Durin' the last six weeks, just lately.

Q You've crawled out of some deep holes in your life.

A Yeah, I just came through the deepest, I think. I have a lot of good friends. And I love a lot of people, but I'm not really *in* love with nobody. And I've never been that way. And, first, it's very lonely. I've *always* been in love with somebody. And when I got over the deal with Leona, it never had happened again, so that left a big void in my writing, as well. And now I'm beginning to get used to it, I guess.

Q In a way, though, isn't it a relief not to have those emotional ups and downs? I've read that you said you married Debbie, your fourth and current wife, out of friendship, and not love.

A Well, I have a lot of dependence already. I didn't realize how much I depended on this lady, but I depend on her a lot. And we talked about it. We confused good friendship for love in the beginning. She was there when I was tryin' to get over this other lady, and it was easy to confuse emotions at that time. And we did, and we got married, and during this last six weeks, I went to her and told her what I thought we'd done. And it answered a lot of questions—freed up a lot of things. Because I really like this lady, and I didn't want to foul up her life. And I was worried about her having to give up friendships with my children that she'd had prior to us being married. Which I'm sure she felt was inevitable if it wasn't going to work. So I went to her and said, "I think it's real simple. We confused our friendship for love. It might make you feel better if we looked at it and admitted it." I said, "Don't you think that's what we done?" And a big smile come over her face. And she said, "Yeah, I think you're right." And I said, "Well, in that case, then you don't have to worry about losin' the friendship of Dana, and Noel, and these people that you've come to love." I said, "As long as we're aware of that . . ." And then a couple of days went by, and I went out to the boat, and she stayed at home. And she called me, and she was cryin'. And she said, "I think the reality of what you said just hit me." I said, "What do you mean?" She said, "Well, I think I've fallen in love with you. I think I'm *in* love with you now." And I said, "Well, maybe I've fallen in love with you. But I think that we should still be aware of the whole thing, so we can be real about it."

Q So where does that leave things?

A Just about where I'm stoppin' here. That's just about where it's at. My life's always been up in the air.

Q Well, being a writer is both a blessing and a curse.

A Oh, yeah. I'm not sure we're supposed to be too happy. It's never been that way for me. I've had things that people would surely gauge as being great that didn't excite me at all. And things that were the most important to me were the ones that people never could understand.

Q Such as?

A Well, I've got a little ol' '77 Chevy pickup that I'm fixin' up at home. It's got a little camper on it. Not a slick truck. It's just an old truck that I've found that's good. And I just drive around in it, go back and forth from the lake to the house, and use it to look at a little property here and there. And I drive it to eat breakfast down at a little cafe every mornin', gettin' to know people in the town. There's a guy there that was a retired almond rancher, a millionaire, who was friends with me. And he's wantin' to buy a bus and go on the road. I said, "Man, why would you want to do *that*?" He said, "Well, why would you want to do *this*?" So it's what you haven't done in your life that you would like to do when you reach maturity, or old age, whichever it may be.

Q Do you still live on your houseboat?

A I have a houseboat, and I live about half the time on that boat, and I have a ranch about fifteen miles from the lake. And I put ten thousand miles on my car and about seven thousand on that pickup in six months, goin' between that lake and that house. And I just go back and forth, because I don't really have anything goin' anywhere. I'm just kinda runnin'. [Interruption from Biff Adams, his drummer]

Adams: You've got to get ready.

Haggard [dressed in scruffy jeans and shirt]: I'm ready.

Adams: Are you? (Laughter)

Haggard: I'm changing my image. To one who gives lesser shit than he used to.

*I*t comes into view as you round the curve of Berry Chapel Road, between Franklin and Brentwood, Tennessee, twenty miles south of Nashville. The long white fences with their stocking-red trim suggest what is to follow, but it isn't until you reach the front entrance, with the high towers and the gatekeeper's box, that you get a full look at Fox Hollow, Tom T. Hall's sixty-acre farm. Something about the layout of the place, with the rippling lake and the ornate, plantation-style house, suggests a scene out of a movie, or maybe even a fairy tale. But aside from that, there is a hint of magic in the air, magic that comes from knowing that while you cannot actually see Sneaky Snake, Ole Lonesome George, the Basset, and the One-Legged Chicken, you know they are there, watching as you drive through the gate and up the slope that leads to the house.

The lord of this particular manor is an anomaly in country music, a man who wanted to be a songwriter, not a singer, and a loner who demonstrates a fair amount of antisocial behavior in a town where playing by the rules often counts for more than talent. And yet Tom T. Hall has been successful in spite of himself. With seven number one hit records, a Grammy, and thirty-six BMI writing awards, "the Storyteller," as he is sometimes called, is responsible for some of country music's most enduring tunes ("Harper Valley PTA," "I Love," "Country Is"). Perhaps the best of his work, however, is the musical journalism of his story songs ("The Year That Clayton Delaney Died," "Ballad of Forty Dollars," "Old Dogs, Children, and Watermelon Wine")—tales of everyday characters caught in humorous, poignant, or ironic situations.

All this has made the 52-year-old Hall a wealthy man. "He could retire from the road right now and be very well off," says his longtime friend and booking agent Tandy Rice. "He's one of the few artists I can say this about . . . he could have a career as a professor, a novelist, or a financial consultant."

Pose this idea to Hall himself, and he sits back, stares out the window for a moment, and then delivers his answer—nothing but a long, slow chuckle. At this moment, Hall, moody and introspective—a man who calls himself the "glorious fool"—is a character out of one of his own creations.

Born into poverty in the eastern Kentucky town of Olive Hill, Hall roamed the country as a traveling disc jockey before moving to Nashville in 1964 as a $50-a-week songwriter. Five of his writing awards arrived before the 1968 success of "Harper Valley PTA," the song that made Jeannie C. Riley a star. The multimillion-selling record also made Hall his first real money ("It was like walking down the street and suddenly bending over and finding $100,000"), earned him one of his seven Country Music Association nominations, and paved the way for his inclusion in the Nashville Songwriters' Association Hall of Fame.

That same year, despite a mediocre voice, Hall the songwriter became Hall the recording artist, his producer, Jerry Kennedy, infusing Hall's records with a distinctive, mostly acoustic ensemble sound and a trademark mournful Dobro. Through the years, Hall's albums have covered a diverse span of styles and subjects, from story songs to children's albums, collections of love songs, a flirtation with bluegrass, and renditions of standards such as "P.S. I Love You" and "Red Sails in the Sunset."

Hall's career as an artist began to cool off in the late '70s, when he left Mercury Records for a stint with RCA. But in 1983, back again with Mercury, he recorded one of his strongest LPs, *Everything from Jesus to Jack Daniel's*. A throwback to Hall's earlier work, the album was stocked with memorable portraits, including those of a truck driver who murders his wife, a traveler who finds a cache of letters in a Bible in a boardinghouse, and a Mac Sledge type [the protagonist in *Tender Mercies*] to whom "you're not allowed to talk about his first wife, Joanne . . . or any-body who ever worked in Elvis's band."

The following interview is a combination of five sessions recorded in 1975, 1977, and 1979, at Fox Hollow, at Hall's studio/office in Brentwood, at Jamboree in the Hills, near Wheeling, West Virginia, and on his cus-tomized touring bus, between shows in Louisville.

Since our talks, Hall has made several changes in his organization, selling much of his real estate, including his Toy Box recording studio and his office building. He also says he gave up drinking hard liquor in 1983 ("I was always a big-friendly-dog-type drunk"), although he still drinks beer.

There is evidence, too, that Hall is mellowing as he moves into mid-life. He spent three years as the host of a syndicated TV show *Pop Goes the Country*—something he told me he had no interest in doing. And at the request of his first idol, Ernest Tubb, Hall rejoined the Grand Ole Opry, which he quit in 1974, not, he says, in a dispute about what instru-mental backing he could use onstage, as was reported, but, as he told *Country Music* magazine, because "when they moved the Opry, I didn't move with it like furniture. I had worked hundreds of places like Opry-land, so I didn't move."

As of 1986, Hall continued to have singles on the country charts, but for the last few years he has turned the bulk of his attention to prose, both as a book reviewer for the Nashville *Tennessean*—for which he once assessed that a particular author's style was "like Hemingway with a hard-on"—and as the author of four volumes of fiction and nonfiction.

His latest book, *Acts of Life* (University of Arkansas Press, 1986), a collection of seventeen short stories about small-town Southern folks (in-cluding Murphy Walls, who got his thumb shot off in Korea but keeps it around in a jar of alcohol), received favorable reviews. In 1982, Double-day published Hall's *The Laughing Man of Woodmont Coves,* a bizarre and disturbing novel about life in a town not unlike that of Olive Hill, Kentucky.

When Hall and I last talked, he had already seen the publication of *How I Write Songs . . . Why You Can* (Rutledge Hill Press published a revised edition in 1987 as *The Songwriter's Handbook*) and the very funny, on-target assessment of the Nashville music scene, *The Storytell-er's Nashville* (Doubleday, 1979). That's where we picked up the conver-sation.

Q You've just published your second book, *The Storyteller's Nashville*. Why did you want to write it?

A Well, sooner or later, one of us had to write a book about the way it was. I felt sort of an obligation to write it. It's not just a book about me. My hope is that it's a book about the way Nashville's changed in the years I've spent here. I think I've succeeded. I took three winters off to do it, and it was quite a project. See, I always wanted to write a book—a real book. That was my ambition as a child—to be an author. I've always loved the strange way that words can be connected, and the way sentences can be punctuated, and how all those little animals run around and bring life to a page. And I must point out that I didn't dictate it, nor did I do it on a tape recorder. I sat down at a typewriter and did the whole thing. It starts on January 1, 1964, when I got to Nashville, and goes through the "outlaw" thing. There's some very colorful language in it, the language of the streets of Nashville then, if it isn't now. I'll probably get a few purists who'll be down on that. 'Cause up front it's pretty rough. It's not a press release, by any means. I finished the thing, and I said, "Good God A-mighty. Can't I even be a hero in my own goddamn book?" But there's some funny stuff in it. I think it's a worthwhile book, if somebody wants to go back and see what it was like from '64 till now. I hope that it's a good picture of what crazy things happen in show business, and where you have to be, and what you have to do to make it.

Q What about your life before January 1, 1964?

A Well, I was born in a log cabin. Abe Lincoln and I have that distinction. Probably a lot of other people. But I was born in 1936, right after the Depression, and the economy of eastern Kentucky didn't recover as quickly as it did in some of the other parts of the country. When my father, whose name was Virgil Lee Hall, decided to get married, he and my mother built a log house out behind my grandfather's house. I was named after my grandfather, Thomas Hall. No middle name. I think it was a family tradition.

Q If you had no middle name, where did the famous "T" come from?

A The "T" was put in later, so no one would confuse me with Tompall Glaser and several other people in Nashville and elsewhere whose names are similar. Besides, what's in a name? A rose by any other name . . . But you know Shakespeare said a funny thing about names. He said, "He that filches from me my good name / Robs me of that which not enriches him / And makes me poor indeed." I've always believed that.

Q Some people thought you just added the "T" to be mysterious.

A No, the mysteries in my life are questions I don't have any answers to. People think I know and won't tell 'em, but I just don't know. On the other hand, a couple years back, they made a movie called *W.W. and the Dixie Dance Kings.* They asked W.W. what the "W.W." stood for. He said, "Nothin'." And I thought, "That guy is usin' my act." (Laughter) It was kind of ironic.

Q How many children were in your family?

A There were eight of us in the house. Six boys. My brother Jack was the oldest, and Quentin, Bill, and then me. I was the fourth son, and the fifth child.

Q Were many of them musically inclined?

A Well, everybody in the family liked music. My older brother Quentin, who was killed in Korea, had a great deal of potential. He was really into music a lot. [Hall's brother Hillman wrote "Pass Me By (If You're Only Passing Through)," and another brother, Jack, has also recorded an album.] But none of them were as much of a fanatic about it as I was. I lived it and breathed it and dreamed it.

Q Your father was a lay preacher who also worked in a brick factory?

A Yes, he worked at the world's largest brick plant, which at that time was in Olive Hill, Kentucky. He worked there until he retired, and then he took up his ministry full-time. They had a thing called the Southern Christian Conference—not to be confused with the Southern Christian Leadership Conference—and I think they had eleven churches. And they would travel around and preach in different churches. I guess I'm a lot like my father. He was a very creative person. And a good preacher, a good fella. Very clever. Very difficult to fool. I tried it a few times. It did not work.

Q Did he approve of your career as an entertainer?

A No. When I was a young man in Olive Hill, I must admit that I was respected, if not admired, by the people in the community. And I was offered several very good jobs—the management of a radio station, the management of a department store—and my father took these to be golden career opportunities. He was somewhat dismayed that I would turn them down when the aristocracy of the community were merchants. But he liked my music, and I did sing for my father on occasion. He passed away a few years ago.

Q Do you have any outstanding childhood memories?

A When I was about four or five, my father moved to Niles, Ohio, so I spent about three or four years there as a very young man. On Pratt Street. I wrote a song about it. There were no blacks in Olive Hill at that time. And the first year I attended school in Ohio, I had a partner, a little black guy. We would go to school together every day. We had to hold hands when we crossed the street, because we had the responsibility of getting back and forth from school alive, which in Niles, Ohio, wasn't an easy thing in those days. But he and I were real pals. And that probably accounts for the fact that I was never prejudiced, which was kind of a blessing.

Q When did you move back to Olive Hill?

A I don't know. I was a real little boy. I just remember that one day we all got in the car and came back to Olive Hill. My father worked in a brick plant in Ohio, too. Maybe he was transferred there. I don't remember. But I remember my pal in Niles, and then I remember when I was four years old, my mother, who died when I was thirteen, would get me up about four o'clock in the morning to listen to Ernest Tubb and all the other guys live from WSM in Nashville. And nobody has ever been able to explain to me, nor have I figured out, why a four-year-old kid would want to get up and listen to the country music radio show out of Nashville, Tennessee. Especially at four in the morning. Maybe I thought this was where I was going. It's kind of a strange thing. And then when I was about five or six, we moved into a new house—new to us, that is—and someone had left a guitar. So my father fixed it up for me, put some strings on it, and I learned to play the guitar. We moved to another house one time and someone had left a piano. So I learned to play piano.

Q So even as a child you knew what you wanted to do.

A Well, I just always gravitated toward music. There's an old expression that says, "You are where your thoughts have brought you." And my thoughts were about music, and entertainment, and pickin' and singin' and writing. So that's how I got here. I had a perfectly normal childhood, other than the fact that I was crazy about music. We'd do a lot of fishin', and we'd hunt possums in the fall, which was a lot of fun, because you could stay out after dark.

Q Didn't you have a grandfather who was wealthy? P. G. Henderson?

A Yes, on my mother's side. P. G. Henderson was tremendously wealthy. He owned all the clay mines around there.

Q But the impression I have is that your family was poor.

A Well, we weren't poor by local standards. But if there are ten thousand poor people in one area, and they all have the same standard of living, it doesn't disqualify the word. I said one time that we didn't know we were poor until we read about it in *The Saturday Evening Post*. We didn't have a lot of anything.

Q Didn't P. G. Henderson help the family out?

A Oh, no, he spent all his money before he died. Which is the thing he should have done. But my grandfather lived in an era before my time, when people traveled by horse and buggy. They had a big plantation house, and they would cater to the traveling senators and governors. It was a very wealthy circumstance for my mother's family. And really, my father's family was well-to-do, too. [Grandfather] Thomas Hall was very well-to-do. He was also a lay preacher. White-haired gentleman. He rode a horse, and would go places and preach. But we weren't poor because of any of the qualifications of my ancestry. We were poor because of an economic circumstance that was prevalent in the whole country. Up until a few years ago, that area suffered from the same dilemma—tryin' to get the economy goin' around again. There was almost no way to make any real money in eastern Kentucky. Bootleggers made a lot of money, and white-collar criminals, but that was about it. It's been pretty rough throughout the history of the state. But the resourcefulness of the people there, in facing some of the dire and unavoidable circumstances they've encountered, is amazing.

Q One of your most famous songs is "The Year That Clayton Delaney Died." I know that you idolized him as a child, but who was he really?

A He was a young man who played and sang real well. He used to work in a nightclub in Indiana, and, of course, I was fascinated to meet a young man who had done professional shows. Clayton Delaney wasn't his real name, though. There's some debate about what his real name was, because I only remember the person. I've had other members of my family tell me he was a different guy. So now I'm almost afraid to say— afraid I'll get the wrong one. But you have to remember this happened when I was seven years old, and I wrote the song when I was, like, thirty. So that's twenty-five years or so that I never thought of the man. He was nineteen or twenty when he died, of lung cancer, or tuberculosis, I'm not sure. But it's a true story.

Q Was he the person who got you interested in playing country music, other than hearing Ernest Tubb on the radio?

A Well, he was the first. Because although I had a guitar and could pick it in some fashion, Clayton was a stylist. He was an original. He did his own kind of pickin' and singin'. If he heard a new Hank Williams record, he didn't sing it like Hank Williams. He sang it like Clayton Delaney. And that knocked me out. Somehow I thought they had thousands of records stashed in Nashville, and they just released one every three months. I didn't know that people wrote them and produced them, and that they never knew what was gonna come next. And then I heard him doing these things, and I realized that you could be an individual, your own person. I think it was the revelation of my entire career—that in addition to people saying, "There's Little Jimmy Dickens," they'd say, "There's Tom T. Hall." I know it was a rash and insolent opinion, but I developed it along in there just the same.

Q Later on, you wrote a song called "Son of Clayton Delaney."

A That's just a figment of my imagination. I was in a little club in Louisville, and I was sitting there listening to this kid pick guitar, and I just adopted him for Clayton's son. I have a son, Dean T. Hall, who's also a good musician, good picker [now part of Hall's touring band], and I wanted Clayton to have a son, too.

Q At the end of the song, the boy introduces himself to the man who made his father famous. Even though the title gives it away, the ending comes as a jolt—almost like an O. Henry story. Did you have that surprise ending in mind all along?

A No, I just started writin' about him, and then at the end, I thought, "Well, maybe it would suit the history of the thing well if we encountered one another for a line." Which is all that happens.

Q You worked as a disc jockey in Morehead, Kentucky, for about seven years.

A Oh, yeah! I was hot in Morehead. I think what people around there remember best about that was the time I went to jail for the March of Dimes. I said I'd stay in jail until the community contributed five hundred dollars. It took a week. (Laughter) Well, you know, people didn't have much money. I overestimated the economy of the thing. This was in '56 or '57. And people just sent a dime at a time. But a thing like that had not been tried in that part of the country. And I really lost a part of my audience, because while I was trying to be a hero, the general consensus was that I had stolen money from crippled children. (Laughter) It didn't work at all. But I've always had to do things in a grand fashion. And it was my idea to go to jail. I was very dedicated about it. I never left. They'd lock me in my cell at night, and in the daytime I'd be out on the block, broadcasting. Some of the kids from Morehead State University would come down and yell, "Hey, you really got a disc jockey in there?" And I'd wave out the window and say, "Yeah!"

Q Bill Whitaker, the general manager there at WMOR, told me you were fired from that disc jockey job.

A No, I quit and joined the Army. I think after I left, Bill told everybody that I got fired, you know.

Q The rumor was that you went on a three-day drunk and came in on the air, and you were fired.

A No, no. I went out to lunch one day, and I passed an Army recruiting station, and I went in and said, "What do you do here?" And the guy said, "You put all these round pegs in square holes, and we count to see if you've got one of everything you're supposed to have, and two of the other things you're supposed to have, and you go in the Army." But I had a friend, a fiddle player, who was in the All-Army Band in Fort Lee, Virginia, where the Quartermaster school was. So I said, "I'll join the Army if you'll let me in the Quartermaster Corps." And they said fine. So I came in and told Mr. Whitaker I was gonna be gone a little while. He said, "How long?" I said, "About three years." I was just on a lunch break, and got bored, and joined the Army. And that worked out well, because I went to Fort Gordon, Georgia, for basic training. Then I went to Fort Lee, Virginia, and the second day I was there, they put me in the All-Army Band. Country band. So it worked out exactly as I planned it.

Q Weren't you also in a band while you were a disc jockey?

A Kentucky Travelers, right. Uncle Curt—he wasn't really my uncle, but that's what everybody called him—was our promoter and manager. We were all children, and he was an adult. Grand old gentleman.

Q How long were you a disc jockey?

A Well, I didn't go there as a disc jockey. I went there as a member of the Kentucky Travelers. We were a bluegrass band. I went over and said, "You guys got a radio station, and you need some talent, and I've got a band." Bill Whitaker said, "Bring 'em in and let me hear 'em." So we went and picked, and he said, "Okay, forty-five minutes a day." Polar Bear Flour wanted to sponsor us. I said, "Well, I'll just write 'em a song, then." Flatt and Scruggs had Martha White, so I figured I'd write the Polar Bear Flour song. And it knocked 'em out. They thought it was great. So we'd open every day with the Polar Bear Flour song. But then the Korean War broke up the band, and Uncle Curt died, and they kept me on as a disc jockey. They said, "Well, your band's broke up, what are you gonna do?" I said, "I don't know." I was only fourteen.

Q What other jobs did you have as a young man?

A I went to work in a garment factory when I was fifteen. Before that, I worked in a graveyard, when I was about twelve or thirteen. But I only did that in the summer. My aunt was on the cemetery committee. She had a brand-new Chevrolet. And when she would take me out to the cemetery to mow the grass, I would ride in the trunk of the car with the lawn mower, rather than ride inside the car.

Q Why?

A I don't know. Maybe I didn't want to get the car dirty. But I remember riding through town in the back of that car with the lawn mower, and I didn't care much about that.

Q How did you like the garment factory?

A Well, it was about a hundred degrees in there, and I was lifting bundles that weighed a hundred pounds—about as much as I did. I was only fifteen, as I said, and when I went to get my work permit, the lady gave me my permit in one hand and a piece of bubble gum in the other. It was one of those little bubble gums that tell your fortune. I didn't read it. Normally, I would have. I'd love to have it back. But I was too excited about goin' to work. I made seventy-five cents an hour, twenty-five dollars a week after taxes. Course, I was rollin' in money, 'cause I'd never had any before. Later on, I worked in a funeral home. And I was a salesman, and a traveling disc jockey. I washed windows for a while.

Q So you earned your success?

A Well, by some fashion I evolved into it. But I had a gift to write. It *is* a gift, you know. It's not something I earned, no. Not at all.

Q Bill Whitaker said the Army changed you, made you tougher.

A Well, it gave me a sense of adventure, because I got to go to Europe—I was in Germany three years—and I made a lot of money playing music. I came out of the Army with a better education, because I finished high school in the Army, and got some college credits. I also got an understanding of how to travel around in the world. I spent a lot of time in France and Italy, because I could afford to. If I'd get a leave, I'd just go to Paris for a couple of weeks. Or go to Venice and check out the food. See, I was in charge of twenty-three guys, and they were all ethnic people. We had some Yugoslavs, and some Orientals, some Czechoslovakians, some Puerto Ricans, some Mexicans, and some black people. And that was a pretty tough job the last year. Because Quartermaster, you know, was all the supplies and stuff. We dispensed the food for all the companies. And these people didn't get along all the time. Some of 'em didn't speak the [English] language. And there were a lot of fights. So to keep my job, I had to fight a lot of the guys in the outfit, because they didn't respect any kind of rank. All they cared about was whether you were tougher than they were. So I spent the last year in the Army in fistfights—about twice a month.

Q Did you go back to Morehead after the Army?

A For a little while. I bought my father a grocery store when I came out of the Army. Because by that time he'd retired and wanted to do something. And one day I came in and said, "Hey, Dad, I don't want to do the radio thing. I've got a friend in Indiana who plays the fiddle, and I'm gonna go up there and get a band together." And, of course, he thought I was crazy. Which I was. Then I loaded all my stuff in an old car and went to Indiana, and worked in nightclubs a couple of years. I wrote a song about it, "Thank You, Connersville, Indiana."

Q That was what Clayton Delaney did.

A Yeah, in fact, I worked the same club that Clayton worked. A place called Buckeye Gardens. That's where I started my career after I got out of the Army. Went right back to where Clayton started. There's an irony there.

Q Consciously?

A Maybe so. Maybe subconsciously, because I always knew where Buckeye Gardens was. Clayton had told me. Clayton said one time, "Boy, you would have really liked our band, Tom. We had shirts just alike." (Much laughter) I couldn't imagine five guys all havin' shirts just alike.

Q What happened to your band?

A Well, one of the guys got tired of it. We'd worked our way up to one of the top clubs in Indiana. I was playin' piano. We had a bass player and a drummer. It was goin' really good, but that was the end of us. I was sittin' one night listening to the jukebox, and I heard Faron Young singing a song, and I said, "There's a new writer in Nashville." I went over and watched the record turning around, and it said, "Hello, Walls," by Willie Nelson. And I said, "Boy, that sumbitch can write songs."

Q Had you been to Nashville before at this point?

A Yeah, I'd been to a couple disc jockey conventions. But I came on back to Kentucky and became a traveling disc jockey. I would go from station to station. If some guy up the road offered me ten dollars more, I'd just put all my stuff in the back of the car. I never bought anything I couldn't haul in a car. And I'd travel up the road a hundred miles. I worked Ohio, West Virginia, Kentucky, Indiana—all those little radio stations. And I read a lot. For about three years, I traveled around and just did disc jockey work and read. I didn't have any romances, I didn't do any drinkin', I didn't have any sports or hobbies. Just worked and read. Wasn't like me at all. It was kind of a phenomenon.

Q Were you a ladies' man then?

A No, I didn't have much goin' for me, and I figured women wouldn't be interested in what little I did have. If they were real ugly, I didn't want to fool with 'em, and if they were real pretty, I figured they had somethin' else to do. So I just left the whole thing alone for a long time. But lookin' back at pictures of myself, I was a pretty handsome little fella, I guess.

Q I'm surprised women weren't crazy over you, especially since you were in radio. That's always been an aphrodisiac of sorts.

A Well, maybe they were, but I didn't have the confidence to pursue it. The traveling disc jockey thing was kind of fun, though, because I was out in the world by myself. I kind of enjoyed being all alone without my family.

Q How did you end up in Nashville?

A Well, I was in West Virginia, at a radio station. And a guy came in, said he was a songwriter. And he was singin' me some songs, and I told him I wrote songs, too. But I had the theory that I would never go to Nashville and knock on doors. I said, "If I've got any talent, somebody will discover it." Which is kind of dumb, but they did, thank God. So, hell, I roamed around until I was twenty-seven years old. Never showed any of my songs to anybody. So this guy comes by, I sang him a couple songs, he took 'em to Nashville, and they sent me a songwriter's contract. Newkeys Music. Jimmy Key. And Jimmy C. Newman recorded my "DJ for a Day."

Q So did you quit your job and move to Nashville?

A No, but, man, I really wanted to write. I didn't know *what* I wanted to write, but at that time, I was writing radio copy. I wrote all the commercials. And that was great training, because a song is about as long as a commercial—a page long. So I wrote radio copy for three or four years. But I said, "I don't know enough about this." So I put an ad in *Broadcasting* magazine, and said I wanted to go to work at a radio station where I could go to school at night. And then I quit my job. But the funny thing was, the guy who owned the station flew up there and fired me. I said, "Why are you firing me? I quit." He said, "I just want it on your record that you're fired." (Laughter)

Q So you went to Roanoke.

A Yes. And it was the best job I ever had in radio, WBLU [in Salem, Virginia]. I just played records. I didn't have to write any copy, and I didn't have to be an engineer. They had a beautiful little campus at Roanoke College, and I stayed there a couple of years. But all the time I was writing songs and sending them to Nashville. And then I got to makin' so much money in Nashville that they said, "Hey, why don't you come down here and write songs?" I said, "Why not?" And I wanted it to be a very auspicious date, so I left New Year's Eve. I got to Nashville January 1, 1964. And the rest is muddy history.

Q When did you marry the first time?

A When I came out of the Army. I came out in March 1961, and I got married in 1962. That's a period that's too personal to talk about. But it all turned out well. I'm very proud of Dean, my son, and happy about that circumstance.

Q Do you wish you had more children?

A No, not really. Raising a kid is really a hassle, especially in this day and time. But I work very hard to support a home for children whose parents are in jail—Bethel Bible School, in Chattanooga. It's not really a Bible school. It's a children's home. I also do a lot of charitable work for adults. I often quote whoever said, "Charity is my church, and example is my best sermon." I try to live in a fashion that would be wise to imitate, if I'm around young people, and give both my money and my time to charities that I think are worthy. But that's not something you talk about. That's something you do for yourself. If you tell everybody in the press what you're doing, then you lose the magic of it. All of a sudden, you have to ask yourself whether you're doin' it for the publicity. I don't want to be questioning my motives.

Q One person you helped was Johnny Rodriguez, who was your protégé of sorts in the early seventies. Have you any more protégés?

A I would help any young person—or old person—who came along and I thought had talent. I didn't go looking for Johnny. He was just a tremendous, unbelievably great talent.

Q When did you marry Dixie Dean [a former music journalist, now a dog breeder of some renown]?

A In 1968. I moved out of my apartment and rented a little house out in the country, and met Miss Dixie. We knew each other for three or four years before we got married. Miss Dixie has a lot of class, you know. She's English, and she can write well and speak the English language, and we're a great contrast to one another. She's a great homemaker and decorator, and she's a good cook. She makes me a nice home. I'm very happy with her. Because when you consider the source of my success, and the haphazard way that I wound up in all these different places doing all these different things, it's really nice to have a home. Some roots. Because I never had any. I never stayed more than a year, from the time I was fifteen until, hell, thirty, I guess. I lived in dozens of places. I was meeting different people, and I had no close friends or relatives. Fifteen years is a long time to be out in the world by yourself. Pretty soon it gets on your nerves.

Q There's a story that says the first time you met Miss Dixie, you told her she was too fat. Is that true?

A Yeah. We were at a B.M.I. dinner, and she was with Mother Maybelle Carter. Miss Dixie was having a potato, and I said, "Is that what made you fat originally?" Mother Maybelle probably thought I was one of the rudest people she'd ever met. But we later became good friends, and it turned out all right. It was one way of getting Miss Dixie to remember me.

Q You've had a lot of diverse friends through the years, including Billy Carter and his brother. Billy was something of a national buffoon for a while. Do you think he got a bum rap from the press?

A Billy and I are very close friends. I don't think he got a bum rap. He never said he was gettin' a bum rap. When he said and did those things, he knew what he was sayin' and what he was doin'. He's very independent. I've never heard Billy say he was gettin' a bum rap from the press.

Q He and his wife, Sybil, came to Nashville and recorded in your studio.

A Yeah, we visited together. We did a session just for the hell of it. But I've recorded with a lot of people just for fun—you just don't hear about it. It's a good record, though. We wanted to put it in an album, but it wouldn't fit in *Saturday Morning Songs,* my children's album, because it's got beer in it.

Q Why did you write all those children's songs?

A Well, it came from a very natural circumstance. I learned that I could communicate with them. I didn't practice or try, or read any books about it. But I found that I could sit around with children, and we had a lot of the same interests. It wasn't in reverse. I didn't write the album and then try to communicate. One day I just found that we got along great. They understood me. Adults don't seem to be able to understand me.

Q Sometimes you're criticized for writing too simplistically. Do you think that's a valid criticism?

A No, if anything, I'm too complicated. Simplicity is what I've always been looking for. I read an article in a newspaper the other day that said I'd written a song that sounded like it had been written by a first-grader— "I Love," about ducks and pickup trucks. And I was very flattered by that. Because it was my intention. And it amazes me the barbs I get in the press that really please me, when people think I'm being insulted by them. I worked Carnegie Hall, and I had a decent haircut, I'd lost about fifteen pounds, and I hadn't been drinking in about three months. I had a good suntan, and I was in great spirits and good health. And I went onstage, and the reviewer said I looked like a high school basketball coach that had made it. Which was a great compliment. It was my intention to look that way. But he thought that's not what entertainers did. So I was inadvertently complimented on my endeavors. "I Love," by the way, probably sold more records than anything else I've ever recorded.

Q Do you think your music has lost some of its depth, its sharpness?

A Oh, I think I'm probably looking for different things. I know what I want to say, and I know when I'm satisfied. Maybe I'm not looking in the same direction, which means I wouldn't have the same perspective on things. But I know what I'm writing, and I know where I'm going, and I'm not writing the same kind of song I did five years ago, ten years ago. Ernest Hemingway said, to paraphrase him, that the death of a creative person was self-imitation. However, the great movie director Alfred Hitchcock said that self-plagiarism is style. But I tend to agree with Hemingway more. I can do a better impersonation of Tom T. Hall than anyone else in the world, but I don't think it constitutes talent. I would rather do something original.

Q You talk about Hemingway often. Also Edgar Lee Masters and Sinclair Lewis. You obviously read a lot.

A Yes, I do read a lot. I read books that get good critical reviews, and they normally turn out to be pretty good books. So critics have a place in the world. Although some pretty nasty things have been said about me at one time or another by a critic, and they're usually right. 'Cause I'm not at my best all the time, but I'm certainly not at my worst all the time. But it's a strange thing that a lot of newspapers will often send out a rock-'n'-roll fan to review a country show, and then a country fan to review a rock-'n'-roll show. I think journalism has a responsibility to send a knowledgeable person on an assignment. I don't like people who come prejudiced to hear me screw up. Because they go back and, sure enough, they say, "Hall screwed up last night." That's not really working at it.

Q Who are some of the people you admire in today's country music?

A I have every admiration for Johnny Cash, Merle Haggard, and Barbara Mandrell. Those are three of my all-time greats, because I know how hard they work. There are so few acts in country music who work these days. They just come out and say, "You're lucky I showed up." They're doin' the crowd a favor. I've never done that, and none of those people I mentioned have done that. They're good spokesmen for country music. Bill Anderson and Harlan Howard have written some tremendously sensitive songs. They're two of my idols, because they've been around so long. I think longevity is to be admired in anything you do.

Q Where do you think country music's going to go?

A Country music has reached a great deal of respectability. I don't know if Nashville as a community—if there is such an animal—is reacting to it properly. Robert Altman said, "Nashville is a huge popularity contest." And I don't particularly care about all the contests they have every year. I think it would be fair to take the top fifty nominees on the first ballot, send them all a letter, and say, "Check if you want to enter a contest that the Country Music Association is having for the number one male vocalist." And if you check no, then you shouldn't be nominated. And it should be made public that you're not running for anything. Then you're not embarrassed if you win, and you're not embarrassed if you lose.

Q You quoted Robert Altman. What did you think of *Nashville*?

A Probably one of the best movies ever made. When it was over, I came out and said, "It's like sittin' in the lobby of the King of the Road [Motel] for two hours during a disc jockey convention." I think you could have filmed it right there. It's a genius movie.

Q How did you feel about it?

A I was embarrassed. It was a little like getting back your wedding pictures and discovering you had your fly open during the ceremony. When Altman was in Nashville, I don't think people knew what kind of movie he was making. They should be embarrassed. Because when a movie producer comes to town, everybody in Nashville just falls down. They flip. They want to be in the movies. But, you know, we have to learn to laugh at ourselves. And I'm sure that a lot of those people who were shocked by it could go back and see it again and have a lot of fun. 'Cause we're all in there. I think any honest person would say, "Yeah, I did that. We do that in Nashville." I don't know what part I was playing, but maybe some of my friends can tell me. The intention was to show our hero worship, our illusions of literacy, creativity. But Altman also devastates the hope we have that there's a meaning to it all. So it's depressing to see it. But then, of course, there's a fine line between love, hate, depression, and happiness. It's a sad movie.

Q Do you think Altman missed anything important?

A Well, yeah, the thing that he missed—and all the people who come here from Hollywood miss it—is how tremendously wealthy and ridiculously powerful some of the people in the movie are, both nationally and locally. Most of these people in the movie are millionaires. He missed that. There is also a segment of Nashville society that is very well informed, very well educated, and highly aristocratic. He missed that, too. But I thoroughly enjoyed it. It's a very serious movie. I thought it had some overtones of the Wallace campaign.

Q Altman inferred that politicians and entertainers have the same purpose in mind. Your songs, however, don't contain as much social and political commentary as they used to.

A No, I used to write some social commentary into my songs, but I quit doing that because I don't think an entertainer has the right to advise people on politics simply because he can play the guitar and sing through his nose. That's probably the reason I quit.

Q Do you think you lost any fans when you did that?

A I don't know who my fans are. The only ones I ever see are standing outside of the bus, and they bring me little sneaky snakes, and cakes, and tomatoes and green onions. But I don't know who buys my records. Bobby Bare told me one time when I found out what I was doing, I'd quit doing it and fall on my ass. So, since I still don't know what I'm doing, maybe I'll hang in there.

Q I've seen several stories that say you're a heavy drinker.

A I'd think that was pretty accurate.

Q Aren't you putting me on?

A No, why?

Q Why are you smiling?

A No, I was smiling because I didn't know the knowledge was that general.

Q You write a lot of songs that have to do with drinking. Do you really drink all that much?

A When I'm under pressure, I do. See, I'm a writer. I've proven that. I've written some songs that have sold. I've made some social comment of significance, maybe. But I'm lazy, as most writers are. And I enjoy being alone. I don't like crowds. I am not a press agent's person. But people call me and invite me to go places, and I always say no. I say it honestly, though. I genuinely don't want to go. So why trouble myself? I was sittin' somewhere a few days ago, and a lady came up to me and said, "You want to dance?" I said, "No, I can't dance." She said, "Well, I can't either." I said, "Then why bother?" But people will invite you to dance even though you can't. And they invite me to go out to parties and be sociable when I can't. Social situations are alien to my nature, and when I'm thrown into something like that, I escape by finding the bar right away. I'm uncomfortable. I sweat. I get nervous, and therefore I get drunk. Then I make an ass out of myself. So why go to all that trouble? You can sit at home.

Q Is it ever a problem?

A Yeah, well, you know, smoking and drinking—any is too much. It's not natural to force stuff into your body.

Q Do you drink every day?

A No. In the winter I don't drink at all. I go two months and never take a drink, because I'm alone writing. It's when I'm pushed out in a crowd that I head for the bar, just to put up with it. And I just sit around and drink and nod my head.

Q I was at your house the other day for a TV taping, and you were having some brandy then.

A There were also five hundred people in the room. When I drink, I don't do things. I don't get in trouble. I don't bother people. And when the crowd leaves, I go straight to bed. Or straight back to my room and watch an old TV show. If there are no people, I don't need to drink. It's the people that make me nervous. Because you're on trial. I'm not a drinking person unless you throw me in a room with six or seven hundred other people, and they're all drunk.

Q Then why do you do songs such as "I Like Beer" and "Whiskey"?

A Well, I do like beer. And drinking is part of life. It's part of the American culture. Country music is traditionally about drinking and being in love. I didn't start it. I have a beer here at the studio sometimes. After five o'clock, we'll have a session upstairs and get a six-pack and sit around. But that's not drinking—three or four beers.

Q What's drinking to you?

A Cocktail parties. They're set up for drinking. That's what they're for. They've got a couple of oysters, two or three pieces of cheese, and four gallons of booze. Why would a person go to a cocktail party? My mother told me why people do that. She would occasionally tell my father, "I'm going into town this afternoon." If he said, "What do you need from town?" she'd say, "Nothing. I want to see and be seen." Well, I have no need to see or be seen. When I get drunk, I'm better off in bed.

Q Are you a hard person to live with?

A I must be the easiest person in the world to live with. I don't do anything. I get up in the morning and have some coffee and work on my songs, then I go down and into my garden. I feed my chickens and my cows, and then I come back and watch a couple of TV shows. Then I sit and read awhile, and work on my writing, and then I go to bed. Anybody could live with me. I'm like livin' with a dog. You just stop and pet me now and then, and go about your business. Who couldn't live with a person like that?

Q I've had people tell me you're a contradiction—that on one hand, you're very tender and good-natured, but that you can also be very cruel, callous, and cold.

A I can be very cruel if someone's trying to push me around. People will underestimate me, and then they'll ask me to do something stupid, thinking I don't know any better. And I know how to say no. I just say, "Bullshit. I'm not gonna do that. You think I'm a damned fool?" Then that makes them mad, because I'm not as easy to get to as they thought I was. That's the people who think I'm cruel and callous and cold. But they call me with some proposition that's just ridiculous. They think I'm sittin' out here drunk or something. People never understand that I have to have a motive for what I do. I have to be motivated by something. They think you should do it because it helps your image. I say, "What image?"

Q For instance?

A Well, some people offered me a television show. I said, "Why should I do a television show?" They said, "Well, this is your opportunity to do one." I said, "That's not enough of an excuse. I know why *you* want to do a television show. You're in the television business. But I'm not." What would I do with a television show? There's nothing in me that needs to be on television every week. You know, you sing some songs. People have seen me do that. And then you smile and introduce the guests. Well, I don't know what all they do on television shows, but I don't want to do it.

Q I've always thought there was a violent temper lurking in you somewhere. Is that true?

A I haven't raised my voice in twenty years.

Q How do you vent your anger?

A I don't get angry very often. But I get disappointed sometimes in people, because I know why they do what they do. So I very seldom say, "I'm mad at you." I say, "I'm disappointed in you. I thought you had more class, more talent than that. And more dedication to your job." It's far more truthful. But I don't get mad.

Q You never erupt?

A No, I'm not a shouter. In fact, when I do get mad, the angrier I get, the quieter I get about it. Because I'm analyzing it. I'm trying to figure out why it happened.

Q Sometimes you look as if you might explode. Or that you're bitter about things.

A No, I'm not bitter. But when I'm uptight and doing something I don't like to do—and one of them is give interviews—my face muscles tighten up. My wife gets on me about this. She can tell when I'm a little upset. When a thing is dragging on, or when people are repeating themselves, I get anxious. I'll say, "Well, what's the point?" And that makes people mad. They say, "Well, I want you to hear the whole story." They don't want to pass on information to you—they want to entertain you. So sometimes I'll say, "Is there an end to this story, a moral, or are you going to talk all day?" And that pisses 'em off.

Q You used to go through a lot of guitars—smashed them onstage like the Who or one of the other rock groups. What was that about?

A Well, that was in the early seventies. If I was touring, and things didn't go right, I would tear up the guitar, break it over the edge of the stage, or throw it in the audience. I did that at one big concert where people were yelling and carrying on. I thought giving them a guitar was the least I could do. But I had to quit doing that because Ovation Guitar Company said nobody can use two guitars a week. One night I gave away my PA set down in Miami. If things don't work, I try to give them to somebody who can make better use of them.

Q Why did you want to do your bluegrass album, *The Magnificent Music Machine*?

A Because I love the music. But I'm just an amateur bluegrass musician. I've had some people say, "If he's a bluegrass musician, I'm a jet pilot." But I had to do a bluegrass album. Not because it would sell records, but because I grew up playing bluegrass. That's the first music I ever did. So I did my album, and I'm delighted with it. I got Jimmy Martin, and Bill Monroe, and J. D. Crowe, and Donna Stoneman to play on the album with me. But that's the end of [making bluegrass records] for me. If it sold, fine. If it didn't, I can't help it. I'm not in the record business. I'm in the music business.

Q Before *The Storyteller's Nashville*, you wrote a book called *How I Write Songs . . . Why You Can*. What kind of response did you get on that?

A Oh, it did great! But it was distributed through a music publishing house, so it wasn't a real book. But it's a pretty good book—has punctuation and everything. And it made money, which I guess is one of the reasons you write books. Not the real reason, but one of them.

Q Didn't you teach songwriting for a while after that?

A Yeah, I've taught songwriting at the University of Tennessee, and Middle Tennessee State University, and a couple of other places. You want to know what country songwriting is? Country songwriting is primitive monophonic poetical composition. It's different from art music, it's different from music to complement the dance, and it's different from classical music, or chamber music. It's primitive poetical composition. I explained that to Hank Cochran the other day, and he said, "Now that I know what I do, I think I'll quit."

Q How do you teach songwriting?

A Well, I have a very good six-hour course about the business of songwriting—how it works and what happens. I worked on the program for about two months. In fact, I have a teacher's certificate of excellence from the University of Tennessee. A lot of the other teachers didn't like me having it, 'cause they'd been there ten years and they didn't have one. But songwriting is not a thing that is widely taught—not to the extent that I teach it. Because I don't lecture, I teach. And that was very rewarding.

Q Is there a difference in writing country songs and other songs?

A Not at all. Depends on the person and what they want to say. I think most hit songs were written by people who were sincere in what they were saying, regardless of the volume, the manner, the form, the fashion, or the fad. They're all songs. People who mean what they say when they're writing and can say it cleverly or entertainingly can have a hit.

Q Do you have to force yourself to write? Are you a disciplined writer?

A No, I'm poorly disciplined as a writer, but I'm a disciplined thinker. If I get an idea for a song, I contemplate it for hours to see if it's something worth saying. And I carry these germs of songs around in my head for weeks. Then suddenly one day it all comes alive and I write it.

Q Do you ever throw away a song because you think it doesn't have enough mass appeal?

A No, I don't do it for that reason. I try *not* to write for mass appeal. That's a trap. That's that "Oh, everybody's gonna love this thing." And everybody can't love any one thing. So if I write a song, and I find myself chuckling about it, or I'm very emotional about it, I think I have a good piece of material. And then I record it.

Q When you write a song such as "I Love," do you instantly recognize that it will be a big hit?

A No, I don't recognize the success. But I recognize the universal thought when I hear one. It dawned on me one day that people had written songs like "I Love Paris," but they'd never stopped with "I Love." They'd gone on. And one day I was trying to figure out what it was that I loved. And I said, "That's not the question. The fact of the matter is that I love."

Q The keystone of your career was writing "Harper Valley PTA," which became a huge hit for Jeannie C. Riley in 1968. Was the woman in the song based on someone you knew in Olive Hill?

A Yes. But I don't remember exactly which lady it was. I honestly don't know her name. I meet these people, but I don't remember names very well to start with. The people are important, but their names aren't. "Harper Valley" is a much bigger story than her, or than me.

Q That single sold five and a half million copies around the world, and the album, which contained several other songs of yours, was a million-seller.

A Yeah. I met a fella in West Virginia who bought a copy of it, and he didn't even have a record player. He just took it home and laid it by his bedside. That's one of the phenomena of the record business—people like an album so much they buy it even if they can't play it.

Q Some people think you're floundering—that you put out all these diverse projects just to meet your contractual obligations until your real inspiration returns.

A Well, I guess I am floundering, whatever that means. Sounds like something that's dying from asphyxiation, doesn't it? But, as I said, I'm not in the record business. I'm in the music business. If I ever end up as a record salesman, I'm *really* floundering. You see, I wrote "Harper Valley PTA" back in the sixties. I've been in decline ever since, in the estimation of people who wanted more songs like "Harper Valley PTA." But I've already written that. I don't admire people who cut a hit, and then recut it twenty-five times in order to have a career. I've seen so much of that. And when I hear it, I go, "Yech." Those people want to sell records. I'd like to sell records, too, but I have to do it with my music. I can't call up and say, "Send me a statistical analysis of what's selling, and I'll do more of that." I couldn't live like that.

Q Then why did you write "Son of Clayton Delaney"?

A I thought it would be nice if Clayton had a son. It wasn't a contrived thing. I was in that club, and it wasn't a very pretty place, as I remember. You had to walk down. And it reminded me of places Clayton probably played. I saw the kid, and the song just started to grow. But the music is completely different from "The Year That Clayton Delaney Died." It's a different song entirely.

Q You said some people think you've been in decline. Do you think that, too?

A Oh, I know the best is yet to come. Because I'm honest about my music. I'm true about it. I'm positive about it. I love what I'm doin'. And that's gotta be reflected. There's always been a market for integrity and honesty and fairness. You know, I started off singing "Ballad of Forty Dollars" and "A Week in a Country Jail." And there were those who thought I was crazy to come out with a song about old dogs and children ["Old Dogs, Children, and Watermelon Wine"] which had nothin' to do with that rompin', stompin' kind of music. I was on the decline when I put that out. So it'll turn out okay. I don't intend to be bullied around by critics, by record companies, and by businessmen. Businessmen have nothing to do with my music. They can count all they want to, but they are *not* going to put me in the numbers business. Let people get to where they don't want to listen. I'll entertain what's left.

Q You write a lot about God.

A But I'm not arrogant about my religion. I don't assume that I was born in just the right spot in the world where all of the great truths of the universe were passed around among the local ladies and the gentry. I think it's stupid of a person to believe that all of the farmers and lay preachers and barbers and doctors and politicians in a specific area were privileged to the truth. I mean, I grew up believing that. But when I got older, I checked the source of their information, and it seemed a little arrogant. Seems that they're not givin' other people in the world a break. My religion is a hope. My poet friend Miller Williams from the University of Arkansas says, "Any sort of faith justified by fact is not a faith." And I would not want to make any classic mistakes with my life.

Q What are classic mistakes, in your opinion?

A Classic mistakes are choosing the wrong religion, dabbling in politics, and hurting people. So I walk around all the probabilities of classic mistakes, although I've made a couple.

Q Such as?

A Oh, they turned out all right in the end. I don't know that I've ever sat down and dwelled on them, or made them specific. But, you know, one day you have to make a decision. Like, you want to be a recording artist. You don't have time to think about it. The offer's there. You can't say, "Well, let me wait ten years and see." You either have to do that or you don't.

Q You think that was a mistake?

A I don't know. There's no way of knowing. I would like to have dedicated my life to some high purpose. We all would. And I don't know if being a country singer is a high purpose or not. It is in the eyes of certain fans, and aspiring young artists. But I wonder how that will set with my ultimate destiny.

Q What would have been something of a high purpose?

A Some high purpose, in my estimation, would have been to have won a just war. I would have liked to have been a general. Not a political general, but a real general, and change the face of the world, if not the course of history. I would *not* like to have been a politician.

Q Is it power you want?

A No. Not over people. But over the events of history.

Q Where do you see your place in all of this?

A I have no idea how history will regard what I've done. I'll be long gone by the time my place in country music has been defined. It could be substantial. I don't know how my songs will fare in the long run. Fifty years from now, I may be a name in the book with the many people who were in the Country Music Hall of Fame. And then again, I don't know. I may be mentioned prominently somewhere for having done something that I haven't even done yet. So there's no way to know. You do what you think is right every day. I would like to grow old gracefully. And be respected for not sticking my nose in everybody else's business. Maybe in time people will forget that I was a kind of recluse.

Q Don't you think of yourself more as a songwriter than an entertainer?

A Yeah. I'm still a little bit sorry that I became an entertainer at all, because I love writing so much. But I had all these songs, you see, and nobody would record them. And Jerry Kennedy said, "Record some of these songs," and I did. And they sold some records, and somebody offered me two hundred fifty dollars to sing for twenty minutes. And I thought, "God, that's a lot of money." You know, I could stammer for twenty minutes. So I did twenty minutes, and now I have a bus and a band. But it's not really what I wanted to do. I wanted to write. But since nobody will sing my songs but me, I get up and sing them.

Q Would you like to quit being an entertainer and concentrate on your writing?

A Um-hum. But I don't know. Maybe I don't have that much to be concerned with. Entertainers come and go. And I've always, throughout my career, had myself situated where I wouldn't have to rely on being an entertainer. I'm not an entertainer type at all. And I know the type. They love it. They love the applause. You can ask some of them to do twenty minutes, and they'll do an hour. I'll go somewhere and they'll say, "We're running out of time. Would you mind cutting your show?" I say, "Christ, no. How much?" I want to get out there and get off. Because, you see, I spend all my life secluded, by myself, writing all of these songs. And it's alien to my nature to go out in front of a thunderous crowd and sing to them. Entertaining to me is a foolishness. It seems like a foolish thing to do. You know, people who whistle, and dance, and do magic, and tell off-color jokes. It amuses me to see them doing it. (Chuckling) And it depresses me to have to do it myself. There's a place for them in the world. But I don't seem to be that kind of person. I'm not moved by any of that. I really like people who have success by way of anonymity. That's the ideal circumstance—to succeed and communicate, but not be bothered with it all the time. But I'm aware that the public will grow tired of seeing me on the road, and then they'll fix all of these things for me.

Q How do you think Music City sees you?

A Well, for one thing, they don't see very much of me. I live in Brentwood, and I don't go to Music City, except maybe once or twice a year. I don't go to functions, except the events that my wife makes me attend. And I don't hang around downtown, and I don't go to awards shows. So I guess there are a lot of wrong opinions about me downtown.

Q Yet people call you the poet laureate of Nashville.

A Well, not because I'm the poet laureate of Nashville, of course. They call me that because I care about poetry, and I care about good writing. And I care about forces that move the world other than country music. You know, we'll be sitting around talking about some very good record that's out, and from habit, or a bit of pedantry, I'll mention something that Shakespeare said in that regard, or that some of my poet friends said, or Mark Twain, and I guess I create an illusion of literacy. (Laughter) But it's all been said, and to hear the same thing said differently is encouraging. To say "I love you," but to say it differently. That's what country music is about. That's what *music* is about.

Q On the other hand, you also have a reputation as a good businessman.

A That's funny.

Q Is that not true?

A My bookkeeper thinks so, and my business manager. I'm a terrible businessman.

Q You had a restaurant for a while.

A Well, I bought the restaurant because it's right next door to my studio. But I didn't want a restaurant. I just wanted the real estate, and it happened to have a restaurant on it. My wife, Miss Dixie, is a very enthusiastic person, so she played with it about six months. But you know, I can make more money in twenty minutes than a restaurant can make in a year. So we got tired of foolin' with it, and closed it up. It was a fun place. But it was a toy. Just another toy.

Q What are your other toys?

A The recording studio. The music business. Life. I call my material possessions toys. You know, I could live in a motel room and look out the window and have my food brought to me. What do I need with houses and stuff? What do I need with a studio? I can rent one. It's a toy.

Q Is Fox Hollow a toy?

A Yeah. I don't need a farm. All these things are toys. You have to know that. Otherwise, you take them seriously and think they're important.

Q Is that why people say you're a little odd?

A You mean slightly insane? Well, that's justified. I *am* slightly insane! I know that. And people know that, and they give me a break because of it. Would a sane person do what I do? No way!

Emmylou Harris

$\mathcal{E}$mmylou Harris shifted the shiny black guitar and cupped her hand to her forehead, screening out a beam of the television lights that separated her from the audience. "This is for all you Marys out there, myself included," she said, launching the down-beat on the big Gibson and sailing into the vocal with hillbilly vengeance:

> Lord, Mary took to runnin' with a travelin' man,
> Left her momma cryin' with her head in her hands,
> Such a sad case, so broken-hearted.
> She say, "Momma, I gotta go, I gotta get outta here,
> I gotta get out of town, I'm tired of hangin' around,
> I gotta roll on between the ditches . . ."

"Leaving Louisiana in the Broad Daylight" by Rodney Crowell and Donivan Cowart (© 1976 Visa Music and Drunk Monkey Music)

It's been fifteen years now since Harris first began rolling on between the ditches in earnest, serving her redneck apprenticeship "in the better hippie honky-tonks of the nation," as she recalls, with the patron saint of country-rock, Gram Parsons.

Parsons, who rode his sorrowful crown to glory on a combination of morphine and booze in 1973, didn't stick around long enough to see the full effect of his musical hybrid. But if Parsons was an original, Harris, 41, has nearly matched him in carving out an identity for herself unique in all of country music. Not only has she carried on Parsons' mission of taking pure, traditional country to a broader audience, but through her own artistry and integrity, she has helped raise the music to a new position of respectability and grace. In the meantime, she established herself as one of country music's premier voices, winning the Country Music Association's Female Vocalist of the Year award in 1980.

Alabama-born, but California-cured, Harris was initially perceived as less hillbilly than hippie, since she came to appreciate country music only in her twenties. Nevertheless, she had a number one country album with her first major-label release, *Pieces of the Sky*, and all along has managed to convey an authenticity above reproach while balancing stalwart country standards with brilliant, and sometimes esoteric, contemporary country-rock. Much as Judy Collins once pushed the work of Joni Mitchell and Leonard Cohen to the forefront of the folk-pop consciousness, Harris and her former husband, producer Brian Ahern, unearthed a treasure trove of offbeat songs and maverick songwriters— Rodney Crowell, Townes van Zandt, Guy and Susanna Clark among them—to provide her with some of the most haunting and intelligent country material of the '70s and '80s.

Aside from an almost innate sense of good song selection, however, Harris has a voice that, it has been said, would melt an all-day Sugar Daddy. In many ways, she is the consummate country artist, as adept with a plaintive country ballad as she is with hard-muscle rock 'n' roll, displaying a distinctive tonality and gift for emotional phrasing with both.

The daughter of a Marine officer, Harris grew up in various parts of the country, mostly North Carolina and Virginia. In high school, she went the cheerleader route, played alto sax in the marching band, and eventually became class valedictorian. While her Woodbridge, Virginia, classmates regarded her as something of a prig, Harris desperately wanted to be "hip and cool," and started singing at parties to gain acceptance. At sixteen, she thought about quitting school "to become Woody Guthrie."

At the time she met Parsons in 1971, Harris was feeling her life had been "relatively uneventful." Then 24, she was a college dropout and the divorced mother of a one-year-old girl. Behind her lay an abysmal first album *(Gliding Bird)*, made during a folkie stint in New York City, an aborted attempt to sing country in Nashville, and a brief, decidedly unhip career as a model home hostess in Columbia, Maryland.

Hearing her sing in a club in Washington, D.C., Parsons, formerly of the Byrds and the Flying Burrito Brothers, thought Harris had a natural feel for country music, and later sent her a plane ticket to L.A. to help with his first solo album, *GP.* A tour and a second album, *Grievous Angel,* followed before Parsons went on to Hillbilly Heaven in a perfect Hank Williams fantasy. He was twenty-six.

From the beginning of her solo recording career, Harris had a hard-core following, culled primarily from Parsons' small, but loyal, country-rock audience. Soon, though, the urgency, intensity, and purity of her recordings won over both the Old Guard Nashville and the mainstream country fans—diverse groups that nevertheless stayed with her through forays into more contemporary material (*Quarter Moon in a Ten Cent Town*), as well as side trips into acoustic, bluegrass-flavored work (*Roses in the Snow*) and rock 'n' roll (*White Shoes*).

Early in the '80s, however, the frustrations of a failing marriage and worries about creativity threatened to overwhelm her, especially when critics judged several of her later albums to be somewhat below her usual standards. In 1984, in what amounted to not only a commercial risk but a creative and artistic rebirth, Harris quit the road and separated from Ahern, leaving their California home to relocate in Nashville. She then began work, with songwriter Paul Kennerley, on her first major composing project, *The Ballad of Sally Rose,* a concept album that stands as a tour de force of writing, singing, playing, and even production.

Based somewhat on Harris' own life, *The Ballad of Sally Rose* is, in effect, a country opera. In the course of thirteen songs, it traces the life of a young woman who opens a show for the Singer, whom she falls in love with, marries, and eventually leaves for her own career. As with any great romance, it incorporates the elements of fate, tragedy, and success tempered by heartbreak and elusive peace of mind. The album, her first without Ahern, the first she co-produced, and the greatest challenge of her career, rivals *Roses in the Snow* as her masterpiece.

The following interview took place at Warner Bros. Records in Nashville in January 1985. It also contains comments from other interviews we did in a Nashville hotel room in October 1981, before an April 1978 club date in Chicago, and backstage at the Grand Ole Opry in October 1975. Since the most recent interview, Harris has married her *Sally Rose* collaborator, Paul Kennerley.

Q Your new album, *The Ballad of Sally Rose*, which you co-wrote and co-produced, must have taken a staggering amount of work—more than any of your previous records.

A A lot of work, yes. It had to be written, which was hard enough in itself, and then I had to actually do [co-produce] the album, so it was kind of like a double-backed project. I mean, I never had to deal with *that* end of it before. No album is a piece of cake. They're all a lot of work. But to have to write the material, too . . . I mean, I had the ideas for the body of the material, giving the nucleus of a story there. But after those songs were written, then there was the problem of filling in the gaps with segues to tell the story, and other songs that also had to be good.

Q This album must have been a catharsis for you, since it got you writing again after a long spell.

A Well, yeah. The reason you write is because there's something you want to say that is important to you—enough to go through all the torture of writing. (Laughter) Because I don't find it a pleasant thing. I *really* don't. I'm glad I don't have to make my living that way. So, yes, it was.

Q The kernel for the story actually came from an experience you and the band had at Mount Rushmore, right?

A Yeah, well, seeing Mount Rushmore is a pretty interesting experience! (Laughter) I mean, it's an amazing thing to think that somebody actually did that. But then, on the other hand, it's just an odd sight. And yes, the character of Sally Rose came from being there. We had a night off, and we were in a bar. It was the night before we played, so we were kind of enjoying the fact that we were in town as just a bunch of people going out to a bar and enjoying ourselves. And Phil [Phil Kaufman, her former road manager], being very protective of me, told somebody who thought they recognized me that no, I wasn't Emmylou, I was Sally Rose. And then we started taking it that she was my sister, or she was a background singer in my band, and between us, she just got to be one of these imaginary characters who became a part of the jargon of the road. I mean, there was a certain point where we called ourselves "Sally Rose and the Buds." (Laughter) But shortly after that, I got the chorus for that song, "The Ballad of Sally Rose," with, you know, "Through the valley of the shadow of Roosevelt's nose," from the Mount Rushmore thing. And then I started thinking, "Well, here's this character," and I had some other song ideas, so I started thinking of approaching it as a story, in order to finish songs, or as a crutch to help me write, if nothing else. I mean, I had some songs that were fictitious, and some songs that were very personal to me, and I just thought of combining them into something else—a concept, an opera, whatever you want to call it.

Q Most people think of this as being extremely autobiographical, with the inside allusions to Gram Parsons. You're probably tired of this question.

A Well, on the other hand, I'm asking for it. I know I am. And obviously, there are autobiographical references. But on the other hand, it *isn't* the story of my life. Some of those things happened to me, and some of them didn't. So I can't call it an autobiography, even if I wanted to, which I don't. But, obviously, Gram is the inspiration, was *always* the inspiration for it. But it is more than the story of my relationship with Gram. First of all, a lot of those things didn't happen, and then it goes into a futuristic thing. I mean, I tried to make Sally Rose a sort of timeless character. You don't really think about when this is happening, or how old she is when she ends up. It could be anything at any time in any place. But that's all, really, that I can say about it. I think anytime anybody writes anything— or, at least, the way I am . . . anything I would write has to be drawn a little bit from something I've at least thought about, or had a limited experience with. A song like "Woman Walk the Line" is much more fictitious. I got the idea for the song, but it's actually based on somebody that I know who had more experiences than that. And Sally Rose's character and the things that happened to her came out of combinations of friends and people that I don't even know very well. But obviously one of those people is *me*. (Chuckling)

Q Is she almost a real person for you now?

A Yeah, she really is. Well, she definitely was when I first got the idea, or rather after I got the three characters, because I had to make definite characterizations in my mind, in order to say, "This song is about this character, and this is what she went through, and why she did this." But then later on, when I realized that the only way the story could really make any sense was through one character, I changed the story line around a little, because the characters had been a bit one-dimensional, and because of how limited you are in the space of one album to tell the story of three people. So she was able to go through more things, mature a little bit more, and be a little more complicated personality. But obviously, she is still pretty one-dimensional. I mean, it *is* just a record. But I'm just saying from my point of view, all the incarnations and all the process of writing and creating that went into it, all of a sudden, there she is. But I have to admit that I'm still haunted by the ghosts of the other two characters. They were so important in creating Sally. They're almost like her alter egos.

Q What were they like? Did they have names, too?

A No, not really. The names weren't nearly as interesting as Sally Rose. But one of them was an older woman who had had a really hard life, and was a very close character to me, because she was based on a couple of people who are very close to me. And she was the most wonderful—I mean, *wonderful* character. I loved her. Then another one was a little more contemporary, based on a couple of friends of mine. It's hard to explain, because when it got time to really develop them and do the project, they were discarded, but they actually helped put Sally together. They helped her become who she was.

Q *Roses in the Snow* is generally considered your masterwork, and yet in a way, this is equal to it. Would you agree?

A Well, it's been a long time coming, and it's a good feeling that it's done. Because sometimes it was the only seed that kept me going when I was feeling overwhelmed by a lot of things. You know, trying to be creative, but on the other hand, just being a working person who keeps twenty-five or fifty people on a payroll. So you've got all that pressure, all the time. But in the back of my mind I was thinking, "I do have an idea, and I know it's something I want to do, and someday I'm going to do it." But what finally happened was, I realized that it wasn't going to happen by itself, that it was going to take leaving the road, letting my band go, and breaking out of a lot of routines which at one point had been very creative, and had become almost destructive. And even *then* I tried to procrastinate. Because we wrote half the album, let's say, and I put it on the back burner and started another album. (Laughter) Which is also, I think, going to be a good album. I mean, I'm still basically a singer of country songs. And that still is a nourishing part for me. But I started it, and it was [pedal steel player and songwriter] Hank De Vito, bless his heart, who is a good friend, who pushed me to go ahead with it. He had heard the songs Paul and I had written, and then I played him the stuff that we had not done tracks on, and then I played him the tracks I had cut [for another album], which I think are very good tracks, and he was very supportive. But at one point, he talked to Paul about it, and he said, "You know, this stuff that you all are writing is the most important thing she's done in a long time, and I really wish you guys would finish it." And, of course, Paul was in agreement, too, but he didn't want to pressure me, because he was a part of the writing of it. So the two of them really sort of approached me and said, "We think that you should go ahead and finish it." And it was that kind of positive, loving concern and pressure that made me put everything aside, once again, but even more seriously. And Paul put his own writing and personal work aside, too. It was just a complete, constant . . . I can't tell you how constant it was. Because we were writing, and going right into the sessions, even to the point of . . . we had written one verse to "Bad News," because it was just going to be a segue, and after we got into cutting it, we realized that it was so exciting that we wanted another verse. So we just cut the verse without even having the words.

Q So you don't want to compare it with *Roses in the Snow?*

A Well, I mean, it's special to me. And I'm hoping that it's special to other people. But it ultimately was done because it was personal, and I wanted to do it. And you do take a chance that it won't make any sense to anybody else. I think anytime you do something that's personal, you run that risk.

Q The reference to "columbine," which actually I mistook for "common vine" . . .

A That's all right. It's me and my enunciation, which has always been bad.

Q I thought it might be part of the same reasoning for bringing in strains from "Ring of Fire," "Wildwood Flower," "You Are My Flower," and "Six Days on the Road"—that those were classic references to earlier works, and you used the columbine image as a reference to "Barbara Allen," the old folk song, where the "rose grew 'round the briar."

A Well, I wasn't thinking of "Barbara Allen," but you're right, in the sense that a lot of my images do come from that, consciously and unconsciously. Because even though I used the word "columbine," it was the same kind of idea, of that image of something entwining around something else. Because I've always been intrigued by those old songs, and I love the poetry of the songs that we don't even know who wrote them, the poetry that became the language of the mountain people, or the folk people everywhere. And then, of course, that led into "You Are My Flower." That just fell out one day. Those words fell out. And then when it says, "You are my flower," and then it just goes into that instrumental . . . that was almost like an accident. But on the other hand it's because I love that old [Carter Family] song, "You Are My Flower," and because I'd had the idea of the fact that "He used to call me sunshine." And then the idea of "You *are* my sunshine." Referring. I love the idea of referring to a line from another song, or referring to a title. Because it brings in kind of a double meaning. It brings in memory and nostalgia, and it sometimes gives me ideas for songs—just what another song might mean to me will give me a feeling for another song, something that I would write.

Q How did you decide who you wanted on the album, as far as Dolly Parton, Linda Ronstadt, Gail Davies, and Waylon Jennings, for example?

A Well, when I first got the idea for the project, I decided that either I was going to do all the harmonies myself or I was going to ask Dolly and Linda to do all of it, or a majority of it. Because there's just a certain sound that we have that is just *real* good. It's a real strong female sound. I definitely wanted to have women singing on it. It's not a feminist thing. It's just a *sound* that you're going for. Women singing with women sound different from women singing with men. That's all there is to it. And of course, there are certain songs that I really felt it was important to have Dolly and Linda on to get a certain sound, and then I was going to do the rest of the harmonies myself. But there were a couple of killers that were *so* high, and my voice just sounded really thin. So I called Gail and said, "Help!" (Laughter) She has a wonderful high "head" voice—real strong. And she came in and just did a great job on a few of those things. And also we have a real good blend. We've been talking about doing a duet together. I think it would be great. And as far as Waylon, there was one song that was written from having been inspired by his particular feel . . .

Q Was that "Rhythm Guitar"?

A Yeah. And we felt that even with everybody who had played on it, the song was still missing something. So we had him come in. And actually, he's really only on that one song, but we just wanted to list everybody who had played. It was going to get so enormous to list everybody who played on every song, because there were quite a lot of people playing on every track. Sometimes we'd have somebody come in just to play a few chords on one chorus. But it adds just that little texture that was needed. It's a very layered album. There are lots of textures, lots of little invisible things that Paul put on there. So it might be misleading to have Waylon's name on there, but he is on the record. It's just that he's really on the one track.

Q Had you wanted your previous records to have these kinds of textures and layers?

A Well, I think of this album as having a certain sound, but I don't think it's that far from the other records. I mean, I have worked with a very brilliant record producer [her ex-husband, Brian Ahern], who I think is one of the best, and who's responsible for bringing certain sounds to country music which had never been heard before. And I think Paul and I both owe a tremendous debt to Brian. So it's not like it's that different. To me, the main difference is that it is original material, so it's more cohesive as a work. That's the difference that I see.

Q When you were with Brian, what did you two aim for when you went into the studio?

A Well, basically it was real simple. I mean, I picked a song, or Brian and I together came up with tunes that we wanted to do, and we came in for the best feel for the track—that thing that's really hard to describe, but when you hear it, you go, "*That's* what I wanted to get." And basically, I worked with the same bunch of musicians for a long time, and we were able to communicate in a special way. Like, John Ware, the drummer— even though I play in and around the beat, and he keeps perfect time, over the years we developed a style of playing together that was kind of creative in a way. (Laughter) So we were able to come up with a song that pulsated with a heartbeat of its own. And from there, Brian and I decided what overdubs we wanted, or who I wanted to sing harmony. We decided later what finishing touches we wanted to put on it. As I say, doing this album was in many ways not that different. I've always been used to that kind of collaboration. But I think sometimes a song tells *you* what it wants. You just have to learn to listen.

Q You've been quoted as saying that you thought you made records for people who don't particularly like country music.

A Well, I've been told that that's what I have accomplished on a certain level. I make records, basically, for myself, and I like to think of myself as performing country music, or that my point of progression is a love of country music. I've never really known who my audience is. They've just always been there, thank goodness. But I do think country music is ap- pealing to more people, and it's reaching young kids and on into older people. There don't seem to be the boundaries anymore. I suppose that's good. Somehow I've ended up making certain people who maybe were not country music fans listen, and from there, hopefully, decide to listen to George Jones and Merle Haggard, and get into the real hard- core, nitty-gritty country performers, of which I don't really . . . I wish I could say I was, but I am what I am. And I progress from the point of "I love this country song, and I'm gonna do it with as much care for the tradition as I can." And somewhere along the line I come up with what- ever it is I come up with, or that they give a lot of labels to but I don't concern myself with. (Laughter) I mean, I really am trying to do this thing right. I believe that I'm a country musician, and that I do as [much] root country music as I can. Sometimes what I do shows that the roots are extending, in that in our live show we do straight country, and we don't water it down, but, well, we do old George Jones stuff and Louvin Brothers stuff, and bluegrass and maybe end with some rock 'n' roll so they can dance. There are nights when no matter what I do, I can't seem to break through. And I blame myself. I feel like "Well, maybe if I'd danced a little bit," but maybe I didn't feel like doing it. So I just retreat into my little shell, and it doesn't work. But the whole show is a collection of songs, done by what I feel is a real traditional country band. This band is a very important part of who I am musically and as an artist. Because I think it's really important to get up onstage and play country music and make it exciting. With some of the songs, the music is sweet and pretty, too. So it's not afraid to be the two extremes—this band is capable of playing a waltz as well as rocking out. And I think that's what I want my audience to get out of it—to really enjoy being able to listen to the sweet, pretty sad songs, and to really get up with the up material, too. I always loved a lot of different kinds of music.

Q But people buy your records and go to your concerts who wouldn't go to see Roy Clark, for example.

A Well, that may be true, but that doesn't really make me happy. Because in a sense, I'm influenced by the real Old Guard country—George Jones and the Louvin Brothers and Webb Pierce and the real stone-hard country. But I can't pretend to be that kind of an artist. I think I'm trying to be true to myself. I'm definitely influenced by those people, and I think it shows up in my records and in the material that I do, but there's no way that I can pretend to be Kitty Wells. But if people could get turned on to Kitty Wells, perhaps, through the fact that she influenced my music, and they could like that music and appreciate it as much as I do, that would be great. But I've learned that you can't hit people over the head with it and say, "You *have* to listen to this, and you *have* to like it." You either love country music or you hate it. I don't think there's any middle ground, as far as that hard-core country. Country music is white blues. I mean, to me, Ray Charles is the father of [modern] black blues, and George Jones is the country singer of the white blues. It's that sound. They're completely different, but they strike the same kind of chord, to me.

Q I'd like to talk about specific albums that you recorded with Brian. *Cimarron* is an album that failed to get your usual glowing reviews. How do you feel about that album?

A Cimarron was, I think, a very country album for me. And I say that because *Evangeline* was purposely not one, only because we had collected these bizarre, left-field songs that I liked a lot and wanted to do. But instead of spreading one or two of them in basically a country album, we decided to put them all on one album, and do something that was sort of a sideline for me. It was fun, and it was very different for me. But with *Cimarron*, I got back to . . . well, I did a version of "Last Cheater's Waltz," and I did a Bruce Springsteen song ["The Price You Pay"]. But to me, the way we did it, and with the lyrics, it's a country song. And I know I can't explain that, and it may not even be true, but in my mind it is, so therefore it becomes my reality. I say, "This is what it is, on my record, to me."

Q *Evangeline* contains the famous Dolly-Linda-Emmylou version of "Mr. Sandman." How did you think that up?

A Well, it was Brian's idea to do it. I was horrified. I said, "I'm a serious *singer*. I can't do a song like *that*," you know. (Chuckling) Now, I love it. It's fun. But it was incredibly difficult. It's a very hard song for a singer like me. I have a hard enough time hearing certain simple harmony parts, much less something that doesn't even sound remotely like a melody to my ear—you know, those kinds of harmonies. I really admire people who can do it, but it never occurred to me that I would be able to do it. Those kinds of parts are like road maps to me. They just make no sense. And the way I learned them was to literally sit down with them, and note for note, just chisel them into my brain until I could sing them in my sleep. And now I know all the parts. Because not only did I do it with Dolly and Linda, and struggled to learn one part, but then they wanted to do the video and put it out as a single, and I had to learn all the harmonies. And now that we do it onstage with the guys, I have to sing all the high parts, which requires a change in the actual structure of the song. [She also sang it with Pam Rose and Mary Ann Kennedy on the *Sally Rose* tour.] So it's fun, but it's so hard that I sort of pat myself on the back every time I get through it.

Q Did Dolly and Linda have trouble with their parts?

A No. (Laughter) I have to say that I think Linda probably knew the parts. I think she probably taught me and Dolly our parts. Dolly got hers right away, while I was sweating off in the back room, where nobody could hear me, just trying to get those intervals I could *not* hear. I would just guess, just *leap* for them and hope that I would make them. And I finally learned them. The "bum-bums" were a bit difficult, because not only were they sometimes strange intervals, but we did them in such a way that they came at different timings. It's like patting your head and rubbing your stomach. It requires mental and vocal coordination that is above and beyond the call of duty. For me. (Laughter) But now that I've sort of got it under my belt, it's fun, but it was hard.

Q You have a talent for collecting left-field songs.

A Well, I look in left field. I spend a lot of time out there. (Laughter) When I used to do four shows a night in bars, I refused to do anything on the hit parade. (Laughter) Which made it kind of hard to make a living, but I managed. I would do them after they'd been *off* the hit parade for several years, but it was just the idea that I was always digging around for relatively obscure material. And I found it.

Q Where do you find it?

A Well, let's see. Give me an example.

Q Well, of course, you were lucky enough to have Rodney Crowell in your band, and he wrote a number of them.

A Right. I was very lucky there. It was like owning my own candy store. I mean, just all these wonderful songs, and nobody knew who he was. I'm really fortunate to have been able to have that experience. He was in my band, and he'd say, "Listen to this, Lou," and all of a sudden, there was "Even Cowgirls Get the Blues." Or he'd say, "Well, here's one," and it was "Leaving Louisiana in the Broad Daylight." And "['Til I] Gain Control [Again]," of course, devastated me, and I'm still recovering from that one. I think it's one of the finest songs ever written.

Q When Rodney left the band to pursue a solo career, Ricky Skaggs replaced him. And then Ricky left for the same reason. Did their leaving cause big problems?

A No, I've been fortunate again, in that I've been able to find people who don't . . . I'm not looking to duplicate, to clone the Hot Band, only in the sense of musical excellence, and being able to duplicate what's gone on in previous records. But as far as progressing into the future with other records and other performances, what I look for with any new member is whether he's going to add a certain, different texture. I mean, Ricky was totally different from Rodney. Ricky added a bluegrass edge, in addition to being able to play a multitude of instruments. We did a different kind of harmony singing. It had a lot more of a bluegrass edge, and there were a lot more specific parts. I learned an incredible amount from him. *Roses in the Snow* was a product of learning how to stick to the right part, instead of doing a duet kind of thing, where you can wander around. I mean, I had to learn, "You sing *this* note, and not that note." I benefited a great deal from having Ricky in the band. But when he left, I didn't look to find another Ricky. Not just because there *isn't* another Ricky around, but I wasn't really sure what I was looking for. I was looking for a kind of "What's next?" in a sense, although part of me wanted to go back to that Rodney Crowell type of honky-tonk thing that the Hot Band started as. And I happened upon an old friend of mine, Barry Tashian. He and I had done the first Gram Parsons record together. In fact, we had discussed starting a band in 1973, after Gram's death, and it was just totally out of the blue that we happened to run into each other. It was almost like a sign that this is what should happen. And Barry joined the group, and it's been really wonderful.

Q He used to play rock 'n' roll.

A Yeah, he had a group in Boston, called Barry and the Remains, that was sort of the quintessential Boston rock group. They opened for the Beatles on that Shea Stadium tour. I mean, he goes back a ways. Well, we all go back a ways.

Q You said it was "almost like a sign." Do you have a sense of fate or purpose about what you're doing?

A Yes, I do. (Hesitantly) And it's something that's just there, and I don't take credit for it. What happened to me and what affected me in my life is what determines a lot of what I do. And you are the bystander, and the bolt of lightning just happens to come up and give you a direction or a sense of what you want to do. Even though you still spend most of your time in the dark, it's a movement toward something. You're not really sure, but at least you're using your instincts to progress.

Q Do you ever think, "I wonder if Gram knows what I'm doing now?" or "I wonder what he would think about it?"

A Well, it's not something I think you can really answer, or that I even concern myself with. The fact that he had a tremendous effect—in fact, he probably had *the* effect—that made me decide what it was that I should do with my time and energy, is really the only response that I can make to that. It doesn't matter whether he knows or not. The fact is, I'm grateful, almost, in a sense, for what awareness I was given through him, and being able to be affected by something very strongly in the sense that I never question at least what I'm trying to do. Maybe sometimes I question whether I'm doing it as well as I should, or what to do, but not the actual content.

Q I read that you said, "When Gram died, I felt like I'd been amputated, like my life had just been whacked off. I'd only been with Gram a short time, but . . . I never realized what kind of music was inside me . . . until I met him. It's amazing how much he changed me, and it's impossible for me to talk about my music, or myself as a person, without talking about Gram to some extent."

A Well, obviously, his death had a big impact on my music, because I had pretty much geared myself to being a harmony singer. I was very happy with being kind of an apprentice, in a sense that we had a very good partnership. We had a natural vocal duet, and we got along very well. He was a very close friend, so his death made me work very hard. I had to make a decision. I had to go on doing a lot of things that before I had depended on him to do. He picked the material, and he did this, and that, and I sort of learned and put whatever ideas I had into it. So it was kind of like being thrown into the water when you don't know how to swim. And I started immediately with the help of very close friends in Washington, D.C., to get together the kind of band that we had had on the road. I had a lot to learn. I mean, I'm still learning, you know. Still working on what I'm doing, trying to find the right songs, do the right arrangements, and learn the right harmonies. It never ends, I don't guess.

Q You have a success that doesn't seem to follow any particular formula, even if some of the early albums had a hint of formula to them, with a traditional classic or two, some Gram Parsons material, a handful of contemporary left-field songs, and a Beatles tune, maybe. Is there a key to this larger success of yours?

A Doing what I want. But I also have to admit that I was fortunate enough to be allowed to do it, in the sense that, for some reason, the records sold enough to give me enough credibility to where even though my records don't go platinum, and I'm not a household word, I can do basically what I want, and get the same number of people to buy the records. That gives me a leverage to be able to experiment, and be able to do what I want. I'm very grateful for that. I really am aware of how important that is, to be able to enjoy what I do.

Q Is there any other woman in country music who has that position?

A Well, it's hard to say. Because it's obviously a personal point of view. It depends. There may be others out there who feel they are as at peace with what they're doing as I am. I don't think you can look at someone on the surface and say, "This is what's happening with them."

Q As a lot of country music gets more pop-oriented, yours continues to stay pure.

A Well, it's interesting, because to me it's obvious that that's what's pop about my music. People say, "She's a pop artist," and somebody else will say, "No, she's a country artist," you know. What turns me on about the music I do is the purity of it. And the traditionalness about it is what is pop about it.

Q I think Warner Brothers doubted that there was anything pop about either *Blue Kentucky Girl* or *Roses in the Snow*, particularly. Was there any actual opposition from them, though?

A No, there's never been any opposition, in the sense that we've never told them what we were doing. It's not like we were secretive or anything. But basically, they've sort of given us a free rein. I admit that they were a bit mystified by it, considering that I was—quote—"successful" on that pop level that we're talking about. Not that I'd had a pop hit. I've never had a pop hit, even though "Mr. Sandman" was played on the Top 40 stations [and went to #37 on the *Billboard* charts]. But the record company assumed that I was heavy crossover potential, which is an understandable assumption to make, in a way. So with *Blue Kentucky Girl*, I gave them what appeared to be an album that had absolutely no chance of crossover, let's say, like *Elite Hotel* might have had a chance, or *Luxury Liner* might have had. But *Blue Kentucky Girl* appeared to have no chance. But once again, I get back to my theory that the more pure and obviously left field, in a sense, you make an album, the more pop it is. To me, *Blue Kentucky Girl* was very cut-and-dried. It had a purity to it that gave it a pop quality. But this is another case of not being able to see the forest for the trees. And even I have to admit that I didn't realize that about it. But it was really clear-cut. Much more clear-cut than *Luxury Liner*, in that there's no way you could call anything on it pop or rock 'n' roll. But they didn't resist it. And with *Roses in the Snow*, I admit there were people who thought it was a disastrous thing to do. To the point of coming out and telling me, you know, because of the way the market was. And they knew I had things in the can that later appeared on *Evangeline* and *Cimarron* that they felt would make a stronger album, a kind of *Elite Hotel* album, that was something for everyone, in a sense. Rather than do something that was basically restricting myself, even more so than on *Blue Kentucky Girl*. But we did that for a reason, you know. We were really trying to make a point, that instead of diversification, we were putting on an even bigger set of blinders, and keeping it in an extremely narrow range. A lot of the reasons were personal, for me. They were clarification reasons. And I have to admit that I was astounded at the success of *Roses*. It's not like I set out to do a failure album, but I was surprised that it seemed to do even better than *Blue Kentucky Girl* or *Luxury Liner*. I still don't understand it, other than the fact that there is an incredible audience out there for bluegrass music that no major record company has capitalized on. I believe that there's an enormous market for bluegrass music. And *Roses* was kind of a tribute to that form of music.

Q "Poor Wayfaring Stranger," from that album, is an extremely evocative track.

A Well, thank you. But I can't take any credit for that at all, and I'm one who isn't ashamed to take credit. But Brian insisted I do the song. I didn't want to do it. I didn't feel I could sing it. And I felt that it had been done, because it's been done very well by much more authentic singers. Ralph Stanley is one of them, of course. So I didn't want to do it. And it was Brian's arrangement, and it turned out to be a live vocal, with everything recorded live. I don't think I could have gone in the studio and over-dubbed it, because I didn't believe I could sing it. Therefore, they caught me. Brian sort of set me in a situation where he knew he could get what he wanted, in spite of the fact that I didn't think that I would be able to do it. And I have come to love that arrangement and everything about it. But that is totally his record.

Q There were no overdubs at all?

A Well, there were some overdubs, but basically, I mean, that's Tony Rice's guitar solo, and that's my live vocal. Brian is really able to get the sound of instruments. He really knows how to record voices and instruments and put it all together. So that album was acoustically, to the ear, a real masterpiece of engineering and mixing.

Q How would you characterize the upcoming album *[Thirteen]*?

A It's just a collection of what I think are pretty basic country songs. But I have to use the word "austere" in a way. Paul called it "blow-down miserable love songs" (laughter), because I mean every one of them was just . . . ohhh! Anyway, I love that kind of song. I always will.

Q But you have another album in mind, too, don't you?

A Oh, yeah, I've always got a few projects in mind. Basically, I'll probably continue to just do albums of country songs, and hopefully there might be one or two that I've written. My only sort of distant hill—longing to do it someday, setting a goal for myself—is my Celtic album, which I do much more talking about than anything else. Except for listening to a lot of Bothy Band records, and Chieftains, and collecting songs that I know, if I knew how to do it, could be done in that style. If I *just* knew how to do it. I don't think it's the kind of thing where you can just go into the studio with a bunch of those really good musicians who play on those records. It's gonna take a lot more homework on my part.

Q How easy will it be for the average country music fan to get into that, do you think?

A Well, it doesn't matter. I mean, I love that music so much. It's also so close to the mountain music that a lot of the real good country music comes from, you know, because of the sound of those instruments. It's more folk music than it is anything else. So I don't think it would be that hard for them to get into. And I think I do have some interesting ideas as far as material. I mean, there's no point of doing it for the sake of doing it. But I can see where it would be an exciting musical project, which is why I'd want to do it. [Other projects recorded since this interview include the award-winning *Trio,* with Dolly Parton and Linda Ronstadt, and *Angel Band,* a collection of gospel songs.]

Q What do you think of your singing these days? *The Ballad of Sally Rose* is probably the strongest vocal performance you've done in a long time.

A Well, it is the strongest. My voice is stronger than it's been in a few years. I'm a lot healthier than I've been. I'm taking a lot better care of myself. But you always think you can do better. You're never satisfied. I don't know anybody who's ever done a record who's completely happy with it. On the other hand, it's funny. Because I'd written the songs, I didn't put as much pressure on myself for the vocals for some reason. I was more concerned with every aspect of the record—the production, the writing, you know. But on the other hand, I guess I do feel all right about the singing.

Q Why is your voice stronger now?

A Well, two years ago, I got nodes on my throat, and I started going to . . . well, not a vocal coach, but somebody who gave me an exercise routine to do. And so on the road, I do it three times a day, and I do regular exercise, too. I just think there's a certain point in your life where you have to start taking better care of yourself, or every aspect of your life is going to suffer. And you don't think of your voice as being a muscle, but it is. And you do have to exercise it and take care of it, and feed it properly and give it enough rest.

Q What about that edge you get to your voice sometimes? Is that something you can control and use for effect?

A I think it's probably gotten to be something that I *can* call up at will. But I'm not sure I really know when to use it and when not to use it. I'm an untrained singer, so if I had to think about what I was singing, or technique, I would just clam up. I don't think I would be able to do it. Once again, I think it's just muscles. You know, the more time you spend in the studio, the more chance you have of knowing what you're supposed to be doing. There are times I think I want to sing with a little harder edge when I hear it back. I say, "I really meeked out on that." Sometimes I accept it and go with it. And then there are times when I say, "Well, I have to go back and try it one more time." But we may be talking about two different things here. Are you talking about the real gravelly sound that has sort of come in my higher register?

Q The way you deliver the phrase "two more bottles of wine" at the end of that song, for instance?

A Yeah. But that was really forced. Now I can get it more . . . even when I'm singing something soft and high, I can get . . . That's much more natural than hitting a kind of a rock-'n'-roll thing. I'm not a rock-'n'-roll singer. I love rock 'n' roll. It's great to play, but it doesn't come natural to me to sing it, and I do tend to hurt my voice for the higher registers and the more delicate sounds when I consistently try to hit it really hard. So it's more than kind of . . . I get kind of a raspy sound in it. But that has to be on the more raspy songs, really. Something like "Drivin' Wheel" is pretty easy for me, but straight-out rock 'n' roll is just . . . I'm too old for it now, anyway. So I don't have to worry about it anymore. (Chuckling)

Q Do you really think that way?

A I think I'm talking more psychologically. (Laughter) No, I shouldn't really say that, because when I'm talking about rock 'n' roll, I'm talking, I suppose, about how we used to think of it as teenagers. Rock 'n' roll has definitely grown up. I mean, if rock 'n' roll is Bruce Springsteen, we can be rock-'n'-rollin' when we're eighty-five. Because that's definitely a very mature music, lyrically and in every other way.

Q Most critics found your rock-'n'-roll album, *White Shoes*, to be quite strong and effective.

A That was sort of a side trip for me, as far as having any, perhaps, cohesiveness. But on the other hand, as just a collection of songs, and the recording of the songs, I thought it was a good album. I thought Brian's production on it was brilliant. "On the Radio" almost made *me* cry, and I don't listen to my records that way. But just the *sound* of that record—the sound of that particular track . . . and, of course, Sandy Denny's song, "Like an Old-Fashioned Waltz," has always torn me up —before she died, even. When I first heard the song, I cried. So I had always wanted to do the song, and then after her death . . . I didn't even know Sandy Denny, but on the other hand, you can't help feeling a certain connection there—your vulnerability and everything else comes in to give another dimension to the song. So there are special moments on that album for me. But on the other hand, I don't consider it a country album, but I think that I have the right, if I want to, to do a side [rock-and-roll] album. I'm not trying to pull the wool over anybody's eyes. I'm just making a record.

Q The title cut—where you talk to yourself, with "Lou, you gotta start new"

—showed a sense of humor that you display in person, but not very often in your music.

A We've worked that up in the show, because it's great having Pam [Rose] and Mary Ann [Kennedy] to do all those Bonnie Bramlett "woah, woahs."

Q Bonnie's one of the great ones.

A Oh, gosh, yeah, she *is* great. I'd love to see her in the mainstream, recording. I don't know why somebody doesn't do a country-blues album with her. A lot of us just sort of play at that kind of sound. But nobody can really sing it like Bonnie can.

Q Why don't you produce it? That would be a good stretch for you, wouldn't it?

A Well, I don't know that I would be the one to produce something like that. But if my involvement in the project was, let's say, executive producer, whatever that is, to get something going, I would certainly lend my endorsement and any energy that I might have toward that. As far as whoever could pull that off, I would think maybe there would be somebody who would be a better producer for it. But there are a lot of good people out there who are tried and true, and who have been through a lot of the bullshit, and who should be taking advantage of the openness of the country market. Sometimes that can be a bad thing, because it loses some of its definition. On the other hand, you can look on it as a positive thing, to where maybe a lot of the people who had some pop success, since pop is so closed right now, could take advantage of having the visibility that country music and country radio and country sales can give an artist. It's a much more staying, lasting thing. I think it would be great. They've got Nicolette [Larson] making a country record. I'd just love to see somebody like Bonnie come back, if she wanted to do it.

Q With a project such as that, and especially the Delia Bell album you produced *[Delia Bell]*, do you see yourself in the role now of being able to foster worthwhile projects and help artists who maybe couldn't get on a big label without your endorsement?

A Well, I don't know how much help I can be. It's just like, I don't know that I helped Delia. I did one album, and now you can't even buy it, you know? Actually, I guess I'm being pessimistic. But eventually that will happen, I'm sure. I mean, I think it's a good record, and I'm glad I got to showcase Delia, because I think she's *the* classic woman country singer of that genre. I think the material was good, but I made certain mistakes on the album that if I did another album with her I wouldn't make. Certain material wasn't suited for her that really *I* wanted to do, but I think that happened on only one or maybe two songs, and the rest of the material was very well suited for her. So I feel that I was a good producer for Delia, but I don't think I would be a good producer for Bonnie. I can almost visualize the kind of record she could make, though.

Q You've just recently moved back to Nashville after living many years in California. But you lived here before, when you were trying to get started. What was it like for you here then? Somebody told me you worked as a waitress across the street from the Greyhound bus station. Is that right?

A It was a very short time. It sounds more colorful than it actually was. I came here in the early summer of 1970. My daughter [Hallie] was about two months old. My [first] husband [songwriter Tom Slocum] and I didn't have very much money, and I had been singing in New York unsuccessfully, doing some local TV, doing a few jobs. The pregnancy kind of hampered that, of course, although I did work right up until my daughter was born. It's actually a lot easier to work before you have the baby than afterwards, so it was very difficult for me to find work singing. And a few times when the cash got really low, I was forced into my only other skill, which is waiting tables. And so I did wait there for a while. Isn't there a Polynesian restaurant, the Mai-Mai, or the Mai-Tai, in town? Every time I mention it to somebody, they say, "I never heard of it." So I wonder if I made it up.

Q Why did you come here? Because you thought you had a better chance to break into country music here than in New York?

A Well, I had been doing some country music in New York, although I was working purely as a solo performer with just myself and my guitar. It seemed to me that there wasn't really room for any country music in New York, although my decision was partly that and partly that it was very depressing in New York. It was very hard. My career was at a standstill, and I guess I just wanted to make a change. And Nashville seemed a lot easier than going out to Los Angeles. But circumstances being what they were, it was really impossible for me to give it a chance. Perhaps if I'd stayed, things would have worked out. But I was only here for way less than a year. Maybe six months.

Q Did you get any singing work here?

A I worked at one concert at Vanderbilt, at their coffeehouse there, and I did a couple of weeks playing a Happy Hour thing at the Red Lion Pub at one of those big motor inns out there on Murfreesboro Road, I think. (Short laugh) It seems like fifty years ago. I went to Washington, D.C., after that. This was the end of '70, around Christmastime. My parents have a farm outside of Washington, in Maryland, and seeing as how I was broke and at the same time my marriage had broken up, I really didn't know what to do at that point. My parents were really concerned about me, and asked me to come home and just collect my thoughts. My family and I are very close, and I went back there and discovered, much to my surprise, a really nice little musical community in Washington. A lot of bluegrass.

Q And then in early '71 you started working the Washington clubs, which is where you met Gram Parsons.

A Yeah. I had a job working as a hostess in model homes in a housing development in Columbia, Maryland, during the day, and then I would go in a few nights a week and sing in these few bars where you would get a young crowd, mostly college students. And I sort of got back into music. Being in New York and going through some hard times had taken the music out of the music, if you know what I mean. Those years I spent in Washington were very good for me. I was able to get back to the reason I went into music in the first place.

Q Originally, though, you did folk music. That Jubilee album you cut in New York *[Gliding Bird]* was more folk than country.

A (Uncomfortable laughter) That was kind of disastrous. But yeah, in college, a guy by the name of Mike Williams and I were like an Ian and Sylvia duet. This was in '66, I think. And I became real dissatisfied with college and quit school and went to Virginia Beach. My plan was to work to earn enough money to go to a real good drama school. So I worked as a waitress and at night I worked in coffeehouses and sang. In the meantime, I got more and more into music and less and less into drama. And at the end of '67, I went to New York to seek my fame and fortune. (Laughter) And I worked the coffeehouses, although the folk scene at that point was really dying out. So I didn't get a whole lot of work. And finally after a couple of years and the birth of my daughter, I just had had enough, and I left for Nashville.

Q So you were obviously interested in country music before you met Gram. But where did that interest come from?

A I listened to country music when I was growing up. I mean, I wasn't raised on a farm in Tennessee, you know, one of twelve children, or anything. I was from Alabama, but we traveled around all my life, because my father was in the Marine Corps. So I have no roots anywhere, but we lived all over the place—North Carolina, Virginia. And we made a lot of family trips from wherever we were stationed at the time to my mother's family in Birmingham. We'd always travel at night, and that's when you get WWVA the best, so that's a sound from my childhood. But I really found a deep love and appreciation for country music. I don't know if it's because I'm originally from the South, and just latently found my roots, or what it is. But it's just a sound, and a feeling that's in the music. And you either hear it and appreciate it, or you don't. It's just a matter of taste. My brother is a country music fanatic, and he was long, long before it was hip for his contemporaries to be into it. He's just a couple of years older than me. So I heard it from him, but it was really my association with Gram that set me in one direction. Believe it or not, I had never heard of the Louvin Brothers, and he turned me on to them, and to George Jones—to all the hard-core country. And he taught me so much about harmony singing. I would say he is responsible for ninety percent of my style. But I had had influences from people like Jerry Jeff Walker, who was in New York at the same time I was, and Paul Siebel, who has written some really fine country songs. And David Bromberg, who does all sorts of material, of course, and has an incredible mind for material. He turned me on to a lot of bluegrass. Some other roots were very, very varied. But country music just makes simple, clear-cut state-ments in a poetic way. That's why I think country songs are so hard to write. Because you can't use anything extraneous. It has to come right to the point.

Q I own a couple of copies of the Byrds' *Sweetheart of the Rodeo* album, but I can't hear Gram on any of them. Why is that?

A Because they took his vocals off. There was some kind of contract hassle, I think. But if you listen real close in the headset, you can hear him, because his phrasing is so different from Roger McGuinn's. It's so strange. It's like hearing a ghost, because his phrasing is the real tradi-tional, Louvin Brothers phrasing, and Roger McGuinn sang it like, you know, Roger McGuinn. And there's such an overlapping that you can hear him in the spaces where Roger doesn't sing, because Gram elon-gates his phrasing. But there are albums that were released before the injunction where you can actually hear Gram, because you can't miss Gram's voice. I mean, things like "The Christian Life." Obviously Gram found that, because he was the one who really brought the Louvin Brothers to the attention of all us non-knowing, non-believing people. (Short chuckle)

Q The first time I interviewed you—in 1975 backstage at the Opry, for a TV special for the Opry's fiftieth birthday—was the first time you had ever even been to the Grand Ole Opry. In other words, the first time you ever saw any kind of Opry performance, you were on it.

A Yeah, the first time. I regret that I never got to see a show at the Ryman. I kept meaning to go when I lived here, but all of a sudden, I didn't live here anymore. It happens, you know. I never saw the Statue of Liberty in New York, and I lived there for two years.

Q And then five years later, in 1980, you were named the CMA Female Vocalist of the Year.

A Right. But I was up for it so many times when I didn't get it that it was almost like they took away my amateur standing when they gave it to me. (Laughter) It was almost like "Oh, no!" And I started to not even go. I was on the road, and I actually did have a day off, but I was way the hell up in Milwaukee or someplace, so I figured I had an excuse. I mean, you know, I didn't think I was going to win. But Eddie [Ed Tickner], my [former] manager, said, "I got a new tuxedo, Emmy, and I'd like you to come to the CMA with me." And I said, "Well, Eddie, you've never asked me to do anything, so if you really want me to go, I will." It was really, *really* exciting. It really was.

Q Have you had any embarrassing moments onstage, on your road show?

A Um, sure. (Laughter) There's the classic one, of falling on my derriere in front of seven thousand people, holding my guitar. This was in the middle of "C'est la Vie," because I stepped in a crack on the stage and went flying up and just landed right on my rear, and, you know, everybody saw it. But as embarrassing as it is, what are you going to do? I got up and I finished the song. (Laughter)

Q You mentioned Hallie, but you have another daughter, Meghann, from your marriage to Brian Ahern. And during that marriage, you also had a stepdaughter, Shannon. How have you been able to balance the nomadic life of an entertainer with a home and children?

A That's something that I have had a bit of difficulty with, and something I've had to work on. I would never take them on the road, and I don't feel guilty about that. And I don't feel guilty about my work and what I do. But sometimes I spend too much time in the studio getting things exactly the way I want it, and that doesn't leave me much quality time with the family. And instead of accepting that, I feel a great deal of dissatisfaction and almost guilt about it. It's just a matter of cutting yourself off at a certain point and organizing your time a little better. Because it really is possible to do it. I think it's important that you set an example for your children that you work hard at what you do, even though maybe when the kids are younger, no matter how hard you try, they might get a distorted view and think you're just having a party all the time. They don't understand how much work is involved. That's something I can't help.

There's no way I can enlighten them to that. I can just hope that eventually, as they reach adulthood and figure out exactly what everything is all about, they're going to gain something from it.

Q In many ways, *The Ballad of Sally Rose* is a much meatier album than you've done in some time. A lot of your hard-core following was frustrated that you hadn't delivered something like this earlier.

A Well, there was no way I could . . . I was at the point where I was feeling those frustrations, too, but it was really traumatic to make the changes I had to make to get to the point where I could even *approach* doing anything like this.

Q Before we turned on the tape recorder, you said you suffered from writer's block for seven years. Has this album gotten you out of it?

A I don't think so. (Laughter) Because, first of all, I haven't really had time to write anything else. I *am* going to approach it again. Obviously not this kind of project, but I have had several ideas since that have been logged in the way that they're always logged, which means the first available piece of paper that I come across. You know, the ideas are jotted down, and then they're carefully preserved and put in a certain notebook where I keep all my bits and pieces of paper. And at some point after this tour is over, and hopefully before I do the next album— or finish it, I should say, 'cause I have started it—I will hit it again. At least I can see the possibility, because all these songs at one point were just pieces of paper in a notebook. I have nothing but admiration for Paul and other real good songwriters who can write about anything and everything, and do. Because I'll never be able to write that way. I can't imagine just sitting down and having to stare at a blank piece of paper. Writing is not the kind of thing I look forward to doing. But at least I feel like I have a start on something. It would be really pathetic for me to never write again just because I happened to do this album. Unless, of course, I stop getting ideas. If *that* happens . . .

The 1985 Farm Aid festivities were rolling right along when George Jones stopped between songs to give the TV audience the toll-free phone number, made up of the letters of the event itself. "If you'd like to make one of your nice donations," Jones said, "it's 1-800-F-A-R-M . . . [long pause] well, I done forgot how to spell, but it's Farm Aid!" It's not  just anybody who can display such bumpkinism and come up a winner, but then you'd be hard pressed to find anyone as ingenuous as George Jones. "You know this ol' world is full of singers / But just a few are chosen / To tear your heart out when they sing," Jones croons in *Who's Gonna Fill Their Shoes*. Surely Jones, 57, is one of the chosen, and even if he can't spell "aid," he administers a little of it each time he sings.

They spend their nights in bars and honky-tonks throughout the South, the lonely and the down-and-out, aching over failed and hopeless love. The beer, they think, helps wash away the memories, but the jukebox is sure to keep them alive, taunting and teasing in the throbbing neon glow. And if there is anyone who understands, who can offer sympathy for the price of a quarter, it is George Jones, the great George Jones, "the eternally troubled George Jones," as writer Patrick Carr once described him, the man some call the greatest country singer of all time. The quarter drops, and out comes the voice of Despair, anxious at first, then desperate, with Jones sliding up a wail meant to caress and exorcise his demons at the same time. He holds the cry as he might the last bottle on earth, and then plunges to the low notes in a moan that leaves no doubt—when you talk about pain and suffering, George Jones has *been* there.

Born in the small southeastern town of Saratoga, Texas, Jones found his first taste of misery the moment he came into the world, when the doctor who delivered him dropped the infant and broke his arm. The family moved frequently in the boy's early years, finally settling in Beaumont, where the elder Jones, a laborer in logging and oil, found wartime work in the shipyards and moved his wife and eight children into a government housing project.

Described as a "hard-living, hard-drinking" man, George Jones, Sr., also played guitar and sang at local square dances. While his Pentecostal wife encouraged their son to sing at church, George Sr. encouraged him to follow in his own footsteps. When his firstborn and favorite child, Ethel, died of a fever at the age of seven, George Sr. began drinking more heavily, and often demanded that his son and daughter Dorothy sing for him.

"It didn't make much difference what time of night it was," George later recalled. "Whenever he'd come in drunk, he'd say, 'Get up and sing me some songs.' We didn't want to sing, but we sang."

Like many of today's big-name country performers, Jones spent much of his childhood listening to the Grand Ole Opry on the family radio, and dreaming of someday performing there himself. "I played hooky a lot, and went out in the woods, where I'd left my guitar out there under the brush," Jones remembers. At the age of twelve, he was both a hardcore country music buff—busking on the streets of Beaumont for spare change—and a school dropout.

At fourteen, Jones ran away from home and took the first of several jobs performing on Texas radio stations. By eighteen, he was a husband and soon to be a father. When the baby arrived, Jones was long gone, only to be jailed for five days for lack of child support. "I didn't want that to happen again," Jones says, "so I decided to go into the Marine Corps." After his discharge in 1953, he signed with Starday Records. His first two recordings, the up-tempo "No Money in This Deal" and the slower "You're in My Heart," foreshadowed the differing styles he would employ throughout his career.

"We had quite a bit of trouble establishing George," Harold W. "Pappy" Daily, co-owner of Starday, was to say later, mainly because Jones tended to sound too much like his idols, Lefty Frizzell and Roy Acuff. He finally got his break in 1955—a year after his second marriage, to a tall blonde who worked as a carhop at a drive-in restaurant—with a song called "Why Baby Why." The record topped the *Cashbox* charts for five weeks, and Jones became a regular on the "Louisiana Hayride." Several months later, in 1956, Jones realized his dream of joining the Grand Ole Opry.

Almost immediately, Jones moved to the more prestigious Mercury label, where he would record the first of his honky-tonk classics ("White Lightning," "The Race Is On") and develop the emotional wail-and-moan delivery that would become his trademark. In time, scores of Jones imitators would be bending or lengthening their notes, and enunciating with Jones's alternating flow—forcing his taut voice through clenched teeth, or singing, as Bill C. Malone describes it, with "rounded, open-throated precision." In the '60s, with such great sad songs as "The Window Up Above" and "She Thinks I Still Care," Jones emerged as a true country star, winning both popular appeal and the awe of his peers, who revered him as "a singer's singer."

With success, however, came a host of anxieties and trials, including the toll that touring takes on the body and spirit. "You get run-down, then when you go home to rest, you can't," Jones remarked during this time. "You're nervous, waiting to go out again." On top of it, Jones developed persistent stage fright, which plagues him to this day.

"Eventually, to cope with all this you start nipping," Jones explained. And that led to countless displays of erratic behavior. One night during this period, when Jones came offstage and found it was too late to buy a can of beer, he flushed his entire concert take —$1,200—down the toilet. By the late '60s, he was beginning to earn his infamous title of "No Show Jones," leaving concert promoters and ticket holders in the lurch. And in 1968 his second marriage came to an end. That same year, his friendship with Tammy Wynette turned serious, and they were married early in 1969. The music press immediately dubbed them country music royalty.

At the end of 1971, Jones signed a ten-year contract with Epic Records, where Wynette was enjoying the peak of her career with producer Billy Sherrill. With the pop-tinged "countrypolitan" sound—a sound Sherrill helped create—dominating country music during the '70s, Jones's classic hard-core style had fallen out of commercial favor. For the last few years his records had failed to make the Top 5. But Sherrill had a plan to record duets with Jones and Wynette, a plan that would simultaneously update Jones's style and rejuvenate his career. The result was a winning combination all around—the duets were commercial hits, Jones cut some of his best solo efforts, and Sherrill remained his producer for more than a decade.

While Jones's career continued to flourish, his personal life once again fell into shambles. To say, in fact, that George Jones has had his troubles is like saying that the *Titanic* had a bumpy voyage. There are those who insist that Jones was never a happy man, and certainly his excessive drinking and unpredictable behavior were well in evidence long before he met and married Tammy Wynette. But when Tammy divorced him in 1975 and eventually married his close friend, producer-songwriter George Richey, Jones's problems began to snowball. His frequent failure to show up for scheduled appearances became the stuff of legend, and his finances deteriorated into bankruptcy. The drinking, meanwhile, continued to the point where Jones was being referred to not only as a sad drunk but as a mean one. Soon there were reports of his having been arrested on assault and battery charges, brought against him by his ex-girlfriend and two other women in separate incidents. But the most dramatic allegation of violence came in 1978 from his good friend Earl "Peanut" Montgomery, a Florence, Alabama, songwriter, who claimed that Jones fired a .38 Smith & Wesson at him during an argument over religion, the bullet missing Montgomery by a scant two inches. Not long after, in 1979, Jones checked himself into an Alabama alcohol and drug rehabilitation center.

The following interview took place in May 1980 in Jones's hotel room in Tulsa, just after he and Tammy Wynette had teamed up again to make records. My first impression was that he looked, well, smaller than life. At five feet seven inches and wearing a blue polyester leisure suit, the effects of influenza, and a weary smile, he didn't seem capable of a lot of those headlines. But he also looked like the survivor of a bad car wreck—scarred, grateful, and leery of getting near the same set of circumstances again. Then I noticed that he carried a drink in his hand —a drink he barely touched the entire time we talked.

Soon, though, Jones was back to his old tricks. In the next three years he was again hospitalized for drug and alcohol abuse (in 1982), arrested for possession of cocaine, charged countless times for drunken driving (including a famous alcohol-related car crash in Mississippi, for which he wrote a $700 rubber check to cover the fines), and sued by an arsenal of ex-wives, ex-managers, creditors, and promoters.

His problems only made him more irresistible to his fans. These same years saw Jones pull out of another career slump—particularly with *He Stopped Loving Her Today*, which won him a Grammy and two CMA Male Vocalist of the Year awards—and secure his status as a country music legend. Perhaps Don DeLillo was right when he wrote in *Great Jones Street:* "Fame requires every kind of excess."

Today, George Jones is said to be a different man, due largely to his 1983 marriage to Nancy Sepulveda, his fourth wife. No matter what happiness this new partnership brings him, the only true constant in his life will probably be music. It is the only thing that has ever sustained him —through an unstable childhood, through the changing fads of the business, and through fits of self-destruction and despair. Jones himself knew it in this exchange.

Q What's brought about this new dedication to your career?
A Well, let's say it's just opening your eyes, maybe for the first time, and really seein' things like it is. Sometimes you get so involved with just one thing—singin' and your career—that you don't stop and consider all the things that helped make it happen, like the people and the fans.
Q But right now it seems as if you've put a lot of extra energy into it—giving it everything you have.
A Yeah, I think we may be overdoing it right now, but it's very important to me, and we've really been hittin' the road pretty hard here lately, what with interviews and recording sessions and TV shows. But there's a lot left undone that I owe the fans, and I feel that this will definitely be the last go-round for me, because I'm not a spring chicken anymore, and I do love country music, and there's lot of things I done wrong that I want to redo.
Q Such as?
A Well, just all the things I was talkin' about—the fans, all the trouble they go to to be at a date, and then you don't show up. That's very, very important to them, much more than we ever realize. And I never did pay much attention to it until lately. That's the main thing I want to do, whether I have any more hits or not. I want to sing country music, and from now on I'm gonna try to do it the right way.

Q You gained quite a reputation as a "no-show" on the concert circuit. But I read somewhere that you said it wasn't always your fault—that you weren't always laid up drunk somewhere and unable to perform.

A Lots of times it wasn't my fault, and there was a few times it was. But it was all based around the people involved—people that should have canceled the dates, who were told to. I was bein' booked in two or three different places at a time, and lot of times I didn't even know about either one of 'em. And the ones I did know about, I tried my best to get canceled out, to no avail. So anywhere that I was supposed to be booked, someone would walk out onstage and say, "George is not here. He's drunk." And who knows? I might have been. (Laughter) But I had my reasons, and we're with the right people now [he was being managed by George Richey's brother, Paul, with the Tulsa-based Jim Halsey Agency handling bookings and network TV appearances], and I think we'll know what's goin' on, and we'll pay more attention to our business than just the singin' part of it.

Q Is this what you thought about when you were in the hospital?

A Oh, yeah. You think of everything in the world, and I think that was the best thing that ever happened to me. Gave me a lot of time to think. And, you know, sometimes you don't take time to think. When you're just hustlin' here and there, sometimes it's good to get off somewhere. And if it takes a hospital to do it, that's good.

Q Did you make the decision to go in by yourself?

A Yeah, along with some friends. Had to have a little encouragement, 'cause I hate hospitals. (Laughter) But I knew at the time I went in that there was really no other choice.

Q How rough was it?

A Pretty rough.

Q I'm surprised that you talk about this so freely.

A Well, I feel like it's the truth, and as long as you tell the truth . . . we've got to live with it ourselves, so why not tell the truth? Might as well be honest with yourself.

Q Tell me more about your hospital stay.

A Well, my body was just down, and could go no farther. My IQ wasn't even enough to register. (Laughter) And I was really just mentally and physically at rope's end—just as far as I could go. Totally.

Q How did you let this happen?

A Well, I let myself, in a way, really get that far gone, but it was the people I was involved with—personal problems. Just weak. And it was so many things, all at one time.

Q I've heard you say before that you think you're weak.

A I think there's a big percentage of us who are. We've got our weak-nesses, and everybody's got one. Of course, some of us can cope with it a lot easier than others of us. I don't know how to explain it.

Q What did you learn about yourself in the hospital?

A Well, just basically what I've been talkin' about. I learned that I've hurt a lot of people while enjoyin' my success, and I've hurt a lot of people in marriage, I've hurt a lot of people just standin' by me—close friends. You do that. You hurt your own kinfolk. You're just havin' a good time, and you don't pay any attention to who you hurt, and nothin' is of any importance except yourself. I've never intended to, or wanted to hurt anyone, but you just do it when you're so high up in success and what have you.

Q How did you find "He Stopped Loving Her Today"?

A Bobby Braddock and Curly Putman wrote it. I carried the song about a year and a half, I guess, and I loved it, but I was too messed up at the time to go in and record. So I held on to it, and they didn't give it to nobody else, and one of my first sessions when I went back in was "He Stopped Loving Her Today."

Q Was it hard for you to go back into the studio?

A Naw, I was happy. I was thrilled to get back in and get involved with the business again, after all the hard thinkin' and the good thinkin'. And the results are payin' off. We're sincere about it, and we're just happy to be doin' what we do best, which is the only thing we know to do, too.

Q With the possible exception of Tammy [Wynette], I can't think of anyone else in the music business whose personal life is so public, and whose life is so mirrored in his songs. Do you consciously pick songs that reflect what's going on in your life?

A Not really. It was just the best things that came along at the time, and they just fit. There were just no other good things presented to me. Like "Someday My Day Will Come"—it was just the best thing I could get ahold of at the time. I would probably think they were wrote with me in mind. And, of course, they got 'em to me at the right time, too, and it just all went together.

Q How about "Grand Tour"?

A Well, "Grand Tour" was before I had any problems. Tammy and I were still married. George Richey wrote it, him and a couple of other guys. And "A Picture of Me," George Richey wrote it. And we've been friends for a long, long time. Did a lot of writing and a lot of sessions together, and kinda been in the same circle together for years.

Q But from what I read, you weren't always such good friends. I'm referring to the time after he and Tammy married, when you phoned their house and he told you not to call anymore.

A Oh, this was when I called to check on my daughter Georgette, and I was asked not to call there anymore. And I don't know. One thing led to another, and everybody jumped off the wrong end. But we got that all straightened out, and everything's fine.

Q You sometimes refer to George Richey now as your husband-in-law.

A My husband-in-law, right. (Laughter) Crazy, isn't it?

Q People always talk about George Jones as being a legend. Do you feel like a legend?

A I don't pay no attention to that. I feel honored with what those words are supposed to mean, but I'm just a down-to-earth ol' country boy, and I love to sing. I love country music, and it's my life. It's the only thing I ever cared for, and it's the only thing I ever will care for. I guess I care for it too much, more than the wives and personal things, but it's very important to me, especially now. And that's the way it is.

Q Why does it mean so much to you?

A There's just a love there you can't explain. Very deep love. A lot of people wonder why I don't try to cross over and record middle-of-the-road and pop. I couldn't enjoy doin' it. Now, there's people that are doin' it that I know don't enjoy doin' it, but their love is stronger for the dollar than it is for country music, or the music that they really love. And I just love it that much. If I could live with shelter and food and a few clothes to wear, I wouldn't care if I even got paid for the dates, because how can you put a price on it? Those people went to a lot of trouble, and they're payin' you back when they're clappin' their hands and hollering. You're doin' what you're enjoyin' at the moment, and they're payin' you back at the same time. So how can you put a price on it?

Q If something happened and you couldn't sing anymore, what would it do to you?

A In the first place, it'd probably break my heart. I don't know that it would kill me. One never knows that. The strong love that I do have for it, who knows, it probably would. You never know. 'Cause it is a pretty strong love.

Q Where do you see yourself in the history of country music?

A Where do I see myself? I don't know how to explain that. It's really not that important to me, as far as glory, popularity, and those things. I just feel like I'm makin' people happy, that they're likin' what I'm doin'. And they durn sure make me happy when I walk out on that stage. That's all that's really important to me.

Q Aside from music, how do you think of yourself? When you look in the mirror, what do you see?

A Well, I see a person that I like a hell of a lot more than what I did. There's a lot of catchin' up to do. I believe from day to day I might like that face in the mirror a little more if things can work out right, and with the help of the good Lord, it probably will. We hope so.

Q How do you look back on your childhood?

A Oh, nothin' wrong. Just had a good one. I had beautiful parents. They worked hard, just like most parents did, and raised us the best way they could. Like most people, we was poor, but we had plenty to eat. Plenty of gravy and biscuits, and everything was fine. I don't think I'd change a thing.

Q Nothing?

A Oh, there were lots of things I'd liked to have done for my parents that I didn't get around to doin', things that made life easier for 'em after it was made easier for me. Right there at the last, I did a little, but that's the first thing you ever want to do if you ever become successful in any kind of business.

Q Do you have any outstanding memories of your childhood?

A 'Bout the biggest day of my life was when Hank Williams came to town [when I was eighteen]. I was on a little radio show in the afternoon, KRIC in Beaumont, Texas, and he was appearing there that night. He had just released "Wedding Bells." And he came by our radio show that afternoon around four o'clock. The program director at the station knew him, and he got Hank to come by and sing "Wedding Bells" on our radio show to plug his date that night. It was a big thrill.

Q Did he give you any advice?

A Oh, yeah. He said Roy Acuff was his favorite back then, and he could imitate him pretty good. When he found out that I loved him and was singin' his songs—you know, someone put it to him that I sang just like him—he said, "I'll tell you, I was a pretty good imitator of Roy Acuff, because he was my favorite, but I soon found out they already had a Roy Acuff, so I just started singin' like myself." And I recall at my first session, the man walked in after about two hours of recording, and he said, "George, we've heard you sing like Hank Williams, Roy Acuff, and Lefty Frizzell, but can you sing like George Jones?" And I said, "Well, I don't know." I thought I was supposed to sell records and sound like all those that was sellin' 'em. So I dropped it down and started singin' like myself, but yet I still had all three of 'em in there.

Q Think you still do?

A Oh, definitely. Roy Acuff, Lefty, and Hank. With what little bit I had to add, with the sound of my voice, I guess. But they're all in there, because they were my favorites. I believe everybody has a couple of favorites back at the time he's growin' up, and if he turns out to be a singer, it's definitely in him somewhere, the influence from his favorites. Or her favorites. You may not mean for it to show, but it shows, and there's no way you're gonna keep it out.

Q One of your most famous songs is "The Window Up Above." How did you come to write that?

A That's a funny situation. I wrote that in about fifteen or twenty minutes. I'd just come off a tour. And I don't know what made me write it. There was no reason for it—no problems at home, or nothin'. I just got home, hadn't been home long, and I got the guitar out in the den and sat down. And the idea just came to me from somewhere. That was back in about 1957, '58.

Q Did you think it was a hit? Did you have any idea it would become a standard?

A No, I didn't know. I was writin' a little bit now and then. I really liked it better than a lot of the stuff that I'd been writin', and a lot of times in a case like that you feel it and do a better job of it. And when that happens, it's a pretty good sign of it bein' a hit. Course, you're really not knowin' that at the time, but you can look back on it and recall there was a very good possibility of that happening.

Q Do most of your songs come automatically like that?

A No. There was a song that I carried for quite a while that I wrote. In Crockett, Texas, they had an old-time fiddlers' contest there every year. And there's a prison there, and there was a few prisoners on the show. They were trusties, and one of 'em was an old man. I got to talkin' to him back there by the stage, and he said he was in for murder. I asked him how long he'd been in, and he said eighteen years. And I said, "Well, when do you get out?" And he said, "I don't. I got a life to go." And I wrote a song called "Life to Go," and I wrote it with Johnny Cash in mind. I couldn't hear no one but Johnny Cash doin' it, but I never could get him to cut it. I wouldn't even cut it myself, and didn't 'til later on, when I put it in an album. But I was on a tour with Stonewall Jackson, and Stonewall said, "Let me have that song!" And I said, "Well, go ahead, if you think you can sing it, but I can't hear nobody sing it but Johnny Cash!" But as soon as he got back in, he recorded it, and it was a number one hit for him. But the idea to write the song was true, and I carried it for a couple of years, maybe, and it kept poppin' up in my mind. And eventually I just sat down and wrote it.

Q So you're not a disciplined writer, where you sit down and make yourself write?

A Naw. You feel the mood comin' on, and you get an idea. Just to sit down right now with a guitar and say I'm gonna write a song, well, I could write it, but it wouldn't be worth a flip. It'd just be "Come back, little darlin' / I love you, you broke my heart." You got to have the idea first, and sooner or later, if you're a songwriter, it comes.

Q Are you writing much anymore?

A Oh, a little bit, every now and then. Been writing some gospel things with a friend of mine. But it's just every now and then. Not a whole lot.

Q Gospel songs—have you turned to religion recently?

A Well, I've changed my attitude. I believe I'm a lot closer in my thinking and ways of trying to change how to live. I'm not a fanatic, and I don't guess I could even say I was saved, 'cause there's lot of changin' I got to do yet.

Q The fight you had with your close friend Peanut Montgomery, where you took a shot at him—wasn't that over religion?

A Naw, but it's a long story, and it's water under the bridge. In fact, I didn't even say what he said I said ["See if your God can save you now"] just before the gun went off. I didn't say that at all. But the way I look at it, if people pretend to be religious, they're not foolin' anybody. They're not foolin' Him, and they're not foolin' theirself. And I figure He'll work that out with 'em, and they'll pay for it eventually. But I know I didn't say that, and Peanut knows it, and the Lord knows it. But I'm not mad at him at all. He's one of the closest friends I've ever had. But sometimes our wants —to be recognized as a songwriter, or singer, or recording artist or what—will cause us to stretch the truth a little bit. But people who do that aren't fooling anyone.

Q I was surprised to see you on *Hollywood Squares*.

A Oh, me! I really enjoyed that. It was the easiest work I've ever done in my life.

Q Even with that first question they asked you—about the relationship between country music and drinking?

A Yeah, that kinda threw me. I had to think of somethin' fast there, which it wasn't much, but I guess we answered it as close as we could.

Q And then you turned up on the *Tonight* show with Tammy, singing "Two Story House."

A Yeah, I forgot my words there, didn't I? I was ready to stop. I thought we could do it over, you know. They didn't tell me that it couldn't be redone, and I didn't know we was actually on the air at the time. And the guy holdin' the cue card on the song—I didn't know the song by heart yet, and he had two lines of the song on each card, and he took the card off before I ever got to the last line that was on that particular card. And I blinked my eyes maybe just for a second, and I looked over and there was new words up there, and I knew they didn't go there. So I said, "We better do that over." And she kept singin', and that was the only thing that saved us, I guess.

Q Yes, after the dog-food commercial, we never saw you again. You went around with a little different hairstyle there for a while—a permanent, I guess. Or at least you had it on the *Tonight* show. Why did you decide to do that?

A Aw, they stuck that on me the day that we did that show. And I didn't like it, but they kept tellin' me it was all right, that it looked good. And I said, "All right." But I wished I'd never done that, 'cause it's not me, and I really felt out of place. Gave me a complex. That's probably the reason I forgot my words.

Q How quickly did you change back?

A Next day. (Laughter)

Q Your album *My Very Special Guests* attracted a lot of national attention and helped to rejuvenate your career to some extent. How did you choose the singers and the songs?

A Well, I just mentioned some of the ones that I liked. I thought of the idea, [producer] Billy Sherrill and I, and he thought it could be done. But it took a little over a year to do it, to get everybody into the studio whenever we could. I went to California and did some of 'em with Linda [Ronstadt] and Emmylou [Harris], and then, of course, in Nashville, with Waylon and Willie. And with Elvis Costello, we waited for him to come over to do his personal appearance there in Nashville, and he done it that afternoon.

Q I think people were surprised to find him on the album.

A (Short laugh) He sent me the song, though, before. And I couldn't believe that anybody in his category of music could write a song that country. But he knew me before I knew him, I guess, 'cause I sure didn't know him. And he sent me the song ["Stranger in the House"] and wanted me to record it. This was before he even knew anything about the album. And Billy kept the tape and he said, "Well, we'll just do this song, and get Elvis Costello on it, too." He's on Columbia Records [the parent company of Jones's label, Epic] over there in England, and I said, "Well, that's great. Let's do it."

Q How did you like him personally?

A Oh, he's fine people. Real nice.

Q Supposedly, none of the guest artists took royalties on the album, to help you out financially.

A No, they didn't, and that was one of the nicest things anybody's ever done for me, really. They were just great. And, of course, the bankruptcy I went through, and still am goin' through, seized that album in particular right away. So it didn't really do nobody any good at all, except the love for each other, and goin' in and doin' the album. And I wouldn't trade that for any of their money, anyway. Let 'em have it.

Q The filing for bankruptcy—what did that do to your pride?

A Well, to start with, I wouldn't have had to do it if I hadn't been involved with the people I was with. But it's just one of the things that happened, and it really bothered me a lot inside when I got a loan, but I couldn't see no sense in not walkin' down the street. We have laws to help us out in those things, and there's a lot of people file bankruptcy. So many that you never even read, except in little small print in the middle of the paper somewhere. But when you're in the entertainment business, or movies, or if you're a celebrity and in the public's eye all the time, when you file bankruptcy, my goodness, it's all over television and the papers and what have you. And it's a big thing. But actually what it boils down to, it's no bigger than you or somebody else that might not make but two hundred dollars a week. But they blow it up, because it's news and it's something for 'em to talk about.

Q Well, the press is always looking for news. Is there anything that you've always wanted to talk about but nobody has asked you?

A I can't think of anything. That I've never told anybody else? Well, you're gonna fall under. Naw, I better not.

Q What?

A Well, when you first come in, my manager told you to ask me about my sex life, to have somethin' different to talk about. You get so involved with music, or somethin', like I was, you can go through life not even knowin' what the hell sex is all about. And in the past two or three years, I woke up to a lot of facts about that—things that you wouldn't ordinarily pay any attention to, or realize, or even know existed. And that's all I'm gonna tell you about it.

Q That's sort of a tease, isn't it?

A Well, that's all. You can fill in between the lines there.

Q How did this reuniting with Tammy happen?

A Well, Paul and George are friends of mine, and all of 'em was concerned—a lot of people in Nashville, too—and they got together to help me out, and they did.

Q Did you ever regard the offer as charity?

A Well, it wouldn't make no difference. I appreciate it very much. No, I don't look at it as charity. They knew my capabilities, and it wasn't to make a lot of money. They were friends, and that's one of the most beautiful things in the world, when you find out you got a friend. Especially when you're down. That's one of the best things about people. But no, charity never entered my mind. It was strictly done as friends, some people that cared, you know. And you really need 'em when you're down like that. If you don't think you do, if you're ever down there, you'll know what I mean.

Q How do you look back over all those years with Tammy?

A Well, they were beautiful, but I just look back over 'em. (Short laugh) Tammy's a fine woman, fine singer, we both had our faults just like everybody does. And I wouldn't swap those years for nothin'. There might be a lot of things we could change, you know, but sometimes we wait too late in life until we find out those things, so they work out for the best.

Q A lot of good music came out of those years.

A Yes, we had some great times.

Q Are you sad about all of this?

A Not really. Yeah, you're a little sad about it, because you'd like to have done certain things better, and hadn't even done a lot of things that you did. Things like that, you're sad about. But I'm just happy we're back recording together again, working some dates together. I'm sad about a lot of things I did to the other marriages. It's just things that you can't do anything about, except not do 'em again, and try to do better.

Q Do you still love her?

A In my own way, I'm sure I do. It's hard to explain that, but we were very, very close, and you don't lose that overnight. That's something you don't lose, but of course, as far as the marriage thing, we know that can never be, and you get that out of your mind, and you just be good friends, and be happy.

Q You seem to have a healthy outlook on the situation.

A Well, I told you, I did a lot of thinkin'. And really, when there's nothing else that you could do with what you've already done, the only thing is just to do what you can do better.

Q Looking back on another part of your life, could you ever be happy singing in those little honky-tonks in Texas again?

A Oh, I could probably be happy. I'd prefer not to, because of the drinking and the drunks, and naturally they're gonna do that in those places, and they smoke and what have you. But I started off in 'em and had some great times. But you have to come up the ladder, and now that you play the better auditoriums and ballrooms and the television work, you naturally wouldn't want to go back to 'em. But if I had to, I could, and adjust myself to it.

Q Can you be around liquor at all now?

A Oh, yeah. I'm around it all the time.

Q But you don't drink at all?

A I don't say I don't drink at all. I might have a beer or a drink occasionally, but nothin' that you could even call drinkin' like I used to.

Q Where do you think country music is headed right now?

A There ain't no tellin'. It's goin' so many different directions, or they're tryin' to make it go in so many different directions. But I think more people are likin' the country music, and other kinds, too. They like the rock, you know, but you still get a hell of a yell out of 'em when you go out there and do a good ol' country ballad. But a few years ago, you know, you didn't have that. You strictly had your category of people. They wouldn't go to hear some other kind of music—they basically had a one-track mind, you might say. But now people are more open, and like all kinds of music. That's what started a lot of the middle-of-the-road ideas, I think, tryin' to sell you pop, and caterin' to a larger audience for the dollar. All I can say is if they enjoy doin' it, if it's what they love to do, then I can't see a thing in the world wrong with it. Because everybody is an individual, and you do what you love to do.

Q There's been a lot of talk about a honky-tonk revival, or a resurgence of interest in honky-tonk music, lately. Do you think that's true?

A A honky-tonk revival? Um, I don't know. I think it's a very small corner that still likes honky-tonk music. I don't think there's very much of it that's actually really sellin' that big, except the plays they might get on the radio, or in a honky-tonk itself. But country music has fought for years to get out of being called hillbilly, and the people called mountaineers and uneducated people, or snuff-dippin', hell-raisin' cowboys. And I don't think unless it's a well-written honky-tonk song that it would take up a lot of room in country music anymore on a large scale. I think it's all about love and more the smoother stuff, more heart and feelin', the stuff that's goin' now.

Q Before you turned to music, weren't you a house painter for a while during your first marriage?

A Yeah, but there isn't much to say about that. I just got to paintin' houses one time 'cause I had to try to make a dollar. I wasn't very good at it, and I did it a couple of years and then went into the Marine Corps [in 1951]. I came out of the Marine Corps [in 1953], and then started recording.

Q When did you realize you'd made it in music?

A Oh, I didn't pay much attention. I was just happy.

Q That seems like a modest answer, doesn't it?

A I don't know. I never did know what that word meant too much. (Laughter)

Q Do you think you've been misunderstood at all?

A I think we're all misunderstood, especially the people that are in the limelight. Because you can't speak out, and they build things up to make a story. Yes, I think we're very much misunderstood, because by the time it gets across town to the press, it's fifteen different versions, you know. And there's been stories out on me that there's no way that they happened.

Q Which ones?

A Well, any of 'em. Most of 'em.

Q Such as beating up women?

A Aw, yeah. All that stuff.

Q That never happened?

A No, sir. No, sir. And that's the honest truth.

Q Do you have peace of mind now?

A A lot more. A lot more. And the way the future looks, I've got more than a lot more.

Q What's going to happen to you?

A I hope good things happen. I just want to see everybody live and be happy, and do their thing. Me included.

*I*n the popular music industry, where careers and fortunes are made with the frequency of Egg McMuffins, the success of the Judds, a red-haired mother-daughter duo from Ashland, Kentucky, is still one for the books. Since 1983,  they have gone from singing around the kitchen table to becoming one of the top acts in country music, winning two Grammy awards, five Country Music Association awards—including three Vocal Group of the Year trophies—earning a full-page article in *Time* and coverage in *Life,* and collecting a host of auxiliary honors usually reserved for their more pop-oriented counterparts.

If the Judds' unique good fortune seems like something out of Hans Christian Andersen, it is in reality a fairy tale of 42-year-old Naomi Judd's own design. Smart, ambitious, and persistent, Naomi is usually regarded as the less talented of the two, mostly because she is uncommonly beautiful—a Southern beauty in the Scarlett O'Hara mold—and because her daughter Wynonna, who sings lead, has such a remarkably mature, expressive voice. Some critics, overlooking the symbiotic quality of Naomi's harmony vocals and her considerable, if still budding, songwriting talents, have unfairly appraised her as "window dressing" for the Judds' sound—an inventive collage of folk, country, be-bop, blues, jazz, early rock 'n' roll, and ballad.

But aside from 24-year-old Wynonna's extraordinary vocal gifts—she has been called the most important new female country voice of the last twenty years—it is Naomi Judd, with her daredevil spirit, her musical eclecticism, and her personal vision split somewhere between that of a '60s flower child and Kentucky pioneer woman, who defines the drive and the imagination behind the Judds' achievements.

The daughter of a filling station owner, Naomi Judd grew up with the given name of Diana. But with a grandfather named Ogden, and two aunts named Mahalia and Watseka, "Diana never seemed quite spiritual enough." In her senior year of high school, Diana married a local boy named Michael Ciminella, dropping out of school when she got pregnant. The day the rest of her class graduated, she gave birth to a daughter, Christina. Another daughter, Ashley, arrived before the family moved to California in 1968.

On the West Coast, Diana found the '60s counterculture more in tune with her personality, and after filing for a divorce in 1972, she held a series of short-lived, but adventurous jobs: working "a couple of months" as a secretary to the Fifth Dimension, modeling exotic footwear, managing a health-food store in West Hollywood, wangling a job on the set of George Lucas' *More American Graffiti*, and, in her spare time, becoming a Brownie troop leader for Christina and the daughters of Western writer Louis L'Amour and the actress Jayne Mansfield. In 1975, however, Diana moved back home to Kentucky, settling in the little town of Morrill, and enrolled in nursing school. Soon Diana Ciminella was legally Naomi Judd—she had not filed for the final decree and so was not actually divorced until 1977—and Christina had become the Indian-sounding Wynonna.

An auspicious thing happened in the little town of Morrill, Kentucky—Wynonna discovered the guitar. And when Naomi and her daughters moved back to California, this time to the hot-tub country of Marin County, Wynonna, then an eighth-grader, cut school and begged and cajoled to stay home to practice guitar, listen to her Joni Mitchell and Bonnie Raitt records, and work out the vocal harmonies with her mother, who was still in nursing school. They were living, they remember, in a one-bedroom apartment over a real estate office, Naomi and Ashley sleeping two to a mattress on the floor. But Wynonna was "eaten up" with music, and in 1977 they cut some demo sessions at a small studio. Naomi never gave up hope—or imagining a life of excitement and fulfillment—even when she couldn't pay the rent.

If all of that sounds like a fairy-tale-in-waiting, the man with the glass slipper was producer Brent Maher, who'd made a name for himself with Dottie West's hit comeback album *(Special Delivery)* by the time the Judds moved to Nashville in 1979. Soon Maher's daughter would come home from high school telling him about a girl "who they don't even allow to sing in the talent contest, she's so incredible." But the timing wasn't right: Maher was busy. And while Naomi worked extra shifts as a nurse to make ends meet, Wynonna, refusing to consider college, boys, a career, or anything except music, stayed home all day watching soap operas.

The turning point came in 1982, when Maher's daughter was seriously injured in a car accident and Naomi Judd was assigned to care for her at a Nashville-area hospital. After the girl's recovery, Naomi took a homemade tape over to Maher on her day off. A month later, Maher listened to the cassette on his way in to work. "It takes me thirty minutes to get from the house to the studio," he was to remember, "and by the time I got there, I was on the phone calling them up."

Naomi and Wynonna worked with Maher and guitarist Don Potter for six months before they put anything on tape, defining their style, building the distinctive country-jazz framework of their sound, and creating the subtle interplay between Potter's acoustic lead guitar and the women's voices. They won their RCA contract with a live audition—something fairly unthinkable with today's music business politics.

Their first single, "Had a Dream (For the Heart)," made the Top 20. The second and third singles, "Mama He's Crazy" and "Why Not Me," went the distance to number one. The die was cast: "Have Mercy," "Grandpa (Tell Me 'Bout the Good Old Days)," "Cry Myself to Sleep," and the title song from their third album, *Rockin' with the Rhythm*, were to follow. But if their first album stressed Appalachian harmony and traditional country themes, their fourth LP, *Heart Land*, with only a nod to country-oriented lyrics and instrumentation, is a record that might appeal more to people named Diana and Christina, growing up in the suburbs, than it would to the Wynonnas and Naomis of the hills.

The following interview took place at the office of their manager, Ken Stilts, in Mount Juliet, Tennessee, in late December 1985—the same day they were interviewed for their full-page story in *Time*. Wynonna's dog, Loretta, kept us company.

Q [to Naomi]: One of the songs you put on your demo tape for producer Brent Maher was a lullaby that you had written for your children. Maher describes it as "a story about an Indian, a little squaw whose husband died and they ended up freezing in the snow." He said, "It tears your heart out. They've got an Indian chant that goes through it—'hi, hi, you, hi, yee, hee / hi, hi, you, hi, yee, hee,' in four-part harmony." Evidently, even Maher thought this was unusual. How did you ever think of such a thing?

A *Naomi:* It's called "The Renegade Song." I wrote it sittin' on a mountaintop in Kentucky, watchin' a storm roll in one evening. The kids were always sayin', "Tell us a story," 'cause we didn't have a TV or anything. I have always had a real affinity, a real place in my heart for the American Indians. When I was a little girl, I thought I was an Indian princess. In fact, when I got out of nursing school, I took the kids to northern Arizona and talked to the Bureau of Indian Affairs about workin' on an Apache reservation up around White River, in the northeast section. Their need for medical help was desperate. They even put nurses on a circuit. I thought it would be good for the kids to learn something about that part of America's crazy-quilt history. But the reason I didn't do it was because I couldn't subject my two kids to their educational system. It was despicable. But I've always been such an incredible, romantic adventurist, you know? Actually, the seventeen-year-old [Ashley], I just found out through reading about her—she was on the front page of our hometown newspaper in Kentucky, with a big article about her and her picture. She told the interviewer that she was going to Mommy's old high school, living with Nana, my mother, living in my old bedroom there in Ashland, and it was the eleventh school that she had attended, and she was in the twelfth grade. And it made me really stop and analyze what a wanderlust I really have—that I have moved these two young'uns around, from [Ashland,] Kentucky, out to Hollywood, back to the mountains of Kentucky, deep down in southeastern Kentucky. We've lived in Chicago, Austin, Texas . . .

Q You've certainly taken a circuitous path to get where you are.

A *Naomi:* Yeah, we just finished playing, believe it or not, Caesars Palace in Las Vegas, with Merle Haggard. And one night I was talking to him backstage before we went on. He said, "Naomi Judd, I hear you and I got a lot of things in common. We're both recluses, and we both have to just disappear sometimes." He was talkin', of course, about Lake Shasta, his getaway up in northern California, which we've been to. We got to play at the Silverthorn. And I told him, "If I don't have a lot of time by myself, I'm just gonna run screaming into the woods and never be heard from again one of these days." But Wynonna and I consider that we aren't just one in a million. I mean, we're one in *millions*, to have been blessed with what's happened to us.

Q But you've also worked hard, you have a fresh sound, and you're an unusual act, in that you're a contemporary mother-daughter team.

A Wynonna: Well, but you have to understand that where we come from, the people that are born poor usually die poor. You know the saying, "You're born, you work, and then you die."

Naomi: One of my favorite quotes—Ernest Hemingway, "Every true story ends in death."

Wynonna: [Gives her mother a mock scowl.] I'm trying to be serious.

Naomi: I am, too.

Wynonna: But it's one thing to be forced to work two jobs. So many people say, "You made it so quickly, and you haven't paid your dues. You haven't played in the honky-tonks for ten years." And I want to get up and go over and shake 'em. Because you have to realize that my mother had to work two jobs to put food on the table. We *have* worked, but it was working to survive. And in my heart, what has happened [for us] musically is something that is completely a miracle, because it's the Cinderella story of the eighties. It's something that people read about and say, "*Man*, I can't believe that really happened," you know?

Q [to Naomi]: But your story is not really as simple as it's been reported. Granted, you were working as a nurse and Brent Maher's daughter was a patient in the hospital, so you were able to meet him and later give him a demo tape. But before that, you had worked for years to try to get something going. In 1977, when you lived in Lagonitas, California [north of San Francisco], you cut some demo tapes in a little nearby studio. So you've been actively pursuing this for a long time.

A Wynonna: Yes and no. Back to what you said about that, you have to realize that by the time we got to Marin County, we had already been to Kentucky, and I resorted back to my creativities and discovered the guitar.

Q This was in Morrill, Kentucky?

A Wynonna: In Morrill.

Q [to Wynonna]: Is it true that when you lived in Morrill, you told the kids at school you were going to Nashville to become a big star?

A Wynonna: Yes, it is. And, of course, they all laughed, and now they all come and see the concerts and say, "Wynonna, I knew you could do it." (Laughter) But when we moved out there [to California], the guy that was givin' Ashley fiddle lessons was the guy that hung out at Tres Virgos Studios in Mill Valley. And he'd take me up there, and I'd just hang out. It was like "Well, there's Wynonna sittin' there. Why not come on in and sing this with us?" It wasn't like Mom and I were planning on this. See, all of this has happened kinda irrelevantly. Because it just all came together. True, out in Marin County, Mom was working, and she was around creativity a lot. Marin County is a very creative area. And I was in eighth grade. I had just begun to get to that place where I didn't want to go to school. I'd rather sit home and play around with my music. So we sang at home, and we sang when we could. But we knew that until I graduated from high school, we were gonna keep it a hobby. I hate that word, but you know, keep it at home. Keep it around the supper table.

Naomi: When we lived up in Marin County, we lived in a one-bedroom apartment over a tiny real estate office, next to the post office. And Ashley and I slept on a mattress in a corner of the tiny living room. Wynonna had the one bedroom, which had all of our clothes in it. We're talking serious poverty. It was very, very hard. We lived under those conditions for a year and a half. And to tell you the truth, there were times when I didn't know how we were gonna eat, or how I was even gonna pay the small rent that I paid. I would go to nursing school all day. Mondays, Wednesdays, and Fridays, I was in class all day. And Tuesdays and Thursdays were what they called "clinicals," where we actually went into the hospitals in the county, under the supervision of our teacher, and practiced what we were learnin' in the classroom. So I had pretty heavy-duty days. I'd go home, fix dinner, do the laundry, clean the house, take care of the kids, do the shopping . . . you know, we had to go to the Laundromat, which was twenty miles away, to wash our clothes. And then at nine o'clock, I'd get the kids settled in bed, and then I'd go to work. I worked as a waitress all night. And I don't . . . it was very, very hard. I think about going on a few hours of sleep like I did, and it still amazes me how I did it.

Q Did you ever lose hope?

A *Naomi:* No, there is some sort of pioneering spirit somewhere in me that just is relentless. And I just knew . . . I think all of these hard times that we've had . . . You know, when we lived on the mountaintop in Morrill, Kentucky, we had very serious hard times. *Very* serious hard times. And I think all these trials, all the struggles that we've had . . . I mean, we've lived so far back in the country that we've had our pipes freeze, and we'd have a well, or a cistern, and we'd get snowbound for days. We'd run out of wood and food. We're talking *survival*.

Q But the impression I have of the time when you lived on the mountaintop is that it was more of an experience you chose—not because you couldn't do any better. You made lye soap, for example, not because you were a product of generations of mountaineers who knew nothing else, but because you were interested in practicing an old skill. In other words, much of the publicity about you makes people believe that you led the eastern Kentucky life with the washing machine on the front porch and you went barefoot all the time—that sort of ignorant poverty—as opposed to someone who made a conscious choice to pursue the pioneer spirit.

A *Naomi:* I always like to have alternatives. And we were there because we wanted to be. No question about it.

Wynonna: You have to understand we'd lived out in Hollywood. We had been there for six years, and Mom realized that Ashley and I were starting to talk about Hollywood as being home. So moving back there, of course, was a conscious effort, because first of all, we were starting to realize that people out there didn't have families, or even family history. No one out there knew about their ancestry. And number two, that's not the kind of place to raise kids. So we packed up and moved back. And we moved into the house where we did because of a miracle that happened. We were living in a little tiny place. So we go to live on top of this incredible mountain in Morrill, Kentucky. We moved there because it was meant to be. This woman named Margaret Allen said, "This house has literally been waiting for you." So that's where we lived.

Q From what I understand, though, the mountain was an estate called Windswept that Mrs. Allen owned, and she had seven cottages there that she rented out. They all had picturesque names such as Paradise, and Avalon, and Chanticleer, the largest one, which is the one you lived in, I believe. Mrs. Allen taught music at Berea College, and her estate was really quite beautiful, with apple trees and the like. What I'm saying is that while it's true that the cottages didn't have phones and televisions, this was a pretty terrific place to live in many respects.

A *Naomi:* Oh, yeah, it was. Our life—I mean, everybody calls it magical. Writers, and people that meet us and all, say, "You all are just unreal!" Somebody even said our story is better than a Judith Krantz novel. (Laughter) I thought that was hilarious. But you know what they were saying, that a Hollywood scriptwriter couldn't have done any better.

Wynonna: I just want to say this. When we first came to Nashville, there were some people who were critical, or at least said, "Now wait a minute, what's the deal?" And it really hurts me.

Q You mean they challenged the validity of your story?

A Wynonna: Well, in a sense, yes. And some reporters have looked for something that wasn't true. Everything we've ever done, we've always been honest about. And our lives are literally a fairy tale. Especially this woman sitting here. I have sat and watched my mother go from Kentucky to California in a U-Haul truck with not even four hundred dollars in her pocket. And I believe that a lot of it was meant to be. I believe that it's in the Lord's will to do certain things.

Naomi: I think one of the greatest gifts that a person can have—and this is going to sound really strange—is to be born poor. I was not born poor. I was the oldest in a family of four kids. My daddy ran a filling station. He was a beloved, respected man in Ashland, Kentucky. And I usually got what I asked for at Christmas. You know, if I asked for a watch, maybe I got a Timex. I remember my brothers asked for a pool table. Well, they got a used pool table, a small one. But we lived in a house with running water, we got a TV in the fifties, and I didn't go without. But when I got [to be] seventeen, and married my hometown sweetheart, that's when the hardships really started. I got the divorce, and I made a decision—here again, all by myself—to stick it out in Hollywood with two babies, one on each hip. And it really taught me what is important about life, what's important *in* life. And the hardships we've gone through, I didn't know at the time how they were gonna come out. And it's real scary doin' stuff, even if you're alone. But when you've got two kids that you're responsible for, it's horrendous. For instance, one time when we lived down on Daniel Boone Road, in Nicholasville, Kentucky, I woke up in the middle of the night. It was so cold. All we had for heat was a potbellied stove in the kitchen, and I'd go out at four o'clock in the morning and bust up chunks of coal to keep the fire going. And we were so cold, we almost froze to death. The pipes froze. It was a bitter Kentucky winter. And the kids had come in and gotten in bed with me, and we had so many quilts on the bed that nobody could move. You had to put your hands on your chest and lift up the quilts to turn over, they were so heavy. Anyway, I woke up in the middle of the night, and one of the kids had wet the bed. We won't use any names. (Laughter) And there was this warm feeling that lasted all of thirty or forty seconds. Of course, I didn't have a washer or a dryer or nothin', and we had slept in our last pair of clean long johns and granny gowns, with two or three pair of socks. So here we are, soppin' wet with pee, and it's down to probably below zero, and no runnin' water or anything. And Wynonna was already running a cold, and had bronchitis. And I got up and wrapped a quilt around me and went in the other room, and just got down on my knees and said, "What am I *doin'* here?" We lived down at the end of a road that didn't get any traffic. A dead-end road, down on the Kentucky River . . .

Wynonna: I had to ride almost an hour to school on the school bus.

Naomi: And I thought, "How in the world am I gonna get out of this one? What happens if Wynonna gets pneumonia?" Not only did I not have any money, but we'd never had medical insurance in our lives. And I piled the kids into this old beat-up car we had, and drove a couple of hours to Ashland to my mom's house. And I nursed Wynonna, and got her over her cold. It's very interesting . . . a game that I learned years ago, quite by accident at the Thanksgiving dinner table, was . . . for instance, when they were kids, I used to eavesdrop on their play, because you can find out a lot about where your kids' heads are at by listening to their pretend games. Because they *will* imitate you in their play. And at the Thanksgiving dinner, I asked the kids what their memories were. You know, "What are your favorite memories?" I really recommend that every parent try that with their kids. It's become a ritual now with us. It's amazing that probably sixty percent of the kids' memories come from those experiences that got us down to a rock-gut, bottom-line love for each other. If you've never had to find out what you're capable of, and just how far you can stretch, and you don't know what you don't want, then you don't know what you *do* want.

Q But did you have a clear-cut goal in mind?

A Naomi: It's not that I always knew what I want. My God, I don't think any of us knows what we want when we're seventeen years old. One of the biggest mistakes I made was to get married at seventeen. But I've always had a good strong sense of what I *didn't* want. I didn't want drugs. I've never been drunk. I still believe in one-on-one relationships. I mean, like in the sixties, when everybody around me was goin', "Who am I? What is the meaning of life?" I thought that was crap. That really irritated me.

Q I read that you said, "I never wanted to be anybody but Naomi Judd from Ashland, Kentucky." Did you say that?

A Naomi: It sounds like something I'd say. But then again, Naomi Judd from Ashland, Kentucky, always had one foot on the ground, but her head in the clouds.

Q The point is, if you always just wanted to be yourself, why did you change your names? What's wrong with Diana and Christina?

A Naomi: They *are* beautiful names. And I'm proud of them. But you have to understand. We were so proud to be from Kentucky, and to have that legacy. And then living out in California, it's almost as if Diana and Christina were California names.

Q This is something you've never discussed publicly before, and the majority of your fans have no idea that Naomi and Wynonna aren't your real names. Why is that?

A Wynonna: We didn't change 'em because of music, so strike that.

Naomi: Oh, no, this was before we discovered music.

Wynonna: I've been Wynonna since I was eleven or twelve or thirteen—somewhere in there.

Q Are you legally Wynonna? Did you actually have your name changed?

A Wynonna: Yeah.

Naomi: And I'm legally Naomi.

Q Where did you get them? Wynonna sounds Indian.

A Naomi: Naomi is from the Bible, and Wynonna means "firstborn," I think. We still have never figured this out. But see, my aunt, my daddy's sister, is named Watseka, and her sister is Ramona. And my granddaddy was Ogden, and we had Mahalia, and these incredibly melodic . . .

Wynonna: Spiritual names.

Naomi: Biblical names, Indian names in our family, and I *really* wanted to identify with them. So that's why I changed those names.

Wynonna: It was a new life.

Naomi: And here again, so many things keep going back to my association with the American Indian.

Wynonna: Naomi is actually a Jewish name.

Naomi: It's from the Bible, that's why. I told Ashley I was going to change her name to Ramona, or something, and she spit her Coke through her nose! (Laughter) She went, like, "Aaaahhhcckk!"

Wynonna: But, you know, I entered high school with my new name.

Q Did you feel like different people when you changed your names?

A Naomi: I've been through so many changes, so many dramatic, no-decompression-chamber changes. And that's one thing I'll give my two kids—they're very resilient. I look at little Ashley, who's living in my old bedroom in Ashland, Kentucky, now, going to Paul Blazer High School, the only high school in town. There's probably two hundred kids in her graduating class. And I think, "This is a kid who was living in Tokyo, Japan, when she was fifteen, as an international fashion model." I'm so proud of her for being so adaptable. But it goes back to having a strong faith in God, and to knowing that there is unconditional love surrounding her.

Q How does Ashley feel about all of your success?

A Naomi: I don't know. I've gotta call her tonight. I'll ask her.

Q [to Naomi]: You and your mother are apparently close. What was her reaction to all this?

A Naomi: I always gave my mom fits, God love her. By the way, I really give my mom credit for any good that's come out of me to this day. Because she's one of the dearest, kindest-hearted, strongest women. I would definitely have to put her on my list of people I most admire. I mean, I always had to get out of that bed on Sunday mornin' and go to Sunday school and church at the First Baptist Church on Winchester Avenue. And she let me know from the git-go how she felt about right and wrong. There wasn't much gray in the way she saw things. They were pretty black and white. And to this day I count her as one of my best friends. She's always lived in Ashland. We bought that house from my grandparents when I was, like, four years old. She never worked outside of the home. She raised four kids and took care of her husband. Until I had to get married, that is. And we lost my little brother to Hodgkin's [disease], and my daddy started drinking, and then her world collapsed. And then she became a cook on a riverboat. I mean, what talent did she have? So it was really hard for her to understand when I'd call her from a phone booth on Route 66 and say, "Hey, Mom, guess where I am now?" But I think deep down in her soul she knew that she had taught me right. Of course, now she's just having the time of her life, with all of our success. She's our number one fan.

Q [to Naomi]: What was the drive behind all these nomadic flights? What was stronger than the fear you must have felt at leaving your husband with no job and two babies to raise?

A Naomi: My favorite word—"imagination." I was watchin' *Miracle on 34th Street* on Christmas Eve, sitting around the fire with my family in Ashland last week, and when Kris Kringle says to Natalie Wood, "There are many nations in the world, but the best one, and the one you can go to at any time, is the imagination," I jumped to my feet and went, "*Yeah*, Santa, tell it like it *is!*" (Laughter) Even when I was a kid, I'd get the kids in the neighborhoods together and we would play . . . I mean, if we had a tea party, man, it was a *tea party!* I was always a dreamer.

Q Does this fall over into your songwriting? We've only seen two examples of it so far, "Mr. Pain" and "Change of Heart."

A Naomi: Fifteen songs! That's how many I've written in my whole, wide life.

Q Why isn't there one on your new album, *Rockin' with the Rhythm*?

A Wynonna: Didn't have time.

Naomi: See, I wrote "Change of Heart" for the very first album. Well, I didn't write it for the album. I wrote it for me. It's based on a true story. "Mr. Pain" I wrote out of camaraderie with my girlfriends. After "Mr. Pain," we were on the road every night, and I barely could get enough sleep. So I haven't written a song since then. But, boy, have I got material for songs now, having lived on the road for a year and a half.

Wynonna: Well, I think everybody realizes that we went from being home to not being home, and so much has happened to us in such a short amount of time that there just wasn't enough time for everything. You had to make your choice. And I think songwriting is the kind of thing that you . . . you can't write about the blues unless you live 'em. And we were so busy learnin' how to get on and off stage that the time for writing just wasn't there. You know, learning how to cope with three or four interviews a day, coping with being in a different state every day . . .

Q Are you writing now, too?

A Wynonna: Yeah. I've taken January as my month to collaborate with some songwriters around town. Well, I helped write the music to "Change of Heart." That's really the only thing. I mean, "Mr. Pain," I just sang it back to Mom, but Mom came up with the majority. And I really am excited about it. I feel like "Who can sing the songs we write better than Mom and I?" And Brent Maher has become my favorite person in the whole world. He writes for us, because he knows us so well. It's like he tailor-makes clothes for us, in a sense. That's the way I feel about his songwriting. "Why Not Me" is such a tailor-made song, it's unbelievable. And a song like "Mama He's Crazy" being a true story, or becoming a true story . . .

Q What do you mean?

A Wynonna: Well, it became a true story before it came out. Before we recorded it, actually. Music has always been my first love. It was always my main focus in high school. I mean, I went to the prom with one of my best friends. It was a guy, but I mean, we used to sit around and jam together. Boys were just not an interest to me. I'd pretty much decided that boys were nerds, especially the ones I went to high school with. But I met a boy that became . . . well, you know the song. It became a true story. And each song since then has really become, well, Mom calls "Why Not Me" our theme song, which is true. And "Love Is Alive" came at a time when I was really suffering. I wanted to be in my own bed. I was really struggling with "What in the world is happening? I love my music. The people that I'm surrounded with I trust and love so much, and I'm learning so much from them. But what else is happening? All this other stuff is freaking me out." And I am just so thankful that our music is real to our hearts.

Naomi: If we weren't sitting here doing an interview, I'll bet you we'd still be sittin' around at home, singin'.

Wynonna: Oh, we would be.

Naomi: What is goin' on in our lives right now is so far beyond our control. I mean, it's absolutely in the Lord's will. We are doin' things that not even in my wildest imagination—which is pretty out there—I would have thought possible.

Q You've mentioned the Lord's will several times now. Do you ever wonder if He meant for you to sing gospel music instead of commercial country? Or working as an instrument of faith in some way?

A *Naomi:* Well, the only way I can answer this question is to be specific and say how this has affected me directly. My little brother who died of Hodgkin's when he was in high school . . . We were both at home. I couldn't go to high school because I was pregnant. He couldn't go to high school because he was dyin' of cancer. So we had the same tutor. I missed high school graduation because of Wynonna's birth. But I'm gonna go home in May and see Ashley walk across that stage. And I have to tell you, it's gonna be a very heavy occasion for me. My mom is head of the scholarship fund, where they give this check to a kid who couldn't afford to go to college. And I know, from what Mom was hinting around, that they're gonna ask me to present the scholarship. And I wouldn't even be able to give donations to the scholarship fund, or to the orphanage outside of Ashland, if we weren't doing what we're doing right now. Music has allowed us to do so many good things.

Wynonna: I have a very strong philosophy from what I've learned this last year about music. And that is, number one, I have probably more of a faith this year than I ever had. I was raised pretty much with goin' to church, and being surrounded by the knowledge of what was right and what was wrong, and what was Christian and what was not. And I tend to believe that your faith is sacred. But we go right ahead and tell people how we feel. It's very hard to sit in a room with people and talk about the Lord simply because people are searching, or maybe skeptical. But I share the Lord with whoever wants to share Him with me. And in terms of gospel music, I've met a lot of people, like Amy Grant, who are doing gospel music. But I tend to take gospel, or what I call "spiritual music," and use that in my personal time. That is kind of like My Thing. If we're sitting backstage on a show with Ricky Skaggs, and he comes into our dressing room and we all sit down and sing [she sings], "Children go where I send thee," and we sing that together, that's . . .

Naomi: It's like church.

Wynonna: Yeah. That's like "Thank you, Lord. Thank you for the feeling in my heart." Our music is very spiritual. My feelings when I sing songs like "Grandpa [(Tell Me 'Bout the Good Old Days)]" are that . . . I mean, I'm overwhelmed with good feeling. It's very hard for people to understand where you come from. Like I said, if you go right out and say, "I'm for the Lord," well, unless you do it in a very subtle way . . . I think it's important to be humble, and if people want to hear it, I want to do a gospel album someday, if not for anybody but just for my kids, and for my heart. [Our guitarist] Don Potter, who's one of my favorite people on this earth, wants us to sing on his next [Christian] album. He's got an album out on Word [Records], and it's wonderful. It's such a godsend. But it's very tough in this world to take the stand and tell people that you're of the faith without sounding . . . you know what I'm saying?

Q That kind of talk tends to turn people away in droves.

A Wynonna: Yeah, I know. But we've known Don a long time. And six or seven months ago, Don got off the road with us. He said, "It's just time for me to be with my wife, and be at my church every Sunday." And, being selfish, that was a very horrible experience for me. See, he was with us almost the first two years.

Q I don't think he's gotten enough credit for the Judds' sound. A lot of what's unique about the way your records sound, and the arrangements of your songs, is in that acoustic guitar framework and filigree.

A Wynonna: He didn't want [the credit], okay? And I'll tell you why I believe that is. You know, when you meet certain people, there is something about them that shines. They blow you away with their presence. That's what Don did to us. Don came into our lives when he had just moved here. He was very skeptical about the business, because he wanted to be a Christian artist, and people were so commercial about it. His heart was heavy about music. Well, he and Brent, together with the two of us, sat down and said, "Look, we love music, and we want to do something." So Don became the strength, musically. We jammed for almost six months before we even put anything on tape. And when I first got out on the road, Don was there underneath my bunk, reading the Bible, and practicing his brains out every day. And I saw a light that shone upon him. And I came over to him, and I found myself wanting to know more about the Lord, asking Don questions, watching him. Just like you say, if someone comes on strong, or if Don had come to me and said, "Wynonna, you're nineteen years old and you need to find the Lord," I would have been, like, "Who are you?" But through learning and experiencing through him, I wanted to shine, too. I wanted to be in that light that he was in. And that's the way I feel about our music, as well as our faith. I think it's very important to try and lead a good life, because people will see that. You can say to everyone, "I'm the most Christian person in the world," but your actions are more important. Don Potter is the kind of man that when you sit down and talk to him, and you mention the Judds, he will never tell you what an influence [he is], simply because that's not the way he is. He's probably the most humble person, besides Brent Maher, that I've ever met. But he is such a big part of the Judds' sound. Every interview I do, I say, "Don Potter Judd, Don Potter Judd." 'Cause he's right there with us, and he helped develop the sense of the jazz-hip style. I require so much from him when we're in the studio, because I am learning about my music, and the lyrics, but when I hear him play his guitar . . . you know, we work so well off each other. It's almost like we're telepathic, Brent, Don, Mom, and I. We can sit in a room and just . . . when we heard "Grandpa" . . . or when we heard "[Workin' in a] Coal Mine," we all just went nuts at the same time.

Naomi: It's uncanny. You know, the four of us listen to everything that comes in. *Everything* that comes in, whether it's from Harlan Howard, the biggest hit songwriter in Nashville, or from the pizza delivery boy. I mean, it's unbelievable. You're eatin' soup beans in a truck stop, and the waitress has got a next-door neighbor who sings and writes songs, you know. But we'll be listening to a demo tape, whether it's a crudely made one from home, or whether it's got some of the master stylists on Music Row in Nashville, and Wynonna, and Brent, and Don, and I will look up at the same time and nod yes or no in agreement. It's really bizarre. We're on that much of a wavelength with each other. But I want to tell you something—talk about three humble men. When you consider how rare humility is these days . . .

Wynonna: Especially in this industry.

Naomi: . . . we have got three of the most humble men I've ever known in my life surrounding us. Brent Maher was the first one we met. He introduced us to Don Potter, and our manager, Ken Stilts. Ken has been a millionaire many times over. But he invested his time, love, and money in us. He doesn't make business decisions based on the checkbook. And we are so totally involved with these three men. We literally trust each other with our lives.

Wynonna: We have been able to walk into a room and make deals and never write it down on paper. But Ken was such a successful businessman that he took us on not really to make money, but as a challenge. He has people calling him every day, saying, "I want you to be my manager."

Naomi: Yeah, I was here one day when Ken turned down two major artists. I'm not gonna say who they are, but they were *major*. He refuses to fool with anybody but us. It's so amazing. Right now, we're sittin' out here at S & S Industries. Ken is from this huge family of sixteen in Hazard, Kentucky, and he built this from scratch, from the ground up. And he just sold S & S Industries to devote himself solely to managing the Judds.

Q Does that scare you at all?

A Wynonna: Yeah. But Ken does things because he loves people. He gave me the chance to have my own apartment, he gave me the chance to buy that BMW sittin' out there, and he's just given so much to us. I feel like I owe my life to Ken Stilts. And what has happened is Ken just had open-heart surgery less than six months ago, and Ken cannot handle what has happened to the Judds and S & S Industries both. And we love Ken so much that we've made a soul deal. Therefore, Ken realizes the need for his part in this. Plus, he and I are very close. He sees a lot of himself in me, I guess.

Q [to Naomi]: How does it make you feel that he sold his company to put everything into the Judds?

A Naomi: Well, it makes me feel good. Because two years ago, Wynonna and I were at a point where she was out of high school, but she had never talked about a career, about getting married, about going to college, or anything. She was loafin' around the house, totally eaten up with her music. You couldn't interest her in anything except music. I'm workin' my butt off at this country hospital . . .

Wynonna: (Laughter) In Murfreesboro [Tennessee].

Naomi: . . . workin' extra shifts and all, just to, well, if Ashley needed a prom dress, or one of the kids had a birthday, then I had to work an extra shift. I could hardly keep a roof over our heads. Then I'd come home, and Wynonna would be laid up watchin' soap operas, with dirty dishes under her bed that looked like science projects, with glowing green stuff all over 'em, and I couldn't get her to do *anything*. We were about to kill each other. Then, enter Ken Stilts, thank you, Lord. Because he became the father that Wynonna never had. I mean, I haven't been married for sixteen years now, whatever. And this man is a father figure to her. Call him a referee, call him whatever you want, he started takin' a lot of the pressure off of me. Here was a third party that she would listen to.

Wynonna: Well, for instance, he'd call me up and he'd say, "Now, Wynonna, do you realize how important tomorrow is? There's a crew of thirty people waiting for you. Please be on time so your mother doesn't have to pull her hair out." He earned my total respect. I respect Ken

Stilts more than I've ever respected even my own father. I've respected him the most of anybody I've ever met. And it's because he's a successful person, as well as a financially successful businessman. He sees me for the dreamer that I am. And we're so much alike. I told him the other day that I want to be a part of some huge charity. I want to someday know that I helped change someone's life. And he sees that, because he's the same way. He's probably given away a third of his earnings. So yeah, it's scary that he's sold the company, but . . .

Naomi: You have to understand, he's totally exhilarated by all this. He likes to give people the chance and the materials to change their lives and fulfill their dreams. That's what he's all about.

Wynonna: We've been so blessed with this team, and when we get awards it really bothers me that we get most of the credit. All these fans assume that the Judds did it all themselves.

Q I'm interested in knowing how the team put the sound together, or how it evolved, especially with Don Potter's input.

A Wynonna: Well, it started with Brent Maher. We gave him a homemade tape, and he told me later that he rode around with it for a month in his car [before he listened to it]. And he said, "I was driving home one day, and I put the tape in, and I almost wrecked."

Q [to Naomi]: Did you lay the tape on him at the hospital when he was there to visit his daughter?

A Naomi: No, I waited. I never even talked to him about it. When you go to work as a nurse, you've got to just totally be a nurse.

Q What did you do, then, mail it to him?

A Naomi: No, I waited until my day off from the hospital, after his daughter was home. I put on my best Sunday dress, walked into Creative Workshop, and said, "Hello, Mr. Maher, do you remember me? I'm Naomi Judd." And, of course, he remembered me. He said, "You're the nurse who was so good to Diana—her favorite nurse who brought her her pain shots on time." (Laughter) And I said, "Well, I've got a daughter that I sing with, and if you have time, please give us a listen. The phone number's on here if you want to call me." And I left immediately.

Wynonna: So he calls. And first of all, he lives, like, three miles from us. So on his way home, he stopped in and we sat around and sang some songs for him. One minute I'd sing him a Bonnie Raitt song, and the next minute we were singin' the Andrews Sisters. I think we threw in an original of Mom's. And he just stopped by every now and then and worked with us, and never really said anything. He would just come by and jam. Brent's a very subtle person. And after a long period of time, say, two or three months, of listening to everything we threw at him—everything from Kentucky mountain harmonies, to Marin County, to Bob Wills and the Texas Playboys, to Linda Ronstadt—he then brought Don over, and we sat around and just started singin' together, jammin' around the table. I remember him almost pullin' his hair out, trying to figure, "What is the *deal* here? One minute they're singin' something bluesy, and the next minute they're singin' 'John Deere Tractor.' "

Naomi: Joni Mitchell to the Stanley Brothers is quite a gap.

Wynonna: So as a producer, he was thinkin', "What is goin' *on* with this?" And I'm sure his mind was tickin'. He'd go home, and his wife told us later that he'd say, "I don't know what to think. I don't know whether they're country, or whether they're this or that."

Naomi: One minute he said he envisioned some kind of female Manhattan Transfer duet . . .

Q [to Naomi]: Because the stuff you were writing was kind of like that.

A Naomi: Yeah, I wrote a song which I still need to pitch to the Manhattan Transfer, if we're not gonna do it. It was on that tape. And the next minute, like she said, we were doin' Everly Brothers stuff.

Wynonna: So he brought Don Potter over, and Don, along with Mom and Brent and I, sat around and started honing in on the things that really hit us spiritually, that really were us. I mean, I can sit at a party and probably sing every one of Joni's songs. I know that much about her music. And Bonnie. They're two of my favorites. So anyway, it just kind of evolved. It was one of those things where he'd bring over a song . . . like he brought over "Isn't it Strange" one day. And we learned it and we sang it. And then we did "John Deere Tractor." So it kind of evolved. We sat and decided, "If you had to do an album, what would you put on it?" Meanwhile, all the people are talking back and forth, like Dick Whitehouse [of Curb Records], and Ken. And we still don't have an eight by ten, still don't have a real tape. And Dick Whitehouse says, "Well, let me hear the product!" So Ken gave us the money to go into a studio and put down three songs on a cassette, and we mailed it out to Dick Whitehouse. He flew to Nashville, and we met him at his hotel and sang to him. He then turned around and took the same tape that we sent him—on a Walkman—and let [RCA's] Joe Galante hear it at a party. So RCA was interested, and we went into RCA, and RCA gave us the rights to do the purple album.

Q The mini-album.

A Wynonna: Right. And we picked eight songs and went in the studio.

Q How do you work in the studio?

A Wynonna: That's a story in itself. Because when we did this first album, we brought in Nashville's finest [pickers]. I mean, we're talkin' [steel and Dobro player] Sonny Garrish and [pianist] Bobby Ogdin—all the guys who have played their brains out on everything you've ever heard out of Nashville. First of all, we go in and do the album completely acoustic. Every song that we've ever recorded is down on that little tape, just with the guitar and the two voices. That way, if it grooves just with that, we know without a doubt that it's great. In other words, we don't have to put a lot of things on it to make it sound great. So when those six players came in, we played them this little cassette. There were no charts, nothin'. We let them hear the tape a couple of times, and we went in and recorded it and gave everybody in that room complete freedom.

Naomi: Well, Don Potter, who's the session leader, had made out charts that first time, remember? And we played 'em the demo, and they all threw 'em up in the air and went, "Holy smoke!"

Wynonna: That's right, he made charts of the chords and everything else, 'cause I saw 'em. He made charts of the whole deal.

Naomi: But they never had anyone do a rough demo like that and play it to 'em. And that's when they all threw 'em up in the air. It looked like a ticker-tape parade.

Wynonna: Yeah. Anyway, that established the spontaneity, number one, and the creative freedom. Don Potter was given the bandleader job, but he's a reluctant bandleader. He would sit there and listen to something that Sonny would play, and be very quiet about it. That's why everybody respected him, because he was there to give them advice. But then Sonny could sit back and feel good about what he played, and in return, I think everybody played better. I think they felt like they could get in there and really hurt themselves on a song, they played with so much feeling. So the first album was so wonderful because it was a collaboration of everybody. And it was so wonderful when it hit, and everything went so great on it. Then the second album, *Why Not Me,* was the same way. They came in, and I remember Brent brought a bottle of champagne, and we all got our little Dixie cups at the studio and said a toast to the studio gang.

[Naomi leaves the room.]

Q Why would RCA only spring for a mini-album that first time?

A Wynonna: I'm glad they did, because it's a great way to introduce a new artist. It's hard to get someone to walk in and buy a whole album on someone they've never heard. Plus, I've always had the belief that you should leave people wanting more. So I'm thankful that was the first album. We were just learning about what to do and how to do it. And the greatest thing is when this album came out, Ken gave us the ability to not have to put together a band and go play honky-tonks to survive. In other words, Ken put us on a budget out of his own money to survive and pay our bills with, and sent us out to visit radio stations. Don, Mom, and I traveled to stations and sang live over the air. We did things like go into hotel suites and have little parties. And we invited all the people from the surrounding area, the radio stations and the press, and we'd sit and sing for twenty-five minutes. We'd go into warehouses where the little guys that get paid four dollars an hour to ship records work, and we'd sit down and they'd order pizza, and we'd sing. So it got to be a personal thing. That's how it all began.

Q Let me ask you this. You are twenty-one years old. Critics have said you are the greatest country voice since Patsy Cline. You've already won a Grammy. [They won another in 1986.] And as you said yourself on one of the awards shows, you've already realized a lot of the things that most people your age are just dreaming about. Some people have suggested that your ego has started to show. Do you think that's true? Or how do you think you've kept your ego in check?

A Wynonna: Well, I think two things. When this first started, I was very shocked that it happened as fast as it did. It was almost overwhelming. I mean, the second single, "Mama He's Crazy," goes to number one. Then the third one goes to number one, and we win the [Country Music Association's] Horizon Award. I was so busy doing interviews every day, and traveling every day, that I didn't really have time to stop and think. But number one, Ken Stilts. I keep going back to him, because he would come to me and say . . . like when he gave me this ring, he said, "Wynonna, you're so blessed, and you're so talented. Do you realize how lucky you are?" And Don helped me to pray about it. He said, "Go to your hotel room at night and say a prayer, and give everything over to the Lord. That way you don't have to take responsibility for it, first of all, and second of all, it will relieve your mind." Because I've had people come up to me, kids especially, who break my heart. I love kids so much. And they'll come up and say, "I'm taking guitar lessons because of you." And it's like I could be the deciding factor of this kid going to college or not. That's heavy. So I had all this taken upon me. And then I met Bonnie Raitt. And I saw one of the greatest talents not doin' a dang thing because of a bunch of crap. And that made me mad. And I realized, "Wynonna Judd, you'd be sitting at home on your butt, playing your guitar, playing your brains out, singing to your family, and working a cruddy nine-to-five job and not fulfilling your dreams if it weren't for Ken Stilts and Brent Maher and Don Potter." That's what did it. That's really the key thing that happened. I mean, there have been a series of things, like when we go back to Kentucky and I see people living in tar-paper shacks, and kids goin' without.

Q Do you still feel overwhelmed by it all?

A Wynonna: Yeah. I felt that way when we did this thing in Las Vegas for these kids that were abused. We were in Las Vegas playing at Caesars Palace, which is supposed to be the best room and the biggest place to play in Las Vegas. I'm there two days, and I get a call from this guy who got involved with some kids who were on drugs, who were thieves, ringleaders, prostitutes, you name it. Las Vegas has a very high number of kids goofin' around. He called me and said, "The kids are askin' for you guys to come over. They're doin' a benefit to raise money for this organization. Would you come and just talk?" I said, "Yes, we will." The kids were my age, why not? And I thought I could minister. I'm really starting to feel like I can minister to kids, because there are a lot of kids coming to our shows. Our fan mail is from people between the ages of eight and twenty-five. So I go over and do this, and here I am, playing at Caesars Palace, and there's this little, humble pastor who opened up his house to all these kids, and they do this little musical thing to raise money. And I went, "Holy crap. Is this not humbling, or what? This incredible town of people spendin' money, and prostitution, and drugs, and gamblin', and here's this wonderful happenin' thing goin' on. How neat to be a part of it." It just freaked me out. So I am constantly overwhelmed by meeting people and talking about music. It's such a spiritual thing to me. I just love music, and everything else is second to me. Nothing else is important. Don and I talked about this one time. Mom and I got into this big, huge thing where it was a constant battle about what to wear onstage. And one night I could not figure out why it was such a traumatic thing to go through what we were gonna wear onstage. I mean, we had, like, two outfits. And Don sat me down later and said, "You know, Wynonna, you could go onstage in jeans and a T-shirt. People are gonna hear your music." I've had so many things happen to me. For instance, going onstage with half a voice—being so hoarse I can barely get through the show. And one night before I went onstage, Don was with us, and I had to sing "Why Not Me," and I was terrified.

Q That's a fairly demanding song to sing.

A Wynonna: Yeah, and I just knew that I had to sing it, and I knew that I was gonna really screw it up. So I got up there, and I was halfway through the show, and I could tell my voice was going. And before I went onstage, I said a little prayer with Don, which I try to do every time I go onstage. So that when I got to that point in the show, doing that song, I just widened my eyes, and just *did* it. I thought, "If it doesn't come out right . . ." I mean, Don kept saying, "They're not gonna know the difference, Wynonna. They've heard this song on the radio. They already know the song. It's in their hearts. You don't have to sell it. You should sing it for the Lord." And I was like, *"Yeah!"* So I got out there and did it, and I got a standing ovation. I've had things like that happen to me that have just really freaked me out. I've had times when I felt like I sang a song the best I've ever sung it in my life. And I've sung it when I felt like I sang it the crummiest, and I've had more people come up to me and say, "I cried for three minutes because of that song." Just things like that, that have genuinely happened to me, you know, I go, "Woahhhh . . . something's goin' on." It's not just a money thing. It's more than that. It's something that's been incredibly blessed.

[Naomi returns.]

Q You reportedly once said that you used to walk into stores singing "Mama He's Crazy," hoping somebody would notice you. Is that true?

A Together: (Laughter)

Naomi [sarcastically]: That sounds like something you would have said, dear.

Wynonna: Yeah, I said that. Because I was talkin' about how people ask us now what these awards mean to us, and I said, "Well, I can no longer go Krogering without any makeup on." And that was what I meant. It used to be, we'd walk around and we'd hear one of our songs on the radio . . . I remember one time drivin' down the street with Ashley in the car, and "Mama He's Crazy" came on the radio, and she rolled down the window and she said, "Do you know who this is? This is my sister, and here she is, Wynonna Judd." And now it's just the opposite. I mean, I went to the Krystal [a drive-in restaurant] the other night, and five kids were leaning out the window wanting my autograph.

Q Not much about your life has been typical. Do you have a feeling of being special?

A Naomi: No, I don't think we're special. I really don't. When I was home last week . . . I don't go to beauty salons. When we were at Caesars Palace, I took my mother in for a facial and a manicure, and I'd never had one in my life. But I wanted to go to Jane's Beauty Parlor in Ashland, Kentucky, on Thirteenth Street, and get a manicure. Because all of a sudden I've got this gorgeous diamond ring from our manager. After all those years that I could only have stubs, workin' as a nurse . . . you know, you can't give somebody a bedpan with these [long] fingernails . . . I'm sitting there in this little beauty shop, gettin' a manicure, flashin' this diamond ring, and it was *wonderful*. Wynonna's heard this story, so she's totally bored. Take your nap, dear. But I found out that these people are so *for* us. They are *with* us. This lady who happened to be in the beauty shop, her sister and I went to school together. And she called her sister on the phone and said, "Get down here right away! Naomi Judd's in the beauty parlor!" Becky was cooking supper for her husband, who's a mechanic down at Fairchild's in Ashland. This poor man had just come in from work, and she's cookin' him supper . . . (Laughter) She left the pots on the stove and ran out the back door, and we sat for an hour and just hooted and hollered over how the teacher used to have to separate us because we were so disruptive, we laughed so much. She wants to take me to the Bluegrass Grill in her '59 Corvette—she has it 'til this day, you know—and she wants me to go play bingo with her on Friday night in Ashland. And this girl looks exactly the same as she did twenty years ago. And here I'm sitting there, and she wants to know what Willie Nelson's really like, and did Conway Twitty really leave his wife for his secretary, and I'm talking a blue streak. You know, I'm as excited as a kid on Christmas morning, being able to share all this gossip in a beauty parlor. I've wanted to do this, and I've wanted to flash my ring and everything, all my life. And I'm talking, and all of a sudden, she reaches over and grabs my arm and interrupts me. She has this incredulous look on her face, and she says, "My God, you have not changed one iota." She says, "Everybody in town that has seen you in the last twenty years says that you were exactly like you were."

Q Do you think that's true?

A Wynonna: Yes and no.

Naomi: Yes. I think our lifestyle has changed, like, three hundred sixty degrees. But I don't think I've changed at all. And it was very reassuring. It was sort of validating, to me, to have someone who had known me . . .

Wynonna: Who knows the *real* you.

Naomi: Yeah. To have her say that. And here I am answering her questions about what Europe's like, 'cause we had just come back from Europe, and tellin' her the nitty-gritty of how you make a video, and all these things that ordinarily I would be sitting in the beauty salon reading about in *Movie Screen* magazine, you know. And here I am telling them from personal experience. It was kind of like being at my hometown awards show or something. It was really weird. *Really* weird. Because my memory is strong, and I can remember bein' Wynonna's age like it was last week. I can remember what I felt, I can remember my favorite outfit, and what I was listening to on the radio . . . just déjà vu everywhere.

Q When did you realize you had made it?

A *Wynonna:* When we were on *Hee Haw.*

Naomi: You know, it's really cute. We will go into some truck stop at three in the morning, and they'll start playin' our songs.

Wynonna: And watchin' us.

Naomi: They'll figure out who we are . . .

Wynonna: By that big bus sittin' right outside the window!

Naomi: Man, talk about when did we know we were a hit? It's been over a year ago. This may have been the night for me. We were sittin' in a truck stop somewhere in the middle of Texas, appropriately enough, at some god-awful hour when the rest of the world was sanely in their beds. And I was eatin' soup beans and corn bread, with a big hunk of onion, surrounded by the Judd Boys, the guys in the band. I had no makeup on, my hair was pulled back in a ponytail, I had a Conway Twitty ball cap on my head, and I was in my wrinkled bus clothes. I'd just climbed out of my bunk. And "Mama He's Crazy" came on. I thought, "Patsy, can you see us now!"

Q [to Naomi]: In 1983, when you were working part-time as a model, you appeared on a Conway Twitty album cover, *Lost in the Feeling.* It was a rather seductive pose—you had your hand inside Conway's jacket and your mouth at his ear. Is that picture embarrassing to you now? How do you feel about it?

A *Naomi:* I can't believe I got *paid* for it! Is that like every girl's dream, or what, to get to whisper in Conway's ear! (Laughter)

Wynonna: It was like he called her up and went, "Hello, darlin', would you be on my album cover?" And she said, "Let me think about it. Okay."

Naomi: Let me show you something real quick. [She reaches for her purse.] You know, on the back of that album cover, I'm in this '53 white Cadillac convertible. Well, I bought the hardtop '53 Cadillac convertible. [She produces a picture from her wallet.] It's turquoise.

Wynonna: I bought a '57 Chevy. Mine's sittin' right up in the driveway.

Naomi [thumbing through more pictures]: I carry around what's important. There's my daddy's fillin' station, the house I grew up in in Ashland . . . I'm puttin' a security system in today for my folks, 'cause it's my fault.

Q The fans won't leave them alone?

A Naomi: Well, everybody knows that's the Judds' house now, and I'd just feel safer. . . . It used to be that they didn't even have to lock their doors at night. But you never know. And it's just to protect them. They've worked so hard all their lives for what they've got now. And I would just die if anything happened to that house. When I go home, I open a drawer of a coffee table, and there's my report card from the third grade, or some coloring book page that Wynonna did when she was five years old, and Mother's Day cards from when I could only print block letters, you know. I think because I've been such a wandering soul all my adult life, it's very important to me that some things never change. Wynonna and I bought video cameras, and when we get some time off, we're goin' back into the hollers of Louisa, Kentucky, to get a permanent record of the old home place where my daddy was born and raised.

Q Have you noticed any resentment from other of the RCA acts that the company has spent so much time and effort on you?

A Naomi: No, not really. People ask us who our favorites are, and to me it's Linda Ronstadt, and Emmylou, and Bonnie Raitt, and Joni Mitchell. And then there's Dolly, and Loretta, and Tammy. I've seen *Coal Miner's Daughter* thirty times, because I identify so strongly with Loretta. And I love Tammy. She came to see us in Vegas, and I really like the lady. But I think the reason we haven't encountered any jealousy is because country music is really like a big family.

Q I think that family stuff has been exaggerated way out of shape.

A Naomi: Well, we'd been around Nashville for a good four years before the RCA contract, before we started doing anything legitimate. And all this time I was goin' with this guy who was always gone out on the road. But I would go down on Music Row on my day off from the hospital, trying to find out which producers were doin' what, and what their sound was like, and what was goin' on. And I really think that because I played it straight—I didn't go out to dinner with the heads of the labels, and I was like "Yes, sir, thank you very much, I've got to go home to my kids now" —I think maybe my reputation had pretty much . . . I still run into producers who tried to take me out, who said, "Well, sure, I'll listen to your tape if you'll go to dinner with me," and all that crap. And for a while I was really bitter. Because when you're practically starving . . . There was a time when I thought, "If we ever make it, I'm gonna tell the truth about some of these guys and how they operate." But there are people like that in everything that you do. What I'm saying is that, now, the secretaries and the people in the restaurants and the bars in Nashville all say, "Good for you. It's nice to know that it can still be done the right way." I would like to think that the other artists who kicked around for ten or fifteen years before they got a label deal might know that we're decent girls. There's been one person that there was a lot of professional jealousy about. And I know I'm weird, but all my life I've had some kind of missionary zeal. I've always felt that if I'm in a situation and I see something that needs to be done, and I see a person trying to get it done who really isn't doing the right thing, it's real hard for me not to speak up. If I know that my idea is going to work, it's always been real hard for me to demur.

Q I'm sure you've told people only a fraction of the stories of what you had to do to get where you are now.

A Naomi: There are a lot of things that nobody knows yet, you're right. I might tell 'em someday. Then again, I might not.

Brenda Lee

$\mathcal{S}$he has been called the best white female rock singer of the '50s, as well as one of the greatest female song interpreters in popular music history, deserving to be ranked with Billie Holiday, Bessie Smith, Mahalia Jackson, Judy Garland, and Edith Piaf. But Brenda Lee, 43, never denies that she started her career in country music, and for more than a decade now she has returned to her country base, where only George Jones, Johnny Cash, and Jerry Lee Lewis equal her status as a performer who is as active today as she was in the beginning of her career thirty years ago.

Born Brenda Mae Tarpley, in Atlanta, the daughter of a construction worker, she spent her formative years in rural Georgia. By the age of three, she demonstrated an extraordinary affinity for music, her mother reporting she could hear a song twice and sing it back word for word. At five, she sang "Take Me Out to the Ball Game" at a Conyers, Georgia, spring festival and won first prize. The performance led to regular appearances on Atlanta radio and television—where she auditioned with the Hank Williams hit "Hey, Good Lookin'"—and to Lee's first professional singing job, entertaining at a Shriner's Club luncheon for twenty dollars.

If the child's family saw her talent as a novelty that brought in occasional money, it took on new importance in 1953, when Lee's father was killed in a freak construction accident, a hammer falling from a carpenter working above him and striking him on the head. From then on, the eight-year-old became her family's principal breadwinner.

Lee's big break came in 1956, when she appeared on an Augusta, Georgia, television show with country great Red Foley. Foley not only invited her to Springfield, Missouri, to appear on his popular weekly ABC-TV program, *Ozark Jubilee*, but introduced her to his manager, Dub Allbritten. Allbritten, impressed with the overwhelming response the child elicited from the TV audience, recognized her potential as a major star. In short order, he had her booked on *The Perry Como Show*, followed by appearances on Steve Allen and Ed Sullivan.

Ironically, then, without ever having cut a record, Brenda Lee was well on her way to becoming a nationally recognized singer and seasoned television performer. Finally, in 1956, the eleven-year-old signed with Decca Records (now MCA), primarily as a rockabilly act. Her first single, produced by Owen Bradley, who would guide her through the biggest years of her career, was a cover of "Jambalaya," backed by perhaps her purest rockabilly recording, "Bigelow 6-2000."

"Essentially a country stylist who was thrust into the role of rock singer," as writer Greg Shaw was to observe, Lee went on to growl and hiccup her way through a number of rockabilly sides, including "Dynamite" (which led to her professional nickname, "Little Miss Dynamite"), "One Step at a Time," and "Rockin' Around the Christmas Tree," now a holiday classic. In 1959 she would expand the style with "Sweet Nothin's," her first real hit, on which, in Robert K. Oermann's words, she "shouted, pouted and purred over a steady beat in a way that can only be described as 'adult.' " The record broke Lee over onto the pop and rock charts, where she would remain throughout the decade.

However, it is for her string of ballads and heartbreak songs, seething with loneliness and vulnerability, that Brenda Lee is best known, hits such as "I'm Sorry" (recorded when she was sixteen), "I Want to Be Wanted," "Emotions," "Fool Number One," "Break It to Me Gently," and "All Alone Am I," which established her on the international pop charts and made her one of the biggest-selling female vocalists of the '60s. To date, she has sold close to 100 million records, at one point remaining on the charts in England for 320 consecutive weeks. Her remarkable voice, unmistakably Southern and possessing a bluesy edge straight out of black gospel music, became one of the most recognizable in the world.

As Lee's pop music singles slacked off in the late '60s, she returned to her country roots, recording Willie Nelson's "Johnny One Time" in 1969. The record became her twelfth million-seller. By 1972, her singles were played exclusively on country stations. Just as she had earned a reputation as a shrewd "song finder" with her pop singles, the diminutive (four feet nine inches) singer drew on Nashville's most respected songwriters for a series of songs that put her high on the country charts in the early '70s: Kris Kristofferson's "Nobody Wins" and Shel Silverstein's "Big Four Poster Bed" among them. Her country singles, one critic wrote, "express strong emotions of pain and tragedy, longings and dissatisfactions—themes of the plaintive woman who retains her raw, wide-ranging and individual emotions above all else."

"The music business has changed, but my sound is still basically the same," Lee says of her return to country. And she insists, quite persuasively, that if her big songs from the '60s—"All Alone Am I" and "As Usual," for example—came out today, they would be country records. "It's just that country grew, and what we knew as rock and pop certainly changed."

As Lee's country career continued, though, she allied herself with producers who hadn't a clear idea of what to do with her, and her albums, in the view of Dave Marsh, became "totally tame [and] formulaic . . . with virtually nothing to recommend them except the odd pleasure of Lee's still-sobbing voice." After a period of experimentation in the late '70s and early '80s, she emerged in 1985 with *Feels So Right,* an LP that celebrated her early rockabilly strength and success. Despite Lee's stellar performance, the album failed to reach its audience, signaling a break with her longtime label. No matter what her future with a record company may be, Lee will doubtless remain one of popular music's most versatile vocalists, and one of Nashville's superior talents.

The following interview was drawn from six sessions recorded at Lee's home in Nashville over a ten-year span, from January 1976 to November 1986. I discovered during that time that she deserves her reputation as one of the smartest, funniest, and most unaffected artists in country music.

Q Your 1985 LP, *Feels So Right,* almost brings you full circle from where you started out, in rockabilly.

A Well, we tried to cut that album in the old way. We didn't use strings. We just used a rhythm group, and not that many background vocalists, and we just sang and played. I really loved it.

Q But MCA didn't promote it very heavily.

A Nope, they didn't. And I don't know why. But you can't fight city hall, and you can't just stop and sit in the corner and be frustrated over things like that. I'm in the process right now of changing labels, I guess.

Q You've been there a long time.

A Thirty years. The only person who's been there longer than me is Bill Monroe, by six or seven years.

Q Part of the public thinks you've retired.

A No, I'm working more than I've probably ever worked. Last year and this year have just been crazy, other than not having anything on the record market. I'm working eight months a year now.

Q Do you feel you belong in a specific musical category—country or pop —or do you feel you transcend classification?

A Well, I don't think that you should categorize artists anyway. When I started out, I was played on all kinds of stations. Rhythm and blues stations played me, country played me, pop played me, rock played me. I just think if something's good, it's everything. Artists never like to be categorized. I know that companies have to do it, because of marketing, and because some artists are strictly one way or another. But I'm not one of those people. And when they put you in the one bag and you can't get out of it, it's frustrating. I think that's true of the new breed of DJs, and the new breed of writers, who are not necessarily aware of what Brenda Lee has done in the past. They only know what I've done in the last couple of years. So they say, "Well, she's country." They don't know about all the awards. I've won every award except the Grammy, but I've been nominated six times for it, the last time in 1979 with "Tell Me What It's Like."

Q Do you feel constricted with the country label?

A Yes, in a way. There's nothin' wrong with [being country]. But it limits what you do, or what you can do. I don't care if you use a steel guitar, or a Dobro, or a fiddle on your records. If the song is there, and it's good, it's gonna go pop anyway. Because what constitutes crossover is not you or the record. It's how much it's selling. The only thing different in country music and pop music is the instrumentation. You could take any pop song and make it country. You could more or less take any country song and make it pop. It's just the way it's sung and the way it's produced. So I don't know what kind of a singer I am. I've never thought of myself as a kind of singer. If somebody asked me what my influence was during my formative years, I'd have to say gospel music. That's all I heard. The funny thing is, that's the one [radio] format I've never been played. But I guess I've always thought of myself as a stylist. That was the goal I always wanted to achieve in my singing. I think if you're basically thought of as that, you can do most anything.

Q Have you ever been ashamed of being country?

A Gosh, no. You can't get rid of your roots. It's either a yoke around your neck or a wreath around your head. Just however you want to make it.

Q There was a time, however, when you didn't want to be promoted country *at all*, only pop.

A Well, my feelings on that have changed. I *am* country. I'm *from* the country. I was born and raised in the country. As far as being a country singer, I don't think that people put me in the category of Loretta Lynn or Tammy Wynette. I think they're great, and I don't want to take anything away from them. But if you were going to compare me with what's happening today in country, I think you would compare me—and this may sound left-field—to Willie Nelson. That's the kind of country that I've done, and I'm going to be doing.

Q You mean in reference to standards?

A Right. Like "Blue Eyes Crying in the Rain." That's the kind of country that I am. If you listen back to my old records—"As Usual," "Too Many Rivers," "Fool Number One," "Johnny One Time" . . . in fact, I covered Willie on "Johnny One Time." That was his record to start with. But there's no sense in fooling oneself. The eighty-five million records I sold between the years '59 and '71 are now considered middle-of-the-road country. Then they were pop. So the business has changed. I may be doing a gospel-country sound. As I say, those are my roots. And I'm proud of 'em. I'm just gonna sing honest, and I'm not gonna try to sound like anybody except me. If I pronounce a word country, it'll just be pronounced that way. I went through a stage where I thought everything had to be correctly pronounced. I wanted to be Nancy Wilson for a while. But I want to be me now. I think that's okay.

Q Has Nashville ever really accepted you?

A [Soft laughter] That's a touchy question.

Q You're often on the board of the Country Music Association, for example, but you're seldom a presenter at the awards shows.

A I think that I'm accepted personally, because I work very hard to further Nashville and its music. I don't think that I have been accepted fully. And when I say "accepted," I don't mean that I'm not respected for my music, and what I've accomplished. But I think that if you didn't start out in country, if you started out in pop and rock, for example, you're not just wholly embraced by Nashville. Like you say, I'm not a presenter. I'm on the board, and I get in the ditches and dig, but sometimes I'm not awarded the fruits of my labor. And I don't mind that. I don't say, "That should be me up there." Because I love this business. And I do what I do, as trite as it sounds, unselfishly. Or else I wouldn't do it. There's no money in being on the CMA board. And there have been no awards for me, certainly. But I do it because I like it, because I want to learn more about it, and because I want to be a part of it. But as far as furthering whatever career I have in country music, I don't think that it has done that.

Q The CMA may not have honored you, but you've gotten some big awards in the last few years, particularly the Governor's Award, in 1984, and "Tribute to a Legend," from the National Academy of Recording Arts and Sciences.

A Yeah, that's voted on by the academy, and they don't give it every year. Red Skelton just received it from the chapter in Los Angeles, and I received it from the chapter in Nashville. That's probably one of the nicest things that's happened to me.

Q You've been around so long that people think you're a lot older than you are. They forget that you were eleven years old when you started recording.

A Oh, yeah. That's a big misconception, and it's been a problem. Because sometimes they think I can't be in with what's happening today musically, because I'm too old. They think, "God, I've watched her for thirty years, so she must be sixty," you know. Like the lady who told me she was so pleased to see me singing again and all, and that I hadn't changed a bit since she saw me at the premiere of *Gone With the Wind.*

Q What?

A Yeah, this woman came up to me and said, "Oh, I just loved your show, and it's so great seeing you again." I said, "Why, thank you." She said, "Do you remember where we saw you?" I said, "Well, no." She said, "At the premiere of *Gone With the Wind.*" Well, I couldn't dispute her. I said, "Wasn't it a wonderful movie? Didn't Clark Gable look great? And how terrible that Margaret Mitchell was killed crossing the street!" I just went right along. Because if you say, "I wasn't there, they're gonna say, "Well, you were, too." You know, that was in 1939, and I wasn't born until '44. But I just made her day, because she really thought I was there. Fans believe what they believe, and you're not gonna shake their beliefs. Sometimes you want to say, "No, I'm not that old." But if that's how old they think you are, it doesn't matter if you show 'em a birth certificate. I do the same thing with people I'm a fan of. Reality lurks in the back of my mind about things, but it gets clouded over by the great American myth.

Q I wonder who they could have confused you with.

A I have no idea. I can't think of any dwarf that was in *Gone With the Wind*. I cannot think of one short person that was in that movie.

Q That's a good story.

A Oh, yeah, I thought that was great, but it shocked me at first. And then one woman asked me if I didn't use to go under the name of Molly Bee. I *loved* that one. That's another of my favorite stories.

Q Back in the seventies, you had a lot of health problems. You had major kidney surgery in '74, three major abdominal surgeries following caesarean sections, and two pulmonary embolisms due to phlebitis. In all, you had seven major surgeries in five years. How is your health now?

A My health is great. Couldn't be better. I've been taking it easy, and not pushing myself like I did in the past. That was the major cause of my health problems, anyway. Other than having a record, I'm doing more than I've ever done, and doing fine. And hopefully, I'll rectify that record situation.

Q You were dubbed "Little Miss Dynamite" when you were a child, and people still refer to that occasionally. How did you feel about that?

A Well, that started in England. It's not so much that I didn't like it, but when you start getting labels, you feel like you have to prove 'em. I mean, if they say, "Frank Sinatra's the greatest singer in the world," and he goes out and hits a bad note one night, it's like the idol has toppled. And if you're called "Little Miss Dynamite," you're supposed to go out on the stage and explode every night. And sometimes you feel like "Oh, Lord." But yes, it's still with me.

Q In 1978, you left MCA for a while, and cut some tracks for Elektra down in Muscle Shoals. They put out one single on you, and that was it.

A Well, the single did nothing because Elektra did nothing for it. It wasn't pushed anywhere.

Q My recollection is that they wanted you to do country-disco.

A They wanted to experiment. So that's what I did. And then, of course, nothing happened. I went back with MCA.

Q I was in the recording studio for some of those sessions, and my memory is that while you were being cooperative with the producer, you were fighting him inside—you knew that music wasn't right for you.

A Yeah. They were trying to discover a new Brenda Lee, and there already was one. And I didn't understand that internally. I understood it in a way, of course. But my gut feeling was that what they were doing wasn't Brenda Lee. It was a creation of other people's ideas of what they thought Brenda Lee should be. And the "me" in me won out, because it was compromising, and I'd never done that. So I said, "Forget it."

Q One thing I remember from that trip is that you came to breakfast with a dictionary and a thesaurus—that you tried to learn a certain number of new words every day. Do you still do that?

A (Laughter) Yeah. I still do my crossword puzzles. And try to learn all the words that I can, so that if I'm ever in a situation where I have to have a philosophical conversation, I can use all my big words. I want to learn everything I can. I want to read every book I can, I want to see every country, every state that I can. I want to talk to every person that I can. Because you can learn something from everybody. That's basically how I got my education. I certainly got more from that than from going to school. Because when I went to school, it was so much fun that I didn't care about studying. I made pretty good grades, but I was certainly no Einstein.

Q How did you manage school traveling around as a child?

A Well, I went to public school up until my junior year. And then things really started happening [with my career]. I was gonna make a movie in Hollywood, so we went out there and I went to Hollywood Professional School for my last two years. Private school.

Q Did you make the film?

A Yes. It was called *The Two Little Bears,* for Twentieth Century–Fox, with Eddie Albert, Jane Wyatt, and Jimmy Boyd. It was a comedy, and I had a fairly large part, in fact. I also had a big hit record out of it, called "Speak to Me Pretty," which was huge in Europe. But I was so fat when they took the promotion pictures! I wore a purple dress, and they painted the walls purple so I would look a little smaller. Those were during my really fat days as a teenager.

Q So you did finish your schooling?

A Yes. It hurts me when somebody in the business quits school to pursue a career. 'Cause I took a year of college by correspondence course. I always wanted to be a doctor. That was my life's dream, to work with handicapped children. And I wanted to be a surgeon, until I found out you had to go to school for fifteen years. I didn't think that I wanted to do that. And of course, I had my singing, and I was supporting my family, so I just couldn't do it. But I love to read, and I guess it started when I was a little girl. Because I was alone all the time, and the only thing there was to do in the room was read or watch television. I would always turn on the TV, just to have the sound in the room, to feel that there was somebody with me.

Q Where was your mother?

A Well, my mom used to go most of the time, but she couldn't go all of the time. And, of course, my manager, being a man, couldn't stay in the room with me.

Q They didn't hire a companion for you?

A I had a private teacher who went. And I didn't like that. I didn't like school on the road. I thought that was ghastly. So I said, "I just can't do this. I've either got to stop singing or I've got to go to a school somewhere." Because education is so important, and those are years that you can't bring back. It's happenings and events that are so special and sacred through your life. You need those years. You really do.

Q Those were the years when you crisscrossed the country doing the big package shows, I guess.

A Yeah. When I was nine, ten, and twelve years old, I'd do those big country tours with Faron Young and Mel Tillis and George Jones—people like that. And my mom and I used to ride with Mel. I was so little that I could stand up on the thing in the middle of the floorboard of the back seat of the car and never touch the ceiling. Mel would drive all night to get to the date, you know, so he'd want me to tell him stories to keep him awake. He was a funny guy. Mel's a great guy.

Q It sounds like a horrendous way to travel, though—covering several hundred miles a night in a car, day after day.

A Oh, yeah, gosh, even up to the middle sixties, we used to travel everywhere by cars. And, of course, back in those days, we didn't have interstates. We'd travel those little main two-lane roads that went through God knows how many little towns. It was great, because you got to see the world. And you don't see that anymore. You don't see those interesting little towns and meet those little people at those stores and stops. But we used to do tours with overnight jumps of, like, five hundred miles. Sometimes never check in for a week at a time. You'd sleep in the car and clean up in the auditorium, and do your shows and get in the car and go again. And I used to go to sleep within five minutes of getting in the car. But then we'd get to the city limits of the next town, no matter where it was, and I'd wake right up and say, "Are we there yet?" My manager said it was uncanny. I must have had mental telepathy. So if I write a book, I'll call it *Are We There Yet?* Because that's how it becomes after a while: "Just get me there."

Q What's the biggest toll your career has had on your life?

A The health, and the relationships. You can't have any relationships, or close friends, period. And your family life suffers. If you've got a marriage, it's got to suffer.

Q I think it would especially suffer if your husband also managed you, which Ronnie [Shacklett] does to some extent.

A Well, Ronnie's tended to some things. And that hasn't been a disadvantage to me personally. But I think it has been for other people [whose spouse also serves as a manager]. Ronnie just makes sure that I'm not getting taken advantage of. He's not really a manager.

Q Didn't Ronnie go over to MCA and negotiate this last record?

A He would go over there with me, but I was the one doing the talking. I may need a manager. I probably do. But I'm happy doing what I'm doing.

Q You mentioned staying in your room alone on the road as a child. Was that a lonely existence?

A Well, sure, because traveling on the road, you have hello/goodbye acquaintances, but you can't just meet somebody on the road and strike up a friendship for a couple of hours. For one thing, if you're a girl, it doesn't look good. And you don't know what kind of people they are. So you just have to be careful. I didn't have any type of a life other than on the stage. I wasn't allowed to because of those factors.

Q You had no friends your own age?

A No. Because there weren't that many in the business at that time. As I said, I did go to public school. When I came back home I was more or less normal, but I felt like I was left out of a lot of things. Because if people were having parties, they'd say, "Oh, well, don't worry about Brenda. She's not gonna be here anyway." So I never felt a steadiness, or any kind of an anchor. There wasn't much for me to hold on to, because I was never anywhere for any length of time. I was at school, and then I was gone.

Q Is that one reason home life means so much to you now?

A I'm sure it is, yeah. But it's nobody's fault. Certainly not my mother's. I was in show business, and I was supporting the family, and that was the way it had to be. But I think kids miss an awful lot if they don't have a good home life, and a foundation to work from. 'Cause then they really never know who they are. They're never really sure.

Q Did you go to your high school prom?

A No. That was one of the big things I missed. Still miss. I wish I could have experienced that. As trivial and trite as it sounds, I think that's a great thing in a girl's life.

Q You married young, though. How did you meet Ronnie?

A Well, I wasn't looking, for one thing. I guess that's probably how you meet the greatest people in your life—when you're *not* looking. I was at a rock-and-roll show. I loved Jackie Wilson. He was always one of my favorites. And I went to see him at the Fairgrounds Coliseum here in Nashville. I don't think I'm forward, but I've always been outgoing. And being raised in show business, you get a lot of those old taboos out of the way. Things like "Wait until the guy calls you." I didn't grow up that way. I thought if you liked somebody and wanted to meet 'em, you just said, "Hey, I'd really like to know you." So I saw Ronnie in the auditorium, and I sent a girlfriend over with my phone number and a message to call me. And about two weeks later he called, and we had a date. I was eighteen, and he was my first single date. I always had to double-date at school functions, and I couldn't even do that until I was sixteen.

Q When was this?

A This was in October of 1962. Then I didn't see him again for about a month.

Q But you got married the same year, right?

A Yes. We married April 24, 1963.

Q So you really didn't know him very long.

A No, and three of those months I was in Europe. I was still eighteen. I was nineteen the following December. Ronnie was nineteen that May. A lot of people ask if it was love at first sight. I don't know. I saw in him some things that I more or less needed—some stability, mainly. I think I probably fell in love with his family as much as I did him at the time, because my father had died. I was crazy about his dad, and I just liked the whole family scene. But then again, it must have been something other than his father, because we're still together. But when I met him, I had no intentions of marrying that young. And surely career-wise it wasn't a good move.

Q Did they try to pretend you weren't married?

A No. It shocked everybody, but I think due to the girl-next-door image that I had, it didn't hurt my record sales. Because guys were not clamoring for me for my sexual appeal, and the girls were certainly not competing with me for their boyfriends' affection. But I think if my manager and the record company had had their say, they wouldn't have wanted me to have done it then. Or they would have wanted me to do it more flamboyantly, one of the two.

Q Is it difficult for you to listen to any of the records you made as a child?

A No, it's not painful to hear the early recordings. It's a little *strange*, because my voice has dropped about two or three octaves since I first started out. My voice dropped a whole octave with each child. *That* was weird! But it's not painful to look back, because I'm very proud of the product that I had out. Although I laugh when I hear my recording of "Jambalaya." I mean, it's *hysterical*. And what is *really* funny is that I'm singing about unrequited love in some of those songs, and I was still playing with paper dolls at the time. I didn't even know what a boy looked like. I really sang like I knew what I was talking about, and I didn't even . . . I mean, I cried my eyes out when I was fourteen years old over a Tiny Tears doll that my mom wouldn't buy me. People still laugh at me for that, but I just wanted that doll so bad. I guess she sheltered me from a lot of things.

Q So all that lust in "Sweet Nothin's" was just pretending.

A Yeah, I don't know where that came from. I really don't. I guess I got it from the guy who sang it to me. Well, the words were there, too. Because you didn't even talk about it when we were that age. I guess I fantasized in that song. I probably wished that I was in that situation, and sang it like that, but I hadn't had any experience, that's for sure.

Q But your delivery added a certain sexy dimension to the lyrics. One critic described your voice there as "part whiskey, part Negroid, and all woman."

A (Laughter) Owen said that it was always uncanny the way I could read lyrics at that age and sound believable. I don't know how I did it. Except that I love lyrics. And I was raised on Edith Piaf. Piaf, and Judy Garland, and Tony Bennett, and Frank Sinatra. And I guess Bessie Smith, and Billie Holiday, and Charles Aznavour. These are the people that I cut my teeth on. Everybody says, "Chuck Berry, Elvis Presley . . ." I had those records, but my manager would always bring these other people to me and say, "Listen to this." So these are the people that I learned my phrasing from. And, of course, they were all innovators, so they helped me a lot. I particularly learned a lot of my phrasing from Sinatra, who I think is the greatest phraser in the business. Bennett, as Sinatra said, might possibly be the greatest *singer* in the business. I don't know. But these are the people I listened to.

Q Did you have any formal vocal training?

A No. My mother took me to a vocal coach when I was fourteen, and he said he wouldn't touch it. He said, "If I even tried, she'd lose what style she has. She doesn't need any vocal training. Maybe breathing and learning to sing correctly, but no voice lessons."

Q You said once that you didn't want to still be singing "Sweet Nothin's" when you were fifty. Do you still feel that way?

A I don't know. After seeing Lena Horne, I don't know that it matters. I mean, who says that you can't do anything if you're able to do it? You think, "Well, fifty!" But, my Lord, there's a lot of people out there who are fifty who love that stuff.

Q How much do you identify with the seminal days of rock 'n' roll?

A Well, I don't know. Because my first record was country. I never said, "I want to be rock 'n' roll," or "I want to be pop." I was one of the people who were inventing rock 'n' roll without knowing what we were doing.

Q You were considered rockabilly for a while, as we mentioned.

A I was rockabilly, along with Elvis, and Carl Perkins, and Jerry Lee Lewis, and Fats Domino. The only thing that says that you're a rock or pop singer is sales. Owen and I always just went into the studio and cut the songs that we thought were good, gave 'em the treatment that we thought they needed, and put 'em out. We never went into the studio and said, "We're gonna cut a crossover record." Or "We're gonna cut a country song." We looked for good material. And we couldn't help it if people said what they were.

Q Were you conscious of trying to "be" a rockabilly singer, or were you just doing what came naturally?

A Just doing what came naturally.

Q What about that growl you got in your voice?

A I don't know where that came from.

Q Nobody coached you on that?

A No. I just always did that.

Q You're probably more popular in Japan than in this country. Why is that?

A Well, I started going over there a long time ago. In fact, I went every year. I've even recorded in Japanese. Actually, I've recorded in six languages, and I've had number one records in Germany, Italy, France, and England, in addition to Japan.

Q And you're a small person, which the Japanese can relate to. That probably helps.

A Well, I don't think it hurts. For once. (Laughter)

Q You've been popular in England for a long time. In fact, the Beatles were your warm-up act over there for a time.

A Yeah, the Beatles used to open for me in the early sixties, throughout Europe, Germany especially. Right before they hit it big in the States.

Q What kinds of memories do you have of them?

A Well, they were crazy. John was always pulling practical pranks. One night, he threw a smoke bomb into the audience. And people just went nuts—thought the whole place had been bombed. But he was always doin' somethin' like that. He was just a funny, funny guy.

Q Did you ever sing with them?

A No. But when Dub [Allbritten] and I came back to the States, we begged Decca to sign 'em. And they wouldn't. Musically, they were very raw, you know, but they were great. You could see that talent, and the depth.

Q You began appearing on Red Foley's *Ozark Jubilee* TV show when you were a tiny child. How did that start?

A Red Foley came down to Augusta, Georgia, where I was livin'. And a little DJ friend of mine [Peanut Faircloth] took me over, and asked Red if he'd let this little local girl sing a song on the show. And he liked me, and he said, "Would you like to come [to Missouri] and make an appearance on *Ozark Jubilee?*" So I did, and I was a big hit on it. Then I became a regular.

Q Was it fairly easy to get a record deal after you became a regular on that show?

A Well, no. 'Cause there were so many years when we paid people just to let me *be* on a show. You know, "*Please* let her sing." (Laughter)

Q You really did?

A Yeah, my managers would say, "We'll pay *you*," or "She doesn't want any money. Just let her be on." Just to get seen, you know. Because it was hard to "sell" a child in those days. Nobody wanted a child on the label. I was turned down by RCA Victor and by just about every label. Decca took me on the strength of Red Foley, and my manager managed Red Foley, so they took me. And it was four years before I had a hit for them. I mean, I had some mediocre things that sold, but it was a good four years before I had "Sweet Nothin's." But Owen never stopped believing, and we just kept on in there. And all this time, I was doin' the major TV shows, because here was a little bitty girl with a big ole voice. So I was salable, but I was not havin' any hit records.

Q You said you began supporting your family after your father died. How many people did you take care of?

A Well, two sisters, a brother, and my mother.

Q What kind of memories do you have of your father?

A Unfortunately, I don't have many. He was an alcoholic. I was goin' on nine when he died.

Q You never talk about your family.

A They have their lives to lead, and they have their identities, and I have never wanted to exploit them as "Brenda Lee's sister" or "Brenda Lee's mother." Because they're fine, hardworking, uncomplicated people, and they like it that way. It's not that they're not proud of who I am. But they want to be who they are, too.

Q Your mother worked in a cotton mill.

A Right. She worked on one of those machines for eighteen hours a day. And the little I was makin' then was a help, even though it wasn't any great amount.

Q An article in the *Journal of Country Music,* published by the Country Music Foundation, says that your mother refused to let you tour with Jerry Lee Lewis when you were a child, "claiming that he was 'an animal.'"

A (Laughter) No, that's not true. I wish she had. But that would have never entered my mother's mind. She wasn't a show biz mother at all. We did do a couple of shows with Jerry Lee in the late fifties, and we were gonna do a tour, but we didn't do it because the kids just tore up the theaters. It was crazy!

Q This was the time *Le Figaro* wrote that you "must be a thirty-two-year-old midget rather than a fifteen-year-old."

A Well, I think I was actually twelve. But it was great publicity for me. Because they had never seen me in France—they'd only heard me. And when we were gettin' ready to go over there, they wanted publicity pictures, and we sent 'em like I looked, you know, twelve. But they didn't believe it. They thought we were lying. So they printed the story.

Q Were you a petulant child star? Did you throw temper tantrums?

A I never threw a temper tantrum.

Q You were well behaved?

A I wouldn't say I was well behaved, but I didn't throw temper tantrums, and I didn't pout if I didn't get my way.

Q What did you do to relieve the tedium?

A I got into everything that I could.

Q Such as?

A Practical jokes—anything that I could do to bug somebody.

Q Did you resent being out there?

A No, I loved it. I thought it was great. I mean, I was gettin' to eat regular, and gettin' to see all these places that I'd only seen in books, and gettin' to go onstage and sing, which I loved to do. And lo and behold, people liked it. Shoot, I thought that was the greatest thing that could happen.

Q You didn't resent having to support the family?

A I didn't know I was doin' it. And if I had known it, that wouldn't have even entered my mind. I would have been happy that I could have.

Q You were a teenager before you had a doll that came from a store—that wasn't homemade.

A Right.

Q Did you feel poor as a child?

A No, I *knew* I was poor.

Q Where did your music come from, except from church?

A I don't know. Because we didn't have a TV or a radio. I always said I was on TV before I *had* a TV. So I don't know where it came from. Well, it came from God, of course. But other than that, I don't know.

Q You didn't hear a local musician or singer, and say, "I'd like to do that"?

A No. 'Cause I didn't hear anybody. My mother used to sing me Hank Williams songs, but other than that, I didn't know any singers. Later on, I guess I did learn Hank Williams songs from the radio. Because I did "Jambalaya," and I did "Your Cheatin' Heart" and "Mansion on the Hill." So he must have been one of the first that I listened to as a little bitty girl.

Q Did you have any psychological problems being so successful so young, especially when your career cooled down in the sixties?

A Well, when I was having all the success, I was going to public high school, and I was a cheerleader. I was on the debating squad, and I was co-editor of the newspaper. I was into all of those activities, and I didn't work except on weekends. I think I was normal as anybody could be and have a career in show business. I'm not saying that people in show business are *abnormal,* but we're a little quirky. (Laughter) And I never really realized that I was having success, because all the money was under the court [in trust], under the Jackie Coogan law. I mean, we lived in a two-room trailer. As I said, the only thing that was different to me was that I was eating a little better. Other than that, nothing changed. Because I never saw any of the money, and I really didn't care. I wanted a nice house for my family, because my mom had sacrificed and worked very hard. But the important thing to me was singing. I don't think that I really took stock in Brenda Lee until I was about twenty-seven.

Q What do you mean by that?

A I mean I don't think that I ever really realized the things that I had accomplished. Because when I did the command performance for the Queen, or when I got a gold record, or some other award, the first thought on my mind was not "Boy, I did good," but "Isn't that nice of them?" I got a lot of my awards out the other day to straighten 'em up, and I don't remember getting a lot of 'em. That's terrible, isn't it? But those things don't mean anything to me. Those are just things to hang up on the wall. Around 1971, I had some very serious throat problems, due to overabuse of my vocal cords, and not knowing how to use them correctly. I just used to dive into everything like it was the last song I was ever gonna sing. I didn't know how to pace myself. When I went to my throat doctor, he said he didn't know how I still had vocal cords, I had damaged them so bad, straining. In fact, I hemorrhaged my cords twice. They thought I wouldn't sing again. And I had to stop singing for six months, and stop talking for three months, and go to a vocal coach and take breathing exercises. Until then, I had taken my talent for granted.

And I think when I thought that I never could do it again, that's when I really got serious about it. And then, too, I think it takes you at least until you get to twenty-five—maybe some people hit it earlier, I don't know, everybody's different—to have some sort of a realization where you're going and what you want to do. And then, at thirty you change again. You have different values. My voice is now, by the way, stronger than ever. Once I learned how to breathe, and the correct placement of my cords, it was a whole different ball game. It's really a joy now.

Q How do you feel about yourself these days?

A Well, I feel now that I know myself, and understand myself, and am as well satisfied with myself as I will ever be. I have to wear so many hats, as I call them. I'm a wife, and I'm a mother, and I'm an entertainer, and then I'm me. It's been hard for me to adapt to all these things over the years. And I've always been one person as a mother, and a different person as an entertainer. It's never been all meshed into one person. But I think it's finally coming together. And it's a terrific feeling, because I've gone through a lot of years not knowing who I was. Not being able to distinguish Brenda Lee from just Brenda. Because I was treated so much like a product, I guess. And I don't mean that to say that the people around me didn't love me, because they did. They cared for me deeply. But I was nurtured as a product, and not as a personality. So I grew up not really knowing who or what I was. I was what I *read* I was.

Q Was it a case of believing your own publicity?

A Yes. Because I lived it every day, and I didn't ever do anything else. When that happens, you say to yourself, "Is that me? Who *am* I?" I really used to ask myself that. I couldn't take the hats off and know just who I was. And I didn't really like either one of me. I was overweight for a long time, and I was very self-conscious about that. And I was short, and that was sort of a hang-up with me. It's not anymore, but it was then. I'd been raised all my life as being Brenda Lee, and it just got confused. I never knew whether people really liked *me* or not. I guess everybody must go through that, to some extent.

Q But you think it was intensified for you, because of your early success?

A Well, yes, because when I wasn't having hit records, I would call disc jockeys and say, "Will you play my record?" And they wouldn't even answer my phone calls. Then, after I started having hit records, the same people would call me, and that would disillusion me. I didn't quite know why, because I was too young. But as I got older, I realized that's the workings of the world, and you must accept that. But I was trying to be something that I was not. I was trying to be what other people wanted me to be, and I had tried to be that so long that I had turned into that.

Q What did they want you to be?

A Well, when I used to do interviews, I would never involve myself in anything other than "When did you start singing?" You know, the same old questions. Because I didn't want to make anybody mad. And I hated it. Because I read a lot, and I am aware of what's going on, and I have opinions. But my interviews would always come out so saccharine. I'd read 'em, and I'd say, "Oh, Lord, that's just horrid." I know people must have read them and said, "Oh, good grief. Nobody's like that." So I just decided I was going to say what I wanted to say. And if I felt like saying, "No, I don't like that," whether it was popular or unpopular, I was going to do that.

Q Was that liberating for you?

A Well, it was hard, because it was such a big change. And I'm a very disciplined person. I'm of that old "The show must go on" school. And a lot of my illnesses have been due to me not thinking of me. I've done shows the day before I went to the hospital for major surgery. Right before I had the kidney surgery, I had a week of dates to do. My doctor said, "We have to get this done within a week, or you'll lose your kidney." And I said, "Well, I can't. I'm booked. I've got to work these dates. I can't cancel them." So I did a week of dates, and I shouldn't have done them, because I almost lost my kidney. I had a very rough time. And then I was up working again three weeks after surgery. Of course, I should never have done *that*. That's carrying discipline just a little too far. But I've learned how to say no. In other words, I've learned to think of me once in a while. And you have to put some other things in life first. And if you don't have the sense enough to take stock in that fact, then people shouldn't have sympathy for you. But it's hard for a lot of people close to me. They don't like that change. They like me the way I was before, because I was very docile, and very agreeable, and never made waves. But I think you grow out of that. Everybody does. You go through a stage of wanting to please. I hated arguments. Oh, I'd do anything to avoid an argument! I don't now, because I realize it's healthy.

Q You now live in a small and very unpretentious house in a working-class neighborhood, right next to your husband's family. People are sometimes surprised by this. What happened to your plans to build a big house?

A Well, I don't know. We've been looking lately. At one point, we bought the land, and we had the house plans drawn up, but we couldn't make the decision. Every time I'd go look, I'd come home and say, "Oh, I like my little house." There's a lot of us here. It's not a grand house, certainly, but it's also by far not the worst house anybody could live in. It's comfortable, and it's more or less me. I don't know that I need anything else.

Who am I gonna impress, anyway? I probably had more people come to this house than I did when I lived in the big Georgian mansion.

Q I thought you were dying to move.

A I thought I was, too, 'til it came down to moving. And then when I think that I won't be here anymore, a big lump comes in my throat. Because a lot of things have happened in this house with my kids—things that are pretty precious. And it's selfish of me, but I don't want anybody else living here. I know that's terrible. I would like for them to be able to know the happiness and the things that have happened, but I'd hate to think that I could never come back. Now, if I could keep this house and build another one and have *both* houses, that would be great.

Q Certainly you could afford to move.

A Well, yeah, sure. We're doin' fine. But you also have to remember that when I was selling big records, from 1959 to 1970, and when I was voted the world's number one female vocalist five years in a row—three of those years overseas—the word "superstar" was not in existence. That is a seventies word. Big money in those days was, God, $1,500 a night, maybe $3,000 a night. That was *top* money for concerts. And club money was $3,500 a week, maybe $10,000 a week. That was big, big money, unless you were Frank Sinatra or Tony Bennett. And you worried about every record that you put out. Like, I remember when we put out "Sweet Nothin's" and it was a hit. Then we were worried about "God, what are we going to put out next?" The one we really worried about was the third record, 'cause if that one didn't make it, it was almost like starting over again. Now you have one record and you're a superstar, and you can work off that for eight years. I know some people who've had *one* record, and they command big prices and they get the TV shows. It's a completely different ball game. I'm glad that I had my success in the sixties, because the field was not as congested. It's harder to break in today. There's a lot more competition, good competition. These people who are playing and singing today don't need hyping.

Q It's almost a different business now.

A Well, there's a lot more to show business. But I learned discipline. That's the main thing the younger breed of entertainers do not have. It makes me mad. I get discouraged about it. Because I don't like to see our business taken advantage of. It puts all of us in a bad light. I don't feel they have the respect for who made them, and they feel like "I did it all myself." And that's not right. Because you don't do it. When it all is said and done, you can have the greatest publicist in the world, you can have the biggest disc jockeys in the nation, you can have everybody in the world in your corner, but if those people out there listening don't like you, you're not gonna go anywhere. So it all revolves around Mr. John Q. Public out there. That's who makes you, and that's who can break you, too. And that's why I say my main objective is to play for those people, 'cause that's who gave me everything that I have. That's why I like to play the little fairs and the small towns that a lot of people won't play. Those are the ones who buy the records. It's not the people who come to Las Vegas to see those shows. They don't necessarily support you, and go buy every record that you have. That's why the country fans are so great. They're so loyal. Unless you get out of doing what they consider their pure music, and their grass roots, that is. Then they'll turn on you. But if you don't, they're very loyal to you.

Q It's been suggested that, aside from Elvis Presley, you will be remembered as the artist who brought national attention to Nashville as a pop recording center in the sixties for your work with Owen Bradley. And yet when you came back from that hiatus, you changed producers. Why was that?

A Well, Owen and I discussed it at some length, because he's always been more to me than just a producer. We've always had a relationship. After all, he's been recording me since I was ten years old. And we've had a lot of success. You're right—we were the first people to record pop in Nashville. We were the first people to use strings on a session. And Owen, of course, is known for building Music City into what it is. He was one of the first innovators here. But [the change] became a thing that the company wanted me to do. They wanted to do a new image with Brenda Lee.

Q Such as?

A Well, they wanted to hit more areas. They wanted to hit country as well as crossover. They thought it was possible to do, and they were looking at my track record, and seeing what records I had sold in the past. They thought I could be very lucrative to them as a company. And so Owen said, "Maybe a change *is* what you need. Maybe you need a new producer." And it was a very big decision for me. One of the hardest I've ever had to make. But we agreed that it might be a way to get recognition in some other fields. Because if a company's not behind you, you really can't do it, you know.

Q So you stopped singing when? 1969?

A I stopped in 1969 for two years. Well, 1967 . . . the next thing I recorded was not with Owen, so I didn't record with Owen for those years [1967 to 1971]. "Johnny One Time" was recorded in New York, and the *Memphis Portrait* album was recorded with Chips Moman. I started back with Owen again in 1971.

Q You're quoted as saying you felt the business was moving away from what you wanted to do.

A Well, there was no real demand, first of all, for female vocalists. Female vocalists have always had a rough time of it, because females are the record buyers. And there was no place for me. And my health had been bad. I didn't want to just keep on putting out product that wasn't going to sell. I felt it could only hurt me. So I just stopped for a while. I wanted to be home. I had a new baby. And I had worked ten years steady, almost ten months a year every year, and I felt it was time to reevaluate what I wanted to do. So when I started back recording with Owen, we put out "Nobody Wins." And it was the same Brenda Lee formula that we'd used for years and years, but it went country. And it went [to] number one on the country charts. I wasn't being played pop, so the smart thing was to record for who was buyin' from me. It wasn't that we were recording that country, but we were recording things that we liked. And it just so happened that "Four Poster Bed" and "Nobody Wins" and "Sunday Sunrise" just went number one country. I don't think there was any calculated move to do that, but I'm certainly glad that it happened. Because I wasn't setting the woods on fire before that.

Q Do you have trouble with people thinking of you as a nostalgia act, or wanting to put you on the Golden Oldies circuit?

A Sometimes. Not as much as a lot of people I started out with. Because I kept having hits, instead of having a few and then coming back when the nostalgia craze hit. But I get a lot of offers to do nostalgia shows. My problem is that I've been around so long. I mean, I was doing all this stuff that Elton John did ten years before he did it. I was the first in the field to use lighted-up costumes and exploding stuff on the stage. And I stopped doin' it because it was goin' over a lot of people's heads, and then it got old-hat. It's just vaudeville dressed up. But bein' around so long works to my advantage sometimes. When my daughter Julie was in her early teens, we went to see the Bee Gees. And of course, I've known them forever. So I called them up and said I was coming, and Barry [Gibb] said he'd leave the backstage passes. We drove up and Julie said, "Mother, how do you *do* this?" I said, "Oh, Julie, I'm popular in some circles." But, you know, when I meet people like that, I never think of me as being a singer. I'm just so pleased to meet somebody that I really admire. And when they say, "Boy, you really sing great," it astounds me.

Q Aren't you being a little disingenuous here?

A No, it really does! I really don't think of them ever thinking of me. When I went to meet Elton John, I was just, oh, Lord, I thought I was gonna faint 'til I could get back there to meet him. And then they told me he was about to die, too, 'cause he listened to me when he was a teenager in England. In fact, he said he wrote "Crocodile Rock" with me in mind. Then when Golden Earring came out with "Radar Love" and had my name in the song ("The radio's playing a forgotten song / Brenda Lee's 'Coming On Strong' "), I couldn't believe it. I guess that's strange, but in all honesty, I really never have. My manager used to get mad at me for that. He'd say, "If you want to be treated like a star, you've got to act like a star." And I said, "But I don't like the way they act. I don't feel comfortable like that." And he used to get so discouraged with me, because I wouldn't go to any of the parties. I thought they were too fast for me. They were doing things that I didn't want to do, and that I didn't believe in. So I guess that I just got left out of that track. Although I do think that I'm well respected in the business. And that's more pleasing to me than anything. 'Cause I want people to say that I did love the business, that I helped it, and I never did anything to disgrace it.

Q Obviously, you're not willing to revamp your entire image to court chart success.

A No, there are certain things I will not conform to. I don't care if it will make me successful or not. I think younger record buyers look at me as sort of establishment, and, of course, they're not into that. But it's not me to go out in a pair of blue jeans and a blouse cut down to my navel. I couldn't do it. If they assured me tomorrow that would make me the number one singer in the world, I'd have to say, "No, I'm sorry, I just can't." The main reason that the Willie Nelsons, and the Kris Kristoffersons, and the Waylon Jenningses are appealing to the younger crowd is that the younger crowd can identify with their dress. They can't identify with a star-spangled-banner Nudie suit. But they can relate to a guy singin' country because he's got blue jeans on and he's got an Indian headband. And they say, "Hey, that music's not bad." When it's not the music that's influenced them at all.

Q You made your reputation, to some extent, as a ballad singer.

A Well, there's nothing I like better than a meaty ballad with great lyrics. After "I'm Sorry" and "I Want to Be Wanted" became number one, I more or less got into the ballad bag, although a lot of my records were two-sided hits. But there weren't that many girl ballad singers. Connie [Francis] was doin' it, and me.

Q What other females from that era are still performing?

A Not many. Connie had all those problems, and she's retired now. She used to be a very good friend of mine. Of course, we were also the biggest of rivals, you know. Or I assume we were. There really wasn't rivalry on my part. I always just loved her. I was never jealous of anybody. I never envied their hits or what they were doing. And I don't think anybody was that jealous of me, really. I mean, I always wanted to look like Annette [Funicello]. Every girl did at that age. I thought, "God, wouldn't it be great?" And then I'd think, "Well, no, then I wouldn't be who I am. And surely I'm gonna shape up in a couple of years. This can't go on forever!" (Laughter) But I guess if any two should have been jealous of each other, it should have been us, because Connie was number one for ages. And then I came along, and we fought it out neck and neck. In fact, we tied in a lot of polls. Those were great times, though. They really were.

Q You knew Patsy Cline, didn't you?

A Oh, gosh, yes. I met Patsy in '56. She became one of my best friends, even though she was twelve years older than I was. I used to go over to her house, and she would let me clomp around in her high heels and dress up in her stage clothes. But we'd never talk show business. I just loved her to death. I thought she was wonderful.

Q How did you meet her?

A I was doing a show somewhere in Texas, and the promoter ran out with all the money. And my mom and I didn't have any money to get home. And Patsy loaded us up in her car and brought us back to Nashville. That's how I met Patsy.

Q Somewhere down the line, Patsy got the reputation as being somewhat coarse and hard-drinking. Does that fit your memory of what she was like?

A I never knew her to drink. But yeah, she could hold her own if she had to come up against men. She didn't sleep around. But she could say some words. (Laughter) Some words could come out of that mouth. Still, it didn't offend you. It was part of Patsy. She was a woman in a man's world. I was in the business before Patsy, but she was one of the first women to star in a show. And she had to deal with those things. Used to be only the men were the stars in a package. But she was one of the first, other than Kitty Wells, to be the head of the thing. She took a lot of grief over that, too.

Q Who, in your opinion, is an example of a woman who has conducted her career in a smart way?

A Well, Dolly Parton, certainly. She's not like anybody else. My manager's booking agency handled her for a while when she first came to town in the sixties. I used to see her at church a lot then. She struck me as being very intellectually aware of what was going on, but she was still able to maintain a very refreshing sort of innocence about everything. I respect Dolly because she goes after what she wants, and because she thinks like a man in a lot of ways, particularly in business. But she still retains her femininity and womanly qualities. And she won't give up her ideals and her values for anybody. I'm sure people must have said, "Dolly, you can't dress like this," and I'm also sure she must have said, "Go sit on it. This is how I want to look." And I respect her for that. Because a lot of people in this business tend to think you have to do what the people in the know want you to do to be a success. And I don't mold to that.

Q You were one of the TV hosts for Farm Aid. How did that come about?

A The [Nashville] Network just called me and asked me to do it. It was only a couple of days before it went on. And for not knowing what I was doing, I think it came off pretty good. I've done a lot of hosting for [the TV show] *Nashville Now*, and I enjoy doing that. I'd like to work on maybe having a talk show of some kind, maybe not even with the Nashville Network, but with one of the others. Or a variety show. I feel comfortable doing that.

Q Does that draw on some different part of you that singing does not?

A Well, I think it shows a little bit more of your personality, and that you like people, and get along well with all kinds of people. It shows another side of you.

Q Did you have any qualms about doing that, or were you confident you could do it?

A I had a lot of qualms. In fact, when they first asked me to host *Nashville Now*, I balked. And Ronnie just *made* me do it. And it turned out to be really good. But I thought, "God, I can't host a show and interview people and talk." (Chuckling) Because there's no script. There's nothin'. You're just *up* there. And it's live—it's not tape, so it was frightening.

Q What kind of material do you think you'll be cutting from here on out?

A I would like to go in and cut an album of old standards.

Q A la Linda Ronstadt?

A Yeah, I had an album like that out in '67, called *Reflections in Blue*. But with most of my big albums, all through the years of hits, half were standards, and half were new things. So I'd like to go back to that formula.

Q What was your mental state during the times you weren't on a label?

A The only thing that bothered me was not being able to create, not being able to be in the studio. The fact that I didn't have anything out there, or that people didn't have anything to buy, didn't bug me. It was being not able to do it for *me*, for my own needs of having to get that out.

Q So you went through a period of depression.

A Well, I don't think I was frustrated about not having a hit record, but I was certainly depressed about my career. I was performing, but I wasn't really happy with what I was doing. I wasn't being directed correctly. There's only so much an artist can do. They can't manage themselves. That's why they have managers and publicists and record companies. So not being with a record company was a little frustrating, yes. If MCA had not called, I probably would have retired. I would have quit. I had really thought about it, and that's the decision I had come to. Because I am not one to go out and hype myself. Not that I think that the past speaks for itself. I don't mean that. Record people today are interested in what you can do today—not what you have done. But I think in show business especially, if you are a proven commodity, that should count for something. And I just didn't feel the need or the desire to go out and convince somebody that I could still sing, or that I could sell records for them. If I had to do that, then I was beating my head against the wall. I mean, I could have gone on a lot of labels. But I would have been in the same predicament. So I had to just give it up.

Q Where do you think you fit into the history of popular music? People always talk about the legendary Brenda Lee.

A They do? I've never heard that. I don't know where I fit in. In England, of course, I was known as the first of the female rockers. In Japan, I'm known as an entirely different commodity. Here, I suppose, as Kitty Wells made it possible for girls to sing country music, I guess Connie Francis and I made it possible for girls to sing pop music. Now, there were people before us—I don't mean to say Connie and I started it—but as far as the craze of the fifties and sixties, when rock 'n' roll started, it was a different music than Patti Page and Judy Garland. It was a completely different mania. I never tried to copy anybody. I've always sung like I do now. And a lot of people have come up and said, "Oh, my daughter sings, and she's never listened to anybody but your records." And that's very flattering. So I hope that I've influenced other girls to make it in the business. But I really don't know where I would fit in, and I don't know if I would be an important fixture in the music business, when you compare me to Elvis and the Beatles, for example. In my mind, I never have been. Maybe I'm looking at it wrong. But if you take into account that it's been thirty years, and I'm here and I'm doin' good, I guess that means a whole lot.

Loretta Lynn

*I*n the last decade, Loretta Lynn has become something of an American folk heroine. A woman whose name is synonymous with rural sensibility for millions of country and non-country fans alike, she is one of the most important stylists—and arguably the most successful traditional female star—in the history of country music. She was also the first female performer to receive the Country Music Association's coveted Entertainer of the Year award, in 1972.

Lynn's story is well-known: born in 1935 and named after movie queen Loretta Young, whose fan magazine photos brightened up the walls of the family's drab Kentucky cabin, she was a wife at thirteen, the mother of four at seventeen ("just a baby with babies," as she puts it), and a grandmother at twenty-nine. She has achieved mass recognition that few other country stars have known, with her 1976 autobiography, *Coal Miner's Daughter*, appearing on *The New York Times* best-seller list for eight weeks, her life story serving as the subject of a major motion picture, and her face turning up on the covers of *Newsweek* and *TV Guide* before Madison Avenue—and Crisco —cottoned on to the idea that country music meant Big Bucks.

In her nearly twenty-five years in the business, Lynn's distinctively earthy music has gone through several cycles as the parameters of country music have changed. She arrived in Nashville at a time when "girl singers" were still something of a novelty—perceived as either a female version of an established male star or as a lesser act on a male singer's show (in her case, the Wilburn Brothers')—and originally sang traditional female country songs in the style of her idol, Kitty Wells. If Wells was not the first female country singer to be a star in her own right, Wells's successor, Patsy Cline, was, and after Cline's death in an airplane crash in 1963, Lynn picked up the torch. In many ways, she has served as a link between traditional and contemporary country thought, since such sharp-tongued songs as "The Pill" and "Don't Come Home A-Drinkin' (With Lovin' on Your Mind)" claim independence for the protagonist of the song, but not for country women in general, who still remain largely true to the confines of traditional female behavior. The irony, of course, is that for all of Lynn's sass and feistiness in song, in real life she appears to be almost completely subservient to her husband, Oliver "Mooney" Lynn. Mooney—from "moonshine"—is also known as Doolittle, a name that friends say explains itself.

While Lynn is probably still the most honest of the country queens, she is also the most tormented. The fruits of her labor notwithstanding—a palatial, antebellum home set on 5,000 acres in Hurricane Mills, Tennessee (a town she and her husband actually own), a nearby dude ranch, property in Mexico, Hawaii, and Nashville, several publishing companies and a talent management company, among other things—Lynn has paid a stiff price for fame. The last few years alone have brought recurrent death threats, more than a dozen hospital stays for exhaustion, bleeding ulcers, undiagnosed blackouts and seizures, and, in 1975, a near-fatal dose of "pills to put me to sleep." In one way or another, she continues to pay the price every time her bus rolls down the highway on an all-night ride to the next town and the next and the next. In 1984, when she again collapsed and was hospitalized for "exhaustion" in Illinois, she awoke to the news that her favorite son, thirty-four-year-old Jack Benny Lynn, had drowned trying to ford a river on horseback.

Probably no one could have been prepared for all that Loretta Lynn would go through, but at the outset of her career, she was naïve about nearly everything. Loretta Johnson, co-president of her fan club, tells the story that when Lynn's first record, "Honky Tonk Girl," was released in 1960, Johnson tapped out a fan letter—now acknowledged as the "first real fan letter"—on a Smith Corona with a script typeface. "Loretta was both alarmed and thrilled," Johnson later learned from Mooney. "Thrilled to get her first fan letter ever, and alarmed because Mooney told her she had to write back. Loretta balked. She said, 'I ain't doin' it! That girl can write so fancy—every letter is perfect! I ain't never gonna let her see my handwritin'!' "

Today, that naïveté is often the subject of Lynn's own humor, and she can be counted on to deliver a funny line as often as a good vocal performance. In 1977, appearing on national television to honor the newly elected President Jimmy Carter, Lynn cracked that she was especially glad to see the Georgian in the White House because it was about time the country got itself a President that didn't talk funny. Several years before, when Nixon was in office, Loretta called him "Richard" to Mrs. Nixon in public. When the wave of protest rolled in, Lynn retorted, "They called Jesus 'Jesus,' didn't they?" And more recently, she and Minnie Pearl were co-hosting TNN's *Nashville Now* when a couple in the audience announced they'd just gotten married. Minnie, talking with Loretta, turned the subject to their own wedding days. "The day was fine," Loretta quipped. "It was the night that got me!"

It is exactly such spirited insouciance that has endeared Loretta Lynn to the American public—that and the straightforward sincerity of her songs. But in the early '80s, after fifty-three Top 10 singles and sixteen number one records, Lynn became frustrated in her career, feeling that her record company, MCA, failed to promote her last five albums. Whether that was true, or whether Lynn was perceived as being too "old-fashioned" for modern country radio, her career had begun to wane as popular taste preferred the more urbanized and pop-influenced Janie Fricke, Barbara Mandrell, and Lynn's own baby sister, Crystal Gayle.

After a two-year hiatus from recording, Lynn came back in 1985, again on the MCA label, with *Just a Woman,* a record that tried both to keep her country and to update her image (i.e., get her records played on contemporary country radio). The brash and goofy formula arrangements that characterized so many of Lynn's earlier records were tempered into a softer backing, and her traditional program was balanced by several slow crossover ballads. But much of the spunk and imagination of old had been repressed—something akin to owning a Ferrari and never driving it over forty. No matter what trends come to dominate country music, however, there will probably always be a market for Loretta Lynn. Her voice is still quirky, graceful, and enormously expressive, an instrument worthy of national treasure status.

The following interview took place in June 1983 at Loretta Lynn Enterprises in Nashville. Lynn's friend and "spiritual adviser," Polly Thomas, says that Loretta is "indestructible," an "old, old soul [who] came up the hard way, life after life after life." Even if one's thinking doesn't run along the tabloid psychic route, in person there is something eerie about Lynn —an almost otherworldly presence, a strange mix of fragility and strength, and an unsettling, stream-of-consciousness way of recounting her life that takes her down dark and menacing paths of memory. It leaves her with a spooky look in her eyes, and it leaves her interviewer thinking of Ronee Blakley's sad, bewildered Barbara Jean in Robert Altman's *Nashville*.

Q You haven't recorded any duets with Conway Twitty in quite some time. Why is that?

A Well, the reason that Conway and I didn't record last year was because my contract with MCA wasn't quite fulfilled. We have so many albums a year to get out, two a year each, and then one with him and me. And I was lazy. I didn't get my second one out. I was so tired. I went to Hawaii and laid around during the wintertime, and then I came out and worked eighteen days and went back to Hawaii. After that, I was working so hard on the road I just didn't get everything together to get my second album out. So I just now got my MCA contract fulfilled. But Conway went ahead and signed with another record label [Warner Bros.], and in his contract, he's got it fixed where he can record with me, no matter what label I go with, or if I stay with MCA. I love him for things like that. I love Conway Twitty as a friend, as a singing partner, as a person. Conway Twitty is a good person inside and out. He's my friend.

Q Why do you think you two have been so successful?

A I think when me and Conway walk in to record we try to outdo each other. We each try to sing better than the other. We fight for it, you know. We've got it up there in the keys we want, and we have that spark.

Q You fight for it?

A Not in the sense of *fighting*, but we really fight for the feel we want. If I happen to think I'm singing a line and I'm not giving it my all, I'll stop and say, "Hey, let's do this over." And he does the same thing.

Q You inspire each other.

A We do. We help each other out. I really need him in the studio when I'm recording. And sometimes, maybe it would do him good if I was standing behind him, saying, "Hey, Conway, you can do it better." Because I know what Conway can do, and he knows what I can do. For a long time, you know, Conway didn't talk onstage. He never even said hello. And I said, "You know, Conway, that's not good." And he said, "But it's different." I said, "Yeah, it's good to be different if it's good. But that's bad." And I said, "Another thing, you didn't sign autographs in the rock field. I understand that. But you're going to have to sign autographs and be down with these fans like me when we're working." We worked seven straight years together. And now you couldn't fight him off. He's signing and selling his albums and he's right down there with the best of 'em. So I think we've been good for each other.

Q You seem to be genuinely fond of him.

A A lot of people thought, "Oh, God, there's somethin' goin' on. Gotta be somethin' goin' on," you know. They would think we were married. Some of them would think we was just living together. Some of them would think we were cheatin' together. But you don't mess in your own nest. You know? Especially when you're in business. And me and Conway, we're in business together. And even though I love him and he's my friend, I just never felt that.

Q How did you meet him?

A How did I meet Conway? Well, I was a big fan of his when he had "It's Only Make Believe." I was just a kid havin' my first four babies. Of course, I had four by the time I was seventeen. And Conway had "It's Only Make Believe" out, and I don't know where I got the poster, but I got a great big poster of his, and that's probably about the only paper that I had on the wall, you know. So I had it hangin' up, and I was always a Conway Twitty fan. And for a long time I didn't hear too much [too many records] from Conway, and I was really tore up about it. So one day I come into Nashville, and I always run in to see my producer, Owen Bradley, who I absolutely love dearly, and he's recorded me for twenty-one years. And he said, "Well, Loretta, would you like to meet Conway Twitty?" And I said, "You're *kiddin'* me!" He said, "No, I'm recordin' Conway." I said, "*You're* recordin' Conway?" And he said, "Yeah, *country.*" And I said, "Oh, you've got to be kiddin' me." And he walked out with Conway Twitty, and I almost passed out. That was my first time to meet Conway. And a couple years later we went to England together. There was a whole tour went over. And Conway and I would sit around in dressin' rooms and do a little harmony together. So, since we's on the same label, when we got back, why Conway said, "Hey, we really do good harmony together. Let's record." And, of course, MCA was for it, so we went in and cut our first session, our first duet ["After the Fire Is Gone"].

Do you remember? [She sings:] "Love is where you find it / When you have no love at home / Nothin' is cold as ashes / After the fire is gone." I had it just as high as you could get it. I sounded like Bill Monroe. And Conway did the harmony. We won the number one, and we got a Grammy award that year, and we took the [CMA] awards just about every year after that.

Q How did you find "Louisiana Woman, Mississippi Man"?

A My husband found that song for us. We walked in the office one day and he says, "Conway, you and Loretta come here. I think I found you a hit." A person by the name of Jim Owen, who plays Hank Williams sometimes, is a great artist in his own right. He wrote the song and brought it in for me and Conway. But Conway Twitty wrote so many great songs when he was just a teenager. I don't think he believed in himself as bein' such a great writer, but he wrote "Only Make Believe" when he was a teenager. Oh, he wrote some great songs. Like "As Soon As I Hang Up the Phone." Of course, I call it "The Telephone Song." That's my favorite song that Conway Twitty and I ever did.

Q What's happened to your songwriting? Why aren't you writing anymore?

A Oh, honey, I *am* writing now! I've just started back writing, because, you know, I had some problems quite a few years back. I signed four lifetime contracts, which MCA was one of 'em, a twenty-year contract. During that time the Loretta Lynn Western Stores started, and that was another deal I got into which I wish I'd never done. But there was a lot of things when I first come to Nashville that I didn't know you shouldn't do, and I did ever' one of 'em. So I'm back to writing, and whoever I record for, my next album will be Loretta Lynn songs. I'm writin', and I'm saying, "Hey, I'm back! Loretta's back and she's writin'." And I don't have to worry now about where I have to go to find a hit song, and I don't have to alter any songs, and I don't have to do this or that to fit Loretta. I'm writin' *for* her.

Q A lot of the songs you've recorded in the past couple of years haven't seemed up to your standards.

A Well, even at that, you know, I was tryin' to alter songs to sound like me and be like me, but with my workin' as hard as I was, I always tried to think that whoever was in the office was tryin' to find songs to fit me. But usually the only one who ever would come up with a Loretta Lynn song was Owen Bradley. The rest of the people at MCA hoped I would cross over and go pop or rock, or whatever. But a singer that can *sing* can do any of it, as far as I'm concerned. But there's always one type of song that they do best. And if I had to, I could probably stand up with the best of 'em and do the rest. But I think I do country best, and I was really kind of tore between the record company and everything else in the last five years because of the change in the music and everything. But as I say, I'm startin' to write again so . . .

Q You're also working on a couple of new books, I understand.

A Well, there's a story behind every song that I've written, and I'm in the process of putting that on paper right now and doing a book for everyone to see. And some of the stories I think will probably surprise some people. Like "Wings upon Your Horns." That was the first one that everybody said, "Uh-oh! What's goin' on?" Right at the time I wrote that, I wrote one called "One of These Days I'm Gonna Get Even, Steven" that was more or less a threatening song. And when it comes down to somethin' like that, you go to thinkin', "What if I *did* do this?" And that's how the song was written. But when I write a song, I have to be alone. I'm another person. I live this person until I have the song written. If it's a honky-tonk girl, I put myself into becoming a honky-tonk girl. If anybody walked into that room when I was writin', they may not even recognize me, 'cause I take on another look.

Q What do you look like?

A I have no idea. My husband gets really upset when he walks in and finds me writin' a song. He knows that I'm so deep into it that it's not me, and he tries to break my concentration and stop me. But this is the only way I can write. And I don't write around him any more than I have to.

Q You and Doolittle appeared on the *Music City News Awards* show, and he acted out the main character in your song "Lyin', Cheatin', Woman-Chasin', Honky-Tonkin', Whiskey-Drinkin' You." How does he feel about things like that, considering his fondness for several of those pastimes in real life?

A Oh, he's the biggest ham in the world! He lives for that kind of stuff! He loves to go out onstage, and he stays at the dude ranch a lot and signs autographs down there. I tried to get him to go out to the Crisco booth at Fan Fair [the annual convention where the fans meet and mingle with the stars], but no, he wouldn't do that. I said, "Hey, if you wanna be famous, you're gonna have to work for it. That's what you always told me." And he said, "Well, I'm not gonna do *that* part of it." But he likes to ham it up.

Q You're one of the few performers who always show up for Fan Fair. Why is it important to you?

A Honey, I *started* Fan Fair! Did you not know that? I started it. Took four years for Nashville to get off their ass. [She covers her mouth, embarrassed, then laughs.] But I'm not kiddin' you. I go around beggin' artists to be on my IFCO [International Fan Club Organization] dinner. I mean, it was my idea to separate the fans from the disc jockeys, 'cause durin' the disc jockey convention we couldn't get to the DJs for the fans. So I said, "Let's have that in June, and then have the disc jockey convention in October." And for five years I worked with it. Then I got so busy that I called my fan club presidents and says, "Take it. I can't do it any longer." You know, I will be with it and I will be there every year I can. I've only missed it once, and I had walking pneumonia and they threw me in the hospital. That was about four years ago. Didn't even know it. But you know, it's got kinda—I don't want to call any names, but there's one singer who charges her fans ten dollars a ticket to go in and eat breakfast with her. And I think there was 16,000 that come to that breakfast, at ten dollars a ticket. Count it up, baby. I feed all my representatives every year, and it costs 'em nothin'. And if they don't have the money to fly in, I fly 'em in. 'Cause they work for me all year long.

Q Rumor has it that you're writing a sequel to your autobiography.

A I haven't started it, because I have so many things that I need to get out of the way. You know, the life of any artist in music is five years. Well, I've been here twenty years. As Roy Acuff says, "I've seen 'em come and go, but I've never seen nobody come and stay like you have!" (Laughter) Well, I feel this way—I have just begun. I am pouring a brand-new foundation, and I will be layin' the first brick soon. I'm really back into writin' now, and I'm gettin' my contract for recordin' straightened out. I'm doin' a lot of new things. I'm gonna be writin' my next story book, my autobiography, because there was so many things that was so much better. You know, how can you put it in a 200-page book? And how can you tell your life story when you haven't even lived? They've been wantin' to write my life story ever since I've been in Nashville. Well, I wasn't old enough to have lived, even if I hadn't been married, you know. So I felt, "What's different about me than anybody else?" Well, there is so many different things that I want to tell the people that was much more important than what was in the book. And I'll have George Vecsey [the co-writer of Lynn's autobiography, *Coal Miner's Daughter*] do the book, because we started out together, you know. That's just the way I am. I would never leave him out. No way.

Q Give me an episode from it.

A Well, there was so many things that happened when I was a little girl, you know. Like my mother. She was the one that taught me more than anybody. And when Jimmy Carter was President, he called and said,

"Loretta, we want you to come up here. Five famous people will come in and bring the teacher that has taught 'em the most." This was from all over the world. And I said, "To tell you the truth, there *was* no teacher." Because where I went to school was in a little one-room schoolhouse, and when I was in about the third or fourth grade, I started helping the teacher and doin' my own report cards and things. Some of the kids would be there because of the government. Before their family would get a check, the kids had to go to school. And they would be like fourteen or fifteen years old and in the first grade. And they would whip the teacher. The teachers would be there maybe a month or two, and the big ol' boys would whip 'em, and they would leave. We'd have three or four teachers a year. I never did get that close to any teacher, even though I built the fires of a mornin', and I cleaned the schoolhouse at night. I swept the schoolhouse, put the benches and tables in place, and erased the blackboard. And I was there and got the kindling and the coal, you know, started the fires an hour before the teacher would come in. She give me a dollar a month. And that was big money. That was almost unheard of in Butcher Holler. I thought that was something else, and I worked really hard for it. So I told President Carter I couldn't bring a teacher. And he said, "Why?" I said, "Well, my mommy was what taught me most." And he said, "Well, there's always got to be a first. Bring her." That was the biggest thrill that my mother ever had. She had been sick, but I thought she had one lung left, you know. They had taken one lung. So I thought the way the doctors talked, she had one lung and it was scarred, but the more she worked with it, the stouter the lung would get. I didn't know that she just had a twenty percent lung. And I guess I'm glad that I didn't know. But if I would have known I wouldn't have said, "Mommy, come on! I want to take you into this room!" When I took her to the White House, she couldn't walk but just a few feet, and then she'd have to sit down. I'd say, "Come on, Mommy! You'll never get to come back!" And I would get upset. But when I found this out when she died, it liked to killed me. It still hangs with me today. If I start thinkin' about it, I try to get off the subject. But my mommy went, and my mommy was very strong. She was the rock of the family. And by the way, I did write a song not long ago called "When the Rock Begin [sic] to Crumble," and that's about my mommy. And when I brought her out onstage, that's the first time I ever seen my mommy cry, except when Daddy passed away.

Q I always hear you talk about your father, but not that much about your mother.

A Well, you know, the third song I ever wrote was about my mommy, "My Angel Mother," on Zero Records. I did a whole album with Zero, and, of course, MCA bought it. They didn't make anything off it, but they bought the album and everybody was able to get it for three ninety-eight or somethin'. It was like a jam session. But "My Angel Mother" was on there, 'cause I wrote ten songs right in a row. I'd already recorded "Honky Tonk Girl" and "Whispering Seas," so I had ten more to do. So I got busy and wrote.

Q You were a close friend of Patsy Cline. What kind of memories do you have of her?

A Oh, I have lots of favorite memories of Patsy Cline. She was really the only close girlfriend that I had when I come to Nashville. There was other girls in Nashville, but we wasn't close. Patsy kind of took me under her wing. The night before Patsy died, her and I was goin' at nine o'clock the next mornin' and shop. And she was gonna buy me somethin' new for my front room. I had nothin' in my front room, and she had bought me curtains and had them hung and ever'thing before I got in. I was in Nashville at Sure Fire Music lookin' for songs. That's who I wrote for, you know. And she called me and said, "I'm at your home and I need to go over some things with you." So I go home and all the curtains are hangin'.

Q What else do you remember about her?

A Oh, we were around the same age, you know, but she was like a big sister, even though she'd been in the business a long time and had worked so hard and been around, and I'd been home raisin' babies. I'd only been singin' six months when I come to Nashville, when I recorded this little ol' record of "Honky Tonk Girl." Let's face it. My sister Peggy Sue and Jay Lee, my brother, was singin' way before I was. My sister Crystal was singin' from the time she was a little tiny girl. I had her on the road with me when I started, you know. I'd take her with me ever' summer and anytime that I could. All three of 'em. And the memories that I have of Patsy are some like this. Some of 'em are really funny, and I have to think of the funny things. Patsy got her a blond wig one time and she called me. This was way before wigs was in, but Patsy was twenty years ahead of her time. On ever'thing. There's never been nobody before her or after her sing as great as Patsy Cline. Of course, I'm a fan. So she called me and she said, "Come over, ol' gal!" Says, "Have supper with us." And gee, I was glad to hear this, 'cause at the time, we were havin' a time eatin' anyway. You know, my husband had gotten a job for, I think, a dollar ten an hour. And that's pretty rough when you got four kids. And the only place we could find to rent was a place for a hundred dollars a month. And it was only a two-bedroom, and it was rough! So over we went. And she just had her new home built. She had her rec room down in, well, kind of like in the basement. And there was two big glass slidin' doors there, you know. *Beautiful* home. And instead of goin' to the glass slidin' doors, I had went to the front door and down the stairs. And there sat this blond girl. She was embroiderin' a table-cloth. And I was always so bashful and timid, you know, so I didn't look at her very good. So I walked into the rec room, and Charlie Dick, her husband, was behind the bar. And I said, "Where's Patsy?" He kind of grinned and looked over at the blond, and I looked back over at the blond and she just kept embroiderin'. And finally she looked up at me and grinned, and I said, "No! What did you do? Get your hair dyed?" That was so funny! We had a big laugh about that. And we had many laughs together. Ever' time Charlie and Patsy'd have a fight, there would always be somethin' that we would laugh about, you know, that they would fight over. They'd always be quarrelin' over somethin' one minute and then lovin' the next.

Q Her death must have been difficult for you.

A Oh, my gosh, yes. Now you've got me rememberin' all kinds of things. Patsy dearly loved [to eat] rabbit. And when we first come to Nashville my husband hunted a lot. In fact, if we didn't eat baloney, it was rabbit. So she would come to my house to eat rabbit. And just Thursday before she was killed, I had fried three rabbits. This was when she had the curtains hung for me, and she went up into the kitchen and she just eat rabbit, eat rabbit, eat rabbit. I said, "Well, now, I have some baloney." And she said, "The kind of meat I love to eat next is baloney." And I said, "Well, looks like we was kind of raised the same way, ain't we, Patsy?" 'Cause she had it rough, too, you know. But we had a lot of laughs. And she'd always tell me how to dress. When I first come to Nashville, I made my own clothes, and I didn't have a lot of money to buy material. So I would make the little fittin' dresses and hang fringe on 'em. I had two dresses. And I always had two shows a day. If it was at night, like in a tavern, I'd have four half-hour shows. So I would take the fringe off one dress after I'd do my first show and sew it on the other. I kept doin' that backwards and forwards. And Patsy give me some clothes and some long danglin' earrings. And I don't know what I would have done without Patsy. But she would say, "Now, Loretta, don't dress in a dress that's too tight. Always get 'em where it just leaves a little bit to the man's imagination." You know, some of the things that I was learnin' at that age I should have learned at fifteen or sixteen. So I guess I was a late bloomer. I thought some of the things was so funny at the time.

Q Was it hard for you to record your tribute album *[I Remember Patsy]* since you were such good friends?

A That was the hardest thing I ever did. I had never done a Patsy Cline song 'til I did that album. I would do shows, you know, and people would holler, "Do a Patsy Cline song! Do 'Crazy'!" And my favorite song that Patsy ever done was "She's Got You." The first time I heard the song, I was down on my knees waxin' the floor. It was on WENO, the station in Madison, Tennessee, where I lived, and the disc jockey said, "That's the new Patsy Cline record, 'She's Got You.'" And I knew it was a smash. But I never sang her songs. I just could not sing 'em. And when somebody'd holler for a song that Patsy had sang and wanted me to do it, it would kind of mess up my whole night, you know. Anyway, when we did *I Remember Patsy*, I started tryin', and the first song I did was "I Fall to Pieces." It took me the whole session to do. I *fell* to pieces. (Laughter) And we didn't do it like Patsy had done it. Owen [Bradley] put it in a waltz so it would sound different than when Patsy sang it. And I couldn't hear the pitch. I was either above the pitch or below it. But we left it like it was. That was the only one that I sang [live] with the music. The rest of 'em they put the track down. And the funny thing was, all the musicians that played on Patsy's sessions was there, except the bass player. He died with a heart attack. But when the musicians was there, I went through the whole session and couldn't sing. So poor ol' Owen said, "Loretta, honey, don't worry about it. Come back and we'll do it some other time." I was in tears. But as I started to leave, I felt that Patsy was around. She said, "I'm ashamed of you! Try it one more time." I said, "Owen, turn everything back on. Let's try it one more time." I went to the microphone, and I went through the songs one right after another. I closed my eyes and I could see Patsy grinnin' and sayin', "You can do it! I'm goin' to be disappointed if you don't do this." And I know a lot of people think this is crazy, but it's not crazy. In my own mind I was seein' her. This is what she would have said to me if she'da been alive. She'd say, "I'm ashamed of you." So I went through that whole album then, the next nine songs. I went flat on "She's Got You," right on the last couple of notes. Maybe no one else noticed it, but I did. On a few of the others maybe, too. But anyway, I've always felt that it would be wrong if I didn't do her songs when I walk out onstage. I never go out there without doin' a medley of her songs, or "She's Got You" or "Crazy."

Q Did you actually hear her voice saying those words?

A No, I just seen her. In my own mind I seen her standing there lookin' at me, you know. And smiling as I was doin' 'em one right after the other. But at first, it was "I'm ashamed of ye! What's wrong with you? You can do it!" One other time, I was in Vegas, and I got "Vegas throat," as they call it. And I just knew I'd never get through her slow medley. I said to the little band director, "I'll never make Patsy's medley tonight, but I'm gonna go out and do my best." And when I started "I Fall to Pieces," I felt someone pat me on the arm. I knew immediately who it was. It didn't make me nervous, and it didn't bother me at all. I knew what it was. I went through the whole medley, and I didn't have any problem at all. She was there to help me.

Q Do you have the sense that Patsy wanted you to carry on for her?

A Definitely. I always feel if someone has passed away and someone has anything to say about 'em and it's not really good, they shouldn't say anything. And I'm always there to defend her. Because a lot of people thought that she was a drunk and all this, and it's not true. I've never seen Patsy Cline drunk in my life. I have seen Patsy take a *drink*. But I have never seen her drunk. I've never seen her do a lot of things that people have said. Patsy at heart was a great person.

Q We got an interesting profile of her in *Coal Miner's Daughter*. What was your first reaction when you saw the movie?

A I had to pinch myself and tell myself it wasn't me up there, 'cause I thought it was.

Q So everything was fairly realistic?

A Oh, yeah. It really was. I didn't watch the filmin', though. That was their baby, and I let 'em rock it.

Q Was there anything in there you'd rather they left out?

A Not really. If there hadda been, it wouldn't have been in the book. If it's in the book, it's true, and it's not private anymore. So I wouldn't change a thing in the movie. Except I woulda made it longer.

Q You managed to get Ernest Tubb in there. What has he meant to your career?

A I imagine that Ernest Tubb has done more for me in country music than anybody. He was the first one that got me on the Grand Ole Opry. The Wilburn Brothers helped me, of course, but Ernest Tubb is special. Very special. I would have to say he means more to me in country music than any other artist. Because when I was a little girl in the hills of Kentucky, I would listen to the Grand Ole Opry. That's the one program we got to listen to Daddy listened to the news. But we'd get to listen to the Grand Ole Opry on Saturday night. And Ernest Tubb was my favorite. I never,

ever dreamed that I would ever see Ernest Tubb. That dream was too big for me, let alone *record* with him. [They did five singles and three albums in the '60s.] You know, "It's Been So Long Darlin' " and "Rainbow at Midnight"—I would sit and cry when I'd listen to him when I was a little girl. And then to grow up and record with him and stand beside of him . . . Ever' time I stood beside of Ernest Tubb—today, even—there is a special feeling that I get that I have never got when I've stood by any other artist. Ernest Tubb has done more—he's had the Ernest Tubb Record Shop and the Midnight Jamboree on [WSM's] 50,000-watt radio for years and years. It comes on after the Grand Ole Opry, you know. And he's done this for ever' artist that's ever hit Nashville, many, many years before they ever got to the Grand Ole Opry. Sometimes I wonder if some of 'em still remember this. [Tubb died a year after this interview, in September 1984.]

Q Tubb was certainly a great influence, then, but Kitty Wells must have been, too.

A Well, Kitty Wells to me is one of the greatest ladies in country music. I don't think that anybody could argue with me about that. I always tried to sing like Kitty Wells when I first started singin'. My husband got me this first job in a little tavern, Bill's Tavern, and I had just started singin' and ever'thing was Kitty Wells songs. "[It Wasn't God Who Made] Honky Tonk Angel[s]" and "Searching," and all the stuff that she did. And one old drunk staggered up to the stage one night just before I started recordin'. I'd only been singin' six months, like I said, before I recorded. And he said [she imitates a drunk cowboy], "Why don't you sing somethin' else?" He said, "There's already one Kitty Wells and there ain't ever gonna be another'un. If you're ever gonna be anything, you better change your tune." (Laughter) From that day on, I tried to sing other people's songs, especially men. You know, all the guy songs, so it would sound different. And I think it helped. And then I tried to get away from the Kitty Wells style as much as I could. But when I come to Nashville, I still had a lot of Kitty Wells in me. You could hear it a long, long time after I come to Nashville, if you listened to my first three or four albums.

Q I read that you went home to Kentucky one time and saw your father sitting on the front porch, long after he'd died. How do you feel when you go back there now?

A Oh, there's a special feelin' that I get. My daddy had a coal bank. Most people who are coal miners know what I'm talkin' about. They had a little coal bank for their own personal use, and that's where they got their coal for the winter. They didn't have to buy it. And most of the time,

I'd tag after Daddy. Mommy always said, "You should have been the boy, and Junior should have been the girl." (Laughter) Junior is the oldest, and Junior would do anything to stay home from school—wash dishes or anything. And I wouldn't. I wanted to go to school. I wanted to be out. I wanted to *go.* But I would tag after Daddy when he was digging the coal. So when I go back home now, there's such a lonesome feeling. It's just like the end of [the song] "Coal Miner's Daughter." You know, "Nothin' lives here anymore / Except the memories of a coal miner's daughter." I feel that Daddy's happy when I'm there. Daddy loved Kentucky and he said way before he died, "I never even want to *die* in Indiana." Daddy *did* die in Indiana, but we took him home to Kentucky to be buried. I was at the gravesite the other day. And I took silk flowers that stood way up high, about three or four feet high. Mommy's was red roses and little tiny white flowers. And Daddy, of course, was color blind. The only color that he would ever buy was yellow, no matter what color Mommy sent him after. So Daddy's flowers was yellow. My brother Herman had cleaned the graveyard off, and it's way back on the hill. There's quite a few buried up there, all related to me. My grandpa, grandma, great-grandma, great-grandfather, and all the cousins. I walked all around the graveyard and looked at the graves and the names and everything. But then I kind of waited, and walked away from the graveyard. And then I went back and I looked at Mommy and Daddy and I said, "I miss you more all the time." And I left.

Q Time hasn't helped?

A Well, no one had ever passed away that was that close to me 'til Daddy, and I almost lost my mind for six months. I went to doctors one right after another. I knew he was dead, you know. I was three thousand miles away. But I knew he was dead before we got the telephone call. One doctor said, "Loretta, the only thing that I can say is you were sleeping at five o'clock in the mornin', and it was eight where your daddy was." But he had gone to work. And he had just hung up his coat when he had a stroke. He had high blood pressure, and the black lung and all. But he was working, and this was the only place Daddy could work without havin' to take an examination. And when he fell, he knew he was dying, and he knew I couldn't make it back to see him. And since I was sleepin', my mind was clear, you know, and we communicated. I knew the color of his coffin, the color of his suit. I woke up screamin' and cryin' and told my husband what I'd just dreamed, and he said, "Oh, just go on back to sleep. When you dream of a death, it's a sign of a marriage." And I said, "Oh, maybe that's it. My sister Peggy is gettin' married." I wanted to believe this so much that I wiped it completely out of my mind. But I went back to sleep and had this same dream, only there was more added to the dream that was true. I thought I was goin' around the coffin wringin' my hands and cryin' and lookin' down into Daddy's face. And [in the dream] my husband said, "You know what caused your old man to die?" And I said, "No, what?" And he said, "He was steppin' out on your mama with a little eighteen-year-old girl, and it was too much for him and he died." This was the only thing that wasn't true. And I thought I looked down at Daddy's face and said, "Well, I should be mad at you for this. But I can't be. You're dead. You're gone." And I started cryin' and wringin' my hands. It took us three days to drive to Kentucky, and we got there just in time for the funeral. My sister Brenda, or Crystal [Crystal Gayle's real name is Brenda Gail Webb], was standin' around grinnin' and wringin' her hands. And Mommy had quite a time with Crystal after that. She was the baby and she just didn't understand what was goin' on. And she don't remember that much. I've talked to her about it, you know, and I think she must have wiped everything out of her mind. She said, "I remember when Daddy bought me some Oreo cookies, but that's just about all I remember." But I know there would have been a lot more that she would have remembered, 'cause Mommy had to take her to doctors, she had such bad nerves about it.

Q You read Johnny Carson's palm one time and told him he was headed for trouble.

A I certainly did. Well, I seen things in his hand, like divorce, and things that I would not say on the air. But I said, "Johnny, I'll tell you more after the show." Well, Ed [McMahon] got with me after the show in the dressin' room and I was with him one hour. Johnny left before I could talk to him. But I seen the divorce in his hand. And I told him he was gonna have problems with his health and with his personal life. I know there was things I said that upset Johnny, 'cause that kind of thing bothers him. So I won't read anybody's palm now unless they want me to, 'cause you never know when you're saying somethin' that bothers 'em.

Q How old were you when you discovered you had this talent?

A I think probably when Doo took me to Washington state when I was fourteen years old. I was seven months pregnant when I went away to Washington, and I didn't even know the world was that big. I cried ever' day. I was homesick for Mommy and Daddy and the kids, you know. I was a little girl, really. And I realized that I had this thing. I would know when Mommy was expecting a letter from me. I would know when to write her, and I would know when she was going to write me. It started like that. We have a home in Mexico, and about six years ago, I would raise up about three o'clock in the mornin' and say, "Mommy?" Because I would hear Mommy say, "Loretty?" I'd be sleepin'. Three o'clock in the mornin'! And I would raise up and say, "Mommy?" This happened three mornings in a row. And I figured that Doo thought I was goin' crazy. So the third mornin' I got up, 'cause I knew Mommy was tryin' to get ahold of me, and I thought I'd better call to find out what she was tryin' to say. And all mornin' the phone was busy. She was tryin' to get ahold of me, and I was tryin' to get ahold of her. So finally I got through. And when Mommy said hello, I said, "Why don't you want me to go to Mexico?" I knew what the connection was as soon as I heard her voice. She said, "Loretty, don't go to Mexico. If you do, you won't come back." I said, "Why don't you think I'll come back?" She said, "Because for three nights and mornings, I've seen a boat and a search party, and they're lookin' for you and they don't find ye. Don't go!" Well, I knew if I told my husband, he'd make me go, 'cause he thinks this stuff is crazy. I'd already started packin', and I knew the twins love Mexico and they really wanted to go, so I didn't know what to tell 'em. So I started sayin', "Honey, I've been gettin' calls from Owen [Bradley] and I've got to record. They want a single out. They've got to have one, and there's nothin' in the can." I really had to start thinkin' up stuff that I had to stay in Nashville for. And after the winter was over, we were on the way in to Nashville from the ranch, and I said, "Honey, you know why I didn't go to Mexico?" He said, "I know there was some reason and you're not tellin' me, and it wasn't to stay to record." I said, "You know when I would raise up in the middle of the night and say, 'Mommy'? Well, Mommy was tryin' to get ahold of me. She said she felt that I wouldn't come back, that I had fallen overboard or somethin'." He said, "If I'da known that, I would have made you went." I said, "I knew that. That's why I didn't tell you."

Q You mentioned Washington state. Was it last summer when the Whatcom County Fair had you back?

A Oh, that was last fall. I went back to Washington to the little county fair where I won all my blue ribbons for my canning, and where I won a talent contest for singing "Since You've Gone," that Ferlin Husky had out. That's when I started singin' all guys' songs, you know. Just before I come to Nashville.

Q Did you enjoy going back?

A It was great! They had so many people they tore the fair down. They may never bring me back again, they had so many people! It was somethin' else. You couldn't believe how it was unless you seen it. There was no room for nobody. Even on the little streets of the town, Lynden, Washington. They had 'em parked for two miles out of town. But it was great to go back. They'd painted a banner, you know, "Our Whatcom County Girl." It just made me feel so good that they love me so much. And remembered me, because that was where I spent thirteen years of my life, from fourteen 'til I started singin'. And at that time, that's when your mind is really developin'. I remember it so much, you know.

Q What projects are you planning for the future?

A Well, I had twelve verses of "Coal Miner's Daughter." That was one of the hardest things I've ever done in my life! It didn't take me long to write it, though. It don't take long when you sit down and just write about what you've done and how you've lived. I could write thirty more verses. But the hard part was when Owen Bradley said, "Loretta, we've already had one 'El Paso.' We don't need another one." That was almost five minutes, I think. He said, "We can't do this. It's a whole album all in its own." I had to sit down and take out six verses. One day I'm gonna rerecord "Coal Miner's Daughter" and put the verses back in that I had to take out. And that will probably be when I have written the second book. There'll be a second movie, too, but nobody knows about that yet.

Q What part of that song means the most to you?

A I think my favorite part is the verse about Mommy readin' the Bible at night, waitin' for Daddy to come in. Me as small as I was, I didn't know why she was readin' and stayin' awake with an ol' coal-oil lamp burnin'. Now I know that she was worried that he *wouldn't* come in. That's one of my favorite parts of "Coal Miner's Daughter." And the other part I think about is, we got one pair of shoes a year, and we saved 'em for winter. And sometimes they didn't last all winter, and I would have to put pasteboard in the bottom of my shoes where I'd worn a big ol' hole. I remember sittin' down beside the road and pullin' my shoes off and holdin' my feet, they were so cold. And sometimes Daddy would come along and take me back home instead of sending me on to school. But I'd better not tell any more, 'cause that's for the second book.

Q But after something of a slump, you feel as if your career is about to be rejuvenated?

A Well, with all the new things that's comin', I feel like I've just begin. Just begin! I'm just *startin'!* And I, well, let's just say Loretta is *here.* And pretty soon, everybody'll know it.

Q A few years ago, you told Roy Blount, Jr., "I think I'm one of the unhappiest people in the world. Never hardly a night goes by on the road when I'm in the back of the bus, and through playing solitaire, that I don't cry. 'Bout half the time I cry myself to sleep." Do you still do that?

A It's funny you'd ask about that, 'cause I got up at daylight this mornin'. And one of the songs that I'm puttin' in my new songbook is "I Wanna Be Free." I'm writin' the story to the song, lettin' everybody know how it was written. Of course, when someone listens to a cheatin' song, they think, "She's cheatin'," you know. But this song come about because I had been in the bus so long. I've had so many death threats that I don't get out of the bus that much. If I get out to eat, I'm feelin' great. I feel like signin' autographs when I go into the truck stops. And my meal is cold before I . . . you know, I don't get to eat when I go in, and I expect it. But ninety percent of the time we're runnin' late, so the bus driver or my road manager brings my meals to the bus. And then we have to have security with so many threats on my life. So I got to where I just stay in the bus. I keep my curtains pulled in the back of the bus and I read. Or I write. And when I wrote "I Wanna Be Free," I got so lonely. It was one of those dreary days, and I was depressed. I was comin' home, and we'd just hit the state of Tennessee. It was cloudy, gettin' fall, just turnin' fall, and I opened the curtains and looked out. Even the leaves were fallin' off the trees, you know. And I was down and I started the song. [She sings:] "Well, I look out the window and what do I see? / The breeze is a-blowin' the leaves from the trees / Everything is free / —everything but me . . ." (Pause) I don't like fall. I like it when the trees is all turnin', but when the leaves is startin' to fall and they're dyin', I don't like it. My part of the year is spring.

Q You've amassed an incredible personal fortune, and you're known all over the world. But with everything you've gone through, has it been worth it?

A Well, right now, let's put it this way. I've missed so much not bein' home with my kids. But I have gained so much by makin' so many friends, and all my fans love me and I love them. So I have gained an awful lot. I guess you'd have to say it all kinda evens out.

Reba McEntire

*I*n October 1984, Reba McEntire came bustling out of the makeup room backstage at the Country Music Association awards, mad as a wet hen. Standing before a mirror, she fished in her purse until she found a Kleenex, and then began scrubbing furiously at her lips.

"They're always trying to give me an upper lip," she said heatedly. "I ain't never *had* an upper lip, and I ain't *gonna* have one."

Later on that night, McEntire, a genuine Oklahoma cowgirl who grew up ropin', ridin', and rodeoin', was named Female Vocalist of the Year—an award she would go on to win four consecutive times, making CMA history and confirming her place as one of the foremost women singers in all of country music.

In 1986, however, when she captured both the Female Vocalist of the Year award and the Entertainer of the Year prize, McEntire was honored probably as much for her grit and personal fortitude as she was for her tradition-based music. In an era when newscasters go to school to lose any trace of regionality, and Crystal Gayle sounds more like the Upper East Side of New York than her native Wabash, Indiana, McEntire stretches her words out in hard Okie style, proud of who she is and where she comes from.

Contrary to how it might appear, McEntire's success hardly came overnight. Her first album, *Reba McEntire*, on Mercury, appeared in 1976, with her first Top 10 hit, "(You Lift Me) Up to Heaven," loping along two LPs later. Finally, she managed a handful of respectable semi-hits, but McEntire didn't score a number one until 1983, with "I Can't Even Get the Blues," followed quickly by "You're the First Time I've Thought About Leaving." Then, with a record label change, it was almost two years before her next number one song, "How Blue," from her MCA album *My Kind of Country*.

One reason it took so long between hits was because radio listeners weren't entirely sure who Reba McEntire was. From the day she landed in Nashville in the mid-'70s, record company executives did their best to obscure McEntire's natural assets. Born in Chockie, Oklahoma, the daughter of a world champion steer roper, she had an accent thick as buttermilk, a desire to sing hard-core "kicker" country music, and an open, friendly, "I never met a stranger" face and personality. Naturally, in line with the Nashville mogul way of thinking, McEntire was originally passed off as a city sophisticate.

Her early album jacket photos showed the grown-up tomboy in silk, lace, and sequined evening gowns, with her hair piled up and her face fit for a Max Factor cosmetics ad. Her music, meanwhile, never seemed to focus on any particular style, making immediate identification of a McEntire record almost impossible.

For a long time, McEntire, now thirty-four, went along with it all. She was, by her own admission, green as gooseberries when she first came to Nashville at the suggestion of veteran country performer Red Steagall. But after her sweetly orchestrated, middle-of-the-road album *Just a Little Love*, McEntire put her cowboy-booted foot down.

No more gussied-up records, she said, and no more dressing up, period, unless it felt natural. The gowns were replaced by jeans, prairie skirts, and the silver belt buckle she got for singing the national anthem at the National Rodeo Finals in Oklahoma City. And the music, beginning with her *My Kind of Country* album, was branch-water pure, yielding her fourth number one single, the emotional "Somebody Should Leave." Shortly thereafter, McEntire found herself winning the respect of her peers and coming in fourth in the country category of *Rolling Stone* magazine's critics' poll.

If McEntire's reputation was sealed with her next album, *Have I Got a*

Deal for You, it was compounded with *What Am I Gonna Do About You.* But her masterwork is undoubtedly her 1986 release, *Whoever's in New England,* in which she revives the woman-to-woman song genre that Kitty Wells established and Tammy Wynette made famous in the late '60s —a woman singing from a woman's point of view to other women, usually about the men in their lives. Here, more than in any other showcase of her career, McEntire proves that she is almost without peer in infusing a song with convincing heartache. But even as she earned her place alongside Wells and Wynette, she also defined herself as a latter-day Loretta Lynn, striking the blow for the independent woman while upholding the traditional values of the past.

That image was to change somewhat in 1988, when McEntire recorded *Reba,* a slow-tempoed, pristinely produced, and largely forgettable collection of contemporary ballads and jazz-pop standards. A waste of an exhilarating voice, the album may also be a disturbing harbinger of the fate of the traditionalist movement.

Early in 1985, McEntire was finishing up her *Have I Got a Deal for You* album when she took time out to talk at her manager's office in Nashville. Since then, she has divorced her husband of eleven years, Charlie Battles.

Q At the time we're talking, "How Blue" has just become another number one record for you. In a lot of ways, it's representative of the kind of music you do as a whole. It has an old-fashioned sound to it, but it's not an old song, is it?

A No it's brand-new. John Moffatt wrote it. I don't know how long he's had it, but it's not an old tune that anybody else has ever recorded before. And that's the kind of stuff I'm looking for. Like on the *My Kind of Country* album, there were six out of ten songs that were old songs, you know, past hits from way back. Some of them were just album cuts that I've always enjoyed. But of the four that were new, "How Blue" was one of them.

Q Why are you so adamant about sticking to hard-core country and not aiming for crossover hits?

A Well, because I have tried the contemporary-type songs, and it's not Reba McEntire. It's just not honest, and I'm an honest person. I'm very blunt, very frank, and when I'm doing country music, I feel like I'm being honest to those people out there. When I say I don't want anything but a fiddle, instead of a violin, on my records, that's exactly how I want it. I'm more comfortable. I don't like a lot of backup singers. If they want any backup singers, I want me and some of my guys who travel with me on the road. That's what I like so much about [producer] Jimmy Bowen. He wants your records to be almost like your stage show. He sets it up so that when you're listening to it and facing the speakers at home, the steel's on the left, the piano's on the right, just like on my stage show. And that's why we're trying to create our stage show to be more like our records, and our records more like our stage show. So when the people leave my stage show and go home and put on my records, it's not such a big difference. Like, "*That* was the girl I just got through hearin'." It's a lot better. They can get it all together.

Q What about your *Just a Little Love* album? There were a lot of strings on there.

A Yeah, a *lot* of strings. *Just a Little Love* was a real contemporary album for me. My most contemporary, I would say. It was an experiment. Well, me and [producer] Norro Wilson had just met for that project, and if me and Norro had gone back again, it would have been a lot different. We probably would have done an about-face, and gone strictly hard-core country. But since he was with RCA and I was with MCA, there was a little conflict there, and it was better just to stay in-house, or strictly independent. So that was that. Norro is a super person, and a great friend of mine, but business things like that get in the way.

Q When you first got with [producer] Harold Shedd to talk about your *My Kind of Country* album, what did you tell him you wanted?

A Straight-ahead country, and no strings. And that's what came out. It's kind of up-to-date, traditional country, but it's not old-fashioned. Or at least that's the way I describe it.

Q Is this a vein you think you'll settle in?

A Well, I'm not gonna say I'll be this way for the next forty-five years, but it's something that I'm real comfortable with. It's just me. I only want to do what I'm real comfortable with right now.

Q A lot of people were moved by your acceptance speech at the CMA, specifically by your reference to your mother. You said that on your first trip to Nashville, your mother, who had wanted to be a singer herself, told you, "I'm living my life through you." Then you held up the award and said, "This is for me and Mama." Are you pursuing this career mainly for her, for yourself, or both?

A Oh, it's a combination of both. When I have temper tantrums and want to quit, or get mad about something in the business, Charlie [her former

husband, Charlie Battles, three-time World Steer Wrestling Champion]
says, "Well, okay, let's just go home. Let's just fire the band, sell the bus,
and quit the whole thing." And I go, "Now, wait a minute. I'm not *that*
upset about things! Let's not get that drastic or hasty." Number one, I do
it for myself. That's the selfish, but the honest thing to say. Number two, I
know that I was put on this earth to sing. Because that's the only thing I
can do pretty good. I've tried rodeoin', and playin' basketball, and ever'
time it comes back to "Reba, just sing!" When I first started entertainin',
Mama would say, "Now, Reba, your jokes are real cute, but just quit
talkin' and sing. That's where you're best at." And I'd say [resolvedly],
"Okay." I'd get up there and trudge through the singin', 'cause I always
thought I was gonna be a comedian of some sort. But God put me on
this earth to sing. Basically He gave the voice first to Mama. But Mama
couldn't use it, so she passed it down to us kids. So that's how it worked
out.

Q Why do you say she couldn't use it?

A Well, it wasn't the right time or place. She didn't have the backing, the
support. She had four kids. You know, everybody thought if you were
gonna take off and go be a singer, you'd be disowned from the family.
You were goin' downhill and we wouldn't love you no more, and that
kind of stuff. They were a real religious family, and they thought that was
the wrong life for a young girl to lead. She was sixteen at the time she
wanted to pursue it, and then she went on to teach school when she was
seventeen, and got married when she was twenty-one, and then had
four kids. So what she did was, she passed it down to us kids. And
supported us.

Q How did your mother feel about the CMA speech?

A Oh, she was cryin'. I don't remember who it was, but somebody was
tellin' me that they were sittin' up in the balcony by my parents. They
said that Mama had her Kleenex out and was cryin', and Daddy kinda
hit her leg, like, "Give *me* a Kleenex," you know. (Laughter) He was
cryin', too! But, heck, I thought I cried enough for everybody. But she
was really moved, and I saw her about an hour later over at the Opryland Hotel. I was runnin' around doin' all kinds of press and things, and
they was over there at the buffet tables eatin' shrimp. She hugged my
neck, and she said, "Well, you finally did it." And I said, "No, ma'am, *we*
did it." So that's the way we settled that.

Q Did you think you were going to win that night?

A Uh-uh. I sure didn't. I didn't think I was gonna win at all. I thought Anne
Murray was gonna get it. She was backstage, and she looked real ready

to accept the award, and it looked pretty much like her night. And I knew I had a lot more to do before I won it.

Q So it was a surprise.

A Oh, you bet! (Laughter) A very *nice* surprise! That standing ovation thrilled me to death. It made me cry so much longer.

Q Part of the reason for the ovation, I think, is that people are impressed by the fact that you stick to your guns about the kind of music you want to make. Most people say, "I just want a hit, and I don't care what I have to do to get it."

A Well, it was a big gamble to take, 'cause I didn't know if the people would really like to hear me sing straight-ahead country. I didn't know if they'd buy it. Thank God they did.

Q What would you have done if they hadn't?

A I don't know. I take every day pretty much [one] at a time, and I pray a lot, so I don't know what would have happened.

Q I've heard that when you have a big decision to make, you go out in the woods and pray. Why out in the woods?

A Oh, that's kinda my church. It's out there close to nature, and I feel a closeness to God there, and I just like to get on a horse and go ridin'. When you're out by yourself you can think better.

Q Is that the way you were raised—to stick to whatever you believe in and not give up until you get what you want?

A Well, I don't just get an idea in my head and bluntly take a stand—plant my feet and say that's it or else. I think about it a long, long time. Me and Charlie, and Bill and Kathy [her attorney-managers, Bill Carter and Kathy Woods—Woods has since split from the firm], talked about goin' straight-ahead country while I was choosin' songs a long time ago. It was a long, building pattern, with us tryin' to make sure this was the right decision. It wasn't only my decision. We all four of us listened, and argued, and talked, and discussed over and over again which was the right direction. It's simple to say, "Oh, well, I decided it, yeah," but that's not really the truth. It was a big decision to make, but we're all glad we went this way.

Q When you did the *Behind the Scene* album, did you want to sound even countrier back then?

A Oh, well, I didn't know that then. I didn't know then what I know now. I've always wanted to kinda go country, but I didn't think it was the thing to do. It's just that I got tired of goin' the contemporary route, and I knew that if I was ever gonna make it in this business and be successful, I had to be me, so that's why I decided to go real country.

Q Did you always think you'd make it?

A Well, I kinda hoped so, yeah.

Q But there wasn't a point where you got so discouraged that you thought you'd give up?

A No, never. I'd get mad, but I wouldn't want to quit.

Q What do you do when you get mad? Scream and kick?

A Yeah, I throw some fits, and temper tantrums.

Q Smash things?

A Yeah.

Q And curse?

A Uh, cuss a little bit, yeah. Vent the anger.

Q I read that you were never ashamed to be "on the rural side of country music." Is that true? Were you ever embarrassed at being more countrified than a lot of today's country singers?

A No. Never. I've never been ashamed of it. I've always lived out in the country. It's three hours to an airport, and heck, we've been on a party line all our life, except here lately. We finally got a private line. It's just something real different. [At the time of the interview, McEntire lived on a 14,000-acre ranch near Stringtown, Oklahoma. She now lives in Nashville.]

Q You come from a background that's fairly traditional, where a woman such as your mother was expected to stay home and raise a family. And yet you've gone off and done what you wanted to do. Did you have any personal conflict about that?

A Well, my mama is a very independent type of person. When she was raisin' four children, Daddy was off rodeoin'. [Her father, Clark McEntire, was three-time World Champion Steer Roper, and her grandfather won the title in the '30s.] But then Daddy'd come in and take care of an 8,000-acre ranch. His daddy was there to help him, and he had one hired hand, but the four kids were just about as much help as that table settin' over there, until we got old enough to learn and keep on tryin'. Alice, the oldest, was five years old when Susie, the youngest one, was born. So to have four kids in that short a period of time, you have to be a tough woman. And to keep us all in line and in school while Daddy was gone took some doin'. Sometimes all the rest of us went with Daddy rodeoin', while the oldest one stayed with Grandma and went to school. So it was one of the most unusual backgrounds I've ever heard of—goin' to school and havin' a normal life, but travelin' all over the United States, rodeoin' and livin' the life we did. But Mama really was—and still is—a very independent type of person. I don't think you'll ever meet another person like her. She's not the type of person that anybody could dictate anything to her.

Q So you come by your independence by example.

A Yeah. She was the one to really instill that in us, to say that you can do whatever you want to do. And when I tried basketball and rodeoin', she'd let me do it, and she'd take me. She'd sit back until I got so humiliated and aggravated at myself when I wasn't winning, and then she'd say, "Don't you think you're really wasting your time at this?" But she knew I was growin' up, and I was bein' a kid. And she didn't push me until it all fell into place, kinda like she knew it would someday fall into place when I was mature enough to handle it.

Q But you never felt guilty that you weren't staying home and having children the way your mother did?

A No, not one bit. I know quite a few women who are having babies for the first time when they're thirty-five and forty. That's not really something I've had a strong feeling about doing—having children. Now, my brother and sisters—all of them have children, and it's something that works in real well with their lives, and they can cope with it. But I give my all to music, and fortunately, I've got a husband who's right in there with me. We love each other very much, and we work hard on the music. If I'm on the road, and he's at home, it's still music. That's what we're thinking about, although he does take care of the home place and run a bunch of cattle. The music is still in the forefront of our minds all the time.

Q When did you realize that you wanted to be a singer and not a comedienne?

A After I got booed off the stage one night. That kinda helped me realize that I wasn't as funny as I thought I was. (Much laughter) That really opened my eyes. What happened was, Ray Wylie Hubbard's band was supposed to back me, and they backed out. They said, "Well, heck, I don't know who she is. I don't want to back her." That was five minutes 'til show time, and I said, "Okay, who's gonna back me?" And they said, "Oh, we've got this rock 'n' roll band that was gonna open the show, but they'll back you." And I said, "Okay." So I ran over where they were, and I said, " 'San Antonio Rose.' You know that one?" They said, "No, sure don't." I said, " 'Faded Love'?" They looked kinda funny. I thought, "Oh, boy." I said, " 'Kansas City'?" They said, "No, don't believe we know that one." I thought, "I don't know what I'm gonna do." We found two or three songs that we both knew, but I finally ended up tellin' jokes to pass my thirty minutes down the drain. John Conlee was on the show, and he had "Rose Colored Glasses" out, and he was a big hit, so while

I was tellin' this joke about a duck, the crowd started hollerin', "Get off the stage!" The acoustics were real bad in the building, and they wanted to hear John Conlee, anyway. So I finished my show and went backstage and did an interview. Mama was sittin' there just real patient like. And when I got through with my interview, I was just about to start bawlin', and she could tell. So we got over to the side, and she said, "What do you think?" And I said, "Well, I think what we need to do is call our bookin' agent, and tell 'em that they'll never book us again without Red Steagall's band, or Jacky Ward's band—I was doin' duets with Jacky at the time—or I'm gonna find a band of my own." So we called 'em up and told 'em that, and the next week we had a band. It was just as simple as that. And we found us a band that we worked with for about a year and a half.

Q Let me hear one of your jokes.

A Uh, you know the difference between unlawful and illegal?

Q What's that?

A Unlawful is against the law and illegal is a sick bird.

Q (Silence)

A That's how it went over all the time, too! (Much laughter) There's nothing worse in the world than startin' off a show and dyin' flat off of a joke. That's so embarrassing. And nobody in the crowd can hurt as bad as that person standin' up onstage, no matter how much the audience is embarrassed for 'em.

Q Was that your worst time onstage?

A Yeah. Well, I fell down one time and ripped my britches. See, our ending was to do a real fast, up-tempo song, and then quit. Then the lights would go out, I'd go offstage, everybody would come offstage, the lights would come on again real light blue, and I'd walk back onstage and sing "Sweet Dreams." Well, while we were doin' our real fast song, the lights went out, and this was in an old theater up in Michigan. And when the lights went out, you couldn't see *anything!* So I was shufflin' to the right, tryin' to get offstage, and I remembered there was somethin' there, a microphone stand, or something, so I had my hands out in front of me. But I was still shufflin', and I shuffled my feet stuck right under a monitor. Well, that tripped me, and I went over the monitor, and my knees just straddled it. Oh, it banged up my knees! Plus, I ripped my britches, and they were so tight that I couldn't get up, so I just crawled off. Tom Bresh had opened the show, and he was sittin' offstage on a stool, and he helped me crawl my way up the stool. He only had one thing to say: "Good show, Reba." I liked to killed him! I said, "Why, you idiot!" But it was really embarrassing. Part of me couldn't keep from laughing, and the other part was almost cryin'.

Q How long ago was that?

A Oh, gosh, about four guitar players ago! (Laughter) Three or four years ago, I guess.

Q You were on television recently singing "Somebody Should Leave." At the end of the song, you started to cry.

A Yeah. I do it every time. The first time I heard it, me and Charlie went out to [songwriter] Harlan Howard's house. I'd never met him before, but Bill Carter called him up and said, "Can they come over?" And he said, "Well, sure." And Harlan and Sharon and Clementyne [his wife and daughter] are just super people. We went over there and was settin', and he was playin' me some songs, and he said, "I want to play you this new song. Just see what you think about it." And I was just settin' back in one of his ol' high-backed leather chairs, bein' real comfortable. I was kinda thinkin' about dinner, 'cause it was gettin' close to dinnertime and I was gettin' hungry. And this song came on, and I just set up. I hadn't heard this kind of a song in *years*. And when the chorus came, I got all choked up. Then when the *ending* came, I was cryin'. And I said, "Harlan, can I have that song?" And he said, "I kinda thought you'd say that." Because he had written songs for Patsy Cline, and I just loved her, you know. He wants to be buddies. And, man, we were buddies 'til death do us part by the time we left that house, the way I felt about it. Just to meet him and see what somebody can do . . . That song will always be a highlight of my life.

Q Harlan's one of the great dinosaurs.

A Shoot, yeah! Writin' songs like "I Fall to Pieces," and helpin' Buck [Owens] write "I've Got a Tiger by the Tail." You know, everything from fluffy songs that are just monsters to serious songs like "No Charge," that Melba Montgomery song—I just love it. He gave me and Charlie a tape of about fifty songs that he'd written, and I was flabbergasted. They've all been my favorites down through the years.

Q So you cry every time you sing "Somebody Should Leave"?

A Uh-huh. It's not hard. What's hard is to hold it back. But you can really get into it. And people come up to me and say, "How do you cry every time?" They never ask me if it's fake. But a lot of them come up and say, "I cried as much as you did." I say, "On the CMA awards show?" They say, "No, on 'Somebody Should Leave.'" So that really makes me feel that the song is an honest song. Even if you've never been through a divorce, if you've got family who've been through a divorce, or you know how *children* are affected by a divorce, or if you know a man and wife who are living together who *want* a divorce but don't get one because of the kids, well, you can just sit back and say, "Man, what a situation." You know, somebody should leave, but there's still some hope. It's a *tough* song.

Q Did you know somebody in that situation? Or does the song itself just affect you?

A Well, basically the song itself. But my sister's been through a divorce, Charlie's been through a divorce, and both times there were children involved. So it's always the kids who get hurt the most. But the parent hurts twice as much for the kids as the kids do themselves. So it's something that anyone can relate to.

Q A lot of critics praise your phrasing, and the fact that you don't take the crossover route. But you also sound as if you've lived these tunes. There's a lot of emotion in your delivery.

A Well, I had very good teachers. The people I listened to for emotion were Dolly Parton and Patsy Cline. My favorite album of Dolly's is *My Blue Ridge Mountain Boy.* Gosh, that song about her daddy datin' a younger woman, "Daddy," and "Gypsy, Joe and Me" . . . I still sing that for my youngest stepson. He loves it, but it's just so heartwarming and tender that he cries. I cry, too. And then Patsy Cline, on "Crazy." You can almost hear her cry from her *guts,* you know. That's the kind of stuff I wanted to do. I wondered, "How do they do that?" And I thought, "Well, they get into a song." And when I record, that's what I look for. I don't look for a fluffy song, as Harlan Howard calls 'em. I look for something that's got meat in it, that's got emotion. In my show, I like to drain every emotion out of my audience. I like to entertain 'em, make 'em feel at ease, and I want to make 'em cry. Then I want to make 'em laugh, and then I want to make 'em feel that they're glad to be there, and then I want to leave 'em drained. That's my ultimate goal—just to leave 'em drained, settin' there thinkin', "Whew, I don't know if I can get out of this chair." That's what I wanna do. That's what we're working towards.

Q But Patsy Cline was your real influence, right?

A Yes.

Q Did she influence your phrasing?

A Naw, I just liked her singing.

Q Yet you turned down a part in "Sweet Dreams," the movie based on her life.

A Yeah, it was just a little bit too risqué. I just read the script—I don't know which writing draft it was—but it was a love story between Charlie Dick, her husband, and Patsy, and it was just a little bit too romantic for me.

Q You mentioned Dolly Parton. There's a lot of Dolly in *My Kind of Country.*

A Yeah, and there'll be a lot more on this new album [*Have I Got a Deal for You*].

Q How so?

A Well, her little trills and the looseness of her vocal cords—that's the only way I can put it—they just kinda run wild. It's just like a little kid in a field of flowers. They just go wherever they want to, and feel free to fly. Dolly's always reminded me of a butterfly, how her voice just kind of floats around and does all those cute little trills and stuff. And when we were makin' this album, Jimmy Bowen said, "Get out there and *sing*. Have a good time." And I just felt so completely at ease with the musicians that he selected. It wasn't like they were studio musicians and I was a vocalist come in to cut an album. After about the first hour, we got jelled into a pattern where we were like a band and singer that had been out workin' together for three or four months. We had a blast. And it gave me a lot of freedom. I didn't have to stop when somebody told me I was flat or sharp, and nobody said, "Don't do this, 'cause you won't be able to match it." Jimmy just said, "Go out there and sing your tail end off." And that's what I did. I just had fun.

Q What's happened to your writing?

A Well, I've got two songs on the new album, one I wrote by myself and one I wrote with my lead guitar player, David Anthony, and my other guitar player, Leigh Reynolds. I didn't tell Jimmy I'd written 'em. I just gave 'em to him. I went out and listened for songs, and I brought all the songs I liked in on a tape. I've got one of them dual cassette players, so I got all the tapes together, and I put 'em in the order of an album sequence, of how I wanted the album to sound, and I just gave 'em to Jimmy. Then when we was listenin' to 'em together, he said, "All right, that's good. I like this one because of the tempo." I said, "You really like it?" He said, "Yeah." I said, "Okay, me and David and Leigh wrote it." And he bragged on it a little bit. And then my song came on, and he said, "*Good* chorus. Oh, that's a good chorus." It finished playin', and I said, "Can we record that?" And he said, "Yeah!" I said, "Okay, I wrote that." And he said, "Well, I'm proud of you." You know, it wasn't "Oh, well, if you wrote it, everybody'll think that's the only reason we recorded it." But since he gave me the okay before I told him it was mine, I had the guts to put it in. Took a long time! (Laughter) An artist who writes their own songs always thinks the producer will say, "Let's get somebody else who's a proven, professional writer first, and then your songs will go in after everything else." So I feel pretty good about it.

Q How many of your songs have you recorded?

A Four. "Daddy" was the first one, from the *Out of a Dream* album, and then "Reasons," from *Behind the Scene,* and then these two.

Q Do you think of yourself as a writer?

A No. One of these new songs, "Only in My Mind," came out real good, though. I wrote it while I was puttin' on my makeup at a concert—you know, writin' while I was thinkin'. It came real fast. And the other one, the one David and Leigh wrote with me, Leigh had written the chorus, and then they brought it in to me. I was sittin' in my room watchin' soap operas, and they banged on the door and said they needed some help. So I wrote a verse, and we presented it to Welk [song publishing company]. But Welk said, "We need another verse." So David took the song home with him and wrote another verse. We each wrote a piece of the song, and put it together.

Q As somebody who doesn't do much songwriting, do you find it difficult? "Reasons," for example, was a very well-crafted tune.

A Well, thank you. I don't know. Somethin' just pops into my mind. I write a lot of little one-verse things, but I don't hardly ever complete a song. I'll keep 'em around, but I hardly ever go back to 'em like I should. But if it doesn't just pop right out, I get bored with it. So if I'm bored with it while I'm writin' it, I'm sure not gonna be singin' it much. So I usually won't ever go back to it. I'll have a better idea come up later.

Q I read a review of your stage show recently that described you as a "saucy songstress." How do you like being referred to as saucy?

A "Saucy." Hmmm. That's okay with me, I guess. Just as long as it's not "boring." (Laughter) It means "got a little fire in you," right? I like that.

Q For years, the stereotypical female country singer was a mousy sort of girl . . .

A Nicey-nicey?

Q Yes, a very sweet, gingham-dressed "girl singer" who stood in front of a haystack and who was passive through and through. There were exceptions—Loretta Lynn at times, Dolly Parton at times, and occasionally Donna Fargo. But on the whole, country music audiences didn't want a woman with fire in her. They seem to want it from you, though. Why is that?

A I don't know what the difference is. I'm not the type to be the next Waylon Jennings, or a renegade. I'm not being rebellious. I'm just doing what I think is my kind of music—my kind of country—and what I feel the best with. And besides that, it's different. Nobody else is doin' it. So why not?

Q It's the same thing with the orientation of the music. There were men doing more traditional material, but there didn't seem to be many women. Emmylou Harris did some, but it usually had a progressive edge. Even Loretta has been doing more contemporary songs.

A Well, it's been real hard to find any country songs here lately, and that's usually where the music is, in the more contemporary.

Q I think people realize that traditional music is a genuine love for you. They can hear it in your accent, if nowhere else. But you can usually tell when somebody's been hyped into an image.

A And when they tell 'em what to say instead of sayin' what comes from their heart. Boy, you can sure tell that. But I get into a lot of trouble sometimes. I say stuff that I shouldn't say, and people get on me about it. And I say, "Well, it was the truth!" So, you know, I get in trouble. But I'd rather tell the truth than not.

Q What have you gotten into trouble over?

A Oh, I can't say it and get in trouble again! (Laughter)

Q You were on *Nashville Now* recently, talking about the big egos a lot of people in this business have. Did that get you in trouble?

A No, that didn't get me in trouble. That was the truth. Very *much* the truth. There are a lot of artists who've got egos so big that you can't get close to 'em. I mean, you literally can't walk up to 'em and speak, because they won't speak to you.

Q Are you still finding that to be the situation, even with the CMA award?

A Oh, sure. The people who did that to me before are pretty much the same. And I don't really care. 'Cause I'm not gonna waste my time on 'em. I feel like everybody in this business, whether they're songwriters or singers, or what some people refer to as superstars, we're all the same. I've seen that especially since I've been coming to Nashville a lot more. We're all creative people, and God gave us a talent that we're all usin'. It's just that some people get bigger breaks than others. But if you have patience, and you're willing to hang in there, your break will come. "Good things come to those who wait." I've always been a firm believer in that. I don't like people who think they're better than you just because they've had bigger breaks. As Minnie Pearl said the other night, "You're gonna meet the same people goin' down that you met goin' up." And Red Steagall's told me that all my life. Look at Harlan Howard, and how long he's been around and all the friends he has. And he's just the same guy he always was, and everybody loves him. Now *he's* got a right to be egotistical, but he's not.

Q Emmylou Harris is someone who's rallied to your side, though.

A Yeah, Emmylou was the different side of the coin. I always loved her music and her voice, but when I met her, it enhanced her singin' to me so much. When I hosted *Nashville Now* and wanted to have her on, she had a job in Maryland somewhere. But she flew in to do the show, and then flew back to Maryland. Most people would say, "I'd rather have a day off in Maryland." But she's the type of person, like Harlan, who believes in havin' friends in the business. And that's what I like. I don't want to fake a friendship on TV or just be nice at certain times. I want to have them people as my friends. And that's why I like the CMA awards shows, and all the awards shows, for that matter. Because you get to be in the dressing rooms all that day, and the real sincere ones will want to sit down and visit with you. The other ones—and you can tell 'em in a second—will be real flighty, real busy. They won't have time for you.

Q You seemed very much at ease hosting *Nashville Now*. Have you had that kind of self-assurance since childhood? What sort of kid were you?

A Well, Alice was two years older than Pake [McEntire's brother, who now has a singing career of his own]. Pake was two years older than me, and I was two and a half years older than Susie. So me and Pake, bein' in the middle, were very close. We were a lot alike, and very competitive. So we were always havin' fistfights. Like, in the mornings, Daddy would send us out to go catch the horses and saddle 'em up before daylight. Daddy would cook breakfast, and all of us kids would stumble in there and eat, and then we'd be takin' out for the north end before the sun came up. I mean, it was real dark, and cold. This was in the fall roundup, to weigh cattle. And me and Pake, in the middle of the day, when we's tired and hot and had already pinned one bunch and goin' after another, if we had to sit and wait for somebody, we'd usually wind up in a big fistfight—on horses! You know, "Get off that horse and I'll go ahead and whup you, and we'll settle this right quick!" Things like that. But if anybody else ever stepped in, it was us two against them. Then when we were at the house, if we were ever bored, it was a competitive thing—anything you can do, I can do better. It would start off, "I can throw a rock farther than you can!" "Well, I can sing better than you!" "Well, I can play guitar better than you." "Well, I can play the piano better than you can!" It just went on and on. "I can play basketball better than you can," and "I can rope better than you can," you know. So I was very competitive, and very much of a tomboy.

Q Do you feel disadvantaged by the fact that your family traveled around from rodeo to rodeo when you were a kid?

A No, I think it helped, because we were on the road so much that it kind of trained me to be on the road now. That's why I don't mind it.

Q As the third kid out of four, did you have to fight for attention?

A Oh, yeah.

Q Do you think that had anything to do with why you decided to become a performer?

A Sure, I wanted more attention.

Q Were you a good student?

A Yeah, I was the co-salutatorian of my graduating high school class. I really liked basketball and 4-H Club real well, and I loved to go to school.

Q How did you do that while traveling around?

A We didn't travel around during school days, just during the summer.

Q Were you the sort of kid who would do anything on a dare?

A Yeah. Most definitely. We'd play Tarzan, but I . . . well, Alice jumped off the barn from a rope and landed in a pile of hay, then Pake did it, and I stood up there on the ledge, holdin' the rope. But I never could get up the nerve to jump off, because I'm scared to death of heights. So I crawled down and went to the house and *told* 'em I jumped off. I had hay poked down in my boots, and I said, "See, I jumped off." And they said, "Reba . . ." I said, "Okay, I didn't." But I could say that bein' a tomboy summed up my childhood pretty well. I still *am* pretty much of a tomboy. I'm sure not one for runnin' around in little frilly dresses and all that kind of stuff.

Q Was there one incident that made you decide you didn't want to be that much of a tomboy anymore?

A Oh, sure. I had a best friend in high school, and she was a beauty queen. She and my brother dated a little bit. She was very athletic, and me and her were big pals. But when Saturday night came, all of us girls went to Kiowa [Oklahoma] to party, or we'd go out to the show and flirt with all the boys. You know, that's when we'd take two hours to prepare and get somewhat *feminine* here. (Laughter) And usually I just turned out lookin' like I did before I started. Really, though, it wasn't until college that I started growin' up. I still didn't wear dresses any at all in college, but when special occasions came along, I did take more interest in dressin' up. I was still rodeoin' at that time. After I got married is when I really had somebody to dress up for, and somebody to tell me how nice I looked when I did dress up. So that makes a big difference. You don't want to dress up and have everybody just kinda ignore you. But Charlie always told me how nice I looked.

Q What first attracted you to Charlie?

A Well, Charlie was a real gruff-lookin' guy. Everybody called him an ol' bear, said he even *growled* like an ol' bear. But all the cowboys liked him. He was quiet, but when he said somethin', everybody paid attention.

And he could cut up, and joke, and play pranks, but he could also be serious. And he always kinda sat back and evaluated everything, where I'm a "yack-yack-yack-yack-yack" kind of person. You know, I have to be right there in the spotlight all the time, and have to have hold of the floor. And we'd go to rodeos, and I'd see Charlie there, and he was real quiet, and I thought he was the best-lookin' thing I'd ever seen. And then when we started datin', back in '75, I just fell in love with him. He's ten years and nineteen days older than me, and I just really needed somebody mature who wasn't into all the little silly games that two people who are young and fall in love go through. He'd been through all that, and he encouraged me on my singin', and was very supportive of it. And I knew with him I could always go on singin' and do what I wanted to. He wouldn't make me stay at home and have ten kids. And he's one of the only people—besides Larry, my bodyguard—who's really ever fought for me. And that's somethin' you don't forget.

Q Your bodyguard has had to fight for you?

A Well, he's sure had to take up for me a lot. I think one ol' guy said somethin' kinda derogatory to me one night, and they had a little scuffle. On the whole, though, my fans, and the people who come to my shows —we're just like friends. Everybody sets and talks. And I don't run out of the building and get away from 'em or hide. I'll just walk out and sit amongst 'em durin' a show. Once in a while somebody'll come up while I'm watchin' the headliner and say, "Oh, Reba, I enjoyed your show," and walk on. Or "Hey, Reba, can I have your autograph?" But then they go on. They don't bother us. They're nice. And they know we're people just like they are. And that's what I like. I've always had people tell me, "No, you're supposed to be put up on a pedestal. They don't want to be able to touch you or talk to you anytime they can." I don't like that. That might work for a lot of people, but it don't work for me. I'm a people person. I'm not a loner.

Q They don't announce, "Reba has left the building"?

A No, they say, "Reba's in the back eating popcorn!" Or "Reba, would you come out to the bus? All your crew's fixin' to run off and leave you!" (Laughter)

Q What was it about you that attracted Charlie?

A He always says it was my money, but I was broke and *he* was broke. (Much laughter) We stayed broke for about four or five years. Lived on love, I guess. If you can do it, that's what we did.

Q And you lived your first three months of marriage in a Chevy pickup with a camper.

A Yeah. It was real nice. It was real intimate. If we had a fight, I couldn't go runnin' back home to Mama, 'cause we were about two or three thousand miles away from home.

Q You were promoting records then?

A No, we were rodeoin'.

Q But you spent your honeymoon promoting a record.

A Yep.

Q *Billboard* magazine calls you "the finest woman country singer since Kitty Wells."

A Great compliment.

Q Is that scary in any way?

A No, you can't be frightened when you're just doing what you're meant to do.

Q You sound like you know what you want.

A Well, it's just taken me eight years to finally realize what they wanted me to do was not what I wanted to do.

Q Was there a time when you thought people weren't taking you seriously?

A Yeah, I guess so. It's just that they thought they were doin' the best thing, because I do have a big range in my vocal. But just because you've got a wide vocal range, that's no reason to go singin' somethin' you're not comfortable with.

Q Is your success indicative of a real swing back toward the traditional, do you think?

A All I can say is I'll sure be goin' more traditional. I don't know if anybody else will. I don't know if mine's traditional, modern-country, or whatever. It's just my kind of country.

Q What do you ultimately want to do with all of this? Are you the sort of person who makes lists and goals?

A No. The biggest goal in my life is to not make a big mistake. The little ones you can get away with and learn from. But my biggest goal is to not make that big mistake, 'cause it'll kill you. It'll set you back. And in this business you can't afford that. As Conway Twitty told me, "It doesn't matter how good you can sing, or what you can do. If you don't have that song, you might as well stay at home. They'll remember you for a while, but if you don't have a song, they won't keep coming back." So if you make that big, bad, major boo-boo . . . well, that's it. It's over. So that's my main goal . . . not to make it.

Q So far, you don't appear to have made many. You've won the Female Vocalist of the Year award from the CMA, the ACM, and the *Music City News* organization. Do you feel like a star yet?

A Naw, not yet. I'm still just a twinkle.

Bill Monroe

*I*f bluegrass music has a face, it is the stoic, taciturn visage of Bill Monroe. Garbed in a gray suit and white Stetson, Monroe takes the stage as both pioneer and patriarch, refusing to make concessions to the audience, concentrating only on melody, harmony, and instrumental prowess, playing his music almost exactly the way he's played it for the last half century.

Through decades of country music evolution, while electric instruments have usurped the original acoustic sound, Monroe has insisted on preserving the old wood-and-steel instrumentation. And as country singing and song structure have inched so close to pop stylings as to often be indistinguishable, Monroe clings fiercely to his "high lonesome" delivery. Along the way, he has created a form of tradition-based music that is as distinctive and mercurial as the man himself.

Now 77, and only recently announcing plans to step back his grueling performance schedule, Monroe was a star when many of today's biggest names were children. The fact that he has outlived a long list of performers—Hank Williams, Elvis Presley, and Marty Robbins, to name a few—testifies both to his strength as a man and to his will to further a music that is as much a personal statement as a stylized genre of entertainment. A member of the Grand Ole Opry since 1939, he still reveres the Opry as the paramount and most important showcase for his music, and proudly wears a ring commemorating the Opry's fiftieth anniversary in 1975.

The son of a lumberman-farmer and his accordion-playing wife, William Smith Monroe grew up in the hills of Rosine, Kentucky, a hamlet in the western part of the state between Louisville and Paducah. Youngest of eight, he describes his childhood as a profoundly unhappy period, due to an affliction of his eyes, the isolation of growing up in the hills, and the fact that he was so much younger than his siblings. His was a musical family, with his brother Charlie an accomplished guitarist and another brother, Birch, proficient on fiddle. By the time Bill was old enough to choose his own musical instrument, only the mandolin remained to fill out the family band. Since he preferred both the guitar and the fiddle, young Bill learned them anyway for his own pleasure. But he bitterly vowed that if he had to play the instrument nobody else wanted, he, as the runt of the litter with the last pick of the choosing, would be the best mandolin player the world would offer.

Like many young men growing up in a rural culture, Monroe acquired much of his musical repertoire and education in church singing (particularly from the old shaped-note hymnals), an experience recounted in his gospel offering "Let the Gates Swing Wide." In time, he would be influenced by Jimmie Rodgers, Gid Tanner and the Skillet Lickers, and fiddler Clayton McMichen. But his earliest and most profound influences were his bachelor uncle Pendleton Vandiver (later the subject of what is perhaps his most famous song, "Uncle Pen"), an itinerant trader and old-time country fiddler, and Arnold Shultz, a black fiddler and guitarist who lived in the area. With Monroe playing mandolin and singing tenor, Charlie on lead vocals and guitar, and Birch on bass vocals and fiddle, the brothers played dances and radio stations around Kentucky, earning a following of their own by the mid-'20s.

At this point, Charlie and Birch never considered music much more than a hobby, and in the late '20s the older brothers went North to find work. For a while, after the death of his parents, young Bill moved in with Uncle Pen before following his brothers to Chicago. There, in 1929, he found work as a barrel stacker in the Sinclair Oil refineries in nearby Hammond, Indiana, for five years turning his paychecks over to his siblings as the sole support of the family. ("He bought a car and then he couldn't even drive it," one of his friends says.)

In time, the Monroe Brothers began playing music together again, eventually landing a position on the WLS *Barn Dance,* more for the square dancing they could do in the WLS touring company. When Birch left the act for a steady job in the refineries, Charlie and Bill followed lucrative radio bookings in the Midwest before settling in the Carolinas, appearing regularly on radio, recording for RCA Victor's Bluebird label, and establishing themselves as one of country music's most popular acts. But with their strong and frequent conflicts, the brothers argued constantly, Charlie, eight years older than Bill, insisting he was the leader of the duo, relegating his brother to a secondary role despite his important songwriting contributions. In 1938, at the top of their career, they parted ways, Charlie to form the Kentucky Pardners, and Bill to organize, for a brief time, a band called the Kentuckians, later the Blue Grass Boys.

From the outset, Monroe was determined to outdo his older brother, to prove his independence and worth with a music that would set him apart from all others. Almost immediately, he developed the sound that would become known as bluegrass, a blend of old-time fiddle music, blues, and jazz. "Bluegrass has got a meanin' to touch your heart," Monroe would later explain. "It's plain music that tells a good story." Most of his themes concern love in its various incarnations and stages— love cherished ("My Little Georgia Rose," "My Sweet Darlin' "), love scorned ("I Believed in You, Darling," "Sweetheart, You Done Me Wrong"), love fulfilled ("Boat of Love"), and love lost ("It's Mighty Dark for Me to Travel"). Other favorite subjects include his Kentucky childhood and culture ("I'm on My Way Back to the Old Home," "The Old Mountaineer"), religious beliefs ("Lord, Protect My Soul," "Remember the Cross"), and preoccupation with death ("The Little Girl and the Dreadful Snake," "I Hear a Sweet Voice Calling"). But while Monroe's lyrics are lyrically rich and uncommonly poetic, his instrumentals are no less important, comprising a primer for every serious mandolinist.

Monroe has dedicated his life to music with an almost missionary zeal ("I don't smoke or drink, to keep my voice in good shape, and I've trained it so's I don't strain it"), resulting in a number of far-reaching innovations not normally credited to him. It was his idea, for example, for instrumentalists to trade off playing the melody, and to alternate with the vocalist—a radical innovation at the time. He also originated the idea of mixing fiddle tunes with vocals. In addition, Monroe takes credit for the first gospel quartet singing on the Grand Ole Opry.

Monroe would become most famous, however, for playing a powerful, close-chorded rhythm chop on his mandolin, effecting a drumlike beat

to hold up the time. More than just a technician, Monroe is revered for
his tone and the emotional power he is able to convey from the melody
alone. When he auditioned for the Opry in 1939, he played traditional
music on traditional instruments, but he performed it with a fast, driving
rhythm that was quite unlike anything else—"country music in over-
drive," as bluegrass would eventually be dubbed. When he cut loose
with a souped-up version of Jimmie Rodgers' "Muleskinner Blues"—the
first song he ever performed in a style that was purely his own—the Opry
directors realized that Monroe, who sang in a surprisingly high, hair-
raising tenor, had created an entirely new and seminal style of country
music. (The bluegrass sound would be finalized in 1945 with the addition
of Earl Scruggs's three-finger banjo style.) In time, a parade of soon to
be famous musicians (Scruggs, Lester Flatt, Carter Stanley, Don Reno,
Jimmy Martin, Mac Wiseman, Sonny Osborne, Byron Berline, Peter
Rowan, Vassar Clements, and Kenny Baker, among others) would move
through the Monroe band before establishing careers of their own. Virtually every great bluegrass musician of the last twenty-five years has
admitted to learning his craft in part from Monroe's recordings.

A man of fierce pride, staunch moral conduct, and extreme reserve,
Monroe stands on ceremony with strangers and colleagues alike. (Minnie Pearl recalls being terrified to talk to him during his first five years at
the Opry.) Rarely seen wearing anything but a suit and tie, Monroe
carries himself with dignity and bearing, cutting a formidable and almost
unapproachable figure—tense, steely, and stone serious. In many ways,
he seems to be a holdover from another era, with an old-school set of
manners and a way of speaking that occasionally dips into the archaic.
His famous temper, which once made him scratch the name "Gibson"
off the peghead of his mandolin when the factory kept it four months for
minor repairs, seems always to bubble just beneath the surface. Yet he
can also be extraordinarily sweet-natured, picking up the lunch checks
for everyone who speaks to him at his favorite diner or stopping to speak
with a small child. Always, he remains mysterious—a loner for life, despite a recent new marriage—bowing to no one, and holding himself
apart from everyone "musically, socially, personally," as his former manager Ralph Rinzler was to observe. However, since his bout with stomach
cancer at the start of the decade, Monroe, who for a time was staunchly
anti-newgrass, now seems more tolerant of the various bluegrass spin-
offs and the musicians who pick them.

Part of the reason for that may be that Monroe was a long time
receiving the credit he deserved, mass recognition outside country music

circles not coming along until the '60s, when the folk music boom introduced a new generation of college students to his legacy. With that, Monroe was in demand for appearances at the University of Chicago Folk Festival and the prestigious Newport Folk Festival, the interest leading also to his first concert performance in New York City. Such appreciation for the music in general led to the sprouting of bluegrass festivals throughout the country, including Monroe's own Bean Blossom festival in Indiana, which celebrated its twentieth year in 1986.

To most observers, the crowning glory of Monroe's career seemed to come in 1970, when he was elected to the Country Music Hall of Fame. But always a man to define things on his own terms—earning the nickname "Bossman"—Monroe founded his own Blue Grass Hall of Fame and Museum in Nashville in 1984. At the time, the museum was touted as "a center for the preservation and promotion of bluegrass music." But initial plans also ensured that Monroe would get his due, with a room reserved solely for his accomplishments and a bronze statue of the man internationally recognized as the progenitor of and driving force behind an original American musical genre.

The following interview took place May 13–14, 1986, at the Nashville offices of Monroe's booking agent, Buddy Lee. Although he is notoriously difficult to interview—reporters tell of Monroe's getting up and walking out of the room, instructing them to come back when they've thought of better questions—our interview proceeded without major incident. Still, interviewing Monroe is disconcerting, mainly because he is uncomfortable in any situation where his music doesn't do most of the talking. The experience is something akin to dancing with a grizzly: while you are delighted you can get the bear to cooperate in the first place, you're never quite sure what he's going to do.

Monroe is undoubtedly still a Kentuckian to the bone, but for business reasons he long ago moved his operation to Nashville, running his office out of a house trailer in nearby Goodlettsville. Typically, he mixes with none of the local musicians, continuing to draw his strength and his influence not from other people but from the land, the hills, and nature. The day we finished our interview, he invited me to join him for supper at his favorite restaurant, a little motel cafe in Goodlettsville where the food is served on light-green sectional plates—the kind favored by grade school lunchrooms—and the jukebox plays "Blue Moon of Kentucky." Near the end of the meal, he asked if we might drive up the road a piece. There, he stopped in front of a shopping center and pointed at the woody hill beyond it. Off in the distance, what seemed only a dot from where we stood, lay Monroe's farm, a 140-year-old house on 288 acres, reiminiscent of the area he plowed as a boy in his beloved Kentucky. "It's the highest hill in the country," he said in almost a whisper, pausing a moment and then repeating the words. With that, he drove off in his Cadillac, the soft curves of his Stetson and the sharp points of the car fins sculpting a bizarre figure in the gray Goodlettsville dusk.

Q At the time we're talking, you're nearly seventy-five years of age. You still write songs, you still keep a full performance schedule, and you still make records. People call you "a living legend." Do you think of yourself that way?

A Everybody else speaks of me bein' a legend, so I guess I go along with 'em. I love to keep on.

Q You're always referred to as the Father of Bluegrass. Do you think you have a mission—a directive of some sort—to play this music?

A I really do, with all my heart. When I was real young, back in the state of Kentucky, I'd be out in the fields, you know, and I would be singin' just to get to hear the tune, and how it would make me feel. So I was gonna be sure that I put Methodist and Baptist and Holiness singin' in bluegrass music, with a lot of the old Scotch bagpipe, goin' way on back. And the way they played years and years ago—Uncle Pen Vandiver, you know —the old Southern blues. And the hard drive was put in there with my mandolin.

Q Is it more than just music to you? Is it something spiritual?

A Oh, yes, that's there. That's spiritual.

Q There's a lot of pride—some would say an arrogance—in your music.

A Yes. This sounds like braggin', but you know, you can hear a lot of different groups on the stage, and bluegrass can go out there, and it's like the music just started there. It's got a music of its own, a hard-drivin' music, you see. It stands to itself.

Q Let me read you something that Butch Robins, who used to play banjo for you, said about you: "A proud man walks with definition. He walks with very sure, confident steps that come down smack on the beat. And Monroe is the one who somehow brought that force into this music. And the music has such focus that even in its weakest moments, it can chill the fiber of a human." What do you think about that?

A Has a lot to do with it. The beat of the different kinds of music plays a big part in me, because I learned all that years and years ago, when I was real young—how to take care of the beat to music, like fiddle break-downs, and marches, polkas, schottisches, the blues, waltzes. I learned all that. A lot of people today don't really know what each of 'em stands for, but they should. Because when you're young, you should learn the time of the music. That means a lot to you.

Q When you first developed the bluegrass sound around 1939, did people take to it from the start?

A Well, the people didn't know what it was, you know. They didn't know what I had put together. They would stand and listen and be just real quiet, and wouldn't say a word. I played a-many place [where] when I'd get through, they wouldn't even speak to me. They didn't even know who I was, or they didn't know whether they liked the music yet or not.

Q Did anybody say, "I want the music you played with [your brother] Charlie instead of this stuff"?

A No, they didn't. Uh-uh.

Q So you were never afraid it wasn't going to go over?

A I really thought it was going to go over. I thought it would be [good] for the good country people, the farm people. But I never did think it would go where it's at today. I just wanted it for my own music, you know.

Q I read something that suggested that after World War II the masses of people around the country were a little bit more sophisticated than they had been, and that the music had to change to keep up with that. Did you have a sense of that when you developed the bluegrass sound, or were you just trying to carve out a distinctive sound, different from what you had with Charlie?

A I was just gonna carve out a music of my own, different from anybody else's music. I didn't wanna copy anybody, and that's what I put together.

Q At first, you sang a different style of tenor from what you had sung with Charlie. How did you arrive at it? Did you do a lot of experimenting with that, or could you hear it in your head?

A Well, I knew what I wanted to do. I could hear it. Back in the early days of the Monroe Brothers, I sung a lot of high baritone, you see. Charlie didn't carry his lead so high. So I would mix the high baritone with tenor. And then when I started the bluegrass group, why, I went on up in tenor, you know, up high. We pitched our music up higher. We sang a lot in [the key of] B natural. In the early days, when I come to the Grand Ole Opry, there was *nobody* on the Grand Ole Opry that played in B natural. Very few played in B flat. You know, you could play in G, C, and D. You could play in C, and you could carry the low part of it, if you wanted to sing to the low part of it. But Bill Monroe carried the high part in C, if he sung in C.

Q Shortly after you and Charlie broke up, you auditioned for the Grand Ole Opry. You were still in your late twenties. Do you remember that audition?

A Oh, yes, I do. I showed up at WSM on a Monday mornin', and I met the Solemn Old Judge [George D. Hay, founder of the Opry]. David Stone was the announcer, and Harry Stone was the president of the company. They's all goin' out to get some coffee, or somethin' to eat, and they told me that they'd be right back, that that wasn't the day—Wednesday was the audition day. So they come right back, and I sang "Muleskinner Blues," "Bile [Boil] Them Cabbage Down"—numbers like that, and a gospel song, and another one—about four. So they told me I could go to work that Saturday, or I could go on lookin' for another job, some other radio station, Louisville, or someplace—maybe I could make more money. And I told 'em, no, I wanted to stay at the Grand Ole Opry. And they said, "Well, you're here, and if you ever leave, you'll have to fire yourself." So I've been there forty-six years.

Q Were you confident that you'd be accepted?

A I was just in hopes I would. I had my group right, you know. They all could play and sing. They knew what they's doin'. And I just thought it would be good for the Grand Ole Opry, and course, the Grand Ole Opry has really done a lot for me and bluegrass music—for the people to hear it all over the world, and know that I was gonna be there Friday and Saturday, when I wasn't out on the road doin' a show. So it's helped give the listeners, the fans, a chance to hear Bill Monroe and the Blue Grass Boys. And you know, through the wintertime, you're there on Friday and Saturday, and it gives people stayin' at home a chance to hear what they want to hear.

Q Were you a fan of the Opry from its inception?

A Well, I heard the Grand Ole Opry way on back in the early thirties, you know. But I never did know whether I'd get to move down South. I was up in Indiana then. We worked our way on around Indiana, Iowa, Nebraska, and into the Carolinas, and then from there into the Grand Ole Opry.

Q So you had perfected the bluegrass sound before you auditioned at the Opry?

A I had it the way I wanted it.

Q Bob Artis, in his book *Bluegrass*, says that at WSM during the early war years, you had a sound in your head that would not let you rest until you found the right musicians to give it expression. Was it difficult telling other musicians what that sound was?

A Well, they heard me playin' and singin', you know, and they knew what I wanted—how I wanted to keep it. If you're gonna be a Blue Grass Boy, you should do exactly the way the music wants you to do it. And if you're workin' for a man, do what he says do, not what you say do.

Q You're supposed to be a difficult man to work for. As one of your former band members said, "He puts up with nothing." Are you a tough taskmaster with the musicians in your band?

A Yes, I have been, all the way. I've tried to keep 'em all sober, you know. Course, some of 'em, it's been hard to keep sober, 'cause they loved it so much. But I believe in bein' sober if you're gonna work. You can't get out on the road and drive and [be] drunk.

Q When twenty-two-year-old Earl Scruggs joined your band with his three-fingered picking style, did you have any reservations about the way it fit your sound? Did you think it had limitations?

A Well, you see, Stringbeans [*sic*, a.k.a. Stringbean, a.k.a. David Akeman] was the first banjo player [in the Blue Grass Boys]. And I wanted the sound of the banjo in my group. So when he went out on his own—I believe he had to go into service for Uncle Sam—then Don Reno would have been the next banjo player. But Uncle Sam called Don Reno, so that put Earl Scruggs ahead of Don. So that give the style of the banjo that helped bluegrass an awful lot. And it really helped Earl Scruggs. You probably would have never heard him, 'cause he was on his way to the cotton mills, you see, if I hadn'ta give him the job.

Q Stringbean called himself "the Kentucky Wonder" early in his career. What sort of man was he?

A He was a fine man. He was a hard worker, and a respectable man, a sober man. Earl Scruggs was a fine man and a sober man, too.

Q Wasn't it your innovation to have the different instruments take the lead in the band, to trade off the lead?

A That's right, yeah.

Q How did you think of that?

A Well, I just thought it would be good for the music—say, the fiddle started first in the introduction, and then the banjo would take the first break, and then the mandolin. I thought it would give everybody a break, you see, and give 'em a chance to let the people hear them. They all deserved that. We could have just cut it down, and let the fiddle done it all. But if you're payin' the banjo player, he ought to get in there and take a break, too, 'cause I knew that the people wanted to hear him. So that's the way I set it all up. I think it helped out a lot. There was a time when a banjo was so popular that they'd rather hear the banjo than hear the fiddle. Because a lot of fiddle players, back in the early days, really didn't know how to play bluegrass music. You had to train 'em, 'cause it was a new music, and the banjo could follow the melody good. A number like "Molly and Tenbrooks" was perfect for the banjo. If it hadn't been for numbers like "Molly and Tenbrooks," the banjo wouldn't have had a lot to do.

Q You changed the structure of the band after Flatt and Scruggs left, to take the emphasis off the banjo.

A Yeah, Don Reno followed Earl. And then followin' Don was Rudy Lyle, and he was a powerful banjo player. He could really tie Earl Scruggs up in knots. Tie Don Reno up, too, because he was such a banjo player. He could really play it, boy. There was some fine banjo pickers come on down through the years. Snuffy Jenkins was the first [finger-picking bluegrass] banjo player. He had his style from down in North Carolina. And that's where Earl Scruggs learned how to play, from the banjo players down in that country. And that's where Don Reno . . . because he was from North Carolina, too, I believe, down below Asheville.

Q But didn't you change the focus of the band to showcase the fiddle and the mandolin and not the banjo?

A Well, I had always taken some breaks on the mandolin, but when you're singin' solos, a lot of times you don't take the break on the mandolin. You let the banjo and the fiddle take it, 'cause you're gonna sing.

Q The defection of Flatt and Scruggs hurt you personally, hurt you financially—because they got bookings that had previously been yours—and hurt your show for a time until you worked out a new one. Are you still angry about that?

A No, no, no. Uh-uh.

Q Well, you have a very famous temper.

A The worst in the world, if you bother me.

Q Is that true?

A Yeah.

Q What makes you mad?

A Well, if you try to shove me, or [use] some bad words, or try to crook me —that makes me mad. If you're gonna be a gentleman, or a lady, be honest. And respect each other, and not call you a name. Use the name that you have, like James Buchanan Monroe, if you're gonna use a name. Now, if you're gettin' ready to fight, you could call somebody anything you wanted to. That would help the fight. But that ain't the way to live through life. I believe in helpin' each other as you go through.

Q Through the years, it probably would have gotten you more radio play, and certainly there would have been career and financial advantages, had you given in and adapted to a more commercial style. Were you ever tempted to concede to the cultural and economic changes in the industry—broaden the confines of your music for wider appeal?

A No, I wouldn't want to go that other way. Bluegrass is the way that I wanted it. And I have never been the kind of man who only had his mind on money. To enjoy life, and play and sing to your friends, and treat them right, like I told you a while ago, respect 'em—that means a lot to me. I've never cared nothin' about bein' rich. I've made a lot of money in my time, but you can't take it with you. Just enjoy life.

Q The rural people particularly respected and revered you because they knew that you would not change the music, you would not bow to what an elite group of people in Nashville said. As a result, in Bob Artis' words again, you had "almost god-like status" in the South, especially when Nashville and the traditional styles of country music began to part ways in the fifties.

A Well, nobody would try to tell me what to do, because they knew that I was a-gonna do what I wanted to in the way of the music. And that was to keep it as near right as I thought it should stay.

Q I know that the word "bluegrass" started showing up in the early fifties. But who gets credit with referring to your music that way? You didn't call it "bluegrass music," did you?

A No. After I formed my group, I thought I'd call it "Bill Monroe and His Blue Grass Boys," to let people know I was from the state of Kentucky. But my music got so popular that they thought it should have a name, and they was right. And then just a year or so, maybe two or three years later, they went to calling it "bluegrass music." But that's a good name for it.

Q I'm not sure that the average country music fan realizes what a prolific songwriter you are, particularly of instrumentals and gospel songs.

A Well, I like to compose. You see now, I've wrote close to a hundred gospel songs. And I'm really proud that I done that. And I've wrote a lot of old-time fiddle numbers, you know. I'd say between eighty and a hundred old-time fiddle numbers, and a lot of mandolin numbers, and a few banjo numbers, you see. And then I wrote numbers like "Kentucky Waltz," and "Blue Moon of Kentucky," and "Uncle Pen"—I've wrote a lot of numbers like that. And like "My Little Georgia Rose," that's a true song. I have some true songs that I'm proud of. But I like to write.

Q How many songs have you written that we haven't heard yet?

A Well, probably twenty or twenty-five.

Q Instrumentals or vocals?

A Oh, they's a lot of instrumentals you haven't heard. Emory [his producer, Emory Gordy, Jr.] made a list of thirty-two of 'em the other day. I need to carry a little tape recorder with me. 'Cause I can put a number together in two, three, or five minutes. And you put it down then, you see, and you don't forget it.

Q How do you decide what's going to be an instrumental and what you're going to put words to? Or do you compose the two together?

A Well, sometimes I put 'em together as I go along, but I have instrumentals that would be fine to have some words with them.

Q Let's talk a little about one of your best-known instrumentals, "My Last Days on Earth," which, as a sort of dance with death, is an extraordinarily moving piece of music. How did you happen to write that?

A Well, one night way along in the morning, around two or three o'clock, I couldn't sleep, and it was cold as it could be, boy. So I thought I'd get up and I'd get my mandolin, and I'd just see what I could come up with. I'd see what different style I could tune. Something new. So I got my mandolin, and I went to comin' up with tuning a different style, where it would harmonize. You could play two strings and one would be harmony for the other string, you see. So I got it tuned up the way that I wanted it, and then I went to playin' some on it, you know, seein' how the one sound would play along with the other sound, and add what notes or the tune I wanted to go with. But it seemed like when I started on it, "My Last Days on Earth" just wrote itself, like it was there already. I was going along with it, and it was really sad.

Q Parts of that are absolutely bone-chilling.

A Yeah. "My Last Days on Earth." Boy, that comes on down there, you know. So then we got it together and people were beginnin' to like it, and MCA wanted to record it. And it really sold good. It sold a lot of records. But I'm really proud of that number there. It's really got the feeling there. It does somethin' to me every time I play it. And then you can hear the waves and the wild . . . what was on it, the birds?

Q Yes. Was that your first time using sound effects?

A Yeah, that's right. I thought that just worked in there wonderful with that number.

Q That record is not really what I think of as bluegrass.

A No, but it's being played in bluegrass style, so bluegrass overrides it, and comes in there to where it kind of works fifty-fifty, you see.

Q Have you written others in this style?

A Not too much, no.

Q You wrote that song in 1980, after you were diagnosed as having cancer.

A That's right.

Q Did you think those were truly your last days on earth?

A Well, you see, what I went through back in 19 and 80, right in there, it could have been my last days. But I had willpower and hope, and a lot of my friends and fans was worried to death. I could tell that. They'd come to the hospital and stand there and cry. You see now, they operated on me, and I was up walkin' that day. They said, "Anybody else— it would have been the next day before they would have got up." So I've just hung in there like that. I don't want to give up. I never give up.

Q Well, you apparently beat it. It's been six years.

A Yeah. That's right.

Q You got married last year, after having been not married for more than thirty years. Can you tell a difference in yourself since you remarried?

A Well, I try to keep the music . . . I practice and listen to a lot of things, and compose. But the music's played its part in the way of both workin' together, I think.

Q So you're happy?

A Yeah.

Q You look happy.

A Well, I just want to live on awhile, and play and sing, and go to church. I go to Brother Jimmy Snow's church on Dickerson Road. And I was baptized in the river Jordan.

Q That was during your trip to the Holy Land in 1983.

A And that was the most wonderful tour. I didn't think I'd ever get to go to Israel. I'd sung about the river Jordan all of my life. But I thought I'd just sing about it. I didn't think I'd ever get to go. So, all at once, Brother Jimmy Snow asked would I like to go on this tour with him, you know. And I said, "It would be the happiest day of my life to get to go with you." So he set it up, and we had three concerts over in Israel. And the people didn't know nothin' about bluegrass music. But they were just *crazy* about it when they heard it. They loved it! So I'd like to go back again sometime, just to get to see the country over there—Bethlehem, Jerusalem, all through that country there. You see a lot of water over there, like the Dead Sea and the river Jordan. And you can see the mountains and hills just *way* back. You forget all about the United States when you get over in that country. You remember about your people back here, like your children, but your work and a lot of other things, you just forget about when you're over there. Your mind stays right there.

Q Did you write any songs out of that experience?

A I might have wrote one or two. I was so busy over there that I didn't get to do a lot. We'd get up of a mornin' around five o'clock, and our tour would start around six. We'd just drive all over the country, seein' different parts. Then we'd come back home that night, around seven or eight, nine o'clock, and check in. But before I ever went to Israel, I had wrote a lot of songs about the countries over there, and the gospel. You know, up in Kentucky, where I was born and raised, the highest ridge in the area there was called Jerusalem Ridge. So I wrote this fiddle number called "Jerusalem Ridge," and I think it's one of the greatest fiddle numbers of all times. We used to fox-hunt back there on that ridge, me and my father and my brother.

Q What was your father like?

A My father could buck-and-wing dance. He was a good dancer, but he didn't play any instruments. But he was a good man, he was a good farmer, and he raised eight children. And you stayed with him and worked there 'til you's twenty-one, then you went out on your own. And when you become twenty-one years old, he would give you a hundred dollars, or he would give you a horse. That's the way he raised all of his children.

Q Are you like him?

A I think about him a lot. He was an honest man, and I believe in standing that way, too. And I know that I got that from my father and my mother.

Q What sort of business was your father in?

A Just farm business. And he cut timber there on the home place. They had a coal mine there, too, where they dug coal in the fall of the year for the people.

Q So that's where you learned to cut timber, and it's also where you learned to dance.

A That's right. And to haul timber, with the wagon and horses. It was right there where I learned all that.

Q What did you learn from your mother? The love of music?

A Well, that's right. She'd be cookin' dinner, and she would have a fiddle laying on the bed, and she'd go by the bed and pick it up and play, maybe one number, then go on in the kitchen and do some more cookin'. And she could play the accordion some. But she could also play the fiddle, and she could sing. She had a good voice. And her hair was red. It had just a little bit of light in it. It come way down her back. And she had blue eyes. My father had blue eyes, and I do, too.

Q You worked as a dancer at one time, in Chicago.

A Yes, at WLS in Chicago. The National Barn Dance there. We danced for them on the road a long time.

Q When you were seventeen, you left Kentucky to follow your brothers North in search of work. At one point, when you worked in the oil refineries in the Chicago area, stacking barrels, you supported your whole family on your small salary. What do you remember from those days?

A Well, there was a time when my brothers couldn't find any work. And my two sisters were there, and they wasn't workin' either. But I worked every day. The people out at the Sinclair refineries, some of 'em was from Kentucky, and they knew that I needed the money to take care of ever'-thing—pay our rent and buy groceries. And they let me work thirty days in the month, 'cause they knew that I needed the work. And I took care of everything. I would work there at Sinclair refinery, and I'd go out on the streetcar to go to work, and my brothers would go out and pick up my check. They'd take it back and get it cashed, and pay all the bills. And I'd hang in there and work.

Q You didn't get to spend any of it?

A I would save about four or five dollars for expenses, you know, for the streetcar, or to get a haircut—things that I would need like that.

Q Was it frightening for you to go to the big city when you were a boy?

A Yes, it was. I didn't know how to get around, or nothin' about it.

Q How did you get over that?

A Oh, just takin' time. I wouldn't be afraid now to go anywhere. Like New York, you know. We know New York pretty good. But you still can't beat Kentucky. Colonel [Harland] Sanders, you know, with Kentucky Fried Chicken—me and him always talked a lot. And he told me, said, "Me and you have done more for the state of Kentucky than any two men." And I do think we done a lot for Kentucky, and I think Kentucky knows that, and all the big people up there in that state, like the governor—they all know that. I'm glad that we done all that.

Q You went to New York to make the Ricky Skaggs video for "Country Boy," where you also got to dance.

A Yeah! (Laughter) I thought that was really good. I enjoyed that. We were there twenty-four hours, and out of the twenty-four hours, I worked twenty-two.

Q Would you like to make more videos?

A Oh, I didn't mind it at all. Everything was set up good, everybody takin' care of their parts in the play. I thought it was fine. Ricky done a good job, and I was just glad to be on it to help him. Don't you think Uncle Pen would have been proud of that? I think he would have.

Q Has Ricky been a sort of messiah for bluegrass? He's certainly integrated the two styles, bluegrass and country.

A Well, I think he was raised on bluegrass music. He came on the stage with me one time when he was around eleven years old and played a number. And a lot of his music today, you can see they's some bluegrass in there, the style of bluegrass, the way they play a lot of it today. Of course, he's got country in his playin' and singin'.

Q Who will carry on for you, do you think?

A All the bluegrass people, all over the world.

Q Is there any one person who does it best?

A No. There's a lot of good bluegrass groups, and I just hope that they'll hang in there, and never let bluegrass die. I don't think it will.

Q Do you think Ricky has helped bring in new fans for bluegrass?

A Well, yes. He's brought in fans for Ricky Skaggs, you see, and his style. 'Cause he uses electric, you see, and bluegrass is not electric.

Q According to *The Country Music Book,* by Michael Mason, you played an amplified mandolin—something that seems sacrilegious for you—on Ricky Skaggs's recording of "Uncle Pen." Actually, you're only credited with having played on "Wheel Hoss," but the mandolin doesn't sound amplified there. Did you at any time play an amplified mandolin on a Ricky Skaggs record, or anywhere else, for that matter?

A Amplifier? What's that?

Q Did you play a mandolin with some sort of an electronic pickup?

A (Amused smile) I don't think so. I might have had somethin' over my eyes and my ears if I did.

Q That was always a rule that was not broken.

A Right.

Q You were never tempted to give in on that either?

A Uh-uh. Never.

Q Well, let's be truthful here. In the early days, you had electric guitar on some of your records—as well as drums, an organ, an accordion, and a vibraphone.

A Well, this company—I believe it was Columbia—wanted me to use electric. They thought it would help sell the music, because electric was tryin' to take over. But I would never let electric take over and rule bluegrass music, because it don't belong in it.

Q The sound of the wood is just so different.

A That's right. You're so right.

Q You want to keep it pure.

A I do, yeah.

Q Let's go back to your early years again for a moment. What about a song like "I Was Left on the Street," that tune about the pitiful little boy. Where did that come from? You don't hear it very often.

A No, it should be sung more. I could picture some little boy, you know, bein' treated that way. So I just wanted to let the people know to take care of their little boys better, and never leave 'em on the street like that, 'cause it would be awful sad. But then this man come by and picked him up, and now he's got the little son and the boy's got a home, you see.

Q Is that song reflective of your own childhood?

A No, no. Uh-uh.

Q I know you had some lonesome years as a child.

A Up where I was raised in Kentucky there was no streets there, just dirt roads and farms.

Q I was thinking more of the spirit of it, because you were orphaned rather young.

A Let's see. My mother died when I was ten years old, and my father died when I was sixteen.

Q I read that you're descended from President James Monroe. Is that true?

A I believe so. I would sure like to claim that. My father was named James Buchanan Monroe. Then when my son came along, why, we named him James William Monroe, taken from my father and me. But the Monroes—their ancestors come from Scotland. And on my mother's side, I believe, they was from Holland.

Q Why do you think you're descended from President Monroe?

A Well, we have a family tree, and I've looked at it quite a bit, but not all the way, you know. A nephew of mine, he borrowed it from me. Maybe he'll bring it back sometime.

Q The two men who are always credited with having influenced your music are Arnold Shultz, the black guitar player around Rosine, and your uncle Pendleton Vandiver. Is there anything significant about either of these two men that we haven't heard before?

A Well, my uncle Pen Vandiver was a wonderful uncle. He was on my mother's side. And after my folks had passed away, why, me and Uncle Pen, we "batched," you know, in this old house away up on the hill there above Rosine. And I was workin', you know, a-haulin' crossties with four horses, and telephone poles. So he was a good uncle. And he'd cook for us, you see. In his last days, he was a crippled man. He got throwed by a horse, or somethin', but he was a good uncle, and he treated me awful good. Give me a home to stay in. I'm really proud of it.

Q What do you think he would have thought of your song "Uncle Pen"?

A Oh, I think he would have loved that. And Arnold Shultz was a good man. He's the black man, and he could really play the blues better than any man I ever heard in my life. But he played the old slow blues, where he could pull the strings and make it really sound blue. But you see, the Methodists and Baptists and Holiness singin' has got the feelin' in it that comes from your heart. So, in singin' the blues, and singin' gospel, why, you can tie it together there. And lot of your songs, like "My Rose of Old Kentucky," will have the same kind of a feeling that your gospel song had, you know, in the way of the blues and the sadness in it.

Q There's an awful lot of sadness in your music. A lot of truly mournful songs.

A Yes, they are. Yeah.

Q Were you really that unhappy, or did you just like the sounds of those chords and the mood they created?

A I just wanted to hear that kind of . . . I just knew that it would come down and touch your heart to hear songs like that. And would make you think how things could happen. So I just wanted to put that in the music.

Q There's almost no other music like it. In fact, John Morthland has written: "Only Hank Williams could match [Monroe] for turning private desolation into art." So many of your songs are so heart-wrenching that even if you didn't hear the lyrics, the melodies would affect you in the same way.

A That's right. You're sure right there. Just the music will touch you, the feeling that you put in it. There'd never been nobody played fiddle in bluegrass style 'til bluegrass come along. Nobody played that style. And without bluegrass music, the five-string banjo would never have made it. He didn't have anything much to play. So you had to play in the bluegrass style to really be somethin' for the five-string banjo. And it's really helped in the way of the mandolin. The mandolin has put a lot of drive in the music. The fast notes work just wonderful for the bluegrass style and the way of playin' the mandolin. So it gives the guitar plenty of time to make his changes, you see, like G, C, and D, and put in a run from one chord to the other. And the bass, you know, helped the time, solid beat. He could change, you know, from G, C, and D.

Q What do you think of the musicians who passed through the Blue Grass Boys and went off to play their own style of newgrass?

A Well, I'm glad that they got their start from bluegrass, and I hope that they'll take care of it, and make a future for theirself, and make plenty of money with it, make a good livin'. If you take care of bluegrass music right, and play it right, it will tell you down through a lot of it what you should do, and how you should treat people.

Q So it's a code of ethics as well as a music?

A That's right. And since I've been at the Grand Ole Opry, I've been late three times in forty-six years. What do you think about that?

Q What were the three times?

A One time I'd started to come in from the farm out here in Goodlettsville, and I had a flat tire just about a half a mile on the other side of Good-lettsville. That really stopped me. Back in those early days, nobody traveled, and I couldn't get that tire changed in time to get to the Opry. Then one time I got on Mount Eagle Mountain, comin' up on the other side, and we's drivin' this long stretched-out car—you know, it had four seats, kind of like a limousine—and I noticed back on the left rear wheel that it was smokin' there, you know, and so I stopped real quick. Got out and went around there, and the wheel was done caught afire. So I jacked that up, took the wrench, and got that wheel off, and throwed it down the side of the road. And everybody else was scared to death. They wouldn't fool with it. It could've went out the gas tank and blown up. But anyhow I got that off. Another time, I was up in the eastern part of Kentucky, and they had a cloudburst there. We was on our way back to Nashville, and you couldn't see the road good, so we pulled off. The water was already high, you see. And then it went down, and we moved on down further, and it would come back in behind us. So we come way on down, and the water got so high that you could look up the river there and see a house comin' down, floatin' on top of the water. It'd come on down to the bridge, and crumble up and go under the bridge. And you could see horses, and mules, and cattle walkin' on that water, you know, swimmin'. Just barely hangin' up there, and taking long steps in the water. And they'd come on down, and we would pull 'em off the road, and turn 'em out another way to where they would come off the road, instead of goin' on toward the bridge. And I believe it was [fiddler] Benny Martin—we had to get out and hold the old stretched-out bus on the road, it was just floatin' ever' ways. Lester [Flatt] and Earl [Scruggs] was with us then. Anyway, we went on. The water went back down in front of us, and we moved on up. And we got on up there and the bridge was washed plumb out. So that stopped us. We never could make it to the Grand Ole Opry. So that was three times out of forty-six years that I missed the Grand Ole Opry.

Q Probably nobody has a record like that.

A I don't believe so. If I'm gonna work, I like to be there in time. I don't like to be late.

Q Some of the Blue Grass Boys had trouble adhering to your punctuality.

A Well, some of 'em wanted to come in fifteen minutes ahead of time, but I told 'em they had to come in forty-five minutes [before time to be on-stage], or they didn't work. They wouldn't get paid on that Saturday. So they said, "Why do we have to do that?" And I said, " 'Cause I said so. Come in forty-five minutes, 'cause fifteen minutes don't give you time to tune up, and it don't give you time to rehearse." I believe in comin' in, and tunin' up, and rehearsin', and gettin' your numbers ready.

Q Wait a minute. As I recall, you got an honorary doctorate from the University of Kentucky.

A That's right.

Q And they were going to give it to you on a Saturday night.

A Uh-huh.

Q And you were torn, because you couldn't decide whether you should go play the Opry or go get your honorary doctorate.

A Right.

Q What did you do?

A I can't remember.

Q Really? Come on. You must have gone and gotten it.

A I went and got it. (Laughter)

Q I've heard you say your favorite of all your songs is "Blue Moon of Kentucky." What inspired that?

A Well, I played in the state of Florida, and I was on my way back to West Virginia. And I was doin' most of the drivin', and I started to writin' that song and just singin' it to myself. And when I got into West Virginia, "Blue Moon of Kentucky" was wrote. It's been a great number.

Q What did you think of Elvis Presley's recording the first time you heard it?

A Well, Elvis had a good voice. I thought he had a beautiful voice. And he come up to the Grand Ole Opry one time and come in the dressin' room where I was at. He was real young then. And he apologized for the way that he changed "Blue Moon of Kentucky." I told him, "Well, if it give you your start, it's all right with me." And I was glad that he picked "Blue Moon of Kentucky" for his first number. We'd sung "Blue Moon of Kentucky" in waltz time all the way. Well, when Elvis come out with this [version] where he had it pretty fast, we moved it on up faster for the second [recording], for the bridge and everything, breakin' it over. So we moved it on up faster to where I think it really helps bluegrass. It's more like bluegrass now [with a syncopated mandolin break].

Q You weren't offended by Elvis' 4/4 version, which jazzed it up?

A No. No. Uh-uh.

Q He probably introduced you to an audience that wouldn't have known of Bill Monroe otherwise.

A I imagine he did, yes.

Q Have you written songs under pseudonyms? Aren't you "A. Price," for example, and "Rupert Jones," and "Joe Arr," and several men with the last name of "Smith," which is also your real middle name?

A (Surprised smile on his face, followed by low chuckling) You're comin' up with some things now . . . I don't know what you're talkin' about. You've got names there, like "Rupert Jones" . . .

Q Yes, and "Albert Price" has written several things.

A What did he write?

Q He wrote "The Little Girl and the Dreadful Snake" and "When the Golden Leaves Begin to Fall."

A Is that right?

Q Yes. And they sound remarkably like songs that Bill Monroe would write.

A I'll bet you Bill helped with that. (Laughter)

Q And maybe "Boat of Love," which "James W. Smith" wrote. You think "Mr. Smith" might have had some help from Mr. Monroe on that one?

A I'll bet you Mr. Monroe told him how it should be done.

Q About "The Little Girl and the Dreadful Snake" . . .

A I thought "Albert Price" done a good job on that. That is a fine song, right there. That's a good story about that song.

Q Did he ever tell you what it was?

A Well, it's right there for you to listen to, and you can tell it yourself.

Q But is that a true occurrence?

A Well, don't you think many a little boy or girl went through that?

Q Went out and got bitten by a snake?

A Don't you think so?

Q I always thought that song was about more than a snakebite.

A No, it was just . . . that's what happened.

Q The end of it says, "Parents watch over your children—"

A That's right. But that's after this has all happened. You see, that's tellin' the parents what to do. The mother of the little girl there is really explainin' that.

Q Have you been a good father, do you think?

A I've tried to be a hundred percent with my children. If I done them a favor, or if I loaned them money, I didn't care whether they ever paid me back or not. And they've stood the same way with me.

Q A couple of years ago you founded the Blue Grass Hall of Fame. Why did you want to do that?

A Well, I just thought it would be a big help to the bluegrass people to have a Hall of Fame. And when we got it all together, we picked the names, you know—Ralph and Carter Stanley, Lester Flatt and Earl Scruggs, Don Reno and Red Smiley, Mac Wiseman, Carl Story, Jim and

Jesse [McReynolds], and the Osborne Brothers. It was just good to put all the old-time bluegrass people in there to start with, I think. And we've moved out to Music Village, U.S.A. Everything is going to really be fine out there. They're gonna have the Walkway of the Stars, and they's gonna be a lot of people come there to see it. I think it'll be a help to all the bluegrass entertainers. And this year there'll probably be two more names that'll go in there that have done a lot for bluegrass music.

Q In the early 1940s, there were three traveling tent shows in country music —Jamup and Honey's, Roy Acuff's, and yours, which lasted quite a while. I read that rather than compete with each other for the same audience, each one would pick out a route and stick to it all summer. But you also coupled your show with exhibition baseball games. What were those days like?

A Well, I think that we would seat around three thousand people in the tent, thirty-five hundred, something like that. And then I had the baseball club, the team that traveled with us, and we would play a ball game in the evening and then the show would start. Then later on, I would put on shows at the ballpark, say a forty-five-minute show, and then the ball game would start following that.

Q What did they charge for tickets back in those days?

A In the early days when I was playin', I believe fifteen and twenty-five cents was the admission. Then it went up to twenty-five and forty-five, twenty-five and sixty, but then we moved on up, and adults would pay ninety cents admission to get in. And that was good money back when we had the tent show.

Q Somebody told me that one of the requirements for being a Blue Grass Boy at the time was being able to play baseball. Is that true?

A Well, it helped out if you could play baseball. Like [guitarist-singer] Clyde Moody and Stringbean—people like that.

Q Stringbean was a shortstop, wasn't he?

A Yes, he could play shortstop, but he could play nearly any position. He was a hard man to strike out, boy. He went one year, and I think maybe they only struck him out a couple of times.

Q Where did you get the idea to combine music and ball games?

A I've always loved to see people play baseball, and I love to play it. I've played it a long time. And a lot of my brothers played baseball. Back before television, baseball was really popular all over the country. Every town had a ball club.

Q I thought you couldn't play as a child, because of your eyesight.

A Well, I could play all right. My eyes was a lot better back in the early days. But I finally got glasses and it went to helpin' me some.

Q Did you finally have surgery on your eyes?

A Yes, ma'am, I did. My eyes was crossed in the early days, so I had to have 'em operated on, you know, get 'em straightened out. That changed my looks a little bit.

Q From what I've read, you were terribly self-conscious about your looks as a child. So much so that when visitors would stop by, you would slip off to the barn behind the house.

A I'd get under the floor, if I could—just anything to get away from 'em, so I could see them and they couldn't see me. I was the most bashful kid in the world.

Q But your music is so full of dignity and self-confidence, even though it's rife with what people call "high lonesome."

A I learned a lot when I got on up in years and got knowin' how to do things. I wasn't ashamed then, you see. I wasn't bashful.

Q Was it all because of your eyes, or were there other factors as well?

A Well, that had a little to do with it. But back in the early days, I didn't have the best clothes. I had to wear overalls when I was young. So I was kind of bashful.

Q And we hear this in your music.

A Yep.

Q Most people don't know that the Everly Brothers were on your tent show for a while in 1957. Do you remember them from those days?

A Yes, I do. They had a good duet. Their father [Ike] was a good guitar man, too.

Q That's right. He also learned to play from watching Arnold Shultz.

A They was from down in Kentucky—pretty close to Central City [Brownie, Kentucky]. But they wasn't with me long 'til their record ["Bye Bye Love"] really went to hittin' the charts. So they had to quit the road—the tent show—and get back playin' in country.

Q From what I read, they did straight country on the tent show, and then for an additional attendance fee, they did some rock 'n' roll. But could they have been real bluegrass singers?

A More country than they would have been bluegrass.

Q DeFord Bailey [the black harmonica player on the Grand Ole Opry in the '20s and '30s] also toured with you for a time. Do you remember him very well?

A Yes, I do.

Q What was he like?

A He was a fine black man. I've known him a long, long time, and he could really play the harmonica—better, I thought, than any man ever played one. Back in the early days, there was three or four fellows that could really play a harmonica. Lonnie Glosson—he was a white man—he could really play a harmonica. But DeFord—he could really play the blues, and he traveled and played shows with me a long time. And the people loved him, because they'd listened to him on the Grand Ole Opry for many, many years. He was a good man.

Q He was also one of the first musicians to record in Nashville. But he never really got his due. [Judge George D. Hay fired Bailey in 1941, ostensibly for refusing to learn any more than about a dozen harmonica tunes. The first black musician on the Opry—he opened the show the night in 1927 when Hay rechristened the WSM Barn Dance the Grand Ole Opry— Bailey is thought to have been treated unfairly. Jack Hurst wrote in his book *Grand Ole Opry*: "There may be a glimmer of prejudice in the Judge's observation that Bailey, whom everybody on the show seems to have liked, was lazy." Unlike other of the Opry stars who parlayed their Opry appearances into handsome incomes, Bailey was living in a public housing project at the time of his death in 1982.]

A No, DeFord didn't never get his due. I was at his funeral, and they had me to get up and talk about him a lot. He should have been in the Hall of Fame. I've always thought that.

Q Another musician we never hear much about is your brother Birch. What kind of man was Birch?

A He was a good brother. He enjoyed life, and he enjoyed his friends and his fans. He played the fiddle—the old-time style—years and years ago. And he learned to sing bass when he was young. He loved to sing bass, you know, gospel singin'. And he worked with me a pretty good while. He played the bass fiddle and sang bass.

Q Let me ask you one more thing about your brother Charlie. It's never really been clear exactly why you two broke up.

A Well, Charlie wanted to move out of North Carolina and come into Tennessee. But we had about thirty days or more already booked, and I didn't want to leave the dates over there, and treat the people that way. So I kept stayin' there, and he just up and pulled out and left, and come on in. He wanted me to come with him, and I was a-gonna stay there and play the dates out like I thought they should be played. 'Cause we had already let the people know that we was gonna be there, you see. So that was our breakup.

Q You and Charlie supposedly disagreed often about a lot of things—one of which was the fact that he always treated you as a little brother. But the rumor was always that you broke up over a woman. Is there any truth to that?

A No, when did that happen?

Q Just before you broke up.

A No, no, no, no. Uh-uh. He had his woman and I had mine.

Q I covered Charlie's funeral for *Country Music* magazine, and I remember seeing you and your son, James, there. The talk in Rosine was that you and Charlie had been estranged for thirty-five years. Did you ever make up with him?

A Oh, yeah, we got along. Yeah.

Q You were talking about Birch singing bass. Somebody told me that you used to sing bass, too.

A I started when I was real young, when I went to singin' school. I thought I would love to sing bass, 'cause I had some brothers that could really sing bass—John Monroe and Birch Monroe.

Q Isn't it rather unusual to be able to sing bass all the way up to tenor?

A Right. There's not many people can do that. That was the first singin' I ever done, was bass.

Q There's a story that says you used to get in fistfights in your shows.

A That's right. We used to box a lot. Ever' evenin' we had boxing gloves, and there'd be different people comin' along that would like to box with you. So I've always done that.

Q But it wasn't out of temper?

A No, just a sport. Somethin' you like to do.

Q Your temper flared a little bit last night during your performance at the Station Inn. You said something to the effect of "Some people say I sing flat. I'd like to see them get up here if they think they can do any better." What brought that on?

A Well, I had heard about some feller from down South—he'd wrote me a letter sayin' some fiddle player had told him that I was singin' flat. The fiddle player worked for me.

Q I see.

A Well, the fiddle player—he's got a lot to learn, because he don't know it all, either. And without bluegrass he wouldn't even be playin' music.

Q Do you consider yourself part of country music as well as bluegrass?

A No, I think I'm bluegrass. I think bluegrass is really the best country music. Country is when you get out in the country, and out around farms, if you're gonna talk about the country. It's not in the city. And I think bluegrass is more like that country out there than what they're writin' today and callin' it country. Now the fans out through the country have changed a lot, but them old-time farmers, back years ago, stood more for bluegrass style than they would have numbers like a lot of people do.

Q You wrote a song about the family homestead in Kentucky, "I'm on My Way Back to the Old Home."

A Yes, ma'am.

Q That's a true song.

A Well, that tells about my old home place and everything. And I was going back up there one time, and as I got right there close to home, there wasn't any light in the house. There wasn't anybody living there. It just kindly tore me down. I always looked forward, you know, when I'd go up there. Somebody would be living there. I could see the light there shinin'. So that's why I wrote the song.

Q There's a reference in that song to fox hunting and to being afraid of being left behind. Did that ever happen to you?

A No, but I would go fox hunting with my father. I was real small, and I would sit down by a fence post, and I would get really sleepy. And he'd be standing up and listening to the hounds run, and I just *knew* I was gonna go to sleep, and I was afraid he'd go off and leave me there. When you're young like that, you look at things maybe the wrong way.

Q I want to ask you about another true song—"It's Mighty Dark for Me to Travel." What was the inspiration for that?

A Well, I was down on Broad Street, here in Nashville, and I was in the barbershop. And this old black man—he shined shoes there. He come up to the door, and I heard him say, "It's gonna be mighty dark for me to travel." So I took that line and wrote the song.

Q An old friend of yours told me that your personal philosophy is to look ahead, and not back, because the amount of time it takes for you to turn around and look at the past is the same amount of time you could have been looking toward the future.

A That's right. You know, you can go on down the road lookin' ahead and thinkin' on what's ahead, but your mind will go back there, and you'll think about the old times, the old days, and what you've done back years ago. You don't never forget a lot of it. It'll stay with you. And the old days —there'll never be any more days like 'em, you know. Just enjoy today, while you're young. Because you get way on up in years and things might not be as good, you see. You don't work as much, so you think back to the good old days.

Q But you work all the time.

A Yeah, I can't quit, you see. I've got to pay bills. But I enjoy hard work. I've always worked hard. The work never got too hard for me. I'm not braggin', but that's the truth. From the time I was real young. And when I was up in my late teens, and on up in my twenties and early thirties, I was a stout man. There was a time when I could carry all the Blue Grass Boys myself, at one time.

Q What do you mean, carry them?

A I could hold 'em all up, and they all weighed nine hundred sixty pounds.

Q Wait a minute. You mean you could physically hold all of these men at the same time?

A All at the same time.

Q How many were there?

A There was four.

Q How would you do that?

A Well, I would put one on top of my shoulders, and one around my back. Then I'd hold one with my right arm, and one with my left.

Q Just to see if you could do it?

A Well, I just thought I could do it, so I did.

Q That's an incredible story.

A Yeah, nine hundred sixty pounds. Clyde Moody is still livin', and he was one of the boys. I'd like for him to tell you that happened sometime, because then you'd have two who'd tell you the same thing. You'd believe it better.

Q I didn't say I didn't believe it. It's just unusual for a man to be that strong.

A Yes, I was. I was strong back in my young days.

Q You had a bad car wreck in 1953.

A Yeah.

Q Somebody told me you walked into the hospital, because you didn't want anybody carrying Bill Monroe into the hospital.

A (Laughter) That's right. I walked in with nineteen broken bones. And my legs was broke.

Q You walked into the hospital on broken legs?

A And it was hard to stand up there, because my back was broke in five different places, and my skull was fractured in three. It's a wonder I hadn't fallen plumb out.

Q How did that wreck occur?

A Well, I'd been a-fox huntin', and I got all my dogs loaded, and I was on my way back to Nashville, gonna work that WSM early mornin' [radio] show. They used to have shows around, I believe, five or six o'clock—something like that. And I was makin' this turn on the road. Well, this drunk come in on the same curve I was on, and he just kept comin' right over in the middle of the road 'til he come right up on me. It was just an awful, awful wreck.

Q And when you got out of the hospital, you went onstage in a back brace.

A That's right. I wore that back brace a long, long time. I've still got that old brace out at the house.

Q You're going to all fifty states this year, in commemoration of your fiftieth year as a performer. Even apart from this year, you keep a touring schedule—two hundred fifty dates in 1983, for example—that would be hard on a man half your age. Why do you do it? You don't need the money. [In 1988, Monroe announced that he would cut back his touring.]

A Well, just like we was talkin' a while back, about respect. I love my fans and my friends. And I like to see 'em all at least once a year. Of course, I don't get to see them every year, but I like to go in different states and different parts of the country. And I live in hopes that I'll get to see some of the old-timers. I don't like to slow down. My health is good now, and I'm ready to go.

Q You have a kind of pride in America that you don't see much anymore. There's a path through your yard that is lined with a big rock from each of the fifty states, for example.

A Yeah, if I can ever get 'em laid where they belong. Like Kentucky—K-Y, up there, T-E-N-N—Tennessee, I-N-D—Indiana. I've taken this little machine that you work on rocks with, and I put that [lettering] in there myself.

Q Somebody asked you to explain yourself one time, and you said, "Just tell 'em I'm a farmer who sings tenor."

A (Laughter) That's right. Back years and years ago, that's what I done. All I would do is sing tenor when I first started.

Q Is that how you think of yourself, as just a farmer who sings tenor?

A No, not now, I don't. But that was right back in the early days.

Q One of the former Blue Grass Boys told me that you would prefer to be remembered more as a songwriter than anything else.

A Well . . . Father of Bluegrass Music. That's a good line there. I appreciate that. I'm really glad and proud that I've done somethin' good for America. And I'm glad that the music was called "bluegrass," comin' from the state of Kentucky, since I was born and raised there. It's spread all over the world, and I'm really proud of that. I don't think bluegrass music will ever die now. So I would just like for people to remember me and what I've done.

*A*t the mere sight of it, a tourist in Nashville would probably become so unglued as to drop his Instamatic. There, jogging up and down Music Row, was none other than Willie Nelson, clad in running shoes and jogging shorts, the likes of which are sold along with T-shirts at his concerts. A bandana tied above his red-orange pigtails held the sweat off his face, a dusty

road map of the places he's been and played in his thirty-year rise from obscurity to superstardom, every mile and every day of his fifty-five years etched there in testament. "I run five or six miles a day. Sometimes I'll run twice a day," he was to say later in his soft Texas drawl. But this morning's run is only for show— a local television personality wants Nelson on the six o'clock news.

Willie Nelson has always jogged to his own pace. In late 1970, after his house burned down, Willie left Nashville, where he'd come in 1959, for his native Texas. Despite the 1962 hit "Touch Me," his eighteen or so albums hardly ever passed the cash register. No thanks, he says, to the record company executives, who had little faith in him as a vocalist, feeling his strange, haunting baritone clashed sharply with the prevalent smooth and sweet Nashville Sound. For a long time, he stuck it out in Music City, playing bass—at twenty-five dollars a day—for Ray Price, and watching the songs he wrote for himself—"Crazy," "Night Life," "Hello, Walls," "Funny (How Time Slips Away)"—become major hits for other people. The songwriting money started rolling in, but finally it came down to either compromising or cutting out for Texas. There, even if he didn't get rich, he was his own man, making his own kind of music, a curious and personal blend of country, blues, gospel, honky-tonk, western, and Texas swing. Nelson opted for Texas, where not even he knew there was an audience waiting for him, an audience made up of folk, country, and rock, of hippies and rednecks, oldsters and youngsters, liberals and conservatives, bound together by an undeniable energy and appreciation of plain good music.

A year after leaving Nashville, Nelson recorded *Yesterday's Wine*, a concept album he still considers his best work. RCA, however, didn't see it that way, and his last two singles went nowhere. In 1973, then, Nelson hightailed it to New York and Atlantic Records, becoming the first country artist to sign with the label. There, he recorded *Shotgun Willie* and the critically acclaimed *Phases and Stages*, another concept LP, about the breakup of a marriage, told from both the male and female viewpoints. The album sold an astounding 400,000 copies. With that, Columbia Records offered him a contract that gave him just what he wanted: total artistic control.

The result was 1975's *Red Headed Stranger*, the brilliant, if flawed, theme album of love and murder. Produced by Nelson in three days on a budget of $20,000, the album used such sparse instrumentation that at first, Billy Sherrill, then the top executive in the Nashville office (as well as a producer well known for his intemperate use of orchestral over-dubs), argued against its release. But Nelson reminded the label of his creative-control clause, and pledged that if the album bombed, he would relinquish his autonomy on future projects. The LP became a best seller on both country and pop charts, yielded the crossover hits "Blue Eyes Crying in the Rain" and "Remember Me," and would eventually sell two million copies. Suddenly, the hottest things in country music were Willie Nelson, the "new breed" of singer-songwriter, and what someone quickly termed the "Austin Sound." The attendance at his annual Fourth of July picnic—which started out at 50,000 paying customers—swelled to twice that number.

If *Red Headed Stranger* was Nelson's breakthrough album, the one that secured his superstar status was RCA's *Wanted: The Outlaws*, released in 1976. Essentially a sampler of "Nashville rebel" music, the album featured Nelson, Waylon Jennings—who got top billing, for contractual reasons—Jessi Colter (Jennings' wife), and Tompall Glaser. Although the company hoped it would do well, nobody foresaw what was to happen: *Wanted: The Outlaws* sold like Gatorade at a chili cook-off, becoming the first country album ever to "go platinum," selling more than a million copies. The irony of the project is that the LP was made up of mostly old material that had appeared elsewhere, often in better versions. But the mission was accomplished. "Outlaw" was now the operative buzzword, and Nelson and Jennings took on a stature of semimythic proportions—that of hairy, hell-raising, nomadic loners who broke all the rules and got away with it.

In the next few years, not only Nashville bowed at Nelson's nylonsneakered feet but seemingly the whole country, including President Jimmy Carter, who asked Nelson to sing the national anthem at the 1980 Democratic National Convention, and went on to become a genuinely close friend. By that time, Hollywood had also beckoned, and Nelson received critical praise for his first acting role as Robert Redford's manager in *The Electric Horseman*. If most of Nelson's subsequent films—*Honeysuckle Rose* and *The Songwriter*, in particular—seem to be just more rehashing of the well-known Nelson saga, enough people still find him fascinating that four biographers—Bob Allen, Michael Bane, Lola Scobey, and Willie's daughter, Lana—have written accounts of his life and career. He is, in the words of musicologist Bill C. Malone, "the hottest commercial property that country music has ever had, as well as one of the most visible figures in American popular culture."

Certainly that is true, but in recent years Nelson has scattershot his musical energies in a variety of projects that teamed him with literally dozens of big names in music, from Julio Iglesias to Neil Young. While there has been no solo LP to rival *Red Headed Stranger*—another theme album, *Tougher Than Leather*, which explores the idea of reincarnation and was released after Nelson suffered a collapsed lung in 1981, paled in comparison—Nelson has continued to turn out albums of quality, a feat for an artist so prolific. So far, his most valuable contribution to the '80s has been spearheading Farm Aid, the concert marathon that raised money for the plight of America's farmers. But he has maintained an excellent showing on the charts for more than a decade, long after most careers have seen their peak.

"I thought I'd peaked several times," Nelson said in this interview, conducted in person, in Louisville and Lexington, Ky., and on the telephone over a five-year span, from 1979 to 1984. "Now I don't think I have peaked," he continued. "Everything just seems to be getting a little bit better every day."

Q As a performer, you've managed, at various stages, to win the youth market, with your duets with Waylon Jennings, the Middle America market, with your collection of standards such as "Stardust," and even the easy-listening market, with a big hit such as "Always on My Mind." Obviously, the response you get in Nashville now is a little different from the one you got when you first went there.

A Yeah! Considerably. I like it better this way.

Q In 1979, you became the Country Music Association's Entertainer of the Year. But your most triumphant return to Nashville must have occurred in 1976, when you performed on the CMA awards show, and you and Waylon Jennings went on to rake in most of the honors. What did that feel like?

A Oh, I enjoyed it. That was a big evening. They threw a big party for us. I sang all night long. At two or three different places. Yeah, I reveled in it.

Q Are you bitter about those early days?

A Well, no. Not really. Not now.

Q How often are you back in Nashville now?

A Every chance I get. When I'm out on the road and I've got a couple of days off and I'm close, I'll fly in there. I still have a farm and a house out there north of town [in Ridgetop, Tennessee], where I used to live, and my nephew lives out there. It's [my sister] Bobbie's son, Freddie. And my son is building a place out there, too. So Nashville is still kinda home.

Q You once tried being a pig farmer in Nashville.

A Yes, I really did. I lost a fortune on pigs. I had the fattest pigs in town, or in the country. I paid twenty-five cents a pound for 'em and fattened 'em up for six months. When I sold 'em, I got seventeen cents a pound for 'em. Lost my ass and all its fixtures. (Laughter)

Q How did you let that happen?

A Oh, I had nothin' to do with it. It was just that I got into the hog business at a bad time. I found out from the old-timers that you can't just get in it one year and expect to make a killin' and get out. You've got to stay with it and raise hogs every year.

Q Had you been a farmer before?

A Oh, yeah. I was raised in a small farmin' town [Abbott, Texas], so I farmed all my life, really. Usually for somebody else, because my grand-parents [who raised me] were too poor to own their own farm. So we were working for the *other* farmer. But I raised for the FFA [Future Farm-ers of America] back in school. I used to raise one pig at a time, to show. But I'd never raised that many before, and I never will again.

Q There are some funny photographs of you taken during that time. You looked like the straightest guy in the world.

A I looked like a young baby boy in some of those pictures. Yeah, that was just about the time that I started raising hogs, and growing my beard back and wearing my overalls again.

Q Do you ever run into anybody in Nashville who gave you a particularly hard time when you first went there?

A I don't really know the answer to that question, because I probably couldn't name the people who gave me a hard time. They were always nameless. They were always in New York, or somewhere. There was a computer somewhere that hated me, I think. But as far as enemies in Nashville, I don't have any. Everybody I know there has always been real good, real nice. I haven't seen any bad guys in Nashville. I've seen some people who were uninformed. But it was out of ignorance; it wasn't intentional. No, Nashville hasn't treated me any worse than any other town.

Q So nobody ever treated you badly—they just weren't anxious to have you do your music your own way?

A Well, sure. In other words, these people had things goin' their own way and they were successful doin' it the way they were doin' it. Some upstart from Texas come running up there, runnin' around sayin', "Well, this is the way I want to do it"—I'd probably have reacted the way they did. Because they didn't have any idea that I knew what I was talkin' about.

Q Was there ever a time when you were tempted to compromise to get ahead?

A No. I honestly can't say there was, because I got mad somewhere along the way, and decided I would not do it, and it got to be fun, not doin' it. I mean, not compromising really got to be a thing, maybe to the point where we went overboard in the other direction. Of course, we were doin' okay, the way we were goin'. We weren't gettin' rich, but we were eatin'.

Q Why did it finally take off in such a big way after all those years?

A The energy, I think, from the young people. When that much energy gets behind any project, it's got to skyrocket. You know, when they got behind the Beatles and rock and roll—and there's millions of those kids out there that buy records. And that audience all of a sudden became a country music audience.

Q But why did they focus on you?

A I don't know the answer to that one. I really don't know.

Q And now kids wear T-shirts that say, "Matthew, Mark, Luke, and Willie."

A Well, that may be carrying it too far. It's a nice thought, though.

Q You give the impression that it wouldn't bother you if the crowds didn't keep coming, as long as you could still play music.

A That's true. We just enjoy playin' for whoever's there. I enjoy playin' in a motel room, just sittin' around pickin'.

Q When did you realize you'd made it?

A I think probably the first time was when I went out—I'd been makin' two dollars a day choppin' cotton, and I went out one night and made eight dollars playin' music. I think I was about eleven years old then. From that day on, I had it made. That was the turning point. That was it. No more cotton choppin' for me.

Q What sort of kid were you?

A Well, when I was a kid, "long hair" meant a long-haired musician. And that was long-haired music, long-haired musician. Of course, I wasn't then. I played country music, but I had fairly long hair, and long sideburns. And my hair was always in my eyes for as long as I remember, except a couple of times when I got a burr haircut. I usually went from one extreme to another.

Q Were you outgoing, active in sports?

A I was very active in all kinds of sports. Played basketball, baseball, football, ran track, was a pole vaulter. I just did anything that I could do.

Q Were you mischievous?

A Oh, yeah. That, too. There wasn't a lot to do in Abbott, so you had to be real creative to come up with something to do on a Sunday afternoon. Which we were.

Q Did you think all this was waiting for you?

A No, I didn't. I didn't really know about any of this. I did know what I wanted to do. I wanted to be a guitar player and a singer. And guys like Ernest Tubb, Bob Wills were my heroes, so I wanted to be just like them. And I wanted to have their lifestyle. And now I do.

Q Did you have a feeling of being special?

A Well, I thought I was better than I was doing. I didn't know whether I was special or not. I wasn't that knocked out over my singing voice back then because I had a real high singing voice, before my voice changed. And when my voice started changing, I sounded like a frog croaking for a few years there. So, no, my singing really didn't knock me out, and it doesn't today. You know, I don't think I'm a bad singer, but I don't think I'm that great, either. But I love to play the guitar, and I thought I could write songs.

Q Does your fame keep you fairly isolated? Can you go out in public and mix with people?

A Sure, I went out and played golf all day yesterday at a country club. I get out all the time. I would hate to think that I couldn't, you know. There are people who come up and want autographs. But that's nice, too. It's a lot better than sitting around in your room all the time.

Q You don't have people tearing your clothes off.

A No, fortunately. I've heard all these things about the Beatles and Elvis. But nobody's even, well, tore a button.

Q What have been the major disappointments of your career?

A Well, I've had some major setbacks, that's for sure. There's a lot of years where it was touch and go financially. Trying to keep a band together when you're not making all that much money is a difficult thing to do, as any bandleader can tell you. So we had some lean years there. With a lot of disappointments. A lot of albums that didn't sell. But as far as any one specific thing, I can't think of anything particular.

Q RCA's handling of your first concept album, *Yesterday's Wine*, which is one of your finest LPs, must have been a disappointment.

A Yeah, I thought that was my best one. Well, all those albums that I did back then when they didn't sell, they were all major disappointments. Because each one of those albums had ten or twelve songs, pieces of my life in them, you know. And I felt very strongly about all those songs, and still do. I think a lot of those songs never had a chance to be accepted.

Q Did you always feel secure about your talent back then?

A Well, that's two different things there. I was never doubtful of my talent, but the odds on anything happening—I mean, there was a time or two that I had a lot of negative thoughts about what my future would be. I wasn't sure whether I might be back pumping gas or picking cotton for a living. Which could have happened. Or really, I think the worst that could have happened was I would go back to playing in small nightclubs around the country again. But that's not too bad, and not a bad way to make a living, either. You can only spend so much money, as long as you're making enough to buy groceries and pay rent and buy a few clothes, and buy a car. That's about all you can expect, anyway. I don't think I would ever have had to go back to picking cotton, but the thought did cross my mind when things weren't going that well. I wasn't going up, but I wasn't going down, either. I was just kind of hanging in space there for years.

Q Where are you now?

A I really don't know. I thought I'd peaked several times. Now I'm not sure. I don't think I have. Everything just seems to be getting a little bit better every day.

Q Do people still call you an "outlaw"?

A I don't know whether they do or not.

Q That term was misunderstood, wasn't it? Originally it meant that your music didn't conform to the Nashville standard, but then some people thought it meant that you beat up people and took a lot of dope.

A Well, some people misunderstood it, I think, or maybe they didn't. (Chuckling)

Q Did you mind that label?

A No, I don't care. It was funny then, and well, I still think it's funny every time I read something where it says "Willie Nelson, the outlaw." But I guess it makes good reading for somebody.

Q How did that get started?

A Oh, I don't know. Somewhere between Tompall [Glaser] and [Jerry] Bradley [formerly in charge of all operations of RCA Nashville], I guess. They thought it might be a good idea, and evidently it was. It caught on.

Q You seem to always be full of surprises. The music industry, for example, thought you were out of your mind when you said you were going to do the *Stardust* album, made up of old pop standards. Did you ever have any doubts about it?

A No, I never did, because those were songs that I've been doin' for people every night nearly all of my life, and I knew that people liked 'em, and I knew I could do "Stardust" and turn around and do "Fraulein" or any kind of music. Those people didn't know whether they were country or pop. Somebody had to tell them later on. They just knew they liked music. They'll sit out there and drink a beer, and they'll dance to "Stardust," and they'll dance to "You Are My Sunshine." They just like music. And I just like music. And those were just songs. They didn't have labels back then. The more I got into the record end of the business, I found out they had music sliced up into a bunch of different categories. And that was very confusing to me. Then I had to start slicin' up what I knew. "Well, you can't play this one, 'cause it's not country," or "You can't play that one, 'cause it's not commercial." So there's a lot of people that still live under the illusion that music is sliced up, but it's not. A G is a G. A quarter note is a quarter note. Whoever's doing it makes it different.

Q Some people think you're largely responsible for bridging country and pop. Would you agree?

A Well, that's a nice thought. Whether it's true or not, I don't know. I may have been partly responsible for exposing both kinds of music to both audiences. *Maybe.* But, of course, I wasn't the only one. There's guys been doin' it all along. I just sneaked some stuff in and caught 'em not lookin', and they liked it before they knew it.

Q But if you didn't look the way you do, with the beard and the long hair, would the kids listen to you sing "Stardust" and some of the older songs?

A Yeah, I think the kids would accept those albums. They're not buying a look, they're buying music. I think the fact that I had long hair and an earring probably got their attention a little bit, and the older people, too. Made some of them pretty mad, I think. But, I mean, there's nothing not to like about those songs. I would question someone's sanity a little bit if they didn't like "Moonlight in Vermont" or "Sunny Side of the Street." A good song doesn't get old. It doesn't die out. A good song just stays and stays forever. There are hundreds of thousands of songs that are still laying there waiting for someone to come along and pick them up again. They were hits twenty, thirty, forty years ago, and they'll be hits in the next twenty to thirty to forty years also.

Q Probably no one else in country music is capable of pulling off these things the way you do. Any idea why?

A Not really, no. I'm not that great a singer. I know the songs and I sing the melody. I don't try to get tricky with them. I think a lot of the singers who know these songs are the pop singers who have such good voices that they usually wind up oversinging those songs. And I think the melody and lyric of those particular songs is so special that it doesn't need anything other than just saying the words and following the melody, really.

Q So you never consciously thought about crossing over?

A That's a term I wasn't familiar with until I got to Nashville. Then I started hearing words like "commercial" and "crossover." Because music had always crossed over. There had never been any divisions in Texas, where I came from.

Q Is music really any different, or played any differently, in Texas, say, as opposed to Nashville? Can there really be a "sound" that's confined to a certain city?

A Oh, no, I don't believe that. I don't believe the Nashville myth or the New York myth. I think they're all musicians travelin' around all over the world makin' music. If they stop in Nashville, they're not gonna sound any different than if they stop in Austin. It just doesn't make sense. Now, there might be some towns where good musicians gather more than they do in other towns. Austin is that place, for sure. There's probably more good bands playing live music in Austin than in any other city in the country.

Q Why is that?

A The climate is good, the attitude of the people is good, the attitude toward strangers is good, and then it's just a nice place to go.

Q Has it changed much through the years?

A No, there's more people down there. It's like Nashville and every place else—it's grown.

Q But did you develop this Austin music scene, or was it already there and you just became the big symbol for it?

A All the ingredients were there. The audience was there. I just happened to stumble onto an audience, really. I just saw that there was a lot of young people who liked country music, and I may have been one of the first ones to see that. And so I started lookin' for the young crowds because I enjoyed that energy. I like bein' around young people. And I thought it was great that they were beginning to like country music and they were beginning to like what I was doin'. So we started seekin' each other out, I guess. But, say, when Leon Russell came out with that album, *Hank Wilson's Back,* that helped a lot, too. Because there was a lot of Leon's rock-and-roll fans that listened to country music for the first time. And they heard "The Window Up Above," "Rollin' in My Sweet Baby's Arms," and "Goodnight, Irene." Leon laid the groundwork for guys like me, who was comin' along singin' those same songs.

Q You did an album with Leon, *One for the Road,* and then you toured together. How did that pairing come about?

A Actually, Leon and I have been friends for a long time, and I'd been tryin' to figure out a way to make records with him for years. And when he did his *Hank Wilson* album, I thought it was great, and I wanted to see him do some more of those. I finally talked him into doin' one with me.

Q When did you first meet him?

A The first time we knew anything about each other was in a studio on the first album that I cut, on Liberty Records. Leon was a sideman, playin' piano, and he didn't know me, and I didn't know him. But we found out later that we'd been on the session together. He recognized himself on one of my records one time, playin' "Mr. Record Man." He said, "Hey, that sounds like me!" Leon is just a genius, I think. He may be the greatest musician I've ever known, alongside of Booker T. Jones.

Q Actually, *One for the Road* sounds as if it were done almost spur of the moment, and that you settled for the first take on a lot of the songs.

A Yeah, it was one of those deals where I was talkin' to Leon and we had a week off at the same time, and he had his studio, so we just sailed into California and spent the week out at his place there, and recorded every day and every night, and filmed it all. We got, I think, a hundred and three songs in six days. And everything filmed. Course, all those are not keepers. *Most* of those are one takes, and there's mistakes that had to be fixed. We had a lot of fun doin' it. One night we did eighteen songs, just he and I and the piano—songs like "Tenderly," and "Stormy Weather," and a lot of those old pop standards that we both knew. So it was easy to do it, and then he took those and went into the studio and put all the other parts on there himself. And there's like ten songs on that album where it's just Leon all the way. He played every instrument on there.

Q Most people consider *Red Headed Stranger* to be your masterpiece. How did you come up with that?

A I really had a movie in mind from the beginning. [A film version of the story, starring Nelson, Morgan Fairchild, and Katharine Ross, was finally released in 1987.] Well, I was thinking about a concept album, too. But I felt like I was writing a sound track when I did it. And I wrote it as if I *were* the guy, which is probably the way I write everything.

Q You've done quite a few films now. How much different is acting from your usual work?

A It's really easier. You've got more time to do what you have to do. The only thing is, you never know how good you did until later.

Q Has anybody accused you of having "gone Hollywood"?

A Oh, I don't care what they say about me. It doesn't really matter.

Q Kris Kristofferson has gotten a lot of criticism that he's gone off and done the movies and ignored his music. Have you heard those criticisms about yourself?

A Oh, I'm sure I'll be criticized whatever I do. While they're talkin' about me, they're lettin' somebody else rest.

Q Is the desire to do movies strong, or do you do them because they're fun to do? Do you want to make a statement with them, for example?

A Oh, no. I just want to play cowboys, is all. I've been wantin' to be in the movies ever since I saw Gene Autry up there, singin' and pickin'. Don "Red" Barry, Whip Wilson, Lash LaRue. I guess I'm like every other kid. I wanted to be in the movies.

Q A singing cowboy?

A Sure! Why not?

Q Did you think you were good in *The Electric Horseman*?

A I thought I was *real* good.

Q You really did?

A Yeah, I really did! What I was doin' wasn't that hard, and there wasn't really that much to do.

Q Did you play yourself? Is it basically your personality?

A Yeah, that's the good part about it. They let you be yourself. In fact, they encourage it. They just let you be natural. Sydney Pollack, the guy that directed it, was real good. He helped any way that he could. But you asked me if it was harder. It isn't as hard physically as doing one-nighters. But when you do the shows, you know how well you did, and you get the audience response immediately. You've got to wait a long time on these movies, I found out. The time between the time that you first think of doing a movie and then you actually see it on the screen is a long, long time. But as long as you've got a lot of patience, I think movies are okay.

Q For a while, you were considered to play in *The Best Little Whorehouse in Texas*.

A Well, I was just one of the guys I think that they had considered for the part. They flew me to New York and I saw the play. And I met with Larry King, the writer. And I met the producers, and at the same time I understand they were talking to Burt Reynolds, and I think he had said no one time, and then he said yes. So it wasn't surprising to me that they had chosen Burt Reynolds over me to do that part. In fact, I'm not sure that that part would have been right for me, anyway. I'm not a very good song-and-dance man, which, for that particular role, you had to be.

Q You haven't done much television. Have you intentionally shied away from the small screen?

A Well, you're always a little afraid of overexposing, you know, if you do too much TV. So that's why.

Q Do you have any specific plans for TV?

A Well, I don't know. I haven't got any plans right now.

Q Surely there are offers every day.

A Well, no, not today . . . (Laughter) Nothing came in today.

Q You apparently aren't afraid of overexposing yourself with records. It seems as if you've got a new one out every time I turn around.

A Well, I'm watching it to see what happens. I know I've got a lot of albums out there, and every time I put one of them out, I think, "Well, maybe this one has no chance at all because it's the ninth album this month," you know. But they seem to all be doing very well. So long as they're selling, I'm not going to worry about it.

Q You also have recorded duets with everyone from Julio Iglesias to Bill Monroe.

A Yeah, I'm up to the M's now. (Chuckling)

Q *Poncho and Lefty,* your duet album with Merle Haggard, was one of your most critically acclaimed albums. How did you and Merle decide which songs you were going to do?

A Well, some of them were my old songs, and some were Merle's old songs. And then for the others, we'd just sit around and start thinking up tunes. We'd record one that I thought of, and then it'd be Merle's time to come up with one. And then Chips Moman, who was doing the producing, would come up with one. So we kind of made it a community project.

Q When you sit down to record, is it a spontaneous thing?

A Well, not really for everybody. The musicians could care less what we play. They're just waiting for someone to tell them what to play. And they let us figure out the tunes that we're going to do. But normally, I know what I'm going to do when I get there. But with Merle or Roger Miller or Webb Pierce, it was easier just to sit around and talk about what we wanted to do next.

Q With those albums with Roger Miller and Webb Pierce and some of the others, were you trying to help people in the industry who had fallen on hard times, or were you just wanting to record with people you happened to like?

A Well, mainly it was to record with people that I enjoyed their singing and I knew that we could sing together. I think it's a shame that all the good singers are scattered around on so many different labels that they never get to sing together. Plus, I knew that there was a lot of people that maybe hadn't been familiar with the songs. Maybe they didn't have a chance to listen to them. Maybe they were too young when, for instance, Webb's songs came out. There's a lot of people, I'm sure, who've never heard "In the Jailhouse Now," one of Webb's songs. Same thing with a lot of Merle's early stuff, and Roger's early stuff. And if it turns out to help them in the long run, well, that's great, too. But I had my own selfish reasons. They have very good songs.

Q Are you still touring two hundred nights a year?

A Yeah, probably that or more. Really, we could do 365 days if they were close enough together. And it really wouldn't be that hard. It's not really that much work to me. I enjoy doin' it. If I didn't play music, if I wasn't allowed to play music, I'd probably get physically sick. It's just something I have to do.

Q What does that do to your private life?

A Well, course, I haven't had one of those in years. I've about forgotten what those are.

Q You call your band the Family Band, and you also refer to your entourage as "family." What makes up the family? Just anybody who happens to drop by?

A Well, the family covers a lot of people. Anybody that likes us. It's pretty open. We'll let anybody in.

Q Many of the musicians in your band have been with you for a long time, and have taken on something akin to cult status themselves. You've known Paul English, your drummer, for example, since 1954, and he's been in your band since 1967. You even wrote a song, "Me and Paul," about your friendship. How did you choose the other members of the group?

A Kinda strange. Most of 'em just kinda turned up. Jody Payne, for instance, turned up one day to play with Sammi Smith, who was on the show with me. Bee Spears showed up one day to take over for somebody who went into the Army. So I really haven't had a lot to do with it. Mickey Raphael I met [in 1974] at a party after a football game in Dallas. [Coach] Daryl Royal was givin' an after-the-game party, and we were all settin' around playin' music, and there was this harmonica player who was just playin' fantastic, so we played together that night, and a few days or weeks later, I did a benefit over in Lancaster, Texas, and Mickey showed up with his harmonica. He's been with me ever since.

Q You do basically the same repertoire every night, and you have for years now. How do you keep the songs fresh after literally thousands of performances?

A Well, we do 'em different each night, basically. When we hit the bandstand, everybody's coming from twenty different directions. I'm always amazed that we ever get a show done. But that's the reason. We never do sound checks, and we never rehearse. That way, it's bound to sound different every night.

Q So there's some improvisation to it?

A Sure. Our show is a lot improvisation. Basically we know the songs, we know the chord progressions, and we've got some head arrangements going. But as far as who's gonna do what, and what notes we're gonna play, we don't really know. I think it makes it more interesting. Everybody looks forward to working that night, because they don't have any idea what they're gonna do.

Q Your guitar has a tone to it unlike any other. How do you mike it? One writer said it sounds like you're playing steel cables.

A (Laughter) Well, that's sort of a bastard setup there. It started out to be a Baldwin guitar with a Baldwin stereo pickup and a Baldwin amplifier. I broke the guitar, and Shot Jackson in Nashville took the pickup from the broken Baldwin and put it in this Martin classical that I've had for years now. I've never been able to get that sound out of any other setup. I don't know what it is. I've tried the same setup with other guitars and other Baldwin amplifiers, and it doesn't work. I guess I just lucked into a real jewel of a guitar. It's like violins. If you happen to get one that's really good, hang on to it, because there's none other like it.

Q You're a strong proponent of positive thinking. How did you get into that?

A Out of necessity, I think. I was so negative and I could see the results of it. And I was very unhappy and I was making myself unhappy, and I'm sure anyone that was around me, I was making *them* unhappy. And I just decided one day that I didn't want to be that way anymore.

Q Did you take a training program?

A No, I read a lot. And I started applying what I'd read, and it worked, so I'm a fanatic about it now. I just can't be around anything or anybody negative. Just refuse to do it. Haven't got time for it. That kind of thing rubs off. There's not a negative-thinking person that I know of on the buses. I don't think he would last long. People would run him off, or he'd have to leave. Because everybody around me knows how I feel, and in keeping those things away from me, consequently they keep them away from themselves. So there are no fights or arguments.

Q Does it keep you from going through periods of depression?

A Yeah, it does. It doesn't keep me from having tendencies—everybody has tendencies to think negative all the time, but it gets easier to turn it around. It's an amazing thing. It snowballs. Just like one negative thought will snowball into a whole big bunch of 'em, a positive thought will do the same thing. And the only thing that'll turn around a negative thought is a positive thought. It helps me continually. Because a negative thought can, and does, produce poisons, releases poisons—actual physical poisons in your body. And they can make you deathly sick. And the first thing you know, you've got stacks and stacks of negative thoughts in your mind. And it gets to a point where nothing is right. You're physically and mentally and spiritually sick. I believe negative thinking causes all kinds of illnesses, including cancer and about any type of ailment you can think of. And it's not easy to turn around in the beginning, because you've spent so many years building those negative thoughts up. And they've been excuses for all your failures. You don't want to start tearing them down, because you don't want to have to admit that you've been that wrong so long. But once you do admit it and start thinking positive thoughts, and replacing the negative ones, then you start having a lot of positive results.

Q Do you sleep easier now?

A I think I could probably sleep the clock around, and do sometimes, but my sleepin' habits are not normal, because I work crazy hours and am not an example of a normal guy. I used to have a lot of bad dreams and nightmares. Maybe fifteen years ago they started fading away and I don't really dream a lot now. Maybe I'm asleep all the time and don't know it.

Q Was that during a non-creative period?

A No, I think I was probably more creative back then. I don't know, there were a lot of negative things going on around my life during that period, so I'm sure that had a lot to do with it, too.

Q Did your career start to turn around when you started practicing positive thinking? Was all this happening at the same time?

A Well, it wasn't that great. I was still successful as a songwriter and an entertainer, but I wasn't happy. It wouldn't have mattered how successful I was, I still wouldn't have been happy. Then when I started turning it around, the first thing that I noticed was that things weren't that good, but they weren't that bad, either. They could have been a lot worse. And I started accepting the fact that I wasn't that successful in all the aspects of my career, but I could still make a living and support my family doing what I do. And there's a lot of people who can't do that. So I started looking at how fortunate I was. "Count your blessings," is how the Baptists and Methodists would explain it. But I started doing that and it started turning my whole life around, and I noticed that things didn't bother me as much anymore. Nothing seems to bother me anymore, really. I've learned to roll with the punches, I think.

Q This is interesting, because your personality has been described as "Buddha-like," but you're also supposed to have a nasty temper.

A Contradictory reports, I'd say. Somebody's lyin'. Or else they're both right, I don't know. No, really, I do have a terrible temper. I can't think of any specific things that *make* me angry, but it used to make me mad when people would try to tell me what to do. Like a guy would blow a whistle and wave a flashlight and try to direct me places I didn't want to go. There must be some significance to that somewhere back in my past. I don't know.

Q How would you like people to think of you?

A Oh, I think everybody likes to be liked. I like people, and there's no reason for people not to like me, really. I don't give 'em any reason to, or I try not to.

Q I saw a show of yours in Waco once, and backstage people were talking about your legendary healing powers. I kept waiting to see a test of that, but it never came up.

A I guess nobody was sick.

Q Do people really believe that?

A I've heard that a couple of times. I'd read that somewhere, but I never did know that I really healed anybody.

Q Isn't there some famous story of some friend of yours sitting in the front row and jumping up and claiming he was healed from a crippling disease?

A I think probably his downer wore off or something.

Q Let's talk some more about your writing. You had a good case of writer's block for a while. How did you get over that?

A I go for a long time when I think, "Well, I'll never write nothin' else. This is it. I've written my last song." And then another idea will come along. Just about the time I give up, I write somethin' else. Oh, I don't give up. I was just kiddin' you, really. I don't worry about it when I don't write. Practically every time that I make myself sit down and rest for a few days, well, I'll start writing. As soon as my mind gets still. That's hard to do these days. I go for months when I can't write my name.

Q Do you go through spells where you'll write one sort of song a lot?

A Yeah, I'd go on house songs for a long time. Every song I'd write would be about a house: "Hello, Walls" was one of them. Probably the rest of 'em you're not familiar with: "Hello, Roof." (Laughter) "Hello, Car" . . .

Q The first project that really got you writing again was *Tougher Than Leather*, right?

A Yeah, that was new material, original material, about a gunfighter who killed this young man, and then got away free. And then he died, and then he was reborn again later as a modern-day urban cowboy, and bad karma caught up with him. And he's sent to prison for something that he didn't do. and the whole theme of it is "Was it something I did, Lord, a lifetime ago? Am I just now paying a debt that I owe?"

Q Do you believe in reincarnation?

A Yes, I do. There's a recent survey somewhere that says that over forty percent of the people believe in reincarnation in this country. Other countries, there's a higher percentage than that.

Q Where do you think you are in the cycle?

A I don't really know. I'm not really concerned about who I was or who I'm going to be. I don't think that's for me. And I haven't spent any time trying to find out or think about it that much. I'm more concerned about what I am today, and I kind of let other people think about what I'm going to be or what I used to be. But I do believe that I was here before, and you were, and we all were.

Q What sort of religious teachings did you have as a child?

A I was brought up as a Protestant, a Methodist. And then I went to the Baptist church later on when I was just in my early twenties. And then I started checking out other religions around the world just to see what other people believed. But if you believe that for all actions there is an opposite and equal reaction, then karma and reincarnation are very real. To me, it's the only thing that does make sense. You can see that everyone is not equal. And you will always find someone who is one of the nicest, finest people in the world who's being miserably mistreated. So in order to justify that, this person has to have something in his karmic past. He's paying for something that he did before. Otherwise, it's all injustice.

Q Do you think of music as being spiritual?

A Oh, I think it's definitely spiritual. All music is. I think it's maybe one of the highest forms of spirituality. Every singer who stands up there is responsible to put across his ideas and beliefs, and I think people expect him to do that, whether he's a preacher with a sermon or a singer with a song. I think basically that's what we all do. We're all teachers, rather than preachers, I think. Each individual has his own little bit of teaching to do each day. If there's a key word, it's "communication." An artist communicates with the audience, and the audience communicates with the artist, and there's an exchange of energies that takes place. And so in that respect, everyone who's standing up there is delivering some sort of message.

Q I read that when you first started out, you played in places so rough that the management had to put chicken wire in front of the bandstand so you wouldn't get hit by flying beer bottles. Is that true, or just another country music myth?

A Yeah, there was a place we used to work in Fort Worth, over on the North Side, on Exchange Avenue, where the musicians had gotten together and decided they didn't want to work this joint unless the guy would put this chicken wire around there. It was too dangerous. You're standin' up there playin', and somebody hits you in the back of the head with a beer bottle. Maybe not intendin' to—maybe he's throwin' it at his wife, or somethin'. Throws your timin' off. But, yeah, it does get a little rowdy in Texas. It's always been that way. Their mothers and dads were that way, so they get it naturally.

Q Probably not too many people realize that you took Charley Pride on a package tour throughout the South when he had only one single out. And this was when the civil rights movement was at its height. What was it like when you were trying to introduce Charley to your audiences? The story goes that you'd give him a big buildup, and then when he came out, you kissed him full on the mouth. By the time the audience got over the shock, Charley already had them hooked.

A (Laughter) Well, it was a little scary, back in those days, and it was, I guess, the first time that a black kid had ever crawled up in front of thousands of white people and started singin' country songs. I wasn't exactly sure how Charley was going to be accepted, but they loved him. And it was sort of controversial. I mean, a lot of people didn't think it was a good idea to put Charley on the show. That took a lot of nerve on his part, too. But when they found out how good he was, and how the people accepted him, then they wanted him on all the shows. Some of the motels wouldn't let him in, and some of the clubs didn't want him to be on the stage, even. So it was interesting going through places like Dallas and Shreveport and San Antonio. But everyone was really very nice, and no one ever said one thing. I guess everyone's imagination was running away with them with what possibly could happen. I still see Charley occasionally. Mostly at golf tournaments. That's about the only place we run into each other these days. He's doin' okay.

Q Do you ever long for those old days, when it wasn't quite so crazy?

A Yeah, I really do. You know, not to the point where I want to go back to 'em, but I think about 'em a lot, where the places were smaller and the crowds were smaller. The reaction was smaller. So I think about it a lot, but I don't really want to go *back* to those days. And I think about why I made it and so many of the others didn't. But I'm not gonna question it. I'm just gonna enjoy it.

Q Are you really having as good a time as you seem to be?

A Oh, yeah. I'm getting to do what I like to do, which is play music and travel. So I'm enjoying myself a lot. I'm having a big time.

Q Do you feel like a legend?

A Well, not really. I'm not sure how I'm supposed to feel.

Q Is it embarrassing to you?

A Not really, because it's kind of an overused word, anyway. It's kind of like "outlaw." It's just another label. I suppose "legend" is supposed to be a positive label. So it doesn't offend me. It's really a compliment in a way. But it sure makes you sound old.

Dolly Parton

The tourist attractions along Highway 441 in Pigeon Forge, Tennessee (population 2,400), rise up out of the foothills of the Great Smoky Mountains like some fantasy carnival from outer space. On the most congested strip this side of Las Vegas, factory outlets, car museums, and outdoor water slides do silent battle for the dollar of the passing motorist. Giant dinosaurs and giraffes—safe in the confines of a handful of miniature golf centers—stare across the road at the façade of an ancient castle, silhouetted against the blue hue of the mountains in an odd, otherworldly scene.

Most of the people who stop here are en route to Gatlinburg, five miles up the highway, where nine million tourists go each year to shop, ski, and camp. In the spring of 1986, the area unveiled another major tourist site—a multimillion-dollar theme park modeled on the life of singer Dolly Parton—Sevier County's most famous daughter—and her Smoky Mountain origins.

Dollywood.

The name, of course, is a Dogpatch play on Parton's own name, her movie career, and the trees that line the Smokies. It came to her, she says, when she first saw the famous "Hollywood" sign sprawled across the Los Angeles hills. If she couldn't sneak up there and change the H to a D, she would simply have to create her own Dollywood—and possibly spread her own sign across the same great mountains that long ago conspired to form the essence of her child-woman personality, and fired her ambition to venture far beyond their smoky rim. It was here that Parton first learned to turn adversity into assets, to believe in the *magic* of believing, and to believe, above all, in herself.

"It's a dream that I have long cherished," Parton told reporters who crowded into Dollywood to ogle her personal tribute to commerce and corn pone. "I love the Smoky Mountains, and I wanted to create a prestigious place and jobs for the people in the area where I grew up. I just felt it was a great thing—a Smoky Mountain fantasy to preserve the mountain heritage."

It was also, as the entrepreneurial Parton knew to the tips of her sculpted fingernails, a very real opportunity to strengthen her grip on the American consciousness while turning a constant and vaguely philanthropic-sounding dollar. If her music and film career has meant that the 42-year-old Parton has realized the American dream on her own terms, she is now carrying the dream to further heights—from Hollywood to Dollywood, and from backwoods singer to commercial real estate developer. And if Parton is successful in her long-range plans for the area—in time, she hopes to expand Dollywood to include a hotel, a Teen Town, a dude ranch, a convention center, and television facilities to accommodate her own production company—she could well become the Donald Trump of East Tennessee, not only erecting monuments to a hometown girl made good, but initiating an economic development project to challenge Sevier County's high double-digit unemployment rate.

Of course, Parton is not the only country singer with her own theme park—Conway Twitty's Twitty City, George Jones's Jones Country, and Loretta Lynn's Dude Ranch immediately come to mind. But Dollywood is far more dazzling, far more show-biz—it opened to a media blitz engineered by Parton's high-powered West Coast management team—just as Parton has always aimed to do her country music colleagues one better, moving her records into mainstream music, taking her cantilevered figure and porcelain-dolled face into the movies (*9 to 5*, *The Best Little Whorehouse in Texas*, *Rhinestone*, and *Steel Magnolias*), and eyeing the distinct possibility of moving her ebullient, but strong-willed, personality into the annals of American folklore.

From the moment she first found success in Nashville, Parton became an ambassador for the East Tennessee hills, celebrating the beauty as well as the hardships of the mountain lifestyle in such songs as "Coat of Many Colors," "My Tennessee Mountain Home," and the profoundly moving "Appalachian Memories."

If anyone has suspected Parton of exaggerating the severity of her childhood, in truth the poverty that she endured in the hollers behind the park that now bears her name was worse than she ever let on. The fourth of twelve children—all of whom slept four and five to a bed—Parton was born in a two-room shack on the banks of the Little Pigeon River. Her father, a sharecropper, paid the delivering physician, Dr. Robert F. Thomas, whom Parton was to immortalize in a song bearing his name, with a sack of corn meal.

Inspired by her mother's singing of folk songs, her father's occasional banjo picking, and the singing in her grandfather's local Chuch of God congregation, Parton began fashioning her own melodies and words at the age of seven. By the age of ten, she was a regular on Cas Walker's Knoxville radio and TV shows, and three years later, she had traveled to Lake Charles, Louisiana, with her uncle to cut a record and to Nashville to make her debut on the Grand Ole Opry. By the time she was in high school, she had wangled a songwriting contract with the prestigious Tree Publishing Co., and cut another single, this time on the major label Mercury Records. Nevertheless, she remained a regular on the Cas Walker programs until the day after graduation, in 1964, when, with a pasteboard suitcase holding her belongings, she boarded a Greyhound for Nashville, vowing to her friends that "I'm never comin' back 'til I make it."

In Nashville, however, Parton discovered that her celebrity status in East Tennessee cut little ice with the big-time record companies. "The day she came to see me," recalls Fred Foster of Monument Records, "she said, 'Everybody in town has turned me down.' " Foster, recognizing the potential of Parton's composing, singing, and interpretive gifts, signed her to a recording contract. They scored with a Curly Putman tune, "Dumb Blonde," before Parton left for RCA. Porter Wagoner, the impossibly pompadoured and sequined hillbilly star, had picked her as the "girl singer" on his syndicated television show and his duet partner on the larger label.

The Porter Wagoner years (1967–74) encompassed, by Parton's account, the best and the worst of what could happen to a young, ambitious, and talented singer-songwriter. While the association with Wagoner's TV show exposed her to millions of country fans who came to her concerts and bought her duet and solo LPs—making her a bona fide star and giving her an annual income of several hundred thousand dollars by the time she was in her early twenties—it also placed her under Wagoner's thumb in the recording studio. The upshot was that while this period saw the peak of Parton's extraordinary songwriting talents ("Coat of Many Colors," "Tennessee Mountain Home," "Joshua," "Down from Dover," "Jolene," and "I Will Always Love You"), she was unable to record her songs the way she originally heard them in her mind. That—plus her boundless ambition to test her talents in other areas—finally led her to break up their award-winning team to pursue an independent career, one that would include an all-out bid for acceptance in the rock, pop, and youth music ranks.

For a short time, Parton toured the country with a group made up of her siblings and cousins, dubbed appropriately the Traveling Family Band. The idea was an admirable one—Parton had always tried to share her success with her family and loved ones—but the cold fact of the matter was that the family had neither the professionalism nor the talent to sustain her. At the same time Parton realized the mistake, she saw that she had also erred in involving herself in a low-budget syndicated TV show that caused more confusion about her change of musical direction. A second ill-fated TV series, this one on the ABC network during the 1987–88 season, would do the same. Nonetheless, the Country Music Association voted Parton the Female Vocalist of the Year in both 1975 and 1976.

By the following year, Parton had generated enormous controversy in the country music industry, largely through her hiring of a Los Angeles-based management firm, Katz-Gallin-Cleary, whose clients included such personalities as Mac Davis, Cher, Florence Henderson, the Osmonds, and Olivia Newton-John, the pop singer who earlier incurred the wrath of Nashville's Old Guard by carrying off the CMA's Female Vocalist of the Year award in 1974. The feeling in Nashville was that Parton had abandoned the people who had both accepted her and made her what she was, a resentment reinforced by Parton's subsequent shift toward a repertoire of overproduced, middle-of-the-road pop music and her reluctance to appear on country-oriented programs, even though she never truly stopped singing country songs. In 1978, partly from grudging admiration, and partly on "good faith" that Parton was not turning her back on country music but merely taking it with her into the larger public arena, the CMA honored Parton with its highest accolade, that of the Entertainer of the Year award. She became only the second woman in history (after Loretta Lynn) to receive it.

The irony of the Dolly Parton story is that the more her California management firm marketed her as a professional personality, and the less interesting Parton's own writing became, the more she began to be acclaimed as one of the great talents of American popular music. But as the transcript of our interview shows, that is something that Parton, a woman of superior intelligence and uncommon instinct, was banking on when she made her move.

The following interview—my only formal meeting with Parton—took place over a two-day span in February 1977 at a house she was renting on Nashville's fashionable Woodmont Boulevard. (She had temporarily moved out of her Brentwood, Tennessee, home, believing that something in the soil or in the well-water supply on the farm was making her ill.) Our talk came at the height of the Parton controversy, when she was most vulnerable to rumors about her intentions, and began on the day after she returned from her first crossover tour, opening for Willie Nelson on a trek through Texas.

Both of us were well aware during this interview that her crossover bid was *the* country music story of the year, Parton saying before we began that she hoped this session—for a cover story in *Country Music* magazine—would clear up any questions the country music audience had about her plans. For that reason, and because, I believe, she wanted to know exactly what Nashville was saying about her, she encouraged me to ask her about all of the rumors circulating about both her career and her private life. One of the funniest—and most rampant—was that her husband, asphalt contractor Carl Dean, was not a real person at all, but a fictitious figure Parton had "made up," since he was never seen with her in public.

I should not have been surprised, then, after we listened to her new country-pop album, *New Harvest . . . First Gathering*, that Parton went out into the yard where Dean was working and brought him in to fix the fire, introducing us in the process. Still, I thought I had enjoyed a somewhat chance meeting with Nashville's most mysterious husband until a short time later, when I picked up Andy Warhol's *Interview* magazine and read a piece on Parton that began with a description of Dean's having been brought in to fix the recalcitrant fire—and meet the visiting reporter.

Looking back over this interview, what emerges with utmost clarity is the fact that if everyone else was confused in 1977 about what she was doing, the savvy Parton, with her goals set firmly in place, knew exactly where she was going and what she had to do to get there. Part of that included giving her husband almost no time at all during the two days I was at the house, since she had told him on the day they met in 1964—the day after she got to Nashville—that her career would always come first. At the end of the second day I told her she was generous to have given me so much time, adding that I probably wouldn't have given anybody two days out of my life if I had just come in off the road. "Yeah," Parton said, fixing me with a steely stare. "But you ain't me."

Q What is going on with Dolly Parton now?

A Well, I tell you what. There's a lot goin' on. I changed management because I didn't have what I needed for the things I wanted to do, or the places I wanted to go. I changed bookin' agencies because I didn't feel that they were bookin' me in the places that I needed to be. Even though they are all dear friends of mine, and God forgive me if I say anything wrong about my friends, because all the people I was with are very qualified for what they do. But I feel that I'm very qualified for what *I* do, and our qualifications for each other were not really jellin' that much. And my group—even though I had wonderful people that I loved, even family—I just didn't think I had musically what I needed to go all the places I wanted to go, and do all the things I wanted to do—cover all the areas I wanted to cover. So I just thought, "Well, I'm thirty years old now. I have held these dreams and plans in my mind for thirty years. I have seen a good many of my dreams come true, and because of some people, I have seen a lot of my dreams turn into nightmares." And I thought, "That's nobody's fault but my own for allowing it to happen." So I said, "If you really want to do these things that you believe you can do, you are gonna have to make preparations for it. You're gonna have to pay a price for it. You're gonna be ridiculed and condemned. But if that's what you really want, then nobody's gonna live for you."

Q How did you go about making the musical changes?

A Well, first of all, I just stopped everything. I changed my organization totally around. I just went to RCA and told 'em I had some ideas in mind I'd like to try. They believed in me and gave me total freedom to work on this album [*New Harvest . . . First Gathering*], and they were willin' to put up the money to promote me into other fields of music, in addition to country. I don't know that this album will necessarily be a big hit, but it's real special to me. But whether it is, or whether it isn't, at least I have the chance now for some musical freedom. I mean, if I cross over [to the pop charts], that's fine. That's great. I already had a following in that area.

It's just a matter of promotion. But I don't want to go as somebody else. I will be me.

Q Where do you want to go, and what do you want to do?

A I want to be a recognized songwriter. I want songs recorded by people in country music and outside of country music. I want to leave things behind for the public. I want to leave things behind for my family. I want to see my records go into any territory that they can go. At least I want a shot at it. I want to do TV, some specials. I want to write some movies.

Q Scores or scripts?

A Both.

Q And act in them?

A Yeah. Well, I never really wanted to be a movie star. That never appealed to me at all. I've always wanted to do a comedy, though. But anyway, like I'm sayin', I don't even know that I will, but if I want to, that's up to me. And I want to. I want to do good. I want to express myself. I want people to accept it. I want to do everything that I possibly can. Ain't that what life's all about? I want to be totally happy with what I do. I'm a big enough person that I can accept success without it affecting me personally, or I'm a big enough person that I can accept failure, if that's what I should see. But I'm also a big enough person that I can be happy either way. Just because I fail at one thing don't mean I'm a failure. But in my mind, I guess really I just want to see what I *can* do. Why not?

Q I was surprised to see you on the *Tonight* show recently. What was that like for you?

A Oh, that was funny. That was the first time I had ever done it with Johnny there. Years and years ago, I was on with Porter, and Joe Garagiola was the host. I didn't say a word. I sat on the panel and slung my foot, as usual. But it didn't seem like the *Tonight* show, because Johnny wasn't there. But this was the first time I had ever done it [alone], and I had a good time. I just really communicated with Johnny, I thought. I was surprised, because I was a little bit afraid. I didn't know if he'd like me or not, and he's so good at what he does. He can do it any way he wants to. He can make you look good or really get you on a spot if he wants to. I was just hoping he'd like me and we just communicated really well.

Q He seemed charmed by you.

A He was just real nice. In fact, he didn't see me at all until I was over there singin'. When he introduced me, I came out. I didn't see him before the show, and I didn't see him after. But it was fun doin' it. I'm lookin' forward to doin' it again.

Q You didn't mind all those boob references?

A Well, I used to. It used to kind of embarrass me, because I didn't know quite how to take it. But I just got to where I kinda play along with it myself, and come up with some funny things. There's no way to hide it.

Q You said you were a little bit afraid. Afraid Johnny wasn't going to like you, or afraid of the fact that it was the *Tonight* show?

A Oh, no, I enjoyed it. In fact, I wasn't a bit scared. It just seemed like a real natural thing to do. Now, I did *Hollywood Squares*, and I don't think I done good at all, because it's not the kind of thing where I get to talk to anybody, you know, make conversation back and forth and communicate. On that, it's like questions and answers, and you don't really get any personality. It looks like a real easy thing to do, but it's not. You have to have a lot of respect for the people who do really well on those kinds of shows, because they're not as easy as they look.

Q I imagine being booked on *Hollywood Squares* and the *Tonight* show is Katz-Gallin-Cleary's doing.

A Yeah. In fact, I think I'm with the best management that I could possibly ever be with. They know just how much to expose you, how much not to, and that sort of thing. But they're real picky about . . . well, I'm gonna be doin' lots of things.

Q So right now you're in a transition period?

A I don't think so. I think I'm just now back at work after bein' off with new management and new organization. I'm just really curious to see how it goes. It's not a matter of tryin' to directly change somethin'. If there's any change, it'll just come from itself. But they're bookin' me in different areas from before. I just hadn't been exposed to that. It's workin' out good. I feel perfectly natural and perfectly comfortable with all the people, like doin' the *Tonight* show. To me, a human being is a human being. Johnny Carson and I are made up of the same things. He just happens to be made up of more of them, I guess. But I'm just sayin' I relate to people as people. We're all the same. We all laugh, we all cry, we all hurt, we all love, and we all hate. We all feel fear, and we all feel jealousy. We all feel excitement, and we all feel nervous about things.

Q You know people are still going to say that you're leaving country.

A Well, we'll just have to wait and see. Because you cannot leave what you are. I'm gonna do country. I'm gonna do things like you heard on the album, in addition to the things I've always done. Why can't I expand? Why shouldn't I try? I hope people don't resent it, but if they do, I really feel bad about that. I truly do. Because all I want is a chance to do everything I want to do in life, which is the same thing every human being wants. Most people don't get to do a whole lot, because they aren't brave enough to try. Well, I'm brave, and I'll try. It's just as simple as that.

Q Do you consider everything on *New Harvest* country?

A Oh, no, no, no. But I consider everything on that album me. Like Tom T. Hall would say, "Country is what you make it." I'm a country person. I love to be country, and I'm glad I was brought up just like I was. I love the old traditional country. I sing it often, and sing it in my show. And I was so influenced by so many people in the business. Well, I wouldn't say so much "influenced" as I just respect them. In fact, on "Applejack," one of the tunes in the album, instead of usin' background people, I wanted to use a lot of the people who had meant a lot to me, and had really influenced me as far as what country is. So I had people like Chet Atkins, Grandpa Jones and Ramona, Carl and Pearl Butler, Wilma Lee and Stoney Cooper, Ernest Tubb and Roy Acuff, and my mamma and daddy. So you see, I really feel like I'm fightin' a battle when I didn't even start a war. You know, I didn't even want to be involved. I'm just gonna do what I want to do, because my music is me, however it sounds. If I wanted to do R&B, it's still me, because it was somethin' I felt I wanted and needed to do as self-expression. But then I turn right around and do somethin' so country that it'll be appreciated by the hardest country people in the world. But I'm not gonna limit myself, just because people won't accept the fact that I can do somethin' else. I'm gonna do both.

Q Do you feel you've been held back, and if so, by whom?

A It's not a matter of holding me back, necessarily, but working in an organization with other people, it's unfair to try to put your own ideas on somebody who is a head of an organization, say like me and Porter. When he was producing me, I got some of my ideas across, and a big part of my ideas were written in the songs, the arrangement ideas and all. But there was so much I wanted to do, and he heard it so differently that we just couldn't agree on so many things. It just took away the joy of recordin' the song at all, because then it wasn't what I created it to be. It took on somebody else's personality. And that would be hard to explain if you were not a writer. But I'm just sayin' that at least this way I write the songs and get 'em down the way I hear 'em.

Q You have a reworking of the old Temptations hit "My Girl" on *New Harvest*, as "My Love." Are you going to be writing in that style yourself?

A Well, I've always done that. In fact, to be honest with you, this album you just heard—only three songs out of that are songs that I've written recently. The rest of 'em I wrote four or five years ago. But I've always written things like "My Girl." It's all a matter of arrangement, but that's where people think you're not country if you use a different instrument on things.

Q People say that you've turned your back on Nashville.

A But I haven't. They'll see. They'll know. I can't preach that now, because I have nothing to show them that I'm not. But I'll be able to do more for the name of country music by goin' ahead and doin' what I felt I should do. I'll be able to do more for Nashville than I could ever have done had I stayed here. Well, I don't mean . . . please let me say this very carefully, because, like I say, it's a real touchy thing right now. I have not turned my back on Nashville. I wouldn't move to L.A. You couldn't give me that place! But it just so happens that that's where the best management I could find happened to be located. It had nothin' to do with the place. If Katz-Gallin-Cleary had been in Nashville, I am sure I would have still wound up with 'em. I wouldn't have had to go somewhere else. I just had big plans, and I just had big dreams, and I just didn't see any reason why a county line should keep me from goin' where I wanted to go. Every country girl wants to go to the city, and every city girl wants to go to the country. But a person that is free to go where they please can go to the country *and* the city. And that's exactly what I'm doin'. I love my home in Nashville. I love the people here. I have dear friends here. I would *never* leave here. Never. I could never live anywhere else. [She has since established additional residences in other cities.] And I still do business here, like interviews and that sort of thing. But, well, like I say, I can't continue preachin' it. I have tried too hard. I'm just gonna have to let my work stand on its own.

Q How do you think you will help country music?

A Well, I think by my being able to become as big as I can in the entertainment field by doin' things like I did on the Johnny Carson show. I know that different times there have been people on there that have really downgraded country music, like . . . what's the drummer's name [Buddy Rich] who said, "Country music is a music with no class"? That makes me furious! You talk about country music in a bad way, and that's like sayin' my mamma is a whore. Them's just fightin' words! So I can help by sayin' that I love country music, and that I am proud to be part of it, I am proud of Nashville, and that I think country music is a music with a lot of class. It's just ordinary stories told by ordinary people in an extraordinary way. And when I become a bigger artist, which I will—I mean, Lord willing, if everything goes well—I'll be doin' big TV shows. But I'll also be able to walk out on the stage of the Grand Ole Opry, no matter where I've been, and have people say, "Well, I saw her on So-and-So, but boy, she's still on the Grand Ole Opry." Well, I'm proud to be on the Grand Ole Opry. I love it. I would like to take it with me everywhere I go, and I do.

Q When you talk about a broader audience, do you have anybody specific in mind?

A Well, I have everybody in mind. That's what I'm talkin' about—universal appeal. I would like to be a universal artist. And I will be someday. If I'm not, it's because I wasn't good enough to be. But if I'm good enough to be, I will be.

Q How much influence were Linda Ronstadt and Emmylou Harris in encouraging you to branch out?

A I don't think any. I admire them, and I love them as friends, and I respect their music, and I think it's pretty well mutual. I mean, they were into my music before I even met either one of them. And I think they're super. But, you see, that is what I was trying to tell you before—I'm not easily influenced by people.

Q I asked you because that's a big theory of people's—that Linda and Emmylou's success in the larger arena, so to speak, inspired you to expand your boundaries.

A I think they have inspired me in many ways. They have made me feel that I should take great pride in the things I do. I mean, not that they are the only ones, but their friendship and the fact that they enjoy my music is great. But you see, what I'm doing is the things I've wanted to do ever since I came to Nashville. I've wanted to be everything I could be ever since I got here. You just have to take it a step at a time. I know one thing. I know that Emmylou and Linda have been great about promotin' me. They have done more for me, as far as their followin', sayin' nice things and talkin' me up to their audiences. I'm sure they've won me a lot of fans that would not have been aware of me otherwise. They've done that—and they've done my songs—for a long, long time. Money can't buy things like that. That's a great compliment. But as far as any of them ever saying, "You ought to do this" or "You should do that," they never said that. [In 1987, Parton, Ronstadt, and Harris would team for the hugely successful *Trio* LP.]

Q Who recommended Katz-Gallin-Cleary to you?

A It was Mac Davis, really. He's with them. He was responsible for me goin' to talk to them, because I happened to see Mac the day I decided I was going to totally change everything. I was going to L.A. to look for management, or I was going everywhere that I needed to go. But he told me how great they were, how happy he was with them, and he thought I should talk to them. I did, and I was just really impressed with them. Anyway, there were several people like that, like Mike Post [the TV theme song writer]. He's a wonderful man, and he's been such a big fan of mine for so many years. I found out later that even before I went with Katz-Gallin-Cleary, he was tellin' Sandy Gallin that they should try to manage me. He just believed that I could really do all these outrageous things, which I hope someday I can live up to. But whether I do or not, it's just great to have people believe that much in you. So there are people like him, and like Bob Hunka, who really believes in you and fights for you. Bob Hunka is a man who works with Emmylou. He works for Happysack Productions, which is their [Emmylou and then husband Brian Ahern's] company, and he works for Warner Brothers. I don't know exactly all the things he does. [Parton later hired him to run her publishing company.] Anyway, he's a dear, dear friend of mine, a brilliant man. And he has been so responsible for gettin' me with so many right people, by helpin' me figure out things when I was changin' agencies. Bob really helped me with good advice. He suggested a lot of things—things I should do and shouldn't do in certain areas. Things like what I needed as far as sound and certain songs he thought would be good for me to include in my show, in addition to my own. When people like Bob and Mike Post believe in you, that means a lot.

Q John Rockwell of the New York *Times* called you one of the great American entertainers.

A Well, he's a kind person, and he's a friend. But it's hard for me to make a comment on that. I don't know what I am myself. All I know is that I try, and I am what I am. And if that's somethin' special to somebody, or anybody, then that's a real special feeling for me to know. But that's somethin' else. I want to improve. I may not be a great entertainer now, but I want to be. So I'll work until I am, if I'm not.

Q Do you think you have that talent?

A To be an entertainer?

Q A great entertainer—one who will endure through the decades?

A I think that you can do anything you want to do. And if I believe I can, I can. And I believe I can. I certainly don't mean it as a vain statement. I am one of those people from the old faith—the old church—that believes that all things are possible, only believe. The Bible doesn't say, "Some things are possible." It says, "*All* things are possible," and I believe that. I grew up with all the faith and belief in the world. It was faith and belief that led us through all kinds of problems when we were growin' up. No doctors—with illness, and believin' that we'd make it, that we'd get well. Believin' in prayer, believin' that there was somethin' bigger than us that would take care of us. I think that's the healthiest attitude in the world. And I believe in my heart that if I've got enough faith, and enough grit and determination, that if there is anything in this business or in this world that I truly want to do, I can give it as good a shot as anybody can. I just believe I can do it, because I work hard enough to do it, if nothin' else. I'll get it done. Let's just put it that way.

Q Do you think of yourself as being ambitious?

A Very. Not in a selfish way, not in a vicious way. It's just I'm very ambitious. I have no time to be idle. I have no time to be lazy. I don't want to be lazy, and I don't want to be idle. I want to leave somethin' good in every day. I want to accomplish somethin', whether it's a song, or somethin' good I can do for somebody, or for myself, or if it's a change I can make for the better. I'm very ambitious, yeah. Not the kind of ambitious person that would just want to do it to say, "Well, now looky there. Showed you, didn't I?" That's not my point. I'm so determined and positive—my attitude is so positive—that it's just hard for me to think negatively.

Q I've heard you say you don't have a negative side.

A I don't. If I do, I've never given in to it enough to know it. They say everyone has a negative side, but I've just never exercised that. I believed I'd have a good marriage, and I do. I believed that I could keep my marriage separate from my business, and I have. I believed that I could be an ordinary person, even bein' a celebrity, and I am. I believed that I could be a star as big as I wanted to be, and I will be. I don't like the word "star" myself, but I just mean "to accomplish" so many things. I just take great pride in what I do. Every time I accomplish somethin', I just feel that much stronger about accomplishin' somethin' else. And that puts that negative side farther and farther away. I'm a real strong person, but yet I'm the most sensitive person you'd ever want to know. I'm very emotional, very sensitive, and very carin' about people. But I'm talkin' about things I can tolerate. I'm very strong with my emotions. I love strong, I work strong, and I endure. I can endure more things without it affectin' me than, I guess, nearly anybody. I just happen to be a strong person. But that all comes from that faith and belief. I've never got so far down I just couldn't see somethin' else. Now, I've been *down*, but I have never been *out*. I'm not a down person. I really have a happy nature. I truly do. The only times in my life that I've ever been sad was because other people were not willin' to let me be what I truly am. There have been times when it's been rough. *Lots* of times, it's been rough. But I always knew that it would smooth out. If I didn't like the road I was walkin' on, I'd start gradin' another one.

Q Aside from the fact that it's given you the chance to demonstrate the different kinds of music you can do, why are you so pleased with *New Harvest . . . First Gathering?* Do you like the fuller production, for example?

A Well, it's an album of joy and love. It was the first chance I had for total musical freedom, to have self-expression with my music, to get all my ideas across. But I also had lots of help from people in the band. I got my own ideas down, and I also had some great ideas provided by the creative people in my group. But it's the first thing I've done of this nature, and it's not that this is the only kind of thing I'm ever gonna be doin'. I just wanted to do these things because I've done the others. And in the next albums to come, I'll be doin' the kind of things I did in this album, in addition to the things I've always done—simpler things, and not so big on production. I'm really proud of the album. I just hope that it's accepted, because it'll always be my favorite.

Q What did you think of the last one, *All I Can Do?*

A I thought it was the best one up to that point.

Q Do you think that of every album?

A Not necessarily. But I think that one was, because I was gettin' the chance and the liberty to get some of my ideas across. It's really hard for me to judge. But I thought musically the last album was the best to date, even though there were some better songs on some other albums.

Q How traumatic was the breakup with Porter?

A Well, I'll tell you. I don't know what information you have on this. I'm sure it wasn't much information that came from me, but I'm also sure there are stories all around. It was not an easy thing for me, nor for Porter. Because any time you're in business that long with people, you laugh together, you cry together, you go through hard times together, you grow together. It's hard to separate. It was hard for me, and it was hard for him. But we disagreed often, because we're quite a bit alike. We're both very creative, very stubborn in our beliefs. It just reached the point where it seemed to make better sense if we didn't try to be partners in business anymore, even though I respect Porter for what he has stood for in the country music business, and for what he has done for me. And even though there were times that were hard, there were times that were good, too. We had problems, but any time two people are in business together and they never disagree, then one of them isn't doin' their job. And we disagreed often. But we made a lot of progress, too. It just reached a point where I had gone as far as I could within a group organization. I felt a need to expand, to try my wings, to have my own organization. That way I didn't have to feel I had to answer for every move I made. I don't like to get too involved in it, because the public don't need to know everything. Some things I don't even like to discuss, because any time you're in business as deep, and hot, and heavy as we were, duet singing partners, as partners on the television show, and recordings, and into production, and trying to express opinions and ideas, it gets a little sticky. But just because we didn't agree on lots of things doesn't make him any less a person, nor me. It's just one of those things. Porter's a brilliant businessman, and especially has been in the past. I don't see Porter much anymore.

Q Are you still friends?

A I suppose so.

Q I've been told that he got a gun after you when you threatened to leave.

A (Loud gasp) Where did you hear that? That's not something written down, is it? Well, even if that *was* the truth, it's not a thing the public should know. Porter's an artist, and so am I. But it's strange, these stories, and even if that had been the truth, I don't think I would have *ever* told anybody anything like that.

Q Did Porter create your sex symbol image?

A (Laughter) Awwwww, I've looked the same since I was just a kid. In fact, that's always been one of the things people have always kidded me about. I started doin' my hair like this when I was in high school, when the style was first out, the teasin' and all, and then it got out of style. But I enjoyed it. I liked it that way. And then, when everything started changing, people got to sayin', "Well, you should change your hairstyle. That's out of style." And I thought, "Well, they noticed, so it may be a gimmick in addition to somethin' I enjoy. I'll just keep it this way to see who all will notice, and to stir up as much interest as I can." And the more interest I stirred up, the higher I put it, the more extreme I got. Then, later on in years, I started wearin' wigs, because I was so involved with my music that I couldn't sit under a hair dryer in a beauty shop. I never go to a beauty shop. But it's just handy to wear wigs, and it's become like a gimmick. But my sex image—what exactly does that mean? I've always worn tight clothes, I've always had big boobs. Well, I've always been well developed. But I don't know exactly what you mean by Porter creatin' my sex image. All he did was put me on television, and I just showed it all off.

Q He didn't try to mold you into a certain image?

A No, he didn't, because he happened to like me as a person. And he happened to like the way I was. Plus, he also knew I was stubborn, and

I dressed as I wanted to. But anyway, I guess because of him I got to makin' enough money where I could buy things.

Q You're aware, I'm sure, that a lot of people thought you and Porter were lovers.

A We were lovers? Well, we were lovers of music, and I suppose we had one of the world's most unique relationships. We were not lovers as you know lovers, but it really wouldn't have mattered whether we were or whether we weren't. Like I say, it was a strange kind of relationship, hard to explain to the public. It was a love of its kind. I think it was more of a . . . ummmm, I never had that one before. Oh, I've heard people think we were married, and all that. In fact, when we split our business, I mean, when I left the show, people would come up and say, "I really hated to hear about you and Porter gettin' a divorce." (A taut laugh) But anyway, I don't know how I could put our relationship into words. We got very angry at each other over workin' things. There was a . . . I don't even think this is somethin' I'd want to put down, so all I want you to write is that we were not lovers, but we loved each other. We were lovers of our music and of our work. But in all truth, I tell you what—I can under-stand how people could have made anything out of our relationship, because we were so involved in business, so involved with each other personally—Porter had no family, and you know, you live together on the road. All the boys in the group are like your family. You're closer than you know. So close that you know each other's moods, and you know certain things that bug you. But it was almost like we depended on each other too much. We were so involved in so many things that we had no separation from each other. To the point where we would even resent each other bein' involved in other things. It was almost like if somebody else . . . I mean, he was so involved with my songs, like, he criticized my songs, and also praised them, and I'd get angry and hurt, knowin' both sides. But like I say, if he really was knocked out over somebody else's writin', or really almost like he was ignorin' mine . . . it wasn't jealousy like lovers. But I don't know. Kind of like a jealousy. It was like, well, how can he criticize my songs so, and then make such a big deal about somebody else's? And then if I liked to hear somebody else sing, or if I was really close to somebody else, it was almost like jealousy. But any time that you give that much of yourself to somebody, and you are as involved as we were—we experienced the joy and sorrow of all the things. We fought in the studio, or at least there was bad times. But we also knew the joy of a song becomin' a hit, especially if we'd fought over it in the studio—that sort of thing. But we didn't have enough separation, which is why it got to be too much for both of us. It got to be *extreme* pressure. But, like I say, it was a relationship that would be very hard to explain.

Q Talk in Nashville has it that you have a business arrangement marriage with Carl Dean—that you married him to counteract Porter's possessiveness, and that you promised Carl half of your earnings in exchange for his name.

A That's really weird, because I was married for a year before I ever knew Porter. Those stories are fun. Now, that doesn't bother me, but it's certainly interestin'. It's fine for it to be written up, but I would just prefer to say that it's never easy to end a relationship, especially where business is involved, and personal feelings and career.

Q *Country Style* magazine recently quoted you as saying that you and Carl lived together for two years before you were married. That was a fairly bold step for a traditional female country music singer to make—admitting it.

A Oh, I did *not* live with Carl! Awww, that's too bad. That's real sacred, my marriage. Because I was brought up—I would *never* have lived with a man before I married him. Oh, I might—years pass, and if it was another time and place, I don't know. But what I said was, "I've been married for ten years, been going with Carl for twelve, met him the day I got to Nashville." Oh, I didn't *live* with him! I made the mistake of sayin' that out of country innocence. I just meant we were *together* for two years before we married. I meant we *went* together. We married exactly two years later from the day we met, but we did not live together. Not that it would matter whether we did or not, because we loved each other. But we didn't. I'm just a bit old-fashioned in my beliefs about things like that. Now, I especially don't like that, because that's a sacred thing to me, our relationship, mine and Carl's. He's just the most precious thing in the world. He's the only thing that remains untarnished in this business. And then people will take what little information you're willin' to give . . . but maybe I made it sound like that. If I did, I didn't mean to.

Q People are fascinated with this marriage, you know.

A Yeah, well, it's a good marriage. It's solid, and it's firm. We've both only been married once, and I'm sure that it will last forever. It's just too right, and too natural, and too comfortable, and too secure for it to ever be anything else. I like it that our marriage is separate from the business, and our personal lives. Although I do mention the fact that I'm married. It's certainly not a business arrangement. If it is it's smart business. But, like I say, I'm a healthy, grown person. It's just fascinatin' some of these things I hear. 'Cause I'd better brace myself. There'll be worse stuff than that in time to come.

Q How do you want people to think of you?

A Often.

Q In what ways?

A A good way. As a person that cares about them. A person who wants to be cared about. A person that wants a chance to be all the things that I can be, given the chance. I want to be accepted as who I am, and what I am—not as what somebody tries to make out of me. I want to be looked at as a real person, even though my look is artificial, as far as the gaudy appearance. Where you can't see is where I want people to see the most. I guess I want to be thought of as an honest person, as a decent person, but with enough character and enough mystery about me to always be fascinatin', or at least be interesting. But I just want them to see me as I am, and they will. I just want to do whatever I can do, and do it the best I can.

Q You talk about what a happy nature you have, but there seems to be an underlying sorrow about you in some ways.

A Really? Sorrow? Well, if there is, then it must be the sorrow I feel for things that are not right with others. I never had that said, but I guess right now what you see as sorrow is concern with the new things I'm doin', and the fact that people are makin' more out of it than it is—and tryin' to make a monster out of somethin' that's *not* a monster. Or maybe I'm just more concerned than I know. How do you say how you are? I don't know what all I'm made of. I do, but I don't know how to say it. I'm very self-critical, so I'm always trying to improve, even though, like I say, I like myself. But because I take pride in what I do, I'm my own best critic. I can see me better than anybody, and I'm honest enough to admit it to myself, even though I don't like to sometimes. I'm capable of just about anything, I guess. Not that I do everything, but I'm honest enough to say that I'm capable of it, under the right circumstances. I have many secret thoughts, and many secret places in my mind.

Q People describe you as being secretive, and shy, and aloof to a certain degree, private, but friendly, and cautious—a little withdrawn.

A Withdrawn? I've never heard that one. I *am* a bit shy, believe it or not, even though I'm an outgoin' person. I'm very modest and I have a shy side. I guess what I started to say before was because I'm modest, I guess that's one of the reasons why when the magazine said we lived together for two years . . . it almost embarrasses me to think that some-body would think that I did that.

Q Do you think of yourself as a businesswoman?

A Yeah, I do. I'm pretty well qualified in that area. I think a good one.

Q How did you learn that?

A By bein' all the things I am, and seein' all the things I see, and doin' all the things I do. I think I know this business pretty well. I don't have to be a business person, and I don't necessarily like to be. But I think I could be a real good business person if I stopped this and just went into business. I feel like I'd be real qualified in a lot of areas. In fact, I am. That's just something I know.

Q Could you be happy if you stopped performing, though? Or are you like a lot of performers, who live for that hour onstage?

A I love to perform. I love the people. I love the excitement of the crowd. I love the excitement of the group, and I love to record, too. I *love* to record. There's nothing sweeter than takin' songs that I've written, and just hearin' 'em on the guitar, and then takin' 'em in the studio and hearin' arrangements and hearin' it all come to life. Oh, it's so excitin'! I guess I love to record as well as anything, but I love to perform, I love to sing, I love to write, and I love the excitement of the people. I even love to autograph. The only times I don't is when there's some reason I can't.

Q Does one outweigh the other?

A Yeah, I'd rather write. I can't help but be partial to that, for some reason. I guess I feel like anybody can sing, and anybody can learn to perform. But I don't think just anybody can write. I think that's a gift that you must exercise.

Q Are you a disciplined writer? Do you make yourself write so many hours a day?

A Oh, no. I'm strictly an impulsive writer. Because I get moods, great moods. You know, really inspired moods, and I just really get involved in what I'm doin' and I just can't stop. I've stayed up as long as three days before, or at least two days, and into the third day, before I could really make my mind stop enough to rest. But I'll tell you somethin' even better than that. The most I've ever written in a day and a night is twenty songs, and out of those twenty songs, fifteen of 'em have been recorded. Be-cause when I get on a wild streak . . . now it depends on the nature of the song. Up-tempo is easier for me to write with simple words. But, anyway, that's the most I've ever written in one sitting. I tell you, a lot of people don't believe that. They think it's a lie, even people who write. Sometimes I don't write but three or four. But I often write ten, or twelve, or fifteen, eighteen. I get excited when I get inspired, because I can't wait to see what I come up with. Really, I do! I get real excited. I can't wait. I just think, "I wish this was day after tomorrow, so I'd have all these on tape, and know what all I came up with."

Q What came out of that twenty-song session? Can you name them?

A Well, I never really tried to break it down, but there was a song—what's it called—"Take Me Back"? "I can still remember Mama washin' on a rub board / On the back porch while us kids played in the yard." And let me think. Well, the song on the new album, "You Are," came out of that batch. Right now, I'd really have to look on some of the albums for titles. I'd know 'em if I saw 'em, but there have been five or six of 'em I haven't recorded yet, so that's why I can't really judge.

Q Will all twenty be recorded?

A Well, I'm sure they will be. I usually won't stop on a song until I'm done with it, and when I'm done with it, it's worth recordin'. I recorded fifteen of them, and I'm sure I'll record the others one of these days, or somebody will. No, I could never record all the songs I write. It just so happened that durin' that time I was recordin', and we were doin' duets, and they were newly written and fresh on our minds. But that's the record of a day and a night.

Q Your songs sound as if you write the words and music simultaneously.

A Yeah, my lyrics and melodies always fall together. I just start right out with both at the same time. I have one song that I think has a terrific lyric, the title and everything, and the melody is good, but it's too simple for the words. They just don't match. I have one song that's real up-tempo, but has real sad lyrics. I guess it's just got its own kind of sound.

Q Do you think about the way people talk about first-generation country, say, Jimmie Rodgers or the Carter Family, and second-generation country, maybe Johnny Cash, and if you're bridging with the third?

A No, you see now with me, I'm only doin' what I do. I'm doin' it the only way I know how to do it. If I can improve it, I will. But you see, I like to think I'm an original. I like to think that I'm a stylist. I know that I am, whether that's good or bad, mainly because I don't dwell in other people's music. I'm too busy making somethin' up, too busy creatin' my own, singin' it the way I sing it and feel it. I'm not tryin' to keep up with the Joneses, or tryin' to sing somethin' like somebody else would sing it, or writin' somethin' like somebody else would write it just because it's the goin' thing. I write from what I feel, whether it's commercial or whether it isn't. But I don't know about that bridge. I guess we'll cross it when we get there, huh?

Q Do you ever feel guilty because you're not having babies and cleaning house all day?

A Never. I've had many babies—there's twelve children in my family, eight children younger than me, and five of 'em I've pretty much raised as my own. Besides, I think everybody has a purpose. I don't feel . . . well, I don't miss havin' children, let's put it that way, because I have children everywhere—nieces and nephews and brothers and sisters and cousins and friends. I love kids.

Q What about staying home and being a conventional wife? Any guilt about that?

A No, I don't want to stay home. I love to travel. I like to *come* home, and I like to *be* home when I'm home, but I don't want to *stay* home. That may sound cruel or silly, but I love to travel. That's one of the great things about me and Carl. Now, he likes to be at home, and he likes to do the things he enjoys doin'. He likes to be alone a lot. But me, I like to travel. He's always welcome to come, even though he don't want to often, but he does sometimes. But at least it's a thing that if we want to see each other, it's just a matter of a phone call to say, "Why don'tcha come up here, or out here, or over here?" Simple as that.

Q In the larger picture of all this, how big a part do you think you've had in making country music acceptable to the mass audience?

A I don't have any idea. I don't know when it started for me, the new followin' and all that. Evidently, a long time ago, because by the time I found out I was hot in other circles, I'd been hot for a long, long time. But I just hope I can always represent my music, and Nashville, and country music or whatever, whether it be rock, or pop or whatever it goes, in a good fashion. I don't know what part I played. I don't know if any. Maybe some. I don't know to what degree.

Q You must have some idea.

A How can I know?

Q Well, you're already a legend.

A As a writer, or singer, or character?

Q Probably more as a character, to be honest.

A Well, that's fine. I just didn't know exactly what you meant. A character never grows old. A character lives forever, just like Mae West, like Zsa Zsa Gabor, like Liberace. I don't know. I guess I *am* a character. I guess I'm a character in more ways than just by looks. I guess I'm a character only because I'm just totally what I am. I'm not afraid to be that, and say what I want to, and I just do what I want to.

Q Do you think about your place in the history of country music? Will you have an influence on the direction country music takes? And will your music endure?

A Well, I hope so, but I won't ever know that, because I'm too busy workin' to try to be one that *will* endure. I probably won't realize that until I'm older, and then look back and see what it is I've done. Right now, I'm too busy tryin' to add to that. I can't just accept it as bein' finished.

Q You're taking a tremendous gamble with your change of direction, risking so much of what you've worked so long to get. Why is this so important to you?

A I just want to see what all I'm made of. I want to see who all I am. I want to know what all I can become, and I will. There'll be lots of mountains that I'll climb, and there aren't any so tall that I'd be afraid to start up. I may not make it all the way on every mountain I climb, but that doesn't mean I'm not going to be tryin'.

Q What'll you do if you don't make it up the mountain?

A I'll get on another mountain. I'll try something a little less treacherous. Oh, I don't know that that's true. I'd probably keep tryin' to climb it over and over, until I either fell off and broke my neck or just got to the top and looked back down on how far I'd come. I've never seen a mountain that I didn't think I could climb.

Minnie Pearl

*I*t is a sight that Grand Ole Opry visitors have relished for nearly five decades. The familiar figure in the old-fashioned summer dress steps to the WSM microphone, the trademark price tag dangling from her flowered straw hat. "How-DEE!" whoops Cousin Minnie Pearl. "I'm just so proud to be here!"

From almost the night she made her Opry debut in November 1940, no one has symbolized the Opry's exuberant spirit better than Minnie Pearl, a.k.a. Sarah Ophelia Colley Cannon, the world's most famous country comedienne. Although she says she never considered herself a superstar, through the years Minnie Pearl has been as responsible for the Opry's enduring popularity as any of its renowned pickers and singers. It is, in fact, almost impossible to imagine the Opry without her.

Now age seventy-six, Sarah Cannon has embodied her famous alter ego since 1936. In the beginning, she says, Sarah Colley was younger than Minnie Pearl. Today, she's older than her counterpart. "But I still have the feeling of being her age when I work her." She describes "the Pearl," as she affectionately calls the character, as the child she never had, and as a sister. "She's a great pleasure . . . When I feel things are getting a little close to me, I can put on that costume and it's all different. I can't describe it, but it's wonderful . . . Minnie is eternal sunshine and boundless optimism; naïve but game; loud but basically shy."

Minnie may be shy, but through the years she's gotten bolder and somewhat racy, starting in World War II, when she entertained American soldiers.

"You know, just the worst thing happened," begins one of Minnie's favorite gags. "I was comin' out of the back of the auditorium, and it was dark, and a feller come up and he had a gun in his hand. And he said, 'Give me your money.' And I said, 'I don't have any money.' And he frisked me up and down, and he said, 'You *haven't* got any money, have you?' And I said, 'No, but if you'll do that again, I'll write you a check!'"

As loud, as naïve and hayseed as Minnie Pearl is, however, Sarah Colley Cannon is cultured and reserved, the very model of a genteel Southern lady. While Nashville society eschews most of the country music performers, it has always considered Sarah Cannon to belong to another category, partly because her mother's great-great-grandfather was an uncle of President James K. Polk, and partly because she has always been active in local civic affairs. Her home, which she shares with her husband of forty years, Henry Cannon, the owner of a charter flying service, is furnished in expensive and tasteful decor, and located next to the Governor's Mansion in an exclusive section of Nashville.

Sarah Ophelia Colley grew up in the small town of Centerville, Tennessee, one of five daughters of a lumberman. She describes her father as "a delightful raconteur, with a great faculty for making things funny." The baby of the family, she was also a daddy's girl. When he died, when Colley was twenty-five, "I thought my whole life had gone." Instead, she was about to begin her new life as Minnie Pearl. In memorial to her father, Minnie's fictitious characters of Brother, Hezzie, and Uncle Nabob reside in Grinder's Switch, Tennessee, the real-life railroad switching station where Tom Colley took his logs and crossties.

As a child, Sarah Colley wanted to be not a comedienne but a serious dramatic actress. Responding to her wish, the Colleys (who could hardly afford the $1,200 tuition—her father had lost his business during the crash of 1929) packed young Sarah off to Nashville's Ward-Belmont College, a prim, but prestigious, two-year finishing school with a strong dramatics department. There, embarrassed at not having the clothes and the niceties the other girls had, Sarah, who played the piano, sang, and demonstrated a flair for comedy, relied on her personality to gain acceptance with her peers.

Upon graduation, Colley taught dancing in Centerville before going to work for the Georgia-based Sewell Production Company, a dramatic troupe that staged plays throughout the South with local talent. As head of Sewell's auxiliary coaching school, Colley spent her summers training new directors. During the winters, she traveled the small Southern towns organizing amateur productions of drama and musical comedy. In 1936, while staying with a mountain family in northern Alabama, Colley happened upon the inspiration for the character of Minnie Pearl, the country girl in the Mary Janes with an eye toward "ketchin' fellers."

Though she no longer plays one-nighters on the road, Sarah Colley Cannon has remained vigorously active in her senior years. In 1980, Simon and Schuster published her autobiography, *Minnie Pearl* (written with Joan Dew), and four years later she opened the Minnie Pearl Museum on Nashville's Music Row. Despite a double mastectomy for breast cancer in 1985, she continues to tape the popular syndicated television show *Hee Haw,* and on Friday nights she appears on both the Grand Ole Opry and the Nashville (Cable) Network's live *Nashville Now* program. Early in 1986, she began writing a weekly newspaper column, "Minnie's Memories," for the Nashville *Banner.* The column deals with her experiences on the Opry and takes a nostalgic look at Americana.

"Folks my age love to reminisce, and I'm no different," says the 1987 recipient of the Academy of Country Music's Pioneer Award. "It's a form of conceit, I reckon, or perhaps escape from a frenetic world, different from the one we knew."

The following is a combination of interviews taped in October 1981 at her home, in October 1975 backstage at the Grand Ole Opry's fiftieth anniversary celebration, and telephone conversations from 1978, 1979, and 1985.

Q There's a fascinating alter-ego relationship between Sarah Ophelia Cannon and Minnie Pearl. You've been quoted as saying, "In all of these years, Minnie Pearl never hurt anybody's feelings, because she was a thoroughly nice person. She still is. She never faced any abrasive situations. She didn't do the traveling. She laid dormant in the garment bag, and when she came onstage, she was rested."

A (Laughter) I'd forgotten I'd said that. That's pretty funny. It's true. I've always said I envied her, and I do. I envy Minnie Pearl. She's a part of me, but at the same time, she never has any worries. She never has any financial concerns. She never has any worries about whether she might have performed less than her best. And because *she* doesn't worry about that, *I* worry about that. And yes, she stays in the garment bag during the traveling. She's carried everywhere she goes. (Laughter) And I have to walk down concourses in airports and take the pressure of deadlines and travel. She just goes where we take her. The odd part about it is that even when I'm tired, she has to come out fresh. So I make the effort, and it's not always easy. But there's never been a tired Minnie Pearl. There's never been an angry Minnie Pearl. There's never been an ugly Minnie Pearl, as far as being unpleasant to people. I get tired, and I get put out with some of the situations that arise that may make me a little short every once in a while with a fan or a friend or somebody. But she doesn't. She's been quite an inspiration to me. And she's been quite a role model. In fact, I'd like to be more like her. I was in the grocery store one time and this woman looked at me and passed on by. Then she turned around and came back and said, "I didn't recognize you. You weren't smiling." (Laughter) I liked that, because it pointed up the fact that Minnie Pearl is a happy character.

Q Do you ever have a conversation with her, just the two of you?

A In a way, I guess. I've had so many occasions when I was uptight, when I was getting ready to go on. It would be an appearance that meant something to me, like a network appearance or a big concert appearance. And I would be a little nervous about it. And I've had the funny feeling from time to time when I'd start to go on the stage that she turned to me and said, "Don't worry, we're going to be all right. Now you leave this to me." That's the way I always think she says it. I always think she says, "Don't get in my way, and we'll both be all right." Which is what I try to do. But it isn't always easy. Because if I'm uptight, sometimes my timing with her is not as good as it might be.

Q You knew Edgar Bergen. Did you ever discuss this with him?

A No. Mr. Bergen tried to sell me to Mortimer Snerd one time, you know. I was at Rutland, Vermont, doing a state fair. And Edgar Bergen was there on the same bill. The fair director took me backstage, and I had dressed at the hotel that summer afternoon. I walked around backstage and Mr. Bergen was in wardrobe. He was sitting there and he was warming up his dummies. He had already limbered up Charlie Mc-Carthy and he was limbering up Mortimer Snerd. Mortimer was this funny old country character that Mr. Bergen had all those years. And Mortimer was sitting on his lap and he was working Mortimer's arms and legs and face and neck. The fair director introduced me to Mr. Bergen, and Mr. Bergen, of course, always treated those dummies like they were people. He turned to Mortimer and he said, "Mortimer, you've been wanting a nice young lady to go out with here in Rutland, and now you're lucky, 'cause here's Miss Minnie Pearl. She'd be a nice person for you to go out with." And he turned the head and the dummy looked at me and Mortimer said [she goes into a Snerd voice]: "No, no, Bergen, no, no. Thanks a lot. No, no. I don't, no." He said, "She's a *lovely* lady." Well, he started in trying to sell me to Mortimer and Mortimer would not have me. He would have *none* of me. And it was certainly a terrible put-down to think that of all the put-downs I had had, this was the worst one. Because Mortimer didn't look like any great shakes himself, you know. We played there three nights, and each night I'd come around back-stage, and Mr. Bergen—we always called him Mr. Bergen, because he was a very dignified man—would try to sell me to Mortimer. And Morti-mer got so he wouldn't even look at me. He said, "No, I . . . I've . . . no." Only he talked real funny, you know. He said [in deep Mortimer voice]: "No, Bergen, I, I, no." And I just thought, "Now that's the worst put-down I ever had." (Laughter) To be turned down by Burt Reynolds was nothing strange. But to be turned down by Mortimer Snerd is *really* bad.

Q You've known a lot of the legends of the music business fairly well. You were a friend of Hank Williams, for example. And in 1961, you got to know Elvis Presley a little when you went to Hawaii with him to do a benefit show. What sort of memories do you have of him?

A Well, I knew Hank a whole lot better than I knew Elvis. Hank was such a lonely man. Henry and I loved him. We were probably as close to him as anybody was. Henry used to fly him, you know. In fact, Hank wrote "Jambalaya" on one of those trips. Now, Elvis—I really only worked with Elvis that one time. And when we went to Hawaii with Elvis, I was not aware of the fact that he was so encapsulated in his fame. I had heard that he couldn't get out and do what he wanted to do, but I hadn't seen it. I didn't know what a prisoner he was, how hounded he was by the public. And we went first-class, of course, flying with him. But when we got to the Honolulu International Airport, there were something like three thousand screaming women trying to get to the airplane, with a number of policemen and security people trying to hold back the crowd. That's the first time I was aware that the man's life might be in danger. And then Colonel Tom Parker came in and said that he wanted me to stay with Elvis because he wanted me in the pictures. He was just doing it to be nice to me, but it was dangerous, because when we got out of the plane, the women were still screaming, and they were about to knock the fence down. And I began to get these chilling feelings that maybe I didn't want to be all that close to Elvis. I was afraid I'd be trampled by that mob of screaming women. Then they brought the car out to the field, and I sat with Elvis in the car as we drove into town. And people all along were screaming and hollering, because they had publicized the route that he was taking in from the airport. Now, you realize this was just after he came back from the service, and he was making *Blue Hawaii* in Honolulu. I would say that he was at his [physical] peak at this point. Very handsome, very boyish, very charming, very nice—a delightful person at that point. Well-mannered, no airs about him, very courteous. And was the rest of the time, as far as I'm concerned. But he hadn't become ill and gained all the weight, and he hadn't gotten into the trouble that he was in toward the end. Well, when we got to the Hawaiian Village Hotel, there was another five hundred screaming women. It was awful. My husband was afraid that we'd be killed trying to get inside the hotel. I felt myself being lifted completely off my feet by all these people. But we went on and we finally got in the hotel and went up on the elevator. He was on the top floor, the fourteenth floor, in this penthouse. They had policemen everywhere you turned. They had them on the fire escape. They had them at the elevator. They had them at the door of his room. Just everywhere. Well, we did the show that night. And, of course, he came out under heavy security, because the women were all over the lobby again. But we came out separately. I'd already decided I wasn't going to stick around and be subjected to that danger. And we raised $52,000 that night for the memorial to the USS *Arizona,* which was lost when Pearl Harbor was attacked. This was on Saturday, and the following Monday, Elvis started filming on *Blue Hawaii.* So he had to stay anyway, but the next day all the rest of us on the show stayed over to get some sun, or whatever. And we were down on Waikiki beach on Sunday afternoon, and we were all cavorting and kidding and having a big time down there. We got to talking about the fact that we wished Elvis could come down and be with us, and we turned and looked up at his penthouse, which was facing the ocean. And he was standing on the balcony of that penthouse, alone, looking down at us. And we hollered and waved at him, and he waved at us. He was just standing there, a solitary figure, lonely-looking, looking down at us having such a good time. He literally was a prisoner because of the fans. He couldn't come down. He couldn't go anywhere. And we sat there on the beach and talked about how it would be—what a price you pay for that sort of fame. And I think that's one of the things that contributed to his death, actually—the fact that he lived such an unnatural life. I felt so sorry for him before he died. He was such a different person than he was on that trip.

Q Did you see him?

A I didn't see him after he became gross. I'm glad I didn't. But he was beautiful—absolutely beautiful—at the time. His skin was so pretty, and his eyes so pretty, and his hair. He was so healthy-looking. So trim and lithe. Oh, he looked good! And he had such charm. Such a tragic man, because he had such potential. And he was so nice.

Q Why do you think he got into the trouble that he did?

A Well, I think everybody has to have somebody to go home to that they care about, and who cares about them. And I think with so many people in our business, like Elvis, their private life gets in trouble, and then when they get off the stage, there's nowhere to go, and nobody to go home to who cares.

Q You mentioned going first-class. Your book talks about when you were a child, and your sister got married and left in a private car, and you realized you wanted to go first-class in life. Was that one of the motivating factors behind your decision to go into show business?

A No, I wanted to go into show business before I ever saw that private car. I've always wanted to go into show business. I spent my whole life when I was just a kid saying, "I want to go into show business." But it was only after I had gotten to be eight or nine years old that I began to be conscious of the fact that there was another world that surrounded people in show business that I wanted to be a part of. I didn't know then about private jets and limos and suites and things like that. But I began to become conscious of it and every time I'd read a book where people were very wealthy, I'd think, "*That* I'd like to have." But it's so tragic that so many people envy the wealthy just because they *are* wealthy. I think that's one of the sad things about young people, that as they become conscious of the fact that so-called stars have all these accouterments of wealth around them, so many of them want that style and that life just because it's rich. And they fail to realize that a lot of these people who have these accouterments are really not all that happy in their personal and private life. I've heard all my life, "Money doesn't bring happiness," and we've kidded about it and said, "Money doesn't bring happiness, but if you have it, you can pick out the kind of misery you want." But really, money doesn't bring happiness, and I think you have to get up in years before you realize it a lot of times. I've tried to tell my nieces and nephews that you can't make a blanket observation and say those people who have money are happy or not happy. Because some that have money *are* happy. And some that have money are *not* happy. A lot of people who don't have any money at all are real happy. When I was growing up, I read or heard this wonderful fable about the unhappy king. He thought if he could wear the shirt of a happy man, he would be happy. And so he offered a large reward to anyone in his kingdom who would bring him the shirt of a happy man. They looked and looked and every man that they thought was happy had something about his life that wasn't happy. And they kept coming back saying they couldn't find the shirt of a happy man. And finally one of the servants came running in and said, "Oh, Your Majesty, I found the happy man." And the king said, "Did you bring me his shirt? Give me his shirt." And the servant said, "Your Majesty, he doesn't own a shirt." Which is the paradox I always think of in connection with the idea that money brings happiness.

Q What's been the biggest disappointment in your life?

A Well, I guess the biggest disappointment in my life was not having children. But career-wise, there have been many. I wouldn't know how to say which was the worst one. That's what show business is made up of, is disappointments. And it's through those disappointments that you grow. As somebody said, "If show business was easy, everybody'd be doing it." If we didn't have the disappointments, we couldn't appreciate the accolades when they come. I've had my share of disappointments, although I never played them up like a lot of people. I never asked for sympathy. I cried a lot to myself. But I've had a lot of disappointments. People don't realize that, because they only see me in a bright concept. But there have been lots of times when I was really upset about things that happened or didn't happen. I always wanted . . . well, I've wanted several things in my career that I haven't got. And I just had to train myself to say, "Well, I missed that one." And just like the brass rings on the merry-go-round, you miss one. But then you wait for the next one to come around, and maybe you catch it.

Q What were some of those things you wanted?

A I always wanted my own network show. And I wanted to do a dramatic role, something on Broadway or on TV or in the movies, some good cameo role. And I always wanted a record [other than my comedy records]. I always thought that somewhere along the line there must be some material that I could find somewhere that I could do, probably a recitation. Because I know I can read lines, or rather I think I can. And I still have an idea in the back of my mind that I'd like to put on record. It's about a woman who struggles along like Dolly [Parton], and Loretta [Lynn], and some of these girls. And somewhere in her life, back in the beginning of her career, she falls in love with a young man who's also in the country music business. And she goes ahead and he doesn't make it. And she's a big star and she comes back and wants to see him one more time. Just to look at him, to see if the old magic is still there. But I can never find anybody to write it for me. I think if I recited something like that with the right music in back of it, it might be poignant. And it might sell. Because this is a situation that truly might have existed.

Q You were nominated for induction into the Country Music Hall of Fame every year for fourteen years before you finally won in 1975. Did you ever lose faith that you were going to make it?

A I had lost faith completely. I didn't think that I'd ever make it. I thought they were going to bypass comics. It had nothing to do with women's lib. I'm not that type. I don't get all excited about women's lib. I think women deserve to have as much pay for an honest day's work as men, but I don't go all to pieces over women's lib. My husband is the boss in our household. He tells me what to do, and I like it that way. I was born and raised in that atmosphere. My father was always the boss in my family, and I think the marriage is happier if the man has the final say-so. My mother taught me that.

Q But did you get bitter about losing so many times before you finally won?

A No, I never got bitter. I'll tell you why. See, the members of the CMA— which is something like 2,000 people—vote for the CMA awards. [As of 1987, the CMA boasted 8,000 members.] But there are two hundred electoral votes that are passed out to people who have been in the business twenty years. And a lot of the people who vote for the Country Music Hall of Fame are not musicians. They're members of the industry, like publishers, managers, and agents—all music-oriented people. So I suspected that it had to be confined to singers and people who were connected with the music end of it, rather than comedy. Nobody of a comedic nature had gone into the Hall of Fame until I went into it.

Q Why do you think that is?

A I don't know. I guess they felt that comedy wasn't all that important. I think it is, because I came along in the years when every country show that went on the road had a comic with them. That's not true now. As country music has grown and the packages go to the bigger houses, unless the comic has a name like mine that's been around a long time, they don't feel that the metropolitan audiences really go for the country comedy. Mine has become camp. I'm so old and my comedy's so old that it's an art form. I don't mean that in a conceited way, but it is. Because there's nobody else coming along in the comedy line. No women. There is not one single girl or woman coming along right now that I can think of who wants to play country comedy. So it's rather unfortunate that when I have shuffled off this mortal plane . . . (Short laugh) When I am gone, I'm sure there will be some more country comedy somewhere with women, but I don't know who it would be right now. [In the years following this interview, she worked with protege Sylvia Harney, who has since developed her own characters.]

Q If there's nobody coming up in the ranks right now, is there anybody already in the business you think could do it?

A Well, June Carter, of course. She has excellent timing, and she's just naturally funny. She's also a born mimic. Her mother brought her to me when she was ten years old, and she went straight into a Minnie Pearl routine. She was fabulous, just great. So the world lost a great comic talent when she married Johnny Cash. And Roni Stoneman is a comic. She used to be with the Stoneman Family and she works on *Hee Haw*. And Roni is a nice kid, and she's got a comedy sense.

Q But she's also a musician.

A Yeah, she's a fine banjo picker and guitar picker. But most women comics don't want to look silly. They don't want to make a fool of themselves, because the glamorous comic is the thing of the day now. Look at Carol Burnett. She's my idol. I think she's the greatest single comic that ever lived. Only she's not a comic—she's a humorist. She's a great pantomimist. She's a great situation comedy expert. Carol can do anything on earth, with her face, with her voice, with her body. She's just fantastic. You have to play comedy as long as I have to really study her and see what an expert she is. She's a craftsman, and not many of the country comics want to be a craftsman. They just want to get up there and act silly. Now, we've got a lot of sidewalk comics. And we've got some people that are pretty funny. Loretta Lynn is really funny. She thinks funny, and she comes off real funny on a talk show or on the stage. Dolly Parton is funny. Now, these are glamorous girls, but nobody wants to put on this silly costume like I did back in those days, and look silly, and be silly, and kid about the way they look. Because they don't want to get down on the level of the country girl who makes a fool of herself. And believe me, I understand that. But what I want them to do is for one time get inside Minnie Pearl's skin and see what fun she has. Because she really has a great time, and she's very happy.

Q Do you think people take themselves too seriously now, as opposed to the thirties and forties?

A Well, I think there's a dearth of material. I don't think people are writing much country comedy anymore. I have a backlog of comedy that I'm too lazy to go back and pick up. I have all the Prince Albert network shows as broadcast, from 1948 to 1954. I could go back and read those gags, and some of them are just as funny now as they were then. But do you think I can remember them? No. So I find myself doing what I did last night, when Grandpa [Jones] and I got on. We had some material written for us. But when we got to the script rehearsal, we said, "Why don't we just tell some of our old material?"

Q How much of your material do you still write?

A Actually, I don't write any of it. I turn phrases occasionally. I do reactions. But I don't sit down and write material. I never did. When I first went on the network, I had New York scriptwriters. But, for instance, last night I was standing by Dolly, and one of the laughs I got was "You should see it from the side." They were looking at her from the front, see. Well, I'm more apt to make reaction remarks than I am to write gags. I like throw-away lines. That's what we call them.

Q What's a throwaway line?

A Well, that's an old vaudeville expression. I guess it means an unpre-meditated gag. It's something that comes up at the last minute and is injected, or interjected, into the bit without previous knowledge of the situation. For instance, if I'm working on the stage and something comes up, like the spotlight goes out or something like that, then I say, "Well, I knew I had a face that would stop a clock, but I had no idea that I'd put out a spotlight." That to me is a throwaway line, and I unconsciously say it to cover a situation. Or if the sound goes off right at the point of my punch line, then immediately I have to think of something to cover with when that sound comes back on. So immediately my mind goes into gear. But I'm so lazy mentally now, from doing these gags so long. It's just like Roy [Acuff] singing "Wabash Cannonball." Every time he's on a show, they want him to sing "the Cannonball," as he calls it. Because people say later, "I wish he'd sung 'Wabash Cannonball.' That's what he used to sing when I was a little girl, listening to him on the Grand Ole Opry." Well, it's the same way with me. They come up after the show and they say, "Why didn't you tell that joke about Brother going through the tunnel, eating the 'nanner?" And I say, "Oh, heavens, that's the oldest gag in the world. I told that one the first night I came on the Opry." Then they say, "I know you did. I know just where I was when you told it." I've tried to analyze that. But they say not to do that. That's what Eddie Cantor had on his desk—a little plaque that said, "Don't educate, entertain."

Q Do you miss working the road?

A No, I don't want it anymore. I never did worry about it, because I worked as long as I wanted to. I was fortunate. Then I decided to get off the road. Since then, I just work whenever I want to, and sometimes I work more than other times, when I find I miss the audience or the camaraderie of show people. My agent would like me to work more, naturally. But I worked for twenty-seven years on one-night stands. At the end of twenty-seven years [in 1967], I decided I'd had enough. And I decided I would wait and rest a while. That's what I'm doing now. I work some, and I work *Hee Haw*. For twenty-seven years, I came back to Nashville from wherever I was out on the road to play the Opry. I live a peculiar life, because I'm not as tied up in show business as I was. I'm living the life now of a suburban matron, which I missed back at the proper chronological time.

Q What's your definition of a suburban matron?

A Well, that's sort of an obsolete term, I think, but it's what people used to call women who had just gotten married, or had been married, say, five or six years. Usually the suburban matron had children, which I don't. She got involved in civic activities. She played a little bridge, and she played a little golf. She cooked and took care of her home, and did the different things that suburban matrons at that time did. So that's what I'm doing. (Laughter) I love it.

Q I'm a little surprised.

A Well, I went into show business when I was twenty-one years old. I left home and joined a producing company out of Atlanta. I went around over the country putting on amateur shows. I worked alone. Each one of the coaches with my company—there were a hundred and fifty of them—went into small towns alone, and they worked with the local organizations, like the PTA, and put on plays. And all the plays that I put on were about country people. They were musical comedies in the thirties. I didn't get married 'til I was thirty-five, and by that time I'd gotten to be Minnie Pearl, and I didn't have any life of the suburban matron. So now, after having been in show business since I was twenty-one, I said, "By Ned, I would like to be a suburban matron." So I learned the things that people learn back when they first marry. I've learned to play bridge and I like it. I've gone back to tennis and I like it. We have a court at my house, and a pool, and I have ladies over for lunch and make homemade mayonnaise. Really, suburban matron is a funny thing to hang this on, because I'm about as much like a suburban matron as an Australian antipode.

Q An Australian what?

A An Australian antipode. That's a form of Australian bird that flies backwards, because he's not interested in where's he's going—he's just interested in where he's been.

Q So why are you doing it?

A Well, I feel like somewhere back in my life I missed the chance to be with my friends. When you work with show people, you learn a certain language, and when you go back and live in the normal world, you learn another language. I decided I wanted to relearn the language of normal, sane, sensible people. Not that our people in show business aren't. Some of them are normal, sane, and sensible. But we live in a life of unreality. And I wanted to get back to the life of reality. I wanted to go to church on Sunday. I wanted to live without the pressure for a while. From the time I was twenty-one until I was fifty-five or fifty-six, I didn't do anything but meet deadlines. That's all show business is—pressure and deadlines. And I was tired of it. So now, the weeks I love are the weeks where I'm just at home, and my deadlines are nothing in the world but getting up, and getting in touch with some of my friends. Playing a happy game of bridge, or tennis, or getting involved with some civic activity. I'm involved with several different civic activities here in town. I'm on the board of several of the charitable organizations. And I've worked with the American Cancer Society for a good while. I'm very much interested in the Humane Society. I think God put these animals here just like He put us, and it's our responsibility to see that cruelty to animals is alleviated. I'm a dog lover. I have a very tender heart when it comes to children and animals. I think every one of us has a social responsibility and a moral obligation to be as kind to people as we can. Because we have a short time here. I'm not a religious fanatic, but I believe in God. And I think He expects us to do the best we can to make this world a little better place in which to live.

Q You mentioned the cancer society. You, of course, underwent a double mastectomy in two separate operations in 1985. How are you feeling now?

A I'm feeling fine. But I don't want to talk too much about it anymore, because I think Henry's gotten a little full of this. He thinks it's been played up too much, probably. I kind of went overboard on the first one —that was in April. And then this one [October], I have talked about on several different shows, and I think he thinks that's enough. I just don't want to push him. Actually, he didn't want me to talk about it at all. I did it against his wishes.

Q Why didn't he want you to talk about it, when you're only encouraging other women to go have mammograms?

A Yeah, and that's really about the only reason I didn't lie about it when I had the first operation. I thought about saying I'd had my gallbladder out, or something. But I wanted to encourage women to have those tests done. Henry just thinks it's a private matter. And you have to kind of observe your husband's wishes somewhere along the line.

Q Tell me more about those days when you produced amateur shows. You did this for six years, from 1934 to 1940.

A Well, I went out of dramatic school—two years of college and dramatic school—to two years of teaching in my hometown. I was killing time until I was twenty-one, when my mother and father would let me go out and see the world and get in show business. Now I've seen the world and been in show business, and now I want to get back in the womb, which isn't easy these days. But when I left college in 1932 and went to work teaching dramatics and dancing in my hometown of, say, a thousand people, all I had on my mind was seeing the world, and being a dramatic actress. I didn't want to play comedy. Never thought of playing comedy. I knew that people had a tendency to laugh at me when I meant to be serious, but I didn't know what God was trying to tell me. I preferred not to listen to Him. Because I thought somewhere along the line there was a place for me in the dramatic world. I realize now that God knew what He was doing. He was nudging me. I had, when I was growing up, acne and greasy hair. Now I work constantly at conditioning my hair. I spend time and money at beauty saloons. (Laughter) I have worked in several cosmetic areas, trying to do away with skin problems that I had. But those things contributed to Minnie Pearl. I knew I couldn't play it straight, but I wasn't ready to let that go until I went on the road, after I worked two years in my hometown. I went on the road, and put on these amateur shows, and I met a lot of Minnie Pearls. I met a lot of country girls who didn't win the beauty contest, but wanted to be funny, and wanted to be loved and wanted to love people. Sort of pathetic in a way, these girls. Because the real thing that a woman wants more than anything else is to be beautiful. I don't care what you say. I don't care whether you grew up in the twenties, like I did, or whether you grew up in the fifties or the sixties or the seventies. What a girl wants is to be pretty. She wants to be a fairy princess and live in a castle. She wants to have a gorgeous, handsome prince come by and grab her up and take her away. So it was a hard comedown for me to realize that wasn't in the script.

Q When did that happen?

A I realized that wasn't in the script when Mama made me be in a beauty contest, 'cause one of the girls fell down and broke her leg. And I had to go on, because they were trying to make money to put the window lights back in the schoolhouse. Little mean young'uns had knocked 'em out. I was seventeen, and I had just lost a dramatic contest. I was a little upset over that, because I lost to my best friend. I lost because she did a comedy reading, and I did an excerpt from *Madame Butterfly*. I was still laboring under the delusion that I was going to be an actress. So Mama made me be in the beauty contest. And I didn't think that the people would laugh at me, but they did. They fell out. One of the best laughs I've ever gotten. I wish I had it now. But that was one of the times when I realized that some of us are not supposed to play it straight. Some of us are born comics. We don't always get laughs, but sooner or later, if we're lucky, we turn that way professionally. Roger Miller is one of my best friends. He's so funny. We were in Hollywood together working a show one time, and we got talking about the fact that we had similar childhoods, that we grew up in comparable atmospheres and circumstances. He was brought up in a little town over in Arkansas, and he was always a clown and acting silly. And I was always a clown and acting silly in a small town in Tennessee. We were *unconsciously* cast as clowns. Neither of us wanted to be cast as a clown, but we were. And he said, "Minnie, when did you find out you weren't cute?" And it struck me that when I found out I wasn't really cute was when I walked into that beauty contest that night. Those good-looking, pretty girls said [tone of utter amazement], "What are *you* doing here?!" If that won't tell it to you, nothing will. And I said, "I'm taking this girl's place who fell and broke her leg." Then they said, "*You're* not going to be in the *beauty* contest?" And you know, they didn't mean to be cruel. They just couldn't believe I'd go out there. But I had brass then, and I knew I had a good figure. I was thirty pounds lighter than I am now. I thought that I could get by with it. I didn't know they'd really laugh. But they had failed to notify the emcee that this switch had been made. They just crossed off the girl's name and put mine in. The emcee was a pretty funny ol' boy, anyway, and he said, "And now representing the Centerville Ice Company . . ." And he looked up and said, "*Ophelia Colley?!*" Well, that didn't help my entrance too much. And everybody said, "Oh, *no!*" and laughed and slapped their thighs.

Q Don't you think that most humor is born as a defense mechanism?

A Absolutely, with women particularly. I think my appearance had a lot to do with it—the acne and the oily hair. I never thought people were laughing at me, actually. I've talked to people in my hometown since the beauty contest, and they've said, "Why, Ophelia, we didn't laugh at you because we were being *cruel*. We thought you were *kidding*." And I did kid, because when I walked out and realized they were laughing, I gave it to 'em. I did the old bit, and then I turned around and walked off. I had a good figure, as I said. I was thin. And I walked off that night and I thought, "God *knows* that hurt. That *hurt*. I'll never make it." But then I went on to college, where my dramatics teacher said, "Colley, you have no sense of humor."

Q Did you think she was right?

A Well, because I was intimidated—terribly intimidated—she scared me out of my gourd. Because I was so impressed with her. She was a beautiful woman, inside and out. She had studied with Maude Adams at the old Currie School of Expression in Boston. She had clichés like "sacrificing everything for your art." But she also said a beautiful thing, which was "Make a fool of yourself for your art." So she must have thought I had a little sense of humor, because she cast me in the Shakespearean plays as Bottom and Petruchio. And one night she kept me onstage until lights out doing the part of Petruchio. And running down steps being Petruchio, and doing the part where he says [in accent], "But I am one who's born to tame you, Kate!" And then she would hurt me and make me cry. She'd say, "You have no talent." And all this time, see, I'm fighting back. Because I knew somewhere along the line there was going be a vehicle. I guess it was my faith in God, I don't know.

Q What else did you learn about yourself in college?

A Well, I found out for *sure* that I wasn't cute. I was away from my family and my hometown for the first time, and I thought I could make an effortless transition from being funny and spoiled and cute in my hometown to a new atmosphere. I thought I would carry it with me. I really did. I thought that I had enough of whatever it took to go ahead and just be as cute and attractive, if you want to put it that way, away from home as I was *at* home. And this was a form of ego that a lot of children don't have. But the ego was completely shattered when I got to Ward-Belmont, because nobody paid any attention to me. And I know why they didn't. It was because I *did* have this ego, and I expected them to come to me. And you can't do that when you go into a strange community. You've got to make the advances and meet people halfway. And I just didn't do that. And then I started crying and being homesick. And, of course, nobody was wanting to be with me then, because people don't want to be around someone who's sad and crying all the time. So I really had quite a struggle the first two or three months I was away—out of my own element and in this college where nobody really cared whether I cried or not. And that was a strange thing to have to put up with. Because every time before when I cried, I had two or three people rush to me to find out what the matter was. And in college, I was a very unattractive figure, I'm sure, moping and crying and not being jolly and funny like I had been all my life. But I think more than anything I missed my mother and father, because they were so supportive and so dear, as they were all of the time, all their lives. I don't know many people who had the anchors, the moorings, and the faith that my mother and father gave me. They gave me great stability. But I got over my homesickness and became, immodestly speaking, one of the popular girls on the campus. Not because I was pretty, or had any clothes or any of the outward accouterments that I thought it took to be popular and attractive. But because I decided I'd just be myself. And that's what's more important than anything.

Q Actually, from reading your book, I thought there was an episode earlier than the beauty contest, where you were receiving for your mother one day and heard the women talking.

A Well, yes, that's right. When I was growing up, all my family flattered me and complimented me. I was the last of five girls, and all the older girls and my mother and father spoiled me and told me I was cute and funny. I think they even told me I was pretty, which, of course, was not entirely true. So one afternoon, one summer—I was about six or seven, I guess —some ladies came to call on my mother. And my mother was not dressed. This was during the time, back in the twenties, when ladies dressed in the afternoon and paid social calls on their friends. So I went to the door, and Mama said to tell them that she would be ready in just a minute, to have a seat. So they had a seat in the library, and I started out through the hall. They couldn't see me and they thought I'd gone on out to play. But I stopped to look at something in the hall, and I heard one of them say to the other one, "She's a plain little thing, isn't she?" Well, it just broke my heart. I couldn't believe that she had said that. She was a nice lady. She didn't mean any harm. And I didn't get mad at her. I was just stunned by the fact that at last somebody had told me that I was plain. I didn't think I was plain, but from then on I began thinking of myself as plain. And I think that's where Minnie Pearl started. She started a lot of different places. But that was one of the contributing facets of the creation of Minnie Pearl. I had always thought that I was pretty up until that point. And after that I never thought so again. But I thought I was pretty funny. And I thought I was cute. I mean, I was making people laugh, and people were telling me I was funny. So if I couldn't be beautiful, at least I was funny. Later on, I realized that some of the most glamorous women are not the pretty women, necessarily. I think if you broke down some of the glamorous movie stars of our time and took their features one by one, they would not be really beautiful. But glamour has nothing to do, really, with facial symmetry or real beauty. Glamour has to do with something that's inside a woman, I think.

Q You said you knew there would be a vehicle for you, from your faith in God. Do you think you were fated to become Minnie Pearl? Were you put here on earth to do this?

A Yes, I think I was. I think that God has a plan for all of us. But He intends for us to work on it, too. I don't think you can come into this world and just sit down and fold your hands and say, "All right, I want this," or "I want that," and He'll get it for you. I think that He equips us when we're born with certain talents and tendencies toward doing certain things, and I think we have to get up and do as much as we can with what we have. Like the parable of the talents in the Bible. I think when He gives us these talents, He intends for us to invest them and make them grow. We have to do our share to make ourselves what we are, what He intends for us to be.

Q Did you listen to the Grand Ole Opry as a child? Were you interested in country music at all?

A It was an accompaniment to my Saturday night, to taking a bath and studying my Sunday-school lesson. Daddy had it on. My father was an outdoorsman, a lumberman. He was a tall, craggy man, like Joel McCrea or Gary Cooper or John Wayne. My mother didn't care for the Opry too much. Mama was a concert pianist—or wanted to be one. She played beautiful classical piano. She was an educated woman. Daddy taught himself, or "learned" himself, as Daddy would say. He was not an educated man, but he had something that was greater than that, which was an understanding of human dignity. And he tried to instill it in his five daughters. Thoreau said, "If a man does not keep pace with his companions, perhaps it is because he hears a different drummer. Let him step." That's on the wall in my home.

Q What do you remember about the Opry as a child?

A I remember the laughter, and the sound of fun. That impressed me. And when I was going out on a date, which was not too rare, I had a pretty good time. The boys always liked to be around me, 'cause I always acted silly. And they knew they'd never get involved with me. Well, they weren't right sure about whether they wanted to get involved or not. So they'd take me. I was pretty stupid along that line, too. Do you know I sat and played the piano while the rest of the girls were smooching? It took me a long time to realize what they were doing. They were around some dark corner kissing, and I was trying to be funny, playing piano. [She sings:] "Yes, sir, that's my baby, no, sir, I don't mean . . ." And I was looking around, and all of a sudden there wouldn't be anybody in the room. But after I left dramatic school and went on the road putting on these amateur shows, I began to collect country stories and country songs. I did a lot of work in the mountains, at consolidated schools. And I loved the sound of country music. I loved the sound of country people who got together on Saturday night and played the fiddle and the unamplified music. I've always had a thing about the unamplified music. And I would listen, and then I began to collect these songs, like "Birmingham Jail," and "The Butcher Boy," and "Red River Valley." And I'd sit at the piano and play them for people. I play a little piano, you know. When I was a little girl, people would say, "Play the piano." And I'd say, "I can't play the piano." And Mama would say, "Don't *tell* them you can't play the piano. Get up there and *show* them you can't play the piano."

Q You're making that up.

A No, I'm not. I played a little piano, and then in 1936 my company in Atlanta sent me to put on a play called *The Flapper Grandmother.* That was a real zinger, too. Up in northern Alabama, Brenlee Mountain. And I stayed in a mountain cabin with a delightful old man and his wife. She'd had sixteen young'uns, she said, and never failed to make a crop. Which I thought was doing pretty well. I came away from there imitating her. Not mocking her, but imitating her. And that's where Minnie Pearl was actually born. I had been collecting the stories, I'd been collecting the songs, and she was kind of like Granny on *The Beverly Hillbillies*—a wonderful old lady. That first night, I said, "What time do you all get up?" She said [in accent], "Well, we don't get up 'til daylight, but we'll get up sooner . . ." I said, "No, that's just fine, just fine." She was cute. And I told her stories when I came away from there.

Q Has the character of Minnie Pearl changed much through the years?

A She's changed some, yes. When Minnie first started out, she was quiet and gentle and nice. She'd say [softly], "Howdy, I'm just so proud to be here." I talked like the old lady up in northern Alabama. She didn't scream, she just talked. And as I said, I imitated her. But then when Minnie started playing the big houses, she couldn't stay quite as gentle. And after I went on the network, those people from the William Esty

Agency in New York came down. And one of 'em said, "Why don't we scream the 'howdy,' and let the audience holler back?" I didn't like that idea at first, but the response was just tremendous. So she got a little more brash that way, and she's gotten a little racier as time's gone by, with some of her gags.

Q The price tag on your hat always reads a dollar ninety-eight. It's become one of the best-known trademarks in the world. How did you think of that?

A Well, it was an accident, really. I had put the hat on Minnie Pearl because back when I was a kid growing up, I saw the girls who came into town on Saturday afternoon to do a little trading and a little flirting, you know. And they always wore a hat to shield their eyes and their faces from the sun. Because back then, if you had freckles and a tan, that meant that you worked in the fields. And that's the last thing girls wanted to look like. So, anyway, they had flowers on their straw hats, and so I put flowers on Minnie's straw hat. And one time, when I'd been on the air about two years, I guess, I had gone to the ten-cent store and gotten some new flowers for her hat, and I put 'em on and forgot to take the price tag off. And I moved my head around while I was working, and that tag fell down on the brim. This was back when we were at the Ryman. And when the price tag fell down, people made fun of it, and I just kept it on. It's been a great trademark.

Q When was your first appearance at the Opry? What was that like?

A Well, I was working, and my father died and I went home to support my mother. My finances went down, and I went to the WPA. And I did a bankers' convention. A nice man [Bob Turner] came back to WSM and said, "There's a girl down in Centerville, and she's working on WPA. I know her family, and they're having a hard time. She needs to be on the Opry." By that time, I was aware of the Opry as a vehicle for Minnie Pearl. I had named her Minnie Pearl because of the two beautiful old country names that I'd heard all my life. So they said, "Come on and we'll give you an audition." So I had an audition. The most significant thing was that they said at first, "You have been directing plays now for the last six years, and you are a graduate of a two-year college in dramatics. These people won't accept you." And I said, "But I came from a country background, and I've worked with country people constantly for the last six years in these mountain places." I said, "They will take me, because I love country people." So the first night I went on, we were down at the War Memorial Auditorium. I can see it just like it was yesterday. Judge [George D.] Hay was handling the Opry. And Roy Acuff was handling the network. We had a relatively small cast. This was in

1940—November. I dressed at home, because I'd never been on radio, and I didn't know how situations would be backstage. And I put on this old hat and the funny old shoes that I wear now. And a dotted Swiss dress, freshly pressed and starched, and the white cotton stockings. And I went up there. Judge Hay said to me, "You're scared, aren't you?" And I said, "I'm scared out of my mind." And he said, "Love them and they'll love you right back." Which sounds like a cliché, but that's the way the man thought, and the way he talked. That's what the Grand Ole Opry was built on—this man's brotherly love. So then I went on the road with Roy Acuff, and I got to know the country performers. They are the most fabulous people in the world. The camaraderie that exists backstage is unbelievable. I've been on practically all the big talk shows, and I know that the camaraderie exists with show people all over. But there's a special type of camaraderie that exists with country music performers. And I'm proud to be a part of it. They kid unmercifully. When I came here, nobody owned their home. They lived in trailers, they lived in two-room apartments, or rooming houses. Nobody had any insurance, and very few of them had bank accounts. There was an expression that they used quite frequently when anything came up. They'd say, "Oh, well, I was looking for a job when I found this one." There was a transience. There was a peculiar feeling about it that I couldn't understand. I had just come off WPA and was broke deader than four o'clock. And I had come from people who saved. My father lost his lumber business in the crash of 1929. So I had had money, and I had lost it. So I wanted to save my money. And these other people didn't seem to have that idea at all. They wanted to spend it and have fun, and that was it. Which probably was what made the Opry sound like it did. They were a fun-loving people. They never talked about capital gain. They never talked about how many dates they could play and not be working for the government. They never talked about anything like that. We'd come in on Saturday night and we'd say, "How did you do in Moulton, Alabama?" And I never will forget . . . Roy Acuff would say, "We done pretty well." Roy is my best friend in the business. And when I was traveling with him, he'd tell us, "Never say anything more than that. Don't brag. Don't complain. Just say, 'We done pretty good.' That way you don't make no enemies. If you come in and you say, 'We killed 'em in Moulton. Had the biggest crowd they've ever had—must have had five hundred people'—then you won't be popular. And if you come in and gripe all the time and say, 'We didn't have no people,' uh-oh. Can't say that. It shows you're slipping—or haven't gotten there."

Q Roy Acuff fired you from his road show. Why was that?

A Well, Roy fired me because I was not willing to turn loose and act silly. I was not accustomed yet to being a clown and acting stupid and doing physical slapstick. I was just holding back, and not giving what I should to the audience. And Roy kept on saying, "Turn loose and have fun! Give the people a show!" And those are the best words in the world to give a comic. But I couldn't see it, so he let me go. And it was the best thing that ever happened to me, because it really jarred me into realizing what I should do. I then went to work with Pee Wee King the following fall, and we had about five years together. It was just wonderful. I learned a lot from Pee Wee. Pee Wee is probably one of the most professional performers. He knows the rudiments of being professional— how to give a show and how to perform onstage. That's the funny part about the country music business. It all looks like everybody's so informal. We call the Opry "organized chaos," because everybody looks like he doesn't know what he's doing. But nine times out of ten, the performers who have been around for a long time know exactly what they're doing.

Q Is the Opry fairly much the same now as it was in the early days?

A Oh, no, no, no. It's fun, and the camaraderie is great. But nowadays, people are business people. If they're not business people, they have agents who are. They figure in thousands, and some in millions. When I came along, most of them carried all the money they had with them. When one of 'em got ready to buy a house, the real estate man would say, "How do you intend to take care of this?" And they'd say, "Will cash do?" They had no idea in the world of how big this thing was going to be. It was a plaything. It was more fun than anything in this world. And everybody loved it. And the main thing people said when we went out on the road was [in accent]: "Y'all sound like you're having such a good time!" And we'd say, "We are! Come up there and see us!" And they would. They'd drive up in every kind of vehicle imaginable. And they'd come in that Grand Ole Opry house and they'd stomp and scream. The mothers would nurse their babies, and they'd bring lunches. And they'd laugh and sing along. They didn't know then that someday this thing would be so big that a movie called *Nashville* would be a hit. And we would become a target.

Q Is that how you see the movie *Nashville?*

A In a way. We are a target.

Q Why do you say that?

A Well, it could be any form of show business. I just felt that we were victims. And I don't blame him [director Robert Altman]. He saw it that way, and I can't see inside his skull. But he missed so much of the country music scene. He made it look like we were all a bunch of freaks. And we're not. We're people who are trying to make a living. And we try to make people laugh. We try to make people happy. I know there's a lot of that in there. A lot of *Nashville* was very true to life. I'm sorry to say that a lot of it was so true to life that we all just couldn't believe that somebody had done that much research. But I'm not going to worry about the movie *Nashville*. I'm not going to worry about anything. Because standing right back of this whole thing is a bunch of the most loyal fans in the world. They're not fickle. And I love every one of them. That's the main thing that bothers me about being in this sort of semi-retirement that I'm in now, where I only work *Hee Haw* and a few of the shows. Twenty minutes was always the amount of time I had onstage, and I miss bringing those twenty minutes of fun to the fans. I miss 'em so much that in '77 I went out and worked harder than I had in ten years. Because Minnie Pearl is just as wild as a can of crab. She's nutty as a fruitcake. She doesn't care whether school keeps or not. She's great. I'm stupid, but she's great. And the reason she's great is because she doesn't try to be serious. She just worries about whether we're going to have the church social on Friday night or Saturday night or Sunday night. And about what she's going to wear, and if a feller is going to kiss her on the way home. Most of the time he doesn't. But she thinks next time he will.

Q What do you think of the criticism that country music has lost its roots, that it's become too homogeneous?

A Well, the young people who are coming up in country music are changing it, because they want things *their* way. Just like we wanted things *our* way when we were young. Young people will always have their way. They will always bring change into everything. They are their own people. People have been saying the younger generation has been going to the dogs for a hundred thousand years. But it's because they don't operate on the same wavelength. And since they don't understand it, they reject it. It's a lack of communication. So they say the young people are ruining country music—they're turning it into something that doesn't even resemble country music. They're not. It's just *their* way. And I don't criticize them. We've had our day. Now let them have theirs.

Charley Pride

Charley Pride grew up picking cotton in Sledge, Mississippi, not far from Memphis, Tennessee. It was in Memphis, of course, that a shrewd record producer named Sam Phillips figured out he could make a pile of money with a white boy who sounded black. A decade later, Pride— perhaps unconsciously —would reverse the formula and become, as a black man who sounded white, one of country music's most popular performers. In 1971, the CMA named him Entertainer of the Year, and by 1975, in an ironic feat, he had sold more records for RCA than anyone except Phillips' old protégé, Presley.

One of eleven children born to a Delta sharecropper, Pride spent much of his childhood listening to the Grand Ole Opry, teaching himself guitar on a Sears Silvertone model, and dreaming, as his idol Roy Acuff had done, of a professional baseball career. Like Acuff, Pride failed to make the major leagues, and turned to music as something of a last resort.

While country music had always drawn on black influences —in fact, one of the early Opry stars, DeFord Bailey, was a black harmonica player—it remained for Pride to break the color barrier as a solo star. When RCA released his first single,

"Snakes Crawl at Night," in 1965, the record company omitted the usual publicity photograph and biographical information, continuing to pass Pride off as white until he had accrued a handful of hits.

Today, as at the beginning of his career, Pride, 50, downplays the racial factor. For years, he reportedly employed very few blacks in his organization, and onstage, where he plays to an almost exclusively white audience, he eschews the flashy clothes, sexual gyrations, and suggestive material that are the staples of many rhythm-and-blues musicians. And while his success may have opened the door for other minority performers, through the years the talent he has signed to his booking agency and used as the opening acts on his shows—Ronnie Milsap, Janie Fricke, and Dave and Sugar, among them—has always been of the overwhelmingly bland variety.

If that formula has made Pride a rich man—he has extensive holdings in music publishing, banking, cattle, oil, and real estate, including the farm he grew up on in Mississippi—it has also prevented him from creating the kind of distinctive personal style that would inspire imitators or wield much influence in the industry—a fact compounded by Pride's inability to write his own material. On the other hand, only Conway Twitty and Merle Haggard have had more number one records.

In 1985, Pride, one of the last bastions of traditional country music, left RCA Records after twenty years with the label. One of his last LPs there, *The Power of Love*, showed him finally opting for the kinds of pop-influenced records that would "keep him contemporary on the charts," as his agent put it. In many ways, the metamorphosis showed Pride to be far more convincing than he had ever been with traditional country, his staid delivery of old giving way to genuine new emotion and verve. What he will ultimately do on his new label, 16th Avenue Records, is yet to be seen, although his first releases, particularly "Shouldn't It Be Easier Than This," have charted well.

The following is a combination of interviews recorded between shows in St. John, New Brunswick, Canada, in 1977, in a hotel room in Nashville, Tennessee, in 1981, and backstage at the Little Nashville Opry in Nashville, Indiana, in 1984.

Q Judging from your current album, *The Power of Love*, your music is a lot more contemporary than it was when you first started out. Did you always want to sing music that had more pop influence, or are you just keeping up with the times?

A Well, I'm just trying to record what fits, you know. And I have a new producer, Norro Wilson. But my thing about contemporary and pop and MOR is this: I think there has been a misnomer about who's been trying to cross over to what, since country music has been the most popular music. We all live by images and symbols, and I'm basically tabbed as a traditionalist. But I feel that a lot of the pop artists have gotten over here with us now. And the people who liked "Kiss an Angel Good Mornin' " can start playin' my records without even talkin' about how contemporary they might sound. "Kiss an Angel" is a clear example of a record that was not recorded to be a crossover record, and all that sort of hocus-pocus, and it became a million-seller. And it's a typical example of where we are today, flailin' around about who's country and who's middle-of-the-road. You know, people at the radio stations say, "Well, Charley's good, but he's country, so we'll have to penalize him for bein' traditional." I knew a guy who had a lot of radio stations, and he told me just before "Kiss an Angel" came out, "As long as you have steel guitars on your records, I'm not gonna play 'em." And then "Kiss an Angel"came out and went to the Top 20 in the pop, because a lot of MOR and pop people decided to play it, and a million people went out and bought it. So there is a lot of so-called experts out there tryin' to put a format together about who's middle-of-the-road, and who's country, and who's contemporary. But all those kinds of music have been borrowin' from each other for so long that I think it's time to stop punishing one another from the standpoint of air play. That's my spiel on that.

Q Do you have more confidence in your singing now than you used to have? Is that one reason you're tackling more ambitious material?

A Yeah, I think I'm singin' better now than I ever sang. And that's not just from a bragadoo *[sic]* standpoint. My fans are writing in and saying the same thing. I quit smoking nine years ago, and I can hold notes longer than I used to, so I'm still learning how to sing and use my voice. And yeah, certain material that I'm doin' now I wouldn't have touched years ago, because of not havin' the confidence that I could do it justice. Now I feel comfortable that I can do it, so I'm doin' it.

Q A couple of years ago, you cut the old Johnny Rivers hit, "Mountain of Love." That surprised a lot of people. Was it your idea?

A I'll tell you how that came about. When I'd be onstage, I'd start talkin' about "Mississippi Cotton Pickin' Delta Town," which Harold Dorman wrote, along with "Mountain of Love." And I'd try to explain the difference between the two songs, and try to show the contrast when "Mountain of Love" came out by Johnny Rivers. And when I'd get into it, the people really loved it. So my producer was out on the road with us one day and saw this, and he said, "Let's cut it." The same thing happened with "Stagger Lee." Norro said, "There's somethin' I've been wantin' you to do since I've been your producer. Would you record 'Stagger Lee'?" So we did that. But there has been sort of a backlash of people sayin' possibly they weren't goin' to play any more oldies, so RCA got afraid and didn't put it out as a single. But the people like it, you know. We close with it, and they like it.

Q What about your larger appeal? What is it about you, for example, that sold a million tickets to concerts in the Houston Astrodome?

A Yeah, they presented me with my millionth ticket on a plaque. It says I've drawn over a million people over the years I've played the Houston Livestock Show. There's no one that even comes close to that. 'Cause, see, I played it durin' the dog days. What I call the dog days are Mondays and Tuesdays, when I was very popular, when the other artists would not play Tuesdays. They all screamed and cried for Fridays, Saturdays, and Sundays. Consequently, I would take my Mondays, Tuesdays, and Wednesdays, and now I've got whatever Saturday I want. I mean, it's kind of an annual thing. I'l either open it up or close it, whatever Saturday I choose.

Q But why do you have such large appeal?

A Well, let me answer you this way. The Mills Brothers were asked one time what they attributed their longevity to, and their answer was: "Simplicity." Simplicity of the song and simplicity of the delivery. No fancy doodads. If you'll notice, many of the biggest songs around are just plain and simple—simple lyrics done with a simple, sincere delivery. That's just about what it boils down to, I think. Even when you meet someone, it's fine to be able to speak elegantly and use highfalutin' words, if you're able to put them in the right context. But there's more people that understand the plain, basic, simple way of talkin'. Like, I remember one time a fella said to me, "Well, we're gonna be comin' up on this confluence pretty quick." I said, "*Confluence,* mmmmm. Listen, now. What's that mean?" He said, "That's the comin' together of things." I said, "I'm gonna remember that, so I can use that sometime." So I like to register those kinds of words, and it's interesting, but I think the most beautiful thing you can do is to be plain and simple. Keep it simple, honest, and sincere, and it'll work.

Q So that's why you've been so successful?

A I think so. I think a great bit of my success is because of how I try to deliver a song and put the feeling in it. Because I am in the business of selling lyrics. I don't think anyone should just go out and sing to be singing a song. If you just open your mouth and say the words without any emotion, it's pointless to try to sing the song, or any song, for that matter.

Q You don't write songs, but what do you think the songs you choose to do say about you?

A Well, music is only a product, like anything else. You pick out what you feel your audience will like, and do it. At first, I recorded a lot of things that I didn't like. After I reached a point where I had some say-so about what I record, I try now to record what I like.

Q Which songs didn't you like?

A Some of the songs I recorded earlier.

Q You won't be specific?

A No, because the people like 'em. I did some of 'em tonight. At least one that they *really* like.

Q But you don't see any theme running through them that reflects who you are as a person?

A Yeah, the feeling that I put into whatever I'm doin'. Because it's a product, as I say, and I try to project those lyrics. If the line says, "She's just an old love turned memory," you've got to put feeling into that, even though it wasn't me hurtin' about this particular woman. I had a few old loves turn memories. They're not cuttin' me like a knife, but I remember 'em, and I have a feeling for those other people that enjoy that particular song to where it makes 'em cry. It's good sometimes to cry and feel good afterwards. But it's puttin' feelin' into your music.

Q What about your love songs?

A I like love songs. I like the positive songs, though. I don't like negative songs. I realize you have to have those other songs, but I prefer to let somebody else sing 'em.

Q You and Conway Twitty and Merle Haggard have had more number one country singles than any other artists. How intentional is this competition?

A Well, like with the awards, I feel that if you just do the job, those things will take care of themselves. I'm not unappreciative of them. But I really wasn't aware of it until someone told me that we were neck and neck for number ones. I don't go around lookin' for those things. But I'm glad it happened. I *am* a competitor. But I'm not out to try to out-sing anybody.

I'm just trying to make good records, and if they happen to go to number one, or win awards, then so be it.

Q I know you're friends with Alex Harvey, the singer-songwriter and actor. I interviewed him one time, and your name came up. Alex said, "Charley's a very smart, very intelligent man. Super-intelligent. But he really plays himself down. If you'd see him perform, you'd think, 'Well, God, that ol' country boy's probably got a seventy IQ,' and that couldn't be more wrong." What's your reaction to that? Do you want people to think you're just a simple sort of person—that not only is your music simple but you're really an "aw shucks" guy?

A Well, I am really. I am a simple guy. But I can be very complex, too. Pisceans are that way. They are simple, yet very complex. They're also basically secretive. They feel that there might be FBI people, or secret phones around. There's a certain intrigue about 'em. Just harmless little things. I don't think so much should be made about it. But they're almost a paradox, and I guess it's because we are the twelfth sign of the zodiac —the things that have been, the sign of death, in one sense of looking at it. A lot of people don't like the sign of death. But it's up to the person that's talking and analyzing it as to how much they're going to see the simplicity or the complexity of things. Let me say it this way. If you ask me a certain question, I'll tell you I don't believe I know nothin'. But I believe I can talk about anything under the sun.

Q What Alex meant, I think, is that you try to make people think you aren't as bright as you really are, so that your fans won't be intimidated or threatened by you.

A It would scare my fans? First of all, I think it's just the opposite. I think the most intelligent people are the rural people, the outback people. What good is education if it ain't worth a hoot? What would you rather have, education or intelligence? You can take any country-music-lovin' person, and give him a big conjecture of words, and he'll still figure it out.

Q I'm not saying that country music fans are stupid. I'm saying that you stress your cotton-picking roots at the expense of your intelligence.

A You're saying that I'm an intelligent man tryin' to put on a façade of bein' a country boy? I don't try to be anything but myself. I have no front, no façade I have to put on. I like to kid around, and I like to watch people and talk to 'em and just analyze 'em. And in the meantime, I can see within 'em. I can see their fears, their hurts, and I'm blessed with an ability to see if someone is puttin' me on. And I do like to kid a lot, but I can be serious, and whatever I'm doin', I'm mostly sincere about it. A lot of times people become so caught up and awed by me bein' so easy to talk to that they tend to overlook that I am just me. And they get so caught up thinkin' that I wasn't that way, or they think, "How can he be just another guy comin' off as he is?" It kinda throws 'em, in the sense that they seem to think that you should be somethin' else.

Q Yes, but you encourage that in a way, too. For example, you seem to take great pleasure in being able to guess people's astrological signs. By doing that, you do seem to want to make yourself look special.

A Well, if I hadn't remembered as far as meeting you [before], I probably would have figured it out pretty close to what you are, anyway. I like to watch people—kind of analyze what they are. I figure that gives me an edge over somebody that don't believe in it. Out of the twelve signs, you look for the most dominant factor you're lookin' for. I miss, but I hit a lot of times, too. So it's just somethin' I'm blessed with, and somethin' I'm interested in. If you are interested in somethin' enough, you work at it and become good at it. That is just one of the things I like to do—survey and analyze people. People are the best things that you can analyze, really. When I used to fly commercial, I used to go down to the check-in desk early and just set and watch people—figure out which ones are goin' to ride first-class and what they might be like. I like to people-watch. It's interesting.

Q The Statler Brothers had a song a few years ago called "How to Be a Country Star," with the line "Get a gimmick like Charley Pride." What did you think of that?

A I liked it! They're funny. It's a pun and it just fits—the humor that it's supposed to be. I liked it.

Q In light of that, how do you recall those days in the sixties when you were on those package tours with Willie Nelson?

A Well, they were an experience. Those were the days when they had what they called the marathons, like the song Willie wrote about "Me and Paul." That was true [the reference in the song], about how he didn't know when he went on the stage in Buffalo. The show started at eight and I was the one closin' the show, and I didn't go on until about one in the morning. There was no concern about stickin' to the time factor, makin' it a good, tight show with each artist. Course, again, havin' so many people back in those days when they did have the marathons, the big package shows, they would just run artist after artist on. They did two or three numbers, and you'd never see the ability of any given artist. You got your chance to see a number of artists, but you didn't see the kind of quality show that takes place today. So those are the things I remember about bein' on the Willie Nelson Show, the Buck

Owens Show, the big package shows when I was a filler, an opening act.

Q The way Paul English, Willie's drummer, tells it, by taking you on that tour, Willie made you a star before you'd even made an album. But this was the height of the civil rights movement, and things got rather hairy for you in places like Louisiana, from what I've heard.

A No, the South was the easiest place for me to play, looking at it from that viewpoint. No matter whether it was North or South, the uniqueness was still there. There was never any adverse or negative response in any way at the beginning of my career, as far as non-acceptance. And that's the truth. Especially the South, because I'm from the South, but I never had any problems, North, South, East, or West, bein' accepted by my fans, once they heard me sing.

Q Well, that's just the point. These people weren't really fans yet, since you hadn't made that many records. Let me read you what Willie told me about that tour: "Some of the motels wouldn't let Charley in, and some of the clubs didn't want him to be on the stage, even. So it was interesting going through places like Dallas and Shreveport and San Antonio."

A I just remember the people acceptin' me on the shows.

Q You seem not to want to talk about the fact that you're a black man who sings white music.

A You see, I've got a way of answerin' this question, and I've done it with you just now, basically. You get with some reporters, and they just want to belabor the point, and elaborate on it until you've chewed your cabbage twice, you know? And I just say, "I am Charley Pride, the man. American." I think that covers it. We can talk until tomorrow about it, but when you get through, it comes down to this: I'm not here to be a symbol or an image, but I'm put in that position by the mere fact of bein' myself. I'm sure that Jackie Robinson would have loved to have been just another ballplayer, but he was specifically told he had to break barriers for his people. He was picked for that particular thing, despite his great baseball ability. Here I am, growin' up singin' country music, and I realize I was preparin' myself, by just bein' myself, to face this type of situation I'm in today. I've had people say to me, "Do you realize what you're doin' for your people?" It all comes down to skin hang-ups. Society's hang-ups. Y'all, them and us. But I don't have skin hang-ups. I'm no color. I'm just Charley Pride, the man.

Q But when you sing, you sound white. Why is that?

A I don't know. First of all, what's soundin' white? I'm an individual. I started listenin' to country music when I was very young, and the people that influenced me were Ernest Tubb, Eddy Arnold, Roy Acuff. They were the biggies after the war. And traditional country music definitely has an inflection, and I don't mean to kick it, like a lot of people do, by sayin' "nasal nuances," and that sort of thing. I don't sing through my nose, but that's what a lot of people hear when they want to downgrade country music and not look upon it as an accepted form of good music. I've heard disc jockeys say, "I love you, son, but I play *good* music." Well, what is country music? Not good music? But anyway, by me bein' young and listenin' to country music, I started to sing and emulate these people and the sound and the inflection I heard that I liked. That's why I've been told that I sound like twenty different artists. I've had 'em tell me I sound like Ernest Tubb, Jim Reeves, Hank Williams, and on and on. But they say that when you're told you sound like more than any one given artist, you're original. So I should be in pretty good shape for bein' original, soundin' like twenty people. But you're sayin' that by lookin' at the pigmentation of my skin, I shouldn't sound the way I sound, 'cause if you put me behind a curtain and never looked—just heard my voice come out from behind that curtain—you'd put my voice with a white skin. True. You would, and so would a person I'm the same color of. Why is that? 'Cause I chose it.

Q It was a conscious effort, then?

A It could have been subconscious. I think it was a little bit of destiny, a little bit of determination to be your own individual.

Q When you initially talked with Jack Johnson, your first manager, did he see the potential you had? Or did he think it was a crazy idea for you to try to sing country music? There was the suggestion of a name change, as I recall.

A Oh, no, he was encouraging. He was the first one who went around Nashville tellin' 'em it could happen, it could be. But when we met, he looked at me and said, "How do they take you up there?" And he said, "We might have to change your name." I think the reason he was sayin' that was just to see if I was for genuine. I haven't ever asked him, but I think he was just testin' me. Like, "I'll just throw somethin' in, see if he'll change his name to George Washington W. Jones III, or do anything, be a freak, if necessary, to get a record." But I said, "No, we ain't gonna change no name now." But no, he was always behind me. We've talked about it, and he felt that it was a certain amount of fate and destiny brought us together.

Q Do you believe in predestination?

A Well, I believe there is a certain amount of that. I don't believe it's precut and dried. I think you can alter it, and that you help it along with the intention of what you're here for, and who you meet. I also think that if you look close enough you can see certain things comin' at you.

Q The first time you were on the Grand Ole Opry, Ernest Tubb introduced you. How did that make you feel?

A Oh, it's hard to explain. It has to happen to somebody. You're frightened, you're happy—so many emotions are going through you at that moment. And you think about when you's little, how you used to listen to the Grand Ole Opry, and now here you are—that sort of thing.

Q How much of an influence was Hank Williams? Was he also someone you listened to as a child, or did you do that tribute album *[There's a Little Bit of Hank in Me]* for some other reason?

A No, other than getting requests from my fans. Most artists do other people's songs in the early part of their career because they don't have any of their own. He was just one of the artists that I used to do his songs. I used to do George Jones, Ray Price, Eddy Arnold, and different ones. So I would get home from off of a tour, and people would write and say, "Well, we liked your show, but we especially liked the Hank Williams songs. Have you ever thought of doing a Hank Williams album?" This was ten or twelve years ago, and we would write back and say possibly we might do that someday. Then the someday finally came, and we put out *There's a Little Bit of Hank in Me,* and it's been a success.

Q I've read that you don't think music should give messages.

A Right. The music ceases to be music then. It's like an entertainer tryin' to be a politician. If you try to be a politician, you cease to be an entertainer. People come to hear me sing. If I didn't give 'em what drew 'em there, they wouldn't be back next time. If they wanted to go hear a politician, they'd go hear a politician.

Q Do you consider yourself apolitical, even though you sang at the Democratic convention and performed at President Reagan's inaugural celebration in 1980?

A I am for the man, whoever it is. I don't consider myself a Republican or a Democrat. So I'm tabbed as a bipartisan follower. In fact, *USA Today* said, "Bipartisan Charley Pride is going to do the National Anthem at the Democratic convention." And I did it, but I was not pleased with my performance on it. I got a little too high, and that was about the second-worst job I've done on it. I think I do it better than anybody in America, but I was singin' a cappella and I got a little bit high.

Q Did you stick around for much of the action?

A Yeah.

Q Did you enjoy it?

A Yeah, it was somethin' different. I had never been to one before. You hear all the jockeying, all the caucuses and this kind of stuff. It's interesting.

Q You mentioned flying commercially. Do you still travel almost exclusively by plane instead of by bus, like most country performers?

A Well, we've just purchased our own plane. We bought a Convair 580. I leased the Fairchild for about ten years, but we own our plane now.

Q You had an accident in the air a couple of years ago.

A Yeah, we had a midair collision on August 6, 1982. We were comin' from Rapid City, South Dakota, and a Cessna 172 hit us. It was an instructor and student pilot, and I think they were flyin' hooded. We were descending from about 19,000 feet. And we were at about 6,800 feet, and they hit our tail section and took our stabilizer off the back, but we got down. They didn't make it. We don't need any more of those. But the percentage of somethin' like that happenin' is so vast that it's hard to believe that it happened. I didn't shake in my boots and tremble and not want to fly anymore, because my career is geared around flyin', and my dates are booked related to my airplane. But I think we've had our quota now. It's happened about three times, and they say those things come in threes.

Q Do you ever ask yourself why you went from being a cotton picker to a millionaire, or why it wasn't you who went down in the plane?

A I don't think about it that way. It was an unfortunate thing that happened, and I'm pleased that I was spared and sorry about the other two people. But I don't read anything else into it. And I don't know why it happened. I take whatever I'm blessed with, and whatever happens to me, and try to keep on keepin' on. I'm goin' to try to live as long and contribute as much as I can. Because I've noticed that most things are geared to dyin', so I thought I'd think about livin' and let the dyin' take care of itself. People say, "You better get yourself some insurance—you might leave tomorrow." But I'm not plannin' on leavin' tomorrow. I'm plannin' on a long extended life. I've got certain priorities set for myself that I believe I'm here to do in this life, and it's gonna take quite a while to do 'em.

Q Such as what?

A Well, I think we're all here for a purpose. I'm here to do what I'm doin to make a lot of people happy. I'm blessed, I'm successful at it, and I'm an instrument. You are, too. It's just how far you want to go with it. I think it would be fantastic to sing in about six, eight, ten, or even twenty different languages, especially the major languages of the world. You got four billion people on the planet. I'd like to sing to about four billion people, to get the response from them that I got from these people tonight.

Q I read a story about a child who would take her medicine only when one of your records was played. In this article, you were quoted as saying, "I believe there is something I've been blessed with that gives me an edge on someone else."

A Yeah, I've even gotten a lot of letters from people who said their relatives had been in comas and they played my records for 'em and they brought 'em out of the comas. But the story you're referrin' to is about a mother and father who brought their daughter backstage in Canada. They told me that she had allergies and took medicine for 'em, but it wouldn't stay down. So one day they were giving her the medicine and they were playin' one of my records, and it stayed down. From then on, they gave her the dosage, they would put my records on, and it would stay down. Then they tried someone else's records—Tom T. Hall and Jim Reeves, I believe—and it didn't work. So they put mine back on, and it worked. Now, if you ask me why, I don't know. But I get letters from people sayin' my voice does somethin' to 'em, other than just the enjoyment of the record. There's somethin' deeper than that, and that makes me feel good, but don't ask me what it is.

Q So what does that do to your self-image? How do you think of yourself?

A As a guy that just likes to be wanted and loved and respected and admired. And accepted as just what he is and who he is, and that's a man, a good American taxpayer. As a person, I fit in anywhere, once I meet anybody. Like even my music. I think I'm the epitome of America. In every sense of the word. Why? Because of the way I project, and my beliefs, what my fans let me be—the total individual.

Q What do you mean?

A Well, I'm an American, I believe in America, and I hope someday we will become the nation that we strive to become. And also because my ancestry dictates what I am. I'm African, Caucasian, and Indian. I'm almost like the flag—red, white, and black. Because by thinkin' in those terms, especially in the way I relate to people, I don't have to sit and wonder about who's better than who, no matter what background anybody comes from. I can only look at myself and feel proud of who I am, Charley Pride, man, American. I mean, I've been on both ends of the stick, as far as the financial part of it. Comin' from the cotton fields of Mississippi, I don't have to ask how it feels to pick cotton, milk a cow, cut wood, get up at five in the morning and make a fire and head bobcats out, too. I've done that. Yet now I can speak in terms of the nice clothes I have, the diamond rings I wear, the financial freedom I have now that I didn't have. So I can converse on all of those, from the bottom of the heap to the top. Someone said, "What did you do before you started singin'?" You name it. I loaded shingles on rooftops for roofers, washed four hundred cars a day, worked as a carhop at a drive-in, did construction, made attic fans, and worked in a wastepaper can factory. I've done it. So I'm the epitome of America.

Q Are there no limitations to your talents?

A There might be a few. But I want to check every avenue that might be beneficial to me. I think I might make a good actor. It's just a matter of having enough time to do so many things I think I could do. I'd love to find enough time to write songs.

Q In this journey from the bottom to the top, as you put it, have you had any ego problems? You probably know that you have a reputation for being somewhat egotistical.

A Well, everyone has to have some ego in whatever they do. But I think everything should balance out. I'm not a person to brag. I'm just a person who is appreciative, but yet proud, too. I'm very happy about my success, and I worked for it. I don't apologize for it. I think that I've been blessed, as I said, to be able to achieve it. If you find your niche in life, and then pursue it, you can be successful. I wanted to be a great baseball player, but apparently that wasn't my niche in life. And as I said before, there is a certain amount of fate and destiny involved in any given endeavor, and everybody is here for a purpose. I was a good baseball player—still am. But it was pointed out to me in the early part of my career that possibly I was here on this planet to do somethin' else. This was told to me by an old man—in fact, the man who owned the place where I grew up in Mississippi, the farm, which I finally bought. He said to me one time, "Have you ever thought that no matter how you tried to get into the major leagues, although you're a good ballplayer, that you're not here on this planet to play baseball, you're here to sing?" So when someone asks what I would tell someone striving, or coming up, I say I have no advice. I'm not an advice giver. But I would like them to try to remember that particular statement. Maybe they would like to be as good and successful a singer as I am, and maybe they can sing just as well. But they might not achieve the success I've had, even with havin' the ability, because they might be a good chemist or architect. But if a person is born with what we call the normal intelligence, or the normal five senses, and can find their niche, they can go on and do things, too, and be successful.

Q I read that at age twenty-six you started asking yourself "why" about a lot of things. You supposedly said, "I lacked the positiveness to move ahead." And yet you seem so confident now.

A I think everyone reaches a point where they have to make a decision not to be afraid to venture into whatever they want to do in life. And they have to find the reason for not venturing, which lots of times is basic fear of failure. Because I used to be afraid all the time. I grew up being afraid to reach out. I had confidence, but not enough. And I started thinking one day, "Do I really believe the Almighty put me here on this planet to be afraid all the time? I should be happy and successful and sure." I figure I was about twenty-six years old when that happened, and it's only been increasing more and more as I get older.

Q So how did you put that into action? Just by saying, "I'm going to be more confident"?

A Well, not by just saying it, but determining that that was the way it was going to be. See, the mind is the strongest thing you've got. Give it enough time, and there's just no tellin' what it can do.

Q Are you satisfied with yourself? Are you happy?

A Yes. Very much so. I think most everything I do is fun. As successful as I am, and with the money I make, a person might think I'd buy fancy clothes. But I don't buy too many clothes—my wife has to make me do it. I'll wear something 'til it goes out of style, and still wear it. On one hand I'm very conservative, but not on the other. I'm a paradox in one sense about certain things. I might give you a hundred dollars, for example. But if you try to squeeze a penny out of me, I just want to get away from you. I want to shun you. It bothers me, 'cause I get scared of anybody who'll take somethin' from me. But if I can't find something good to say about somebody, I don't bother with 'em. I won't be around 'em. I'll just stay to my side and leave them to theirs. You won't find me runnin' anybody down, or bein' mean to anybody. If there's somebody I have a little friction with, I stay as much uninvolved as I can. Because I don't like to be disliked.

Q You prefer to live in Dallas instead of Nashville. Why is that?

A It has everything I need. Schools for the kids, country music, the people.

Q Have people in Nashville resented the fact that you don't live there?

A Resented it? No, why should they?

Q I don't know that they should, but other performers who live elsewhere have said that their record labels resented it because they didn't live in Nashville and couldn't be at their beck and call.

A Naw, that hasn't happened.

Q You have a reputation for being a smart businessman. Do you think you are?

A I'd like to think so. I'm into a little bit of this, a little bit of that, numerous things. But I don't want to discuss 'em except in generalities. Whatever I can see to make my money work. So far, it's lookin' pretty good. I want to be a good businessman. Gettin' to be much better all of the time.

Q How important is money to you?

A It's not. See, I've never been poor. I mean, what's poor? You don't miss what you never had. I was a happy kid who had plenty to eat. No luxuries with bicycles and that sort of thing, but I was rich. I've always been rich. I'm not tryin' to play nothin' down. Everything that you see that I am, what made me the way I am, is where I grew up and the people that influenced me as I grew up in my environment. I've always been a thinker. I didn't even finish high school, but I feel I have a lot of degrees. I'm not a philosopher, I'm not a psychiatrist, but I've been around a whole bunch. I try to meet and talk to everybody I can. I learn from them. They're all my subjects. That's where you get your knowledge. See, I told you I don't know nothin'. I'm a believer, so whatever I get, I have to take it in the computer and decipher it out. I want to try to sample everything I can, to help me along in this life, you see. And I feel that everything I've accomplished has been with the help of everyone that I've met, includin' my mother, my father, my brothers and sisters, and all the friends I went to school with. And all the things I was told as I started to grow.

Q We were talking about money, however.

A Yeah, I used to hear people say, "Money is the root of all evil." Then I heard somebody say the correct way was: "The *love* of money is the root of all evil." Now, I said to myself when I started to grow up, "Money is the root of what you make it." I don't care about money, other than what it's good for. If I didn't have to have it for means of exchange, I'd care less about it. But I'm gonna get some as long as I'm breathin', and there's some out there to get. I truly believe this. This quarterly tax system, though —man, they charge me a lot. I pay a *bunch*. It's tough. I remember they used to let you keep it at least a year. They changed the rules on you, you know. Guys like Howard Hughes, J. Paul Getty, and the Rockefellers and the Rothschilds—they used to go out and make a hundred grand, or fifty grand, twenty-five . . . and they took basically that home. How you ever gonna catch 'em? They used to call it the good old days. Some things *were* the good old days back in the good old days, when you didn't have as many taxes to pay. I'm not against taxes. It's just the way they're doin' it now, and what they're doin' with it when they take it. So that's my answer to that.

Q Some performers are terrified that it will all end tomorrow. Are you like that?

A I never have been the kind of person to worry about what might happen *tomorrow.* I used to be quite afraid in general, when I was younger. I used to be afraid all the time. You say, afraid of what? Pretty near everything. Again, of what people was tellin' me. I remember when Hitler was raisin cain, and I was helpin' Daddy pick up scrap iron to keep him over there, because if he was burnin' the Jews, he didn't have me in his plans to hang around, you see, if he'da won. So I'm just sayin' these things made me think. Songs like "Comin' In on a Wing and a Prayer" meant somethin' to me as a kid, when I heard about Hirohito, along with Hitler.

Q People sometimes call you a legend. How do you react to that?

A Just like pickin' cotton. It's just as natural as sayin', "Well, here he is. He just picked a hundred pounds of cotton, and he's fixin' to go to town and buy him some ice cream now."

Q So you do feel like a legend?

A No. I don't think about things that boggle the mind. I believe that if you want something, then basically you'll get it, and you don't make no big thing about bein' a successful singer. I like it, but I don't sit around and think about bein' the Great Charley Pride, the Legend. And I'm not tryin' to be humble or nothin'. That's just the way I do it. I appreciated those folks tonight, but I think I'm just one of 'em. It just happened to be me up there instead of them. Well, in a way I'm not just one of them. I'm glad they enjoy meeting me and everything, but I don't want them to look upon me as some sort of god, or something overly big. But sometimes they do. I hope it don't hurt 'em.

Marty Robbins

*W*hen Marty Robbins died in late 1982, country music lost one of its smoothest vocalists and best-loved entertainers. Although it was the gunfighter ballads—primarily "El Paso"—for which he was best known, Robbins, who struggled valiantly to keep the "western" part of country-and-western music alive, sang and wrote songs drawn from all aspects of American popular music. Many of his love songs and ballads—including "A White Sport Coat," "Big Iron," "Don't Worry," "You Gave Me a Mountain," and "My Woman, My Woman, My Wife"—have enjoyed a timeless popularity and appealed to an audience outside of country music, earning new fans for the country fold. In his eulogy, veteran country music disc jockey Ralph Emery called Robbins' death "the most devastating blow to country music since Hank Williams died."

Born Martin David Robinson to an itinerant Arizona family, Robbins, one of nine children, endured a hardscrabble childhood on the desert outside of Glendale. His father, a first-generation Pole, drank to excess and drifted from job to job during the Depression. "My father did a lot of things, but he really didn't make too much money," Robbins once said, "I remember once he owned a hog ranch and was doing pretty well. Next thing I knew we were living twenty miles across the desert in a tar-paper shack."

When Robbins was twelve, his parents separated, and the boy moved to Glendale with his mother. He spent his teen years getting into minor scrapes with the law and pursuing a variety of romantic, high-spirited interests—amateur boxing, herding wild horses, and hanging out at the stock car races, the latter pastime sparking a lifelong obsession.

Never much of a student, Robbins nevertheless demonstrated a flair for storytelling, rooted in the tales his maternal grandfather, a medicine-show barker, shared from his travels. With the help of a high school English teacher, Robbins began to set his stories on paper and fashion them into songs. At seventeen, he enlisted in the Navy, where he taught himself to play guitar.

Upon his discharge from the service in 1945, Robbins returned to Glendale and worked as a truck driver and electrician's helper, playing guitar in a supper-club band at night. In time—using the pseudonym Jack Robinson because his mother disapproved of his new profession—he signed on as a singer-guitarist at radio station KTYL in Mesa, Arizona, and formed his own group. From there he took a disc jockey job at KPHO in Phoenix, run by former Grand Ole Opry announcer Harry Stone.

While Stone arranged for Robbins to appear on the Prince Albert NBC segment of the Opry in 1948, his real break came when Opry regular Little Jimmy Dickens dropped by the KPHO studios in the spring of 1951. Impressed by Robbins' clear, commanding voice, Dickens urged Columbia Records to give the young singer an audition. Within weeks, Robbins was signed to the label, and in 1952, "I'll Go On Alone," an original song from his second recording session, climbed into the Top 10.

With that, Robbins' rise was meteoric. He became the youngest writer signed to the Acuff-Rose Publishing Company, and in only six months' time, an official member of the Grand Ole Opry, an honor he would enjoy for nearly thirty years. From the outset, however, he showed himself to be an artist of remarkable versatility, his earliest records embracing not only country music but gospel, Hawaiian, Mexican, and rockabilly. "A White Sport Coat," which won Robbins his first gold record in 1957, has become a classic of '50s pop.

Ironically, although he won two Grammy awards and countless other citations, Marty Robbins never won a Country Music Association award, largely because of industry politics. As an artist who insisted on doing things his way—he was his own manager, booking agent, press agent, and, sometimes, his own producer—he refused to involve himself in most of the Music City power plays, for a time even eschewing membership in the CMA. Nevertheless, he was a clear favorite at the fan-voted *Music City News* awards and, just two months before his death, he was awarded country music's highest honor—induction into the Country Music Hall of Fame.

Whenever he appeared on the Grand Ole Opry, Robbins traditionally closed the show. One of his rituals—to the delight of the audience—was turning back the hands of the Opry clock to give himself more time. Time finally ran out for the fifty-seven-year-old Robbins on December 8, 1982, following a massive heart attack and quadruple bypass surgery. Fourteen months before, Robbins sat for the following interview, which is supplemented with comments from five previous interviews, conducted from October 1975 to October 1981.

Q We haven't talked since your last heart attack [on New Year's Day, 1981]. How are you feeling?

A If I was feeling any better, I'm sure the police would come and get me. I feel great.

Q That was your second heart attack, right?

A Third. See, one time I had one that I didn't even know about, but it was real bad. The first one I had was in 1968. It was *bad*. Bad enough, probably, to put me in the hospital, but I didn't know that's what it was. But it was as bad as the one that *put* me in the hospital. And I got over that one by myself, without ever going to a doctor. The pain in my chest was absolutely terrible for about two and a half hours, but I thought I had just a real giant case of indigestion. You know, if you don't drink, you don't smoke, and you're not on dope, then you think automatically that you have a good heart. Well, let me change that around. I *do* have a good heart, but I have a cholesterol problem. Or I *had* one. That was my problem, the foods that I was eating, and that caused a blockage. But the first one was in October of 1968, and it was just as painful as the one in 1969 that eventually caused me to go to the hospital and have [triple bypass] surgery in 1970. Then the one that happened New Year's Day this year was just a small one. In fact, I didn't really think that I was having a heart attack, because I had it for . . . Let's see, New Year's Day happened on a Thursday, and I waited Friday, Saturday, and Sunday, and then Monday evening I finally called the doctor and made an appointment for Tuesday. So that was five days that the heart attack was going on. And when I finally called the doctor and said I'd like to come see him, he said, "You get over here!" (Laughter) I said, "Well, I was planning to come tomorrow." He said, "Get over here *now!*" So I went to his office and he gave me an electrocardiogram, and shipped me off to the hospital. Man, I didn't even get to do anything. I was laying on that stretcher, and I had my boots on, my cowboy hat, and they put me in the ambulance. The doctor wouldn't let me drive, wouldn't take me, called an ambulance for me, and I had to leave my car there at his office and have somebody pick it up for me. They shipped me right up to intensive care at St. Thomas Hospital here in Nashville. But I guess all heart attacks are serious, whether they're small or whether they're big. There's something wrong with your system. So again, you see, it was a case of not eating the right things. But for ten years everything was going just fine. Then I kind of strayed away from the diet that I was supposed to be on, and went back to what I liked, which was all sweets, and that's something I can't handle. I don't suppose anybody should eat the amount of sweet things that I was eating. That's what caused the last heart attack.

Q How does something like that affect your outlook on life?

A Well, it never bothered me too much. What I was worried about—I wasn't even worried, more concerned, I guess—was about the test that I had to take to see if I needed an operation. So I got all ready for that, you know, and made myself believe that everything was all right, and no operation was necessary. And so they gave me the test, and that's how it came out. I didn't need it. Then I was sort of depressed, really, because I *didn't* get to go through with the operation, because I was so ready for it, see. (Laughter) So I didn't have to have the operation, although I did have a little damage done to my heart, because a little clot of cholesterol had gone through a vein that replaced the artery and stopped right at the end of it. And just this small little portion of the heart was all that was injured. And it made me get back on the right kind of diet, but, of course, here I am again. [He is eating a bag of cookies he spied in my satchel.] I wander away from it and eat things I shouldn't eat. But that's life. (Chuckling)

Q So aside from today, you're basically watching your diet?

A Well, the doctor tells me to do certain things. And I don't want to absolutely refuse to do what he tells me, but then I don't want to stop living. I don't want to die, but I would die if I couldn't do some of the things I want to do. I mean if I can't do what I want to do, then why should I be here? There's got to be another place. So I'll get away from the diet once in a while, and then I'll go back to it. But that's better than getting off of it like I did.

Q I guess an armchair psychiatrist would say that the reason you race cars is because you know that any day that could be it.

A No, but I do know that one day it *will* be it, you see. But I don't know if it's gonna be today, or tomorrow, or the next day. And it could be any day. I don't think of it that way. I mean, that's not why I race, and that's not why I live and have fun. I live and have fun because I enjoy life. And I understand death. So I'm not afraid of death. I might be a little concerned about how it happens, but I'm not afraid of it. So that's why I do the things I do. I do anything I want to do. I have motorcycles, and if I want to ride 'em at 110 miles an hour, I do it. If I want to race a car, I race a car. Because I *do* have a good heart. I just have high cholesterol. Well, I don't have right now, and I'm sure I could pass the physical anywhere to race automobiles. But I enjoy life, and there are certain things I have to do to enjoy life. I can't *sit down* and enjoy life, for instance. I'm enjoying this right now, but if I wasn't talking to you, I wouldn't see any reason to be sitting here. I'd be somewhere doing something, if it's nothing other than riding around the block. Because I want to keep moving.

Q How often do you race?

A I really don't get to do it as much as people think I do. People think I do it all the time, just because I race a few times a year. One year, I wrecked three times and totaled three cars. It's not that I got worried about being killed or being hurt, but man, that was three cars and they cost a lot of money, and just to completely start all over again . . . I don't know. I had some bad luck.

Q You were badly hurt at the Charlotte Speedway in 1974, going into the wall head-on at 150 miles per hour.

A Well, I had thirty-seven stitches up here [he points to his head], four broken ribs, and a broken tailbone. But see, I really love it, so that didn't bother me. Then, at Talladega [in May 1975], we had a wreck. I guess we were doin' about 185 miles per hour when I hit one car, and we had slowed down to about 160 when another car hit me in the side. And something flew off his car, or else it just hit me so hard that it just knocked me out. And I don't remember anything until we got into the field hospital. I remember I came to on the stretcher as we were goin' through the door. And I couldn't remember where I was, I couldn't remember what racetrack it was, what turn it was. But I remembered who I was, and I got to thinking, "Well, I might have really done the wrong thing today." (Chuckling) Then I thought, "What if I forgot the words to my songs?" So I just sat on the edge of the car by myself and did "El Paso" all the way through, which is four and a half minutes. Without forgetting the words. Then I knew that everything was all right. So, of course, I figured that it'd be all right to race again. And everybody keeps saying to me, "Why do you race?" So to save a lot of talking, because I really wasn't in the mood for it—I was real dizzy—I told this TV reporter that I was going to quit racing, because I thought that way I wouldn't be hassled any more that day. I knew I couldn't answer some of their questions, see, because I couldn't remember. Well, boy, I got just a flood of telephone calls and letters—"Are you gonna *quit?*" So it was even worse then than it was before. People really can't understand why I like it, but they probably have a sport that they like, and they like to do it. I like to race, and that's it.

Q As long as we're on grim subjects, you heard a loud buzz in the sky some years ago, and it turned out to be Jim Reeves's plane going down. What do you remember about that?

A Well, I was outside. This has been almost twenty years ago, but I'd always heard, you see, that rainwater was good for your hair. And it was raining that day, and these big, big drops of water were coming down. so when it started raining, I ran outside with some shampoo. Had my bathing suit on, and I was standing out in the rain, and the rain was just *coming* down. You couldn't see ten yards, it was so heavy. It was one of those summer rains. And I heard this plane going over, and I said to myself, "Boy, that guy should not be there flying around in this kind of weather." And maybe three or four seconds later, I heard the crash. It was on a Friday, I remember, because I had a race that evening. So I went out and raced, and I came back that night around eleven-thirty or twelve, and Franklin Road was just covered with cars. And I thought, "There's been a bad accident somewhere." And I turned up the street to go to my house, and I asked somebody, "What's happened?" They said, "There's been an airplane crash, and Jim Reeves was on it." They were looking all over and never could find him. I knew just about where he was, and I told a police helicopter, "If you'll take me up, I can show you where he is." And they said, "Well, we're gonna be looking over here." And they were looking two or three miles away from where he was, see. But they finally found the plane. It went straight down, I think, in a clump of trees in the backyard of some people who were away on vacation. And it was hard for them to see the plane. But that was a funny feeling when they told me that it was Jim Reeves. You get to know somebody, whether you work with them a lot or not, you know them. And it doesn't make any difference whether you like them, because you know them. And when they go, you know . . . It's the same thing in the case of [Elvis] Presley, even though I didn't know him as well as I knew Jim. And Hawkshaw Hawkins, the whole bunch. I knew them all well. And it's not really a funny feeling, it's a sad feeling, I guess, because it's somebody who probably enjoyed life as much as I did *[sic]*. And though I know that there is a time to go, you don't want it to come any sooner than it has to. You want to be ready for it, and you want to have lived your life out and enjoyed all the life you can. And when it's through, then you want to go quietly, in sleep. (Chuckling) That's how I want it to happen. Not in a race car.

Q That would be fairly dramatic, though, wouldn't it?

A Well, to go out like that, yeah, that would be something. But that's not the way I want. I don't want to be in twisted metal. You see, I'm not *afraid* of dying. I'm afraid of the *way* I'm gonna die, you know. (Chuckling) Because I'm afraid it's gonna hurt. And I can't take pain. I can't stand pain! I want it to be an easy way. So if God is listening, let me go in my sleep when I'm about a hundred years old, and I'll be happy.

Q Speaking of God, do you ever wonder why you lead this extraordinary life, while some other guy works on telephone lines all day long?

A Oh, sure, I've wondered about it. But I know why. It's because I prayed for it. I started praying for this long before I ever got it, and long before I ever got into the business. Because I do believe in prayer. And I prayed for all these things, and God gave me the strength to get them. I have never set up any particular goal. Never. I just let it happen. Because I knew it was going to happen. I first started praying to be a cowboy singer, you see. I wanted to be like Gene Autry. I wanted to ride off into the sunset. And then later on in life I found out that Gene *owns* the sunset, and I couldn't ride off into it unless I asked him. So I settled on being a country-and-western singer.

Q You mentioned Elvis a while ago—you were on one of those very early tours that he did, weren't you?

A Let's see, the first show I remember with him—well, there were a number of shows. We did Tampa, Jacksonville, Orlando, Daytona Beach, a tour of about seven or eight days down in Florida. That was the first tour with him, and we did some tours out of Texas. This must have been the early part of '56.

Q How was the billing?

A Well, I was on the Opry, but I didn't have "Singing the Blues" until the latter part of '56. So Hank Snow was the big dog on that tour in Florida. I think Hank always closed the show, or he did a couple of nights and he might have found it a little too rough, and I think Presley started closing the show. Because he was a very exciting act. And though he was younger than I, you know, I wasn't so stupid about the business. There are certain people you can follow, and certain people you can't. I wouldn't be afraid to follow anybody now, but at that particular stage, it would have been kind of silly for me to follow Elvis Presley. Because I remember the first time I saw it happen, where they really mobbed him. It was in Jacksonville. I couldn't imagine that happening, you know. They chased him in the dressing room. We played the football stadium, I think it was, and we dressed underneath the stands in a shower room. And he was on top of the showers trying to get away from people—guys and girls, trying to grab a shoe, or trying to grab anything, you see. I just stood there watching. Nobody noticed me. I was getting a big kick out of it.

Q What did you think of him personally?

A He was a nice-looking young kid. He had a manly look, and that's what I liked about him. Well, I liked him mostly as a person. Presley was a fine kid. I remember on this particular trip, we were sitting there backstage —Hank was on and I was singing songs to him—and he told me that I was his favorite singer. Later on, when he got big, he changed. Frank Sinatra and Perry Como were his favorite singers. But I think Colonel Tom Parker had something to do with that, because I don't believe they would allow Presley to really become involved with country music, be-cause it would bring him down. And he *loved* country music. He knew all the songs. He knew *everybody's* songs.

Q Were you at the Grand Ole Opry the night Elvis made his debut?

A Yes, I was. Up until just before that, I thought he was black, you know. But he didn't do too well that night. Country people weren't acquainted with what he was doing, and they weren't that much into rock and roll. I remember I talked with him and told him how really great I thought he was. It was after that that we did some tours together. I knew that sooner or later he was going to be big, because in Daytona Beach, we hadn't even played there—people didn't even know Elvis Presley—and when we went out on the beach to go swimming, the girls were all looking at him, just like, "Boy, there is *something!*" He had everything in his favor. He had youth, good looks, he had talent, he was single, and then he got Colonel Tom Parker on his side. That was it. He was the best manager a person could get.

Q Did you know Colonel Tom?

A Oh, yes, I knew him through Hank Snow. This was before he had Presley. [Parker also managed Snow.] Colonel Tom got me out of a contract one time that I didn't want to be in. He did it as a favor. I was really hung up bad. This guy really had me. Colonel Tom said, "Do you want out of that contract?" I said, "Yes, sir." He said, "I'll get you out of it." And sure enough, he did.

Q Was it an ironclad contract?

A Oh, I was hung up for six years! At a big percent. And all it cost me was a thousand dollars to get out of it, and it would have cost me many, many thousands of dollars if I had stayed. In fact, it was to the point where I even wanted out of the business. So, see, he was a good man.

Q He didn't want anything in return?

A He asked me if I would be interested in being under contract, and I said, "I really don't want to be under contract to anyone, but I'll work for you anytime you want me to. I just don't want to be under contract." He said, "That's all right." So I didn't have to sign with him. I worked show dates in Florida for him after that.

Q You always hear about these incredible stunts that Colonel Parker would pull. Are those stories true?

A I don't know about the stunts. I've heard a few things that were funny. I don't know if this is true, but I think it's a real great story. It seems Colonel Tom went down to a small town in Mississippi, and he bought the big billboard on each end of town. And on each billboard it said, "It's coming." That's all it said. Ten days later, he changed it to say, "It'll be here—December 4." That's all you could see, you know, on both ends of town. Now, by the time the date was announced, everybody got to wondering, "What *is* it? What's going to be here?" (Chuckling) So the time came for *it* to be onstage. The theater was packed, the money had already been put in the black bag, the back door was open, and the driver was in the car. And Colonel Tom goes in and pulls the curtain back, and there's a big sign that says, "It's gone." (Chuckling) Colonel Tom goes out the back door, and that's it! (Much laughter) I really don't think that's true, but that's how far people would say Colonel Tom would go to get something done. He knew every angle.

Q If Elvis had stayed with country music, what do you think would have happened?

A Well, he definitely had to have another style of song, and he got it in "Heartbreak Hotel." Then he had to go on with that particular type of song, with that little bigger sound than he was getting with that three- or four-piece group he had. I think Colonel Parker, or whoever changed his style of music, did the right thing. It was the best move for Elvis, because at that time country music was as far down in the dungeon as it could be thrown. I mean, *nobody* was buying it. Even I cut some rock and roll back in those days, '54, '55.

Q You mean "Singing the Blues," which didn't come out until '56?

A Well, that was the first hit. I had it number one in the country field, and Guy Mitchell had it number one in the pop field. But I cut some things before that that I had written, plus I did a couple of Little Richard's things, and one of Chuck Berry's, because I was searching. I wasn't doing any good cutting the country songs then. I wasn't getting any play. I did "That's All Right (Mama)," Presley style, except I had a fiddle on it. And it was a number one country song. So that kind of stuff helped me. But I was never ashamed of singing country music, and I was never ashamed of buying it. The same as I was never ashamed to say I liked Perry Como. I used to sing Perry's songs, or Eddy Arnold, or Hank Williams, or Fats Domino or anybody else. Music is music. It's either good or bad. That's the way I feel about it.

Q Do you think Elvis was a country musician?

A I think he was the first country-rock artist, because of things like "I'm Left, You're Right, She's Gone," and a lot of those early ones. I could be wrong, but I don't know why. I've never been wrong in my life. You won't write that, will you?

Q Of course not.

A Really, though, I don't know what country is. I haven't figured it out yet. Everybody who complains, "Let's keep country country," well, what the hell *is* country? I don't know what country is. Once you pass Roy Acuff and Bill Monroe, you've passed country. There are ten different categories of music. You put Ernest Tubb in one category. How are you gonna put Ernest Tubb in country? That's not country. That's Saturday Night Jukebox Texas Barroom music. That's Ernest Tubb-type music. I think every artist has his own particular type of music. I do Marty Robbins-type music. If you wanna call it country, that's fine. If you don't, that's fine.

Q Really?

A I mean, you can't hardly call the songs I've been doing lately country. They don't get any crossover play, mainly because they weren't strong enough. Or if they *were* strong enough, the record company didn't see to it that they were put out and made available for the fans to buy. I search for new fans with almost every album I release, because I don't think there are enough people who like just strictly country music. They'll bitch about it all day long, about nobody doing country music. And then somebody goes and cuts an album of country music, and either the record company doesn't put it out, or the people don't buy it, because it doesn't sell. The industry continues to change all the time. Not in favor of country music, but it changes. It never has been in favor of country music. If it is, I'd like to know. I fail to see it. I've never heard a record company say they were gonna do anything for country music unless it was a country music banquet, or something like that. It's like a politician saying what all he's gonna do, until it gets right down to it, and then it isn't done. But that's business, and I understand it, and I don't complain.

Q You usually make a point of saying "country-and-western" music. Does it bother you that people have dropped the "western"?

A No, the only reason that I say "country-and-western" is, you know, that's what they call it. "Country" and "western" are, I think, two different types of music. Western music, to me, is the cowboy music. They had western swing, which was Bob Wills's style of music. But western music to me has always been cowboy music, and country music was a type of music that Roy Acuff did. There are a lot of people in that category who don't go quite as country as Roy Acuff, but they're still country. But then there are so many different categories that you can't find a name for everybody. Like, what kind of music do I do? What is a gunfighter ballad? You see, that's not country-and-western. That's cowboy music, or western music. And what is a song like "A White Sport Coat (and a Pink Carnation)"? That isn't country-and-western. That's more pop. And what about "Devil Woman"? That's calypso. That's not country. You see? They call me country-and-western, but I don't really cut country-and-western.

Q What about "El Paso"?

A I don't consider "El Paso" a country-and-western song. It's a cowboy song, early American folk music from the western United States. It's not an old song—I wrote the song—but it's the type of song that you would have heard eighty years ago. That's not country-and-western. It's the same as Vernon Dalhart's music, which was early American folk music. You probably don't remember him. I don't remember anything but his records. See, I'm not that old. But he had true-to-life songs, songs about train wrecks ["The Wreck of the Old 97"], disasters at mines, that sort of thing. Folk music is songs about what happened in this country. Bluegrass is folk music, and I'm quite sure that Dixieland is American folk music. And your cowboy songs, such as the Sons of the Pioneers used to do—like "Cool Water," "Tumbling Tumbleweeds"—that's American folk music. And "El Paso" is American folk music. Even if it didn't really happen years ago, it's on that order. It's something you would read about in a western story in the days of Billy the Kid. So I don't consider it a country-and-western song. And I don't consider "A White Sport Coat" country-and-western. But I really love the cowboy songs. That's my favorite.

Q So how do we categorize you?

A Like I said: I do Marty Robbins-type music. I mean, just by the standards of today or yesterday, my music is not really country-and-western. I use trumpets in most of my things, and I do more of the "border" type of music. But I *have* done the old pop standards, and I've done country-and-western. I've had eighteen number one records. In fact, I'm not blowing my own horn, but for a period of time from August of 1959, when "El Paso" came out, to late 1962, everything that I recorded and released went into the Top 100 best-sellers of the world, plus the country charts. Now, that's not every *other* song. That's *every* song. Elvis Presley and Fats Domino were the only other people who had anything like that going. Elvis had it going in all three charts—country-and-western, rhythm and blues, *and* pop—and Fats had it in rhythm and blues and pop, and I had it in country-and-western and pop. People don't realize how many records I have had in the Top 100. But I think the only two records that I had that really were country were ones called "Begging to You" and "Singing the Blues." The way I did "Singing the Blues" was *really* country. But Guy Mitchell had the big recording on it. In fact, I read a piece in the paper a few months back that said that Guy Mitchell's recording of "Singing the Blues" stayed number one longer than any record by the Beatles, or Presley, or anybody else. But I had the first recording of it, and my version got up in the Top 30 in the pop charts way back in 1956. [It got to number seventeen, according to Joel Whitburn's *The Billboard Book of Top 40 Hits*.] So that was something there.

Q Aside from the fact that you're from Arizona, and grew up hearing about the great western lore, doesn't part of your fascination with gunfighters stem from the tales your grandfather, Texas Bob Heckle, used to tell?

A Oh, he could tell the tales! He was a good storyteller, yes, but I was a baby then. Later in life, I kind of felt that he had been putting me on a little bit with his stories, even though he was what he said he was. He was a Texas Ranger at one time, and he had two little books of poems that he sold on a medicine show. He'd sell the medicine, and then he'd sell the little books of poems. He wasn't educated, except by life, but he was pretty wise. And I could tell by the words that he used that he was a pretty intelligent man. But the stories that he would tell me were cowboy stories that he heard around the campfire. That's how the stories were related back in the early days of the American West, just like in England, you know. Stories were told by different people. News went around by word of mouth, and that's the way the early American cowboy songs were done. Actually, as far as news was concerned, I guess one rider would take it from one cowboy camp to another.

Q Was your grandfather the inspiration for your career?

A No, Gene Autry was really the inspiration for almost everything. But the talent that I do have came from my grandfather, because he was able to write. I had a brother—he's passed away now—who wrote on the same lines as my grandfather, but he could not write melodies, you see. I saw a lot of my grandfather's writing in my brother's writing. But my grandfather only inspired me to be a cowboy, I guess. That's what I wanted to be. Because I thought a lot of him, and he was a cowboy, you know. Of course, he died when I was six years old, so I don't remember seeing him a lot. I remember visits to his house. About once every three or four months, we'd go to see them. They lived in town, and we lived way up out in the desert, so we wouldn't get in too often. But when we did, I'd sing for him and he would tell me stories.

Q Tell me more about your childhood. What kind of kid were you?

A Well, when I was six? I was a good kid.

Q When you got older.

A Oh, I was a bad boy, *bad* boy! When I was older, I just about turned into a Johnny Cash or a Merle Haggard! (Laughter) Of course, now they've straightened up, so I can say that. But they were bad boys, see. And I almost turned into one. Stopped just short of it. Things changed when I realized that I was not going to get what I wanted in life by living the life that I was living.

Q Were you a juvenile delinquent?

A Yes, absolutely. Because, you see, at one time in the little town of Glendale, Arizona, the word was out that they were going to get up a petition and have all the people in the town sign it and send three of us boys to the reform school because we were unwanted citizens. We were really bad. (Laughter) This was like when I was fourteen and fifteen years old. And I did pull some good ones, boy. I couldn't tell you the things that I did, because they could still be after me. So I'm not going to confess now. That's too late in life.

Q How about just one?

A No, no. If I did, then you'd lose all respect for me. So I just can't do it.

Q Is it true that you once tried to rescue a cow that had fallen off a bridge and broken her back?

A That was a strange situation. I was all dressed, you know, just like I am now, with a tie and everything. I was coming into town. And I had to cross over the bridge to the property, and there was a bull standing on the bridge, and he wouldn't get off. So I had to scare him off that bridge so I could drive my car across. Well, when I did, I heard this "mmmmuuuuuhhhh" [great lowing sound] down under the bridge. And I looked, and there was this cow down in the water. And there were a lot of cottonmouths and copperhead snakes that stayed under there where it was cool in the summertime, see. Well, I saw her under there, saw her legs underwater, and I could tell she was off balance. Because she would swing her head around and get it going in a circular motion, and give herself some leverage and straighten up. And then she'd get weak and go back, and just about get her head underwater. I thought, "Well, that water is just not that deep." And I couldn't figure out what was wrong. So I took off my coat and tie and went in there. I was keeping my eyes open for snakes, you know. And I was trying to scare her, or do anything to get her to go forward a little bit. But her back legs were paralyzed. So, evidently, she had fallen off that bridge and broken her back, because she could pull herself along on her front legs. And I got her out from under the little bridge, but during that time she was swinging her head, I didn't dodge it one time, you see. And the hard part of her head hit me right in the chest and in the right shoulder. But it didn't bother me at the time, and after I got her out far enough, I went down and got the tractor and fashioned a big belt to put under her, and I used the tractor to lift her out of there and place her up on dry ground. But she couldn't move. And we got the veterinarian out there, and he couldn't do anything for her. So we gave her water and hay right there for a couple of days. But she didn't get any better, so we had to have her put away.

Q But you were okay?

A Well, no. My shoulder started hurting, see. And it wasn't long before I couldn't move my right arm. And then it got so bad that in order for me to get out of bed, I had to reach over with my left arm and take my right arm and put it over on the top of my head and hold it. That's the only position that I could get in that wouldn't hurt. And it was that way for thirty days. Well, when I finally felt good enough to go to a doctor, because I was laying in bed with nothing to ease the pain, he told me I had a shoulder separation. He said it'd be eight months before I'd raise the arm all the way. And when I did raise the arm, I checked back and it was eight months exactly that I had been hit! And we were going to do a movie in Arizona called *Motorcycle Joe,* but I couldn't do it because I couldn't use my right arm. So by the time I got ready to do it, the people had cooled on the idea. And I had the lead in that one. Too bad, because it was a good movie, too. [Robbins appeared in a number of B-grade westerns, finally to win a role in a major motion picture, Clint Eastwood's *Honkytonk Man.* He was scheduled to attend a screening the day of his massive heart attack.]

Q Didn't you at one time want to make one of your songs into a movie?

A Let's see, I've had a number of those now, so I don't know which one you're talking about. But the songs that could be made into films would be, say, "El Paso," "El Paso City," "Small Man," "Mr. Shorty," "Pride and the Badge." You know, there are about five or six long western songs that could be made into great movies. But they're not making westerns right now, and haven't made any westerns for quite some time. But it could be that they will make a motion picture with "El Paso" as the theme. They'd use the song, or mostly the melody of "El Paso" with new lyrics. But that isn't certain, because the networks have to approve. And they won't do anything until they feel that the public is ready, which they won't ever know, because Madison Avenue doesn't know any more about it than I do. They have feelers out there to find out what the public wants, but they don't *know* what the public wants. The public is ahead of Madison Avenue. Has been and always will be ahead of the industry. So you give them something you *think* they want. And they might buy it, you see.

Q This goes back to what you were saying about music.

A Absolutely. There are many, many different categories of music. And they're not cutting all the different types of music that could be cut, and which would supply all the different wants. Because, believe it or not, there are still people who like old-fashioned country-and-western music. There are people who still like the rock 'n' roll from the fifties. There are still people who like the big-band sound or progressive jazz. But like in your early country-and-western, only a small portion of the buying public is in that group. So your big record companies don't worry about that small group. They only worry about what will sell a million, and about an artist who might be good for two songs that sell a million and then he's gone. That's the way it is right now, and that's the way it's going to be from now on. There might come a time when they cut a few more

country-and-western songs styled in the sixties. That style of country-
and-western was a little more advanced than the Roy Acuff or Hank
Snow or Ernest Tubb style of music. But I think someday that they will
have to go back, when they get as far away from country music as they
can possibly get and have nowhere to go. Then they will have to come
back and start over. Because there is a limit to everything. They go back
and start over again. Only you don't go back quite as far, maybe.
Sometime, you know, they'll go back to nothing but the ballads, and
back again to the waltz. And back again sometime to the midwestern
things like the polka and the different styles of folk dances and music.
But right now, that's not what is selling, so they don't worry about that.

Q Some people think that's already happened, you know. Isn't that George
Jones with you in that picture on the shelf?

A Yes. That's George Jones, Faron Young, and Marty Robbins. That's the
Good, the Bad, and the Ugly, and I'm not saying *anything*. (Laughter)
Well, now, George—I don't know if he's good, bad, or ugly, and I don't
think Faron's bad *or* ugly. I think I'm good, you know, so I got me in the
middle and the bad and the ugly got to be on each side of me. I can
talk about them like that because they're my friends. And they both have
different lifestyles than I have. They do different things for kicks, you see.
Like, well, they're both a little feisty. Faron especially. Kind of cocky, you
know. I like him, though. I guess that's why I *do* like him. And I like George
because he's like he is. Just because he does what he wants to do. Faron
does what he wants to do, too. And I do what I want to do. See, I don't
get the publicity that they get at times. Because I'm more of a conservative. I just race cars. (Chuckling)

Q People have an absolute fascination with George Jones.

A Well, it's probably for real country. I would say there's three real great
country singers—George Jones, Hank Williams, and Roy Acuff. And of
the three, I wouldn't know which one I would like to listen to most. Because I like them all. And George Jones is a modern Roy Acuff. If you'll
listen to him and then listen to Roy Acuff's early recordings, or recordings
of just fifteen years ago, you'll hear quite a lot of Roy Acuff in George
Jones's style of singing. But he's one of the top three, I would say.

Q You recently went to the White House to sing. Anything special happen
there?

A Well, the agency that handles their entertainment called and said the
President had requested that Marty Robbins come and sing on the
Fourth of July. So you know, I'd never been to the White House. Never
been to Ford's Theatre. And there were a lot of acts that did that little

thing [a concert performance, later a television special] for President Carter when he was there. But I was never asked to go, and about the only reason I can figure out is because I'm not a Democrat. I'm not really a Republican, either, you see. I'm an American. And I feel that a man should be more interested in the country than in the party. I had nothing personal against President Carter. Obviously, he was a good man, or he wouldn't have been elected. But I just feel we needed the change. Maybe we'll need another change three years from now. I don't know that much about politics. But back to the White House, we got to sing for the President and his wife and a crowd of about three hundred people out on the south lawn. Mr. Reagan got up and made a little three-minute speech, and I got to do about twenty-five minutes, you know. I guess I could have gotten more time, but I would have had to have the House pass a bill for more time for Mr. Reagan. If he'd have been singing, he might have gotten more time, you see. So if I get to go again, I'm going to teach the President some country-and-western songs so he'll get more time on the bandstand.

Q That's very generous of you. Did you get a chance to speak with him?

A I didn't get to speak with him long, because they won't let him stand in one spot too long. And there are guards all around. I got to shake his hand, and he told me how much he enjoyed the show. He made a special request for "A White Sport Coat (and a Pink Carnation)." And, you know, to me he has the cowboy image. And when I went up, I thought, "He's going to like the cowboy songs." So it was a big surprise when I found out that he had made a request for "A White Sport Coat." Because, you see, President Eisenhower's favorite song was "El Paso," and Eisenhower didn't have the cowboy image that Reagan does. But he liked the cowboy songs. [According to wire service reports, Reagan sent Robbins a telegram during his last hospitalization.]

Q You have a reputation for having a good time onstage, but you're also criticized for acting too silly. Critics say you carry the cutting up, the jokes, and the mugging too far.

A Well, some of the entertainers take it too serious. I believe they leave having fun up to somebody else.

Q Did you begin working the comedy into your show at the beginning of your career? How did that evolve?

A Well, when I first came to the Grand Ole Opry, I was playing a theater in Miami, Florida, with Hank Snow. We did three shows a day. I didn't have any kind of hits, so I was allowed fifteen minutes. The people didn't know my songs, so I'd go out and sing and I wouldn't really get much of a hand. And I really didn't know what to say, except "Now, for my next selection, I would like to do . . ." (Laughter) Well, it didn't make any difference what I did—they didn't know it. So I had about a day of that, about three shows, and then I said to some of the guys in Hank Snow's band, "Give me a couple of jokes so I can go out and tell 'em." And I started telling more jokes than singing. I was doing better as a comedian than as a singer! Then I used to do imitations of a lot of different people, also because I had no hits. I could imitate Ernest Tubb, Hank Snow, Gene Autry, Tex Ritter, Al Jolson, Perry Como, Johnnie Ray—quite a few people. But, you know, I have such a good time onstage that I feel I should go out and pay to get in. But then I've seen my act before, so I don't really need to pay to see it. Actually, one time in California I *did* have to pay to get in. I went around the back, and this guard didn't know me. Course, there are a lot of people in the world who don't know Marty Robbins. There's millions and *billions* of them who won't *ever* know Marty Robbins. And this was definitely one of 'em. (Laughter) I don't think he even knew who was on the show. I told him I was Marty Robbins and I was on the show, and I said, "I'd like to get in the back gate, sir, rather than go around the front." And he said, "I don't care who you are. You're not gettin' in here." So I had to go around front and pay two-fifty to get in. Honest! But I made the guy give me back my two-fifty.

Q You have an album called *The Legend*, which you wanted to call *Super Legend.*

A (Laughter) Oh, please, please . . .

Q There was some opposition to that title at the record company. Do you feel like a legend?

A No, I don't feel like a legend. I feel like a *super* legend. (Much laughter) Isn't that funny? You know, I wanted to call it *Super Legend* because, well, just because I like to do things that will cause attention. And that title would definitely have caused a lot of attention. Because pretty soon somebody's going to start calling somebody a "super legend," just watch. And if Columbia Records had named that album *Super Legend,* from now on, people would have said, "Here he is, ladies and gentlemen, *super legend* Marty Robbins!" That would have been just another name, you see. Because anybody who has a record in the Top 10 is a superstar now. Everybody is a star, and about ninety percent of them are superstars. But there are really very few superstars. You could probably count them on both hands. The rest of them are stars. If you're a superstar, you last. You know, you stay around and you're in the business twenty-five years, and the people still come to see you. You have nice crowds, and you sell a fairly decent amount of records.

Q Is the fact that you crave attention the reason you're in this business?

A Yes, I guess so. I love it! Because I like attention. That's why I race, too. I race for the fun of it, but I also race because I get attention. I get write-ups. People don't believe it's the singer Marty Robbins racing. But yes, I love attention. I like it when people call my name. I don't care what they say, if they just call my name. And I hear it, you know, going through airports. My ears are tuned for the name Marty Robbins. Regardless of what they say, they can say [he mimics a crowd whispering] "Marty Robbins!" Everything else can be mumbled, but I can hear "Marty Robbins" so plain, you see. (Chuckling) I'll go through an airport sometimes and people will look at me, and I'll just look at them out of the corner of my eye. I don't want them to know that I'm looking at them. I'll just act like I'm occupied with something else. But all the time I'm watching and listening. And finally one of them will get up enough nerve to come over and say, "Are you Marty Robbins?" And I'll say, "No, but you're about the third person that has asked me that in the past hour!" And they'll say, "Well, you look enough like him to pass as his twin brother!" And so I'll talk with them a little while and tell them how great I think Marty Robbins is, and I'll say, "You know, he's my favorite country-and-western singer." (Laughter) I just have a great time with it. And then when I've got them talked out of the idea that I *am* Marty Robbins, I tell them the truth. Then they don't know *what* to think, you see. (Laughter) And so it's a lot of fun.

Q Does ego ever get in the way?

A My ego? I don't have any ego problem at all. If I wasn't recognized, that wouldn't drop me down. I wouldn't feel bad over that, because, like I said, I realize that everybody is not familiar with Marty Robbins. Everybody was not familiar with Elvis or the Beatles or even Jesus Christ. So it doesn't bother me that everybody's not familiar with me, when there's eighty jillion people in this world, probably. How can I be known to all of them? No way, you see. So I take what I can get, and I'm happy with it. If I can get a little more, I'll try. If I can't, well, that's all right.

Ricky Skaggs

To proponents of "neotraditionalism," the wave of musicians returning to "old-time" country sounds, thirty-four-year-old Ricky Skaggs is something of a country music messiah. A performer who almost single-handedly revived interest in the traditional hard-country and bluegrass sound—paving the way for such performers as Randy Travis and Dwight Yoakam —he is also a supremely gifted musician, capable of playing almost anything with strings on it, and turning out brilliant interpretations and arrangements of little-known classics.

Skaggs's first Epic LP, *Waitin' for the Sun to Shine*, released in 1981, was the sleeper of the year, yielding four hit singles and demonstrating the formula that will probably earn him a place in the Country Music Hall of Fame. Blending honky-tonk, old-time country, jazz, white gospel, and bluegrass in a way they'd never been integrated before, he managed to turn the old-style elements into a commercial, contemporary form without sacrificing the purity of the mountain style. Skaggs himself describes it as "bluegrass instrumentals with country lyrics," or "mixing the sweet flavor of '50s country songs with the fire of bluegrass instrumentals."

Whatever you call it, Skaggs's music is a high-energy sampler of what smart country music can sound like—old-fashioned and traditional enough to entice Bill Monroe to join him on record and in a music video, and yet progressive enough to inspire England's Elvis Costello to jam with Skaggs in concert. Merle Haggard has said Skaggs is "the brightest thing that has happened to country music," with similar plaudits coming from Chet Atkins and Roy Acuff. But Emmylou Harris issued what has to be the ultimate superlative: "He's as good as chicken-fried steak."

These days, with Nashville emerging as "the Mayo Clinic of the Music Business," where such acts as the Osmonds come to rejuvenate their careers and invent their country roots, Ricky Skaggs is obviously the real McCoy, a country boy from the top of his carefully coiffed, hayseed hairdo to the lapels of his loud, thrift-store zoot suits. No matter how many rough edges CBS has managed to smooth away, his body still looks as if it were nourished on an all-starch, beans-and-taters diet, and his thick jaw and neck serve as a testament to his hillbilly heritage. But if Skaggs's diction and grammar are one hundred percent hill country ("We was real poor. We was just farm people. We was real happy with what we had"), his is also a perfect bluegrass voice—a high, clear, lonesome tenor, the kind that's born and bred, not acquired. Which may explain why Skaggs once appeared on network TV in a tuxedo with the sleeves rolled up.

Skaggs grew up in the mountains of eastern Kentucky, near the town of Louisa. The son of a welder, he began singing at three and picking the mandolin at five. By the age of seven, he had already performed with Lester Flatt and Earl Scruggs, but when his parents tried to get him on the Grand Ole Opry, they were told he was too young. His career opportunity came at fifteen, when his hero, Ralph Stanley, invited him to replace his late brother, Carter, in his group. Skaggs dropped out of high school in his senior year to tour full-time, and in the next decade, he would work with such eclectic bluegrass groups as the Country Gentlemen, J. D. Crowe and the New South, and his own band, Boone Creek, which experimented with a fusion of bluegrass, folk, jazz, and rock.

In late '77, Skaggs replaced Rodney Crowell in Emmylou Harris' Hot Band, and immediately gained mainstream recognition for his proficiency on guitar, mandolin, fiddle, and banjo. When he left Harris' band in 1980 to begin a solo country career, he played with the Whites for several months, later marrying Buck White's daughter Sharon. [The husband and wife team would win the Country Music Association's Vocal Duo of the Year award in 1987.] All the while, Skaggs had been releasing bluegrass records on various independent labels, and by the time he took his tapes to CBS/Epic, he was a pro at both performing and producing his own material.

There was a lot of excitement about Ricky Skaggs when we did our interview in October 1981. His debut Epic album had only been out a few months, but his credentials, his superior musicianship, and his musical integrity had the town abuzz. He was already perceived as the bright hope for saving true country music—something not everyone wanted done. While the CMA was to name him 1982's Best New Artist and Best Male Vocalist, he was overlooked in '83 and '84, an act as unthinkable as Bill Monroe hanging up his mandolin to become a heavy-metal star. Skaggs believes the slight was directed by rival record companies who had no comparable old-time country acts—and therefore wouldn't benefit from a back-to-basics movement in country music—or who feared the rise of traditional country artists would kill the country crossover market. In 1985, one of his singles, a reworking of Bill Monroe's "Uncle Pen," became the first bluegrass tune recorded by a solo artist to hit the number one position on the *Billboard* country charts.

Today, with the 1985 Entertainer of the Year title safely under his belt, Skaggs is crusading against country radio station programmers who say his music is too country to be played on country radio. If that is likely to get him in trouble, it is not as controversial as his Born Again Christianity, which has alienated some of his mainstream followers. In his Entertainer of the Year speech, he cried and thanked the Lord effusively, adding, "This is everything I've worked for all my life." And then, in reference to his heroes, Ralph Stanley, Bill Monroe, and Flatt and Scruggs, he said, "They ran the race and have had to slow down—now a fresh runner has grabbed the torch." He was already talking that way when we met at a Nashville hotel to tape the following interview.

Q Your music appeals to country music fans of all ages. Yet a lot of young people enjoy your music thinking it's "the latest thing," not knowing that it's rooted in a style that their grandparents probably liked. If they knew that, they might think they weren't supposed to like it.

A Yeah, I know what you mean. I'm very lucky, because I've been able to take the love that I have for traditional and old-time country music, or bluegrass—whatever you wanna call it—and get it across to the people in a way that it is marketable, fashionable, commercial. I always hate that word "commercial." But it's definitely not crossover. (Laughter) And I'm very glad that I get a chance to do that, because there's not very many artists that want to do it. They're so afraid it ain't gonna sell. They end up wantin' to do more commercial-sounding music, more pop-oriented music, because they think that the younger people, or more of the record-buying age, is gonna grab it and buy it. And it's so funny because the younger kids are saying, "Hey, man, I like that new music you're doin'." And it's older than the hills, you know. (Laughter) Which is nice. I say, "Thanks, you know. I'm glad you like it." What else can you say? I mean, I tell 'em that it's old-time music, and it is, but it really ain't, too. Because it's done in a new fashion, and it's done in a way that not anyone else is doin' right now. I'm not sayin' that in a boastful way, because people like Emmylou [Harris] and people like Gene Watson and John Anderson are doin' *great* country. Good, pure country music. And I think it's great. But I feel like I'm reachin' back a little bit farther into more bluegrass and more old-time country music and diggin' out my material. Blowin' the dust off of it, so to speak, and then runnin' with it.

Q What's the atmosphere in the record industry that's allowed you to be able to do this? I'm surprised, for example, that CBS gave you full artistic control on your first album.

A Yeah, well, I don't think they would have stuck their neck out had they not believed in the music and seen somethin' had already happened. Like, I had done an album on Sugar Hill records called *Sweet Temptation* back when I was workin' with Emmy. There was a single off that album, "I'll Take the Blame," with "Could You Love Me One More Time?" And "I'll Take the Blame" was a smash hit in Texas. It was number one on KIKK radio in Houston for five or six weeks in a row—you know, a completely unheard-of artist with a new song out. So I have a lot of fans in Texas. Well, now we're gettin' a lot of fans all over the country. But Texas has been a real good place. But I think seein' that, and hearin' that, CBS knew that there's somethin' happenin'. And hearin' a lot of talk on the street—you know, "Ricky Skaggs is doin' this," and "Ricky Skaggs is doin' that, and boy, you better watch him. He's gonna do somethin'." That's the kinda talk that was happenin', which I was totally unaware of at the time. I was just tryin' to play music, tryin' to make a livin'. I was workin' with Emmy, and doin' things on my own—tryin' to record albums, and tryin' to do things. Naturally we all want the kind of position that I've got right now, but few of us really get it. I just didn't know anybody that could produce and work with my kind of music like I could, because I felt like I really had self-control, but yet I had a leader ability to be able to show other people how to play my music and add somethin' to it without takin' the heart and soul out of it, you know. But I think CBS checked me out pretty thorough. Rick Blackburn [formerly senior vice president and general manager of CBS Nashville] told me that anyway. He said, "I talked to Brian [Ahern], I talked to Emmylou, I talked to Rodney [Crowell], and I talked to Rosanne [Cash]." And I said, "Well, that's good, Rick, 'cause I had you checked out, too." (Laughter) From then on, we just hit it off really well, you know. We understood that we was both into it to make it the best that we could and *sell* it, you know, and really try to go for it.

Q And yet I read that when you showed up to play a concert somewhere, you got a note that said, "Your bluegrass fans are here tonight. Don't disappoint us."

A Yeah, we got a few of those when we first started. And we still have a certain amount of folks that send up little notes saying, "Hey, play some bluegrass," or, you know, "Get out the fiddle! Play the fiddle some." And I use the fiddle in my show. I'd be a fool not to. I mean, people has known me for the last five or ten years as a session musician, workin' with Emmy, and recording with all kinds of different people playing fiddle, mandolin, guitar, and banjo, and doin' vocals. So it's real hard for people *not* to wanna hear me play fiddle, and I'm glad they do, because it just adds that much more to the show. We try to put on a good show to entertain, as well as do the kind of music that's on record, you know. I don't think I played any fiddle on my *Waitin' for the Sun to Shine* album. I've got one of the finest fiddle players in the country, Bobby Hicks, playin' with me, so I don't really feel like there's any need for me to play fiddle, other than just to do it for a show piece. Bobby's worked with Bill Monroe for five or six years, so he has that real bluegrass, that good fiddle background, you know. But it hurts me when they tell me that they want me to play bluegrass, and eventually I'll wanna add more acoustic music in my show. The main reason I haven't right now is because most of my band has come from a more electric, semi-acoustic kind of background. My steel player, Bruce Bouton, played some acoustic music up in the Washington, D.C., area. And my guitar player, Ray Flacke, is from London, England. So he never really heard any acoustic bluegrass music until he moved over here three or four years ago. Course, he'd heard a few things over there, but never really tried to play any, you know. And now I have him playing some acoustic guitar on the shows. We do some fiddle tunes and stuff like that, and I have him lay his Telecaster down and pick up his acoustic guitar. And it's great, 'cause he enjoys doin' it. It's somethin' new for him to get into, plus it's just somethin' else that adds to the show. But I don't want to do any bluegrass until I can do it right. 'Cause I've always tried to play the bluegrass and the acoustic, old-time music as good as I possibly could play it. And right now I don't feel I could do it as good. If I had maybe another musician or two I could, but right now I can't financially afford it. Maybe someday, you know. Eventually I would love to get another musician that plays banjo and fiddle and mandolin, some acoustic guitar, and could sing. I'm not askin' for too much, am I? [The Ricky Skaggs Band received the CMA's Instrumental Group of the Year award each year from 1983 to 1985.] But if I could find someone like that, it would free me up. Jesse Chambers, my bass player, plays electric bass, and he has wanted to play some more acoustic bass, you know. And that would be able to give us some more acoustic musicians so that we could play some more bluegrass in the shows. But like I say, right now I just really can't. Because I don't want to do it 'til I can do it right. I just take a pride in that, especially, more than anything. That's music that I was raised up on, that I *know* how to play. And I know the ingredients that it takes to play that music *right*. And right now I don't feel like me and my band could perform it right. We could *fool* the people. We could make 'em *think* we was doin' it. But there'd be some people out there that we wouldn't be able to fool, and I'm not gonna try to fool myself. Because I take pride in *all* kinds of music that I'm doin'. I mean, we do western swing, we do rockabilly, we do gospel, we do country, and we do some bluegrass on our shows. But it's things that we've really practiced on and had the time to work on. It's not really what you'd call traditional old-time bluegrass. We do a fiddle tune called "Sally Goodin" where I play fiddle, and my fiddle player plays banjo, and my guitar player plays acoustic guitar, and my steel player plays Dobro on some stuff, and that's fine. But I still use the drums on it, and I use piano for the rhythm and stuff, so it's not really like old-time traditional bluegrass like I'd eventually like to do.

Q Let me read you something Walter Carter wrote in *The Tennessean*. "His acceptance as a country artist stems in no small part from his leaving behind a couple of key bluegrass elements of vocal phrasing and the banjo. He softened and evened out the attack of the typical bluegrass tenor, so lyrics are easier to understand. The lack of a banjo keeps him from being tagged as a bluegrass act, and at the same time opens the door to every country style from waltzes to rockabilly."

A Hmm. He's also the guy that said I was seventeen, right? (Laughter) Well, he made a little mistake. Just ten years off. (Laughter)

Q It's probably a typo.

A Yeah, he said it was a slip of the finger, instead of a slip of the tongue. (Small laugh) No, I guess that sums it up pretty good. I feel that'a way, you know. I used the banjo on my new album *[Highways and Heart-aches]* that I'm gonna be cuttin' Sunday. Well, I'm gonna be usin' banjo on *one* cut ["Highway 40 Blues"], but it's a *country*-style banjo. It's not what you'd call a bluegrass-style banjo. And I think it'll be accepted. I think the bluegrass fans are gonna say, "Hey, he's using a *banjo!* That's great!" But I think the country folks are gonna say, "Hey, that's really nice. That really blends in there." I try real hard to blend music together. Like the engineer that I use, Marshall Morgan. He and I work real good together. I feel comfortable with him. He does a lot of work for [producer and executive vice president of Warner Bros. Records] Jim Ed Norman, and he's producing some records, too. [Morgan has produced albums for the Whites, Lacy J. Dalton, the Nitty Gritty Dirt Band, and others.] So he really knows what things are supposed to sound like, and that's what I like about his engineering. He makes a banjo sound like a banjo, he makes a mandolin sound like a mandolin, and he makes an acoustic guitar sound as big as a truck. (Laughter) And that's what you usually *don't* hear on records. That's one thing I really like about the *Waitin' for the Sun to Shine* album. The acoustic instruments are just as loud as the electric instruments. There's nothin' that's any louder than the other. You know, the Dobro's as loud as the steel. And the piano is right in there with the fiddle and everything. I really want to get that happening, because there's so many times that you hear acoustic instruments on record and the electric guitar is "Ruuurrr", you know. Sounds like a chain saw cranking up, or a motorcycle. And then you hear the drums just *overriding,* and the bass *real* loud. And when you do that, the vocals get lost. And the acoustic instruments, because they're not amplified, and because they're natural wood instruments, they get lost. So it becomes a competition. So from letter A we always try to make sure everything is acoustically *right there.* And I feel like we did that with the *Sweet Temptation* album, with an engineer I used in California. We did tracks here in Nashville, too, but when we mixed it in California, we did it at the Enactron Truck, and Stuart Taylor was the engineer. And I brought to his attention that one thing I wanted *very much* was to have those acoustic instruments up, you know. And a couple of times he said, "Boy, I think that guitar is a little bit *loud.*" And I said, "Naw, I like it up there." (Laughter) And now we've heard it and lived with it all these years, knowin' that it's right. It's blended in there, you know.

Q Sometimes that raises goose bumps, like the close-up mixing of Tony

Rice's acoustic guitar solo on Emmylou's "Wayfaring Stranger," for example.

A Yeah. You know, a lot of people's takin' a chance on havin' an intro for a song on an acoustic guitar, 'specially somethin' that's really rockin', like "Don't Get Above Your Raisin'." You know, the acoustic guitar started out, and it was just right up there punchin' away. Then when the drums and the bass came in, you could still hear the guitar. That's what I really consider being part of my sound—that I really call mine. Personally, that's just the way I always wanted it. But now it's just a real part of my sound because I've used it that'a way for the last few years. I've done it so long that when people—'specially somebody that's been a Ricky Skaggs fan for a few years—hear one of my records come on the radio, they pretty well know who it is, just knowin' the blend of the music. I'm not talkin' about somebody sayin', "Oh well, yeah, that's 'I'll Take the Blame,' because I know the way it kicks off," or "I know the solos in it." They know the acoustic and the electric joining in together. And I guess that's what you consider the bluegrass and country joined together—tryin' to blend the two together. I *guess* that's what I'm tryin' to do.

Q How did you hit upon the idea to do "Don't Get Above Your Raisin' " in that faster, jazzy tempo?

A Well, I already had most all the material together, in my head and on cassette, and I was sittin' in my livin' room workin' on the stuff. I needed an up-tempo song, somethin' that would be powerful, medium-speed, not "Rollin' in My Sweet Baby's Arms" or "Rocky Top." Nothin' like that. No, thank you. And I had a list of old songs that I keep in a notebook—songs that I thought someday I might want to redo. And I saw "Don't Get Above Your Raisin'." I was just settin' on the couch, thinkin' how I could do that song, you know. So I started workin' with it and kinda jazzed it up a little bit—brought the tempo up more than what it was on the original record of Flatt and Scruggs. That's not a real interesting story, I don't guess. (Laughter) But that's really how it came about. It wasn't by mistake or anything. It was just one of those songs that had possibilities of bein' bluegrass crossover, or whatever you call it. (Short laugh) No, I don't guess you could really call it bluegrass crossover. But it just had the potential of bein' somethin' other than what it was. Lot of songs you can work with 'em, and it seems like the way they were recorded is all they'll ever be. They're just destined to stay that way. I also did a song called "Head Over Heels in Love with You", an old Flatt and Scruggs tune, that'a way. I just changed the tempo—put more of a rockabilly feel on it. That'll be on a new Sugar Hill album that I had to finish up before the CBS stuff was released.

Q Rockabilly has enjoyed a resurgence of popularity lately, with everybody from Johnny Cash to Joe Ely to Eddie Rabbitt cutting a couple of rockabilly sides. Is it because after Elvis Presley died we heard so much of his early music again?

A Well, I guess in a way you can kinda thank New Wave. I don't really thank New Wave for a whole lot of anything, but you've gotta say that they've taken some old rockabilly tunes and rockabilly artists and tried to copy them in their own sick fashion (laughter), so to speak. And it's really become popular again. I think rockabilly has always been pretty strong in England and Europe—that part of the world. Even after it died out over here, you know, George Jones did rockabilly years ago. That's a place that I'm gonna search for some material. I've got some friends that's got some really old George Jones stuff—before he was even on Starday [Records], I think, which was a long time ago. But I think people want to hear that rock-and-roll beat, you know, the energy and the aggression of rock-and-roll music. But lyrically they don't like a lot of it. Because lots of times they can't understand the words, and they don't make sense. There's some good rockabilly tunes that has some really good lyrics, you know—good messages about 'em. And I think that sets aside the country from the rock and roll. Like, there's a couple of Beatles tunes that I want to do. Matter of fact, there's a Beatles tune I wanna do on my new album for Epic. Lot of folks won't know it's a Beatles tune, because it'll be a different arrangement, naturally. But it's worded real nice. We slipped one out onstage once. We was just messin' around. It was out in California, and my guitar started feedin' back, you know. The strings started buzzin', and it sounded just like the intro on "I Feel Fine." So my British guitar player started playin' it—"A oop, da da da, da da da da." And the band came in and just started playin' it away. And I just started singin' it, you know, and the crowd *loved* it. It was just a small place, about two hundred and fifty people there, and we was just havin' a good time. It was on our second show, and we was real loose. I didn't even remember all the words to it. I used to sing it when I was a *kid,* you know—seven, eight, nine years old, when the Beatles was big and hot and popular, when Paul McCartney didn't play for Wings. (Laughter) You know a lot of the young kids today say, "Oh, Paul McCartney, yeah, I remember him. He's in a group called Wings." I say, "Did you ever hear of the Beatles?" "Oh, yeah. Didn't Paul McCartney use to play for them?" *God,* I mean, how kids have grown up not to remember things.

Q Emmylou has done several Beatles songs. What do you think you learned from her, and what did she learn from you?

A I think I learned more of a country approach—how to work with country music. I had never worked with a drummer, and a piano player, and a full band like that before I went to work for her. And I don't think she ever had anyone in her band that was as much of an authority on old-time mountain country music as I was. Kind of a walkin' dictionary, you know, of old tunes. And explanations of what makes this harmony work, and what makes this sound. You know, "It's weird, but it sounds great." Like real old-time mountain harmonies, where they would sing a major seventh harmony against a 1 chord, or somethin', which gives it a real weird sound. Or against a 4 chord, you know. All those things were really interesting to her, and Brian [Ahern, her former producer/husband], too. So I think what I learned from her was very helpful to me. And I think what she learned from me—and bein' around me, bein' associated with the kind of stuff that I loved—was important to her. Especially from [the] *Blue Kentucky Girl* [album] on down to the Christmas album [*Light of the Stable*], which is a great record.

Q You must have been a great influence on *Roses in the Snow,* her bluegrass-flavored album. How much did you contribute to that?

A Well, I could talk to you a lot about that, and a lot of things I wouldn't want printed. I brought Emmy a lot of material for that record—probably six or eight songs. And playin' mandolin, fiddle, banjo, and guitar, and doin' vocals, naturally if one person does all that it's gonna have to sound some like the personality of that person. There was a lot of direction, a lot of producing, that I feel like I did. But it was real good to work with people that all that was so new to. There was a lot of "Hey, this sounds great!" you know, and "Isn't that nice?" That's what country music was built on—the love for that old kind of music. Naturally, we have all kinds of music. It's kind of like Christianity. Christianity was built on Jesus Christ bein' the Son of God, you know. But now there's all kinds of different Christian beliefs and faiths. It's just like old-time country music, and I don't mean to be sacrilegious when I compare the two. Because there's a lot of religion in music. I know that there is in *my* life, and it's very strong. If I didn't have it, I couldn't sing the songs that I sing. I couldn't sing 'em with the conviction and the authority that I have. But hearin' people talk about country music in that'a way, you know—they hear the old-time music and they say, "Oh, that's so nice," and "So pure and so refreshing." But it's always been there. It's always been right in the center. It's the *roots,* you know, and there's all kinds of people who've poured water to the roots and made 'em grow branch roots and everything—made the music branch out and go in different places. But if you cut all the branches off, you'd still have that root right there, and that's what good, solid, old-time country music is. That's why I feel real good about what I'm doin'. Because it's from the core, the rooted part of country music.

Q You played on the very first sessions for the famous Dolly Parton, Emmylou Harris, and Linda Ronstadt trio album. What was that like?

A Well, that's when I first joined Emmy's band. I had known Linda and Emmy for four or five years before that. But goin' out and meetin' Dolly was a real treat. We hit it off real well, you know. I'm sure she hits it off well with a lot of different people, because she's got that ability. But for some reason we got along exceptionally well, I guess because I was just very country, very common and very plain, and I was very proud of that. And I think she's proud of bein' country and bein' from where she was born and raised, too. It shows, it comes through. And it's made her millions of bucks, too. But we had a lot of songs in common that we knew, a lot of old gospel songs and things. And we said, "Hey, let's record some of this stuff," you know. And she recorded two songs for my Sugar Hill album. But RCA wouldn't give her a release on it. That was very sad, because it was gonna be me and Dolly and Ralph Stanley. Which would've been one of the most beautiful things. It makes you want to cry. I mean, I *did* cry about it, just to be honest. Ralph was really into it, you know. And Dolly already had her parts down for both the songs. One song was "Don't Step over an Old Love," that was gonna be a duet between me and her. And she really enjoyed doin' it. The other was "A Vision of Mother." [Both songs later ended up on Skaggs's *Don't Cheat in Our Hometown* LP on the Epic label.] We had a great time. But record companies are that'a way. It doesn't matter what Dolly wants. There was something in her contract, I guess. And I kind of understand in a way now, because CBS . . . They own me. I mean, in so many words, they really do—they own Ricky Skaggs. They own the rights to me. That's what a contract usually is. They own my voice. I have a lot of flexibility. They're real good with me. I mean, I can tell 'em, "Say, I'd like to go sing on Reba McEntire's record [on another label]." And they'll say, "Sure, fine." Or Janie Fricke. Course, Janie's on Columbia, which is in the family, you know. And bein' a background singer is one thing. But singin' a duet with someone and sharin' the spotlight, where people's gonna say, "That's So-and-So and Ricky Skaggs . . ." Well, CBS feels like they've put money into me to help me grow. And I in turn have produced good music for them to be able to get out on the market and sell. So we have a great understanding. They know what I've done for them, and I know what they've done for me. But back to the trio project. I know that the album cut of "Mr. Sandman" that Emmylou released had Dolly and Linda on it. Emmy had to go in on the single version and sing all the parts herself. And Emmy's [title cut from] *Evangeline* had the girls, the trio project. And "Even Cowgirls Get the Blues" was recorded at that time. There's a lot of songs that they did. In fact, there was a song that Dolly and Linda and Emmy had worked on that I was considerin' pitchin' to the Whites, my wife and her family, to see if they would like it. Also, me and Dolly and [vocalist-banjoist] Herb Pedersen tried to do it. But it apparently didn't come out in the studio to suit 'em, and it wasn't released.

Q What do you think your best work with Emmy was?

A Everyone says "Darkest Hour Is Just Before Dawn." And I feel the same way. I think that ought to go in a national archive, and in two hundred years from now they oughta dig it up and play it for everybody—even on the moon. So yeah, I feel like it's probably my best work with her. It was just one of those songs that was *magic*, you know. It didn't take many takes to get it—it's just so good the way it is. You could've added all kinds of stuff to it, but you would've taken so much away by doin' that. I feel real good about that song. That's a great one. I talked to [bluegrass musician-songwriter] Ralph Stanley the other day, and I said, "Ralph, are you gettin' any royalties on these songs?" He said, "Yeah, I got some money in on 'Darkest Hour' here not long ago." I said, "I'll bet you did." (Laughter) That's got to have sold a lot of records for him. But Ralph Stanley is probably my biggest fan. And I'm so happy about that. Because he was the first artist that I ever worked for professionally. And he was a real cornerstone, a real solid musical piece of ground for me to grow in. I had studied the Stanley Brothers' music all my life. Well, it wasn't just the Stanley Brothers' music. It was Appalachian mountain music. My mom and dad was singin' Appalachian music, or eastern Kentucky old-time music, back before it was called bluegrass—back before it was nothin' but just ol' hillbilly, back-porch, livin'-room, kitchen (laughter), whatever you wanna call it, pickin' music. You know, you just set around and play and sing. And the Stanley Brothers were lucky enough to be able to get it on record, and then go out on the road and perform it.

Q You worked as a boiler operator for a while between stints as a musician. Why did you leave music?

A Well, I had worked with Ralph Stanley for about two and a half years, and I was *burnt up* on the road. I was just *fried*. I wasn't makin' very much money, and the accommodations were terrible—four or five in a motel room together. It was just *very* hard times financially. So I kinda wanted to get my head together and see if I was man enough to stick this thing out. You know, "Just how good do you think you are, Skaggs? Do you really think you're good enough to make it?" I wanted to give it careful consideration and thought. And naturally the Lord was up there guiding me around somewhere. And I just decided later on that I would go ahead and get back into music. I only was out of it for like two or three months, 'cause I hated workin' in that boiler operation job. God, what a . . . gig. (Laughter) It was awful. *Noisy!* And I hate noise, you know.

Q What do you think your music would have sounded like had you not grown up in eastern Kentucky?

A Gosh, who knows? I never had a question asked to me like that. I don't know. Maybe like Ted Nugent, you know? (Laughter) No, he was in Detroit, right? I have no idea. Well, [steel guitar player] Buddy Emmons is from Indiana. Actually, a lot of good country artists have come from Indiana.

Q Bobby Bare once said he wouldn't have been the person or the musician he is had he not grown up in Kentucky and in southern Ohio.

A Yeah, he grew up around Lawrence County, Kentucky. He lived in Louisa for a while, right close to where I lived. But yeah, I know that what I'm doin' now reflects so much on how I was brought up—the atmosphere and the whole element, you know. That's why I wish that I could raise my kids up in the same kind of atmosphere, gettin' out and gettin' fleas and ticks on 'em, you know. (Laughter) And bein' able to go fishin', walk around in the hills, and go see a coal mine, you know. And bein' able to go out and pick tomatoes off the vine, instead of goin' to a store and gettin' 'em. I didn't know that you could buy tomatoes in a store until I was fifteen years old. (Laughter) You know, I thought everyone just naturally had a garden. And I thought everybody had horses, and chickens, and cows, and coon dogs, and rabbits and beetles. You know, it was just a way of life for me. And I just took it for granted that ever'body was raised up that'a way. But boy, the more I talk about it to people, the more I break their hearts, because they wish so much that they had what I did. And I feel sorry for 'em, because I wish they had it, too, seein' how tragic their lives have ended up, you know—drugs, drinkin', broken-up homes, and not knowin' where to go, which way to turn. It's a hard life for people sometimes, when they haven't had that good family, that Christian upbringing, you know. And I know that if you raise your kids up with that solid Christian life, they won't ever forget it. It'll always be in the back of their mind. 'Cause the Bible says that: if you raise your children up with it they'll never fall away. Even though they might not live by it. I mean, I've had Jesus Christ in my mind *forever*. I've known who He was, you know, and because my mom and dad told me that, therefore I believed it. But it wasn't until about a year ago that I had Him in my heart. And that's what makes the difference, when you accept that, and live that. And now, ever'thing is just *so* much easier. People think you have to give up so much to be a Christian, you know. They think, ''Well, I've gotta quit *livin'* if I do that. I can't drink anymore, and I can't get out and gamble and play poker.'' (Laughter) But the Lord gives you so many things that's so much better than all that. You don't even remember that you done 'em. Well, you remember, but it changes your ''want to's,'' put it that'a way. (Laughter)

Q What was the incident that made you feel the Lord in your heart?

A Well, I just knew that I wasn't right. I knew that if I died, I was gonna be lost in eternal damnation. Because readin' the Bible and knowin' what's said in there, I knew that I wasn't anyways *close* to what God told the disciples and the prophets how to live, and in turn had His son, Jesus, go to the cross for, for all of our sins. I mean, He died for me, just like He died for you, or for anyone else. He went right up there on that cross, and He didn't die for just a certain amount of people—He died for the whole *world. Everyone.* And when I knew how good He had been to me all these years, and how He gave me a talent, you know, I felt like I was the luckiest person on the earth. I still do, because I feel like, why did He just give it to me? I know He gives talent to everybody, and to a lot of different people in certain special ways, but why did He give *me* so *much?* Why did He give me the abilities to be a bandleader, which a lot of people don't have? A lot of people are great musicians, but they can never have that personality to go out there and lead a band and be the head of a show. And why did He give me the abilities to play four or five different instruments? Most people can barely play one, and yet I can play so many. And why did He give me the abilities to sing so many different harmonies? Lots of people can only sing lead, you know. They think tenor is lead, only high and loud. (Short laughter) But He's just been so great to me. Why shouldn't I want to live for Him the rest of my life? Especially after I really accepted Him in my heart, and said, ''Lord, come in and just be the Savior of my life, and I'll be whatever You want me to be. You just show me and *lead* me.'' And I was also baptized, which I think is very essential. Because the Bible says, ''Saved and be baptized.'' John baptized with water, but Jesus baptizes with love and the Holy Spirit. And when I was baptized, I *felt* Him come into my life. I mean, it was just a feeling I've never felt before. I felt a warmth, and I felt His presence enter my body. Now that's real heavy, I know, but it's true. And I'm sure that anyone that's ever been saved and baptized can say they felt that same thing. There's so many songs written about " . . . and then I felt the Holy Spirit." But when you're saved, whenever you're baptized, you've done what the Lord has asked you to do. Then it's "Go on and be a servant." You know, serve the world. Don't *be* the world, but come here and serve your brothers. Because Jesus was the servant when He came here. He was the King of the Jews, but He was a servant. And, well . . . didn't know I was gonna start preachin' today. (Embarrassed laughter)

Q Speaking of serving your brothers, a couple of the reviews of *Waitin' for the Sun to Shine* take you to task for recording "So Round, So Firm, So Fully Packed." They accuse you of being sexist. How do you feel about that?

A Yeah, well, that kinda surprised me. 'Cause it's a very *mild* song. I think people's sick minds take stuff and start twistin' and turnin' it around to try to make something sexual and somethin' real nasty out of it. But me and Merle Travis was talkin' about it the other night. He's the guy that wrote "So Round, So Firm, So Fully Packed." Me and Merle got to meet during Disc Jockey Week, and we was talkin' about the whole concept of the song. But see, "So Round, So Firm, So Fully Packed" was a Lucky Strike slogan back in the forties and fifties. And "Just ask the man that owns one," another line that's in that song, was from a Packard ad. So it's just full of old slogans, you know, like "the toothbrush smile they mention on the radio." That was Colgate toothpaste. It's so easy for people to take potshots at somethin' like that. I think there's probably a few stations that wouldn't play it. I don't know why. That really hurt me, because I would *never* record anything that I thought was *bad,* you know. I won't even record a song about drinkin'. I've recorded a song called "Don't Cheat in Our Hometown" that says, "If you're gonna cheat on me, don't cheat in our hometown." But that's not me gettin' out and cheatin' on you. I try real, *real* hard, you know? I mean, I get so many songs sent to me. I guess me and [wife] Sharon get an average of three cassettes a day in the mail. So I know that there's a lot of [cheating and drinking] songs on the radio that do real well and stuff, but there ain't enough money to make me record one of 'em. I'll just make what I'm supposed to make, and do what I'm supposed to do. I'm not sayin' that what those other people do is dishonest. It's just not the way I live, and it's not the way I believe. I don't want to do anything on record that I wouldn't do in my own life. And I can't really see anything wrong with "So round, so firm, so fully packed / That's my gal." That's just a guy braggin' on his girlfriend. And they were talkin' about it bein' a sexist song, with the line "Just ask the man that owns one," like, "I own this woman, she's my slave." That's so yucky and stupid. That's so *sick*. I don't know why anyone would take . . . well, that's the press. (Tense laugh) I'm not saying that it's all that'a way. 'Cause most of the reviews on the record has been real, real good. *Rolling Stone* is the only one that really said that, I think, and that particular review was real good. The best one CBS has ever gotten on a country record from them, they said. But they *had* to say somethin' a little negative, you know. But that's good. That keeps it all spicy and everything. (Short laugh)

Q So on the whole you're optimistic about the future?

A Yeah, I feel there's a real respect at CBS for me and the music that I'm doin'. And people really seem to just appreciate me as a person. I love that as much as anything. I'm glad that they respect me for what I am, for how I believe, for my living standards, my morals, plus my music too. That makes it all pretty good.

Mel Tillis

*A*s a child, his stutter brought him the pain of separation and the taunts of his classmates. As an adult, when he used it to make people laugh, it brought him financial security and acclaim. But in the final analysis, Mel Tillis' famous speech impediment has obscured the depth and breadth of his accomplishments, and diverted attention away from what Tillis really is: one of country music's most versatile and underrated talents.

Seldom flashy, sometimes ponderous, Tillis nevertheless excels in at least four obvious performing arenas. He is foremost, of course, a singer, one who has mastered the slim groove between gut-level honky-tonk and mainstream Nashville Sound. When he opens his mouth, there is no doubt that he is the genuine article, someone who cares about the music and its evolution. Initially a songwriter, and one of the best of the honky-tonk genre, Tillis has distinguished himself as a comedian as well. And now that Bob Wills and Ernest Tubb are gone, Tillis has become, at the age of fifty-six, with thirty years in the business, one of the last real *bandleaders,* his group, the State-siders, earning a reputation as one of country music's finest show bands.

Born Lonnie Melvin Tillis in Tampa, Florida, the son of a baker, Tillis grew up in the hamlet of Pahokee. At the age of three, he contracted malaria, which left him with his lifelong stammer. The child suffered another trauma at age seven, when his father, who periodically deserted the family, once again left his wife and four children to work on a dredge boat in Puerto Rico, staying nearly five years.

A drummer in the high school band, Tillis also played violin at an early age, but gave it up for football. At sixteen, finding he didn't stutter when he sang, he made his first public appearance as a musician, singing and playing guitar in a Pahokee talent contest. He got his first paying job in music in the Air Force with a band called the Westerners, playing evenings and weekends in local clubs. After the service, where he'd been a baker like his father, Tillis took a series of colorful jobs—working as a strawberry picker, as a fireman on the railroad, as a milkman, and as a driver for Harry's Cookies—while honing his skills as a performer.

But just as the Air Force told Tillis they "didn't need any stuttering pilots," when Tillis first went to Nashville in the mid-'50s and announced his intention to become a vocalist, record company executives laughed at the idea. In 1956, after writing "I'm Tired," for Webb Pierce, Tillis finally broke into the business as a songwriter, earning a $50-a-week draw with Cedarwood Publishing Co. Through the years, Tillis went on to write some 1,000 songs, 500 of them recorded, ranging from poor-boy blues to honky-tonk misery and vague social consciousness, including two of country music's most enduring classics—"Detroit City," made famous by Bobby Bare in 1963, and "Ruby, Don't Take Your Love to Town," a huge hit for Kenny Rogers and the First Edition in 1969. Both songs depicted characters and situations that were far more complicated and ambiguous than those in most country music of the '60s.

It was his voice—distinctive and free of gimmicks and ornate embellishments—that made him a star, however, Columbia Records signing him in 1958 and quickly releasing "The Violet and the Rose," a Top 30 hit. In the years to come, Tillis would switch labels often, earning thirty-five Top 10 hits, including "Who's Julie," "Good Woman Blues," "I Believe In You," "Coca Cola Cowboy," "Southern Rain," and "In the Middle of the Night." In 1976, the Country Music Association named him Entertainer of the Year, as much for his self-mocking comedic flair as his music.

As the '80s got under way, Tillis began to look less like a honky-tonk singer-songwriter and more like an all-purpose entertainer, appearing frequently in Las Vegas and on the Johnny Carson show, cutting a duet album with Nancy Sinatra, and putting more energy into his occasional acting roles and his business enterprises than his recording career. When he connected on a hit such as "Send Me Down to Tucson," though, he proved his mastery of the country idiom. "As time passes," critic John Morthland was to write of him, "Tillis sounds more and more like the real thing, and one of the last of them."

The following is a compilation of three interviews that took place in November 1978 at the Tulsa International Music Festival, in the summer of 1983 at the Little Nashville Opry in Nashville, Indiana, and in August 1985 in Louisville. Tillis was surprisingly guarded and out of sorts during our first interview, but pleasant and cooperative on the second. For the third, he was giddy with excitement over his new movie production company, and proved the perfect interviewee—talkative, open, and unaware of the clock.

Q You've just moved over to RCA Records, and your first album, *California Road*, is a more traditional-sounding record than most people are doing now. Why did you want to do that?

A Well, somebody has to do that. Ricky Skaggs [who had a hit with Tillis' "Honey, Open That Door"] and George Strait can't do it all by theirselves. And it looks like everything is becoming so . . . it's a new input, you know, and there's nothin' I can do about it. And I want to keep traditional country, or a more traditional country sound, alive as long as I can.

Q Do you really think it's swinging back that way, with Reba McEntire's success, and George Strait's?

A I think that's what the people want to hear. They're so tired of "seven in a row" that they want to puke. FM radio has hurt traditional country music. And they didn't do it intentionally, I don't think. But "seven in a row," I mean, you play seven in a row of the New Country, and you don't know who's coming up. All of these people were singing, the Nitty Gritty Dirt Band, and Julio and Willie, and Lionel Ritchie—there's a good one for country—they might play a George Strait song next, and then they'll play Earl Thomas Conley and Reba McEntire, and then they might play Olivia Newton-John, who hates country music.

Q You don't think Lionel Ritchie belongs on country radio?

A Naw, it's not right! I can't fight it, though. I shouldn't even be criticizing, but I can't help it. And in order for traditional country music to survive, they have to put some personality on the radio. And we've got to start recording with our bands. Everybody records with the same studio musicians, because the producers are from L.A. and New York. Here they come in town, and they say, "No, we won't use the band. We want to slick up country music." They slicked it up all right. They slicked it right out of the business. Country music is as low as it's been since 1974. And they're tryin' to figure out what's goin' on. I'll tell you what's goin' on. You tune in to the Nashville Network, and you'll see what the people are wantin' to see. They want to see *Nashville Now*, and they want to be a part of it.

Q It's the most popular show on the network.

A Right! And you can't forget those country people out there. And that's what happened. The country fans that we had—with *Urban Cowboy* and all the ones that we gained, all of a sudden they said, "Boy, look at all these people! Country music did that, so let's kinda slick it up a little bit and see what happens!" I'll tell you what happens. Country music has lost a lot of its popularity. It's bad. The new acts—I think they're great. They've got a tremendous amount of talent. And I'm not knockin' these kids, because that's their input. I'm not sayin' don't record like that. Record the way you want to record. If it's New Country, if it's traditional, I think it's all got a place on country radio, if you're gonna call it country radio. I think that you can play a Bill Monroe record, and you can turn around and play a Lee Greenwood record, and you can play an Eddy Arnold record every now and then if you want to. But that's not happening. They're playing the goldie oldies.

Q Well, you own a station down in Mobile.

A I own three stations.

Q All country stations?

A Yes.

Q What kind of rotation do they play?

A I don't even know. I stay out of it. But I know in Texas, where I am, in the panhandle, in Amarillo, you can't get very far away from Bob Wills. And I know they do play the New Country, but at the same time, though, they play traditional. You've got to play Ernest Tubb in Texas. You've got to play Hank Thompson.

Q Didn't you used to carry another fiddle player?

A I used to have four fiddles. I had a big band at one time. I had seventeen [pieces]. I always wanted to have me a Bob Wills band. And I had me one, and I really enjoyed it for a couple of years, and then it just got too expensive to carry everybody, so I cut down to nine.

Q How long have you had nine?

A About two years [since 1983]. And before that I had ten.

Q Aside from the Bob Wills idea, why did you want such a large band?

A Ego. I had more pickers out there than Count Basie. I don't know, I just like a big band. I like to get it as close to the record as I can get it. And I love the fiddles. I could get by with five [instruments]. But I think that you should give the fans as much as you can without breaking yourself, you know. I think they deserve a big band, if that's your style. And it is my style. And I ought to be able to use my band when I go into the studio, because they know me as well as anybody in the world. Because we travel together. And we eat together, we sleep together—not in the same bunk, everybody has their own bunk—and that's who I should record with. That's where you get your personality, from your band. Your band gave you your style. Like the Drifting Cowboys and Hank Williams. It was a marriage. Ernest Tubb and the Texas Troubadours—that was another marriage. Bob Willis and the Texas Playboys—that was his style, and you knew the minute they come on who it was. You knew Hank Thompson, and you knew Carl Smith. You *knew* those guys. And you knew Lefty Frizzell, boy. And Little Jimmy Dickens, with the twin guitars. Everybody had their style. Bill Monroe had his style. And *that's* who you should record with.

Q Why don't producers want to do that?

A They say that it takes too long, for one thing. And then they can go in there and record, put you on with just a skeleton band, and then you sing, and they add on all this other stuff a week or two later when you lose all the feeling, and then you'll come back in and sing it over and over again. I want to do it live, at one time, with my band.

Q Records made that way usually sound as if they're made that way. You can hear it.

A Oh, yeah. Onstage, my boys are as good as any band. And hell, we can't even get nominated [for CMA Band of the Year]. Our band can play circles around most of 'em. I'll guarantee you that. Boy, I'm just bitchin', ain't I? I want to write a book. I started on it the other day. *The Rise and Fall of Country Music.* As I see it.

Q Rawson Associations, the publisher of *Stutterin' Boy*, your autobiography, didn't seem to do much to promote that book.

A Naw. All they wanted was a paperback. They had three printings, I think. Sold 30,000. And they strung that out. You couldn't even get it in my hometown [Pahokee, Florida]. Or in Palm Beach County. I don't think they had the money to do it.

Q How did you think the book itself turned out? Were you happy with it?

A Well, they took out 268 pages. [Sadly:] And they *sanitized* me.

Q What did they take out that disappointed you?

A Oh, they were right, possibly. But, you know, I've got a lot of stories. I didn't tell everything, 'cause it'd be three volumes. But I told some good ones in there, and I heard a lot of other good ones, and they took 'em all out.

Q The story about the time you answered your hotel-room door wearing a woman's negligee is a famous one, but as you said in your book, it usually includes a naked girl or two. What are some of the ones they left out?

A Well, I can't tell you that. I'm saving them for my next book, and I've got a pretty good start on it.

Q Not too long ago, you bought Cedarwood, the music publishing company where you started out as a writer. How did that feel?

A Great! It was a dream come true. I went there and they paid me fifty dollars a week on a draw against my earnings, and then I had my big run-in with Webb [Webb Pierce, who, Tillis says in his book, expected half the credit and half the royalties of any Tillis-written song he recorded]. I went in one day, and I wanted to buy some property in Florida, and I went in and I signed a twenty-year contract. So I was always with them as a writer, and later on I got them to split the publishing when I started my company, Sawgrass, and Mel Tillis Music. And after that, I didn't do too much writing, because I got busy on the road, and I just didn't have the time to write. I was too busy makin' money, and my God, did we make money in them days!

Q Well, clear that up for me. Tom T. Hall says it's a myth that people make money on the road. But your book says that's where you *do* make your money.

A Oh, yeah, that's where you make your money. What's he talkin' about?

Q He says the overhead just eats it up.

A Gol-lee. Yeah, you make your money on the road. That's your cash flow. And you're lucky if you break even on the records.

Q How many publishing companies do you have now?

A I've got Sawgrass and Cedarwood, Sabal, Mel Tillis Music, Guava, and Tuffy Music.

Q Do you only record songs out of your publishing companies?

A . . . And I've got an old company that was owned by Johnny Horton, called Cajun Music. We've got "North to Alaska" in there, and "Squaws Along the Yukon," and all them songs. I've got a great catalogue of songs now. It's all computerized.

Q But do you only record songs that you own?

A [Jerry Reid, Tillis' guitar player, interrupts to ask Mel if he wants a pork-chop sandwich. Tillis again ignores the question.]

Q Do you think you'll be cutting more traditional material with RCA?

A Yes. And I'm gonna use my band. I done told 'em. If they don't want me to do it, I'm just gonna have to go to TV to sell my music.

Q Have you talked to [vice president and general manager of RCA Nashville] Joe Galante about it?

A No, I haven't talked to him yet about it. He may not let me. But I want to do it! I'm gonna do it! If I'm goin' out, I'm goin' out on my terms.

Q Well, RCA let Leon Everette do it. And several other acts—Gene Watson, Ricky Skaggs, John Anderson, and the Bellamy Brothers, for example—have recorded with their own bands on other labels.

A Well, I'm gonna use 'em. I don't think [producer] Harold [Shedd] wants me to use 'em. I don't think Galante will mind. [Apparently he did. Several months after this interview, RCA and Tillis decided to discontinue their relationship after only one album. Tillis now has his own independent record label.]

Q You have a way of putting across a song, particularly "Send Me Down to Tucson" or "A Cowboy's Dream," so that it sounds as if you've lived it. What do you think about when you're singing? Are you conscious of trying to "sell" a song?

A Well, if a song is meaningful, if the words are good words and it has a good melody, it makes you put that in there, put the feeling into it, if you like it. It does for me. I don't know about other people. Some people are just natural singers. They can sing anything and put feeling into it. But I have to work at it. I love it, though.

Q What's happened to your songwriting? You don't seem to record many of your own songs anymore.

A Well, I'm so busy anymore. And I think the good Lord only gives you a certain amount of songs, especially if you're doing other things, like personal appearances and all that stuff. And if you look back at the writers that came along the same time I did, like Harlan Howard, and Hank Cochran, Roger Miller, Willie Nelson, most of those guys aren't writin' neither, because they're too busy. And then, too, I think you run out of songs. But I got some that I've been workin' on, you know.

Q How did you come to write "Ruby, Don't Take Your Love to Town?"

A Well, that was a true story. But it was about World War II, instead of the Vietnam War. I knew this particular guy, and I knew his wife. She was from England. And he brought her to the States from England after the war. They moved to Pahokee, Florida. They were our neighbors. And they had their problems. And I remembered that story, and I kinda changed it up a little bit. Changed the war to the current war.

Q Supposedly, the real-life inspiration for "Ruby" killed himself.

A Uh-huh. The third wife after "Ruby." He killed that wife and himself.

Q His paralysis was really only temporary, though.

A It was some kind of war wound, and they come home and they moved in a little three-room house behind our house. And his paralysis happened . . . He went over and they gave him a spinal, and something happened to him, and he was paralyzed for a year or two, maybe three, I don't know. I moved off after that.

Q In "Detroit City," did you realize the line "I want to go home" was going to be the magic line, the one that really grabbed people?

A No, I didn't. But, you know, I wrote the song first as "Detroit City." And then comes along Billy Grammer. And he records it, and he changes [the title] to "I Wanna Go Home." Along come Bobby Bare, and changes it back. I said, "Bare, why did you change it [back]?" And he said, " 'Cause everybody on the road was askin' me to sing that song 'Detroit City.' "

Q How did you get the inspiration for that song?

A Well, I was goin' around singin' the old song "The Sloop John B.," and it has "I wanna go home / I wanna go home / Oh, I'm so broke up / I wanna go home." And I was singin' that one day, and I had the idea. Me and Danny Dill got together and wrote "Detroit City." When I was in the Air Force, I had met guys all over the world who said, "Boy, when I get out, I'm gonna head for Detroit. I got a cousin up there, and boy, he's just a-makin' all kinds of money." And then I went to Detroit, and I found out that that wasn't so. A lot of 'em were laid off. Everybody had seniority and stuff, and some of 'em were laid off, and all kind of hardships, and then they became social problems to Detroit. And they would get drunk, and they were on welfare, their pride was hurt, and they missed the cotton fields of home, the Southland, and all the openness of it, you know. And that was the reason it was such a big hit. We didn't know it, though, when we wrote it.

Q Was that a song that came quickly, or did you labor over it?

A No, we wrote that song in about two hours. "Ruby," about thirty minutes.

Q But you wrote "Ruby" on your own, right?

A Right.

Q What was Nashville like when you first went there as a Cedarwood staff writer?

A Well, there was only three publishing companies around in those days

[Acuff-Rose, Tree, and Cedarwood], and there was only about four or five writers that I would call full-time writers—Boudleaux and Felice Bryant were there, and Danny Dill was there, and Vic McAlpine was there. And that was about all of the writers. So the field was completely open for new writers to come in. I'd never written a song before. And I tried it, and luckily I found that I had that talent for writing songs. And I think there were only a couple of studios at the time, RCA and Bradley's Quonset Hut. They didn't have the Music Row at that time. The offices of the different artists were scattered all over Nashville. Cedarwood was down on Seventh Avenue, right behind the Krystal [hamburger stand]. And they had a little ol' shoe store down there, I believe it was Florsheim's or Bell, or something, and I used to go in there and buy shoes from Curly Putnam [one of Nashville's top songwriters] and Lloyd Green [now a well-known pedal steel guitar player]. But it's changed so much now. There's thousands of hopeful writers and performers and pickers there now. And publishing companies, recording studios, and now they're doin' a lot more television and movies. It's really changed a lot.

Q Have you changed much since then?

A Oh, yeah, I think I have. I've gotten older. I'm more independent now than I was then. Well, I was always independent, but I worked for somebody else at that time, Cedarwood. And I feel I had rather be independent, work for myself.

Q If I took all the songs you've written, and even the ones you've chosen to record, would I find clues to your personality in them? Do you strongly identify with your songs, or do you choose most of them strictly for entertainment?

A I do so many different type songs, you know. I'll sing "A Coca-Cola Cowboy" and then turn around and do "I Believe in You." So I don't think so. Not like Hank Williams. I mean, his were all sadness, you know. Grant Turner asked him one time, "Hank, why do you suppose all your songs are so sad?" He said, "Well, Grant, I suppose you just might call me a saddist." (Much laughter) That's so beautiful. Now, that's pure, right there. He didn't know what that meant.

Q What do you think about the recent crackdowns on suggestive country music song lyrics?

A Well, I haven't responded to it. I guess, mainly because I had out a song that, well, a lot of my songs kinda fit into that category. I had out a song, "I Got the Hoss, If You've Got the Saddle." And it's got two meanings. And the little kids that hear that song love it, because they only hear the good side of it. The other, older people, most of 'em like it, but there are a lot of people that consider themselves "holier than thou" that hear the down side, as they call it. I got out one now called "Your Body Is an Outlaw." I had one song out one time about a couple—it was a duet—where we sang, "Darlin', let's go all the way tonight / You go tell him / And I'll go tell her." That's all it was. "We're gonna get this thing straightened up," you know. And I got all kind of mail from little ol' ladies at home. But if everybody did the same kind of songs, you wouldn't need but one guy singin'. That's all you'd need. Everybody can't be preachers.

Q You were a regular on Porter Wagoner's [TV] show for a while. How do you look back on those days?

A Well, I look back on 'em as an opportunity that came along and introduced me to the country people as a performer who stuttered. And it helped me. And then later on I went on out to L.A. and I did *The Glen Campbell Goodtime Hour*, and he sort of introduced me to the world, because his show was all over—Australia, England, Britain, Japan—everywhere. I look back on it as a blessing, a great experience.

Q Was that your first national show?

A No. I was asked to be on a major television show by Jimmy Dean. He was the co-host of *The Mike Douglas Show*. They called me from Philadelphia and asked would I like to be on. I said, "Yes, *sir*, I'd like to be on." My first time ever on a national show. So I went out and bought me a new guitar, and I went to Philadelphia, and I went in for the rehearsal with their band, and I opened up the guitar, and it didn't have a string on it. I was scared to death! So I didn't have a guitar. That was pretty funny to them. I'd just forgotten about putting any strings on it when I bought it.

Q Didn't you use to wear rhinestone suits?

A Yes, as a matter of fact, I wore 'em up until I met David Allan Coe, and he pulled up to my office in an ol' hearse. And he had my name all over it! "I am a friend of Mel Tillis." So I gave him all my rhinestone suits. That's how he got the name the Rhinestone Cowboy.

Q Truly?

A Yeah.

Q Had you decided to stop wearing them before that?

A I think when I left *The Porter Wagoner Show* and I went out to L.A. and started appearin' on the talk shows, I sort of looked around at other people, so I changed up to just suits. Or sometimes just a slack outfit or something. Not square suits, but somethin' just a little more like other people were wearin'.

Q What have been the highest and lowest moments of your life so far?

A I think the happiest professionally was when I won the Entertainer of the Year award. The happiest personally were when my children were born. That's a good feeling. The saddest times, I guess, were the times when I was rejected because of the stutter, you know. Well, for instance, the high school play. I wanted to be in it, and they wouldn't let me be in it. That was a sad time.

Q How did the kids at school treat you?

A I was always doing things, ad-libbing, in class. I could ad-lib without stuttering, so I did a lot of that, and I was always getting into trouble on account of that. But I had good teachers. School—I grew up with the kids I went to school with, so I was more or less taken for granted. What really hurt was when I finished high school and I went off to the University of Florida. I had to make all new friends again, and be embarrassed again, and everything. That was hard. And then I left college and I went into the Air Force, and I had to do the same thing over again. Those were some of the hard times.

Q Didn't the Purina Company hire you for a commercial one time and then change their mind because of your stuttering?

A Well, that wasn't them. It was the networks. It wasn't me; it was the contents of the commercial. It was written out in the stutter, and that's no good, 'cause I don't stutter on the words they write, anyway. And it went over a desk in New York, and the commercial layout had me and Jerry Clower in there, and it had the stutter in there. So the girl, she was doin' her job, and rejected it. We got a telegram right on the set. And I read it, so I decided to sue 'em if we didn't get an apology. I believe one of 'em apologized—well, maybe both of 'em did. Anyway, the commercials were run.

Q The *Music City News* poll named you Comedy Act of the Year seven times. Has your image as a clown gotten in the way of people taking your music seriously?

A Well, sometimes I think it has, yeah. But I love comedy. I mean, that's part of me. I learned to love the comedy when I was a kid. I learned how to use it, and the stutter, to make people laugh. So I guess I became a comic. I don't know.

Q Has any record company or management agency tried to create a special image for you?

A Naaa . . .

Q What's your self-image? How do you think of yourself?

A Well, I draw a Lawrence Welk audience. (Laughter) No, in Texas, and

Oklahoma and New Mexico, I draw a younger audience. But mainly I get the people who watch [Johnny] Carson, and Mike Douglas, and Dinah [Shore], along with the country fans that I have, you know. I sort of have the Good Ol' Boy image, I guess. I'm not an outlaw image, you know? And I'm not a pop image. Just Country Boy image.

Q What do you think your style is?

A Country.

Q Strictly country?

A Yeah.

Q But sometimes there's honky-tonk mixed in, sometimes there's Bob Wills, which is almost jazz.

A Yeah, yeah, we mix 'em up. I do a little bit of all of it, actually. I had a song out called "I Believe in You." I knew the song was either a hit for me or it would be a bomb. I had the strings, the flutes, and everything. And it went number one in seven weeks. So I feel like I'm a singer that can do MOR or country music or western swing. I don't do any rock. I do the honky-tonk music, though.

Q Do you remember the first time you played Las Vegas?

A Yeah.

Q Was that frightening at all?

A Naw, not really. You mean the main rooms? Oh, yeah, I was scared to death. I thought it would be people in evening gowns in the audience. I went and I hired an arranger, 'cause I had to use their orchestra with my band. And I got arrangements on all my songs, and strings and everything, and I started singin' with all that mess. But they didn't want to hear that mess. They wanted to hear country music. And I learned. Now I only perform with my band out there. I had so many complaints. They'd say, "Shit! I come all the way from Oklahoma, and I don't want to hear this bunch of stuff. I want to hear 'Heart Over Mind.' " So you learn, you know.

Q Do you have a temper?

A Yes.

Q What makes you angry?

A Well, one time I was over in Oklahoma City, workin' a private party. And there were about two thousand people there, and they were all pretty well-to-do people. They were "oilies," you know. [Oil money.] And up comes a lady with a cigarette in her hand, on a holder, and a drink in her hand, and a pencil and a piece of paper. Well, she come and she got the end of that cigarette right almost on my nose, and spilled her drink on me. "Can I have your autograph, please?" I said, "Yes, ma'am, if you will remove the cigarette from my nose." And her friend there with her, a lady, she was in her late forties, said, "Well, get mad! Get mad!" That made *me* so mad! I just turned around and split. I wasn't mad at her, but I don't like that. That's ignorance.

Q Did you give her the autograph?

A No, I didn't. I hate that kind of stuff. Or somebody come up to me and say, "Hey, M-M-M-M-M-Mel!" [An exaggerated, imitated stutter.] You know? That's ignorance.

Q People will do anything.

A Yeah, they will. Or they'll come up to you, about half drunk, and say, "Get up there, boy, and let me get your picture. If you don't, I ain't *never* gonna get another one of your albums!" (Long pause) I don't like that. And people say, "He's so stuck-up." Well, that's the reason. Now, the majority of the people are good people, and they've got manners. But there are some that are just completely rude.

Q You've made some cameo appearances in several of the best-known "good ol' boy" movies, such as *W.W. and the Dixie Dancekings, Every Which Way But Loose,* and *Smokey and the Bandit II.* But now you're gearing up to produce movies of your own.

A Yeah, I just produced a movie, *Uphill All the Way,* that Roy Clark and I are in. It's a family movie, but it's funny, sort of a chase. It's Mel Tillis and Roy Clark as Laurel and Hardy, or Abbott and Costello.

Q Is this a true story?

A Well, it's based on a true story from when the revolution was over in Mexico, when Pancho Villa had gone to Mexico City, and bandits were attacking the border. They just put the stumbling, bumbling con men, Mel Tillis and Roy Clark, into that little story there. And it's a cute little story. You'll leave the theater with a happy feeling. I know you will. It's got some good songs on it. Waylon Jennings does "I Never Meant to Be an Outlaw," Glen Campbell does "The Unlikely Posse," and when Burl Ives does "Old Gun," boy, the tear'll come to your eyes.

Q I get the impression from your book, *Stutterin' Boy,* that you're planning to go into moviemaking in a big way.

A I sure am. I wanted a small project to begin with. This one cost three and a half million, and it's our movie. We own the negative. I found out it's just like making a record. I went to the people with a prospectus, and I told 'em about the movie, and they trusted us with their money.

Q This seems like more than just another challenge for you. Why do you want to do this so much? Is it a transition out of music?

A Now, it probably goes back to when they wouldn't let me be in the play, when I had to be the curtain puller. I guess that's given me the drive. Most of the people in the country business came from, well, not *tragic* backgrounds. Some of 'em did, like Hank Williams, you know. But I think that if there's a large family, you may feel like that you didn't get as much attention as the other kids did, and maybe that's right. I think the stutter made me work harder to become an entertainer. I would have done anything. Well, I did. I was a writer in the beginning. I wrote songs. Because they didn't want any stuttering singers. And I said, "Well, what *do* you need?" And they said, "Well, we need a writer." So I said, "Okay, I'll write some songs." So that's how I started in the business.

Q Your daughter, Pam Tillis, is also a professional singer. Did you give her any advice when she started her career?

A Yes, but she won't take any of it. She's a Leo, like me. I told her, "Art is one thing, but you have to make a living. And you need to treat our business as a job, an eight-hour job." But it's not eight hours, it's twenty-four. I tried to get her to cut country, but she didn't want to do that. Although I think she's finally decided to come over to country, if you want to call it country. It's New Country. I wish her all the luck. I back her. I push her. But she'll be okay. She's a great singer. And I mean, it's their input, the new generation. I favor the more traditional, but when it was my time, I had my input. Roger Miller, Willie Nelson, Harlan Howard, Hank Cochran, all the guys our age, we were different from the Hank Williams writers. When we come on, we were writin' social songs, and didn't even know it. You know, "Detroit City" and "Ruby, Don't Take Your Love to Town."

Q Could you live off of "Ruby" and "Detroit City" if you hadn't had your other investments? Have those songs been that successful?

A Yeah, it's *incredible*. I could quit right now and draw six figures for the rest of my life just off the songs that I've written. I've really been a blessed man.

Q You must have done something right in your last life.

A (Laughter) I must! I wonder if I could talk right back then?

Conway Twitty

*A*lthough his lubricious pompadour was finally tamed into a civilized curl job at the end of the last decade, 55-year-old Conway Twitty still remains the most consistent artist in country music—as well as the record holder for the most number one singles. Beginning with the million-selling "It's Only Make Believe" in 1958, Twitty staked his claim at the pinnacle of the music business thirty years ago, and one way or another, he's held it ever since. Never handsome, and never a dynamic stage performer, Twitty can credit his longevity to primarily two factors— an uncanny ability to understand the psychology of the country music fan, and the knowledge that it is the song—and not the singer—that really matters. As Twitty himself has admitted, "It's my instinct more than my voice that keeps me on top."

A performer with an almost "religious hold" on housewives— "he's responsible for more middle-aged women's fantasies than the entire series of Harlequin Romances," wrote Larry Nager of the *Cincinnati Post*—Twitty understands what women want. His lyrics manage to do what most other country songs don't, which is to acknowledge a woman's sensuality *and* her desire to be treated with respect.

But Twitty also understands the mystery it takes to *keep* a fan, something he achieves by not talking onstage, by limiting his interviews and avoiding overexposure on TV, and by singing about romantic fantasy—as well as about adultery, lost love, guilt, and regret. His efforts won him a Grammy in 1971, but strangely he has never won an award from the Country Music Association, except for his duets with Loretta Lynn (Vocal Duo of the Year, 1972–75). The slight doesn't bother him, he says, because he knows his fans will see it as an injustice and lobby the radio stations to play his records all the more.

Born in Friars Point, Mississippi, and named Harold Lloyd Jenkins for the silent screen star, Twitty picked his stage name from the towns of Conway, Arkansas, and Twitty, Texas. The son of a Mississippi riverboat pilot, he learned the rudiments of guitar before he was six. By the age of ten, he had his own band, and at twelve, he was appearing regularly on local radio in Helena, Arkansas, where his family relocated. Like Roy Acuff and Charley Pride, Twitty initially wanted to be a baseball player. But just when the Philadelphia Phillies offered him a contract, the draft intervened, and when he got out of the Army, music—particularly the jumpy, raw sounds of Elvis Presley—turned his head instead. An attempted career with Sam Phillips at Sun Records failed when Twitty wanted to emphasize the country side of rockabilly, an irony considering that out of all the singers recording for Sun at the time—Presley, Jerry Lee Lewis, Johnny Cash, Roy Orbison, and Carl Perkins—only Twitty continues to have regular chart activity and pursues his career with such zeal.

Although he also recorded for the Mercury label, Twitty's real success came at MGM Records, with the now famous "It's Only Make Believe," one of the most powerful vocal performances of the '50s. The record eventually sold 8 million copies, scoring the number one spot on the charts in twenty-two countries. With Elvis in the Army, Twitty became one of the most recognizable figures in rock 'n' roll, allegedly inspiring the character of Conrad Birdie in the Broadway musical *Bye, Bye, Birdie*. Three gold records and an impressive string of rock hits followed, but then in 1965 Twitty switched to country music, even though it meant making only two hundred dollars a day, as opposed to the thousands he made doing rock shows. In the long run, of course, country music paid off as his rock career never could have. According to *Billboard*, he racked up thirty-six consecutive Top 5 hits from 1968 to 1977, and he currently holds the record for the number of chart-topping singles—fifty, as of early 1986. At one point, for a span of ten years, every Conway

Twitty single reached the top position in at least one of the major music trades.

Despite his success, Twitty has occasionally been accused of a certain inflexibility in his overall career. But in the late '70s he made two savvy policy decisions—changing his trademark hairstyle and adapting his wardrobe to a more modern look. His music, too, has changed. From his first number one country single, an unadulterated honky-tonk number called "The Image of Me," he has moved through various styles, including the heavily orchestrated Nashville Sound, R&B-influenced country-rockers, and even modified outlaw music. Of late, he has shied away from the ultra-commercial, slightly corny mainstream material to record smooth, well-crafted ballads and country blues that appeal to a somewhat broader audience. Whatever the material, Twitty doesn't just sing it—his strong, passionate baritone throbs and growls and squeezes all the nuance out of a lyric, explaining in part why he is so popular with women. But men like him, too. He is probably the only country music star to be made an honorary chief of the Choctaw nation, receiving an Indian title of Hatako-Chtokchito-A-Yakni-Toloa, or "Great Man of Country Music." And when the Americans teamed up with the Russians for a joint space mission some years back, the hillbilly strains of "Hello, Darlin' " wafted out into the galaxies.

All of this has meant vast wealth for Conway Twitty, money he has invested and mined in a myriad of businesses, including a restaurant, a travel agency, health clubs, a resort in the Cayman Islands, several music publishing companies, and a talent booking agency. And if Twitty was once torn between baseball and music, he now has the best of both worlds, since he owns twenty percent of the Nashville Sounds, a Double-A ball club, and holds interests in several other minor-league teams. Whenever the Sounds are at home and Twitty's not out on the road, the singer can often be found sitting behind home plate at Greer Stadium, cheering his team, eating hot dogs, and signing autographs.

However, his biggest investment—and one of Nashville's premier tourist attractions since it opened in 1982—is Twitty City, his nine-acre theme park consisting of a multimedia museum, gift shops (with items bearing the picture of Twitty's own mascot, the Twitty Bird, a guitar-slinging parakeet in cowboy clothes), botanical gardens, Twitty's business offices, and, incredibly, the Twitty family compound—his private residence, the separate homes of his children, and a guesthouse for his mother.

If Twitty City—modeled on a Southern plantation—is a wonderfully vain and exploitative monument to the singer, his fans, and country music in general, it also traps its residents in a fishbowl existence, a factor said to have contributed to Twitty's 1985 divorce from Mickey, his wife of nearly thirty years. In March 1987, Twitty married his longtime secretary, Dee Henry, who had received co-producer credit on Twitty's recent records, and reportedly oversaw much of the growth of Twitty Enterprises. Two months before the wedding, Twitty announced that he was combining Twitty City and nearby Music Village U.S.A., a complex of museums honoring Marty Robbins, Ferlin Husky, and Bill Monroe, into a single forty-seven-acre, $20 million attraction.

This interview was done before all that, however, in 1980. We met at United Talent, the Nashville booking agency Twitty owns with Loretta Lynn.

Q Your music has taken on a more contemporary feel with the last couple of albums. Was there a moment when you realized you had to make changes?

A Yeah, well, I've made a bunch of changes in twenty-five years, but this last one didn't come at the time country music in general started changing, which was back in '73 or '74. I've never been much for fads. I change when I feel like it's time for Conway Twitty to change. I've been in this business for a long time, and a couple of years ago, I began to feel it was time for another change for Conway. Because if you're going to live and grow, you've got to change. When you stop changing, you die. Anything is that way. So I thought it was time to make some changes. I had been produced by a gentleman named Owen Bradley ever since I'd been in country music. But I felt like I needed some new ideas, and some fresh input—change the pickers I'd been using for so long, the studio I'd been recording in—just something to give Conway Twitty a fresh new sound. And I did it. I made the change. My last two albums [*Cross Winds* (1979) and *Heart and Soul* (1980)] have been different from what I've recorded since I've been in country music.

Q Some of the tunes on *Heart and Soul* are very heavily rock- and R&B-influenced—"Smoke from a Distant Fire," "Turn on Your Love Light," and "Night Fires."

A Yeah.

Q A lot of this sounds like an update from your rock-'n'-roll days.

A Well, it is. The title of the album is *Heart and Soul*, and what it means is that it covers the whole spectrum, as far as Conway Twitty's musical career is concerned—the country thing that I've been doing since 1965 and some of the rock and soul stuff I did back in the fifties.

Q Have you lost or gained any fans with the change?

A I don't think we lost anybody. That was my main concern. My main worry wasn't *gaining* new fans—it was not losing the ones I had, because they've stuck right with me all these years. They've been loyal. And I certainly don't want to do anything to offend those people. Because without those fans, you can just hang it up. If you don't pay attention to 'em, it all collapses. But that's the beautiful thing about country music. Once somebody becomes a fan, they'll stay right with you until you're seventy. When you're about twenty-five, you know, you sort of start settling into a certain groove, and your likes and dislikes don't change as much as they did when you were thirteen, fourteen, fifteen, or sixteen. And the people who happen to like country music remain country fans for years. And they'll remain Conway Twitty fans for years, unless I do something to alienate them. That was my main concern. And naturally, at the same time, I wanted to pick up some new fans. That's what I tried to do with the *Cross Winds* album, and this new *Heart and Soul* album that we have out.

Q I read that your record sales had fallen off somewhat, and that was the reason behind the change.

A No, that's not true. Here's what happened. I had ten years of number one records. I had a song called "Georgia Keeps Pulling on My Ring" that went to number two and stayed number two for, I think, five weeks. Dolly Parton's first crossover hit, "Here You Come Again," was number one, and it stayed number one for a long time. So all I did was go from number one to number two. I had about three or four records in a row that went to number two. But there's nothing wrong with having a number two record. I think that's pretty good, especially right in the middle of all the crossover stuff, when country music has been undergoing a change. But this [change in my music] took like a year or a year and a half. No, it had nothing to do with [sales or chart activity]. The records were still selling just as good. I was just fighting crossover things.

Q Do you think of yourself as a crossover artist now?

A No, I think of myself as a country artist. That, first and foremost. As long as I can have country hits, I don't care what else happens.

Q It's only recently that I've seen your co-producing credit on your albums. Why haven't you done this before?

A I don't know. I was always just as involved in [picking] my own material as I am now. But I never thought about co-producing before, and I wouldn't have, I don't think, with Owen. Owen Bradley, in country music, is just a giant.

Q How did you tell Owen you didn't want him to produce your records anymore?

A It was one of the hardest things I ever did in my life. It really was. And being the kind of person I am, I might never have done it. But had I not known him so well—you know, being produced by this man for all these years, I knew him, or felt like I did. I just knew he'd look at me and say, "Conway, if it's better for you, then do it." And that's exactly what he said. He was a dandy, you know. He was a good 'un. (Small laugh)

Q You hold the record for the most number one singles, supposedly more than anyone else in popular music, including Elvis, Sinatra, and the Beatles. How many have you had now?

A Something like thirty-three, I think. [By early 1986, he had fifty.]

Q Was there ever a tendency to think, "I don't really have to work so hard on this one, because it'll go to number one anyway"?

A Nooooo, uh-uh. I don't care if you've had forty in a row—that next record is only as strong as the song is. It's not Conway Twitty [that makes a record a hit], and I know that. Sometimes you think, "Well, I'll just write one and put it out." I've written a lot of my songs, but when I write one, it's in competition with the other things that I find, just like any other song is. I'm going to record the best song I can find, and I have a good ear for a country music song, because I'm a big country music fan. And the fans are going to let you know in the end whether you've got a hit or not. All the promotion in the world is not going to help and all the hype in the world is not going to do you any good if that song's not there. If the song *is* there, then you've got a chance.

Q What's happened to your songwriting? Do you still work at it the way you used to?

A Maybe not quite as hard as I used to. Every year you get a little bit busier, you get involved in too many things, and it's hard to get into that mood with so many other things on your mind. Every year the writing gets a little harder, too, but I still think about it and I work at it. I just haven't written anything I think is good enough. When I do, I'll put it on there.

Q You've said that the central theme of your work is that the man is usually in the wrong—that you seldom blame the woman for the trouble in a relationship.

A I've never recorded a song that put a woman down. I don't think I ever will. Women are special to most men, I think. They are to me. Men make most of the mistakes, in my opinion. In all the years I've been in this business, I've always recorded songs that are positive as far as women are concerned. That's just the way I feel.

Q For an entire generation, you were almost as famous for your heavily lubricated pompadour as you were for your music. Now you have a more modern look—a new, curly hairstyle. What did you think when you looked in the mirror and saw it for the first time?

A (Laughter) I kind of liked it. I was a little bit scared to change my hairstyle at first, because that was the most dominant thing about my personal appearance. When people draw caricatures, you know, they always take one feature and overdo it. And when they drew one of me, it was always my hairstyle that they used. I guess it was a unique hairstyle. I'd had it for a long time, and that was a big decision for me. Again, it goes back to what I was saying a while ago about not doing anything to offend people. If you've got a good thing going, why change it? But the time to change is before your career starts going down the tubes, when things are still hot. It's hard to do sometimes. You know, it's easy to do when things aren't going so well. But I decided to change the hairstyle a little bit, and the reaction was tremendous everywhere we went. People would say, "Man, you look ten years younger." When I heard that, I decided to leave it like that. (Laughter)

Q Conway Twitty seems to be a separate entity—almost an alter ego instead of just a stage name. Could Harold Jenkins have accomplished what Conway Twitty has?

A (Long pause) That's a good question. I've always tried to separate Harold Jenkins from Conway Twitty. I think you have to do that to stay within the boundaries of reality. Conway Twitty, in my opinion, is nothing more than what a country fan thinks Conway Twitty is. Conway Twitty is a very fragile, living thing. He lives within the imagination of millions of fans out there. The only way they have of knowing Conway Twitty is to know his music. They listen to the songs he records, and they get all involved in them. And you have to be careful about what you record. Loretta and I recorded a song—the biggest record we've ever had as a duet—called "The Telephone Song," or "As Soon As I Hang Up the Phone," which was a song I had written. And that song was so big that people would actually call me and ask me, "What's wrong with you and Loretta? Why are you breaking up?" I mean, that's how involved they get! They really believe it. And I'm guilty of it myself when I hear another artist I don't know. I listen to their music and I try to imagine what that person is really like. But to me, that's what Conway Twitty is. It's a very fragile, living thing in the minds of people who like Conway Twitty's music. It's not real. It's *not,* and I know that. So to keep your sanity, you have to separate the two things. You've got to be Conway Twitty when it comes time to be Conway Twitty, and when you walk off that stage, you've got to be Harold Jenkins again. Because that's what's real. I think that's what happened to Elvis. He totally separated himself from reality. He created his own world. But it wasn't real, and nobody can exist in that for long. All the things around you fall apart. You can see it happen to a lot of people in our business—not just the music business, but in the movies. Those people box themselves into situations where there's nothing really real. They begin to believe all the things that are written about them, and things that people think about them. And there's no way you can measure up to that. I think it's the reason that certain singers get drunk before they walk out onstage. They've got to have a bunch of drinks, or take some dope or something, to put them in the frame of mind to where they believe it. I mean they really believe that they're Conway Twitty, or George Jones, or whoever they might happen to be. That's the only way they can go out there and do it. Whereas I try to do it without drinking or taking pills or anything. I've known for years that there's a tremendous problem there, and you have to separate those two things. You can't exist without that.

Q When you wake up in the morning, are you Harold Jenkins or are you Conway Twitty?

A (Laughter) Well, I hope I'm what's real, and that's Harold Jenkins. Anytime that I'm not actually on the stage performing, I'm Harold Jenkins. That's the only time you go into that make-believe world, and really, there's a very thin line there. It's not really make-believe, 'cause it's a part of your life, too. But the way I've approached it down through the years has worked really good for me. Most of the people who work for me have been working for me for twenty years or more. I don't want to ever lose things like that.

Q You've thought about this a lot.

A Well, I just know that you can't be all things to all people. Nobody can. Only in make-believe, like Conway Twitty and your records you put out there. There may be ten thousand different people that think Conway Twitty is ten thousand different things. As long as you don't get on some talk show somewhere and blow all that—say things that you shouldn't say, and destroy that fragile little image in that one country music fan's mind—then you *can* be all things to all people. I've seen it. I've been offended many times by different people I've seen on the *Tonight* show, or some talk show. Baretta [Robert Blake], for instance. I was always a big Baretta fan. I saw him on there and he said, "I'm not like that character at all. I'm tired of doing that character." That hacked me off! I don't think he's got a right to destroy something that entertained me. I can't accept that Baretta character anymore. He destroyed it for me, and I never want to be guilty of that. I think that's one of the reasons that Conway Twitty has had the longevity that he's had. It's because I respect that image that each fan out there creates individually. I try to never do anything that will destroy that image.

Q Do you work at being mysterious?

A Well, the very fact that I don't do many interviews helps keep that mystery alive. You know, people don't really know what Conway Twitty's like. They conjure up what they *think* Conway Twitty's like. If you remove all doubt and you just lay your life out there on the line, it's no good. Yeah, I work at it, and I think it's important. Not for my own ego, but to protect this image that each person out there has.

Q If I took all your songs and I laid them end to end, would I find clues to your personality?

A Sure. I can't speak for any other artist, but in all the songs I have recorded. Yeah, you can find Conway Twitty in there somewhere.

Q Such as?

A Hmmm. (Laughter) Well, everybody does that in a way. They'll listen to all the songs you've done down through the years, and they'll come up with what they think Conway Twitty's really like. They'll probably find one part of what you're really like, and somebody else will find another part. But it would take all those people getting together and discussing it to come up with what a person is really like. Because there are so many facets to a person's character and personality—just jillions of different little ol' things that make you what you are. Each one of those songs is one of those facets, so it takes a lot of them. But somewhere in there, you'd definitely find me, because I've never done a song that I didn't really like. It's got to be a part of you somehow, for you to really like it.

Q Let's talk about some specific records. How did you decide to cut "I'd Love to Lay You Down"?

A "I'd Love to Lay You Down." (Small chuckle) I was sitting in my office listening to songs. I'll go through a thousand songs to find ten for a new album, you know. And I heard this little song. Someone was in the office with me running the tape machine. About halfway through, they stopped the machine and went on, and I said, "Whoa, back it up." And they said, "You don't like *that!*" And I said, "That's my next single. Back it up and play it again." Whoever was in the office with me, I can't remember who it was, just couldn't believe it. But it was kind of hard to hear the words. And I got a pencil and wrote the words down and listened to it four or five times. Then when I recorded the song, people started commenting, "Don't you think this is a little strong? Don't you think people are going to object to this song?" And I said, "I really don't see why." I mean, that's what a country song is all about. It's taking a page out of somebody's life, and writing about it and singing about it. In this particular song, you're talking about your wife. If it was just about anybody, then it would throw a different light on the song. But it's about your wife, and I definitely don't see anything wrong with it. I think it's a beautiful love song, and there's nothing about it that offends me. I've had to defend a couple of songs that I've done, and that's one of them. (Laughter) I still believe in it, and I think the track record of the song proves it. Women understand things like that more than men, you know. With a man, the first thing he thinks is "That's a dirty song." Women don't look at it that way, thank goodness. But I would never record a song I thought was filthy or didn't have any class, you know.

Q You got a lot of flak about "You've Never Been This Far Before."

A Oh, yeah! That got a lot of reaction from program directors and disc jockeys around the country—people that were *friends* of mine, even. They would call my office and say, "Conway, we can't play this record." And I'd say, "Why?" They'd say, "'Cause of the lyric." And I'd say, "What's wrong with the lyric?" Well, they'd pick a line, you know. I'd say, "What do you think this song is about?" And they'd say, "Well, it's about some young girl that's never been out with a guy before." I'd say, "No, no, no. That's not what the song is about." And they'd say, "Well, what's it about?" So I'd tell 'em. The song's about a married woman who's never been outside the boundaries of her marriage before. Here's a woman that this guy has admired for years, but she's been off-limits to him. She's married to somebody else. And there's a line in there that says, "I don't know, and I don't care, what made you tell him you don't love him anymore." That line sets her free from him. In other words, she's left this guy, and for the first time she's with you. You have to think about it. Here's a woman that's been a friend—probably her husband has been a friend—somebody that you've really admired all these years. And she's never been outside the boundaries of her marriage before. That's what the line "You've never been this far before" means. And naturally, you're going to be nervous about it. You're with her for the first time, and she's with you. But the one line that really got them was the one that said, "As my trembling fingers touch forbidden places." Well, to me, that was the tenderest line in the song. You know, simply holding her hand is a forbidden thing. It was something that you've been wanting to do all these years. Just putting your arm around her would almost make you pass out, you know. That's what the line meant to me when I wrote it, and most women understood that. But those guys, those disc jockeys and the program directors, the first thing they think is something else. That's just the way guys are. But women understood it, and women forced them to play the record. (Laughter) It was one of the biggest records I've ever had.

Q I've heard you talk about being shy. If that's true, how can you sing some of these steamy lyrics, or go onstage and sing a cheating song such as "Linda on My Mind"? Is that Conway Twitty, too?

A Yeah, that's Conway Twitty, too. I can talk about things in a song that Harold Jenkins normally wouldn't, you know. But I'm not *excessively* shy. I've just been sort of a shy person most of my life. The longest walk I ever took was the first time somebody introduced Conway Twitty, and I had to walk from wherever I was to that microphone. Even today, it's still a long walk for me. Once I get there, and get the guitar on and start singing the songs, there's no problem anymore. But that walk, from the time you're introduced until you get there . . . I guess there's a transformation taking place, or something. I don't really know how to explain it. But once I get the guitar on and start doing that thing, there's no problem.

Q I would assume that most of your fans are women. Do you try to write from the woman's point of view? Do you actually try to think like the woman, or more like the cheating husband?

A I *try* to think like the woman, yeah. But I don't want to make it sound like all my fans are women. That's not true. I have just as many men fans, because in my songs I say things that men want to say but most men have trouble saying—things that women like to hear. This way, all the men have to do is drop a quarter in the jukebox and play the song. It's letting Conway say it for you, you know. That way, you've got the man *and* the woman as a fan. I try not to offend either one with a lyric.

Q You've been described as "a master of fantasy," and a lot of your tunes deal with fantasy—"It's Only Make Believe" and "I've Already Loved You in My Mind," for example. Do you have an active fantasy life yourself?

A Sure. I think it's important to most people to be able to dream. Where would this world be without dreamers? It's the dreamers who have come up with most of the things that are important to us. When I think, or fantasize, or dream—whatever you want to call it . . . well, yeah, I'm a dreamer.

Q You started to say something else. What's one of your fantasies?

A Aw, there's no one certain thing. You just listen to my songs and you can tell. Course, women are one of them. And I always loved baseball. I always dreamed of being a Mickey Mantle or somebody like that. You just picture yourself doing different things. No one certain thing. Just everything.

Q You went for seven years without ever saying anything onstage. Now you do a little bit of talking. What was the idea behind all of that?

A Well, again, it was the—what was the word you used?—mystery. People had different opinions as to why Conway Twitty didn't talk, you know. They had all kinds of ideas, and I think that's good. Let each one of 'em think whatever they want to think. In the first place, when it comes right down to it, I know they like my singing. They buy my records, and they come to my shows. But I don't know if they like my philosophies, so I don't say nothin'. I just do what I know they like. Plus, too, I had been in the rock thing. I had a lot of things that I could do in rock music, 'cause I had been out there a long time. But in country music, I chose just to sing the songs. I had somebody else in my band that would step up there and introduce the song. He'd talk and do whatever any emcee did. Then I'd step up there and sing it. Nobody else did it like that. It was different. I stood right in one spot. Everybody else would walk up and down, and they'd do different things. I didn't move. I just stood there and did those songs. And I did it for a long time that way. But then when I *did* do something a little different, like talking a little bit on the stage—not a whole lot, just a few words—it was a big deal. The disc jockeys would say, "Come out to the show tonight. We understand Conway talks now." And with a little ol' thing like that, people would just flock out there to hear what you're goin' to say. It was just part of the mystery.

Q So why did you change?

A Well, you can't keep something going forever. I mean, simply standin' there for your whole career and not ever saying anything is not going to work. You need something new every now and then to help keep it a little different. So by not doing everything all at once, you always had a change you could make. It was a little thing—not much—but that made your show new and fresh to them, see? And I had promoters who would say, "Take the guitar off, set it down, do this, do that." And I said, "No, someday I will." You just don't do it all at once. If you do, how are you going to follow it? Like right now, there are some entertainers in country music that are traveling around the country with huge lighting things, with all kinds of smoke bombs going off on the stage. I'm not bad-mouthing it, but what are they going to do next year when they go back to that town? How are they going to follow that? Anything they do less than that is going to be a letdown. It's better to slowly build up to that than to do it all at once and come down. That's how I try to pace my career.

Q How did you hit upon that famous growl that you get in your voice?

A That growl has been part of my singing style for as long as I can remember, from the first time I recorded. Well, I don't know if it was there the first time, but I had it when I recorded "It's Only Make Believe." That was my first recording session for MGM. I had a producer named Jim Vienneau, and we ran through the song a couple of times, and then we put it down on tape. And Jim came down and said, "It's going to be a good song. We're going to have to work on it a little bit, but it's going to be good." Then he said, "What was that little thing you did in there?" And I said, "What?" And he said, "Well, let me play it back." And he played it back, and he said, "There—that." I said, "Aw, I didn't mean to do that." I thought he didn't like it, see. And he said, "No, no, I like it. Does it come natural to you?" I said, "Yeah." He said, "Then leave it in there." So we did, and it's been in there ever since.

Q You and Loretta have been a hit duet team for a long time. This new duet you have out now, "True Love," is one of the most believable of all the love songs you've done. How many takes did you need on it?

A Not many. I think the really good, solid records come pretty quick. Because everybody realizes it's a good song—Loretta, and the pickers, and the [background] singers, and the engineers, and the producer—just everybody knows almost instantly that it's something special. All kinds of little magic things happen in there.

Q What did you think of Loretta the first time you met her?

A Well, I was a Loretta Lynn fan when I first got into country music, in 1965. Course, I recorded and played rock music for ten years. But I listened to country music all the time, and I was well aware of everybody in country music. And when I got into the country music field myself, I got with Decca Records, which is MCA now. And I knew Loretta was on the same label, and we had the same producer. I had told Owen a couple of times that I wanted to meet Loretta, and he told me that she'd said she was a Conway Twitty fan, and she wanted to meet me, too. She didn't like rock-'n'-roll music. But she loved the song "It's Only Make Believe," which was a big country record, too, back in 1958 and '59. That was before

Loretta even got into the music business. So when she was just a house-wife, she was a Conway Twitty fan—had a poster up on her wall and the whole thing. And, of course, that knocked me out to hear that. So finally, through our producer, we met. Either she was doing a session and I got there to do one right after hers, or vice versa. But I remember Loretta was standing there facing Owen, and I was standing right be-hind her. He said, "Do you still want to meet Conway Twitty?" And she said, "Yeah!" And he said, "Well, he's right behind you." She turned around, and I was standing right there, and she jumped straight up! She's a character anyway, you know. She was just slapping her leg, and saying, "I can't believe it! I met Conway Twitty, blah-blah-blah." So we were friends really, just right off the bat. And shortly after that we went on a tour to Europe together. We did the very first Wembley Festival that they ever had, and we stayed over there for three weeks. We got to know each other better, and I can't remember which one said it, but one of us wondered what it would be like to record together, since we liked the same kinds of things, and since our voices seemed to be compatible. And we decided we wanted to try it. There were a lot of objections to it from different people, and we had a lot of obstacles to overcome. But we were determined to do it, and we went in the studio and recorded our first album together in 1969.

Q Why do you think you've been so successful together?

A That's a good question. There were a lot of people who said, "It'll never work. It may last for a year or two, but you're going to wind up being enemies because of egos." But Loretta, in my opinion, doesn't have an ego problem, and in her opinion, I don't have one either. I might have, but I don't think I have. As far as our duets are concerned, we've just released what we call our *Diamond Duet* album, our tenth-anniversary album. And in all those ten years, we've never had a problem. Not ever. We're in business here together at United Talent, our booking agency, and in other things. But we've never had a cross word, and I don't think we ever will. It's just one of those natural things. And it just seemed like it was meant to be that way.

Q A Canadian critic, Dave Mulholland, has described your music as "blues for the middle class," meaning that you've cleaned up the rough edges but kept the heartache.

A "Blues for the middle class." Hmm. Well, I think there's a very close relationship between blues and country music. I was born in a little town called Friars Point, Mississippi, about eighty miles south of Memphis, right on the Mississippi River. It had about five hundred people, and about eighty percent of 'em were black people. And I grew up right there with them. When I was growing up, I never knew that there was a difference in black and white, until I got older and started hearing people say there was. You know, the people I grew up with were friends of mine. They were just like anybody else to me. The old [black] gentleman that lived next door to me played guitar and harmonica. He was a blues singer, and I learned a lot from him. I called him Uncle Fred. There was an old Negro church right down the street from my house, and I'd go down there on Sunday night, or Wednesday night, and sit on the ditch bank out there and listen to the choir singin'. Boy, you're talking about some good singin'! Then, of course, on Saturday nights, I listened to the Grand Ole Opry. That was my total exposure to music for the first ten years of my life. I think a lot of [the blues] is evident in my vocal style, even in the straight country.

Q "Talkin' 'Bout You"?

A Yeah, "Talkin' 'Bout You." That was one of the things from one of my albums. I wrote that song. That's definitely got some blues in it. It's got a little bit of everything in it—just like Conway Twitty. It's got a little bit of blues, and you can hear some religious music in there, if you listen. Course, the country sound would be the dominant thing, but the other stuff is in there, too.

Q Tell me more about your childhood. Any special memories come to mind?

A Aw, the whole thing is strong in my mind, and always will be, I think. It was kind of a Huckleberry Finn type of childhood. I lived right on the Mississippi River, in a houseboat. It was an old barge-looking thing, not very big—two rooms, you know—and it was right there in the river, pulled up against the bank, by the levee. You had a big gangplank that went from the boat out to the bank. I lived on that. My dad was a pilot on a Mississippi River boat. I used to sit up in the pilothouse and practice on the guitar and sing songs. Growing up there really helped make me turn out the way I have, you know, good or bad. It's a definite part of what makes Harold Jenkins Harold Jenkins.

Q Was there a moment when you realized that you had made it?

A No, I don't think there was ever one thing in my life that made me come to that conclusion. And maybe I still haven't come to that conclusion, because I really don't look at it like that. Success, to me, is doing something you love to do and being able to make a living at it. There are a lot of people I know who make a lot of money and they're miserable. You hear this, and you think, "Aw, that's a bunch of junk." But it's true.

They're doing something they detest, but they're caught up in this thing. You're successful when you can do something you love to do. It's not measured in how much money you make. It's measured in mental freedom and happiness—being happy with your life, no matter what it is. A beach bum is a successful person to me if he's happy with himself. Because he is accomplishing the one thing that we all want to accomplish subconsciously, and that's to be happy with your life. I was happy with my life a long time before I started making any money, 'cause I was doing something I love to do.

Q You've been described as "the ultimate businessman." Do you have a natural acumen for business?

A Naw, not really. There's an old saying, "A good executive is one who can successfully pick people who can handle things for him." And I've always been fortunate that way. I know people pretty good, and I've surrounded myself with people who know those kinds of things. I wouldn't be happy doing that. You get bogged down awful quick. If you've had some hit records, and all of a sudden you picture yourself a big businessman, you can go down the tube right quick. One of the main things in life is knowing what you can do and knowing what you can't do. And if you stay away from those things that you can't do, then everything is going to work out. That's what I always tried to do.

Q If tomorrow nobody wanted to hear a Conway Twitty record anymore, could you be happy?

A Yeah, and I could understand that, you know. I've had a few people say that. Not in my presence, but to some of my kids who tried to get into the music business. A couple of them did for a while, and they had disc jockeys and program directors say, "Your dad's been around long enough. It's time he got out and let somebody else get in there." I can understand that kind of thinking, in a way, but that's wrong. One person, or even ten people, don't make that judgment. It's the fans out there. When the fans decide it's time for Conway Twitty to sack it up, I can accept that. And that day will come. I know it will. But I don't think it'll come for a long time, for one reason. I've done a lot of thinking about this. When I was growing up, some of my heroes in country music all of a sudden quit having hit records. Some of them quit havin' 'em after five years, some of 'em after ten years. But at some point, they quit having hit records. And in my opinion, they sing just as good today as they did back then. And I wondered why. But at an early point in my career, I figured out why. I know where to put the emphasis—not on Conway Twitty, but on that song. I think somewhere along the line these people somehow destroyed that little image that we were talking about, through the type of songs that they recorded, or through publicly doing or saying the wrong thing somewhere. But they did *something*. The fans didn't just quit liking 'em. People who like country music *stay* country music fans. That's just the way it is. And they'll stay with it right on down through the years. In rock music, it's different. A kid thirteen or fourteen years old likes, well, whoever, you know. But when he gets sixteen or seventeen, he begins to think a little different, and his tastes change along with it. You don't find that many kids that like country music, because they don't really understand the lyric. 'Cause most songs are about cheatin' and about hurtin'. They don't understand those kinds of things, because they haven't lived 'em yet. And in country music, you have to live it. I mean, it's real. You've got to live it to really understand it.

Q This was what was going through your mind, as I recall, when you were trying to get something going with Sam Phillips and Sun Records. Except you wanted to do country music, and Phillips didn't.

A Oh, yeah. The rock thing was brand-new in 1956, when I first got out of the Army and was trying to get into music. There had never been anything like it, you know, and you didn't have anything to compare it to. Every vocal lick, every guitar lick, every drum lick, had to be created right on the spot. That was a tremendous problem for Sam Phillips with some records he did with Elvis and with some other artists he had. He'd record a song with Elvis, and then he had to look for something else that would fit that kind of sound. They didn't have anything they could just say, "Well, we'll use part of this, and part of that." They had to invent it right there. And all I'd ever done was country music. And that was strictly as a hobby—never professionally. So naturally, my mind pointed more toward country music than anything else. But they were just all dead set against that. Especially Sam Phillips, because he had a new thing going. And I don't blame him. When I got with MGM and recorded the song "[It's Only] Make Believe" after about six or seven years, I tried to get MGM to let me do country music. The biggest star they ever had was a country music artist—Hank Williams. But they just refused to let me do it. They said, "We've got a good thing going. Why change it?" They had their point, you know. So when my contract ran out with MGM, it took me a couple of years to get away from all those people that make a Conway Twitty work—like managers, and booking agents, and record company people and all. But I finally got rid of all that and came to Nashville. And there was a guy named Harlan Howard who was a songwriter here. He had been to see some of my shows, and he told me I should be in country music. Period, you know. He said, "Get out of that rock stuff, and get into country music where you belong." And I had been trying to *do* that. (Laughter) So Harlan took some of the songs that I had written over to Owen Bradley at Decca. He listened to the songs and said, "Who's that singin'?" And Harlan said, "Well, that doesn't matter. Do you like the songs? I'm pitchin' you some songs." He said, "Yeah, I like the songs, but who's that singin'?" And, course, Harlan knew that I was lookin' for a label that would let me do country music. And he said, "Well, you're not going to believe it, but it's Conway Twitty." Owen said, "Awwww, Conway Twitty, the rock singer?" And he said, "Yeah." Owen said, "I just don't believe that." And Harlan said, "Well, it is, and he's lookin' for a label, and he wants to do country music." Course, Owen loves all kinds of music, but he said, "Okay, he sold me. If he wants to do country music, tell him to come on and we'll do some." So I signed with Decca in 1965, and I've been doing country music ever since. I never looked back. I love it.

Q You said once that you had to work your way up to country.

A Yeah, and I don't mean that as a slam to rock music. Back in the fifties, I liked it. But I didn't love it like I do country music, and I didn't think I was good enough to do country music back then. Course, I was younger then, you know. Like I said, I think before you can sing it, you've got to live it. Back when I got into rock music, I hadn't had a chance to live it yet. In the nine or almost ten years from the time I started singing rock music until I recorded my first country song, I think I *did* work my way up to it. To me, it takes just as much talent to sing country music as it does to sing any kind of music. And I really did have to work at it to experience all the things that a country song is about.

Q You apparently wanted to be an actor at one time. You made a couple of movies—in fact, one with the illustrious title of . . .

A *Sex Kittens Go to College.* I know, 'cause that was my favorite. (Laughter) That was 1960. I did three movies [*Platinum High School* and *College Confidential* in addition to *Sex Kittens Go to College*] early in my career, and I was fascinated just by the thought of it, you know. But in the course of doing these movies, something happened to me that changed my whole thinkin' on it. The main thing was, when we got ready to do each one of them, a director would go out on the lot at Universal, or MGM, and there'd be maybe two hundred people out there. These people were extras—people that you just see in the movies. Some of them have one or two lines. And the director would walk up and down in front of these people and he'd say, "Okay, I want you and you, and that one over there, and that one over yonder," you know. The first time I saw that, it really made an impression on me. Every one of them, without exception, worked hard to get into that business. They studied it, they knew way more about it than I did, and here I was taking up a spot that one of these people could have had. I mean, I'd done nothin' but sing a song, you know. And I thought, "What am I doing here? Why am I doing this?" That really affected my thinking. But I did three pictures, and there were certain people that said mine was the best performance turned in by any rock singer up to that point. Sal Mineo—remember him?—was one of 'em who said that. And I refused to do any of those beach pictures. I had an acting part in each movie. So it wasn't just one of those singin' things, although I wrote the title songs to all three of them. They were all definite acting parts. I was a killer in one called *Platinum High School.* And I think I could have done more movies. Any entertainer is an actor, of sorts. You have to be, because you're dealin' with something that's not real. That was fascinating to me. But that other part— takin' up somebody else's spot who worked hard for it—that really affected me. So after the third one, I decided not to do any more, and I never have. I've had opportunities to do 'em, and to do acting parts on TV. It seems to lure a lot of people. They just jump head over heels to try to do one of those things. Me, I can't see it. I've been doing this for twenty-five years, and if I do it another hundred years, I'll never really get it right. There'll always be room for improvement. I'd rather stick to one thing, and always try to do it a little better, and let those other people do those things that they're trained for. I don't condemn anybody for wanting to do that, because I know it's a tremendous lure in our business to get in some movie or play Las Vegas, which is another fantasy land.

Q Do you enjoy playing Las Vegas?

A I enjoy it for two or three days. I enjoy the fantasy part of it, you know. You can go out there and be anybody you want to be, and nobody's going to pay any attention to you. 'Cause everybody else is being what they want to be. (Laughter) They lose all touch with reality, and the people in Las Vegas make it that way. If you start remembering real things, like the house payment next month, or all those bills you got waitin' on you, you won't put that dollar down. Right? So they create this fantasy, and they want you to forget all those things. But I can't do that. So I enjoy bein' out there about two or three days. But playing out there is a different thing. You try to stay out there for two or three or four weeks —I can't take it. It just runs me nuts. I've got to get back out where there's real people and real things going on. Besides, I don't think it does you that much good as a performer, or even as a recording artist. It just takes away, instead of adding. So it has no lure for me. Like the movies and television. You can burn yourself out really quick that way. Every time you pick up a magazine or turn on the television, you see the same people on there. They'll use you up, and they don't care, 'cause there are others standin' in line right behind you. Television feeds off of people like Conway Twitty or Loretta Lynn or Mac Davis—whoever. It really can't exist without these people. But I refuse to let them feed on me. If I can use TV like it uses me—at the right time and on the right show—then I think it's good for Conway Twitty, and I'll do it. But I won't just go do a show because it's got big ratings. I've turned tons of 'em down through the years because I didn't think they knew anything about country music, and I didn't think they could present a country music artist the way he should be presented.

Q But does Las Vegas?

A Well, it's beginning to present country music properly. Just startin', though. Out there, they have these tours that come in from all over the United States and Canada. And when a country music artist plays Caesars Palace, or wherever, there should be somebody at Caesars Palace who says, "Three months from now we have Conway Twitty coming here." Or Loretta Lynn, you know. 'Cause there are certain parts of the country where Conway and Loretta are going to be stronger, right? Let's get our tours coming from Texas, and Oklahoma, and Mississippi, and Louisiana during that two-week period, instead of New Jersey and Maine, where they might not be quite as strong. There needs to be some thought put into it. But for a long time that wasn't the case. They didn't have a talent coordinator who understood country music. They'd have tours coming from New Jersey, and all these people would be goin' around sayin', "Conway *who?*" (Laughter) But they're beginning to handle it the right way now.

Q There's a lot of correlation between what a preacher does and what an entertainer—particularly a country entertainer—does. Do you agree with that, and did you ever think about going into organized religion?

A Oh, that was one of the biggest decisions I had to come to grips with. You know, when I was fifteen or sixteen years old I *was* a preacher. I always felt like I wanted to do something with my life where I was in direct contact with people—where I could help people, like a preacher or a doctor. But I didn't have the smarts to be a doctor. I would have loved that—bein' able to help somebody one on one. Same way with a preacher. So I tried that for a couple years. I preached at youth revivals, and I worked with young people a lot. But that just didn't work out. It wasn't really what I wanted to do. Baseball was another thing I loved. Right in the middle of the preaching thing, the offer to sign with the Phillies came along, and I decided, "Well, I'll try that." Course, this is when I was young, you know, like eighteen. And then I got drafted and had to go into the Army. When I came out, the Elvis thing was just beginning—that type music—and I got into that. After I was in it three years, I began to wonder, "What am I doing in this? This is not anything like what I've always wanted to do." It really bugged me that I was doing something that wasn't helping people. And then, not too long after that, people started coming up and saying, "Hey, Conway, man, you don't know what 'It's Only Make Believe' meant to us." They would tell me different stories, about where they were and at what point in their lives they were when they heard this song. They remembered it, you know. Then with other songs after that, they'd say stuff like "Man, 'Hello, Darlin' ' straightened out our lives. We were having problems, and that song came out and we applied it to our problems and our life, and it helped straighten us out." And I began to realize that I *was* doing the right thing. And today, there's no doubt in my mind. I believe I'm doing the right thing, you know. I *know* it. But that's the reason you have to be careful what song you record. (Laughter) That song is so important to people.

Q Then there's the other side of fame. You had a bomb scare a few years back. What was that all about?

A Boy, I don't know. I forget what year that was, but it was three or four years ago, I think. I was booked on a tour in England—that big show they have over there, the Wembley Festival—along with a lot of other artists. And we were walking out the door to go to the airport when I got a frantic phone call from my office. They said they just had a bomb threat. A guy had walked into the office right underneath mine, which is a doctor's office, and told the two nurses that they'd better get out, because he had planted a bomb in Conway Twitty's office, and it was due to go off shortly. Well, the whole office building evacuated. They called the bomb squad, and naturally, I was about to go to England and leave my kids here, and I had to make a really quick decision. And I never miss shows. I've missed three in twenty-one or twenty-two years. But I had to cancel that particular show, because I had to have the bomb squad come out to my home and check everything out—all my cars, and of course the office. They never did find anything, but the FBI told us that had it been a phone call, it still would have been serious, and you've got to check it out. But when someone actually walks in and shows his face and says, "There is a bomb," then you've *really* got to take it serious. But I never heard any more about it.

Q Do you ever have any guilt about having so many rewards heaped upon you, financial and otherwise?

A Yeah, I do. Sometimes I think, "Boy, it's got to be a sin to do something that you love so much, and to get paid this kind of money for it." You know, when another guy's out there on an assembly line, working at something he doesn't like. He ought to be paid way more than me, because he suffers. Yet I'm fortunate enough to be doing something I love to do, and it just happens that the thing pays a lot of money. Yeah, I feel funny about that sometimes.

Q Do you feel like a legend?

A I don't really know what a legend is. I just feel like Conway Twitty is an entertainer that's happy with his life and with his career. I feel like I've been very successful at it. I don't think I've done it all, by any means. I've still got a lot I want to do, and I need more years to do it. I feel like I'm trying to put back—and it's important to put back—at least some of what I've gotten out of it. I would never be able to put back everything, but I feel a need to put back more than I have.

Q By doing what?

A I don't really know. There's not any one certain thing. Maybe by bein' honest about this business, helping to make country music grow, and by having good records. It's just little things here and there that you can do to make country music more acceptable to a lot more people. By being the kind of person you are, by recording the songs you record. By always trying to make it better. Only longevity can help you put more back into it.

Q What do you think about when you're onstage? Do you really think about the songs? Some performers say their minds are a thousand miles away while they're up there.

A Well, see now, that takes away [the impact] to me. I know that there are some entertainers who stand up there and sing songs and think about going fishing and various other things. But if I really felt that way, I'd never admit it. Because again, you're helping to destroy that image. These people know you through your music, and if they think you're thinking about going fishing or playing football when you're singing a great love song, it's like . . . Well, it's like a woman laying there eatin' an apple if you're making love to her. It's going to take something out of it, you know? Songs are sort of like a love affair between you and those fans out there, and if you do anything to take away the guts of it, then you're helping to destroy the thing that you're trying to make grow. I've never felt that way. I've never recorded a song I didn't like, and when I reach the point when I get tired of a song that we're doing onstage, I take it out of the show. I'll put another song in there that maybe I haven't done in a long time, something that I still get that feeling for. "It's Only Make Believe" is a unique example of what I'm talking about. There's a song that I've been doing since 1958. Twenty-two years, now. It's still in my show. I never, ever get tired of singing that song. But if I ever get to where I can't sing it—and mean it—then I'll take it out of the show, no matter what.

Q There's a funny story about a trip to Columbus, Ohio, to promote that song when it first came out.

A Yeah, well, when "It's Only Make Believe" was released in February or March of 1958, it was out about three months and nothing happened. The record company started pushing the B side, a song called "I'll Try." And I told them that I thought they were on the wrong song, that although the B side was a good record, I definitely thought the other side was a much better song. And, of course, a new artist and a brand-new record —nobody's going to pay any attention to you. So after three months, nothing happened, and I thought, "Well, I know it's not the song. I believe in this song, so it must be me." So I quit and went home.

Q To drive a tractor.

A Yeah, on my father-in-law's farm. I was out there on the farm one day, and somebody came out there and said, "There's some radio station in Columbus, Ohio, that's trying to get a hold of you." You know, back then, that was a big deal in Marianna, Arkansas. So when I got home that night, I called this guy back, and it was a *big* rock station. He began to tell me what kind of a smash hit record I had in Columbus, Ohio. He said, "I honestly believe that it's going to be the record of the year. It's one of the biggest records we've ever had." Well, I just couldn't believe all that. But he finally convinced me, and he wanted me to come there and do a promotion with the radio station. I got all my band rounded up and we went to Columbus, Ohio. And they really rolled out the red carpet. I had never been treated like that before. I just didn't know what to *think,* you know. And this radio station had a disc jockey they called Dr. Bop. He did his show from the top of a drive-in restaurant. It was a big flat-top drive-in, with a lot of area around there for people. So this Friday night, he told us what time to be there, and we got in this old car I had and started headin' that way. And we turned on the radio, and we were listenin' to this guy, and he was sayin', "Well, he's going to be here pretty soon." And he was playing my record just one time after another. So about a mile from the restaurant, we started seeing all these people walking in that direction. They were out in the street, over in people's yards—just people everywhere, as far as you could see. And we were trying to drive down through all this. Of course, when they saw the name up on this rack we had on top of the car, they started grabbin' the car and bouncin' it, and screamin' and yellin', and tryin' to get in. We were all scared to death, you know. We had never *seen* anything like that. And there was no way out, and we couldn't move any farther. We were just stopped. It looked like miles of people to me, and it *was*. (Laughter) Finally, the police got there. And they couldn't get the doors open, because the people were jammed just as far as you could see in every direction—behind us, in front of us, and on both sides. We could see the restaurant way on up the road, and we could see the guy up on top and we could hear him on the radio tellin' people what was going on out there, you know. But we couldn't do anything else. (Laughter) So there were about seven policemen, and one of 'em said, "Roll the window down." And I said, "Nooooooo. (Laughter) I'm not rolling this window down." And he said, "Roll the window down. We can handle it." So I rolled the window down and climbed out, and six of those policemen held me way up in the air and carried me from there to the steps of that restaurant. And it was a *long* way, and I just can't tell you what was going through my mind. I thought, "What in the world am I getting into?" I had to get up there and pantomime this record, and I was up there all by myself. (Laughter) They played this record ten times in a row, and I stood there and pantomimed this thing with people as far as you could see. It was a tremendous experience. It's something I'll never forget.

Q It sounds like a dream.

A It *does* now. It's like it never happened, and yet I know it did. But if I had to go through that again, I don't think I'd do it. (Laughter) It's just hard for me to realize that I did that. I *did*.

Q It was Conway Twitty.

A It was Conway Twitty, that's right.

Q Country music, as we knew it when you started, is probably gone forever. Do you hate to see it go?

A Well, I don't think it's gone forever. I think there's parts of it in things that are being done today. When you're writing or recording a song, you think about different licks you've heard down through the years, or different little things that go into it. You've got all these things to subconsciously—or maybe consciously—pull from. But you're right, the total sound from around 1960 is probably gone forever. And there's nothing wrong with that. It's sacrificed so that country music can grow. It's like your children. When I was on the road, I'd go home and one of them was two years old. I'd come back five months later, and he'd be two and a half years old. That little part in the middle was gone for me forever. But I really liked what I was seeing in the two-and-a-half-year-old. Same thing with country music. Sacrifices had to be made for it to grow. But I think parts of it will always be around in whatever's going on. I hope so, anyway.

Hank Williams, Jr.

*I*n Lexington, Kentucky, Hank Williams, Jr., is a *star* these days, just as he is about everywhere else on earth. He is so much a star, in fact, that the folks in Lexington want to give him the red-carpet treatment when he flies into Bluegrass Field in his private plane. Of course, the red carpet is no bigger than a bath mat, but Bocephus doesn't mind. In fact, he loves it. The plane lands, the door opens, and out pops Hank, grinning for the crowd.

"Aah," says Williams, arms outstretched, "Hillbilly Heaven!" The comment draws a chuckle from the crowd, especially from the hospitality girl, a shapely blonde who's already caught Williams' eye. "C'mon over here, darlin'," he says, his arms open to infinity, "I'm so lonesome I could cry."

It's been thirteen years now since Williams climbed up Montana's Mount Ajax and fell headfirst off the top of the world, losing literally his face and nearly his life in the process. Today, some nine operations later, including one in recent years to correct the alignment of his eyes, Williams, now 39, is virtually a new man—with a new face, a new music, and a new attitude toward life and living. Before the accident, Williams, who spent his teenage years as a clone of his late, great daddy, looked as if he were bent on riding his father's ghost right into the grave—boozing, pilling, and partying to excess in the time-honored country music tradition.

"I used to cry all the time," he remembers. "But takin' a bottle of Darvon and tryin' to kill yourself and gettin' pumped out is not fun . . . Back then, there's no doubt that I was haunted by Daddy . . . I'd sit in front of a record player, play Daddy's records, get the biggest bottle of Jim Beam I could find, and try to communicate with him. Like about my divorce, I'd say, 'Why did we have to go through this, Daddy? Why is it?' *Wallowing*, you know."

All that's changed now, along with his self-destructive, hell-raising ways. Or at least that's what Williams said in our 1981 interview, having just cut "All My Rowdy Friends (Have Settled Down)." Of course, it was only a matter of time before he amended that to "All My Rowdy Friends Are Coming Over Tonight." And today, his concerts are still full of hillbilly mayhem, as Williams, a powerful and affecting showman, uncorks his personal brand of country, blues, and Southern rock—an amalgam that has alienated most of Nashville's Old Guard. Until 1987, when he was named the Entertainer of the Year, it also kept him from reaping the Country Music Association awards he both craves and deserves. In accepting his trophy, he joked, "I got to looking for this one so long, I thought I was gonna run out of glasses for a few years."

This interview—with guest appearances by George Jones and Williams' then-wife, Becky—took place in Williams' hotel room in Nashville, in between recording sessions for *The Pressure Is On*. Just before we started, Williams, a man of irresistible charm and wit, if also redneck obsessions, took off his cowboy hat to scratch his scalp. The first thing I noticed was that he's almost completely bald on top. The second was the wide scar where half the contents of his skull spilled out on the Continental Divide.

Q You've had a lot of producers through the years, but you seem to have found your niche with Jimmy Bowen.

A Yep. He does everything inside that glass, and I do everything outside. When we met, he said, "Hey, you've made enough records. You play some instruments, and you know what you want to do. You produce out there, and I'll produce in here." It wasn't a [producer] Ray Ruff situation, you know. Of course, only half of *[Family] Tradition* was Ruff. The other half was Muscle Shoals and Jimmy and me. He rides a real loose bridle with me, and he's probably the best mixer in town. I kinda get down when there's horns and marimbas or mandolins. See, I'm the one that's doin' all that. I make the music, and he makes the mixin' of it, and it's workin' out real good. [Williams is currently produced by Barry Beckett and Jim Ed Norman.]

Q One of your more controversial songs is "The American Way." What was the impetus for writing it?

A Well, the Eastern Airlines terminal in Atlanta, just like it said. I was waitin' in line, and there was a guy there dressed up. I needed some help with a flight, and he got attention, and I didn't. You know, 'til they know who you are. You know what I mean? What does that say—"If you fly in from Birmingham, you'll get the last gate / If you flew in from Boston, though, you sure won't have to wait." Boy, I got hot. Now I fly on Williams Airlines. And that one airline that had the bird on the tail, I said, "You know, you need to change that over a little. That should be a turkey on there instead of a goose." That's how it happened. And the high-society lady was at Cabo San Lucas, Baja. Me and Becky was down there. I got the flamenco guitar, boy, I'm drinkin' those piña coladas, and boy, I felt good! Yeah! Just havin' a ball down there. This was where Hemingway did it, you know. And there was this ol' woman there. She said, 'Hey, cowboy, where's your horse?" I said, "He's right here between my legs, hon." (Laughter) Boy, her girlfriend looked at her like, "Any other brilliant remarks to make?" And I thought about that. I enjoyed puttin' her down so much I had to put it into that song.

Q What was the look on her face?

A Blank. Just blank. 'Cause I was lubricated anyway. Havin' a good time, and some rear end had to come along, as usual. But her girlfriend laughed right out loud. That's one of my favorite songs. And it's a good one in the show. There's a lot of folks who find it easy to relate to that. Maybe they don't think it happens to Waylon Jennings or Hank Williams, Jr., or George Jones, but it does. Until "Oh, Mr. *Williams*," you know. And that's a turnoff, for them and me, too.

Q What about "Texas Women"? Why did you write that song?

A I sat around with Merle [Merle Kilgore, Hank's best friend and current manager], and we were sellin' albums and shows and T-shirts in huge amounts in the state of Texas, and I said, "Man I'm gonna write somethin' about Texas. Those girls who are at the shows and all, God, I believe you could have took a medium in some of their pants." (Laughter) And that's how it came about. And I wanted some kind of an anti-*Urban Cowboy* song. Because I'm not into urban cowboys much. I'm into

Idaho and Montana cowboys. That's how it came out—"I'm a country plowboy / Not an urban cowboy / I don't ride bulls / But I have fought some men / Drive a pickup truck / Trust in God and luck / And live to love Texas women." It was pretty easy. But it was a big surprise. I thought, "That's a good album song."

Q You had no idea it would be as big as it was?

A No. That shows you what writers know.

Q Any idea why it went so well?

A 'Cause I told the truth, I guess. I think there's a lot of country plowboys, and not urban cowboys. I think that's what it was, and there must be a lot of Texas women. But it was a big play song, too. See, there's a lot of mine that some stations aren't gonna play. And this was the first one in a long time that everybody just added as soon as they got it. Some of 'em are not gonna play "Women I Never Had," or WHN in New York's not gonna play "Dinosaur," about gay guitar pickers. But if you worried yourself about that, you'd write commercialized songs, I guess. But that's what they told me—it was just played everywhere, played a lot.

Q That song, like many of your songs, uses wit to push the point home.

A I love to do that. I *am* a smart-ass in my songs, but see, I want this guy drivin' along in his pickup truck or that little girl goin' along in her [Mercedes] 450 to get excited about somethin', and say, "Thank gosh that's right. I like that." "I Got Rights," or "The American Way," or "If You Don't Like Hank Williams," although I didn't write that, or "Women I Never Had," well, I think Daddy's [music] had a lot of that in it. Not in the same way that mine do, but his was sure easy to relate to. If you can't relate to 'em, there's no use puttin' 'em out. That's the key to hit songs, I think. They've got to relate to 'em. So if you write it, and you get excited about it, or hot about it, and you relate to it yourself, it's a lot easier for them to relate to it out there.

Q "Family Tradition" had that same kind of wit.

A Oh, yeah. I didn't realize that a lot of kids weren't thinkin' about [my] daddy in that song. They were thinkin' about Harold who used to own the plant and Harold died and now they run it this way. Or Dad used to run the gas station, but now I run it this way. I met a lot of people like that. They said, "Man, I know what you mean." And I never thought about that side of it. I was just thinkin' about Daddy and me, that's all. I was tired of hearin', "Hey, your daddy woulda never done this and done that." And Merle Kilgore said, "No, he wouldn't have done that. He would have told you to kiss his butt." There's a lot of people that love to tell you Hank Williams stories, and they ain't never seen him. He was here in '49, and he was gone in '53. That was it. Ernest Tubb summed it up perfectly—"If he'da had a drink and gone to school with everyone who says he did, he'd have been the most educated alcoholic in the world."

Q Somebody told me that the Old Guard was offended by "Family Tradition."

A Yeah, they might have been.

Q You didn't hear any feedback on it?

A Naw, I don't think they'd want to tell me, do you? I don't think they'd want to say, "I didn't like that." Let's see [quoting the song], "Country music singers have always been a real close family / But lately some of my kinfolk have disowned some of the boys and me." Well, wouldn't there be quite a few of us that they would put down? Williams, Waylon, Willie, Dolly, Tanya, you know. There's a right and a left in country music, for sure. I love Minnie Pearl. She's one of my favorite people. I don't think she would ever put me down.

Q She seems to be a levelheaded woman.

A Her and Daddy were pretty close, too. I'm sure there are some others [who criticize me], but I don't hear about that. I think that's under their breath when I walk by, which is not very often around here. I don't know why they should be offended by it, though, if they really knew Daddy. I can show 'em some newspaper clippings. Like when me and Waylon wrote "The Conversation." I didn't make up anything. In fact, we left out a lot. A *whole* lot. (Laughter) There's two Hanks that people have in mind. I'm talkin' about Daddy now. There's the one on record, and then there's the mythical one, the image. And a lot of big American folk hero superstars are like that. They're not really what people want them to be, or think of. And Daddy didn't sit around all the time with a big bottle of bourbon and cry, believe me. That ain't the way it was. And it was nice to meet all the Faron Youngs and the Lefty Frizzells and the Ernest Tubbs that weren't afraid to tell you how it was. Like the old Hadacol Caravan on the train that they used to go in. They say, "Y'all think you're so wild now and the music business is so great. Hoss, you shoulda been around back then. All those chorus girls dancin', and Bob Hope's comin' out there and Jack Dempsey and Carmen Miranda—that was a heck of a show." There was a Golden Age of Hollywood, and I think that was a golden age. There weren't many stars in Hollywood at a certain time, and there weren't many country music people at that time. That would be kind of a dream tour, to just go across the country on a train like that. I don't think that'll ever happen.

Q You mentioned people wanting their heroes to be one way, when they're actually another. Has this happened to you? Have people wanted you to be something you're not, other than a reincarnation of your father?

A Oh, gosh, yeah! Has it! You know, I read one magazine where I think they thought Hank Williams, Jr., was a guy who sat around in an opium den all night long. They just don't know how it is, you know. I've got a song about that on my new album *[The Pressure Is On]*. I nearly got killed in 1975 in that fall. I got new blood and a new face and new teeth and . . . a lot of new things. (Laughter) And "OD'd in Denver" happened, too. I just couldn't handle all that stuff anymore. Course, I had a lot of it from '71 on, several years there, but I'm not near as wild as some people think I am. Just because my songs drive a point home . . . Ted Nugent's a wild man, too. He doesn't smoke a cigarette, he doesn't drink a drop of alcohol, no cocaine, no nothin'. You watch that son of a gun on his show and you say, "Man, he is on some kind of *stuff*. He is on some high *octane* tonight!" (Laughter) You know, he's out there doin' his thing, and he doesn't do a thing in the world, but he gets pretty high on that git-tar, and I get high on ol' Nadine, too. But you know, I puff a little wacky-backy now and then, and a little Jim Beam is good for you, I think, to clean you out. But I can't do any of the big stuff anymore. The body just don't like it, and that Denver thing was kinda scary. Well, "All my rowdy friends have settled down / The hangovers hurt more than they used to / Corn bread and ice tea's took the place of pills and 90 proof / Nobody wants to get drunk and get loud / And all my rowdy friends have settled down." That's a new song of mine. ["All My Rowdy Friends (Have Settled Down)."] There's a lot of times when I pull in, I've got old friends comin' to a show, and they say, "Hey, man, let's get *high!* Let's get *wild!*" I say, "Naw, me and Merle's just gonna sit back here and watch y'all now. We've put our time in, so y'all could go crazy." (Laughter) It's nice to get over that stage, too. It really is. It's amazing how many people stay in it. I was lucky.

Q What do you think you'd be like today if you hadn't fallen off that mountain?

A Um, have a lot less headaches. (Laughter) I think it'd be the same thing. People have got that mountain thing like it was some big renaissance; some big deal that happened to me where I saw the light. That ain't the way it was. I'd left Nashville, the *Friends* album *[Hank Williams, Jr., and Friends]* was made, and I was sweepin' out the closets. What that mountain did was just knock the hell out of me for about two and a half years, and eight operations. Me and [writer] Michael Bane was talkin' about this, and what happened in '79 might have happened in '77. But I nearly never sang again, and that's for sure. And it'll give you a new outlook. You know that you can be dead just like that, after you face death one time. But it'll make you go out and enjoy life, too. And you know, I was still doin' all kinda goodies after that mountain fall. But the move had been made. I'd made up my mind. I was gonna stay home and open Acuff-Rose checks, or I was gonna do things my way, one or the other. If I'd died on that mountain, Daddy's royalty check wouldn't have been no smaller. And when I finally got that across—when I sat down with managers, record people, road people, and said, "Okay, if I'da died, you think Daddy's check woulda been any littler?" They'd say, "Naw, I guess not." I'd say, "Does he need me to keep him alive?" "Naw, I guess not." That really did get that point across. In fact, we went to a honky-tonk in Birmingham when I was still all wired up, and J.R. [his former manager, James R. Smith] was sittin' there, and somebody was up there singin', and somebody came up and said, "Hey, sing this song . . ." that the guy had just sung, you know. And I said, "How many people in here is gonna go buy a record in the next month, you think?" And J.R. had the funniest look on his face. He looked over at me and said, "Not very many." I said, "Now we can do business." I said, "I'm not gonna play for listeners no more. I've already done that." Except the kind that are really listenin', you know what I mean. 'Cause there are listeners and there are buyers. There's two different worlds.

Q There's an interesting song on the *Rowdy* album, "You Can't Find Many Kissers."

A Yep. I got one in there, though, Miss Becky. [He motions toward the bedroom.] "You Can't Find Many Kissers"—that's a hit song for a girl. I really like that song, 'cause it kinda gets the point home. Just the way the world is. I noticed in one review where a guy said that was a strange song for me to be doin'. I didn't think it was strange at all. 'Cause I'm old-fashioned. I like all the blankets on the ground and candlelight and all that good stuff.

Q You're a romantic?

A Oh, am I! One of the best, may I say. (Laughter) [He yells to the bedroom.] Right, babe? ["Yeah!" shouts Becky.]

Q There are several definitions of that word. You can be a romantic in a lot of ways.

A Well, maybe I'm new-generation romantic. I just believe in havin' a good time. I love to send flowers and all that stuff. Little presents and stuff to people who appreciate them.

Q Are you a romantic in the sense that you cry easily?

A No, I used to cry a lot. All the time. '73, '74, '75, man, it was . . . I had to get pretty tough to write in that time. I had the divorce, the MGM thing [his record label, MGM, didn't like the Southern rock direction his music was taking], the manager thing, my mother died, and you know, I was in a little lake house in Cullman [Alabama]. There wasn't no time to sit around and cry, 'cause I had done that so much. That time, I was really into this Hank Williams-clone-type, self-sorrow, self-destructive-type thing. Really *wallowing* in it. And I met with a doctor up here, and we talked about that a lot.

Q In "Family Tradition," you quote the three questions that people allegedly ask you all the time, beginning with "Hank, why do you drink?" I'll ask you a couple of the same questions.

A A lot of times when we're on the road, they'll come to get you in a jeep, me and the pilot and Merle and the guitars and stuff, or they'll come in a hatchback. And we look at other and say, "And they wonder why we drink." Or there'll be some little problem and that's what we usually say —"And they wonder why we drink." I do that with Merle.

Q "Why do you roll smokes?"

A I don't do that much anymore. You know, I'm the oldest thirty-one-year-old around, I think. The frame has been rewelded several times. (Laughter) The period I'm talkin' about now back then, that was pretty strong. I was strictly in a self-sorrow-type thing. I was really into it. But this song was the other side, the fun part, and that's where the whole song came from. We were tired of all these sad, morbid Hank Williams things. It was time for "Whiskey Bent and Hell Bound" and "Family Tradition." It was time for some pluses instead of all these sad, morbid things.

Q "I am into happy and I don't like sad."

A Yeah! That's right! Course, George [Jones] does all those, well, like, "If Drinkin' Don't Kill Me." If I heard that song by anybody else, I'd say, "That's the most rottenest, hillbilly, stagnant piece of . . . material . . . I ever heard in my life." And when he does it, it's the *greatest* thing I ever heard in my life! It's just the difference. I'll bet there's a lot of people out there that just wouldn't think of me and George [together] at all. And we did some shows together.

Q And you've recorded together.

A Oh, yeah, hell, the guy's a dinosaur. He is *the* dinosaur. And he don't even care about fishin'. One night I got my Thompson [submachine gun] out and shot down all the tomato plants when he was down there visitin'. It scared him, and he ran over in the corner and pouted. That was '76

or so, and I thought, "Well, he don't like guns at all, I can tell that."
(Laughter) And I thought it was all over then, but we talk about music a
lot when we're around [each other]. I don't think he'd want to go crappie
fishin' on Kentucky Lake at five-thirty in the mornin'. I respect artists and
writers, and that guy is an artist. There's no doubt about it. A lot of
people just command respect when they come in the room. They don't
demand it—they command it. And he's one of 'em. He may be a little
squirrelly sometimes, but he still commands it. And you know this thing
he's got about Daddy.

Q Didn't you use to be an honorary deputy, or a full-fledged deputy somewhere?

A Yeah, I *am* a deputy. I used to deputy at Paris [Tennessee] all the time.
That was a big thing for me. I'd ride around with 'em, get ideas for
songs, stay around the jailhouse. [He whistles.] Boy, that's the wild side
of life! That poor sheriff took every kind of abuse in the world. "Come out
here and get this so-and-so. He's beatin' him up. I want you to put him
away." Two hours later: "Please let him out." God, I could never do that.
I don't see how those guys do it. What an overworked, underpaid job
that is. Well, I believe in doin' things right. I'm not gonna walk around
New York City with no .45 stuck in my belt. No way. I've got a permit right
here in Nashville, in Alabama, and up at Paris, Tennessee, and Florida.
The places I'm goin', I'm bonded. I believe in doin' it right, 'cause there's
a right way and there's a wrong way to do it. And if you go down to your
sheriff and you got a pretty good reason, they'll give you a permit. But if
you don't got no reason, you don't need it.

Q Is your love of fishing and hunting strictly for sport?

A Well, it's for sanity. You know, I got that from my granddaddy. When the
eight-year-old Hank Jr. went down to Troy [Alabama], it was a lot more
fun to spend summers at Granddaddy's with his ol' sixteen-gauge and
those cottonmouths and cans than it was at camp in Nashville. It was a
lot different. And a lot of people don't realize that Daddy, man, he *loved*
those guns. He had a pile of 'em! And he shot 'em! He shot 'em at *people!*
And he shot 'em off in *hotels*. He nearly hit [Nashville songwriter] Danny
Dill one night. He was sittin' there with Faron Young, and he had his feet
propped up, and he was mad, and drinkin', and he said, "I think I'll just
shoot my god-dang foot off." Faron said, "Go ahead." BOOM! He said,
".357." (Laughter) And Faron got nervous and went over there and he
said, "Gimme that. You can't even hit your own toe." (More laughter)
Him and Mama done some shootin' out on Franklin Road. I don't think
they wanted to hit each other, though. But he did blast away. George
[Jones] likes to shoot sometimes. Jerry Lee [Lewis] likes to shoot, too.

(Laughter) My shootin' and theirs is two different things, though. (Laughter) I ain't never shot at nobody, and I don't plan on it. If I do, it'll be very serious, as it should be. You know, Daddy would carry around suitcases full of 'em, just like I do. He'd trade around, and give 'em to people. I remember when he had two double beds full of guns right here in Nashville. Most of 'em nickel-plated Smith and Wessons and Colts. But I didn't know him at all, so I don't know how I coulda got it from him. I got it from Granddaddy. I enjoy reloading, and makin' 'em, and you know, just like buildin' a git-tar—flintlock, black powder, anything like that. Some people like machine guns and military stuff. I don't like that at all. And I imagine it's got a lot to do with the Old West. This is America, and it's only been a hundred years ago when everybody was packin'. I think Louis L'Amour summed it up perfect about his books. People say, "Why are your books such big sellers?" And he says, "Well, because we're all frontiersmen, or we want to be." Why is cowboy so big? It's because we're Americans, and part of that is Colt .45s and Winchesters. That's just part of it. It's in a lot of people, I guess. Some of 'em want to look at 'em, wall-hang 'em, some of 'em want to build 'em, some of 'em want to shoot 'em, some of 'em don't. I know a lot of guys with fantastic collections, and they never shot one in their life. But they like to collect 'em. Like Buddy Hackett, Mel Tormé.

Q Let's get back to your songs. "Give a Damn," for example, ties in with what you were saying about doing things the right way.

A Oh, that was room service. "Give a damn about your job." Well, that happens every day, too. You need somethin' fixed or somethin' worked on, and it don't get fixed. If my monitors ain't right, or my guitar ain't right, people in my organization know I get just *bad* bent out of shape. "Man, this is *not right!*" And the Japanese that make all this video equipment. I think that's what "Give a Damn" is all about. I've got some older Martin guitars and Smith and Wesson pistols and Winchester rifles, and man, there's no comparison with today. Are the resources runnin' out, or is the patience or the pride? I think there should be pride in anything you sign your name to. "Give a Damn" is kind of a gospel song. I just think it's another song about today. But that was from room service, when they'd bring me all this crap up in the room, and leave the ketchup off, or the honey, or something. So I wrote a song about it.

Q It's the opposite of "Take This Job and Shove It."

A Oh, yeah, I don't like that kind of stuff.

Q David Allan Coe wrote that song. What did you think of his recording of "Hank Williams, Junior-Junior"?

A Oh, I thought it was one of the greatest songs I ever heard in my life.

(Laughter) Mostly because my friend Dickey Betts wrote it [with Coe and Bonnie Bramlett]. That's a good feelin' to be sittin' there and hear some-body sing a song about *you,* especially when your first two names are "Hank Williams." Odds on that is bad. Course, in '74, the odds of me havin' four albums in the charts right now would have made some money, too. But, you know, it's just hard to believe that it all would happen. Me and Merle ride around and talk about it and he says, "Man, it's just like when I was with [Johnny] Cash. It's *happening!* You're hot! You're hot! You're blowin' wide open!" And I think, "Yeah, I'm hot, I'm blowin' wide open, I don't have my pack of hounds anymore, and I got two boats that are sittin' there on lakes and not bein' used." There's the other side of the coin, too. But I was damn proud when Dickey brought me that tape and played it for me. I would venture to say that Daddy probably had two hundred and fifty songs written about him, and I've had one about me. (Laughter) That's about average for tryin' to keep up with him.

Q Well, you could take "If You Don't Like Hank Williams" and apply it to yourself.

A (Laughter) Boy, *could* you! You sure can!

Q I read, though, that you said you didn't want to be a legend, only a man.

A Um-hum.

Q But songs such as "Hank Williams, Junior-Junior" could contribute to the legend making.

A Well, it could contribute to you bein' your own man, too. I don't have any illusions, though. There's not many Hank Williamses passed around every century. Not many. [Kris] Kristofferson summed that up perfectly. He was on a talk show one time when he was really smokin', you know, and they said, "Do you think you're the Hank Williams of today?" This was like 1970, and he said, "I don't know. Why don't we wait until 1990, and then we'll know." God, what an answer! In other words, "If I'm sellin' 'em out twenty years later . . ." You know, me and Waylon talked about it when we did that thing ["The Conversation"]. He said, "Hell, you think they're gonna be singin' 'Luckenbach' twenty years from now? Hell, no!" (Laughter) We were just sittin' there kiddin' about it. He's got a hell of a track record to follow! You know, you come in '49, you're gone in '53, and Greg Allman can sing you "You're Gonna Change (Or I'm Gonna Leave)" word for word when he comes to do the show. God-dang! He's known everywhere! He's a John Wayne! I read in a magazine that of everybody—Gershwin and all of 'em—I think the Beatles were first, somebody else was second, and Daddy was either third or fourth. And when you look at these things, he was a *hoss!* (Laughter) He was a hoss. And that opened a lot of doors for me, too. It closed a lot, about doin' any other kind of music in the sixties and seventies, but it opened a lot, too. Maybe it was cool to hang out with Hank Williams, Jr., where it might not have been with other types. Because a lot of 'em look at Daddy as one of the first rockabillies. That's without a doubt. "Move It On Over" and "Rock Around the Clock"—there could be a good copyright suit on those two, when you listen to 'em. And I've got films of him doin' those legs around on "Lovesick Blues" and all. He was fluid onstage. (Laughter) I don't think I even realized until a few years ago how big he was. I took it all for granted until I was doin' my thing. And to have a catalogue go on and on and on, like his goes on! And it seems like there's an album out all the time—"There's a Little Bit of Hank in Me," the Charley Pride, or Glen Campbell, or Ray Price, or George Thorogood and the Destroyers—whoever. He's got copyrights that just go on and on. You would probably say, "Well, nobody's gonna cut 'Your Cheatin' Heart' " or one of those again, but it'll be out. Somebody'll do it. The man was a genius. There's just no doubt about that. And his songs are not dated. They're not Jimmie Rodgers songs. They're not water tanks, or trains, or thirties or fifties, because those same feelings are timeless. Like the one me and George [Jones] did, "I Don't Care (If Tomorrow Never Comes)," or "Hey, Good Lookin'," or whatever. I think that's the key to his songs. They're truthful, they're real life, and they're not dated.

Q Do you get tired of reading things that say you're haunted by your father's ghost?

A Yeah, I really do. I *really* do.

Q Except that you're your own worst enemy about that. You go on and on about him.

A Well, I *was* now. I *certainly* was. All the way through that period I'm talkin' about. But I don't do that no more. Thank goodness, because I would have been dead. There's no doubt about that. This doctor up here said, "You've been taught to look like, act like, sing like, be like Hank Williams all your life." And he said, "You've nearly made the whole circle. He died at twenty-nine, and you're gonna die at about twenty-six." Then he put me in the hospital. Boy, he was the only one that had the guts to say that. And boy, did he sum it up for me. He made me understand *perfectly.* (Laughter) There's no doubt that I was haunted back then, but nobody was writin' about me then. But there's no doubt I was. You know, when we started doin' our own thing, and I got serious about the music business, I don't think it was haunted. It was more like blessed.

Q People were fond of saying that you were as self-destructive as your father.

A Well, I *was* now, but look at any other hillbilly. Johnny Cash, George [Jones]. I don't have to name a bunch of names. You know, "I'm gonna show you how much cocaine, how many pills, how much stuff I can do. I'm the greatest super-hillbilly of all time." Isn't that really the bottom line on a lot of it? That's what I was doin'. Maybe Daddy was the original prototype. George sat many, many times—he'll tell you—drunk [he goes into a drunk routine], "I'm gonna be jus' like your daddy." (Laughter) You know, I'd try to straighten him up or somethin', say, "Oh, you couldn't even shine his boots, little pal." Then he'd say, "That's right! That's *right! That's what's wrong!*" (Lots of laughter) *That* didn't work, either. But he don't do that no more, either, much. I'm glad to see that he's out of it. But I've seen him do that—"I'm gonna be just like your daddy." I said, "No, you're not. You're gonna be George Jones, 'cause you are *also* a hoss." You know, there's no doubt, whether it's me or anybody else, some of Daddy's songs can get you. Kris Kristofferson, about a year ago, said, "You know, I never really realized what 'I Can't Help It (If I'm Still in Love With You)' meant until Rita [his ex-wife, singer Rita Coolidge] informed me she wasn't gonna be living at my address anymore." That's some words from a pretty heavy writer about another one. He said, "I never realized what 'Cold, Cold Heart' or 'You Win Again' meant until that happened." And that's true. You know, that's what had happened to me when that divorce was goin' on. It's easy to drag those albums out and get *down.* All the *way* down.

Q Everybody does that to some extent. And then finally you ask yourself, "Why am I doing this?"

A Yeah, I could be in Montana right now, or fishin' in Florida! I'm not having a good time! (Much laughter) That's what I told Merle. Takin' a bottle of Darvon and tryin' to kill yourself and gettin' pumped out is not fun. That's not where it's at. That's what I did with the help of this fella up here [he gestures heavenward]: "Why am I doin' this?" But I guess it was kind of "Well, who cares?" It's like "Stoned at the Juke Box." Who cares about it? Nobody cares. They don't care about me. They only care about Daddy. I'm tied to him, you know? I guess that's why I was doin' it. But when I had Toy Caldwell and Dickey Betts and Charlie Daniels on that *Friends* album, there was other people. And then of course Waylon in the middle seventies, when we were doin' those shows, helped a hell of a lot. And I said, "Well, there *is* other people."

Q How do you answer the charge that you're exploiting your father's name?

A Well, let's see. We got four albums that add up to three years on the charts, and Daddy's name ain't mentioned too many times in all them songs. But I'm pretty proud of it. I'm not gonna say, "Hey, I'm severed from him." I'm not gonna pull some of these other famous parent-child relationships and say, "Ugh, let's don't talk about them, let's don't mention them." Huh-uh. We do some of his songs on every show, but we don't do the whole catalogue. I don't know. My first two names *are* "Hank Williams." And a lot of people said I should change it, in '75. They said, "We need to just drop that." And I said, "Are you kidding? No way!"

Q Aren't you Randall Hank Williams?

A Right. That's what it says on the birth certificate—Randall Hank Williams, Jr. And they say, "Well, how can you be a junior if his name wasn't Randall?" I don't know, but that's what's on there—Randall Bocephus Hank . . . (Laughter) Rockin' Randall. That's what we got on the bus— Rockin' Randall and the Rockets. We put that up on the thing in the front, 'cause that's what it was at Overton, when we were Rockin' Randall and the Rockets, with my crew cut and white [guitar] strap.

[At this point, there is a knock at the door. In walks George Jones, who asks, "Junior here?" Hank yells, "Yeah, yeah, little pal, come on in." Jones says, "I won't be in the way, will I?" "Naw, we're just talkin' about you anyway," Hank says. Jones disappears into the bathroom. When he returns, he ducks out the door, saying he'll be back.]

Hank: He's shy, you know. That song we did ["I Don't Care (If Tomorrow Never Comes)"], God *almighty,* that thing come out good! That's the first one I've done like that in many moons. My voice and his just worked out.

Q How did you decide to do it?

A We'd been doin' it on the bus, on those shows we did. And we just said, "Hell, let's cut that thing."

Q Do you think you're a good singer?

A I'm not a technically perfect singer. I've got a good range, but I can get flat and sharp right along with Johnny [Cash]! (Laughter) I can get up there on some [Roy] Orbison stuff, and down on "Understand Your Man," some of it. But since that fall, it got deeper, I know that. All that stuff made it deeper. But like a Gordon Lightfoot, you know, just perfect . . . hell, I don't have perfect pitch. But boy, there's a lot of people in this business that aren't good singers that have sure been big stars! Gosh! I don't think that means anything in country music. Now, Becky's a good singer. She can do that opera stuff and make the glass just bust. That's like the *National Enquirer* came out with that story when I was sixteen. This guy asked me, "Are recording qualities better today than in your father's time?" I said, "Yeah, we got sixteen tracks—he had one. Everybody'd gather around the mike, and they'd do it." Article came out, picture in front of the Nudie car, the big white Nudie suit, with a headline, "Hank Williams, Jr., Says Sings Better Than Father Ever Did." I never forgot that, either.

Q The cover photo for your album, *Habits Old and New*, shows you sitting on the hood of the Cadillac your father died in. Was that your idea?

A I love that cover. I looked at that, and I loved it. And what the album said, *Habits Old*, the front of it, *and New*, the back picture. That's just somethin' I wanted to do on the cover. You know, he was on the cover, and "Kaw-liga" was a single, but it didn't sound like his "Kaw-liga." And "The Blues Man." Whew!

Q Your version of "Kaw-liga" was pretty souped up. Did you get complaints about that?

A Oh, yeah. Sure. You can't get a seven if you don't ever throw the dice, though.

Q You've mentioned Waylon a few times today. What has his friendship meant to you through the years?

A A lot. I've got some clippings of "Audrey Williams and the Caravan of Stars," and it was Hank Williams, Jr., Duke of Paducah, somebody else, and Waylon Jennings and the Waylors at the bottom of the page. And I would ride that ol' Dodge motor home and smoke cigarettes over there on Waylon's bus, you know, and then zoom, we were apart. And then we got together after that *Friends* album, which was a great thing for Richie [Richie Albright, Waylon's drummer for years] and him to call and say, "We're lookin' for somebody to open our show, and we think you can do it." That meant a hell of a lot at that time, and then we started doin' shows. There's no doubt in my mind that his friendship has meant a lot to me personally, and it sure has meant somethin' in the music business, too. And when me and Becky would come up here, we stayed at their house. Jessi [Jessi Colter, Waylon's wife] is a sweetheart, and Waylon is, too. And he liked to shoot .22 Colts at cans and stuff. We went out to Johnny Cash's one day and fooled around, and he was just about it up here, as far as friends go. Probably Minnie Pearl and him. I think he talked to me like he wouldn't talk to other people. You know, he produced that album on me *[The New South]*, and he's been a friend all the way through. Jessi, too. And he thinks Becky's the sweetest thing in the world, with her Louisiana accent. They came to the wedding down there in Mer Rouge, Louisiana, and he looked around at the big place, and there were some people in white jackets runnin' around and he said, "This is the real thing, ain't it?" (Laughter) He tickled the heck out of me. "This is the real thing!" We went to Florida and fooled around, and lots of stuff. He helped me a lot, there's no doubt, and he's mighty good. *Real* good. And hey, if they want to talk about Daddy, I do a lot of his [Waylon's] stuff on shows. Too much sometimes. I get into that [he pretends to play guitar] doom-tuck-tucketa, doom-tuck-tucketa. You know, he gave me that guitar, and I get into those Waylon licks sometimes and I can't stop. And we'd end up those shows with "Are You Sure Hank Done It This Way?" and gosh, they threw babies in the air when we got through.

Q What's really important to you at this stage of your life?

A Becky and Hillary and Holly [his daughters]. And my huntin' and fishin' places up there in Paris. [Williams has since moved his residence and business headquarters to Paris, from Cullman, Alabama.] And when I get onstage I like havin' those monitors right. It's hard to put the pressure on yourself and say, "I gotta produce, I gotta produce, I gotta produce." We're at a point now where it could get too busy, if I don't watch it. I don't want to get like that. A little more time right now is most important. And just sellin' records, maybe be [CMA] Entertainer of the Year sometime. Maybe I won't have to wait until I'm forty-somethin' like several of the other boys.

Q Didn't you use to say you'd quit at thirty-five?

A Yeah, and the way it's goin' now, I might be able to. (Laughter) But those Montana ranches are so expensive. God, they're high!

[Hank's wife, Becky, comes into the room.]

Hank: C'mere, honey. Come talk about the first time I met you—how I tried to get in your pants and you wouldn't let me, and how I called Merle and told him how excited I was.

Becky: I can't talk. I'm so sleepy now.

Hank: C'mon, we're gonna talk to my Jessi now, Jessi Jr.

Q [to Becky]: Has this new fatherhood changed Hank?

A *Becky:* Has it! He was a little wild, and she [Hillary, their firstborn] settled him down a good bit. Made a big difference in him, really. Don't you think it did?

Hank: Oh, sure it did. Yeah. It's hard to hold them little ones [he also has a son, Hank Williams III, better known as Shelton, from another marriage] and look at 'em and come in and be kinda spaced or speeded. That's just no good. Just no good when they want to play, or somethin'.

Q [to Becky]: Does he help you with the children—change the baby's diapers?

A Yeah, he feeds her sometimes. He got up with her two nights when he was home.

Hank: I've changed two.

Becky: Gave her her bottle a couple of times in the middle of the night. He's pretty good, if you can believe that.

Hank: Yeah, Waylon does [his son] Shooter, too.

Becky: Yeah, he helps around the house when he's home.

Hank: Hillary helps me load bullets in the gun room. She picks up those brass frames and goes, "Pow! Pow! Pow!" And, you know, when I get the powder and the primer in there, she stands down there and hands the bullets up and thinks that's the greatest thing in the world. I might load a hundred fifty rounds, and she'll hand up a hundred fifty bullets, and I'll put 'em in there, load it. She loves that gun room in the basement. And she loves it outside. I know where she's gonna be livin'. She's gonna be an outdoor girl. But Holly, now, she's got the black hair. I think Holly's coloring came from Daddy. She's got that black hair and olive skin. Hillary looks like me. Holly's different. She's kinda loud.

Q [to Becky]: What did you think of Hank when you first met him?

A Becky: Well, I was surprised. I didn't know who he was. I knew about his daddy, but I didn't know there was a junior.

Hank: Isn't that humiliating?

Becky: I'd never heard of him. I asked the lady I worked with, "What does he do for a living?" I'd heard he was in town buyin' an airplane. I said, "Oh, does he travel a lot? Is he a salesman?" She said, "Are you kidding?"

Hank: God, I hate for my fans to hear that!

Becky: (Laughter) I'd worked in the music business a year.

Hank: See, I got this airplane, and I was so down on everything else, I said, "I'm gonna learn to fly." So I bought me this plane, boy, and I saw her picture on this airplane salesman's desk. She had pigtails and a softball outfit on. I said, "Who's this girl?" He said, "No, no, no. Man, I need to line you up with So-and-So. It's great. (Wolf whistle) Fantastic!" And I said, "No, who is this?" He said, "You don't want her, believe me." I said, "Yeah, who is *this?*" So I called her up. And I said, "I just bought a plane. I don't have any money. Would you take me to dinner?"

Becky: Yeah, right. And you were gonna come in a limousine, and I almost died!

Hank: I did, didn't I?

Becky: No, you had Merle come. But I would have been embarrassed to death!

Hank: Where did we go?

Becky: Somewhere to eat with Merle and his wife at the time. [To me:] But he was really down-to-earth. I thought he'd be real conceited. He wasn't at all. I liked him the first time I met him. (Laughter)

Hank: I liked her, too. Then the next time we went out and heard some black guy playin' the sax, and I got ripped.

Becky: And then I started backin' down a little bit. I thought, "Hmmm." (Laughter)

Hank: The second night, oh, I had a ball! Played that piano! And then we went back to her apartment and I wrestled with her for about an hour or two and left.

Becky: (Laughter) *Wrestled* with me?

Hank: Yeah, that's all there was to it. I called Merle, and I said, "Man, I can't believe this! She don't want to do no *business*, man. See if you can check her out. See if you can find out anything about her." He said, "Man, I've called everybody. She does *nothing!*" (Laughter)

Becky: (Laughter) Can you believe that? Isn't that *awful?*

Hank: He said, "Well, I've called all these guys, and that's it." So we went out eight days in a row. Went to see *Jaws,* and man, that's the first time I've stood in a line for a long time. And then I was goin' to Montana on the mornin' of the seventh of August, and we were out here in one of the Halls of Shame of Nashville, havin' a few drinks, and I was tryin' to tell her, "You know, I think I love you, but I'm not tryin' to say we're goin' steady or anything." And she said, "I don't want to get into any serious thing, but I think I love *you* . . ." So I tried real hard that night. I said, "Hey, I have *got* to taste the wine!" (Laughter) And man, there was no way in the *world!* I said, "What is goin' *on* here?" It just wasn't gonna happen at that time. And twenty-four hours later, I was nearly dead, when I went out there [Montana]. And I said, "It is all over but the cryin', now. I found somebody that I liked, and now I look like—" I knew I looked bad, but I hadn't seen myself. But that's the way it happened.

Becky: The main thing was whether he would live or not. I just couldn't believe it. I'd just met him, and I really did like him a lot, you know. I just couldn't believe it.

Q I read you were afraid his face wouldn't look real.

A Becky: Well . . .

Hank: You and me both.

Becky: I never really understood plastic surgery, I guess, and he told me he'd had a lot of plastic surgery, and I just couldn't imagine what it was going to be like when he got back. I wasn't really worried about what he was going to look like. In fact, when he got back, he looked real good to me. It didn't bother me. He thought I was just gonna be grossed out, but it really didn't bother me at all.

Hank: See, I was over here havin' some physical therapy in a Whirlpool, and they snuck her in there. And I was wearin' a hat that was way down, flat brim, and I was all wired together. This eye was way down here [on his cheek], glasses on, a hundred sixty pounds. And I got out of this Whirlpool, got dressed, and was ready to leave, and this woman who's a good friend of ours said, "Becky's out here." I said, "Naw, I don't want Becky out there." And so I walked out, and she was standin' there. And I said, "I told you, I don't want you to see me." Now this was her answer. Talk about puttin' butter in fire, she said, "Well, I want you to see me, 'cause I've lost weight, and I've got my fingernails fixed like you like 'em . . ." That's her answer for somebody who's nearly dead. Well, that did it. That did it right there. So we went on back to her apartment, and she nursed me back to health. Right?

Becky: Yeah!

Hank: Milk shakes through a straw, and soup and stuff. And a lot more physical therapy, and operations, and goin' to hospitals. And I got to thinkin' about it, 'cause I've had some previous wives, you understand, and I thought, "If this is the bad times, what would the good ones be like?" I said, "Self, the good ones would be unbelievable!" (Laughter) And it worked out. See, she had a previous very famous football player, pro quarterback friend who decided he was too good for her, and I had had a wife who decided she was too good for me. So it worked out perfectly. Worked out so wonderful. [Hank and Becky were divorced several years after this interview.]

Q Do you think Becky was the main reason you pulled through?

A Oh, yeah, ain't no doubt about that. But really, I was thinkin' it's over, you know. But she would call me, and we would write letters back and forth. I'd just get better and better, and then when this special nursing care started, I healed *real* quick! Of course, those people in Montana helped me a whole lot. I couldn't have been in a more perfect place to recuperate. I'm sittin' in a house with a big glass front, lookin' out at Flathead Lake and the Bob Marshall wilderness. Oh, it was beautiful! Swans, bald eagles, black bears—it was my kind of place. I learned about every Indian tribe from all the books I could read in that area, and we'd go messin' around up in there. Dick's wife [Dick Willey, the

friend with whom he went mountain climbing] would give me these vita-
min milk shakes—all this stuff. I had two months there until I could come
back.

Q [to Becky]: I'm sure you know that Hank has something of a "wild man"
reputation.

A Becky: Well . . .

Hank: (Laughter)

Becky: A lot of people think he's really awful, you know, from the songs
he writes. (Laughter) But he's really not. Not that bad. Well, a little bit.

Hank: She loves it.

Becky: Well, I don't know what he does, 'cause I don't go on the road
with him very much.

Hank: Hey, lawdy! Heh, heh, heh! It's the challenge. It's the *thought* of it!

Becky: Yeah, but he's not that bad.

Hank: Well, she told me she'd dated some other folks, and that they were
just too nice.

Becky: Yeah, I like a little bit of the wild in a person.

Hank: Well, that's the man.

Becky: Yeah, keeps you interested. Or guessin'.

Q So when he comes up with a song like "Women I've Never Had," how
do you feel about it?

A Hank: You wouldn't believe it!

Becky: It doesn't bother me. (Laughter) I'm pretty cool about everything.

Hank: Naw, tell her what you said the first time I sang it to you. You
thought it was great, remember?

Becky: Oh, *yeah!* "Texas Women" was my favorite one on the whole
album.

Hank: But "Women I've Never Had," she thought that was a *great* song!

Becky: Yeah, it doesn't bother me. I was at the picture session for the
"Rowdy" cover [where Hank is fraternizing with two women].

Hank: Dammit!

Becky: And the photographer died when I walked in.

Hank: Did he!

Becky: He thought I was gonna be really hot about it. But I just sat there
and watched the whole thing. Well, some of it I didn't, but . . .

Hank: He was nervous. Those girls were havin' fun, too. They were tryin'
to make you mad.

Becky: I'm not real jealous, I guess.

Hank: Yeah, but she thinks she is the plainest of the plain—a little ol'
country girl from LSU [Louisiana State University]. She was a homecom-

ing queen at LSU. She plays classical piano and sings opera, but like her daddy says, "I spent twenty thousand dollars on you, and you won't sing one damn song." She can put that Rachmaninoff up there! And I say, "God, I wish I could do that!" And then I sit down and do Fats Domino, and she says, "Oh, I wish I could play like that!"

Becky: I *do!* (Laughter)

Hank: And she does that heavy stuff, you know. But she don't know what men think about her. And I know, 'cause some of 'em has told me.

Becky: I know.

Hank: They say, "Boy, she is a peach! She is a real *peach!*" We are so different in some ways. She wouldn't do anything in the world to hurt anybody's feelings. You can be real mean to her, and she won't be mean back. I don't like that.

Q So you're a good balance.

A Hank: I guess. She makes me mad about that sometimes. But she's learnin' a little bit. She can be mean sometimes.

Becky: 'Bout twice a year.

Hank: Yeah, 'bout twice a year. One time I come in about four or five in the morning, about half ripped, and she come up shakin' her finger in my face, and I got ahold of that arm and shook her a little bit, and everything was fine after that. But I thought it was gonna be a Bad Day at Black Rock. (Laughter) She gets mad, and I get mad, but it's over so quick. That's the best part—gettin' over it.

Q You think this marriage is going to last?

A Hank: I hope so.

Becky: I hope so.

Hank: Yep. I've had all the wives I can stand.

Tammy Wynette

*T*he actress in the daytime soap opera seemed familiar. No, it wasn't the waitress's garb that gave her away, but rather the role itself, a bit of type-casting in reverse. In 1986, before low rat-ings forced *Capitol* off the tube, Nashville's own Tammy Wynette played the recurring role of Darlene Stan-kowsky, a waitress and would-be singer who gave up her career to stand by her man—a thankless lug who's standing by someone else these days. She may be waitressing now, Darlene insists, but it's just a matter of time before she meets that big producer and goes on to make country music history.

Tammy Wynette in a soap? The idea was so obvious it's amazing no one thought of it before.

"My whole life's been a soap opera, anyway," Wynette ad-mits. And there isn't a woman in the world who can doubt her.

It's coming on dusk in Hendersonville, Tennessee, and the year is 1980. I am watching *Gilligan's Island* on TV in Tammy Wynette's living room. Tammy isn't here. She's on her way home from the hospital, where she's been the last two days, having fallen down the stairs at her office "on her tailbone," as her sister-in-law, Sylvia Richey, puts it. Meanwhile, I'm getting the once-over from Wynette's cat, Melody Man, a huge gray hulk of a beast.

In time, Wynette appears at the top of the stairs, moving slowly, a woman in pain. She makes her apologies and disappears into her bedroom—once correctly described as "early Vegas hotel." But Wynette has been sick so often that her illnesses and accidents arouse more suspicion than sympathy, and she knows it. In a little while, she comes to the door, changed into a copper lace nightgown, and invites me in. She asks if I mind if she lies down while we talk, then stops en route to the canopy bed. "I guess I got pretty beat up," she says, and then, for proof, slides the straps off her shoulders and slips the gown to her backside. Wynette does a half turn. "Have you ever seen anything so ugly in your life?"

Tammy Wynette has had her trials. And continues to have them, bruises of one kind or another showing up just as the last ones have faded. There was the alleged kidnapping from a Nashville shopping center in 1978—lots of bruises there, of course—and the fires and the vandalism, not to mention the celebrated five marriages, the stormy divorces, the frequent hospitalizations, the death threats, the shock treatments for depression, and the $37 million lawsuit filed by former husband Don Chapel over passages in Wynette's autobiography that accused him of trading nude photos of his wife through a pornographic club.

All of this is pretty exciting stuff for a girl who started out life as Virginia Wynette Pugh in Itawamba County, Mississippi. But if Wynette, now forty-six, has learned anything during her years in the business, it's that the talk and the weirdos and the nicknames ("the Heroine of Heartbreak") come with the territory. Especially when you build your career around the image of a long-suffering, somewhat masochistic housewife, feigning complacency, but aching for release—though certainly not for divorce. The irony, of course, is that until she married producer-arranger George Richey in 1978, Wynette never really stood by her man at all. Instead, she threw out a succession of husbands—four to be exact—almost as soon as she acquired them.

The man behind the Tammy Wynette myth is Billy Sherrill, a shrewd CBS Records executive and producer, who took one look at "a pale, skinny little blond girl at her rope's end," heard the sob in her voice, and instantly knew that if he found the right songs for her, Virginia Wynette Pugh, a divorced beautician and the mother of three, could move out of a government housing project and into the psyches of millions of frustrated and lonely blue-collar women. But first this Svengali would have to rechristen her ("You look like a Tammy to me") and make sure she understood that, as the puppet master, he controlled the strings.

"If we were recording tonight," he is reported to have said of her, "and I said, 'Your next record is "Three Blind Mice,"' she'd say just three words: 'What key, Billy?'"

The Wynette-Sherrill collaboration was one of the most successful in country music history, earning Wynette more number one singles than any other female country singer—thirty-five in all—and making her the first woman to sell a million copies of an album (*Tammy Wynette's Greatest Hits*). But in the months following this interview, Wynette and Sherrill parted professional company, just after Tammy's much-publicized musical reunion ("Two Story House") with ex-husband George Jones.

In 1986—six years later and the twentieth anniversary of Wynette's recording career—Sherrill announced that he would once again produce her records, although he has yet to do so. [Steve Buckingham produced her 1987 LP, *Higher Ground,* a collection of performances with some of the industry's biggest names.] As a real force in country music, however, Wynette's glory days may be over, and not just because her voice has lost some of its upper-range power. Her strongest appeal was never really musical, but cultural. The women who bought 30 million copies of her records looked to her to mirror their own lives, and in the late '70s, when she was no longer perceived as a professional victim—and, more importantly, when she seemed to have finally made a good marriage—the old legions of the record-buying public turned against her. Whether Sherrill, or any producer, can restore Wynette's status as "the First Lady of Country Music" depends largely on how much of an anachronism Wynette appears to be to a new generation of fans.

If the early '80s were not hit-making years for Wynette, there were other things to occupy her. In 1985, wearing a new, younger face and a remarkably streamlined body, she became a director and founding member of the Touchstone Foundation, a Stetson-and-sequins version of the Betty Ford Foundation, geared to rehabilitating performers and music industry executives with alcohol- and drug-dependency problems. The following year she began her appearances on *Capitol,* which, although they ended almost as soon as they began, opened the doors to new career possibilities.

Looking back over her problems, Wynette muses, "I'm a better person for having gone through what I did." And her husband, George Richey, who hopes "I'm part of the happy ending to her life," believes the bad times are finally over. But Wynette, the soap opera queen extreme, has her finger on the pulse of daytime America. "The sad part about happy endings," she says, "is that there's nothing to write about."

Wynette milked it to the hilt in this 1980 interview.

Q Where do you think you are now in your career?

A I don't think I've reached my limit yet. My career for the last four years has been blah, as far as I'm concerned, and as far as records go. But half of it has been my fault, and half of it has been my producer's fault. I can't stay home and look for material, because I work the road. Billy and I have been together for fifteen years. I love him like a brother. But he cannot get out and look for material because he doesn't have the time. He's got ten or twelve artists that he's recording. And to try to find material for Johnny Paycheck, for me, for [George] Jones, for Johnny Duncan, Janie Fricke—it's so hard to do. So it's been slack on both our parts and it has become *very* stale, record-wise. I think my personal appearances have improved a hundred percent. Because I feel more at ease onstage now than I ever have—free to be me. When I was married to Jones, he didn't inhibit me in any way, other than when he was drinkin', and I was just worried, not really knowing what to expect from him. But I felt inadequate with him to even develop my own personality. Because he was so great. He did most of the talking, and I just leaned on him and let him carry the show. He'd say, "Sing," and I'd sing. And I didn't realize how much I really did depend on him and lean on him until after the divorce, when I started makin' some shows on my own. And I thought, "God, what do I say now? What would George say? What are some of the things he used to say?" It was really hard to make that change. But we've been working together better since we divorced than we ever did while we were livin' together. Somehow that always seems to happen. But I don't know. We may never cut another duet together, and again, we may. Right now, it's just kind of in limbo.

Q That's a surprise.

A We found it's very difficult to have a duet out with both of us having singles out. One of those three records, possibly two of 'em, are gonna suffer. Even if we stagger them. Because, say, I had one that was [number] 40 with a bullet, Jones had one that was 30 with a bullet, we had a duet that was 6 with a bullet—all in the Top 40. So they're givin' us more air play than some other artists, and they get complaints on that. So one or two have to suffer. Maybe we'll just do one album a year, like Conway and Loretta do, and pull one single from that. And that would be it, and we wouldn't have that much competition with our own single records. I really don't know right now. We haven't sat down and talked with Billy about it. I know he feels we're oversaturating the market when the two of us have three products out. It's hard for the CBS people to work three products. They go in with "Hey, you've gotta play this new song by George, but you've gotta play this one by Tammy, and they've got a duet, too." So it's kinda hard to do.

Q The rumor is that the impetus for the George and Tammy reunion was not so much to help George get on his feet again as it was to help Tammy get a hit, since you haven't been in the Top 5 or even the Top 10 in quite a while.

A Well, I haven't had anybody say that to me. It's probably been said. I'm sure it has. But no, that wasn't the reason. With my hand to God almighty, the only reason that [George] Richey and Paul [Paul Richey, George Richey's brother and George Jones's manager] and I did anything at all was because the doctors told us he had maybe two months to live, more than likely a week. And that his IQ was [that of] a babbling idiot when he went in [the hospital]. And due to the bankruptcy thing, which was never settled, you know, he couldn't own anything. So we tried in every way we could to help him. And if there was anybody that felt that way about it, I kinda pity 'em. Because I'd hate to think that the only thought that I could have about somebody would be negative, instead of a positive thought like "Hey, they still want to try to work together and do duets." Because we did the duets before "He Stopped Lovin' Her Today" came out. So I wasn't ridin' on "He Stopped Lovin' Her Today." Jones hadn't even recorded in two years. So I think both of us needed it. I didn't do it because of his popularity, and he didn't do it because of my popularity, or lack of popularity. He hadn't had any good records in a couple of years, because he just hadn't recorded, and mine had been the slowest time of my whole career. And it just happened at a time when we decided that we wanted to do some duets together. And it didn't help any of our singles, because Jones himself made "He Stopped Lovin' Her Today." Nobody could have sung that song like he did. And nobody could have put any more feeling into it than he did. And he deserved the recognition. I think he was twenty-five years too late in getting his [CMA] award. But I didn't do it for any other reason than to help him. I will help George always, as long as George wants to help himself. But if the time comes that George doesn't want to help himself, then I will bow out. Because if he doesn't want to do it, God knows I don't want to try to make him. That was one of the problems when we were married—my naggin' and his nippin'. And I don't want to go through that again.

Q Three nights ago, he was supposed to sing for the Nashville Songwriters Association, in an appearance at the Exit/In, Nashville's most prestigious club. Except that he didn't make it, and you filled in for him. What happened?

A Drunk. I'll just be very honest with you. I don't know any other way to put it. He missed four days, two in Canada, two in Ohio, and I worked an hour and a half each show, three hours a night, to pacify the promoter to try to keep them from suin' him. Two I think are gonna sue anyway. But he gets off and gets these wild, weird . . . I guess when he's so strung out he thinks the FBI's chasin' him, and he has to hide out. It's so pathetic. Got a million-dollar voice and can't use it. And Paul asked me if I would consider . . . Well, no, before he ever asked me, I told him I would do the show. And then he came back and asked me if I were serious, and I said yes. Because people like Frances Preston [of BMI] and Maggie [Maggie Cavender, executive director of the Nashville Songwriters Association] and all those people have been so good to me. And I've never really been recognized as a songwriter, though I've written a lot of songs. Mine has been basically just singin'. I wanted to do it for the songwriters because I believe they're the most underrated, underestimated, under-paid, underprivileged people in the business. When a hit record comes out, people say, "Did you hear Don Williams' new song? It's fantastic!" But they don't say, "Did you know So-and-So wrote that song?" So I told 'em, yes, I would do the show. Jones was in town, but he was in no condition to work.

Q How did you come to write "Two Story House"?

A Well, I had had the idea of "Two Story House," just "I've got my story, and you've got one, too," and that was about all that I had to it. I had a session the next day, and Jones did, too. Mine was at ten, and his was at six. And the title had come from two guys. Right now, I can't even tell you their names, but of course, they got credit for the song, even though I wrote it. But I wanted to do somethin' with Jones, and Jones wanted to do somethin' with me. And at two o'clock in the mornin', I got Richey up out of bed and I said, "Go play the piano for me. I've got to finish this song, because I think it'll be a good song for us to do tomorrow, since we're only gonna do one duet." And it's so funny—Pops, Richey's father, has been a Baptist minister for fifty-one years. And he's just the greatest old guy in the world. And when I got Richey up out of bed to play the piano, Pops comes down the hall. And he's lookin' at his watch, you know. And he says, "Son, whatcha'll doin'?" Richey says, "Well, we're tryin' to write a song." And Pops says, "Be a good time to get some sleepin' done."

Turned around and went back to bed. Next mornin' we got up, we cut the song, brought it home that afternoon, and listened to it. And he said, "Son, that's a good song. Dad didn't really want you to go back to bed last night. I knowed you could do it." (Laughter) He is such a funny old man. But the lines to the song just came really simple. Once I sat down at the piano with Richey playin', I knew exactly what I wanted. I wanted him to have his story, and me have my story. But that we tried to make it, we climbed to the top, but we couldn't make it, because success really destroyed us. I was proud of that song.

Q So you think it teaches a lesson?

A Yes, in a way.

Q What's the hardest lesson you've had to learn?

A Self-discipline, I guess, because I'm very stubborn. If I make up my mind to do somethin', come hell or high water, I am not gonna change my mind if I can help it. If I am wrong, I hate so bad to have to admit I'm wrong. I will, but it kills me. I want to be right so bad, that self-discipline, just makin' myself say, "It's not all a bed of roses, and not everything you do is always right," is hard. And my stubbornness, I guess.

Q What's the story behind the writing of " 'Til I Can Make It on My Own"?

A That would have to be my favorite song of anything I ever had a part in writing. I wrote it with George Richey and Billy Sherrill. I had a session at two o'clock, and Richey said he had an idea. Billy said, "Well, sit down at the piano and see if we can put it together." But we just didn't have enough time. So Richey said, "Come over to the house tomorrow, and we'll finish that song." So we went over, and his ex-wife was poppin' popcorn, and we all sat around. I sat on the floor, and Richey sat at the piano, and we got it every bit down, except two lines. We called Sherrill, and he said, "I'll come over in the mornin' and help you do it." He came over the next mornin', and was watchin' football games, runnin' from one room to another to see who was winnin', and finally we got him to sit down long enough to help us get the last two lines. But Richey said a line that just blew my mind. He said, "If this happened to you, how would you feel? You've been with a guy for so long, and all of a sudden now you find yourself all alone, and you don't know what to do." And I said, "Well, you fool, that just happened to me! Don't you remember Jones?" And he laughed. And I said, "The only thing I can think of to say there is 'Til I get used to losin' you, let me keep on usin' you.' " He said, "Write it down." So I did. And in a few minutes, his face lit up like a star, and I said, "Say it! What is it?" And he said [she sings], "You were never in my class, so just kiss my rotten —." (Laughter) And it broke my train of thought for two hours. I could not get back on that song. We had so much fun doin' that. And it is, of all the singles, my favorite. Even more so than "Stand By Your Man." But that doesn't say very much, because I didn't like "Stand By Your Man." I had no faith in that song at all. I think I should record another that I don't like, and maybe that would do it.

Q There's a lot of pain in " 'Til I Can Make It on My Own."

A Yes. So true. Because I did call on Jones several times after the divorce, to ask what his opinion was, or what I should do. He left home on December 13, our divorce was final on March 13, and I saw him on the CMA awards show on October 13. Then in November or December, shortly after that, is when we wrote that song. It hadn't been that long since he left, and I had just gone through it all.

Q So many of your songs are based on events in your life, and a number of them are extremely personal. One in particular is "That's the Way It Could Have Been," which is said to be about a brief affair you had with a married man, allegedly one of the Statler Brothers.

A Well, I can't tell you who inspired the song. I'd get some people in trouble. But I was working the road with three groups, and I got off the bus one night, and this one guy said, "That looks like a prom dress." And I said, "Yeah, if I'da had it way back then, it would have been a prom dress." And he said, "Wear it again tomorrow night." And I wore it again the next night, and he said, "If I had taken you to the prom, that's what I would have wanted you to wear." And I sat down on the bus and I got to thinkin' that had things happened sooner than what they did, it would have been the other way around. Because it was a hopeless situation for both of us. And it was the only time in my life I've ever had that kind of problem. And I admire him so much for stickin' to his beliefs, and I'm proud of myself for doin' the same thing. He's still a very good friend, and always will be.

Q You seem to have some contradictions. Your autobiography stresses how much you need your privacy, and yet you'll tell the most intimate things about yourself in your music.

A I do want my privacy, yes, but what I really mean by wanting my privacy is I want time alone with my husband, time alone with my family, trips with my family, picnics with the kids. But when it comes to writing, it's the only way I can get it out. Because some things I can't talk about, but I can write about, and pretend it's a third person. And that way I get it off my chest, and I know what it means. But the average public has no idea what I'm talkin' about. And there's just been many songs that I've written that way. I had rather tell the public what the truth really is than for them to hear somethin' from somebody else and it be totally untrue. Because my life has not been a bed of roses. I have been no saint, and I have not ever tried to imply that I ever was, or ever will be. And I couldn't have written a book, or song, or anything, had I not been totally honest with myself first. "To thine own self be true."

Q Everybody talks about your life as being a soap opera. Do you resent that?

A No, 'cause I like soap operas. It doesn't bother me.

Q Even when they say "Tammy Wynette, Tammy Wynette," like "Mary Hartman, Mary Hartman"?

A As long as they call the name, I don't care. A lot of people put down soap operas, but we get in crowds of people—friends from Tucson, friends from Texas or Florida—and before the night is over, somebody will bring up "Did you see *Another World,* or *Days of Our Lives,* or *General Hospital* today?" And maybe it *is* like a soap opera, but those things in those soap operas are everyday things that really happen. It's just that those people have the guts enough to get up and act it out. It happens to a lot of other people, too, but they're not in the spotlight, and it doesn't matter. It isn't known about them, but all our mistakes are made in public, so everybody has to know what mistakes we make.

Q Two of your mistakes were husbands Michael Tomlin, the Nashville Realtor, and Don Chapel, a desk clerk who wanted to be a singer, right?

A Yes, Don was working at the Anchor Motel when I met him. That was the nicest cheapest place, if there's a good way to say that, that I could stay when I came to Nashville lookin' for work. And he took me out to his sister's, because I was very lonely with none of my family here. At the time, none of my kids were with me. They had gone back to my mother's for three weeks until I could find a place. I ran into an awful lot of problems. Landlords didn't want to rent to a single woman, and they definitely did not want children. And they wanted no part of entertainers. So I had a rough time findin' a place for us to live. Mother came and got the kids, and while she was takin' care of them, Don took me out to meet both his sisters—Jean Chapel, who's a great songwriter, and his other sister, Martha Carson, one of the greatest singers ever. And they really made me feel at home. Jean did some sewin' for me, and made me some clothes, because she knew I didn't have much money. And Martha and Jean and I went to church and would sing together, and I just fell in a pattern where Don was always around, and he was company. And I thought, "Well, at least it would be somebody to help me take care of the kids." Because he's not really a singer, and he wouldn't be on the road with me, and I'd feel secure leavin' the kids at home with him." But it didn't work out that way.

Q His story about the nude pictures is that you posed for them.

A Oh, I've heard all kinds of tales on the pictures. But I think that's [offering the photographs to others] just about as low as you can get. Because I didn't think anything about bein' in my own bedroom without any clothes on. There was nobody in there except my husband and myself. And I thought nothin' about walkin' to the bathroom nude and steppin' out of the shower. And he made it sound so ugly and so vulgar and so, ahhh . . . He's just a loser, and that's all you can say about him.

Q Aside from that, do you feel misunderstood in any way?

A No, not really. I don't believe I feel misunderstood. I think the press has been very lenient with me, and very good to me, considering all the things that have happened to me, and all the things that I've gone through they've written about. But I don't think that anybody has been really unfair to me, other than with the kidnappin' situation. That hurt me more than anything ever has in my life. Because I picked up a couple of papers, and it said, "Was this a publicity stunt?" Well, if they had seen the broken cheekbone, the terrible knots on my throat, my neck swollen, my face beat all to pieces, I don't think they would have thought it was a publicity stunt. Because I believe I could create a publicity stunt a whole lot easier than that. That hurt me an awful lot. And in Tulsa, shortly after that happened, I was doin' a press conference, and I was still shaky. It was only three weeks after it happened, and I was still nervous, not knowin' who it was, where to look, or what the man or person wanted. And I had a lady come up to me and stick a microphone up in my face and say, "Oh, so you really *are* here! One of the guys out there told me to come in and see if I could see the rope burns on your neck." And I crumbled. I went to pieces. I told Richey, "I'm a victim, I'm a suspect, and now I am totally nothin' as far as they're concerned." And I absolutely couldn't take it. They can be very cruel when they want to be.

Q You certainly have had your share of troubles. Do you feel like a victim?

A No. I did for a while. I had seventeen break-ins within nine months in my house before the fire, and the kidnappin' and the threats on my daughter Georgette's life, and they were all tied in together. But I don't feel like a victim all the time. I feel very free now. It took me a long time before I would even drive again after the kidnappin'. I wouldn't go anyplace by myself. But, like I said, the thing that hurt me worst was people sayin' it was a publicity stunt. And then they even called my husband in to ask him to take a lie detector test, to prove he didn't do it. And they said, "If you'll take one—" And his exact words were "We'll be givin' 'em whole-sale. Anyone remotely connected with her will take a lie detector test." Well, needless to say, he was the only one who took a lie detector test. There was a note left on our door, and we were the only two who took a handwriting test to prove that we didn't write the note. We had no help. It was the most disorganized thing I have ever seen in my life, and I lost a lot of respect for the Nashville Police Department. An awful lot. And I hate to say that, because there's been many times I've had to call on 'em. But there were so many different directions they could have gone to investigate. One, for instance, was that I told 'em the guy got into a dark blue station wagon with another man. And when I started runnin', there was an old pickup truck comin' from the other direction. Of course, I thought it was them comin' back after me, and I rolled down in a ditch. And when I got up, I saw it wasn't the blue station wagon, it was an old beat-up pickup. And I told the police that. In that little area, it couldn't have been that hard to have found an old beat-up pickup, and it had to have met the blue station wagon. But they just didn't investigate. They found six phone taps on seven lines—two of 'em under lock and key in the basement. All my burglar alarm wires were cut, all my telephone wires were cut, but it was all unrelated, as far as they were concerned.

Q When you first went into this business, did you have any idea how horrible the underside could be? Why did you want to do this?

A Well, I've never really thought of that, exactly. Part of it was to have a better life, but it was more of an escape from the real world. Because I could go out on the road and leave my problems behind me, and sing and enjoy what I was doing. Come home, and the problems were still there, but I'd had a little time to work on 'em. And it's a great escape, because you're in another world.

Q You must have realized early, though, that there would be untold pres-sures, even in the best of circumstances.

A Well, yes. I'll never forget the first time I was put on the spot so badly— I'm speaking professionally now—after I got here. I had my first record, "Apartment No. 9," and Sherrill said, "Take it up to the Ralph Emery show [on WSM] tonight. I want him to play it." I said, "Okay." And bless his heart, Tex Ritter was workin' with Ralph on that show, and Tex had had a little bit too much to drink that night. And the record had already been cut by Bobby Austin on the Coast, but the label was so small they said they couldn't get any distribution. They wanted to sell the master to somebody who would do somethin', but nobody would pick it up, so CBS said they wanted me to do it as a female version, not a cover. Because I don't think a female can cover a male, or a male cover a female. It's two different versions. But I took my record up there. And Ralph Emery looked at it, and he said, "What's your name?" And I told him and he said, "Okay. Let's listen to the song." And he listened, and I was just really nervous. And when he finished it, he said, "It's a great song, but the name'll never make it. Tammy Wynette—that's a strange name." And Tex said, "Wait a minute. I'm not through with her. I want to know: Why did you cut this song? Do you think you did a better job than Bobby Austin did?" This was my first time ever in a station. At 50,000 watts of dead silence. And it seemed eternity, but I know it was only a few seconds until Ralph came to my defense. He said, "Tex, I don't think it's fair to ask her that. This is her first record. She's new in the business, and she doesn't even know Bobby Austin." And Tex said, "Oh, well, okay." And everything was all right. But God, I didn't know what to say. That's the worst I've ever been put on the spot, and if he had really put me down —if Ralph had come back with "Yeah, answer that. Why did you do that?"—I just would have had a coronary and gotten it over with. (Laughter) No way!

Q You said he didn't think the name would ever work. Do you ever feel like Virginia Wynette Pugh?

A Only when I go home. Then I feel like I'm back with everybody who called me Wynette all my life. I have relatives or friends come by and say, "Hey, Wynette! How you doin'?" Many members of my family still will not call me anything else. My mother doesn't call me Tammy. She still calls me Wynette. That's about the only time I ever feel like Virginia Wynette Pugh. I do want to go back, though. I fully intend to do this before too long. I want to go back to Birmingham and go to the beauty shop where I worked. Three of the girls that I was workin' with are still workin' there, and I saw 'em the last time we were in Birmingham. So I want to go back and fix hair with them, all day long. I'd love every minute of it. And Richey said he thought it was a great idea. I think it'd be fun. 'Cause I still have my license.

Q Are they two separate people, Wynette Pugh and Tammy Wynette?

A Yeah, they're two separate people. Wynette Pugh was a scared little farm girl that got a high school education, married very young, and made a lot of mistakes. And then there's Tammy Wynette, who has learned an awful lot, got most of her education on the road, learned how to work out problems, and be what the name Tammy Wynette implies—a singer—when I go out onstage. So there's definitely two, yes. Most of the time it's Tammy, 'cause I'm not back in Alabama that much, to where I feel like I'm back home and I got no shows to do, nothin'. That happens very rarely, but when it does, I'm very pleased with it. I enjoy it.

Q You wrote a song early on called "The Only Time I'm Really Me."

A I wrote that when I first came to Nashville, when I was travelin' with the kids so much. I didn't have much money, and I had to take the kids everywhere I went. Durin' the day I would think, "Gosh, I'm a mama, I take my kids with me, I'm a singer, I'm a driver—I drive every place we go. I guess the only time I'm really me is when I go to bed at night." And that's how that came about.

Q You're often in the news for one kind of illness or another. How many times have you been hospitalized in the past five years?

A In the past five years? One, two, three . . . In the past five years, I've had five major operations, two minor operations, and I was also hospitalized for starch peritonitis, which is poison from the surgeon's glove. (Laughter) Now, that *does* sound like a soap opera, doesn't it? I got it from the doctor who did my surgery in New Orleans. Course, it wasn't his fault. He couldn't help it. But I got very badly infected intestines. In fact, I got gangrene by the time I finally found out what was wrong with me, and it was poison from the surgeon's gloves. And I've had my little finger broken three times, and it will never grow back. They had to fuse the end of it, and it's deteriorating now. But none of mine have been bad diseases, just gallbladder, hysterectomy, appendectomy, cystic mastitis, and things like that. Nothin' like cancer or heart problems. Mine have just been freak things that have happened.

Q Do you think life on the road has contributed to your illnesses?

A Yes, definitely. I went back to work ten days after I had the gallbladder operation, and I went back to work twelve days after I had the complete hysterectomy. I never gave myself time to heal, and then I formed adhesions, and I had those taken out, and they came right back. I never did take the proper time off to get myself in good shape. And I think that's why this year has been so good, because I haven't worked that hard. The past three months have been rough, but that's been the roughest of the whole year.

Q By looking at the progression of your music, it's possible to look at the progress of Tammy Wynette, too. Early in your career, you sang motherhood and good-wife songs, such as "Stand By Your Man" and "I Don't Wanna Play House." Then you graduated to modern songs of independence and liberation—"Womanhood" and " 'Til I Can Make It on My Own," for example. Are you aware of these changes in yourself?

A Do I feel like I have grown like that? Yes, I do. I think it's a mistake when people don't grow with their music. There's very few people that can get by without doin' that. Jones is one of 'em. 'Cause he never has to change. He's Jones, and he's idolized. I don't try to change what I do, but I do try to keep up with what's modern, and what's goin'. Even though I'm just a country singer. I never proclaimed to ever be anything other than a country singer. When my records are played on pop stations, believe you me, I'm the first one to say, "Why?" Because usually the ones that are played are so country that I don't understand anybody else playin' 'em. But I do try to keep up with modern lyrics. I think we have Kris Kristofferson to thank for that. He helped broaden the lyrics of country music so much with "Help Me Make It Through the Night." And Freddie Hart. Nobody had ever said a line in a song like "So sexy-lookin'," until he did that. And I think little by little, we have grown up with our music. We started out with train songs and railroads and cotton fields, and now we've grown up to big cities. And I'm sure it's gonna change again. I was listening to some of the old Elvis records the other day. And I swear, they sound as country as what country is now. The only people I remember hearing as a child, other than George Jones, Webb Pierce, Kitty Wells, Jim Reeves, and Patsy Cline, were the Drifters and the Coasters. And they even sound country-flavored now. But they didn't back then.

Q After you became successful and started making money, what kinds of things did you try to do for your mother and grandparents?

A My grandparents raised me, and I called 'em Mama and Daddy. Mother remarried when I was four, and she moved across the road from us in another house, but I stayed on with my grandparents for a while. And we were poor, but we didn't know we needed anything, because we just didn't know anybody else had any more than we did. But when I became halfway successful, I wanted to do all I could do for my family. So the first year, I helped my mother. She still has a home down there. We put a new roof on the house, added another bedroom and a bath, put carpet throughout the house, and a dishwasher and everything. Well, I had bought a washer and dryer for my grandparents, because Mama was gettin' really disabled, and Daddy was, too, at the time. And Daddy pitched a fit, because he did not want it on the inside of the house. He wanted it on the back porch! And I told him, "You can't put a washer and dryer on the back porch, Daddy. It's gotta go in the house." And he said, "I ain't never heard of a washin' machine bein' in the house." I said, "Well, this one has to go in the house." So I finally got him to let me cut out some cabinets, or get it done, and put the washer and dryer in there. Then the next Christmas, I thought, "Mama's too old to be washin' dishes." And she wasn't really gettin' the dishes clean, because her eyesight was bad. Before we would eat, we'd have to go in and rewash all the dishes, because she'd leave little particles of food on 'em. So I told my mother I thought Mama and Daddy needed a dishwasher. So I ordered it, paid for it, and told 'em to deliver it. They brought it that afternoon. A guy that Daddy has dealt with for years, Mr. Cashin, took care of it. And when the truck pulled up, Daddy said, "What's old man Cashin doin' down here? What's he bringin'?" I said, "I've got a surprise for you." He said, "What kind of a surprise?" I said, "I bought you a dishwasher." And Mama was standin' in the kitchen at the sink, and her mind was gone by that time. She would even ask me, "Who are you, honey? Do you have little girls?" And I'd have to say, "Yes." It broke my heart. Liked to killed me. My grandmother's name was Flora, but Daddy always called her Flor. And we got the dishwasher up on the front porch, and Daddy said, "Flor, come and look at this contraption they've brought up here." And she didn't hear him. And I said, "Daddy, it's a dishwasher. It's gonna save Mama havin' to do so much work." And he said, "It's the only thing she's got left that she can do, and I ain't takin' it away from her. I don't want that contraption in my house." So I told 'em, "Load it back up." And I said, "Well, what would you like to have?" And he said, "You know, that rug you put down in the livin' room sure did make a difference." And I said, "Carpet?" So I carpeted his bedroom, Mama's bedroom—she was in a hospital bed by then—the living room, the dining room, and another guest bedroom. Which only left the bath, and the little ol' bath is just a tiny thing. And I went back down there a couple of years later, and he said, "Girl, that rug is the best gift you ever got us, ever. But I'm tellin' you, when I get up to go to the bathroom at night, my feet get cold in that bathroom." I went back and bought a little ol' piece of material to carpet the bathroom with, just so they'd have it and it wouldn't be cold when they walked in. (Laughter) I had a good childhood.

Q Let's talk about vanity for a minute. Would you ever consider having a face lift?

A Oh, heavens yes, in a split second I would! I think that's very important. I hope mine doesn't come for a while. I got to lookin' at my eyes the other night, and I thought, "Ooh, what's this? I'm beginnin' to get some flab hangin' down here. But I wouldn't hesitate at all. I think it's very important for anybody in the limelight, whether it be a hair transplant, a boob job, a face lift, nose changed, eyes—whatever, I would do it. Because I think a show is exactly what it says—"a show." They want to hear you sing, but they want to see a show, too. They want to see what costumes you wear, what you look like—everything about you. And I think you should live up to that to a certain degree. You can't look like you've stepped out of a hatbox all the time. But you can have cosmetic surgery and use preventive creams to keep your skin from dryin' out so much, so you don't have to age as fast. I religiously take my makeup off every night. I go through a ritual that takes twenty or thirty minutes. And that's the one thing I started my girls out on. I had mudpacks on their faces every night. We have laughed so much about that.

Q What do you think of your looks?

A My looks? My neck's too long, my nose has a hump in it, and I have to use mustache wax on my eyebrows to keep 'em in place. They fall down like that. I like my lips, my mouth. All my kids have big, full lips, and most all my people on both sides do. I'm satisfied with my eyes. My boobs are too saggy, and the kids call me "Weenie Butt," 'cause I have no rear end. They laugh and say, "Mama, you've got such a weenie butt, no wonder you have to wear clothes so little." But I think I'm . . . Let's see, how can I say this so it sounds right? I had rather think that I look classy than to think that I'm beautiful. I'd rather look nice, and have somebody say, "Gee, you really looked nice last night," instead of "Man alive, did you see what she was wearin'?!" I'd rather just dress more conservatively with my streetwear, and just be classy, not flashy.

Q People talk about you as being a sex symbol.

A (Laughter) Oh, God, no! I've never ever thought of myself as a sex symbol, and never will. No way. I guess that goes back to my childhood again, too. I played basketball, and Daddy would never let me wear the shorts. I always had to wear blue jeans with a jersey. I took the shorts home one day and begged and pleaded. I said, "*Please* let me wear the shorts. Everybody else does." I was the only one that dressed differently on the basketball court. Daddy took one look at those shorts, and they were cut square across the legs, and he said, "Flor, put some elastic in them legs, and she can wear 'em." I was *still* the only one dressed different on the court! (Laughter) From blue jeans to elastic in the legs, but at least I did get to wear the trunks. But no, I don't think there's anything sexy about me. I like to think of myself as bein' a good listener when I have friends that have problems, or my kids have problems. And there's nothin' that means any more in the world to me than for my kids to come spend the day with me, like they did today in the hospital. And I tell 'em, "Hey, go on, I know you're gettin' bored up here." But they say, "No, no, Mama. We'd just as soon stay up here." I feel like I raised the kids by myself, up until Richey and I got married, and it's always been us. And the kids feel that way. It's very strange. Gwen said today, "You're more like a sister than a mother, 'cause we all kinda grew up together." And I guess if I wanted to be anything, it would be a good mama. I think that would please me more than anything else in the world.

Q Is that why you wrote "Dear Daughters"?

A Well, when I wrote that song, I was feelin' guilty about being away from my girls. If I was gone for more than three or four weeks, they'd fly and meet me someplace, or they'd go with me. But I sat down and talked to them, and one of my daughters, who was then sixteen, said, "Mama, if you were here every day, we'd probably climb the walls, and we'd be on your nerves so bad you couldn't stand it. We don't know any other way of life." I don't think I'd given 'em enough credit for bein' as well adjusted as they are. But when I missed something, when they did something when I was gone, I felt like "Well, doggone, if I had been here . . ." You know, I'd missed a very important part of their life. So the song I wrote about the girls I wrote while I was drivin' to Florida. I finished it by the time I got there. And I called my mother, and told her, "I've just written a thing about the girls. I don't know if I'll ever record it or not, but I will have it put on a plaque for 'em, and I'm gonna do it onstage." And before I got through half of the first verse, she started cryin'. I said, "Okay, okay, that's it. Forget it." But it's the most important thing to me that I've ever written, because every line is true. And it is all the things . . . well, I guess it's just a few of the things, because I've missed many more things, but it's a few of the important things that I felt that I had missed. When my oldest daughter had her first date, I was in California, and I called home three times to make sure she was home on time. It's just little things that I'd like to be there to see and can't.

Q You obviously had a strict upbringing. What did your grandparents think about the kind of music you sing, and about the songs that deal with drinking and divorce and assorted carrying on?

A You know, I don't think Daddy and them really thought anything at all about it. It's the strangest thing in the world—like I said, Richey's father has been a Baptist minister for fifty-one years, and "Your Good Girl's Gonna Go Bad" is his favorite song. When I appeared at the Exit/In, he came to see the show, and I told the audience, "I'd like you to meet my father-in-law. He's been a Baptist minister for fifty-one years, but he likes 'Your Good Girl's Gonna Go Bad.' " And the crowd just laughed, and Pop was goin' [she nods her head up and down], "I like that song." So I guess I feel it's okay as long as I don't make a fool out of myself in a barroom, by bein' drunk or disorderly or foul-mouthed. I can't stand that. I cannot take dirty, filthy language in front of my kids, and I don't like it in front of myself. If it's two couples sittin' around tellin' jokes and laughin' and havin' a good time, that's great. I'll go all the way. I'll laugh as loud as anybody. But in mixed company, I don't. If there's any strangers around, or people I don't really know, and if my kids or my family are present, I don't like that. I guess I'm very old-fashioned. The one thing that makes me madder than anything, that I could preach on every time I start, is the old double standard—"He's a man, so he can do it." I hate that, I guess because I'm raisin' five girls and one boy. [George Richey has a son and daughter, in addition to Wynette's four daughters.] And I've been liberated. I'm a *very* liberated woman, because I've never been placed in that position. But I have had friends and relatives that have been put in that position, of doin' the same job that a man does, and makin' less money. And I think that stinks. But what irritates me more is if a girl gets pregnant, it's totally all her fault. That is so wrong! If my children haven't learned how I expect them to conduct themselves by now, then it's too late for me to try to teach 'em now. And if somethin' happens to them, I am with them all the way. If they do somethin' wrong, that does not mean that I don't still love 'em. If they commit murder, I'll tell 'em, "It was wrong, but I love you, and I'm still with you." I cannot stand the thought of my girls bein' put down because they're girls, and boys are more important. They aren't more important to me.

Q Is there any subject that would embarrass you to sing about?

A No, I don't think so. I would never sing about abortion, things like that. But off the top of my head, I can't think of anything else. I've cut cheatin' songs, love songs, Bonnie-and-Clyde-type songs, and even "Rocky Top" [bluegrass music]. In the music that I do, I don't think there's any subject that I wouldn't sing about.

Q You said that if you could be anything you wanted, it would be a good mother. How do you think of yourself? What's your self-image?

A How do I think of myself? I'm very stubborn, as I said before. That's somethin' I'm workin' on, tryin' to get it to where I don't fly off the handle. One of my worst faults is not sayin' what I think when somethin' happens, and get it off my chest so that it's over with, said and done, and nobody's feelings are hurt. But I have a tendency to brood about it for a couple of days. Then something else happens, and it makes it that much worse. By the time I'm really mad, I bring up everything that's happened for the last six months. And I hate myself for bein' that way, and I *am* tryin' to change. God only knows. I'm thirty-eight. I've had plenty of time. I think I'm mellowing a little bit.

Q What kinds of things make you angry?

A The *National Enquirer*.

Q Have they been after you?

A Oh! They hounded me so bad when I dated Burt Reynolds. They hounded us until it was unbelievable. And when Richey and I got married, one of them stood on a ladder on the beach to take pictures of the wedding. Then we had our reception at the Hilton Hotel in Jupiter [Florida], on the eighth floor. And poor Pops, he's just so naïve. He looked up and he said, "Son, what are they doin' washin' windows this time of day?" And Richey said, "Dad, they're not washin' windows. Everybody just stay where you are. That's the *National Enquirer*." And you know what's even funnier than that? I buy it every week, and read it. And *love* to read it! Until I'm in it. And then I'm furious. And that is so ridiculous. I know that stuff isn't true when I read it. I buy the *Star*, I buy the *Globe*, I buy the *Enquirer*—every ol' tabloid that I can buy. And I read 'em religiously. I was readin' something to my adopted daughter in California the other night, and I said, "Ohhh, do you believe this?!" And she said, "What are you readin' that out of?" I said, *"National Enquirer."* She said, "And you believe all that?" And I said, "Well . . . maybe not all of it." We went out on the set the other day to visit Burt, and he asked me who was playin' him in the movie *[Stand By Your Man]*. I told him it wasn't goin' that far. And he *laughed!* (Laughter) That's one thing that makes me mad. I picked up a magazine the other day and it said, "Burt Sizzles As Singer Tells All!" Oh, I hit the ceiling! Because I called Burt, asked his permission to use the poem in the book, asked his permission to write about us. And he said, "I wouldn't want you to *not* put me in the book, because I was part of your life, and you were part of mine." But when I told him the movie was gonna end before it got to us, he said, "Oh, good, that'll give us a chance for a sequel. I'll play me, if you'll play you." And he laughed, and put his arm around Richey, and he said, to me, "You've got a hell of a husband. I'm so glad he knows we're friends." And it *is* great. Richey thinks the world of him. And we are good friends. We always will be. We just had fun together. He likes Southern women, down-to-earth, plain ol' girls that don't demand an awful lot, and who are happy to be who they are. But I'm the luckiest person in the world with George Richey. He's got to be the most wonderful father, other than my [grand]father, that I've ever known. The only thing the man really wants out of life is just to be loved. The rest he can take care of, as long as he knows the kids and I love him, respect him, and believe in him. He has done so much for me, career-wise, everything. After twelve years of bein' in the business, I was still workin' some of the worst joints that could have possibly been worked. And I didn't know that I didn't have to do that, until Richey came along and started sayin', "No, you've got to make some career moves." And I said, "What do you mean by career moves?" And he said, "A job that's prestigious—a job where you'll benefit from it, instead of goin' back to the same old honky-tonks night after night." And he's such a genius with music. And he's always been around when I've recorded. He's overdubbed me many times, and he's produced me many times. He puts all my Vegas shows together. I write down the list of the songs I want to do, and he works out all the arrangements himself, conducts for me. And the band absolutely loves havin' him around, because he's got such an ear for music. He can hear one bad note that five boys won't hear. And he points it out, and then they all say, "Oh, *that's* what's been soundin' strange in that song!" And he's so good. He's not jealous of me and anybody. He knows my past like the palm of his hand, and I know his. The greatest thing we have goin' for us is that we like each other, and we're buddies. And I think sometimes that's even more important than bein' in love with somebody, to really like 'em. Because I like what he stands for. He's very old-fashioned in some ways, but he's very broad-minded in other ways. And I kinda like that. (A smile) I kinda like him.

Q So you think this is it—no more husbands?

A Oh, I don't think—I *know!* No more. This is it. I'd be a fool. I could never find anybody that would love me the way he does, and treat me the way he does, and love my family and children the way he does. He was in love with my children long before he was ever in love with me, because his were in California, and he tried to substitute my kids for his. He would come by and pick mine up and take them out for a pizza or whatever.

Q A lot of big names in popular music—people who have been wonderful songwriters—seemed to lose that creative spark when they got married, almost as if they needed unhappiness in their love life to come up with those songs. Could this be part of the problem you've had in the last few years with your career?

A Richey hasn't written anything in three years, and I've only written a couple of things—"Two Story House" and "We'll Talk About It Later." We've been laughin' about it. The day we went in and told Billy Sherrill we were gonna get married, he laughed and said, "Well, there goes the slow, sad ballads. Now I guess everything you write is gonna be up-tempo and happy." (Laughter) I guess he's been right. We haven't even written up-tempo and happy. We just haven't had time to write.

Q Do you write better when you're sad?

A Oh, yeah. Because when you're down, things look so much worse than when you're up. You can't even see the bright side of anything when you're down. So everything's negative, and you think of all the sad things in the world. But when you're happy, everything is wonderful, and what is there to write about? Nothing bad's going on. It's all good. And it's hard to write a song like that. Donna Fargo is one of the few who did, with "Happiest Girl in the Whole USA," which was a positive, up-tempo song. But there's not many of them. If I wasn't happy in my real life, I couldn't come across to the people happy, 'cause it would show. And it did many times with Jones and me—the bitterness, where we had argued. I could see it. And as much as we tried to make light of it, some of it had to come out, and the people out there could see it.

Q Have you had many embarrassing moments onstage?

A Ohhh! (Groan) Yeah, I've had several of those. My bra strap broke one night, and another night I had on a strapless dress and a guy caught me around the waist to pull me over to him. I was shakin' hands out in the audience. And he got ahold of this black strapless dress, and it's just knit, and he had it almost all the way down. I was just about to panic. Then, another time, I went onstage freezin' to death. It was an outside fair date, and I was determined I was not gonna be cold. I put on two pairs of pajamas underneath my dress to keep from freezin', and I forgot about it. And when I lifted my dress to walk up onstage, all you could see was blue and green pajamas underneath my dress. Oh, Lord! I bent over to shake hands with a guy in Vegas the other night, and the zipper popped in the top of my dress. And I had to sit down in this woman's lap and say, "Would you please zip my dress?" 'Cause I open up [the show] in the audience. I walk out and talk to the people, and then go up onstage.

Q I've seen you do that, and I wondered then if it had ever gotten unmanageable.

A A couple of times. Well, more than a couple of times. But the security in places like Vegas is always pretty good. They don't get to me nearly as much. Outside country festivals and parks are the worst. Boy, they want anything. Blood. Just anything to take a sample home with them.

Q Has it ever become dangerous?

A No, not really dangerous. There's been a couple of times when I've been a little bit uneasy. I had a guy pull a knife out of his pocket one night when I was out, but he wanted to cut the stones off my dress. So it was totally harmless. But I didn't know that at the time, and I panicked.

Q Do you ever feel guilty about the material wealth your fame has brought you?

A I don't really feel guilty. I think I feel more or less like I don't deserve what

I have. I feel very undeserving, but I don't feel guilty. And the reason I feel undeserving is because members of my family were just as talented as I was and could have made it, too, had they had the opportunities. But they didn't, and I did. But I feel real good that I've been able to be as successful as I have, and been able to give them the things they couldn't buy for themselves. I am a very strict mother, in that I don't want my kids to say, "Hey, I'm So-and-So's kid. I'll do what I want to do." They would get their butt busted quicker than they could turn around if I ever knew they were guilty of doin' that. Because I want my kids to be normal. I expect them to make an F, or a D, or a C, and I expect them to get grounded. But I love giving more than getting, anytime. This year, I have given away at least two complete housefuls of furniture. Because we had the house on Hillsboro Road furnished, this house was furnished, and the house in Florida was furnished. We took what we wanted, and we gave living-room and dining-room suites away. One of the little girls who work with us got married to a boy who also works with us, and we gave them a dining-room suite. It makes me feel good to be able to do that, because it's their very first home. They came on the road last week and said, "Well, we've got our dining-room suite and a water bed. No chairs yet, but a dining-room suite and a water bed." I love to play Santa Claus. Christmastime is really a special time for me. That's the one time when I really do splurge.

Q One writer has suggested that your illnesses are an unconscious reaction to the fame and the money—that you feel you have to pay for it all in some way.

A Well, I never liked to have to cancel shows. I feel sorry for the promoter, first, because he's going to lose money. Then people drive heaven knows how far to get to the shows, and I feel guilty even when I'm sick, having to cancel. But the old saying "The show must go on" does not apply to me anymore. I've tried that, and I've broken my health down. The show must go on as long as I am able.

Q Do you think you're a good singer?

A I don't think I'm a great singer, no. I think I'm average.

Q Are you a good writer, in your estimation?

A Yes, I think I'm a good writer, because I write from my heart. And I've never been recognized—well, very little—as a writer. But the things I do write, I'm proud of, and I think I'd have to say yes, I do think I'm a good writer.

Q If all of a sudden people didn't want to hear Tammy Wynette anymore, could you be happy?

A Well, I hope I don't have to quit until I'm older than Roy Acuff. But if the time comes, and they don't want to hear me anymore, I can accept that. I may not want it to happen, but I can accept it. Because I've been extremely lucky, and if I keep on bein' extremely lucky, somebody else is gonna fail. There's only room for so many. Somebody has to go down for somebody else to come up. So I know I can't stay popular forever. And I don't expect that. I just want to write enough and record enough to be able to work a few days a month, and just be happy.

Q How do you think the history books will record you? How do you think you fit into the scope of country music?

A I hope I've contributed honesty, sincerity, something that I feel in my heart. I hope I get that across to people. I never asked for a title of any kind. CBS gave me a party, long before they were givin' out the [gold and platinum] awards, for bein' the first female to sell a million copies of an album. And there was a lot of controversy about that a couple of years ago. But they finally verified that I was the first to do that. And that didn't mean that much to me, other than the fact that the day I walked in Billy's office, and he said, "You're the first lady to so-and-so," the name stuck. And Jones and I even had out albums, *Me and the First Lady, The First Songs of the First Lady,* and *The First Lady and the King.* And I'm not saying I'm deserving of that title, but I hope they write me up as bein' . . . well, I think one guy said it better than I could say it—"the Edith Piaf of Country Music." I like that. I just hope I get across what I feel—my emotions, and my sincerity, and my honesty—on record.

Q And if they call you "the Heroine of Heartbreak"?

A That's all right. I have no objections to that. I've been called a lot worse. I have had a lot of heartbreak, and a lot of other people have, too. But if that's what they consider me, then that's fine with me.